Wide Area Networks

Patrick Regan

Taken from:

Wide Area Networks, First Edition
by Patrick Regan

PEARSON
Custom
Publishing

PEARSON
Prentice
Hall

PEARSON CUSTOM PUBLISHING
75 Arlington Street, Suite 300, Boston, MA 02116
A Pearson Education Company

This book is dedicated to my good friend Diane. A wonderful person, who I could see as my mom.

Preface

When first learning WAN material, I was often faced with books that were inadequate in depth of the material or books that were written for electrical engineers. In addition, after reading several books and performing research on the Internet, I felt that there were large areas where knowledge and understanding should be better. This book was designed to give an overall study of WANs and WAN technology and should help clarify those areas.

To make sure that readers have had the basics, the first chapters review the OSI model, Ethernet, and Token Ring. Next comes a thorough review of TCP/IP and IPX/SPX protocols/ standards with an emphasis on TCP/IP addressing. The book then starts looking at switches and bridges and how they affect network performance and security.

After gaining a good understanding of how LANs work, you will be ready to connect them together with routers and other WAN devices. Therefore, the book moves into WAN technology, including T-Carrier and E-Carrier systems, ISDN, X.25, Frame Relay, ATM, routers, and routing protocols. The book then finishes with an overview of WAN security and voice communications (including VOIP) and wireless technology.

To reinforce the material, each chapter contains review questions. In addition to configuring protocols on Windows machines and reviewing scenarios, the book presents hands-on experience with WAN technology in the chapters on Cisco switches and Cisco routers.

As you go through the book, you will notice that a lot of information is repeated. This allows the chapters to be taught out of order and helps to complete the overall picture. In addition, I have found that the best way to teach this material is to repeat the information as often as I can.

I would always recommend that, before taking a course on WAN technology, the reader should have had a course in LANs or networking technology or have equivalent knowledge of the COMPTIA Network+ exam. In addition, they should already be familiar with the Microsoft Windows environment and how to connect a computer to a network. For a review, however, many of the necessary LAN components that affect WAN connectivity have been discussed.

ACKNOWLEDGMENTS

I would like to thank the following reviewers for their valuable feedback: David Beach, Indiana State University; Phillip Davis, DelMar College, Texas; Samuel Guccione, Eastern Illinois University; Jeffrey L. Rankinen, Pennsylvania College of Technology; Robert Robertson, Southern Utah University; and Timothy Staley, DeVry University–Irving, Texas.

Brief Contents

Contents

CHAPTER **3**   **Voice and Data 66**

CHAPTER **4**   **Network Technology and Protocol Review   116**

CHAPTER **5**   **IP Addressing   148**

CHAPTER **8** **Using Cisco Switches   248**

CHAPTER **9** **WAN Technology   288**

CHAPTER **10** **Packet Switching Networks   330**

CHAPTER **11** **Cell Relay Networks   354**

CHAPTER **12** **Introduction to Routers and Routing   370**

CHAPTER 13   Introduction to Cisco Routers   402

CHAPTER **17** **Voice Communications   552**

CHAPTER **18**   Wireless Technology Used in WANs   **584**

CHAPTER 1

Introduction to Networks

Topics Covered in this Chapter

Introduction

As PCs became more popular, there was an increasing need for people to share data between computers. This need lead to the networking of computers. One type of network is a local area network (LAN). A LAN includes computers that are connected within a geographical close network, such as a room, a building, or a group of adjacent buildings. Soon there was a need to connect the smaller LANs into a wide area network (WAN). Some of these WANs span the world. This chapter introduces the basic concepts of networking, LANs, and WANs.

Objectives

- Differentiate between LANs, MANs, and WANs.
- List and describe the components that make up a network.
- Given a network problem scenario, select an appropriate course of action based on a general troubleshooting strategy.
- Describe the importance and use of documentation.
- Identify the purpose, features, and functions of hubs, switches, bridges, routers, gateways, and network interface cards.

1.1   NETWORK BEGINNINGS

Early computers, before PCs were called **mainframes;** they were large, centralized computers used to store and organize data. To access a mainframe you used a **dumb terminal,** which consisted of a monitor to display the data and a keyboard to input the data. Different from a PC, the dumb terminal did not process the data; instead all of the processing was done by the mainframe computer (centralized computing).

As computers became smaller and less expensive, **personal computers (PCs)** were introduced. Unlike mainframe computers, personal computers are meant to be used by one person and contain its own processing capabilities. As PCs became more popular, a need grew for people to move data from one computer to another. This was initially done with a "sneaker-net," where a person would hand carry the data from computer to computer on a floppy disk. Unfortunately, this method was relatively expensive and time consuming when disks had to be transported over long distances.

As the need to share data between different computers grew, distributed computing was developed. Distributed computing connected several computers together with cable. Different from centralized computing, the processing in a distributed computing system is done by the individual PCs. In fact, the distributing computing system is typically more powerful than the centralized computing system because the sum of all of the processing power of the individual PCs is more than a single mainframe.

1.2   NETWORK DEFINITIONS

A **network** consists of two or more computers connected together to share resources such as files or a printer. For a network to function, it requires a network service to share or access and a common media or pathway to connect the computers. To bring it all together, protocols give the entire system common communication rules (see Figure 1.1).

1.2.1   Network Services

The two most common services provided by a network are file sharing and print sharing. **File sharing** allows you to access files that reside on another computer without using a floppy disk or other form of removable media. To ensure that the files are secure, most networks can limit the access to a directory or file and what kind of access (permissions or rights) that a person or a group of people have. For example, if you have full access to your home directory (personal directory on the network to store files), you can list, read, execute, create, change, and delete files in your home directory.

Depending on the contents of a directory or file, you can specify who has access to the directory or file and you can specify what permissions or rights those people have over the directory or file. For example, you could specify that a group of people will not be able to see or execute the files, while giving a second group of people the ability to see or execute the file but not make changes to the files and not delete the files. Lastly, you could give rights to a third group so that they can see, execute, and change the files.

Print sharing allows several people to send documents to a centrally located printer in the office. Therefore, not everyone requires his or her own personal laser printers. Net-

Figure 1.1   Computers Networked Together

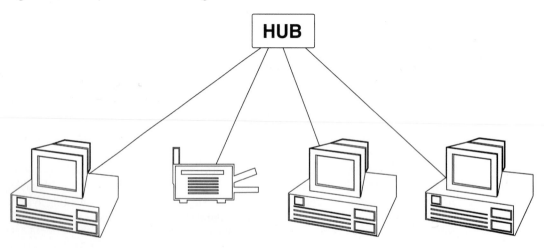

Figure 1.2   E-mail with Microsoft Outlook

works can limit who has access to the printer. For example, if you have two laser printers (a standard laser printer and an expensive high-resolution color laser printer), you can assign everyone access to the standard laser printer while only assigning a handful of people access to the expensive printer.

Internet services provide businesses with important tools. **Electronic mail** (e-mail) and World Wide Web access are two popular services. E-mail is a powerful, sophisticated tool that allows you to send text messages and file attachments (documents, pictures, sound, and movies) to anyone with an e-mail address (see Figure 1.2).

Much like the mail from the post office, e-mail is delivered to a mailbox (delivery location or holding area for your electronic messages). An Internet mail address will include the user name, followed by the @ symbol, followed by the name of the mail server. When you connect to the network, you can then access your e-mail messages. Other features may include return receipt so that you know that the e-mail message was read or delivered. You can also reply to e-mail messages by clicking on the reply button, send e-mail messages to several people at the same time, or forward a message to someone else.

Because the Internet is essentially a huge network, it is possible to make your network part of the Internet or to provide a common connection to the Internet for many users. You can create your own web page on the Internet to provide products and services to the public, or you can perform research on the Internet.

1.2.2   Network Media

If you have something to share, such as a file or a printer, you must then have a pathway to access the network resource. Computers connect to the network by using a special expansion card called a **network interface card (NIC).** The NIC will then communicate by

Figure 1.3   A Network Card with an Unshielded Twisted Pair (UTP) Cable Attached to a RJ-45 Connector and an Unused BNC Connector

sending signals through a cable (twisted-pair, coaxial, or fiber optics) or by using wireless technology (infrared, microwaves, or radio waves). The role of the NIC is to prepare and send data to another computer, receive data from another computer, and control the flow of data between the computer and the cabling system (see Figure 1.3).

1.2.3   Protocols

Protocols (TCP/IP, IPX, and NetBEUI) are the rules or standards that allow computers to connect to one another and enable computers and peripheral devices to exchange information with as little error as possible. Common protocol suites (also referred to as stacks) are TCP/IP and IPX. A suite is a set of protocols that work together. Today, the most popular protocol is the TCP/IP protocol suite because it is the protocol that is used for the Internet.

1.2.4   LANs, MANs, and WANs

Today, networks are broken into three main categories: (1) **local area networks (LANs),** (2) **metropolitan area networks (MANs),** or (3) **wide area networks (WANs).** A LAN has computers that are connected within a geographical close network, such as a room, a building, or a group of adjacent buildings. A MAN is a network designed for a town or city, usually using high-speed connections such as fiber optics. A WAN is a network that uses long-range telecommunication links to connect network computers over long distances and often consists of two or more smaller LANs. Typically, the LANs are connected through public networks, such as the public telephone system.

Figure 1.4 A WAN

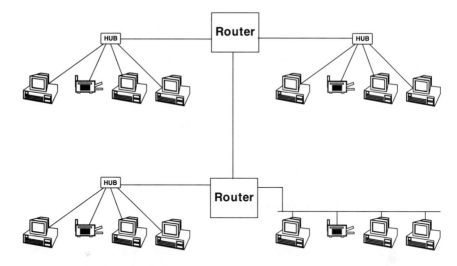

Figure 1.5 The Internet

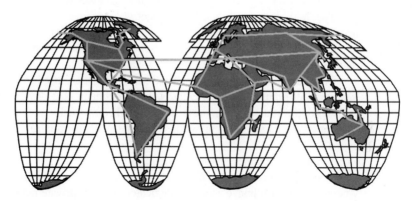

The WAN can be broken down into either an **enterprise WAN** or a **global WAN.** An enterprise WAN is a WAN that is owned by one company or organization. A global WAN is not owned by any one company and could cross national boundaries. The best known example of a global WAN is the Internet, which connects millions of computers. As of February 2002, there are over 544.2 million users on the Internet and the number is growing rapidly (see Figures 1.4 and 1.5).

Internetworking is the art and science of connecting individual LANs to create WANs, and connecting WANs to form even larger WANs by using routers, bridges, and gateways. Smaller LANs are known as **subnetworks** or **subnets.** Internetworking can be extremely complex because it generally involves connecting networks that use different protocols.

Today, when dealing with networks, you will often hear two more terms: (1) intranet, and (2) extranet. An **intranet** is a network based on TCP/IP protocols (an internet) belonging to an organization, usually a corporation, accessible only by the organization's members, employees, or others with authorization. An intranet's websites look and act just like any other websites, but the firewall surrounding an intranet fends off unauthorized access. Like the Internet itself, intranets are used to share information. Secure intranets are now the fastest-growing segment of the Internet because they are much less expensive to build and manage than private networks based on proprietary protocols. *NOTE:* An Intranet could have access to the Internet, but does not require it.

Extranet refers to an intranet that is partially accessible to authorized outsiders. Whereas an intranet resides behind a firewall and is accessible only to people who are members of the same company or organization, an extranet provides various levels of accessibility to outsiders. You can access an extranet only if you have a valid username and password, and your identity determines which parts of the extranet you can view. Extranets are becoming a very popular means for business partners to exchange information.

1.2.5   Public and Private WANs

A WAN can be a government-regulated public network or a privately owned network that crosses into the public network environment. It doesn't matter whether the area being bridged is across the country or across the street. If the geographical separation crosses over a public thoroughfare, a WAN is required to make the connection.

The WAN is typically used to connect two or more LANs. LANs that are interconnected by a WAN may be located in the same geographical area such as an industrial park or campus setting, or in geographically separate areas such as different cities or different regions.

There are a number of transmission services that are used to support WAN communications, all running across the hardware components that physically connect different LANs. For the attached user, these services and components work in tandem to create the illusion of one large virtual network. Thus, the WAN is often represented in diagrams as a cloud.

WANs can be either private or public. A private network is a network that belongs to a particular person or group. Of course, when you own the network, a private WAN is one where you have exclusive access to dedicated links. A private network is much more expensive than public networks.

While a majority of LANs connect to WANs through a public interface, an increasing number of WAN connections are privately owned. Private network operators typically lease lines from public network providers while maintaining control and management of the network from their own facilities. Most private WANs include a separate connection to the public WAN. Government regulation of private WAN operations is relatively limited. Because many corporations and universities base their internal networks on leased lines, they may be making interstate and intrastate calls from one site to another.

If leasing a physical WAN connection does not make economic sense, private WAN operators have several other options to consider. Wireless WAN connections, such as satellite or laser line-of-sight between buildings are common solutions, but they are subject to potential environmental interference and breaches of security.

Another non-lease WAN option is a **virtual private network (VPN).** A virtual private network (VPN) is a network that is constructed by using public wires to connect nodes. For example, there are a number of systems that enable you to create networks using the Internet as the medium for transporting data. These systems use encryption and other security mechanisms to ensure that only authorized users can access the network and that the data cannot be intercepted.

A key component of a public WAN is the presence of government regulation, which not only dictates the telecommunications services that are provided by public WAN operators, but also determines how which services are subject to tariff and at what rate. In the United States, the Federal Communications Commission (FCC) is the primary regulator of the public network environment. In addition, there are a variety of national and international organizations that define the format standards for telecommunications.

The best example of a public WAN designed for voice is the **public switched telephone network (PSTN),** while the Internet is the largest public WAN designed for data. In North America, telephone services across a PSTN are provided by a telephone company, commonly known as Telco. Telco may be used to refer only to local telephone companies, or it may represent the telephone industry in general, including both local and long distance carriers. In many European countries, a governmental agency known as the **Postal, Telegraph, and Telephone (PTT)** is responsible for providing combined postal, telegraph, and telephone services. A similar centrally-controlled system is used in China.

Another distinguishing characteristic of the public WAN is the tariff, which is the rate charged for a variety of telecommunication services that are provided to Telco customers. Unlike the private WAN, where the network owner pays the full cost of leased or owned connections, public WAN operators provide shared facilities where link ownership and payment is distributed among all connected users.

There are several categories of WAN service providers, but the two most common groups provide a majority of WAN services:

- A local exchange carrier (LEC) is a company that owns the "last mile" telephone wire that runs to your house and provides telephone service within the local exchange. When you need to call long distance, the LEC typically intercepts long distance calls and hands them off to your specified long distance carrier.
- Long distance services are typically provided by an inter exchange carrier (IEC or IXC). These are the well known telecommunication giants including AT&T, Sprint, MCI/WorldCom, and GTE, who own the interstate connections of the PSTN. In some cases, the IEC may also be your LEC.

1.3   INTRODUCTION TO TROUBLESHOOTING

When comparing PC problems to network problems, network problems can have a much more devastating effect on network users. This is because users in corporations tend to store many of their documents on the network, and they require access to many network services such as file and print sharing and e-mail. In addition, a network problem can affect many users, not just one.

Network problems could be server problems, network problems, client problems, or user problems. The only way to get good at troubleshooting computers and networks is to practice, practice, practice. Experience is what will make you a good troubleshooter.

When encountering a computer problem, you should follow certain guidelines. First, your mind must be clear and rested. You must be able to concentrate on the problem. If you are not able to concentrate, you may overlook something that is obvious, such as the power cord being unplugged.

Don't panic, don't get frustrated, and do allow enough time to do the job right. If you panic, you may do something that will make the situation worse. If you start to get frustrated, take a break. You will be amazed how five or ten minutes away from the problem will clear your mind and will allow you to look at the problem a little differently when you come back. Lastly, make sure that you have enough time to properly analyze the problem, fix the problem, and properly test the system after the repair. Again, if you rush a job, you may make the problem worse or overlook something simple.

1.3.1   Computer Problems

If it is a server problem or a client work station problem, everything that applies to a PC problem also applies to a server or client problem. The problem could be hardware failure, compatibility issues, improper configuration, a software glitch, environment factors, or a user error (see Table 1.1). Some examples could be a faulty component such as a hard drive, floppy drive, power supply, cable, or modem. In addition, problems can be caused by a virus, software that isn't compatible with a screen savers, BIOS setup program settings, power management features, control panel settings, software drivers, hardware settings, power fluctuations, or electromagnetic interference.

1.3.2   Network Problems

Dependency on network resources has grown tremendously over the past ten years. In today's world, a company's success is highly dependent on its network availability. As a result, companies are increasingly less tolerant of network failures. Therefore, network troubleshooting has become a crucial skill to possess.

Not only has the dependency on networks grown, but the industry also is moving toward increasingly complex environments that involve multiple media types, multiple protocols, and often interconnection to unknown networks. These unknown networks may be defined as a transit network belonging to an Internet service provider (ISP), or a telco that interconnects with private networks. The convergence of voice and video on data networks has also added to the complexity and the importance of network reliability. Of course, the more complex a network environment is, the higher the potential for connectivity and performance problems. In addition, it makes it harder to troubleshoot.

Table 1.1 Computer Problem Classifications

Reason for failure	Description
Hardware failure	When one or more computer components fail.
Hardware compatibility	This may appear to be a hardware failure, but it is when a hardware component is not compatible with another hardware component.
Improper hardware configuration	This error will often appear to be a hardware failure, but it is when the hardware has not been installed or configured properly. This happens often when the user does not read the manual or does not have the knowledge to make use of the manual.
Improper software configuration	This error may appear to be a hardware failure, but it is when the software (operating system or application software) is not installed or configured properly. This happens often when the user does not read the manual or does not have the knowledge to make use of the manual.
Software failure	This may appear to be a hardware failure, but it is when there is a glitch in the software. This can range from corrupted data to a programming flaw.
Software compatibility	This may also appear to be a hardware failure. The software may not be compatible with the hardware or other software.
Environment	This problem may appear to be a hardware failure. The location of the computer and its environment (temperature, air flow, electromagnetic interference, or magnetic fields) may affect the reliability of the PC and have a direct impact on the PCs life.
User error	A very common situation where the user hits the wrong keys or is not familiar with the computer and/or software. It could be something as simple as the user hitting the zero (0) key rather than the letter O.

A network problem would include problems with the media that connects a server and/or client to the network and anything else the media connects to, including switches and routers. For example, most computers are connected to a network through a cable that is connected to a hub. Then the smaller networks can be connected together to form a larger network by using routers. Therefore, the cables, the hub, or the router could be faulty, a cable may not be connected properly, or a hub or router may not be configured properly.

In addition, for a computer and a server to operate properly, the computer's protocol has to be configured properly. In addition, you must be given proper permissions to use a network resource; the network may require services provided by other servers such as a DNS server to provide name resolution for your network to function properly. For example, when you type in http://www.acme.com, a DNS server will look up the IP address for www.acme.com so that it knows how to contact that web server. Network communications can also be interrupted by external environmental factors such as electromagnetic interference.

1.3.3 General Troubleshooting Strategies

To troubleshoot a failed network, you must be able to characterize certain symptoms. These symptoms might be general (such as clients being incapable of accessing specific servers) or more specific (routes not existing in a routing table). Each symptom can be traced to one or more problems or causes by using specific troubleshooting tools and techniques. After being identified, each problem can be remedied by implementing a solution consisting of a series of actions.

When you're troubleshooting a network environment, a systematic approach works best. An unsystematic approach to troubleshooting can result in wasting valuable time and resources, and can sometimes make symptoms even worse. In addition, you can easily get frustrated as you cannot figure out the problem because you missed something. Therefore, to start troubleshooting problems, you should first define the specific symptoms, identify all potential problems that could be causing the symptoms, and then systematically eliminate each potential problem (from most likely to least likely) until the symptoms disappear.

Cisco, a leader in switches and routers, uses a general troubleshooting strategy that consists of the following eight steps:

Step 1: Define the problem.
Step 2: Gather detailed information.
Step 3: Consider possible scenarios (brainstorm and come up with several possible or probable causes of the failure).
Step 4: Develop a plan to solve the problem.
Step 5: Implement the plan.
Step 6: Observe the results of the implementation.
Step 7: Repeat the process if the plan doesn't fix the problem.
Step 8: Document the changes after the problem is solved.

When analyzing a network problem, you must define the problem by making a clear problem statement (see Figure 1.6). You should define the problem in terms of a set of symptoms and potential causes. To properly analyze the problem, identify the general

Figure 1.6 Cisco Troubleshooting Model

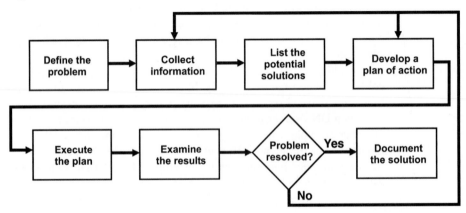

symptoms then ascertain what kinds of problems (causes) could result from these symptoms. For example, hosts might not respond to service requests from clients (a symptom). Possible causes might include a misconfigured host, bad interface cards, or missing router configuration commands.

Next, collect information by gathering facts that will help you isolate possible causes. You can start by asking the affected users some questions. In addition, you can talk to network administrators, managers, and other key personnel to check the status of the network and see if anything has been recently done to the computer and network. In addition, you may need to determine if the problem is affecting anyone else. This determines the scope of the problem. You will also collect information from sources such as network management systems, configuration commands, or protocol analyzer traces.

You would then list the potential causes and their solutions from the facts that you have gathered. Of course, using the facts, you can eliminate some of the potential problems from your list. Depending on the data, you might be able to eliminate hardware as a problem so that you can focus on software problems. At every opportunity, try to narrow the number of potential problems so that you can create an efficient plan of action. Of course, don't forget to check the obvious causes of a problem, including cables being connected properly on both ends, devices being turned on, and devices having their power connected.

After your action plan has been developed, begin with the most likely problem and devise a plan in which only one variable is manipulated. Changing only one variable at a time enables you to reproduce a given solution to a specific problem. If you alter more than one variable simultaneously you might solve the problem, but identifying the specific change that eliminated the symptom becomes far more difficult and will not help you solve the same problem again if it occurs in the future. Whenever you change a variable, be sure to gather results. In addition, keep in mind that some situations may have more than one cause. If the problem has not been resolved, you must then move to the next most likely cause on your list.

1.3.4   Preparing for Network Failure

It is always easier to recover from a network failure if you are prepared ahead of time. One of the most important requirements in any network environment is to have current and accurate documentation of your network available to the network support personnel at all times. If not, troubleshooting becomes much more difficult and the troubleshooting problem will take much longer to solve. In addition, always document any changes being made. When you solve a problem, be sure to document the problem and its solution so that you can refer to it in cases that have similar problems and to look for trends in the future.

To determine whether you are prepared for a network failure, answer the following questions:

- Do you have an accurate physical and logical map of your network?
- Does your organization or department have an up-to-date network map that outlines the physical location of all the devices on the network and how they are connected, as well as a logical map of network addresses, network numbers, subnetworks, and so forth?

■ Do you have a list of all network protocols implemented in your network?

■ For each of the protocols implemented, do you have a list of the network numbers, subnetworks, zones, and areas that are associated with them?

■ Do you know which protocols are being routed?

■ For each routed protocol, do you have correct, up-to-date router configuration?

■ Do you know which protocols are being bridged?

■ Are any filters configured in any bridges, and do you have a copy of these configurations?

■ Do you know all the points of contact to external networks, including any connections to the Internet?

■ For each external network connection, do you know what routing protocol is being used?

■ Do you have an established baseline for your network?

■ Has your organization documented normal network behavior and performance at different times of the day so that you can compare the current problems with a baseline?

NOTE: Don't worry if you don't know what some of the terms mean. One of the goals of this book is to explain these terms and to show you how they relate to troubleshooting network problems.

Lastly, before moving on to the next chapter, you must be reminded to perform backups on a regular basis and to store those backups in a safe place. This is because the best method of data recovery is to make sure you have backups. In addition, be sure to test your backups from time to time by trying to restore a nonessential file.

SUMMARY

1. Early computers, before PCs, were called mainframes. They were large, centralized computers used to store and organize data.

2. To access a mainframe operators use a dumb terminal, which consists of a monitor to display the data and a keyboard to input the data.

3. As computers became smaller and less expensive, PCs were introduced. Unlike mainframe computers, PCs are meant to be used by one person and contain its own processing capabilities.

4. A network consists of two or more computers connected together to share resources such as files or a printer.

5. For a network to function, it requires a network service to share or access a common media or pathway to connect the computers. To bring it all together, protocols give the entire system common communication rules.

6. Computers connect to the network by using a NIC. The NIC will then communicate by sending signals through a cable (twisted-pair, coaxial, or fiber optics) or by using wireless technology (infrared, microwaves, or radio waves).

7. The role of the NIC is to prepare and send data to another computer, receive data from another computer, and control the flow of data between the computer and the cabling system.

8. Protocols (TCP/IP, IPX, and NetBEUI) are the rules or standards that allow computers to connect to one another and enable computers and peripheral devices to exchange information with as little error as possible.

9. Today, networks are broken into three main categories: (1) LANs, (2) MANs, or (3) WANs.

10. A LAN has computers that are connected within a geographical close network, such as a room, a building, or a group of adjacent buildings.
11. A MAN is a network designed for a town or city, usually using high-speed connections such as fiber optics.
12. A WAN is a network that uses long-range telecommunication links to connect the network computers over long distances and often consists of two or more smaller LANs. Typically, LANs are connected through public networks such as the public telephone system.
13. An enterprise WAN is a WAN that is owned by one company or organization.
14. A global WAN is not owned by any one company and could cross national boundaries.
15. An Internetwork is a network that is internal to a company and is private. It is often a network consisting of several LANs that are linked together. Smaller LANs are known as subnetworks or subnets.
16. A repeater, which works at the physical OSI layer, is a network device used to regenerate or replicate a signal or to move packets from one physical media to another.
17. A hub, which works at the physical OSI layer, is a multiported connection point used to connect network devices via a cable segment.
18. A bridge, which works at the data link OSI layer, is a device that connects two LANs and makes them appear as one or is used to connect two segments of the same LAN. The two LANs being connected can be alike or dissimilar, such as an Ethernet LAN connected to a Token Ring LAN.
19. A switching hub (sometimes referred to as switch or a layer 2 switch) is a fast, multi-ported bridge that builds a table of the MAC addresses of all the connected stations.

20. A router, which works at the network OSI layer, is a device that connects two or more LANs. In addition, it can break a large network into smaller, more manageable subnets.
21. A brouter (short for bridge router) is a device that functions as both a router and a bridge.
22. A gateway is hardware and/or software that links two different types of networks by repackaging and converting data from one network to another network or from one network operating system to another.
23. When comparing PC problems to network problems, network problems can have a much more devastating effect on network users, can cost the company many hours of productivity, and can cause a loss of revenue.
24. If it is a server problem or a client work station problem, everything that applies to a PC problem also applies to a server or client problem. The problem could be hardware failure, compatibility, improper configuration, software glitches, environmental factors, or user error.
25. A network problem would include problems with the media that connects a server and/or client to the network and anything else the media connects to, including switches and routers.
26. Cisco, a leader in switches and routers, uses a general troubleshooting strategy that consists of the following steps: (1) define the problem, (2) gather detailed information, (3) consider possible scenarios, (4) devise a plan to solve the problem, (5) implement the plan, (6) observe the results of the implementation, (7) repeat the process if the plan doesn't fix the problem, and (8) document the changes after the problem is solved.
27. It is always easier to recover from a network failure if you are prepared ahead of time.

QUESTIONS

1. A network needs all of the following components except:
   a. protocol
   b. services
   c. media
   d. dedicated server

2. The _____ is used to connect to network's media.
   a. hard drive controller
   b. SCSI card
   c. motherboard
   d. network card

3. What are the rules or standards that allow computers to communicate with each other?
   a. media
   b. client software
   c. services
   d. protocols

4. Which type of network is made for a single building or campus?
   a. LAN
   b. global WAN
   c. MAN
   d. enterprise WAN

5. A _____ is a network that uses long-range telecommunication links to connect network computers over long distances.
   a. LAN
   b. WAN
   c. MAN
   d. NOS

6. Which of the following connectivity devices can be used as protocol translators between different networking environments?
   a. routers
   b. repeaters
   c. bridges
   d. gateways

7. Which of the following best describes the difference between bridges and routers?
   a. Bridges can segment network traffic while routers cannot segment network traffic.
   b. Routers can choose between multiple paths while bridges cannot choose the best path among multiple paths.
   c. Bridges can only be installed on an Ethernet network while routers can only be installed on a Token Ring network.
   d. Routers can link dissimilar physical media while bridges cannot link dissimilar physical media.

8. Your company has two LANs. One is a Windows NT network and the other is a Novell NetWare network. Users need access to resources and the ability to transmit data between LANs. Which of the following devices would you use to enable communications between dissimilar LANs that use different protocols?
   a. bridges
   b. gateways
   c. routers
   d. repeaters

9. A repeater is a device that regenerates signals so that they can travel on additional cable segments. Which of the following statements are true of repeaters?
   a. Repeaters can be used to solve the problem of crosstalk.
   b. Repeaters can be used to solve the problem of attenuation.
   c. Segments joined by a repeater must use the same physical media.
   d. Segments joined by a repeater must use the same media access method.

10. Which connectivity devices should be used in a complex Ethernet 10BaseT network that uses both TCP/IP and NetBEUI protocols?
    a. amplifiers
    b. brouters
    c. routers
    d. terminators

11. Which device can be used with all media types and can provide flow control, broadcast management, and multiple communication paths?
    a. a bridge
    b. a gateway
    c. a router
    d. a repeater

12. There is excessive traffic on your Ethernet 10Base2 network. Which of the following devices can be used to split the network and reduce the amount of traffic on each segment?
    a. a bridge
    b. a gateway
    c. a repeater
    d. a terminator

13. Which connectivity device operates at the data link layer and joins two different networks to make them look like one network?
    a. NIC card
    b. router
    c. bridge
    d. gateway

14. You have a network that has very heavy traffic. You need to do something to segment the network. You want to keep certain work stations communicating with another group of work stations, which need to communicate with another group of work stations. What type of hardware would you implement to arrive at this configuration?
    a. router
    b. bridge
    c. brouter
    d. hub

15. You are setting up a network that uses both routable and nonroutable protocols and you need to minimize the amount of investment in equipment as well as the amount of equipment that will go into your rack. What type of connectivity device will you choose to implement?
    a. router
    b. bridge
    c. brouter
    d. switching hub

16. Which of the following troubleshooting steps is the LEAST important?
    a. Define the problem.
    b. Document the solution.
    c. Execute the plan.
    d. Develop a plan of action.
    e. None of the above.

17. Which of the following steps immediately follows *Examine the results* (Step 6) in the troubleshooting method?
   a. Collect additional information or develop a new plan of action.
   b. Determine if the problem has been resolved.
   c. Document the solution.
   d. Iterate the process.

18. Which two of the following actions are associated with *Define the problem* (Step 1) of basic troubleshooting (select 2 choices)?
   a. documenting symptoms
   b. narrowing possibilities
   c. listing possible causes
   d. recording details

CHAPTER 2

Introduction to the OSI Model

Topics Covered in this Chapter

Introduction

In the early days of networking, networking software was created in a haphazard fashion. When networks grew in popularity, the need to standardize the byproducts of network software and hardware became evident. Standardization allows vendors to create hardware and software systems that can communicate with one another, even if the underlying architecture is dissimilar. For example, you can use the TCP/IP protocol to access the Internet on an IBM-compatible PC running Windows or an Apple Macintosh running OS X.

Objectives

- Describe the OSI model and how it relates to networks.
- Recognize the different logical or physical network topologies (star, bus, mesh, ring, and wireless) given a schematic diagram or description.
- Specify the main features of 802.2 LLC and MAC.
- Identify the purpose, features, and functions of hubs, switches, bridges, routers, gateways, and NICs.
- Given an example, identify a MAC address.
- Identify the seven layers of the OSI model and their functions.
- Identify the OSI layers at which the hubs, switches, bridges, routers, and NICs operate.

- Explain the need for standardization in networks.
- List the differences between the de jure and de facto standards.
- Define *virtual circuit.*
- Define *sessions* and explain how they relate to networks.
- List and define the types of dialogs.
- List and define the 802 Project standards.
- Define *signaling, modulation,* and *encoding.*
- Define *bandwidth* and compare *baseband* and *broadband.*
- List and describe the different connection services.

2.1   THE NEED FOR STANDARDIZATION

To overcome compatibility issues, hardware and software often follow **standards** (dictated or most popular specifications). Standards exist for operating systems, data formats, communication protocols, and electrical interfaces. If a product does not follow a widely used standard, the product will probably not be widely accepted in the computer market and will often cause problems with your PC. As far as the user is concerned, standards help you determine what hardware and software to purchase and it allows you to customize a network made of components from different manufacturers.

As new technology is introduced, manufacturers rush to get their products out so that their product has a better chance of becoming the standard. Often, competing computer manufacturers introduce similar technology at the same time. Until one is designated as the standard, other companies and customers are sometimes forced to take sides. Because it is sometimes difficult to determine what will emerge as the true standard and because the technology sometimes needs time to mature, it is best to wait a while to see what happens.

There are two main types of standards. The first type is called ***de jure* standards** (by law standard). The *de jure standard* is a standard that has been dictated by an appointed committee such as the International Standards Organization (ISO). Some of the more common standard committees are shown in Table 2.1.

The other type of standard is the ***de facto* standard** (from the fact standard). A *de facto* standard is a standard that has been accepted by the industry just because it was the most common. These standards are not recognized by a standard committee. For example, the *de facto* for microprocessors are those produced by Intel while the *de facto* standard for sound cards are those produced by Creative Labs.

When a system or standard has an **open architecture,** it indicates that the specification of the system or standard is public. This includes approved standards as well as privately designed architecture whose specifications are made public by the designers. The advantage of an open architecture is that anyone can design add-on products based on the architecture. Of course, this also allows other manufacturers to duplicate the product.

Table 2.1 Common Standard Committees

American National Standards Institute (ANSI) http://www.ansi.org	ANSI is primarily concerned with software, has defined standards for a number of programming languages such as C Language, and has developed protocols for the SCSI interface.
Electronics Industry Alliance (EIA) http://www.eia.org	The EIA is a trade organization composed of representatives from electronics manufacturing firms across the U.S. EIA is divided into several subgroups: the Telecommunications Industry Association (TIA); the Consumer Electronics Manufacturers Association (CEMA); the Joint Electron Device Engineering Council (JEDEC); the Solid State Technology Association; the Government Division; and the Electronic Information Group (EIG).
International Telecommunications Union (ITU) http://www.itu.int/	ITU defines international standards, particularly communications protocols. Formerly called the *Comité Consultatif Internationale Télégraphique et Téléphonique* (CCITT)
Institute of Electrical and Electronic Engineers (IEEE) http://www.ieee.org	IEEE sets standards for most types of electrical interfaces including RS-232C (serial communication interface) and network communications.
International Standards Organization (ISO) http://www.iso.ch/	ISO is an international standard for communications and information exchange.

The opposite of open architecture is a **proprietary system.** A proprietary system is privately owned and controlled by a company that has not divulged specifications which would allow other companies to duplicate the product. Proprietary architectures often do not allow mixing and matching products from different manufacturers and may cause hardware and software compatibility problems.

2.2   THE OSI REFERENCE MODEL

With the goal of standardizing the network world, the **International Organization for Standardization (ISO)** began development of the **open systems interconnection (OSI) reference model.** The OSI reference model was completed and released in 1984.

Today, the OSI reference model is the world's most prominent networking architecture model. It is a popular tool for learning about networks. OSI protocols, on the other hand, have had a long "growing up" period. While OSI implementations are not unheard of, OSI protocols have not yet attained the popularity of many proprietary and *de facto* standards.

The OSI reference model adopts a layered approach where a communication subsystem is broken down into seven layers, each one of which performs a well defined function. The OSI reference model defines the functionality that needs to be provided at each layer but does not specify actual services and protocols to be used at each one of these layers. From this reference model, actual protocol architecture can be developed (see Figure 2.1 and Table 2.2).

The ISO model separated the various functions so that a vendor did not have to write an entire protocol stack. One vendor could write device drivers for their device, and not worry about higher layers, and the work can be contained and modularized. This also speeds up the process of bringing a product the market as it minimizes code that a vendor needs to write. It also prevents changes in one layer from affecting other layers, so it does not hamper development.

To facilitate this, ISO has defined internationally standardized protocols for each one of the seven layers. The seven layers are divided into three separate groups: (1) application oriented (upper layers); (2) an intermediate layer; and (3) the network oriented (lower) layers.

> *NOTE:* For an easy way to remember the order of the OSI reference model, you should use the following mnemonics:

Please	Do	Not	Take	Sales	People's	Advice
Physical	Data link	Network	Transport	Session	Presentation	Application

All	People	Seem	To	Need	Data	Processing
Application	Presentation	Session	Transport	Network	Data link	Physical

When a computer needs to communicate with another computer, it will start with a network service, which is running in the application layer. The actual data that needs to be sent is generated by the software and is sent to the presentation layer. The presentation layer then adds its own control information called a header, which contains the presentation layer's requests and/or information. The packet is then sent to the session

Figure 2.1 The OSI Reference Model

OSI Reference Model

Application Concerned with the support of end user application processes	• Supports the local operating system via a redirector/shell. • Provides access for different file systems. • Provides common APIs for file, print, and message services.
Presentation Provides representation of the data	• Defines common data syntax and semantics. • Converts to format required by computer via data encoding and conversion functions.
Session Performs administrative tasks and security	• Establishes sessions between services. • Handles logical naming services. • Provides checkpoints for resynchronization.
Transport Ensures end-to-end, error-free delivery	• Breaks up blocks of data on send or reassembles on receive. • Has end-to-end flow control and error recovery. • Provides a distinct connection for each session.
Network Responsible for addressing and routing between subnetworks	• Forms internetwork by providing routing functions. • Defines end-to-end addressing (logical – Net ID + Host ID). • Provides connectionless datagram services.
Data Link Responsible for the transfer of data over the channel	• Sends frames; turns received bits into frames. • Defines the station address (physical); provides link management. • Provides error detection across the physical segment.
Physical Handles physical signaling, including connectors, timing, voltages, and other matters	• Provides access to media. • Defines voltages and data rates for sending binary data. • Defines physical connectors.

layer where another header is added. It keeps going down the OSI model until it reaches the physical layer, which means that the data is sent on the network media by the NIC (see Figure 2.2). The concept of placing data behind headers (and before trailers) for each layer is called **encapsulation** by Cisco documentation.

When the data packet gets to the destination computer, the NIC sends the data packet to the data link layer. The data link layer then strips the first header off. As it goes up the model, each header is stripped away until it reaches the application layer. At that time, only the original data is left. It is then processed by the network service.

What is so great about this system is that it allows you to communicate with different computer systems. For example, a Windows NT server can send information to a UNIX server or an Apple Macintosh client.

Let's follow the steps of communication between two computers from initial contact to data delivery. A computer wants to request a file. The process would start with a network

Table 2.2   Common Technologies as They Relate to the OSI Model

OSI model layer	TCP/IP	Novell NetWare	Microsoft Windows
Application	FTP, SMTP, Telnet	NDS	SMB
Presentation	ASCII, MPEG, GIF, JPEG	NCP	NetBIOS
Session		SAP	NetBEUI
Transport	TCP, UDP	SPX	NetBEUI
Network	IP	IPX	NetBEUI
Data link	Ethernet, 802.3, 802.5, FDDI, Frame Relay, ISDN	Ethernet, 802.3, 802.5, FDDI, Frame Relay, ISDN	Ethernet, 802.3, 802.5, FDDI, Frame Relay, ISDN
Physical	10Base-T, 100Base-T, UTP 4/16 Unshielded Twisted Pair, SONET	10Base-T, 100Base-T, UTP 4/16 Unshielded Twisted Pair, SONET	10Base-T, 100Base-T, UTP 4/16 Unshielded Twisted Pair, SONET⁻

Figure 2.2   Layer Interaction of the OSI Reference Model

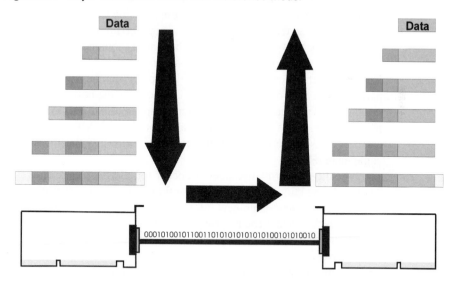

application on the client computer. Before the request can be made, the client had to first determine the address of the computer. Therefore, it sends a request out to resolve a computer name to a network address.

If the client already knows the server's network address, it will make its request in the form of a data packet and send it to a presentation layer protocol. The presentation protocol would encrypt and compress the packet and send it to a session layer protocol, which would establish a connection with the server. During this time, the packet would include the type of dialog (such as half-duplex connection, discussed later in this chapter) and determine how long the computer can transmit to the server. The session protocol will then send the packet to the transport layer, which will divide the packet into smaller packets so that it can be sent over the physical network. The transport layer protocol will then send the packets to the network layer where the source network and destination network addresses are added. It will then send the packets to a data link layer so that it can add the source and destination address and the port number that identifies the service requested and prepare the packets to be sent over the media. As you can see in Figure 2.2, the packet is much bigger than it was when the process was started. The packet is then converted to electrical or electromagnetic signals that are sent on the network media.

When the packets get to the destination server, the NIC sees the signals and interprets the signals as 0s and 1s. It then takes the bits and groups them together into frames. It will then determine the destination address of the packet to see if the packet was meant for the server. After the server has determined that it was, it will then remove the data link header and send the packet up to the network layer. The network layer will remove the network header and send the packet to the transport layer. If the data packets have reached the server out of order, the transport layer protocol will put them back into the proper order, merge them into one larger packet, and send the packet to the appropriate session layer protocol. The session layer protocol will authenticate the user and send the packet to the presentation layer protocol. The presentation layer protocol will decompress, decrypt, and reformat the packet so that it can be read by the application layer protocol. The application layer protocol will read the request and take the appropriate steps to fulfill it.

Before the packet is actually sent, the sending computer must determine if the packet is to go to another computer within the same network or to a computer in another network. If it is local, the packets are sent to the computer. If it has to go to another network, the packet is sent to a router. The router will determine the best way to get to its destination and then send the packet from one router to another until it gets to the destination network. If one network route is congested, it can reroute the packet another way and if it detects errors, it can slow down the transmission of the packets in the hopes that the link will become more reliable.

In reality, encapsulation does not occur for all seven layers. Layers 5 through 7 use headers during initialization, but in most flows, there is no specific layer 5, 6, or 7 header. This is because there is no new information to exchange for every flow of data. Therefore, layers 5, 6, and 7 can be grouped together and the layers actually used can be simplified into five layers: (1) application (equivalent to the application, presentation and session layer); (2) transport; (3) Internet (equivalent to the network layer); (4) network interface (equivalent to the data link layer); and (5) physical layer (see Figure 2.3).

When encapsulation with TCP/IP is used, the order in which information blocks are created is data, segments, packets, frames, then bits. The user application creates the data and a variety of parameters and passes the segment to the network layer. The network layer places the destination network address in a header, puts the data behind it, and transmits a packet (datagram) to the data link layer. The data link layer creates the data link header, which includes the destination MAC address. The datagram is converted to a frame and is passed to the physical layer. The physical layer transmits the bits (see Figure 2.4).

Figure 2.3   Encapsulation that Actually Occurs on Today's Networks

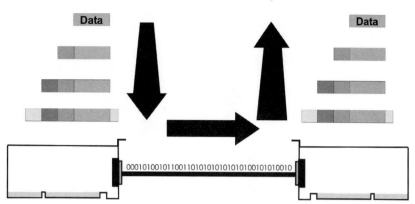

Figure 2.4   Information Blocks Associated with the Simplified OSI Model

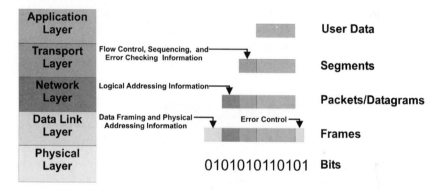

Many protocols will have the destination computer send back an acknowledgment stating that the packet arrived intact. If the source computer does not receive an acknowledgement after a certain amount of time, it will resend the packet.

Example:

Let's say you are running a word processor and you decide to access a file that is located on a remote computer's shared directory. A shared directory is a directory on a computer that provides the directory to clients over the network. The user clicks on the open button so that they can view the files of the remote computer. The word processor initiates the entire process by generating a network request. The request is sent through a client/redirector, which forwards the request to a network protocol such as TCP/IP. The packet is then forwarded to the NIC driver and sent out through the NIC where it is sent through the network to the remote computer. Of course, as the request is being sent down from the word processor to the NIC, the request becomes bigger as the packet is encapsulated (see Figure 2.5).

Figure 2.5   A Network Request Going Through the Simplified OSI Model

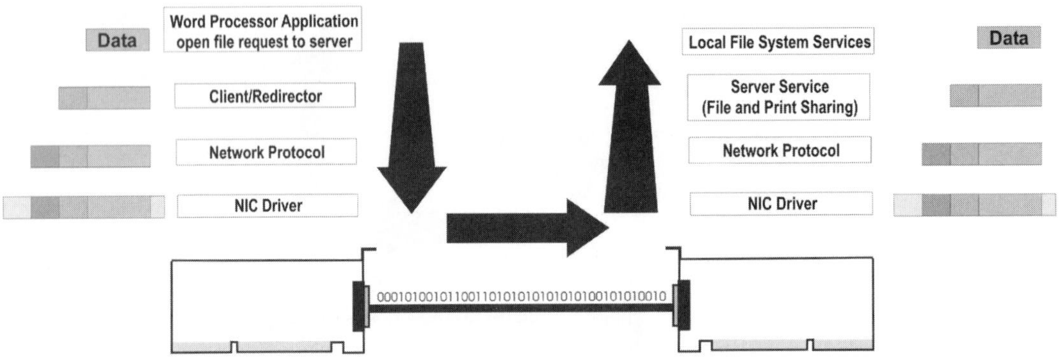

When the packets are received at the remote computer, they are processed by the driver on the remote computer. They are then forwarded to the network protocol, which is then forwarded to the server service (file and print sharing). The server service then uses the local file system services to access the file. As the packets go from the NIC to the local file system services, they are stripped back to the original request. The file is then sent back to the requesting computer.

2.3   THE PHYSICAL LAYER

The network oriented/lower layers are concerned with the protocols associated with the physical part of the network, which allows two or more computers to communicate. The **physical layer** is responsible for the actual transmission of the bits sent across a physical media. It allows signals, such as electrical signals, optical signals, or radio signals to be exchanged among communicating machines. Therefore, it defines the electrical, physical, and procedural characteristics required to establish, maintain, and deactivate physical links. This includes how the bits (0s and 1s) of data are represented and transmitted. It is not concerned with how many bits make up each unit of data, nor is it concerned with the meaning of the data being transmitted. In the physical layer, the sender simply transmits a signal and the receiver detects it. Lastly, the physical layer is also responsible for the physical topology or actual network layout. The physical layer includes the network cabling, hubs, repeaters, and NIC.

2.3.1   Point-to-Point and Multipoint Connections

All physical topologies are variations of two fundamental methods of connecting devices, point-to-point and multipoint (see Figure 2.6). **Point-to-point** topology connects two nodes together through direct cabling. For example, two computers connected together using modems, a PC communicating with a printer using a parallel cable, or WAN links connecting two routers using a dedicated T1 line. In a point-to-point link, the two devices

Figure 2.6   Point-to-Point and Multipoint Connections

monopolize the communication medium between the two nodes. Because the medium is not shared, nothing is needed to identify the two nodes. Whatever data is sent from one device is sent to the other device.

Multipoint connections link three or more devices together through a single communication medium. Because multipoint connections share a common channel, each device needs a way to identify itself and the device to which it wants to send information. The method used to identify senders and receivers is called **addressing.** SCSI devices connected on a single ribbon cable are identified with their SCSI ID numbers. NICs connected on a network are identified by their media access control (MAC) address.

Topology describes the appearance or layout of the network. Depending on how you look at the network, there is the physical topology and the logical topology. The **physical topology** (part of the physical layer) describes how the network actually appears. The **logical topology** (part of the data link layer) describes how the data flows through the physical topology or the actual pathway of the data. While the physical topology is easy to recognize, the logical topology is not. The logical topology describes how the data flows through the physical topology. The physical and logical topologies are not always the same.

2.3.2   Physical Topology

As stated above, the physical topology describes how devices on a network are wired or connected together. The types of physical topologies used in networks are as follows (see Table 2.3):

- bus topology
- ring topology
- star topology
- cellular
- mesh topology

A **bus topology** looks like a line and data is sent along the single cable. The two ends of the cable do not meet and the two ends do not form a ring or a loop (see Figure 2.7). All **nodes** (devices connected to the computer including networked computers, routers, and network printers) listen to all of the traffic on the network but only accept the packets that are addressed to them. The single cable is sometimes referred to as a segment, a backbone cable, or a trunk. Because all computers use the same backbone cable, the bus topology is very easy to set up and install and the cabling costs are minimized. Unfortunately, traffic

Table 2.3   Physical Topologies

Topology	Installation	Expansion/ reconfiguration	Troubleshooting	Media failure
Bus	Relatively easy	Moderately difficult	Difficult	Breaks in the bus prevent transmission
Ring	Moderately easy	Moderately difficult	Easy	Breaks in the ring prevent transmission (partial for dual rings)
Star	Easy but time consuming to install	Easy	Easy	Break in one cable only affects one computer
Mesh	Difficult	Difficult	Easy	Very low
Cellular	Easy	Easy	Moderately easy	Very low

Figure 2.7   Two Examples of Bus Topologies

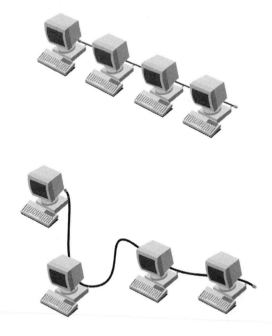

easily builds up on this topology and it is not a recommended topology for large networks. An example of a bus topology includes Ethernet (10Base2 and 10Base5).

Typically, with a bus topology network, the two ends of the cable must be terminated. This is because when signals get to the end of a cable segment, they have a tendency to bounce back and collide with new data packets. If there is a break anywhere or if one sys-

Figure 2.8 Two Examples of Ring Topologies

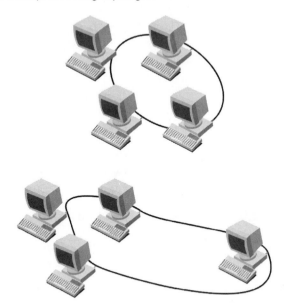

tem does not pass the data along correctly, the entire network will go down. This is because a break divides the trunk into two pieces, each with an end that is not terminated. In addition, these problems are difficult to troubleshoot because a break causes the entire network to go down with no indication of where the break is.

A **ring topology** has all devices connected to one another in a closed loop (see Figure 2.8). Each device is directly connected to two other devices. Typically in a ring, each node checks to see if the packet was addressed to it and acts as a repeater (duplicates the data signal, which helps keep the signal from degrading) for the other packets. This allows the network to span large distances. Though it might look inefficient, this topology sends data very quickly because each computer has equal access to communicate on the network.

Traditionally, a break in the ring will cause the entire network to go down and can be difficult to isolate. Today, some networks have overcome these pitfalls by allowing computers to continue communication with their connected partners by using dual rings for fault tolerance and by programming computers to act as beacons if they notice a break in the ring. Lastly, because each node is a repeater, the networking device tends to be more expensive than other topologies. IBM token ring and fiber distributed data interface (FDDI) are examples of ring topologies.

A **star topology** is the most popular topology in use. It has each network device connect to a central point, such as a hub, which acts as a multipoint connector. Other names for a hub would be a concentrator, a multipoint repeater, or a media access unit (MAU) (see Figure 2.9).

Star networks are relatively easy to install and manage, but may take some time to install because each computer requires a cable that runs back to the central point. If a link

Figure 2.9 Star Topology

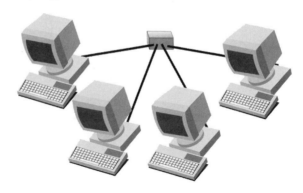

Figure 2.10 Mesh Topology and Modified Mesh Topology

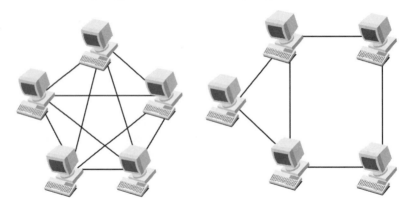

fails (hub port or cable), the remaining work stations are not affected like work stations in a bus and ring topology are. Unfortunately, bottlenecks can occur because all data must pass through the hub. An example is an Ethernet (10base-T and 100Base-TX).

Another topology is the **mesh topology** where every computer is linked to every other computer. While this topology is not very common in LANs, it is common in WANs where it connects remote sites over telecommunication links. This is the hardest to install and re-configure because the number of cables increases geometrically with each computer that you add.

NOTE: Some networks will use a modified mesh topology, which has multiple links from one computer to another but doesn't necessarily have each computer linked to every other computer (see Figure 2.10).

Many wireless technologies use a **cellular topology** where an area is divided into cells. A broadcast device is located at the center and broadcasts in all directions to form an invisible circle (cell). All network devices located within the cell communicate with the network through the central station or hub, which is interconnected with the rest of the network infrastructure. If the cells are overlapped, devices may roam from cell to cell while maintaining connection to the network (see Figure 2.11). The best known example of cellular topology is a cellular phone.

The **hybrid topology** scheme combines two of the traditional topologies to create a larger topology. In addition, the hybrid topology allows you to use the strengths of the various topologies to maximize the effectiveness of the network. Examples of a hybrid topology would be the bus star topology and the star ring topology (see Figure 2.12).

Figure 2.11 Cellular Topology

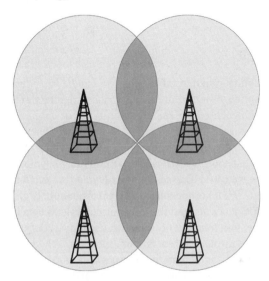

Figure 2.12 Hybrid Topologies (Bus Star and Star Ring)

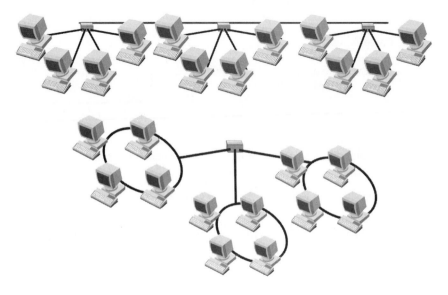

2.3.3 Segments and Backbones

A segment could be a single cable such as a backbone cable, or a cable that connects a hub and a computer. A logical segment contains all the computers on the same network and contains the same network address such as networks with a backbone cable or a hub used in a logical bus topology.

A backbone can be used as a main cable segment such as that found in a bus topology network. This would include a long single cable with patch cables used to attach the computers or smaller cables connected together with barrel and T-connectors. In addition, a backbone can be referred to as the main network connection through a building, campus, WAN, or the Internet.

2.3.4 Cables

The cabling system used in networks can be considered to be the "veins" of the network. The cabling system connects all of the computers together and allows them to communicate with each other. The common types of cabling include UTP, shielded twisted pair (STP), coaxial, and fiber optic (see Table 2.4). The UTP, STP and coaxial cables use copper wire to carry electrical signals and fiber optic cable carries light signals.

Frequency (bandwidth) is the number of cycles that are completed per unit of time and is generally expressed in hertz (cycles per second). Data cabling is typically rated in kilohertz (KHz) or megahertz (MHz). The more cycles per second, the more interference the cable generates and the more susceptible to data loss the cable is.

The data rate (or information) capacity is defined as the number of bits per second that move through a transmission medium. When you choose a cable, you must choose one that will handle your current network traffic and you must allow for growth.

With traditional cabling, there is a fundamental relationship between the number of cycles per second that a cable can support and the amount of data that can be pushed through the cable. For example, Category 5 and Category 5e cables are rated at 100 MHz. To im-

Table 2.4 Cable Types

Cable type	Cable cost	Ease of installation	Installation cost	EMI sensitivity	Data bandwidth	Comments
UTP	Lowest	Very simple	Lowest	Highest	Lowest to high	Used in more than 80% of LANs
STP	Medium	Simple to moderate	Moderate	Moderately low	Moderate	Usually found in older networks
Coaxial	Medium	Simple	Moderate	Moderate	High	Often used as a backbone cable
Fiber optic	Highest	Difficult	Highest	None	Very high	Uses light instead of electrical signal

plement a 100Base-TX network, you must be using Category 5 cabling because the cable must support a frequency of 100 MHz. During each digital cycle, a single bit is pushed through.

While this is a good way to think of the relationship between information rate and cable bandwidth, the IEEE recently approved the 803.3ab standard (1000Base-T), which covers running Gigabit Ethernet over Category 5 cabling. Category 5 does not operate at 1 GHz. Instead, the cable uses four data pairs to transmit the data and uses sophisticated encoding (multiplexing) techniques to send more bits of data over the wire during each cycle.

In copper wiring, a signal loses energy during its travel because of the electrical properties at work in the cable. The opposition to the flow of current through a cable or circuit is called impedance. Impedance is a combination of resistance, capacitance, and inductance and is expressed in ohms. A typical UTP cable is rated at between 100 and 120 ohms. All Category 3, 4, 5, and 5e cables are rated at 100 ohms.

Attenuation is when the strength of a signal declines over distance on a transmission medium. This loss of signal strength is caused by several factors such as the signal converted to heat due to the resistance of the cable and the energy is reflected as the signal encounters impedance changes throughout the cable. Low decibel values of attenuation are desirable because that means less of the signal is lost on its way to the receiver.

Interference occurs when undesirable electromagnetic waves affect the desired signal. Interference can be caused by **electromagnetic interference (EMI)** caused by large electromagnets used in industrial machinery, motors, fluorescent lighting, and power lines. **Radio frequency interference (RFI)** is caused by transmission sources such as a radio station. Another term used to describe instability in a signal wave is **jitter,** which is caused by signal interference.

Besides looking at the capacity and electrical characteristics of the cable, you also need to look at two other factors when choosing a cable. First, you should look at cost. If you are installing a large network within a building, you will find that the cabling system can cost thousands of dollars.

> *NOTE:* The cost of installing the cable (planning and hourly wages) is many times the cost of the cable itself. Therefore, you must make sure that you have the financial resources available to install such a system.

Second, you should look at the ease of installation of the cabling system because this affects your labor costs and can indirectly affect the reliability of the network. In addition, you should look at the ease of troubleshooting, including how it is affected by media faults and if the cable system offers any fault tolerance.

A **twisted pair** consists of two insulated copper wires twisted around each other. While each pair acts as a single communication link, twisted pairs are usually bundled together into a cable and wrapped in a protective sheath (see Figure 2.13).

Figure 2.13 Twisted Pair Cable

Question:

Why are the wires twisted around each other?

Answer:

The reason that they are twisted is because copper wire does not constrain electromagnetic signals well. This means that if you have two copper wires next to each other, the signal will induct (law of induction) or transfer from one wire to the other. This phenomenon is called **crosstalk.**

The circuits that send data on the cable are differential amplifiers. Twisted wires ensure that the noise is the same on each wire. The common noise is then canceled at the differential amplifier. Because the data is inverted on the second wire, the data is not canceled. Therefore, by using twisted pair, the crosstalk is canceled.

Twisted pair can be either **unshielded twisted pair (UTP)** or **shielded twisted pair (STP).** Of these, unshielded twisted pair is the same type of cable that is used with telephones and is the most common cable used in networks (see Figure 2.14). UTP cable consists of four pairs of wires in each cable. Each pair of wires is twisted around each other and used together to make a connection. Compared to other cable types (unshielded twisted pair, shielded twisted pair, coaxial cable, and fiber optic), UTP is inexpensive and is the easiest to install. The biggest disadvantages of UTP are its limited bandwidth of 100 meters and it is quite susceptible to interference and noise. Traditional UTP has had a limited network speed, but more recently UTP can be used in networks running between 4 Mbps and 1 Gbps. There are some companies such as Hewlett-Packard that are working on a 10 Gbps network standard.

In 1995, UTP cable was categorized by the EIA based on the quality and number of twists per unit. The UTP categories are published in EIA-568-A (see Table 2.5).

Early networks that used UTP typically used Category 3, while today's high-speed networks typically use Category 5 or Enhanced Category 5 cabling. Category 3 has three to four twists per foot and could operate up to 16 MHz, while Category 5 uses three to four twists per inch, contains Teflon insulation, and can operate at 100 MHz. Enhanced Category 5 is a higher quality cable designed to reduce crosstalk even further and support applications that require additional bandwidth.

While Category 6 was recently approved, Category 7 has not yet been approved. Therefore, no vendor can promise complete compatibility for Category 7 for future networks.

As network applications increased network traffic there was a need for faster networks. One way to increase the performance of the network is to use more expensive fast

Figure 2.14 UTP Cable

Table 2.5   Unshielded Twisted Pair Cable Categories for Networks

Cable type	Bandwidth (MHz)	Function	Attenuation	Impedance	Network usage
Category 3	16	Data	11.5	100Ω	10Base-T (10 Mbps), Token Ring (4 Mbps), Arcnet, 100VG-ANYLAN (100 Mpbs)
Category 4	20	Data	7.5	100Ω	10Base-T (10 Mbps), Token Ring, Arcnet, and 100VG-ANYLAN (100 Mpbs)
Category 5	100	High speed data	24.0	100Ω	10Base-T (10 Mbps), Token Ring, Fast Ethernet (100 Mbps), Gigabit Ethernet (1000 Mbps), and ATM (155 Mbps)
Category 5E (enhanced)	100	High speed data	24.0	100Ω	10Base-T (10 Mbps), Token Ring, Fast Ethernet (100 Mbps), Gigabit Ethernet (1000 Mbps), and ATM (155 Mbps)
Category 6	250	High speed data	19.8	100Ω	10Base-T (10 Mbps), Token Ring, Fast Ethernet (100 Mbps), Gigabit Ethernet (1000 Mbps), and ATM (155 Mbps)
Category 6E (enhanced)	250	High speed data	19.8	100Ω	10Base-T (10 Mbps), Token Ring, Fast Ethernet (100 Mbps), Gigabit Ethernet (1000 Mbps), and ATM (155 Mbps)
Category 7 (not yet approved)	600	High speed data			

electronic devices. A cheaper way is to increase the amount of usable bandwidth by using all four pairs of the UTP cable instead of using just two pairs.

While your telephone uses a cable with 2 pairs (4 wires) and a RJ-11 connector, computer networks use a cable with 4 pairs (8 wires) and a RJ-45 connector (see Figure 2.15). In a simple network, one end of the cable attaches to the NIC and the other end attaches to a hub (multi-ported connection).

With UTP wiring, you must be very careful about the quality of the RJ-45 connector crimping. Bad crimping can lead to intermittent connections or pulled out wires. You also must make sure that the pairs stay twisted right down to the connector.

In a larger network, one end of the cable will connect the network card of the computer to a wall jack. The wall jack is connected to the back of a patch panel kept in a server room or wiring closet. A cable is then attached to the patch panel and connected to a hub. The cables that connect the computer to the wall jack and the cable that connects the patch panel and the hub are called patch cables.

Figure 2.15   UTP Cable with a RJ-45 Connector and a UTP Cable with a RJ-11 Connector

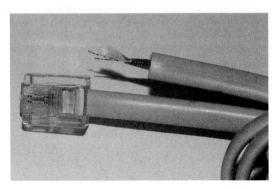

Figure 2.16   Shielded Twisted Pair Cable

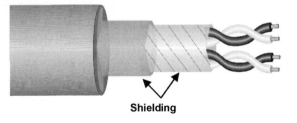

Shielded twisted pair cables are similar to unshielded twisted pair cables except that a STP is usually surrounded by a braided shield that serves to reduce both EMI sensitivity and radio emissions (see Figure 2.16). Shielded twisted pair cable was required for all high-performance networks such as IBM Token Ring until a few years ago and is commonly used in IBM Token Ring networks (see Figure 2.17) and Apple's LocalTalk network. STP is relatively expensive compared to UTP and is more difficult to work with.

Coaxial cable, sometimes referred to as coax, is a cable that has a center wire surrounded by insulation and then a grounded shield of braided wire (mesh shielding) (see Figure 2.18). The copper core carries the electromagnetic signal, and the braided metal shielding acts as both a shield against noise and a ground for the signal. The shield minimizes electrical and radio frequency interference and provides a connection to ground. Coaxial cable is the primary type of cable used by the cable television industry and is widely used for computer networks.

For computer networks, coaxial cables are usually used for the backbone cable for Ethernet networks. The network devices are attached by cutting the cable and using a T-connector or by applying a vampire tap (a mechanical device that uses conducting teeth

Figure 2.17   IBM Shielded Twisted Pair Cable

Figure 2.18   Coaxial Cable

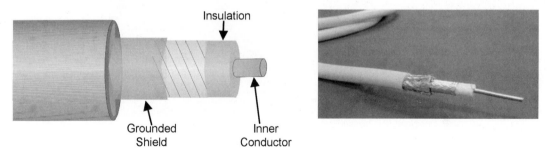

to penetrate the insulation and attach directly to the wire conductor). To maintain the correct electrical properties of the wire, you must terminate both ends of the cable and you must ground one end of the cable. The termination dampens signals that bounce back or reflect at the end of the cable. The ground completes the electrical circuit. Not grounding can lead to an undesirable charge in the coax, whereas grounding at both ends can lead to a difference in ground potential and cause an undesirable current on the coax, especially if they are between two buildings.

BNC Connector is short for British Naval Connector, Bayonet Nut Connector or Bayonet Neill Concelman. It is a type of connector used with coaxial cables such as the RG-58 A/U cable used with the 10Base-2 Ethernet system. The basic BNC connector is a male type mounted at each end of a cable. This connector has a center pin connected to the center cable conductor and a metal tube connected to the outer cable shield. A rotating ring outside the tube locks the cable to any female connector.

BNC T-connectors (used with the 10Base-2 system) are female devices for connecting two cables to a NIC (see Figure 2.19). A **BNC barrel** connector allows two cables to be connected together.

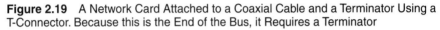

Figure 2.19 A Network Card Attached to a Coaxial Cable and a Terminator Using a T-Connector. Because this is the End of the Bus, it Requires a Terminator

Question:

You have two Ethernet hubs that you must link together as one network. Each hub contains a single BNC connector that allows you to connect the hubs together. Therefore, you take a coaxial cable and connect it directly from the BNC connector to the other BNC connector. Unfortunately, the hubs do not function together. What is the problem?

Answer:

The problem is that anytime you use a coaxial cable with Ethernet, you must always connect network devices using a T-connector. In addition, the two ends must be terminated with the proper terminating resistor.

A **fiber optic** cable consists of a bundle of glass or plastic threads. Each bundle is capable of carrying data signals in the forms of modulated pulses of light. While glass can carry the light pulses (several kilometers) even further than plastic, plastic is easier to work with. Because each thread can only carry a signal in one direction, a cable consists of two threads in separate jackets; one to transmit and one to receive. The fiber optic cable uses cladding that surrounds the optical fiber core, which helps reflect light back to the core and to ensure that little of the light signal is lost. Lastly, the cable contains kevlar strands to provide strength.

The light signals used in a fiber optic cable are generated by light emitting diodes (LEDs) or by injection laser diodes (ILDs). ILDs are similar to LEDs but produce laser light. Because laser light is purer than normal light, it can increase both the data rates and transmission distances. Signals are received by photodiodes, which are solid state devices that detect variations in light intensity.

Over the past five years, optical fibers have found their way into cable television networks—increasing reliability, providing a greater bandwidth, and reducing costs. In LANs, fiber cabling has been deployed as the primary media for campus and building backbones, offering high-speed connections between diverse LAN segments.

Fiber has the largest bandwidth (up to 10 GHz) of any media available. It can transmit signals over the longest distance (20 times farther than copper segments), at the lowest cost, with the fewest repeaters, and with the least amount of maintenance. In addition, because it has such a large bandwidth, it can support up to 1000 stations and it can support the faster speeds that will be introduced during the next 15 to 20 years.

Fiber optic cable is extremely difficult to tap, making it very secure and highly reliable. Because fiber optic cable does not use electrical signals running on copper wire, interference does not affect fiber traffic, and as a result the number of retransmissions is reduced and the network efficiency is increased.

Fiber optic cables use several connectors, but the two most popular and recognizable connectors are the straight tip (ST) and subscriber (SC) connectors. The ST fiber optic connector, developed by AT&T, is probably the most widely used fiber optic connector. It uses a BNC attachment mechanism similar to the Thinnet connector mechanism (see Figure 2.20).

The SC connector (sometimes known as the square connector) is a typically latched connector. This makes it impossible for the connector to be pulled out without releasing the connector's latch (usually by pressing some kind of button or release).

Figure 2.20   Fiber Optic Cable and Common Connectors (ST, SC, and MT-RJ)

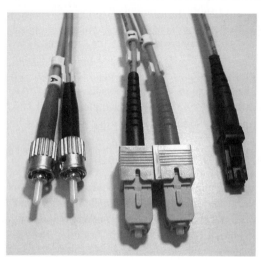

A new connector called the MT-RJ uses a connection that is similar to a RJ-45 connector. It offers a new small form factor two-fiber connector that is lower in cost and smaller than the duplex SC interface.

The main disadvantage of fiber optics is that the cables are expensive to install and they require special skills and equipment to split or splice cables. In addition, they are more fragile than wire. Fortunately, in recent years, while fiber optic products are being more mass produced, the cost gap between the high grades of UTP have closed significantly and there are many premade products available.

2.4   THE DATA LINK LAYER

The **data link layer** is responsible for providing error-free data transmission and establishes local connections between two computers. This is achieved by packaging raw bits from the physical layer into blocks of data called frames, and sending these frames with the necessary synchronization, error control, and flow control. Each frame includes a checksum (CRC) or some other form of error control information, a source address, a destination address, and the data. Each packet sent is a piece of a message. Because a package contains the data and destination address, each packet travels the network independently from other packets.

The data link layer is divided into two sublayers, the **logical link control (LLC)** sublayer (IEEE 802.2) and the **media access control (MAC)** sublayer. The media access control (MAC) sublayer is the lower sublayer and it communicates directly with the network adapter card. It defines the network logical topology, which is the actual pathway (ring or bus) of the data signals being sent. In addition, it allows multiple devices to use the same media and it determines how the NIC gets access or control of the network media so that two devices don't trample over each other. Lastly, it maintains the physical device address, known as the MAC address, which is used to identify each network connection so that a device can transmit a frame to another device. Lastly, it builds frames from bits that are received from the physical layer. Some examples of media access control sublayer protocols include CSMA/CA, CSMA/CD, token passing, and demand priority.

The LLC sublayer manages the data link between two computers within the same subnet. A subnet is a simple network or smaller network which is used to form a larger network. In addition, if we were operating a multi protocol LAN, each network layer protocol would have its own service access point (SAP), which is used by the LLC to identify which protocol it is. For example, TCP/IP, IPX/SPX, and NetBIOS would all have different SAPs so that it can identify which was which.

2.4.1   Physical Device Addressing

Because many network devices share the same transmission channel, the data link layer must have some way to identify itself from the other devices. The physical device address or **media access control (MAC) address** is a unique hardware address (unique on the LAN) burned onto a ROM chip assigned by the hardware vendors or selected with

Figure 2.21   Three Networks Connected Together with a Router. Each Computer is Identified by its Eight Hexadecimal Digit MAC Address. Notice the MAC Address 22-33-A3-34-43-43 is Used Repeatedly but on Different Networks

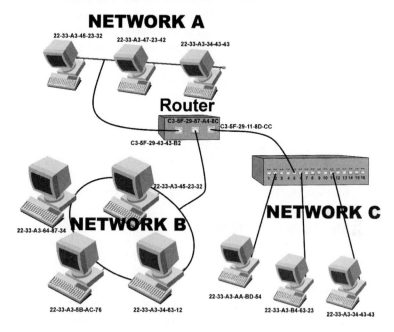

jumpers or DIP switches. It identifies a house or building within a city. Much like a street address within a city, you cannot have two NICs or nodes with the same MAC address on the same network. You can have the same MAC address on two separate networks. For Ethernet and Token Ring cards, the MAC address is embedded onto the ROM chip on the card (see Figure 2.21).

The MAC address is 48 bits (6 bytes) in length and is usually represented in format. The first 24 bits of a MAC address are referred to as the organizationally unique identifier, or OUI. OUIs are sold and assigned to network hardware vendors by the IEEE. The last 24 bits are assigned by the individual vendor. A MAC address is ordinarily expressed as 6 pairs of hexadecimal characters separated by colons. An example of a MAC address is 00:53:AD:B2:13:BA or 00-53-AD-B2-13-BA.

2.4.2   Logical Topology

As introduced with the data link layer, **topology** describes the appearance or layout of the network. Depending on how you look at the network, there is the physical topology and the logical topology. The **physical topology** (part of the physical layer) describes how the network actually appears. The **logical topology** (part of the data link layer) describes how the data flows through the physical topology or the actual pathway of the data. While the physical topology is easy to recognize, the logical topology is not. The physical and logical topologies are not always the same. There are two logical topologies: (1) bus and (2) ring.

Let's look at an example of Ethernet that uses a backbone cable. It is a network that is physically a bus topology. The pathway of the signals or the logical topology is also a bus topology. If you compare that to an Ethernet network using a star topology, the physical network is a star topology. Yet the pathway or logical topology is a bus. This is because each cable attached to the hub has two wires. One wire is used to carry data from the hub to the network device and another wire is to carry the data from the network device to the hub. The hub then connects the pairs of wires with each other creating a large bus pathway. Of course, the bus has two ends that are each contained within the hub (see Figure 2.22).

Another example would be to look at an IBM Token Ring network. One form of Token Ring is connecting the network devices using a star topology. While this network has a physical star topology, the pathway or logical topology is a ring. This difference between the Ethernet hub and the Token Ring MAU is that while the hub contains two cable ends, the Token Ring MAU connects the two ends to form a ring (see Figure 2.23).

2.4.3   Media Access Methods

The set of rules that define how a computer puts data onto the network cable and takes data from the cable is called the **access method.** The access method is sometimes referred to as **arbitration.** While multiple computers share the same cable system, only one device can access a cable at the same time. Of course, if two devices do use the same cable at the same time, both data packets sent by the card become corrupted. Typical cable access methods are:

- Contention
- Token passing

Figure 2.22   Two Examples of a Logical Bus Topology

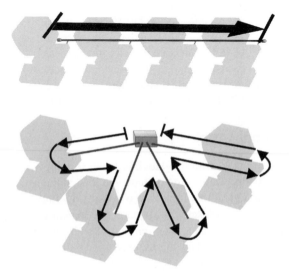

Figure 2.23   Logical Ring Topology

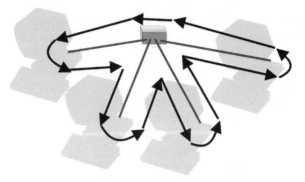

- Polling
- Demand priority

Contention is when two or more devices contend for network access. Any device can transmit whenever it needs to send information. To avoid data collisions (two devices sending data at the same time), specific contention protocols requiring the device to listen to the cable before transmitting data were developed.

The most common form of contention is called **carrier sense multiple access (CSMA)** network. Even though each station listens for network traffic before it attempts to transmit, it remains possible for two transmissions to overlap on the network or to cause a collision. As a result of collisions, access to a CSMA network is somewhat unpredictable and CSMA networks can be referred to as random or statistical access networks. To avoid collisions, CSMA will use one of two specialized methods of collision management: (1) collision detection (CD) or (2) collision avoidance (CA).

The collision detection approach listens to network traffic as the NIC is transmitting. By analyzing network traffic, it detects collisions and initiates retransmissions. **Carrier sense multiple access with collision detection (CSMA/CD)** is the access method utilized in Ethernet and IEEE 802.3. Collision avoidance uses time slices to make network access smarter and avoid collisions. **Carrier sense multiple access with collision avoidance (CSMA/CA)** is the access mechanism used in Apple's LocalTalk network.

While contention is a very simple access method that has low administrative overhead requirements, high traffic levels cause more collisions, which cause a lot of retransmitting, which causes even slower network performance.

Token passing uses a special authorizing packet of information to inform devices that they can transmit data. These packets, called tokens, are passed around the network in an orderly fashion from one device to the next. Devices can transmit only if they have control of the token, which distributes the access control among all the devices. Token Ring uses a ring topology, and each station passes the token to the next station in the ring. ARCnet uses a token passing bus as it passes the token to the next higher hardware address (MAC address), regardless of its physical location on the network.

Token passing is deterministic because you can calculate the maximum time before a work station can grab the token and begin to transmit. In addition, you can assign priorities to certain network devices that will use the network more frequently. If a work station has an equal or higher priority than the priority value in the token, it can take possession of the token.

Polling has a single device such as a mainframe front-end processor designated as the primary device. The primary device polls or asks each of the secondary devices known as "slaves" if they have information to be transmitted. Only when it is polled does the secondary computer have access to the communication channel. To make sure that a slave doesn't hog all of the bandwidth, each system has rules pertaining to how long each secondary computer can transmit data.

The newest access method is called **demand priority.** In demand priority, a device makes a request to the hub and the hub grants permission. High-priority packets are serviced before any normal-priority packets. To effectively guarantee bandwidth to time-sensitive applications such as voice, video, and multimedia applications, the normal priority packets are promoted to a high priority after 200–300 ms.

2.5   THE 802 PROJECT MODEL

In the late 1970s, when LANs first began to emerge as a valuable potential business tool, the IEEE realized that there was a need for certain LAN standards, specifically for the physical and data link layer of the OSI reference model. To accomplish this, they launched Project 802, which was named for the year and month it began (1980, February). These standards have several areas of responsibility including the NIC, the WAN components, and the media components. They are shown in Tables 2.6 and 2.7 and Figure 2.24.

Of these, probably the two most popular 802 standards discussed are 802.3 CSMA/CD LAN (Ethernet) and 802.5 (Token Ring). When these two standards were originally created, the 802.3 standard performed better on smaller networks and the 802.5 standard performed better on larger networks. While both networks will slow down as more computers are added because of the increased traffic, the 802.5 network runs more efficiently as the number of collisions increase with the 802.3 network. Fortunately, the 802.3 network performance has been increased with increased bandwidth and enhanced with switches.

NOTE: Recently the 802.3u working group updated 802.3 to include Ethernet 100BaseT implementation. Another popular, more recently discussed 802 standard is the 802.11, which covers wireless networks.

2.6   THE NETWORK LAYER

The **network layer** is concerned with addressing and routing packets or datagrams in order to move the data from one network (or subnet) to another. This includes establishing, maintaining, and terminating connections between networks; making routing decisions;

Table 2.6 802 Project Standards

Standard	Category
802.1	Overview and architecture of internetworking including bridging and virtual LAN (VLAN)
802.2	Logical link control (LLC)
802.3	Carrier sense multiple access with collision detection (CSMA/CD) LAN (Ethernet)
802.4	Token bus LAN
802.5	Token Ring LAN
802.6	Metropolitan area network (MAN)
802.7	Broadband local area networks (BLAN)
802.8	Fiber optic technical advisory group
802.9	Integrated voice/data networks
802.10	Network security
802.11	Wireless networks
802.12	Demand priority access LAN, 100BaseVG-AnyLAN
802.14	Coaxial and fiber cable such as those found on cable television to support two-way communications

Table 2.7 Popular 802 Standards

Technology	Speed(s)	Access method	Topologies	Media
Ethernet (IEEE 802.3)	10, 100 or 1000 Mbps	CSMA/CD	Logical bus	Coax or UTP
Token Ring (IEEE 802.5)	4 or 16 Mbps	Token passing	Physical star, logical ring	STP or UTP
FDDI (IEEE 802.8)	100 or 200 Mbps	Token passing	Physical star, logical ring	Fiber optic or UTP (implemented as CDDI)
Wireless (IEEE 802.11)	1 or 11 Mbps	CSMA/CA	Cellular	Wireless

and relaying data from one network to another. The OSI model classifies a **host** as the computer or device that connects to the network that is the source or final destination of data and routers (intermediate systems) perform routing and relaying functions that link the individual networks. Therefore, routers are network layer devices.

Figure 2.24 The 802 Standards

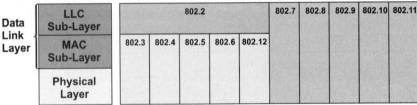

2.6.1   Network Addressing

For a device to communicate with another device, the device will require two pieces of information: (1) a logical address associated with the source and destination stations and (2) a path through the network to reach the desired destination. Both of the required bits of information are stored in the device's routing table. The addresses within the routing table are logical network addresses that contains two parts: (1) one part that identifies the network and (2) another part that uniquely identifies the host on each of those networks. If the address of the destination device is known to the device, it will broadcast the packet to the remaining interfaces.

For each network to operate on an internetwork and to identify themselves to each other, each network must be assigned a network ID. Therefore, at the network layer, networks are identified with a unique **network address.** This means that every computer on an individual LAN must use the same network address. Of course, if the LAN is connected to other LANs, its address must be different from all of the other LANs. Physical device addresses (MAC address) and logical network addresses are used jointly to move data between devices on an internetwork.

When planning out a network, assign logical addresses to each host. For example, when you use the TCP/IP protocol, the administrator assigns IP addresses to each computer. The IP address contains the network address for the subnet that the host is on and a host address to represent the host on the subnet.

As a packet is sent to a remote host several networks away, the packets are sent to the first router. The router looks at its destination by looking at the logical address. It then determines which way to send the packet, strips off and rebuilds the data link layer source and destination address information, and sends the packet to the next router. When the packet gets to the next router, the router reads the logical address to determine its destination. It then determines which way to send the packet, strips off and rebuilds the data link layer source and destination address information, and sends it to the next router. It will keep doing this until it gets to the destination network and sends it to the destination computer.

Remember, the data link layer provides for the transmission of frames within the same LAN. The network layer performs the much more complex task of transmitting packets between two network computers or devices in the network, regardless of how many data links/routers exist between the two. Examples of network layer protocols that connect the networks together include IP and IPX. Examples of protocols that determine which route to take include RIP and OSPF.

A network computer or other networked device can perform several roles simultaneously. The term "entity" identifies the hardware and software that fulfills each individual role. Every entity must have its service address so that it can send and receive data. This address is usually referred to as a **port** or **socket,** which is used to identify a specific upper-layer software process or protocol. Multiple service addresses can be assigned to any computer on which several network applications are running.

For example, when you try to read a web page, the packet from the Internet is routed to your computer using a TCP/IP network. Because today's operating systems are multitasking environments, they can be running or accessing several different network services. The port, which is included in the packet, would be used to identify the type of packet so that the system would know which software on the host is needed for the packet.

Because a network computer can handle multiple conversations with other computers at the same time, the system must be able to keep track of the different conversations. Computers distinguish conversations by using either connection identifiers or transaction identifiers.

A common term that you will hear about when dealing with Windows and networking is the Windows Socket or WinSock. A Windows socket is a Windows implementation of the UC Berkeley Sockets application programming interface (API) that is used in TCP/IP protocols to connect to the appropriate TCP/IP service such as HTTP, FTP, or Telnet. The WINSOCK.DLL file is the Microsoft Windows interface for the TCP/IP protocol.

2.6.2   Routing Protocols

To determine the best route, the routes use complex routing algorithms, which take into account a variety of factors including the number of transmission media, the number of network segments, and the network segment that carries the least amount of traffic. Routers then share status and routing information with other routers so that they can provide better traffic management and bypass slow connections. In addition, routers provide additional functionality, such as the ability to filter messages and forward them to different places based on various criteria. Most routers are multiprotocol routers because they can route data packets by using many different protocols.

A metric is a standard of measurement, such as a hop count, that is used by routing algorithms to determine the optimal path to a destination. A hop is the trip a data packet takes from one router to another router or a router to another intermediate point in the network. On a large network, the number of hops a packet has taken toward its destination is called the "hop count." When a computer communicates with another computer, and the computer has to go through four routers, the packet sent from the first computer to the second would have a hop count of four. With no other factors taken in account, a metric of four would be assigned. If a router had a choice between a route with four metrics and a route with six metrics, it would choose the route with four metrics over the route with six metrics. Of course, if you want the router to choose the route with six metrics, you can overwrite the metric for the route with four hops in the routing table to a higher value.

To keep track of the various routes in a network, the routers will create and maintain routing tables. The routers communicate with one another to maintain their routing tables through a routing update message. The routing update message can consist of all or a portion of a routing table. By analyzing routing updates from all other routers, a router can build a detailed picture of network topology.

The various routing protocols use different metrics, including path length, hop counts, routing delay, bandwidth, load, reliability, and cost. Path length is the most common routing metric. Some routing protocols allow network administrators to assign arbitrary costs to each network link. In this case, path length is the sum of the costs associated with each link traversed. Other routing protocols define hop counts.

Routing algorithms can be differentiated based on several key characteristics. First, the capability of the routing algorithm to choose the best route is very important. One routing algorithm may use the number of hops and the length of delays, but may weigh the length of delay more heavily in the calculation. To maintain consistency and predictability, routing protocols use strict metric calculations.

Routing algorithms are designed to be as simple as possible. In other words, the routing algorithm must offer efficiency with a minimum of software and utilization overhead. But while being efficient, the routing algorithm must be robust so that it can quickly change routes when a route goes down because of hardware failure or a route has a high load (high amount of traffic). Of course, when this is happening, the routing algorithm must be stable.

Routing algorithms must converge rapidly. Convergence is the process of agreement by all routers of which routes are the optimal routes. When a route goes down, routers distribute the new routes by sending routing update messages. The time that it takes for all routers to get new routes in which they all agree on should be quick. If not, routing loops or network outages can occur. A routing loop is when a packet is forwarded back and forth between several routers without ever getting to its final destination.

Routers use distance vector-based routing protocols to periodically advertise or broadcast the routes in their routing tables, but they only send routing tables to their neighboring routers. Routing information exchanged between typical distance vector-based routers is unsynchronized and unacknowledged. Distance vector-based routing protocols are easy to understand and configure. The disadvantage is that multiple routes to a given network can reflect multiple entries in the routing table, which leads to a large routing table. In addition, if you have a large routing table, network traffic increases as it is periodically advertised the routing table to other routers, even after the network has converged. Lastly, for distance-vector protocols to traverse large internetworks can take several minutes. An example of a routing protocol that uses the distance vector algorithm is the router information protocol (RIP).

Link-state algorithms are also known as shortest-path-first algorithms. Instead of using broadcast, link-state routers send updates directly (or by using multicast traffic) to all routers within the network. Each router, however, sends only the portion of the routing table that describes the state of its own links. In essence, link-state algorithms send small updates everywhere. Because they converge more quickly, link-state algorithms are somewhat less prone to routing loops than distance-vector algorithms. In addition, link-state algorithms do not exchange any routing information when the internetwork has converged. They have small routing tables because they store a single optimal route for each network ID. On the other hand, link-state algorithms require more CPU power and memory than distance-vector algorithms. Link-state algorithms can be more expensive to implement and support and are harder to understand. Examples of a routing protocol that uses a link-state algorithm is TCP/IP's OSPF and IPX/SPX's NSLP.

2.7   THE TRANSPORT LAYER

The **transport layer** is the middle layer that connects the lower and upper layers together. In addition, the transport layer is responsible for reliable, transparent transfer of data (known as segments) between two end points. Because it provides end-to-end recovery of lost and corrupted packets and flow control, it deals with end-to-end error handling, dividing messages into smaller packets, numbers of the messages, and the repackaging of messages. In addition, if packets arrive out of order at the destination, the transport layer is responsible for reorganizing the packets back into the original order. Examples of transport layer protocols include SPX, TCP, UDP, and NetBEUI.

Computers and network devices often use long strings of numbers to identify themselves. The transport layer is responsible for name resolution where it can take a more meaningful name and translate it to a computer or network address. Examples of name resolution protocols would include domain name system (DNS) and Windows Internet naming service (WINS).

2.7.1   Connection Services

Networks are divided into connection-oriented and connectionless-oriented networks. In a **connection-oriented network,** either you must establish a connection using an exchange of messages or you must have a preestablished pathway between a source point and a destination point before you can transmit packets.

Handshaking is the process by which two devices initiate communications. Handshaking begins when one device sends a message to another device indicating that it wants to establish a communications channel. The two devices then send several messages back and forth that enable them to agree on a communications protocol.

To establish a connection in a connection-oriented service, the three steps are: (1) call setup (also known as a three-way handshake), (2) data transfer, and (3) call termination. Establishing a connection before transmitting packets is similar to making a telephone call. You must dial a number, the destination telephone must ring, and someone must lift the telephone receiver before you can begin communicating.

Connection-oriented services provide flow, error, and packet sequence control through acknowledgments. An **acknowledgment (ACK)** is a special message that is sent back to the sender when a data packet makes it to its destination. You can compare this to a letter sent at the post office with a return receipt that is sent back to the sender to indicate arrival at its destination.

While TCP and SPX are two examples of connection-oriented protocols, Frame Relay, when using Permanent Virtual Circuits (PVCs), does not require any message be sent ahead of time. Instead, it requires predefinition in the Frame Relay switches, establishing a connection between two Frame Relay attached devices. ATM PVCs are connection-oriented, for similar reasons.

The exchange of messages before data transfer begins is called a call setup or a three-way handshake:

1. The first "connection agreement" segment is a request for synchronization.
2. The second and third segments acknowledge the request and establish connection parameters (the rules) between hosts.

3. The final segment is also an acknowledgement. It notifies the destination host that the connection agreement has been accepted and that the actual connection has been established.

The data is then transferred. When transfer is complete, a call termination takes place to tear down the virtual circuit.

The disadvantage of using a connection-oriented network is that it takes time to establish a connection before transmitting packets. The advantage of using a connection-oriented network is that the connection can reserve bandwidth for specific connections. As a result, connection-oriented networks can guarantee a certain quality of service (QoS). By using quality of service to guarantee bandwidth, connection-oriented networks can provide sufficient bandwidth for audio and video without jitters or pauses and the transfer of important data within a timely manner. Lastly, the connection-oriented network can better manage network traffic and prevent congestion by refusing traffic that it cannot handle.

Connectionless protocols do not require an exchange of messages with the destination host before data transfer begins, nor do they make a dedicated connection (virtual circuit) with a destination host. Instead, connectionless protocols rely upon upper-level, not lower-level protocols for safe delivery and error handling. Because data is segmented and delivered in the order the data is received from the upper OSI layers, connectionless protocols do not sequence data segments. Therefore, connectionless protocols are best suited for situations where high data transfer rate and low data integrity is needed. An example of a connectionless protocol is UDP.

The data link, network, and transport layers offer connection services which define how two devices form a connection. The connection services determine the level of error detection, recovery, and flow control that is used in communicating data between two network devices. The data link layer is concerned with connection services from one device to another device within the LAN, while the network layer is concerned with connection services from one device to another device on different LANs. The transport layer is concerned with an end-to-end connection service (a type of overall quality assurance).

NOTE: To speed communication, most network layer protocols are connectionless-oriented and do not bother with sending or receiving acknowledgements. Instead, they let the transport layer handle acknowledgments and provide error control.

2.7.2   Error Control

Error control refers to the notification of lost or damaged data frames. This includes the following:

- The destination does not receive the data packet.
- The checksum does not match. A checksum value is mathematically generated before the data packet is sent, attached to the data packet, and is sent. When the data packet gets to its destination, the same mathematical calculation is performed. If the same value matches the value that was sent, the data is assumed intact.
- The packet size does not configure to minimum or maximum size requirements for the frame type used.

■ Noise, interference, and distortion, which scramble the data
■ The capacity of a channel or network device is exceeded, causing a buffer overflow.

Before continuing on, you need to differentiate between error detection and error recovery. Any header or trailer with a frame check sequence (FCS) or similar field can be used to detect bit errors in a protocol data unit (PDU). Error detection uses the FCS to detect the error, which results in discarding the PDU. Error recovery implies that the protocol reacts to the lost data and somehow causes the data to be retransmitted.

Regardless of which protocol specification performs the error recovery, they all work the same way. The transmitted data is labeled or numbered. After receipt, the receiver sends signals back to the sender that the data was received, using the same label or number to identify the data. If the data was not received, it will either tell the sender to resend the data or if no acknowledgement is received, it will assume that data was not received and resend the data.

2.7.3   Flow Control

Flow control is the process of controlling the rate at which a computer sends data. Depending on the particular protocol, both the sender and the receiver of the data (as well as any intermediate routers, bridges and switches) might participate in the process of controlling the flow from sender to receiver.

Flow control is needed because data is discarded when congestion occurs. A sender of data might be sending the data faster than the receiver can receive the data, so the receiver discards the data. Also, the sender might be sending the data faster than the intermediate switching devices (switches and routers) can forward the data, which also causes discards. Packets can also be lost due to transmission errors. This happens in every network, sometimes temporarily and sometimes regularly, depending on the network and the traffic patterns. The receiving computer can have insufficient buffer space to receive the next incoming frame, or possibly the processor is too busy to process the incoming frame. Intermediate routers might need to discard the packets based on temporary lack of buffers (holding space) or processing.

Flow control attempts to reduce unnecessary discarding of data. Flow control protocols do not prevent the loss of data due to congestion; these protocols simply reduce the amount of lost data, which reduces the amount of retransmitted traffic, which reduces overall congestion. However, with flow control, the sender is artificially slowed or throttled so that it sends data less quickly than it could without flow control. There are three methods of implementing flow control:

■ buffering
■ congestion avoidance
■ windowing

Buffering simply means that the computer reserves enough buffer space in memory so that a burst of incoming data can be held until processed. No attempt is made to actually slow the transmission rate of the sender of data. In fact, buffering is such a common method of dealing with changes in the rate of arrival of data that most of us would probably just assume that it is happening.

Congestion avoidance is the second method of flow control. The computer receiving the data notices that its buffers are filling. This causes either a separate PDU or field in a header to be sent toward the sender, signaling the sender to stop transmitting.

A preferred method might be to get the sender to simply slow down instead of stopping. This method would still be considered congestion avoidance, but instead of signaling the sender to stop, the sender would slow down.

The third category of flow control is called *windowing*. A window is the maximum amount of data the sender can send without getting an acknowledgement. When you have configured a window size of 4096, the sending machine waits for acknowledgement for 4096 bytes before transmitting another byte. If you have configured a window size of 8192, it's allowed to transmit 8192 bytes before an acknowledgement is received. This cuts down on the amount of traffic because the number of acknowledgements is reduced. If your network is stable, you will use a higher number for the window. If the network is not very stable, it best to use a low number to focus more on reliability instead of performance.

NOTE: Window size (in bytes) ranges from 0 to 1,073,741,823 bytes. The default value is 4128 bytes.

2.7.4   Multiplexing

Transport level communication protocols can use techniques called multiplexing and demultiplexing. This technique allows data from different applications to share a single data stream. When multiplexing occurs, the only way to tell one application from another is by identifying each unit of data with a transition mechanism such as a port number or a sequence number. Sequence numbers assure proper reassembly while port numbers assure appropriate application destination. Demultiplexing occurs when the destination computer receives the data stream and separates and rejoins the application's segments.

2.8   THE SESSION LAYER

Application-oriented layers are concerned with protocols that provide user network applications and services. The **session layer** allows remote users to establish, manage, and terminate a connection (a session). A **session** is a reliable dialog between two computers. In addition, the session layer enables two users to organize and manage their data exchange and to implement dialog control between the source and destination network devices, including the type of dialog (simplex, half duplex, full duplex) and how long a computer transmits. Simplex, half duplex and full duplex are explained later in this chapter. When establishing these sessions, it creates checkpoints in data streams. If a transmission fails, only the data after the last checkpoint must be retransmitted. Lastly, it implements security, such as the validation of usernames and password. Examples of session layer protocols include SQL, NFS, RPC, NetBIOS, FTP, NCP, and Telnet.

Data can flow in one of three ways: (1) simplex, (2) half duplex, and (3) full duplex. Simplex dialog allows communications on the transmission channel to occur in only one direction. Essentially, one device is allowed to transmit and all of the other devices receive. This is often compared to a public address (PA) system where the speaker talks to an audience but the audience does not talk back to the speaker.

Half duplex dialog allows each device to transmit and receive, but not at the same time. Therefore, only one device can transmit at a time. This is often compared to a CB radio or walkie-talkies. A full-duplex dialog allows every device to both transmit and receive simultaneously. For networks, the network media channels would consist of two physical channels: one for receiving and one for transmitting (see Figure 2.25).

2.9 THE PRESENTATION LAYER

The **presentation layer** ensures that information sent by an application layer protocol on one system will be readable by the application layer protocol on the remote system. This layer, unlike lower layers, is simply concerned with the syntax and the semantics of the transmitted information. Therefore, it acts as the translator between different data formats, protocols, and systems. It also provides encryption and decryption of data, compression and decompression of data, and network redirectors. Examples include NCP and SMB.

In addition, the presentation layer deals with character set translation. Not all computer systems use the same table to convert binary numbers into text. Most standard computer systems use the American standard code for information interchange (ASCII). Mainframe computers (and some IBM) network systems use the extended binary coded decimal interchange code (EBCDIC). They are totally different. Protocols at the presentation layer can translate between the two.

Another form of translation performed by the presentation layer is byte order translation. In big-endian architectures (used by PCs with Intel processors), when representing

Figure 2.25 Simplex, Half Duplex, and Full Duplex Communications

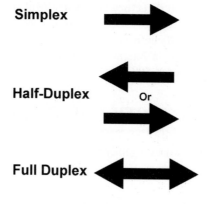

a multi-byte value, the leftmost bytes are the most significant. In little-endian architecture (used by systems based on Motorola processors), the rightmost bytes are the most significant. For example, the big-endian architecture would represent a 16-bit binary number as 11111111 01010101, while little-endian would represent the same 16-bit binary number as 01010101 11111111. To allow both of these types of systems to connect to the same network, the presentation layer will translate from one format to the other.

2.10   THE APPLICATION LAYER

The **application layer** represents the highest layer of the OSI reference model. It is responsible for interaction between the operating system and the network services and provides an interface to the system. It provides the user interface to a range of network wide distributed services including file transfer, printer access, and mail. Some examples of upper layer protocols would include File Transfer Protocol (FTP), Simple Mail Transfer Protocol (SMTP), AppleTalk and NFS.

NOTE: The application layer does not provide interface for software applications such as word processors and spreadsheets.

Directory services are network services that identify all resources on a network and make those resources accessible to users and applications. Resources can include e-mail addresses, computers, and peripheral devices (such as printers). Ideally, the directory service should make the physical network, including topology and protocols, transparent to the users on the network. They should be able to access any resources without knowing where or how they are physically connected.

There are a number of directory services that are widely used. The most common is the **X.500,** which uses a hierarchical approach in which objects are organized like the files and folders on a hard drive. At the top of the structure is the root container with children organized under it. X.500 is part of the OSI model, however, it does not translate well into a TCP/IP protocol environment. Therefore, many of the protocols that are based on the X.500 do not fully comply with it.

Lightweight directory access protocol (LDAP) is a set of protocols for accessing information directories. LDAP is based on the standards contained within the X.500 standard, but is significantly simpler. Unlike X.500, LDAP supports TCP/IP, which is necessary for any type of Internet access. Because it's a simpler version of X.500, LDAP is sometimes called X.500-lite.

2.11   CONNECTIVITY DEVICES

To connect networks together, there are several devices that can be used. These include repeaters, hubs, bridges, routers, brouters, and gateways.

Figure 2.26   A Repeater

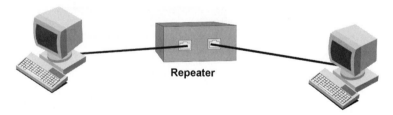

Repeater

2.11.1   Repeaters

A **repeater,** which works at the physical OSI layer, is a network device used to regenerate or replicate a signal or to move packets from one physical media to another.

> *NOTE:* A repeater cannot connect different network topologies or access methods. This can be used to regenerate analog or digital signals distorted by transmission loss over the length of a cable connection. Analog repeaters usually can only amplify the signal (including distortion) while digital repeaters can reconstruct a signal almost to its original quality (see Figure 2.26).

2.11.2   Hubs

A **hub,** which works at the physical OSI layer, is a multiported connection point used to connect network devices via a cable segment. When a PC needs to communicate with another computer, it sends a data packet to the port that the device is connected to. When the packet arrives at the port, it is forwarded or copied to the other ports so that all network devices can see the packet. In this way, all of the stations "see" every packet just as they do on a bus network. A standard hub is not very efficient on networks with heavy traffic because it causes a lot of collisions and retransmitted packets (see Figure 2.27).

Hubs can be categorized as either passive hubs or active hubs. A passive hub serves as a simple multiple connection point that does not act as a repeater for the signal. An active hub, which always requires a power source, acts as a multiported repeater for the signal.

> *NOTE:* When installing an active hub, make sure that the fan (which provides cooling) is operational.

The most advanced hub is called an intelligent hub (also known as a manageable hub). An intelligent hub includes additional features that enable an administrator to monitor the traffic passing through the hub and to configure each port in the hub. For example, you can prevent certain computers from communicating with other computers or you can stop certain types of packets from being forwarded. In addition, you can gather information on a variety of network parameters, such as the numbers of packets that pass through the hub and each of its ports, what types of packets they are, whether the packets contain errors, and how many collisions have occurred.

Figure 2.27   A Hub

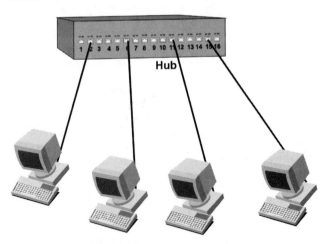

Hub

2.11.3   Bridges and Switching Hubs

A **bridge,** which works at the data link OSI layer, is a device that either connects two LANs and makes them appear as one or connects two segments of the same LAN. The two LANs being connected can be alike or dissimilar, such as an Ethernet LAN connected to a Token Ring LAN.

> *NOTE:* Bridges can connect dissimilar network types (for example, Token Ring and Ethernet) as long as the bridge operates at the LLC sublayer of the data link layer. If the bridge operates only at the lower sublayer (the MAC sublayer), the bridge can connect only similar network types (Token Ring to Token Ring and Ethernet to Ethernet).

Different from a repeater or hub, a bridge analyzes the incoming data packet and will forward the packet if its destination is on the other side of the bridge. Many bridges filter and forward packets with very little delay, making them good for networks with high traffic (see Figure 2.28).

Bridges that connect Ethernet networks are known as spanning tree bridges. Bridges that connect Token Ring networks are known as source routing bridges. Token Ring bridges usually do not do any filtering, but Ethernet bridges do.

A **switching hub** (sometimes referred to as a switch or a layer 2 switch) is a fast, multiported bridge that builds a table of the MAC addresses of all the connected stations. It then reads the destination address of each packet and forwards the packet to the correct port. A major advantage of using a switching hub is that it allows one computer to open a connection to another computer (or LAN segment). While those two computers communicate, other connections between the other computers (or LAN segments) can be opened at the same time. Therefore, several computers can communicate at the same time through the switching hub. As a result, the switches are used to increase performance of a network by segmenting large networks into several smaller, less congested LANs while providing necessary interconnectivity between them. Switches increase network performance by pro-

Figure 2.28   A Bridge

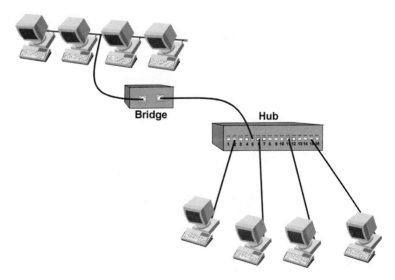

viding each port with dedicated bandwidth, without requiring users to change any existing equipment such as NICs, hubs, wiring, or any routers or bridges that are currently in place.

Many switching hubs also support load balancing so that ports are dynamically reassigned to different LAN segments based on traffic patterns. In addition, some include fault tolerance, which can reroute traffic through other ports when a segment goes down.

A new network layer device is the layer 3 switch. Layer 3 refers to the network layer of the OSI model. The layer 3 switch performs the multiport, virtual LAN, data pipelining functions of a standard layer 2 Switch, but it can also perform basic routing functions between virtual LANs. Virtual LANs are explained in Chapter 3.

2.11.4   Routers and Brouters

A **router,** which works at the network OSI layer, is a device that connects two or more LANs. In addition, it can break a large network into smaller, more manageable subnets. As multiple LANs are connected together, multiple routes are created to get from one LAN to another. Routers then share status and routing information with other routers so that they can provide better traffic management and bypass slow connections. In addition, routers provide additional functionality, such as the ability to filter messages and forward them to different places based on various criteria. Most routers are multiprotocol routers because they can route data packets using many different protocols (see Figure 2.29).

NOTE: Routers cannot pass non-routable protocols such as NetBEUI.

A **brouter** (short for bridge router) is a device that functions as both a router and a bridge. A brouter understands how to route specific types of packets (routable protocols), such as TCP/IP packets. For other specified packets (nonroutable protocols), it acts as a bridge and forwards the packets to the other networks.

Figure 2.29 A Router

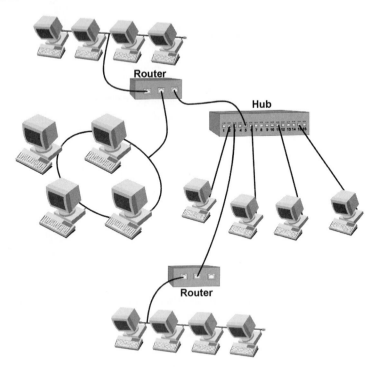

When you send a packet from one computer to another computer, a brouter first determines if the packet should be sent locally to another computer on the same LAN or if the packet should be sent to a router so that it can be routed to the destination LAN. If the packet is meant to go to a computer on another LAN, it is sent to the router (or gateway). The router will then determine what is the best route to take and forward the packet to that route. The packet will then go to the next router and the entire process will repeat itself until the packet gets to the destination LAN. The destination router will then forward the packets to the destination computer.

2.11.5   Gateways

A **gateway** is hardware or software that links two different types of networks by repackaging and converting data from one network to another network or from one network operating system to another. An example of a gateway would be a computer or device that connects a PC to a mainframe or a mini computer, such as an AS400 midrange computer. This can be done by adding either an Ethernet card or a Token Ring card to the AS400 computer and adding software to the client computers, adding a special expansion card to the PC so that it can communicate with the AS400 directly, or by using a gateway computer to act as a translator between the AS400 network and client networks.

NOTE: A gateway can be used at any layer of the OSI reference model but it is usually identified with the application layer.

Table 2.8 Connectivity Devices and
Their Associated OSI Layers

OSI layer	Device
Application	Gateways
Presentation	Gateways
Session	Gateways
Transport	Gateways
Network	Routers Brouters Layer 3 switches
Data link	Bridges Layer 2 switches
Physical	NICs Transceivers Repeaters Hubs MAUs Cables

In Chapter 1, network devices used to connect a network together were introduced. These include network cards, repeaters, hubs, bridges, routers, brouters, and gateways (see Table 2.8). Network cards, hubs, repeaters, and cables operate in the physical layer; bridges and layer 2 switches operate in the data link layer; and routers operate at the network layer. In addition, devices that provide and/or use network services operate at all seven layers of the OSI model so that they are able to perform their functions. This includes network hosts (including networked PCs, network printers, and servers) and network management.

SUMMARY

1. To overcome compatibility issues, hardware and software often follow standards (dictated or most popular specifications).
2. A *de jure* (by law) standard is a standard that has been dictated by an appointed committee.
3. A *de facto* (from the fact) standard is a standard that has been accepted by the industry just because it was the most common.
4. When a system or standard has an open architecture, it indicates that the specifications of the system or standard are public.

5. A proprietary system is privately owned and controlled by a company that has not divulged specifications that would allow other companies to duplicate the product.
6. The OSI reference model is the world's most prominent networking architecture model.
7. The concept of placing data behind headers (and before trailers) for each layer is called *encapsulation.*
8. The physical layer is responsible for transmission of bits sent across a physical media.

9. *Bandwidth* refers to the amount of data that can be carried on a given transmission media.

10. A twisted pair consists of two insulated copper wires twisted around each other.

11. Cables in twisted pairs are twisted to reduce crosstalk.

12. *Crosstalk* is when a signal inducts or transfers from one wire to the other.

13. UTP cable was categorized by the EIA based on the quality and number of twists per unit.

14. Early networks that used UTP typically used category 3 wire but today's high-speed networks typically use category 5 or enhanced category 5 cabling.

15. While your telephone uses a cable with 2 pairs (4 wires) and a RJ-11 connector, computer networks use a cable with 4 pairs (8 wires) and a RJ-45 connector.

16. A straight-through cable, which can be used to connect a network card to a hub, has the same sequence of colored wires at both ends of the cable.

17. A crossover cable, which can be used to connect one network card to another network card or a hub to a hub, reverses the transmit and receive wires.

18. STP is similar to UTP except that it is usually surrounded by a braided shield that serves to reduce EMI sensitivity and radio emissions.

19. Coaxial cable, sometimes referred to as coax, is a cable that has a center wire surrounded by insulation and a grounded shield of braided wire (mesh shielding).

20. A BNC connector is a type of connector used with coaxial cables, such as the RG-58 A/U cable used in 10Base-2 Ethernet systems.

21. BNC T-connectors (used with 10Base-2 systems) are female devices for connecting two cables to a NIC.

22. A BNC barrel connector is for connecting two cables together.

23. A fiber optic cable consists of a bundle of glass or plastic threads, each of which is capable of carrying data signals in the form of modulated pulses of light.

24. Fiber optic cables use several connectors, but the two most popular and recognizable connectors are straight tip (ST) and subscriber (SC) connectors.

25. Point-to-point topology connects two nodes directly together.

26. Multipoint connection links three or more devices together through a single communication medium. Because multipoint connections share a common channel, each device needs a way to identify itself and the device to which it wants to send information. The method used to identify senders and receivers is called *addressing*.

27. A bus topology looks like a line where data is sent along the single cable. The two ends of the cable do not meet and the two ends do not form a ring or loop.

28. A ring topology has all devices connected to one another in a closed loop.

29. A star topology is the most popular topology in use. It has each network device connect to a central point such as a hub, which acts as a multipoint connector.

30. Most wireless technologies use a cellular topology, where areas are divided into cells.

31. Mesh topology is where every computer is linked to every other computer. While this topology is not very common in LANs, it is common in WANs where it connects remote sites over telecommunication links.

32. The data link layer is responsible for providing error-free data transmission and establishes local connections between two computers.

33. The MAC sublayer is the lower sublayer that communicates directly with the network adapter card.

34. The LLC sublayer manages the data link between two computers within the same subnet.

35. The physical device address or MAC address is a unique hardware address (unique on the LAN/subnet).

36. *Topology* describes the appearance or layout of the network. Depending on how you look at the network, there are always the physical and the logical topologies.

37. The physical topology (part of the physical layer) describes how the network actually appears.

38. The logical topology (part of the data link layer) describes how the data flows through the physical topology or the actual pathway of the data.

39. The set of rules defining how a computer puts data onto the network cable and takes data from the cable is called the *access method*. The access method is sometimes referred to as *arbitration*.

40. *Contention* is when two or more devices contend (compete) for network access. Any device can transmit whenever it needs to send information. To avoid data collisions (two devices sending data at the same time), specific contention protocols, which require the device to listen to the cable before transmitting data, were developed.

41. The most common form of contention is called CSMA.

42. CSMA/CD is the access method utilized in Ethernet and IEEE 802.3.
43. Token passing uses a special authorizing packet of information to inform devices that they can transmit data.
44. Polling has a single device, such as a mainframe front-end processor, designated as the primary device.
45. The network layer is concerned with addressing and routing necessary to move data (packets or datagrams) from one network (or subnet) to another.
46. Networks are identified with a unique network address.
47. A Port or socket is used to identify a specific upper layer software process or protocol.
48. To determine the best route, the routes use complex routing algorithms that take into account a variety of factors including the speed of the transmission media, the number of network segments, and the network segment that carries the least amount of traffic.
49. The transport layer can be described as the middle layer. It connects the lower and upper layers together. In addition, it is responsible for reliable transfer of data (known as segments) between two end points.
50. Flow control is the process of controlling the rate at which a computer sends data.
51. The session layer allows remote users to establish, manage, and terminate connections (sessions).
52. A *session* is a reliable dialog between two computers.
53. The presentation layer ensures that information sent by an application layer protocol of one system will be readable by the application layer protocol on the remote system.
54. The application layer represents the highest layer of the OSI reference model.
55. Directory services is a network service that identifies all resources on a network and makes those resources accessible to users and applications.
56. A repeater, which works at the physical OSI layer, is a network device used to regenerate or replicate a signal or to move packets from one physical media to another.
57. A hub, which works at the physical OSI layer, is a multiported connection point used to connect network devices via a cable segment.
58. A bridge, which works at the data link OSI layer, is a device that connects two LANs and makes them appear as one or is used to connect two segments of the same LAN.
59. A switching hub (sometimes referred to as switch or a layer 2 switch) is a fast, multiported bridge that builds a table of the MAC addresses of all the connected stations. It then reads the destination address of each packet and then forwards the packet to the correct port.
60. A router, which works at the network OSI layer, is a device that connects two or more LANs. In addition, it can break a large network into smaller, more manageable subnets.
61. A brouter is a device that functions as both a router and a bridge.
62. A gateway is hardware or software that links two different types of networks by repackaging and converting data from one network to another network or from one network operating system to another.

QUESTIONS

1. Which model is the most well known model for networking architecture and technologies?
   a. OSI Model
   b. peer to peer model
   c. client/server model
   d. IEEE model
2. Which describes the correct order of the OSI model layers from bottom to top?
   a. physical, data link, network, transport, session, presentation, application
   b. data link, physical, network, transport, session, presentation, application
   c. physical, data link, network, transport, presentation, session, application
   d. application, presentation, session, transport, network, data link, physical
3. What happens to the data link layer source and destination addresses when packets are passed from router to router?
   a. They are stripped off and then recreated.
   b. They are stripped off and replaced with MAC addresses.
   c. They are stripped off and replaced with NetBIOS names.

    d. They are reformatted according to the information stored in the routing table.

4. Which layer of the OSI model determines the route from the source computer to the destination computer?
    a. the transport layer   b. the network layer
    c. the session layer   d. the physical layer

5. Bridges are often called MAC bridges because they work at the MAC sublayer. In which OSI layer does the MAC sublayer reside?
    a. the transport layer   b. the network layer
    c. the physical layer   d. the data link layer

6. Which layer of the OSI model provides synchronization between user tasks by placing checkpoints in the data stream?
    a. the transport layer   b. the network layer
    c. the session layer   d. the physical layer

7. Which layer of the OSI model adds header information that identifies the upper layer protocols sending the frame?
    a. the presentation layer
    b. the MAC sublayer
    c. the network layer
    d. the LLC sublayer

8. Which layer of the OSI model defines how cable is attached to a network adapter card?
    a. the cable layer
    b. the hardware layer
    c. the connection layer
    d. the physical layer

9. Many applications use compression to reduce the number of bits to be transferred on the network. Which layer of the OSI model is responsible for data compression?
    a. the application layer
    b. the network layer
    c. the session layer
    d. the presentation layer

10. Which of the following connectivity devices typically work at the data link layer of the OSI model?
    a. routers   b. repeaters
    c. bridges   d. gateways

11. Which layer of the OSI model packages raw data bits into data frames?
    a. the physical layer
    b. the presentation layer
    c. the network layer
    d. the data link layer

12. Which layer of the OSI model is responsible for data translation and code formatting?
    a. the application layer
    b. the presentation layer
    c. the network layer
    d. the data link layer

13. Which layer of the OSI model provides flow control and ensures that error-free messages are delivered?
    a. the transport layer   b. the network layer
    c. the session layer   d. the physical layer

14. The data link layer of the OSI is responsible for what tasks?
    a. creating, maintaining, and ending sessions; and encryption
    b. reliable delivery of data and error control
    c. transferring and routing of packets on the network
    d. addressing and reassembling frames

15. The IEEE 802 project divides the data link layer into two sublayers. Which sublayer of the data link layer communicates directly with the network adapter card?
    a. the LLC sublayer   b. the LAC sublayer
    c. the MAC sublayer   d. the DAC sublayer

16. What is the term for two computers acting as if there is a dedicated circuit between them even though there is not?
    a. virtual circuit   b. gateway
    c. physical circuit   d. dialog path

17. The Project 802 model defines standards for which layers of the OSI model?
    a. the physical layer and the data link layer
    b. the network layer and the data link layer
    c. the transport layer and the network layer
    d. the application layer and the presentation layer

18. Which Project 802 model specification describes Ethernet?
    a. 802.2   b. 802.5
    c. 802.3   d. 802.10

19. Which Project 802 model specification adds header information that identifies the upper layer protocols sending the frame and specifies destination processes for data?
    a. 802.2   b. 802.5
    c. 802.3   d. 802.10

20. What does the 802.5 specification specify?
    a. Ethernet   b. fiber optics
    c. Token Ring   d. Arcnet

21. Which of the following allows for two devices to communicate at the same time?
    a. simplex   b. full duplex
    c. half duplex   d. complex

22. Which of the following allows for two devices to communicate to each other, but not at the same time?
    a. simplex   b. full duplex
    c. half duplex   d. complex

23. The address that identifies a NIC to the network is known as the _____.
    a. MAC address   b. port address
    c. MAC identity   d. I/O address

24. When you have different networks that are not physically separated, you must have a unique configuration for each network. What has to be unique, besides the node address on the network, to tell the networks apart?
    a. the network ID
    b. the IP address
    c. the computer name
    d. the workgroup or domain name

25. Connection-oriented and connectionless-oriented communication are the two ways that communication can be implemented on a network. Which of the following is often associated with connectionless-oriented communication?
    a. fast but unreliable delivery
    b. fiber optic cable
    c. error-free delivery
    d. infrared technology

26. There are two ways to implement communication on networks: (1) connection-oriented communication and (2) connectionless-oriented communication. Which of the following is associated with connection-oriented communication?
    a. fast but unreliable delivery
    b. fiber optic cable
    c. assured delivery
    d. infrared

27. What type of communication ensures reliable delivery from a sender to a receiver without any user intervention?
    a. communication-oriented
    b. connectionless
    c. connection-oriented
    d. physical

28. What layer of the OSI model functions as a router?
    a. data link   b. transport
    c. network   d. physical

29. Which of the following is characteristic of a mesh network?
    a. It keeps cable cost down.
    b. It offers improved reliability.
    c. It needs a system to perform polling.
    d. It needs a token to operate.

30. What is the order in which information blocks are created when encapsulation with TCP/IP is used? (Select the best answer.)
    a. segments, packets or datagrams, frames, data, bits
    b. data, segments, packets or datagrams, frames, bits
    c. bits, frames, segments, packets or datagrams, data
    d. packets or datagrams, frames, segments, bits, data

31. Which of the following best describes the function of a connectionless-oriented protocol? (Select the best choice.)
    a. A connectionless-oriented protocol requires an exchange of messages before data transfer begins.
    b. A connectionless-oriented protocol is a faster transfer method than a connection-oriented protocol.
    c. A connectionless-oriented protocol relies upon lower level protocols for data delivery and error handling.
    d. A connectionless-oriented protocol creates a virtual circuit with the destination host.

32. Which of the following functions are performed by the MAC sublayer of the data link layer? (Select 2 choices.)
    a. It adds a source service access point and a destination service access point to the header.
    b. It provides media access.
    c. It isolates upper level protocols from details of the application layer.
    d. It builds frames from bits that are received from the physical layer.

33. Which of the following is a true statement regarding IP and MAC addresses? (Select the best choice.)
    a. An IP address is 6 bytes long and is usually represented in decimal format.
    b. A MAC address is 48 bits long and is usually represented in hexadecimal format.

c. An IP address is 48 bits long and is usually represented in hexadecimal format.

d. A MAC address is 6 bytes long and is usually represented in decimal format.

34. Which of the following does TCP/IP implement at the transport layer to manage flow control? (Select all choices that are correct.)

a. the use of buffering

b. the use of "ready" and "not ready" indicators

c. the use of packet switching

d. the use of windowing

35. A packet is the protocol unit for which layer of the OSI model?

a. the data link layer   b. the session layer

c. the presentation layer   d. the network layer

e. the transport layer

36. If a window size is changed from 3000 to 4000 during the data transfer state of a TCP session, what can a sending host do?

a. Send an acknowledgement before sending 4000 bytes.

b. Transmit 4000 packets before waiting for an acknowledgement.

c. Transmit 4000 bytes before waiting for an acknowledgement.

d. Transmit 4000 segments before waiting for an acknowledgement.

37. What are four functions or characteristics of the network layer of the OSI model? (Choose four answers.)

a. It uses a two part address.

b. It maintains routing tables.

c. It uses broadcast addresses.

d. It establishes network addresses.

e. It provides access to the LAN media.

f. It provides media independence for upper layers.

g. It provides path selection for internetwork communication.

38. What is a function of a reliable transport layer connection?

a. route selection

b. session checkpoints

c. acknowledgement

d. system authentication

39. What is the advantage of using a connectionless-oriented protocol such as UDP?

a. Packet acknowledgement may reduce overhead traffic.

b. Loss or duplication of data packets is less likely to occur.

c. Packets are not acknowledged, which reduces overhead traffic.

d. The application relies on the transport layer for sequencing the data packets.

40. What is a key use of a device hardware address?

a. To obtain a vendor code/serial number from the user.

b. To transmit a frame from one interface to another interface.

c. To transmit a packet from one local device to another local device.

d. To transmit data from one local device to a remote device across Internet.

e. To contain logical information about a device to use in end-to-end transmission.

41. What are the two sublayers of the data link layer? (Choose two answers.)

a. MAC   b. LLC

c. SAP   d. LCP

e. NCP

42. What are the generic parts of a network layer address?

a. an internetwork number and a URL

b. a vendor code and a serial number

c. a network number and a host number

d. a broadcast number and a unicast number

e. a domain identifier and a device identifier

43. Which two statements about a reliable connection-oriented data transfer are true? (Choose two answers.)

a. Recipients acknowledge receipt of data.

b. When buffers are filled to capacity, datagrams are discarded and not retransmitted.

c. Windows are used to control the amount in outstanding acknowledged data segments.

d. If the segment's time expires before receipt of an acknowledgement, the sender drops the connection.

e. The receiving device waits for acknowledgement from the sending device before accepting more data segments.

44. Which three functions are supported by connection-oriented services? (Choose three answers.)

a. Connection parameters are synchronized.

b. Any loss or duplication of packets can be corrected.

c. The data packet is independently routed and the service does not guarantee that the packet will be processed in order.

d. A data communication path is established between the requesting entity and the peer device on the remote end system.

45. What is an example of a valid MAC address?

a. 192.200.23.243   b. 19-22.02.54-34

c. 000.1223.FED   d. 00-00-12-34-FE-AB

46. A network administrator is verifying the configuration of a newly installed host by establishing an FTP connection to a remote server. Which layer of the protocol stack is the network administrator using for this operation?

a. the application layer

b. the session layer

c. the data link layer

d. the presentation layer

e. the transport layer

f. the internet layer

47. In contrast to connectionless-oriented services, which of the following are generally regarded as characteristics of connection-oriented network services? (Choose two answers.)

a. nonreliability

b. less bandwidth intensive

c. reliable

d. handshaking

48. Which OSI layer ensures reliable, end-to-end delivery of data?

a. the application layer

b. the presentation layer

c. the session layer

d. the transport layer

e. the network layer

49. What are the advantages of using the OSI layered network model? (Choose three answers.)

a. It allows multiple vendor development through standardization of network components.

b. It creates a list of communication rules that all companies must implement to get onto the Internet.

c. It allows various types of network hardware and software to communicate.

d. It prevents changes in one layer from affecting other layers, so it does not hamper development.

e. It allows companies to develop proprietary interfaces.

50. Which of the following are application layer protocols? (Choose two answers.)

a. ping   b. FTP

c. IP   d. telnet

e. TCP

51. At which OSI layer is the best path to a network determined?

a. the data link layer

b. the network layer

c. the physical layer

d. the presentation layer

e. the session layer

f. the transport layer

52. Which of the following devices operate at layer 2 of the OSI model? (Choose two answers.)

a. router   b. SMTP server

c. transceiver   d. switch

e. bridge   f. hub

53. Identify the name of the OSI layer next to its description.

a. _____ This layer segments and reassembles data into a data stream.

b. _____ This layer manages devices addressing, tracks the location of devices on the network, and determines the best way to move data.

c. _____ This layer transmits the data and handles error notification, network topology, and flow control.

54. Place the data encapsulation steps in the proper order by placing a number (1 through 5) on the step.

a. _____ Synchronization of a pattern of 1s and 0s with some clocking function allows transmission on a medium and recognition of data bits.

b. _____ Data is segmented and packaged with information to allow the sending and receiving hosts to communicate reliably.

c. _____ Alphanumeric user input is formatted for sending over the internetwork.

d. _____ A frame is built to allow communication over and interface to the network.

e. _____ Data is encapsulated with a network header specifying source and destination logical addresses.

CHAPTER 3

Voice and Data

Topics Covered in this Chapter

Introduction

Before diving into WANs and the technology that makes up a WAN, you must have a good understanding of what a network that includes a WAN is supposed to carry. Understanding the characteristics of network traffic will help you design an effective network. To explain and demonstrate some of the concepts shown in this chapter, there is a discussion on modems, one of the earliest devices used to send data over a voice network.

Objectives

- Given a number, convert it between decimal, binary, and hexadecimal.
- Differentiate between digital and analog signals and give some examples of each.
- Define *bandwidth* and compare and contrast between *baseband* and *broadband*.
- Define *multiplexer* and compare and contrast between *frequency division, time division,* and *statistical time division multiplexing.*
- Compare and contrast between *circuit switching, packet switching,* and *cell relay switching.* In addition, give examples of each.

- Identify the characteristics of voice, data, and video traffic.
- Explain how to convert an analog signal to a digital signal.
- List the characteristics of a modem.
- Explain how baud rates relate to bits per second.
- Define *handshaking* and compare and contrast *hardware handshaking* and *software handshaking.*

3.1   BITS AND BYTES

The most commonly used numbering system is the **decimal number system.** In a decimal number system, each position contains 10 different possible digits. Because there are 10 different possible digits, the decimal number system contains numbers with base 10. These digits are 0, 1, 2, 3, 4, 5, 6, 7, 8, and 9. In order to count values larger than 9, each position away from the decimal point in a decimal number increases in value by a multiple of 10 (see Table 3.1).

Table 3.1   The Decimal Number System

7th place	6th place	5th place	4th place	3rd place	2nd place	1st place
10^6	10^5	10^4	10^3	10^2	10^1	10^0
1,000,000	100,000	10,000	1000	100	10	1

Example:

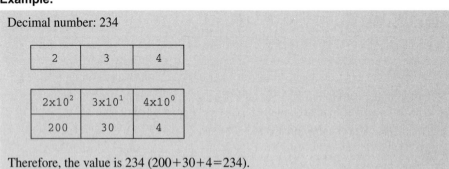

Decimal number: 234

2	3	4

2×10^2	3×10^1	4×10^0
200	30	4

Therefore, the value is 234 (200+30+4=234).

3.1.1   The Binary Number System

The **binary number system** is a different way to count. The binary system is less complicated than the decimal system because it has only two digits: (1) a zero and (2) a one. A computer represents a binary value with an electronic switch known as a transistor. If the switch is ON, it allows current to flow through a wire or metal trace to represent a binary value of one. If the switch is OFF, it does not allow current to flow through a wire, thus representing a value of zero (see Table 3.2). The ON switch is also referred to as a high signal while the OFF switch is referred to as a low signal.

If you use two wires to represent data, the first switch can either be ON or OFF and the second switch can either be ON or OFF, giving you a total of four combinations or four binary values (see Table 3.3). If you use four wires to represent data, you can represent sixteen different binary values (see Table 3.4).

Because each switch represents two values, each switch you use doubles the number of binary values. Therefore, the number of binary values can be expressed with the following equation:

Number of binary numbers $= 2^{\text{Number of binary digits}}$

Therefore, one wire allows $2^1 = 2$ binary numbers: 0 and 1. Two wires allow $2^2 = 4$ binary numbers: 0, 1, 2, and 3. Four wires allow $2^4 = 16$ binary numbers.

Table 3.2 One Digit Binary Number

Wire 1	Binary equivalent	Decimal equivalent
OFF	0	0
ON	1	1

Table 3.3 Two Digit Binary Number

Wire 1	Wire 2	Binary equivalent	Decimal equivalent
OFF	OFF	0 0	0
OFF	ON	0 1	1
ON	OFF	1 0	2
ON	ON	1 1	3

Table 3.4 Four Digit Binary Number

Wire 1	Wire 2	Wire 3	Wire 4	Binary equivalent	Decimal equivalent
OFF	OFF	OFF	OFF	0 0 0 0	0
OFF	OFF	OFF	ON	0 0 0 1	1
OFF	OFF	ON	OFF	0 0 1 0	2
OFF	OFF	ON	ON	0 0 1 1	3
OFF	ON	OFF	OFF	0 1 0 0	4
OFF	ON	OFF	ON	0 1 0 1	5
OFF	ON	ON	OFF	0 1 1 0	6
OFF	ON	ON	ON	0 1 1 1	7
ON	OFF	OFF	OFF	1 0 0 0	8
ON	OFF	OFF	ON	1 0 0 1	9
ON	OFF	ON	OFF	1 0 1 0	10
ON	OFF	ON	ON	1 0 1 1	11
ON	ON	OFF	OFF	1 1 0 0	12
ON	ON	OFF	ON	1 1 0 1	13
ON	ON	ON	OFF	1 1 1 0	14
ON	ON	ON	ON	1 1 1 1	15

Table 3.5   The Binary Number System

8th place	7th place	6th place	5th place	4th place	3rd place	2nd place	1st place
2^7	2^6	2^5	2^4	2^3	2^2	2^1	2^0
128	64	32	16	8	4	2	1

Question:

How many values do 8 bits represent?

Answer:

Because a byte has eight binary digits, a byte can represent $2^8 = 256$ characters.

Much like decimal numbers, binary digits have placeholders that represent certain values, as shown in Table 3.5.

Example:

Convert the binary number 11101010 to a decimal number.

1	1	1	0	1	0	1	0
1×2^7	1×2^6	1×2^5	0×2^4	1×2^3	0×2^2	1×2^1	0×2^0
128	64	32	0	8	0	2	0

Therefore, the binary number 11101010 is equal to the decimal number 234 $(128+64+32+8+2=234)$.

Example:

Convert the decimal number 234 to a binary number.

Referring to Table 2.7, you can see that the largest power of 2 that will fit into 234 is 2^7 (128). This leaves the value of $234 - 128 = 106$. The next largest power of 2 that will fit into 106 is 2^6 (64). This leaves a value of $106 - 64 = 42$. The next largest power of 2 that will fit into 42 is 2^5 (32) which gives us $42 - 32 = 10$. The next largest power of 2 that will fit into 10 is 2^3 (8) which gives us $10 - 8 = 2$. The next largest power of 2 that will fit into 2 is 2^1 (2) which gives us $2 - 2 = 0$.

$$
\begin{array}{rl}
234 & \\
\underline{-128} & 2^7 \\
106 & \\
\underline{-64} & 2^6 \\
42 & \\
\underline{-32} & 2^5 \\
10 & \\
\underline{-8} & 2^3 \\
2 & \\
\underline{-2} & 2^1 \\
0 &
\end{array}
$$

Therefore, the binary equivalent is 11101010.

1	1	1	0	1	0	1	0
2^7	2^6	2^5	2^4	2^3	2^2	2^1	2^0

In computers, one of these switches is known as a **bit.** When several bits are combined together, they can signify a letter, a digit, a punctuation mark, a special graphical character, or a computer instruction. Eight bits make up a **byte.**

Because bytes are such small units, kilobytes (KB), megabytes (MB) and gigabytes (GB) are used. The prefix "kilo" indicates thousands, "mega" indicates millions, "giga" indicates billions, and "tera" indicates trillions. With computers, the measurement is not exact. A kilobyte is actually 1024 bytes, not 1000. This is because 2^{10} is equal to 1024. Like the kilobyte, a megabyte is 1024 kilobytes, a gigabyte is 1024 megabytes, and a terabyte is 1024 gigabytes.

1 kilobyte = 1024 bytes
1 megabyte = 1024 kilobytes = 1,048,576 bytes
1 gigabyte = 1024 megabytes = 1,048,576 kilobytes = 1,073,741,824 bytes

3.1.2   The Hexadecimal Number System

The **hexadecimal number system** has sixteen digits. One hexadecimal digit is equivalent to a four digit binary number (4 bits, or a *nibble*) and two hexadecimal digits are used to represent a byte (8 bits). Therefore, it is very easy to translate between hexadecimal and binary and hexadecimal is used primarily as a "shorthand" way of displaying binary numbers (see Table 3.6). To designate a number as a hexadecimal number, it will often end with the letter *H*. In order to count values larger than fifteen, each position away from the decimal point in a decimal number increases in value by a multiple of sixteen (see Table 3.7).

Question:

What is the hexadecimal equivalent of the binary number 1001 1010?

Answer:

Because 1001 is equivalent to 9 and 1010 is equivalent to A, the hexadecimal equivalent is 9AH.

To convert a hexadecimal number to decimal number, you could first convert from hexadecimal to binary and then convert from binary to decimal. Another way to convert is to multiply the decimal value of each hexadecimal digit by its weight and then take the sum of these products.

Table 3.6 Hexadecimal Digits

Decimal	Binary	Hexadecimal
0	0000	0
1	0001	1
2	0010	2
3	0011	3
4	0100	4
5	0101	5
6	0110	6
7	0111	7
8	1000	8
9	1001	9
10	1010	A
11	1011	B
12	1100	C
13	1101	D
14	1110	E
15	1111	F

Table 3.7 The Hexadecimal Number System

7th place	6th place	5th place	4th place	3rd place	2nd place	1st place
16^6	16^5	16^4	16^3	16^2	16^1	16^0
16777216	1048576	65536	4096	256	16	1

Example:

To convert EAH to a decimal number, you would multiply A by 1 and E by 16 and then add them up.

E	A
$E\times16^1$	$A\times16^0$
14×16^1	10×16^0
14×16	10×1
224	10

Therefore, the hexadecimal number EA is equal to the decimal number 234 (224+10=234).

Example:

To convert the decimal number 234 to a hexadecimal number, you would refer to Table 2.9 to find the largest power of 16 that will fit into 234 is 16^1 (16). 16 goes into 234 14 (E) times, leaving a 10 (A).

$234/16 = 14.625$
$234 - (14\times16) = 10$
$14 = EH$

16^1	16^0
14×16^1	10×16^0
E	A

Today, TCP/IP addresses (IPv4) are based on 32 bits divided into 4 groups of 8 bits. The groupings of eight bits are sometimes referred to as **octets.** Because a hexadecimal digit consists of four bits, it takes two hexadecimal digits to express an octet.

3.1.3   The ASCII Character Set

In order to communicate, you need numbers, letters, punctuation, and other symbols. An alphanumeric code represents these characters and various instructions necessary for conveying information. One commonly used alphanumeric code is the **ASCII (American Standard Code for Information Interchange)** character set. Because ASCII is based on eight bits, there are a total of 256 different combinations of 0s and 1s, allowing 256 ($2^8 = 256$) different characters. A partial listing of ASCII characters is shown in Table 3.8. For example, if a byte had the binary code 01000001, the byte would represent the letter A (see Figure 3.1) and 01100001 would represent the a.

Table 3.8 A Partial List of the ASCII Character Set

DEC	BIN	HEX	ASCII	DEC	BIN	HEX	ASCII	DEC	BIN	HEX	ASCII
32	00100000	20	space	64	01000000	40	@	96	01100000	60	
33	00100001	21	!	65	01000001	41	A	97	01100001	61	a
34	00100010	22	"	66	01000010	42	B	98	01100010	62	b
35	00100011	23	#	67	01000011	43	C	99	01100011	63	c
36	00100100	24	$	68	01000100	44	D	100	01100100	64	d
37	00100101	25	%	69	01000101	45	E	101	01100101	65	e
38	00100110	26	&	70	01000110	46	F	102	01100110	66	f
39	00100111	27	'	71	01000111	47	G	103	01100111	67	g
40	00101000	28	(	72	01001000	48	H	104	01101000	68	h
41	00101001	29	)	73	01001001	49	I	105	01101001	69	i
42	00101010	2A	*	74	01001010	4A	J	106	01101010	6A	j
43	00101011	2B	+	75	01001011	4B	K	107	01101011	6B	k
44	00101100	2C	,	76	01001100	4C	L	108	01101100	6C	l
45	00101101	2D	–	77	01001101	4D	M	109	01101101	6D	m
46	00101110	2E	.	78	01001110	4E	N	110	01101110	6E	n
47	00101111	2F	/	79	01001111	4F	O	111	01101111	6F	o
48	00110000	30	0	80	01010000	50	P	112	01110000	70	p
49	00110001	31	1	81	01010001	51	Q	113	01110001	71	q
50	00110010	32	2	82	01010010	52	R	114	01110010	72	r
51	00110011	33	3	83	01010011	53	S	115	00111011	73	s
52	00110100	34	4	84	01010100	54	T	116	01110100	74	t
53	00110101	35	5	85	01010101	55	U	117	01110101	75	u
54	00110110	36	6	86	01010110	56	V	118	01110110	76	v
55	00110111	37	7	87	01010111	57	W	119	01110111	77	w
56	00111000	38	8	88	01011000	58	X	120	01111000	78	x
57	00111001	39	9	89	01011001	59	Y	121	01111001	79	y
58	00111010	3A	:	90	01011010	5A	Z	122	01111010	7A	z
59	00111011	3B	;	91	01011011	5B	[	123	01111011	7B	{
60	00111100	3C	<	92	01011100	5C	\	124	01111100	7C	|
61	00111101	3D	=	93	01011101	5D	]	125	01111101	7D	}
62	00111110	3E	>	94	01011110	5E	^	126	01111110	7E	–
63	00111111	3F	?	95	01011111	5F	_	127	01111111	7F	Delete

Note: "DEC" stands for "decimal," "BIN" stands for "binary," and "HEX" stands for "hexidecimal."

Figure 3.1 A Byte Representing an ASCII Character

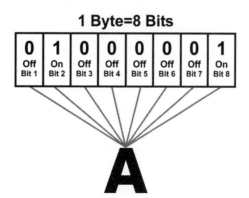

3.2 REPRESENTING DATA ON THE NETWORK

To represent data on a network, you will need to use some form of **signaling.** Signaling is the method for using electrical, light energy, or radio waves to communicate. The process of changing a signal to represent data is either called **modulation** or **encoding.** The two forms of signaling are digital signaling and analog signaling.

Both the data and the signals used to transmit the data can be in either analog or digital form. As a result, you may have the following:

- analog data to analog signal: involves amplitude and frequency modulation technique
- digital data to analog signal: involves encoding techniques
- digital data to analog signal: involves modulation techniques
- analog data to digital signal: involves digitization techniques
- analog or digital data to analog signal: involves spread spectrum technology

Each of these five combinations occurs quite frequently in computer networks, and each has unique applications and properties, as shown in Table 3.9.

3.2.1 Digital Signals

Digital signals (the language of computers) is a system that is based on a binary signal system produced by pulses of light or electric voltages. The site of the pulse is either ON/high or OFF/low to represent 1s and 0s. Binary digits (bits) can be combined to represent different values.

In digital transmission, the bit error rate (BER) is the percentage of bits that have errors relative to the total number of bits received in a transmission, usually expressed as ten to a negative power. For example, a transmission might have a BER of 10 to the minus 6 (10^{-6}), meaning that out of 1,000,000 bits transmitted, one bit was in error. The BER is an indication of how often a packet or other data unit has to be retransmitted because of an error. A too-high BER may indicate that a slower data rate would actually improve overall

Table 3.9   Data Being Encoded Into Signals

Data	Signal	Common conversion technique	Common devices	Common systems
Analog	Analog	Amplitude modulation or frequency modulation	Radio tuner, TV tuner	Telephone, cable TV, broadcast TV, AM and FM radio
Digital	Digital	NRS-L, NRZI, Manchester, differential Manchester, 4B/5B	Digital encoder	LANs, digital telephone systems
Digital	Analog	Amplitude modulation, frequency modulation, phase modulation	Modem	Connect to the Internet or other computer via phone lines
Analog	Digital	Pulse code modulation or delta modulation	Codec	Telephone systems, music systems
Analog or digital	Analog	Spread spectrum technology	Spread spectrum technology	Cordless telephones, wireless LANs

Figure 3.2   A Digital Signal Distorted by Noise and then Regenerated with a Repeater

Figure 3.3   Measuring Data Bits by Using Both Current State and State Transition Methods

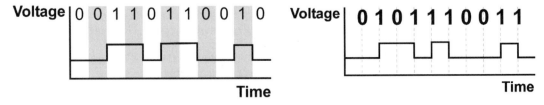

transmission time for a given amount of transmitted data because the BER might be reduced, thus lowering the number of packets that had to be resent.

Because the values of a digital signal can only be ones or zeros, if noise that raises, lowers, or distorts the signal is added, as long as the values are within a certain range it can be interpreted correctly. When the signal is regenerated, the signal is actually recreated and then sent out. Because the signal is recreated, the noise is removed (see Figure 3.2).

A digital signal can be measured in one of two ways: (1) The **current state** method periodically measures the digital signal for the specific state, (2) the **transition state** represents data by how the signal transitions from high to low or low to high. A transition indicates a binary 1 while the absence of a transition represents a binary 0 (see Figure 3.3).

3.2.2   Analog Signals

An **analog signal** is the opposite of a digital signal. Instead of having a finite number of states, it has infinite number values that change constantly. Analog signals are typically sinusoidal waveforms characterized by the waveform's amplitude and frequency. The **amplitude** represents the peak voltage of a sine wave.

The **frequency** indicates the number of times that a single wave will repeat over any period. It is measured in hertz (Hz) or cycles per second. The length (time interval) of one cycle is called its *period*. The period (*t*) can be calculated by taking the reciprocal of the frequency (*f*):

$$t = 1/f$$

Another term used when talking about modulation is *time reference* (phase). A **phase** is measured in degrees. Phase can be measured in 0°, 90°, 180°, and 270° or 0°, 45°, 90°, 135°, 180°, 225°, 270°, 315°, and 360° (see Figure 3.4).

Much like digital signals, analog signals can be measured by either the current state or the state transition method. For example, it can measure the amplitude at set intervals or it can measure the transition from one amplitude to another. In analog signals, **signal-to-noise ratio** (S/N or SNR) is a measure of signal strength relative to background noise. The ratio is usually measured in decibels (dB).

NOTE: Analog signals degrade as noise levels increase. In addition, when an analog signal is amplified to regenerate the signal, the noise is also amplified and regenerated (see Figure 3.5).

Figure 3.4   A Sine Wave Showing the Amplitude, Frequency (Cycles Per Second), and Phase

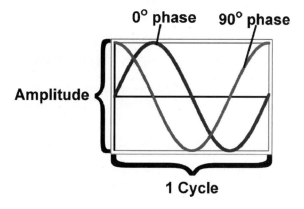

Figure 3.5   An Analog Signal Distorted by Noise and Then Amplified

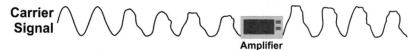

By varying the amplitude, frequency, and phase, data is sent over telephone lines. The earliest form of encoding data over telephone lines is **frequency shift keying (FSK),** which is very similar to the frequency modulation used in FM radios. FSK sends a logical 1 at one particular frequency (usually 1750 Hz) and a logical 0 is sent at another frequency (often 1080 Hz) (see Figure 3.6). Today, this technique is used with low rate asynchronous modems (up to 1200 baud only). Its disadvantages are (1) the rate of frequency changes is limited by the bandwidth of the line and (2) distortion caused by the lines makes the detection even harder than amplitude modulation.

The **amplitude modulation (AM)** technique changes the amplitude of the sine wave. In the earliest modems, digital signals were converted to analog signals by transmitting a large amplitude sine wave for a "1" and zero amplitude for a "0," as shown in Figure 3.7. The main advantage of this technique is that it is easy to produce and detect such signals. However, the technique has two major disadvantages: (1) the speed of the changing amplitude is limited by the bandwidth of the line, and (2) the small amplitude changes suffer from unreliable detection. Telephone lines limit amplitude changes to some 3000 changes per second. The disadvantages of amplitude modulation renders this technique no longer usable by modems; however, it is used in conjunction with other techniques.

Phase modulation (PM) is a process where two sinusoidal waveforms are compared with each other. When two waveforms are going in the same direction at the same time, it is known as *zero phase shift*. With a phase shift of 180 degrees (as in Figure 3.8), waveform *B* starts at the midpoint of waveform *A*. When waveform *A* is positive, waveform *B* is negative, and vice versa. Two phase states allow the representation of a single bit of digital data, which can have the value "0" or "1" (see Figure 3.9). Additional 90 and 270 degree phase shifts pro-

Figure 3.6   Frequency Shift Keying (FSK)

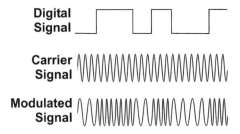

Figure 3.7   Amplitude Modulation (AM)

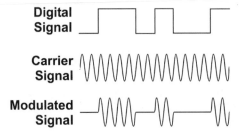

Figure 3.8   Phase Modulation (PM)

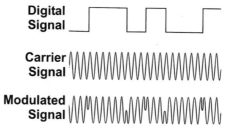

Figure 3.9   Phase Shift Keying (PSK)

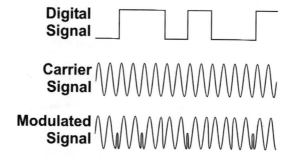

Table 3.10   Data Bits Interpreted from Phase Signals.

Phase	Data Bits
0°	0 0
90°	0 1
180°	1 0
270°	1 1

vide four phase shift states and the capability to represent four digital data representations. Therefore, a 1200 baud modem using PSK can transmit data at 2400 bps (see Table 3.10).

Phase change is neither affected by amplitude change, nor intermodulation distortions. Thus, phase modulation is less susceptible to noise and can be used at higher frequencies. Phase modulation is so accurate that the signal transmitter can increase efficiency by introducing multiple phase shift angles.

A submethod of the phase modulation is called *differential phase modulation.* In this method, the modem shifts the phase of each succeeding signal a certain number of degrees for a "0" (for example, 90 degrees) and a different certain number of degrees for a "1" (for example, 270 degrees) (see Figure 3.9). This method is easier to detect than the previous one. The receiver must detect the phase shifts between symbols, not the absolute phase. This technique is also called phase shift keying (PSK). In the case of two possible phase shifts, the modulation is called binary PSK (BPSK). In the case of four different phase shift possibilities for each symbol, which means that each symbol represents two bits, the modulation is called QPSK. In the case of 8 different phase shifts, the modulation technique will be called 8PSK.

Quadrature Amplitude Modulation (QAM) allows the transmission of data using both the phase shift of PM and the signal magnitude of AM at the same time. When more phase shifts and magnitude levels are used, more data can be transmitted. However, multibit technology eventually runs out of steam. As the number of tones and phases increases, it becomes more and more difficult to differentiate between similar combinations. For example, to get sixteen different combinations (four bits), you can use eight phase angles with a single amplitude or four phase amplitudes with double amplitudes. Therefore, a 2400 baud line can support up to 9600 bps. Trellis coded quadrature amplitude modulation (TCQAM or TCM) encodes six bits for every baud, so a 2400 baud signal can carry 14,000 bps.

3.2.3   Synchronous and Asynchronous Connections

As mentioned earlier in this chapter, data bits are encoded on a network media and the receiving NIC interprets the signal by taking measurements of the signal. Therefore, the receiving NIC must use a clock or a timing method (either synchronous or asynchronous) to determine when to measure and decode the signal and to decode the data bits.

Synchronous devices use a timing or clock signal to coordinate communications between the two devices. If the sending and receiving devices were both supplied by exactly the same clock signal, then transmission could take place forever with assurance that the signal sampling at the receiver will always be in perfect synchronization with the transmitter.

In synchronous communications, data is not sent in individual bytes, but as frames of large data blocks. For example, frame sizes vary from a few bytes to many bytes. Ethernet uses 1500 byte packets. The clock is either embedded in the data stream encoding, or it is provided on a separate clock line so that the sender and receiver are always in synchronization during a frame transmission.

Asynchronous signals are intermittent signals; they can occur at any time and at irregular intervals. They do not use a clock or timing signal. As the data frame is sent, the data frame consists of a start signal, a number of data bits, and a stop signal. The start signal is sent to notify the other end that data is coming, while the stop signal is sent to indicate the end of the data frame. While asynchronous signals are simpler electronic devices than synchronous signals, asynchronous signals are not as efficient as synchronous signals because of the extra overhead of the start and stop signals. An example of an asynchronous device is a modem.

3.2.4   Bandwidth

Bandwidth refers to the amount of data that can be carried on a given transmission media. Larger bandwidth means greater data transmission capabilities. Bandwidth use schemes based upon the availability and utilization of channels. A channel is a part of the medium's total bandwidth. It can be created by using the entire bandwidth for one channel or by splitting up multiple frequencies to accommodate multiple channels. For example, if a medium can support 10 Megabits per second (Mbps), two channels can be created at 5 Mbps each.

Baseband systems use the transmission medium's entire capacity for a single channel. Baseband networks can use either analog or digital signals, but digital signals are more common.

A **broadband** system uses the transmission medium's capacity to provide multiple channels by using **frequency division multiplexing (FDM).** Each channel uses a carrier signal that runs at a different frequency than the other carrier signals used by the other channels. The data is embedded onto the carrier channel. As data is sent onto the transmission channel, one **multiplexer (mux)** sends several data signals at different frequencies. When the various signals reach the end of the transmission media, another multiplexer separates the frequencies so that the data can be read.

Although baseband can only support one signal at a time, it can be made into a broadband system by using **time division multiplexing (TDM).** TDM divides the single channel into short time slots, allowing multiple devices to be assigned time slots.

TDM works well in many cases, but it does not always adapt to the varying data transmission needs of different devices or users. Regardless of the needs of the devices that transmit data, the same duration of time to transmit or receive data is allocated. A derivative of TDM is **statistical time division multiplexing (STDM),** which analyzes the amount of data that each device needs to transmit and determines, on a case-by-case basis, how much time each device should be allocated for data transmission on the cable or line. As a result, STDM uses bandwidth more efficiently.

3.3   DATA SWITCHING TECHNIQUES

Because large internetworks can have multiple paths that link source and destination devices, information is switched as it travels through the various communication channels. Data switching techniques can be divided into **circuit switching, packet switching,** and **cell relay.**

Circuit switching is a technique that connects the sender and the receiver by a single path for the duration of a conversation. Once a connection is established, a dedicated path that always consumes network capacity exists between both ends, even when there is no active transmission taking place (such as when a caller is put on hold). Once the connection has been made, the destination device acknowledges that it is ready to carry on a transfer. When the conversation is complete, the connection is terminated (see Figure 3.10). Therefore, circuit switching networks are sometimes called connection-oriented networks. Examples of circuit switching include phone systems and data that need to be transmitted in live video and sound.

In **packet switching** methods, messages are broken into small parts called packets. Each packet is tagged with source, destination, and intermediary node addresses as appropriate. Packets can have a defined maximum length and can be stored in RAM instead of on a hard disk. Packets can take a variety of possible paths through the network in an attempt to keep the network connections filled at all times. However, because the message is broken into multiple parts, sending packets via different paths adds to the possibility that the packet order could get scrambled. Therefore, a sequencing number is added to each

Figure 3.10   Circuit Switching

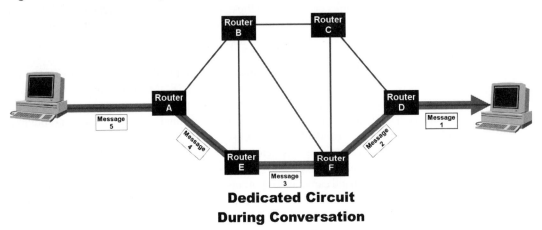

Dedicated Circuit
During Conversation

Figure 3.11   Packet Switching

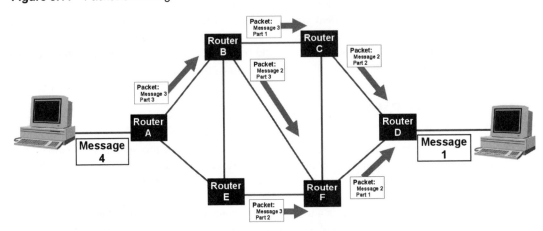

packet and packets are sent over the most appropriate path. Each device chooses the best path at that time for every packet. Therefore, if one path is too busy, it can send the packet through another path. Because some packets may be delayed, which causes the packets to arrive out of order, the device will reorder them by sequence number to reconstruct the original message (see Figure 3.11). The Internet is based on a packet switching protocol. Other examples include Frame Relay and X.25. Message switching is typically used to support services such as e-mail, web pages, calendaring, or workflow information.

Cell Relay is a data transmission technology based on transmitting data in relatively small, fixed size packets (**cells**). Each cell contains only basic path information that allows switching devices to route the cell quickly. Cell relay systems can reliably carry live video and audio because cells of fixed size arrive in a more predictable way than systems with packets or frames of varying size. Examples of cell relay are asynchronous transfer mode (ATM) and switched multimegabit data service (SMDS).

Figure 3.12   A Virtual Circuit as a Cloud

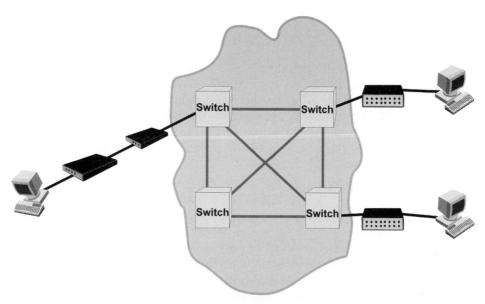

Connections between two hosts in a packet switching network are often described as virtual circuits. A **virtual circuit** is a logical circuit created to ensure reliable communications between two network devices. To provide this, it provides a bidirectional communications path from one device to another and is uniquely identified by some type of identifier. A number of virtual circuits can be multiplexed into a single physical circuit for transmission across a network. This capability often can reduce the equipment and network complexity required for multiple device connections.

A virtual circuit can pass through any number of intermediate devices or switches located within the virtual circuit. In this case, the two hosts can communicate as though they have a dedicated connection even though the packets might actually travel very different routes before arriving at their destination. While the paths may vary, computers neither know this nor need to know it.

Virtual circuits are sometimes graphically depicted as a cloud because the user does not worry about the path taken through the cloud. Users only worry about entering the cloud and exiting the cloud. A virtual circuit acts as a direct connection even though it may not be directly connected (see Figure 3.12).

3.4   TYPES OF NETWORK TRAFFIC

Before this book jumps deep into WAN technology, let's take a look at the three major types of traffic that are found in the WAN environment:

■ Data, which refers to electronic information found in files, databases, documents, and images as well as in digitally encoded voice and video.

- Voice, which is the term collectively used to identify live voice that is transported across the network.
- Video, which is the term collectively used to identify live moving images that are transported across the network.

Networks were originally designed to carry one specific traffic type: either voice or data. In today's business environment, approximately 80% of communication is voice and 20% is electronic data (for example: e-mail, database updates, file transfers, web page displays, and telnets). Recently, voice and data transmission, the different technologies, and the departments responsible for them have begun to merge. Therefore, it is important to consider the unique traffic requirements of voice and data networks separately.

3.4.1   Voice Traffic

Sound is produced by vibrations of compressed air. As sound starts out, it travels in all directions away from the source. When the sound reaches the human ear, it causes the eardrum to vibrate, which allows you to hear the sound.

Sound is characterized by its amplitude and frequency. The amplitude (loudness/intensity) is measured in decibles **(dB),** which are based on logarithmic curves. This means that if there is a sound that is 100 times as intense as another, the first sound is only 20 dB larger. A whisper is 10 dB, normal conversation is 65 dB, and a rock band with amplifiers is typically 110 decibels.

Frequency (pitch) is the rate of the vibration. It is measured in Hertz **(Hz),** or cycles per second. Very few people can hear lower than 16 Hz or more than 20 kHz. The lowest note on the piano has a frequency of 27 Hz, while the highest note has a frequency of approximately 4 kHz.

The human voice can produce sounds in the range between 50 and 1500 Hz, while most of what a person can hear is in the range between 300 and 3400 Hz. To carry a voice signal on a digital carrier, the analog voice signal needs to be converted to a digital signal. **Nyquist's theorem** states that, to ensure accuracy, a signal should be sampled at least twice the rate of its frequency. Therefore, the voice signal is sampled (measured) 8000 times per second. Each measurement is then quantized or converted into an 8-bit number (256 different combinations). As a result,

$$8000 \text{ samples/second} \times 8 \text{ bits/sample} = 64 \text{ Kbps}$$

to represent a digital voice signal. The method of digitizing analog voice signals is called **pulse code modulation (PCM).**

If you want to convert a sound (an analog signal) into a digital signal, you would digitize the sound by converting the signal into data that the computer can understand. Digitizing is done by taking samples of the electrical signal and assigning a binary value to the amplitude of the signal. This process is also known as **sampling.** If the number of samples increases, the recorded sound will be closer to the real sound. Unfortunately, sound files that contain more samples are larger.

If you follow Nyquist's sampling theorem and the human range of hearing is about 20 kHz, you should sample at 44 kHz (if you double the 20 kHz and add some more for error). Therefore, 44 kHz is often referred to as CD-quality sampling. The number of bits that represent the binary number is known as bit resolution. Therefore, if you have an 8-bit card (a card with a bit resolution of 8 bits or 1 byte), it can store 256 combinations of eight 0s and 1s. Therefore, when the amplitude is measured during a sample, it is assigned a specific binary value indicating how loud the signal is. A 16-bit card gives greater accuracy because it allows for 65,536 combinations of 16 0s and 1s. Today, most sound cards are 16-bit cards. The device that performs this analog to digital conversion is known as an **analog to digital converter (ADC)** (see Figures 3.13 and 3.14).

Today, PSTN is the largest voice network. Originally, PSTN was designed to handle voice only, but it has adapted rapidly to meet a variety of data needs. While the demand for data services will continue to increase, voice continues to be the largest source of revenue for WAN providers.

Voice networks have several common characteristics that are designed to meet the needs of voice traffic:

■ If a voice transmission does not arrive in the proper order, it is not likely to be of any use because it may not be understood. As a result, voice networks are usually circuit switched because voice requires consistent timing to prevent jitter. Jitter will be

Figure 3.13   Original Signal

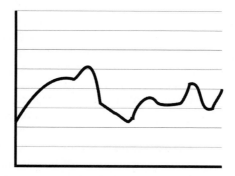

Figure 3.14   Two Examples of Sampling. The Second One Consists of More Samples, therefore, the Reconstructed Signal is Much Closer to the Original Signal than the First One

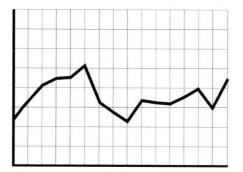 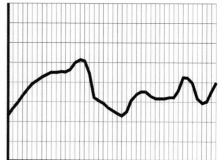

explained later in this chapter. In general, packet switched networks are not suited for voice traffic because prioritization can cause delays.

■ Because timing restraints do not allow time to retransmit lost or damaged information, voice networks usually have minimal error control and no error recovery. Fortunately, voice traffic is very forgiving of errors.

Voice traffic is also supported by a wide variety of network types, including SONET/SDH, wireless, frame relay, ATM, TCP/IP, and ISDN, but the vast majority of voice traffic is carried across the PSTN.

Traditional broadcast media like radio, television, and PSTNs use analog technology that is typically represented as a series of varying sine waves. The term "analog" can be traced to the similarity between the actual fluctuations of the human voice and the "analogous" or comparable modulation of a carrier wave.

Telephone systems use analog switched lines to provide voice communications by converting sound waves (vibrations that move in the air) into electrical signals. Each telephone handset contains a transmitter covered by a diaphragm and a receiver composed of a coil attached to a speaker cone that vibrates to produce sound waves. When a person lifts the telephone handset to make a call, switchhook contacts are closed, which energizes a relay and prompts a device called a line searcher to find an open line. A connection from customer to the telephone central office is then established and a dial tone is generated. The line searcher then prepares the telephone company switching equipment to receive a telephone number. When a person speaks into a telephone handset, acoustical energy vibrations caused by the voice apply varying amounts of pressure to the diaphragm. In response to the natural rise and fall of human speech, the diaphragm converts the pressure into different amounts of current or electrical energy. This variation in the current is an electrical representation of the human voice. The resulting output of this process is an analog electrical signal.

The transmitted signal then flows through the voice coil in the handset of the person receiving the call. The coil attached to the speaker cone in the receiver vibrates in response to the signal to reproduce sound waves, and the person listening to the telephone hears the other person's reproduced voice. To allow the person speaking into the telephone to hear his or her own voice, a small amount of current called a *side-tone* is applied to the transmitting station's receiver; this also helps control the loudness of a person's voice. Telephone systems use a pair of twisted pair copper wires. Telephones are connected to the cable by a RJ-11 jack.

When an analog phone call is made, it goes through the following steps:

Step 1: Both telephone sets are on-hook and circuits are open.

Step 2: A handset is lifted, the switch is closed, which completes the circuit, and current begins to flow. This sends a signal to the telephone company's Central Office (CO) and their system generates a dial tone.

Step 3: The customer dials a destination telephone number and the resulting signals are received "in-band" by the CO switch.

Step 4: The CO that handles the destination phone sends a ringing signal to the destination receiver and a ringing signal to the sender to let him or her know that the call request has been completed and the call is going through. The time it takes for the CO to complete the connection between the person calling and the person called is referred to as "call setup time."

Step 5: When the call is answered, another signal is sent to the CO to stop ringing, and the initiator and the receiver can begin communicating.

Step 6: When the telephone is put back onto the cradle, the switch is again opened, current stops flowing, and the dial tone stops, which terminates the connection.

When voice is transmitted over a network, losing or altering a few bits does not cause a problem. Minor data loss is not even noticed. Of course, what is more important is to deliver voice content promptly and in order. Therefore, a constant bandwidth along a fixed (connection-oriented) circuit is required.

3.4.2   Data Traffic

When you think of networks, you most likely think of networks that carry data back and forth to provide file and print sharing and e-mail support. Because data does not have to be delivered in real time, data networks are more concerned about reliable transportation of information so that data is neither lost nor corrupted. As a result, data networks are typically packet switched or cell switched to ensure the error control and recovery needed to ensure a reliable transfer. The use of a fixed path with constant reserved bandwidth is not required for data communications.

To make sure that the data is delivered, each data packet sent on the network is numbered and includes a timer. The timer is used to determine when to drop the packet if the packet is not delivered within a certain amount of time. This way, the packet will not aimlessly traverse the network forever if it cannot find its destination. When the data packet is sent and is received, the destination will send back an acknowledgement. If the acknowledgement is not received by the end of the time out period, the packet will be resent. Because you are using either a packet switched network or a cell switched network, there is a chance that the packets can be delivered out of order because each packet could take different routes. The numbering system will allow the packets to be put back into the proper order.

To ensure that the data does not get corrupted, the sender performs a cyclic redundancy check (CRC) on each data packet and the result is added to the end of the packet. When the packet is received at its destination, the same CRC (a form of mathematical calculation) is done and compared with the one that was sent. If they are different, the packet has become corrupted, the data is discarded, and the receiver does not acknowledge that it was received. After the time out period, the packet will be resent.

3.4.3   Video Traffic

Video traffic is similar to both voice and data in that it requires reliable end-to-end transport while sharing the timing requirements of voice traffic. The ideal network type for video information is a cell switched ATM network that provides quality guarantees and fast delivery.

3.4.4   Packet Loss, Latency, and Jitter

When a voice or video call traverses an IP network, the stream of audio and video data is broken up into small "packets" of information. **Packet loss** refers to sent packets that don't arrive at the receiving end. This can create a "blip" or "clipping" in the audio quality and freeze up the video quality. A videoconference will express noticeable quality degradation in communication at even .25% percent packet loss.

Latency, which plays a role in the cause of jitter, can be defined simply as the time it takes for a packet to cross the network. Varied latency will cause **jitter.** Acceptable levels of latency for a packet to get from one end of a video conference to the other averages around 150 milliseconds. Anything above 200 milliseconds will cause the human ear to detect the delay in conversation, thus making interactive communication difficult.

For example, if two video endpoints are communicating and receiving one packet every 20 milliseconds for a period of time, then at some point in the communication one packet arrives in 160 milliseconds, the next packet arrives in 200 milliseconds, and the third packet arrives in 20 millisecond, the varying of latency of the packets is called jitter. The destination prefers that packets come in at a constant rate. So when packets experience jitter, the destination codec can use system resources to smooth the media stream. Of course, an excess of jitter will cause poor quality voice or video transmission if there are not enough system resources to continuously smooth out the stream. Generally, a 10–30 ms variation is considered acceptable.

To have quality voice or video communication, you must keep the sum of packet loss, latency, and jitter within optimal range. In comparison, the public Internet does not have centralized administrative control, so there is no way to control jitter, latency, or packet loss levels. This is why attempting to make a high-quality voice or video call on the public Internet is trickier. Of course, voice would be easier because voice requires much less bandwidth than video.

Quality of Service (**QoS**) refers to the capability of a network to provide better service to selected network traffic over various LAN and WAN technologies. The primary goal of QoS is to provide priority, including dedicated bandwidth, controlled jitter and latency, and improved loss characteristics. Making sure that providing priority for one type of traffic does not make others types fail is also important.

When designing your network, you must make sure that the network has enough bandwidth on all segments. In addition, you must have network packet management that gives priority to time-sensitive packets, which is usually done by routers. In addition, at the network endpoints, additional corrections such as packet loss concealment (PLC), adaptive jitter buffering (AJB), and latency reduction give reasonable voice quality under adverse and unpredictable conditions.

3.5   MODEMS

A **modem (modulator/demodulator)** is a device that enables a computer to transmit data over telephone lines. Because computer information is stored and processed digitally, and the telephone lines transmit data using analog waves, the modem converts digital signals to analog signals (modulates them) and analog signals to digital signals (demodulates them).

Modems can be either an internal or external modem. Internal modems are an expansion card that gets plugged into an expansion slot, while external modems can be attached to the computer using a serial port. In either case, modems have at least one RJ-11 connector used to connect the twisted pair cable between the modem and the wall telephone jack. Some will include a second RJ-11 jack to connect a phone.

3.5.1   The RS-232C Standard

RS-232c was designed for the interface between data terminal equipment (DTE) and data communications equipment (DCE). The EIA-232F interface standard is the current incarnation of the RS-232 standard, which is an interface standard for connecting a DTE to a voice modem for use on analog public telecommunications systems. Although the RS-232 and EIA-232F standards are a little different, they are also similar in some ways.

The electrical component of EIA-232F incorporates ITU's V.28 standard, which describes the electrical characteristics for an interchange circuit. With V.28, voltage levels are detected at the receiving modem by the relative voltage difference between two different circuits. A voltage difference of more than +3 volts is considered to be a value of 1, and a voltage difference more negative than –3 volts is considered to be a value of 0.

To define functional and procedural components, EIA-232F incorporates the ITU's V.24 standard. V.24 defines a list of 43 interchange circuits that can be used by other standards to define an interface. An interchange circuit is the signal that is transmitted over a wire and connected to a particular pin in a connector. Each of these interchange circuits defines a particular function. By using the appropriate functions in the proper sequence, a computer and modem can create a connection between themselves and between the remote modem and the remote computer. EIA-232F, using the common DB-9 connector, uses nine of those 43 interchange circuits.

RS-232 circuits all carry bipolar low voltage signals, measured at the connector with respect to signal ground. Signals within the range –3 volts to +3 volts are considered invalid (noise). For data lines, binary 1 (a high) is represented by –3 volts to –25 volts, while a binary 0 (a low) is +3 volts to +25 volts.

> *NOTE:* The hardware handshaking and flow control signals (DTR, DSR, CD, RTS, and CTS) are negative true. This means that the signal of a negative voltage means that the signal is ON. For control signals, the ON signals are represented by +3 volts to +25 volts, while the OFF signal is –3 volts to –25 volts. Because most computers use 12 volt power supplies, RS-232 signals are usually represented by 12 volt signals rather than ±25 volts.

3.5.2   How a Modem Works

When the calling computer wishes to call another computer (such as one used by an Internet provider or through a bulletin service (BBS)), the calling computer activates the modem and dials the telephone number. The receiving computer will hear the ring and answer the call. As the receiving modem answers the call, it immediately transmits a **guard tone.** A guard tone is a certain frequency used to identify the device on the other end as a modem. This way, different tones can be used to distinguish between faxes, modems, and voice (no tone). Next, the second modem sends an **unmodulated carrier tone.** The communicating devices use the unmodulated carrier tone to query each other about capabilities such as speed. In addition, the two modems send several signals to measure the quality of the line. When both modems agree on a speed, they then determine the appropriate error control and compression. Finally, the modems turn on the **carrier detect signal,** which remains on throughout the modem connection. If the carrier is gone, the connection is broken.

> *NOTE:* Both carriers use different frequencies so that they can exist at the same time.

Sending data through a modem begins with the receipt of digital data from the computer. The modem then converts the digital signals into analog signals. The UART of the modem then adds the start and stop bits and any error control bits, such as parity. When the data reaches the modem, the UART strips the start and stop bits, checks for errors, and converts the analog signal to a digital signal, which is then processed by the computer. As the modem is communicating, it continuously monitors the status of the line, the quality of the signals, and the number of errors encountered. When the modems register excessive problems, they interrupt the carriers and reevaluate the line, thus reducing the speed of transmission. If the reduced speed decreases the number of errors, the line will be reevaluated again to see if the speed can then be increased. The two communicating computers must be set to the same number of bits used for data, the length of the stop bits, and the type of error control. If they are not, the receiving computer would misinterpret the data which would result in errors or garbage. It is usually the calling computer that will be configured to the settings of the receiving computer.

Example:

You need to download some technical information, which is not available on the Internet but is available on a BBS computer. Therefore, you are given the phone number to the BBS computer and the following information:

9600 baud at 7E1

The 9600 baud is the speed of the modem on the other end. The *7* indicates that seven bits are used for data and the *E* indicates that it uses even parity checking (*O* would represent odd parity). Lastly, the *1* indicates that it has one stop bit.

3.5.3	**Baud Rate versus Bits per Second**

Baud rate refers to the modulation rate or the number of times per second that a line changes state. This is not always the same as **bits per second (bps).** If you connect two serial devices together using direct cables, then the baud rate and the bps are the same. Thus, if you are running at 19,200 bps, then the line is also changing states 19,200 times per second to represent 19,200 logical 1s and 0s. Much like the data and stop bits, the sending and receiving devices must agree on the baud rate. The speed of a normal serial port is 115.2 Kbps.

An example of different baud rates and bps rates is telephone communication. Telephone lines are actually limited to a maximum of 2400 baud. However, because they use analog signals and not digital signals, the bps can be increased by encoding more bits into each line change. Consequently, 9600 bps encodes 4 bits at the same time, 14,400 encodes 6 bits, and 28.8 encodes 12 bits. In addition, bps can be increased by using data compression.

Two formulas express the direct relationship between the frequency of a signal and its data transfer rate. Nyquist's theorem, which was discussed earlier, calculates the data transfer rate of a signal given its frequency and the number of signaling levels:

$$C = 2f\log_2 L$$

C is how fast the data can transfer over a medium, in bps (the channel capacity)
f is the frequency of the signal
L is the number of signaling levels.

For example, given a 3100 Hz signal and two signaling levels, the resulting channel capacity is 6200 bps ($2 \times 3100 \ \log_2 2$). A 3100 Hz signal with four signaling levels yields 12,400 bps.

Shannon's formula calculates the maximum data transfer rate of an analog signal (with any number of signal levels) and incorporates noise:

$$S(f) = f\log_2(1 + S/N) \text{ bps}$$

$S(f)$ is the data transfer rate in bits per second
f is the frequency of the signal
S/N is the signal to noise ratio (S-power of the signal in watts, N-noise level).

If you have 0.2 Watt power and 0.00002 watts using a 3100 frequency, you would have:

$$S(f) = 3100 \times \log_2(1 + 0.2/0.0002)$$

$$= 3100 \times \log_2(1001)$$

$$= 3100 \times 9.97$$

$$= 30,901 \text{ bps}$$

NOTE: Error correction codes can improve the communication performance relative to uncoded transmission, but no practical error correction coding system that can approach the theoretical performance limit given by Shannon's law exists.

If you look at the formulas closely, you will see that the greater the frequency of a signal, the higher the possible data rate. This also means that the higher the desired data transfer rate, the greater the needed signal frequency.

The decibel is a relative measure of signal loss or gain, and is expressed as:

$$dB = 10\log_{10}(P_2/P_1)$$

P_2 and P_1 are the ending and beginning power levels of the signal expressed in watts.

If a signal starts at a transmitter with 10 watts of power and arrives at a receiver with 5 watts of power, the signal loss in dB is calculated as follows:

$$dB = 10\log_{10}(5/10)$$
$$= 10\log_{10}(0.5)$$
$$= 10(-0.3)]$$
$$= -3$$

There is a 3 dB loss between the transmitter and receiver. In other words, any time a signal loses half its power, there is a 3 dB loss.

3.5.4   Parity

Parity provides an error check on the bits that are being sent. For example, if you specified that you are using eight bits to represent your data, the bits are evaluated by counting the number of 1s in a byte. If you are using odd parity, the parity generator/checker will count the bits and store the appropriate bit as the parity bit to make the total number an odd number. If it is an even number, the parity bit will be a 1 and if it is an odd number, the parity bit will be a 0. Then the data and parity bit will be sent through the communication channel. When it gets to its destination, the same count is done on the bits. If you are using odd parity, the parity bit will be assigned to keep the total an even number.

Example:

If you are using the following configuration

    9600 baud at 8E1

you have configured your communication as even parity. If you are sending an ASCII lowercase "a," you would be sending the binary pattern of 0110 0001. If you count the number of bits, you should come up with a value of 3, which is an odd number. Because even parity is specified, the parity generator/checker will use a 1 for the parity bit. Again, if you add data bits and the parity bit together, you have a value of 4, which is an even number. The bits representing the letter "a" and the parity bits will be sent. The same parity calculation is done when the data gets to its destination to make sure all of the bits, including the parity bit, are still even. If not, it considers the data invalid.

There are two disadvantages of using parity for error control. First, only errors with 1, 3, 5, or 7 bits have changed. It will not discover a problem if two bits have been changed because the two bits cancel each other out. Second, it detects the error but does not correct it.

3.5.5   Modulation Schemes

Data is sent over telephone lines by using analog signals, specifically sinusoidal waveforms. A sinusoidal waveform is characterized by its amplitude and frequency. Another term used when talking about modulation is *time reference* or *phase*. A phase is measured in degrees. Phases can be measured in 0°, 90°, 180°, and 270° or 0°, 45°, 90°, 135°, 180°, 225°, 270°, 315°, and 360°.

By varying the amplitude, frequency, and phase, data is sent over the telephone lines. The earliest form of encoding data over telephone lines is FSK. FSK was usually used with 300 baud modems. PSK is the varying of the phase angle to represent data. Because the phase has four different values, it represents two bits of data. Therefore, a 1200-baud modem using PSK can transmit data at 2400 bps.

QAM combines phase and AM to encode up to six bits onto every baud, although it usually encodes only four bits onto every baud. Therefore, a 2400-baud signal can carry up to 9600 bps. Lastly, TCQAM (or TCM) uses the full 6-bit encoding for every baud. Therefore, a 2400-baud signal can carry 14,400 bits per second.

3.5.6   The Command Set

When a computer sends data using a modem, it sends a command to control the modem. The instructions that the modem understands are referred to as the **Hayes command set** or **AT commands.** Today, virtually all modems are Hayes compatible and follow the same set of basic commands. Most of the time, users do not have to know these commands because most communications software packages know them. A small handful of programs, however, require the user to enter these commands.

AT commands that must sometimes be entered by the user can be divided into the basic command set, an extended command set, and register commands (see Table 3.11). Basic commands begin with a capital character followed by a digit. Extended commands begin with an ampersand (&) and a capital letter followed by a digit. Register commands access small memory locations (registers) within the modem. The order in which the commands are issued is important, and every command must begin with "AT." In addition, there are no spaces between any of the commands or the numbers specified.

Examples:

To make sure that the cables are connected properly and that the baud rate is set properly, you would type the following command and press the Enter key. If everything is fine, it will respond with an OK.

```
AT
```

To dial a number using a touch-tone telephone, you would type the following command and press the Enter key:

    `ATDT2633077`

To dial a number using a pulse telephone, you would type the following command and press the Enter key:

    `ATDP2633077`

To hang up the phone, you would type the following command and press the Enter key:

    `ATH`

To show all of the ampersand commands, you would type the following command and press the Enter key:

    `AT&$`

To perform a hardware reset for the modem, you would type the following command and press the Enter key:

    `ATZ`

Table 3.11   Common AT Command Parameters

AT	The AT command tells the modem that you are going to send it a command. You must type "AT" before you issue any other command. If you issue "AT" as a command all by itself, the modem should respond "OK". This indicates that your cables are connected correctly and the baud rate is set properly.
D	"D" tells your modem to dial the numbers following the *D*.
H	Hang up the telephone.
P	"P" is a subcommand of the "D" command. This tells your modem that you want it to dial in pulse mode. Use this if you do not have a touch tone phone line.
Z	Resets the modem to the default state
~	Makes your software pause for half a second. You can use more than one ~ at a time.
^M	Sends the terminating carriage return character to the modem.
AT$	Command quick reference
&$	Help for ampersand commands
D$	Help for dial commands
S$	Help for "S" registers

3.5.7   **Faxes and Modems**

"Fax" is short for **facsimile transmission.** A fax machine takes a piece of paper, digitizes the text and pictures, and sends the data over a telephone line. A fax machine on the other end reassembles the text and images and prints the text and images on paper. Today, many machines have a fax/modem, which can take a document (such as Microsoft Word document) and send the document to another fax machine. If the other fax machine is a fax/ modem, the image can be either displayed on the screen or printed to paper.

Today, most fax/modems are group 3 fax/modems. Group 3 fax/modems provide various levels of processing based upon their service class. Class 1 devices perform basic handshaking and data conversion and are the most flexible, because much of the work is done by the computer's central processing unit (CPU). Class 2 devices establish and end the call and perform error checking.

3.6   HANDSHAKING

Handshaking is the process by which two devices initiate communication. Handshaking begins when one device sends a message to another device, indicating that it wants to establish a communication channel. The two devices then send several messages back and forth, which enable them to agree on a communications protocol.

Handshaking can be done either with hardware or software. Essentially, a handshake consists of codes or signals to ensure that both the sender and the receiver are ready for the transmission, that the transmission has taken place, and that both ends can get ready for the next transmission. Hardware and software handshaking can both be used. One simple form of a hardware handshake consists of a transmitter raising a line to logical HIGH to indicate it is ready to send. The receiver detects the ready-to-send signal and when it is ready to receive, it sends a logical HIGH clear-to-send signal to the transmitter. The receiver then reads the data that the transmitter sends. Both ends then remove the signals until they have each made themselves ready for the next transmission. This sequence could be repeated byte by byte or for each block of bytes. Mechanisms can also be developed in software for blocks of bytes. Assume a full duplex channel exists. When the receiver is ready it sends a code, which could be a single byte, to the transmitter. The transmitter then starts sending. When the receiver starts to fill up it sends a "stop" signal to the transmitter. Codes can also be used to indicate whether the material sent arrived intact. Thus, handshaking and data integrity start to overlap.

In telephone communication handshaking precedes each telephone connection. Handshaking is: (1) the exchange of information between two modems and (2) the resulting agreement about which protocol to use. Handshaking makes the "crunching" and other sounds that occur when you make a call from your computer. Because the modems at each end of the line may have different capabilities, they need to inform each other of their capabilities and settle on the highest transmission speed they can both use. At higher speeds, modems have to determine the length of line delays so that echo cancellers can be used properly.

While many books may discuss handshaking associated with serial ports, handshaking functions can be used for any communication system. This can be applied to data busses, networks, serial links, and so forth to perform the following tests:

- System active/available
- identify nodes (for networks)
- control the flow of data
- request/take control of the communication link
- contribute to data integrity

With hardware handshaking, there are pins on the peripheral chip that are dedicated to controlling the communication. Some of these lines are placed there by the chip designers and sometimes the pins are general I/O pins that are controlled by the software for the purpose of controlling the communication.

When two types of equipment communicate over a standard RS-232C serial link, the two devices will be DTE and DCE. The DTE is usually, but not always, the computer. The 16450 chip, which is part of the serial interface, is designed as a data terminal. The DCE is traditionally the modem.

3.6.1 Hardware Handshaking

When the RS-232C interface transfers data between the computer and the modem, it uses the TD (transmit data) and RD (receive data) lines. The other signals are essentially used for flow control, in that they either grant or deny requests for the transfer of information between a DTE and a DCE. Data cannot be transferred unless the appropriate flow control lines are first asserted or turned ON. The following is a list of common EIA RS-232 hardware handshaking signals:

- **transmit data (TD)**—The line where the data is transmitted one bit at a time.
- **receive data (RD)**—The line where data is received one bit at a time.
- **request to send (RTS)**—The signal line, which is asserted by the DTE to inform the DCE that it wants to transmit data. If the modem decides this is OK, it will assert the CTS line. Typically, once the computer asserts RTS, it will wait for the modem to assert CTS. When CTS is asserted by the modem, the computer will begin to transmit data.
- **clear to send (CTS)**—The signal that is asserted by the modem after receiving a RTS signal indicating that the computer can now transmit.
- **data terminal ready (DTR)**—The signal that is asserted by the computer and informs the modem that the computer is ready to receive data.
- **data set ready (DSR)**—This signal line is asserted by the modem in response to a DTR signal from the computer. The computer will monitor the state of this line after asserting DTR to detect if the modem is turned ON.
- **Carrier Detect (CD)**—This signal is asserted by the modem, informing the computer that it has established a physical connection to another modem. It is sometimes known as data carrier detect (DCD). It would be pointless to have a computer transmitting information to a modem if this signal line was not asserted. If the physical connection is broken, this signal line will change state.

Table 3.12 RS-232 Signals

Signal	Description	DTE 25 pin	9 pin equivalent
Tx	Transmit	2	3
Rx	Receive	3	2
RTS	Request to send	4	7
CTS	Clear to send	5	8
DSR	Data set ready	6	6
GND	Ground	7	5
CD	(Data) carrier detect	8	1
DTR	Data terminal ready	20	4
RI	Ring indicator	22	9

The RS-232 serial interface pin out is shown in Table 3.12. The EIA RS-232 interface can send data either way (DTE to DCE or DCE to DTE) independently at the same time. This is called a full duplex operation.

Let's go through each of the steps necessary to transmit and receive characters across the serial interface. To transmit data from a DTE to a DCE, you would have to:

Step 1: Assert DTR and RTS.
Step 2: Wait for DSR and CD.
Step 3: Wait for CTS.
Step 4: Transmit data as long as CTS is asserted.
Step 5: Pause and wait whenever CTS drops until asserted again.
Step 6: Steps 1 and 2 are essential to ensure that the modem is on-line and connected to another modem. Waiting for DSR and/or CD checks that the modem is on-line.

To receive data from a DCE to a DTE, you would have to:

Step 1: Assert DTR and RTS.
Step 2: Wait for DSR and CTS.
Step 3: Receive the data.
Step 4: If you need to pause incoming data, drop RTS. Reassert RTS when ready to commence receiving.

So an example of a modem exchange would involve a dozen steps. The basic steps would be similar to the following:

Step 1: The telephone rings when a remote modem wants to make a connection. The data set sends the ring indicator signal to the data terminal to warn of the incoming call.

Step 2: The data terminal switches ON or flips into the proper mode to engage in communications. It indicates its readiness by sending the data terminal ready signal to the data set.

Step 3: Simultaneously, it activates its RTS line.

Step 4: When the data set knows that the data terminal is ready, it answers the phone and listens for the carrier of the other modem. If it hears the carrier, it sends out the DCD signal.

Step 5: The data set negotiates a connection. When it is capable of sending data down the phone line, it activates the DSR signal.

Step 6: Simultaneously, it activates its CTS line.

Step 7: The data set relays bytes from the phone line to the data terminal through the RD line.

Step 8: The data terminal sends bytes to the data set (and then to the distant modem) through the TD line.

Step 9: Because the phone line is typically slower than the data terminal to data set link, the data set quickly fills its internal buffer. It tells the data terminal to stop sending bytes by deactivating the CTS line. When its buffer empties, it reactivates CTS.

Step 10: If the data terminal cannot handle incoming data, it deactivates its RTS line. When it can again accept data, it reactivates the request to send line.

Step 11: The call ends. The carrier disappears, and the data set discontinues the DCD, CTS, and DSR signals.

Step 12: Upon losing the DCD signal, the data terminal returns to its quiescent state, dropping its RTS and DTR signals.

In a nutshell, the data terminal must see the DSR signal as well as the CTS signal before it will send data. In addition, the data set must see the DTR and RTS signals before it will send out serial data. Interrupting either of the first pair of signals will usually stop the data terminal from pumping out data. Interrupting either of the second pair of signals will stop the data set from replying with its own data.

3.6.2   Software Handshaking

Software handshaking (sometimes called character-oriented protocols) involve sending flow control signals as signal bytes embedded with the data bytes. Therefore, no hardware handshaking lines are necessary. This is necessary because the hardware handshaking lines only extend from the DTE to the DCE and cannot send flow control to the other computer at the other end of the line.

In software handshaking (character-oriented protocols), some characters have special significance (control characters). These control characters will have preagreed upon flow control, terminal control, and/or error control significance. Software will have to be present to determine if a byte received is either a data byte or a control byte.

In the most common software handshaking scheme (Xon/Xoff), instead of the DTE device dropping the RTS signal to pause, the control byte Xoff (^S) is sent. When ready to resume, the control byte Xon (^Q) is sent.

NOTE: Data usually flows in one direction and control bytes (software handshake) usually flow in the other direction.

To transmit data from DTE to DTE via flow control, you would:

Step 1: Check for a valid communication link (comm link) (DTR, DSR, and CD asserted).
Step 2: Make sure intermediate DCE devices are ready (RTS and CTS asserted).
Step 3: Transmit data, but watch the receive data line closely.
Step 4: Transmit the data as long as an Xoff has not been received.
Step 5: Pause and wait whenever Xoff received until Xon received.

To receive data (DTE to DTE) you would:

Step 1: Check for a valid comm link (DTR, DSR, and CD asserted).
Step 2: Make sure intermediate DCE devices are ready (RTS and CTS asserted).
Step 3: Receive the data.
Step 4: If you need to pause incoming data, transmit the Xoff character. When you are ready to commence receiving, transmit Xon.

In FTP data bytes are packaged into small chunks called packets, address fields are added at the front (header), and checksums are added at the rear of the packet. Communication takes the form of a handshake between the sender and the receiver. Communication of a message from sender to receiver takes the format of this datagram.

This is a half duplex method of communication. Long messages are broken up into a series of data packets and transmitted one at a time across the link. Each packet is acknowledged before the next packet is transmitted. If a packet is not acknowledged, the sender will time out and then retransmit the packet. If the packet is acknowledged by the receiver, the sender sends the next packet and so on until the entire message has been sent. If a packet that contains errors is received, the receiver will send a negative acknowledge, which requests the sender to send it again.

Data bytes can contain data according to the ASCII code (for text), or simply a value between 0 and 255 for binary data. Control bytes are only treated as control bytes if they are in the proper position (field) within the packet. Control bytes or complete response packets can be used to determine the behavior of the communication link and are used for a range of different purposes.

Some systems may utilize software codes so that information may only be transmitted in one direction at a time (half duplex), which requires software codes to switch from one direction to another.

Some examples of control bytes are:

■ **ACK**—Positive acknowledge. This is sent by the receiver to indicate successful receipt of the previous message block or a successful response to a selection (multipoint) or line bid (point-to-point).
■ **NAK**—Negative acknowledge. This is sent by the receiver to indicate the unsuccessful receipt of the previous message block. It is also used to indicate a negative response to a selection or line bid.

- **SOH**—Start of header. This is transmitted before header characters that specify routing or priority information for the message.
- **EOT**—End of transmission. This concludes the transmission.
- **ETB**—End of transmission block. This indicates the end of the text block that started with STX or SOH. The receiver will then send ACK or NAK depending upon the correct receipt of the message blocks.
- **SYN**—Synchronize character. This establishes and maintains character synchronization prior to a message block and during transmission. Also used as a fill when there are no messages to be sent.
- **STX**—Start of text. Transmitted before the first data characters. Signifies that a block of data bytes follows.
- **ETX**—End of text. Terminates a data block begun with SOH or STX and terminates the end of a sequence of blocks. The receiver will then send ACK or NAK depending upon the correct receipt of the message blocks.

See Table 3.13 for the list of ASCII codes used for software handshaking.

Table 3.13 ASCII Codes Used for Software Handshaking

Hex value	Code	Full name
1	SOH	Start of heading
2	STX	Start of text
3	ETX	End of text
4	EOT	End of transmission
5	ENQ	Enquiry
6	ACK	Acknowledge
10	DLE	Data line escape
11	DC1/XON	Device control 1 (transmit ON)
12	DC2	Device control 2
13	DC3/XOFF	Device control 3 (transmit OFF)
14	DC4	Device control 4
15	NAK	Negative Acknowledge
16	SYN	Synchronize
17	ETB	End of transmission block
18	CAN	Cancel
19	EMS	End of medium

3.6.3   **Flow Control**

Flow control is the ability to slow down or speed up the flow of bytes in a wire. For serial ports, this means the ability to stop and then restart the flow without any loss of bytes. Flow control is needed for most external modems to allow a jump in instantaneous flow rates.

For example, consider the case where you connect a 33.6 Kbps external modem via a short cable to your serial port. The modem sends and receives bytes over the phone line at 33.6 Kbps. Assume it's not doing any data compression or error correction. You have set the serial port speed to 115,200 bps, and you are sending data from your computer to the phone line. Then, the flow rate from the computer to your modem over the short cable is 115.2 Kbps. However, the flow from your modem out the phone line is only 33.6 Kbps. Because a faster flow (115.2 Kbps) is going into your modem than is coming out of it, the modem stores the excess flow (115.2 Kbps – 33.6 Kbps = 81.6 Kbps) in one of its buffers. This buffer (which is common for all communication devices) would soon overrun (run out of free storage space) unless the high 115.2 Kbps flow is stopped.

But flow control comes to the rescue. When the modem's buffer is almost full, the modem sends a stop signal to the serial port. The serial port then passes on the stop signal to the device driver and the 115.2 Kbps flow is halted. The modem continues to send out data at 33.6 Kbps, drawing on the data it previously accumulated in its buffer. Because nothing is coming into the buffer, the level of bytes in it starts to drop. When almost no bytes are left in the buffer, the modem sends a start signal to the serial port, and the 115.2 Kbps flow from the computer to the modem resumes. Flow control creates an average flow rate in the short cable (in this case, 33.6 Kbps) which is significantly less than the ON flow rate of 115.2 Kbps. This is called *start/stop* flow control.

So far in our discussion we assumed that the modem did no data compression. This would be true when the modem is sending a file that is already compressed and cannot be compressed further. Now, let's consider the opposite extreme, where the modem compresses data with a high compression ratio. In such a case, the modem might need an input flow rate of 115.2 Kbps to provide an output (to the phone line) of 33.6 Kbps (compressed data). The compression ratio is 3.43 (115.2/33.6) which is much higher than average. In this case, the modem is able to compress the 115.2 Kbps PC to modem flow and send the same data out on the phone line at 33.6 Kbps. There's no need for flow control here. But such a high compression ratio rarely happens so that most of the time flow control is needed to slow down the flow on the 115.2 Kbps PC to modem cable. The flow is stopped and started so that the average flow is usually well under the ON flow of 115.2 Kbps.

In the previous example, the modem was an external modem. But the same situation exists (as of late 2000) for most internal modems. There is still a speed limit on the PC to modem speed, even though this flow doesn't take place over an external cable. This makes internal modems compatible with external modems.

Flow control can also be used for the opposite direction of flow; from a modem (or other device) to a computer. Each direction of flow involves 3 buffers:

1. in the modem
2. in the UART chip (called first in first out (FIFOs))
3. in main memory managed by the serial driver

Flow control protects certain buffers from overflowing. The small UART FIFO buffers are not protected in this way but rely instead on a fast response to the interrupts they issue. FIFO stands for *first in, first out,* which is the way it handles bytes. All 3 buffers use the FIFO rule but only one of them also uses it as a name.

3.7   COMMUNICATION STANDARDS

While the modem interface is standardized, there are a number of standards and protocols that specify how formatted data is to be transmitted over telephones lines. The ITU, formerly known as the CCITT, has defined many important standards for data communications. Most modems have built-in support for the more common standards. V.22bis, V.32 and V.32bis were early standards that specify speeds of 2.4 Kbps, 9.6 Kbps, and 14.4 Kbps respectively (see Table 3.14).

The V.34 standard was introduced at the end of 1994. It supports 28.8 Kbps, and is now considered the minimum acceptable standard. V.34 modems are able to drop their speed to communicate with slower modems and interrogate the line, adjusting their speed up or down according to the prevailing line conditions. In 1996, the V.34 standard was upgraded to V.34+, which allows for data transfer speeds of up to 33.6 Kbps, is backwards compatible with all previous standards, and adapts to line conditions to eke out the greatest usable amount of bandwidth.

Error correction is the capability of some modems to identify errors during transmission by embedding some error checking scheme into the data being sent. If the data at the receiving end seems corrupt, it is automatically resent. Because the error correction information is sent by one modem and interpreted by another modem, both modems must agree on the same error correction method.

The most successful proprietary protocols are the **Microcom Networking Protocols (MNP).** The MNP standards go from MNP Class 1 to MNP Class 10. They do not stand alone, but operate in conjunction with other modem standards. MNP 1 is half duplex. MNP Classes 2–4 deal with error control and can transmit error-free data by resending blocks of data that become corrupted in transmission. Today, when modems negotiate operation parameters during initialization, the modems will try to agree on the V.42 standard. If one of the modems can not use the V.42 standard, it will try MNP 4, followed by MNP 3, MNP 2, and MNP 1. If the modems can't use any of the error control methods, then it will use none.

> *NOTE:* While the error detection technique is effective, it is still possible to experience data loss or corruption due to buffer overflow, interrupt conflicts, loose connectors, faulty cables, and faulty modems.

MNP Class 5 and V.42bis support data compression. Data compression refers to the modem's ability to compress data as it is being sent. Because the data can be compressed to one quarter of its original size, the effective speed of the modem is quadrupled. A 28,000 modem can yield a transfer rate up to 115,200 Kbps. Some of the newer protocols, such as V.42 and MNP Class 4, use synchronization bits on the line to act as clock pulses. The data is then sent between the clock pulses, which enhances error control and leads to faster speeds. Of course, the modem on the other end must have a UART chip that can

Table 3.14   Communications Protocols

Protocol	Maximum transmission rate	Duplex mode	Comments
Bell 103	300 bps	Full	Used FSK. Bell 103 is the only standard for which the baud rate is equal to the data rate.
CCITT V.21	300 bps	Full	
Bell 212A	1200 bps	Full	Uses QAM.
ITU V.22	1200 bps	Half	
ITU V.22bis	2400 bps	Full	Uses QAM at 600 baud
ITU V.29	9600 bps	Half	Data transmission standard for Group III facsimile (fax) transmission.
ITU V.32	9600 bps	Full	Uses TCQAM at 2400 baud.
ITU V.32bis	14,400 bps	Full	Uses TCQAM at 2400.
ITU V.34	28,800 bps	Full	Most reliable standard for 28,800 bps communication.
ITU V.34bis	33,600 bps	Full	Enhanced V.34 standard
ITU V.42	33,600 bps	Full	An error detection standard for high speed modems.
ITU V.42bis	38,400 bps	Full	Uses data compression protocol
ITU V.90	56,600 bps	Full	The fastest transmissions standard available for analog transmission, it is capable of 56,000 bps.
ITU V.92	56,600 bps	Full	Transmits at the same speed as V.90 but offers a reduced handshake time and an on-hold feature.

translate from synchronous to asynchronous. The 56 Kbps standard allows for the fastest data transmission. When possible, 56 Kbps modems do not translate information from digital to analog, making maximum use of the digital circuits available in most PSTNs.

MNP Classes 5–10 address various modem operating parameters. Class 5 was already discussed. Class 10 is Microcom's proprietary error control protocol. It provides a set of *adverse channel enhancements,* which help modems cope with bad phone connections by making multiple attempts to make a connection, and adjusting both the size of the data packets and the speed of the transfer according to the condition the line. The most common MNP protocols are numbers 2–5, and 10 is often included.

The 56 Kbps modem became available in 1997, despite the absence of an international standard for this speed. The K56Flex group of companies, including 3Com, Ascend, Hayes,

Motorola, Lucent, and Rockwell, used Rockwell chipsets to achieve the faster speed, while companies like US Robotics used its own x2 technology. The two systems were not compatible, forcing users and Internet Service Providers (ISPs) to opt for one or the other. Moreover, there are basic limitations to 56 Kbps technology. It uses asymmetric data rates and thus can achieve high speeds only when downloading data from an ISP's server.

Most telephone COs (exchanges) in this and almost every other country around the world are digital, and so are the connections between COs. All ISPs have digital lines linking them to the telephone network (in Europe, either E1 or ISDN lines). But the lines to most homes and offices are still analog, which limits bandwidth and suffers from line noise (mostly static). They were designed to transfer telephone conversations rather than digital data, so even after compression there is only so much data that can be squeezed onto them.

56 Kbps makes the most of the much faster part of the connection—the digital lines. Data can be sent from the ISP over an entirely digital network until it reaches the final part of the journey from a local CO to the home or office. It then uses PCM to overlay the analog signal and squeeze as much as possible out of the analog line side of the connection. However, there is a catch: 56 Kbps technology allows for one conversion from digital to analog, so if there is a section that runs over analog and then returns to digital, it will only be possible to connect at 33.6 Kbit/s (maximum).

> *NOTE:* Analog lines can reach a maximum speed of only 53 Kbps due to FCC regulations that restrict the power output.

The reason that it's not possible to upload at 56 Kbps over analog lines is simply because analog lines are not good enough. There are innumerable possible obstacles to prevent a clear signal getting through, such as in-house wiring anomalies, varying wiring distances (1–6 Km), and splices. It is still theoretically possible to achieve a 33.6 Kbps data transfer rate upstream, and work is being carried out to perfect a standard that will increase this by 20 to 30%. Another problem created by sending a signal from an analog line to a digital line is the quantization noise produced by the analog to digital conversion (ADC)

Digital to analog conversion (DAC) can be thought of as representing each eight bits as one of 256 voltages—a translation done 8000 times per second. By sampling this signal at the same rate, the 56 Kbps modem can, in theory, pass 64 Kbps (8000×8) without loss. This simplified description omits other losses, which limit the speed to 56 Kbps.

There is also some confusion as to the possible need to upgrade the PC serial port to cope with 56 Kbps operation. These days, the serial port usually uses the 16550 UART chip, itself once an upgrade to cope with faster modems. It is rated at 115 Kbps but 56 Kbps modems can overload it because they compress and decompress data on the fly. In normal Internet use, data is usually compressed before being sent, so compression by the modem is minimal.

On February 4, 1998, the ITU finally brought the year-long standards battle to an end by agreeing to a 56 Kbps standard, known as V.90. The V.90 standard uses techniques similar to both K 56 Flex and x2, and the expectation was that manufacturers would be able to ship compliant products within weeks rather than months. The new standard was formally ratified in the summer of 1998, following an approval process that lasted several months.

The V.90 standard is neither x2 nor K56Flex, although it does use techniques from both. It is actually two standards in one: The specification defines (1) a digital modem and (2) an analog modem capable of transmitting data at up to 56 Kbps downstream and up to

33.6 Kbps upstream. In this case, downstream means from the digital to the analog modem. The former is connected to the PSTN via an ISDN line, and will usually be part of a bank of modems connected to a multiple-line ISDN at an ISP. The analog modem plugs into the PSTN at the subscriber's end.

The key to V.90's 56 Kbps capability is the PCM coding scheme introduced by the standard's proprietary forerunners. PCM codes are digital representations of audio signals and are the telephone system's native language. The exchange generates these on receipt of analog signals from the subscriber's handset. They are eight bits long and are transferred at a rate of 8000 per second—a total throughput of 64 Kbps. A V.90 digital modem uses a large subset of these codes to encode data and delivers them to the telephone system via an ISDN link. At the subscriber's end, the codes are converted to an analog signal by the exchange—as if they had been created in the usual way—and these tones are sent to the subscriber's modem.

Most of the work in creating V.90 went into the line probing and signal generation schemes. When a V.90 connection is first established, the two modems send each other a list of their capabilities. If V.90 communication is possible, the analog and digital modems send test signals to each other to check the quality of their connection and establish whether there are any digital impairments in the telephone system that might prevent the PCM codes from arriving correctly. For example, on some long distance or international calls, the 64 Kbps signal is compressed to 32 Kbps (or more) for reasons of economics, which ruins V.90.

If there are no impairments, the analog modem analyzes the signals from the digital modem and informs it of the best way to encode its data. The two modems also sort out what the round trip delay is and work out what equalization to apply to the line to get the best possible frequency response.

Coding the information into PCM is a complex business. The telephone system doesn't treat PCM codes linearly. Instead, it allocates more PCM codes to lower signal levels and fewer codes to higher levels. This corresponds with the way the human ear responds to sound, but it also means that the receiving modem might not be able to distinguish between some of the adjacent codes accurately. Also, the signal synthesized by the digital modem must be able to be accurately converted to analog and sent through the analog parts of the telephone exchange.

Error connection and detection systems also limit the sequential permutations possible. In short, there are sequences of codes that can't be sent and others that must be sent, but these are dependent on the data being transmitted. A final complication is that the American and European telephone systems use different sets of PCM codes.

The V.90 standard was formally ratified on September 15, 1998. Beyond V.90, an ITU study group is looking into the next generation of PCM modems, with the intention of achieving a 40–45 Kbps transmission speed from the analog modem.

Announced in 2000, the ITU's V.92 analog modem standard has the same download speed as the V.90 standard (56 Kbps) but increases the maximum upload speed from 33.6 Kbps to 48 Kbps. The new standard also introduces a couple of user convenience features:

■ QuickConnect shortens the time (by up to 30 seconds) it takes to make a connection by reducing handshake procedures by up to 50%. The reduction is accomplished by having the modem "remember" the phone line characteristics, which are then stored for future use.

■ Modem-on-Hold allows users, provided they subscribe to their phone company's Call-Waiting service, to be connected to the Internet via a given phone line while concurrently using it to receive or initiate a voice call.

3.8   SERIAL LINE PROTOCOLS

Serial line protocols are used for a computer to connect to a server (such as those used by an ISP) via a serial line such as a modem to become an actual node on the Internet. Serial Line Protocols include the **Serial Line Internet Protocol (SLIP),** the Compressed Serial Line Internet Protocol (CSLIP), and the **Point-to-Point Protocol (PPP).**

3.8.1   The Serial Line Interface Protocol (SLIP)

The first protocol used for carrying IP packets over dial-up lines was the Serial Line Interface Protocol (SLIP). SLIP is a simple protocol for which you send packets down a serial link delimited with special END characters. SLIP doesn't do a number of desirable things that data link protocols can do. It only works with TCP/IP, therefore it cannot be used with other protocols such as IPX. It doesn't perform error checking at the OSI data layer and it doesn't authenticate users dialing into an access router. Also, you have to know the IP address assigned to you by your service provider. You also need to know the IP address of the remote system you will be dialing into. If IP addresses are dynamically assigned (depends on your service provider), your SLIP software needs to be able to pick up the IP assignments automatically or you will have to set them up manually. Lastly, you will have to configure certain parameters of the device such as the maximum transmission unit (MTU), the maximum receive unit (MRU), and the use of compression.

3.8.2   The Point-to-Point Protocol (PPP)

One of the oldest data communications protocols still in use today is IBM's Synchronous Data Link Control (SDLC). SDLC defined rules for transmitting data across a digital line and was used for long distance communications between terminals and computers or between pairs of computers. IBM submitted SDLC to standards organizations, which led to the **High Level Data Link Control (HDLC)** protocol.

HDLC is a group of protocols, or rules, for transmitting data between network points (or *nodes*). In HDLC, data is organized into a unit (a *frame*) and sent across a network to a destination that verifies its successful arrival. The HDLC protocol also manages the flow (or *pacing*) at which data is sent. HDLC is one of the most commonly used protocols for layer 2 of OSI. (Layer 1 is the detailed physical level that involves actually generating and receiving the electronic signals. Layer 3 is the higher level that has knowledge about the network, including access to router tables that indicate where to forward or send data.) On sending, programming in layer 3 creates a frame that usually contains source and destination network addresses. HDLC (layer 2) encapsulates the layer 3 frame and adds data link control information to the new, larger frame.

PPP is a protocol for communication between two computers that uses a serial interface, typically a personal computer connected by phone line via a modem to a server.

For example, your ISP may provide you with a PPP connection so that the provider's server can respond to your requests, pass them on to the Internet, and forward your requested Internet responses back to you. PPP uses the Internet protocol (IP) but has the capability to encapsulate multiple network LAN protocols. It is sometimes considered a member of the TCP/IP suite of protocols. Relative to the OSI reference model, PPP provides layer 2 (data link layer) service. Essentially, it packages your computer's TCP/IP packets and forwards them to the server where they can actually be put on the Internet.

PPP is a full duplex protocol that can be used on various physical media, including twisted pair, fiber optic lines, or satellite transmission. PPP supports asynchronous serial communication, synchronous serial communication, and ISDN. Furthermore, a multilink version of PPP is also used to access ISDN lines and to inverse multiplex analog phone lines and high-speed optical lines.

PPP uses a variation of HDLC for packet encapsulation. PPP is usually preferred over the earlier *de facto* standard SLIP because it can handle synchronous as well as asynchronous communication. PPP can share a line with other users and it has error detection that SLIP lacks. Where a choice is possible, PPP is preferred.

To enable PPP to transmit data over a serial point-to-point link, three components are used (see Figure 3.15). They are:

- **HDLC protocol**—Encapsulates its data during transmission.
- **Link Control Protocol (LCP)**—Establishes, configures, maintains, and terminates point-to-point links (including Multilink PPP (MP) sessions) and optionally tests link quality prior to data transmission. In addition, user authentication is generally performed by LCP as soon as the link is established. It can also increase throughput using compression.
- **Network Control Protocols (NCPs)**—Used to configure the different communications protocols including TCP/IP and IPX, which are allowed to be used simultaneously.

Figure 3.16 shows a PPP packet.

A series of PPP control protocols provides features for a particular layer 3 protocol to function well across the link. For example, IP Control Protocol (IPCP) provides for IP address assignment; this feature is used extensively with Internet dial-up connections

Figure 3.15 PPP Protocol

Network Layer	Upper-Layer Protocols (such as IP, IPX, AppleTalk)
Data Link Layer	Network Control Protocol (NCP) (Specific to Network Layer Protocol)
	Link Control Protocol (LCP)
	High-Level Data Link Control Protocol (HDLC)
Physical Layer	Physical Layer (Such as EIA/TIA-232, V.24, V.35, ISDN)

Figure 3.16   PPP Packets

1 byte	1 byte	1 byte	2 bytes	Variable	2 or 4 bytes
Flag	Address	Control	Protocol	Data	Frame Check Sequence (FCS)

today. An ISP or other provider of remote connectivity services can use Dynamic Host Configuration Protocol (DHCP) as the source of IP addresses that NCP hands out.

There are three distinct phases of negotiation of a PPP connection. Each of these three phases must be successfully completed before the PPP connection is ready to transfer user data. The three phases of a PPP connection are:

1. **Link establishment**—LCP packets are sent by each PPP device to configure and test the link. Each device on both ends of a connection negotiates communication options that are used to send data. It includes PPP parameters address and control field compression and protocol ID compression, which authentication protocols use to authenticate the remote access client and multilink options. An authentication protocol is selected but not implemented until the authentication phase. If no configuration option field is present, then default configurations are used.
2. **Authentication**—After LCP is complete, the authentication protocol agreed upon by the remote access server and the remote access client is implemented. The nature of this traffic is specific to the PPP authentication protocol.
3. **Network layer protocol**—During the network layer protocol phase, PPP uses the NCP to allow multiple network layer protocols to be encapsulated and sent over a PPP data link.

3.8.3   PPP Authentication Methods

When a client dials in to a RAS server, the server must verify the client's credentials for authentication by using the client's user account properties and remote access policies to authorize the connection. If authentication and authorization succeed, the server allows a connection.

There are a number of PPP authentication protocols, some of which are supported by the RADIUS protocol. Each protocol has advantages and disadvantages in terms of security, usability, and breadth of support (see Table 3.15).

Password Authentication Protocol (PAP) is the least secure authentication protocol because it uses **clear text** (plain text) passwords. The steps when using PAP are:

Step 1:   The remote access client (RAC) sends a PAP Authenticate-Request message to the remote access server, containing the remote access client's user name and clear text password. Clear text is textual data in ASCII format.

Step 2:   The remote access server checks the user name and password and sends back either a PAP Authenticate-Acknowledgement message when the user's

Table 3.15 Various Security Protocols

Protocols	Security	Use when
PAP	Low	The client and server cannot negotiate by using a more secure form of validation.
SPAP	Medium	Connecting to a Shiva LanRover, or when a Shiva client connects to a Windows 2000 based remote access server (RAS).
CHAP	High	You have clients that are not running Microsoft operating systems.
MS-CHAP	High (most secure)	Used on clients running NT v. 4 or Windows 95 or later. MS-CHAP is the most secure form of authentication.

credentials are correct, or a PAP Authenticate-No message when the user's credentials are not correct.

Therefore, the password can easily be read with a protocol analyzer. In addition, PAP offers no protection against replay attacks, RAC impersonation, or RAS impersonation. Therefore, to make your RAS more secure, ensure that PAP is disabled. Another disadvantage of using PAP is that if your password expires, PAP doesn't have the ability to change your password during authentication.

Shiva Password Authentication Protocol (SPAP), Shiva's proprietary version of PAP, offers a bit more security than PAP's plain text password with its reversible encryption mechanism. SPAP is more secure than PAP but less secure than CHAP or MS-CHAP. Someone capturing authentication packets won't be able to read the SPAP password, but this authentication protocol is susceptible to playback attacks (i.e., an intruder records the packets and resends them to gain fraudulent access). Playback attacks are possible because SPAP always uses the same reversible encryption method to send the passwords over the wire. Like PAP, SPAP doesn't have the ability to change your password during the authentication process.

Historically, **Challenge Handshake Authentication Protocol (CHAP)** is the most common dial-up authentication protocol used. It uses an industry Message Digest 5 (MD5) hashing scheme to encrypt authentication. A hashing scheme scrambles information in such a way that it's unique and it can't be reversed back to the original format.

CHAP doesn't send the actual password over the wire. Instead, it uses a three way challenge-response mechanism with one way MD5 hashing to provide encrypted authentication without sending the password over the link. The steps when using CHAP are:

Step 1: The RAS sends a CHAP Challenge message containing a session ID and an arbitrary challenge string.

Step 2: The RAC returns a CHAP Response message containing the user name in clear text and a hash of the challenge string, session ID, and the client's password, using the MD5 one way hashing algorithm.

Step 3: The RAS duplicates the hash and compares it to the hash in the CHAP Response. If the hashes are the same, the remote access server sends back a CHAP Success message. If the hashes are different, a CHAP Failure message is sent.

Because standard CHAP clients use the plain text version of the password to create the CHAP challenge response, passwords must be stored on the server to calculate an equivalent response.

Because CHAP uses an arbitrary challenge string with every authentication attempt, it protects against replay attacks. However, CHAP does not protect against RAS impersonation. In addition, because the algorithm for calculating CHAP responses is well known, it is very important that passwords be carefully chosen and sufficiently long. CHAP passwords that are common words or names are vulnerable to dictionary attacks if they can be discovered by comparing responses to the CHAP challenge with every entry in a dictionary. Passwords that are not sufficiently long can be discovered by brute force by comparing the CHAP response to sequential trials until a match to the user's response is found.

Microsoft Challenge Handshake Authentication Protocol (MS-CHAP) is Microsoft's proprietary version of CHAP. Unlike PAP and SPAP, it lets you encrypt data that is sent using PPP or PPTP connections using Microsoft Point-to-Point Encryption (MPPE). The challenge response is calculated with an MD4 hashed version of the password and the NAS challenge.

> *NOTE:* The two "flavors" of MS-CHAP (versions 1 and 2) allow for error codes including a "password expired" code and password changes.

The steps when using MS-CHAP are as follows:

Step 1: The RAS sends a MS-CHAP challenge message containing a session ID and an arbitrary challenge string.

Step 2: The RAC must return the user name and a MD4 hash of the challenge string, the session ID, and the MD4-hashed password.

Step 3: The RAS duplicates the hash and compares it to the hash in the MS-CHAP response. If the hashes are the same, the RAS sends back a CHAP Success message. If the hashes are different, a CHAP Failure message is sent.

MS-CHAP v1 only supports one-way authentication. Therefore, MS-CHAP v1 does not provide protection against RAS impersonation, which means that a client cannot determine the authenticity of the RAS server it connects to.

MS-CHAP v2 provides stronger security for remote access connections and allows for mutual authentication where the client authenticates the server. The steps when using MS-CHAP v2 are as follows:

Step 1: The RAS sends a MS-CHAP v2 Challenge message to the RAC, which consists of a session identifier and an arbitrary challenge string.

Step 2: The RAC sends a MS-CHAP v2 Response that contains the user name, an arbitrary peer challenge string, a MD4 hash of the received challenge string, the peer challenge string, the session identifier, and the MD4 hashed versions of the user's password.

Step 3: The RAS checks the MS-CHAP v2 Response message from the client and sends back a MS-CHAP v2 Response message containing an indication of the success or failure of the connection attempt. An authentication response is based on the sent challenge string, the peer challenge string, the client's encrypted response, and the user's password.

Step 4: The RAC verifies the authentication response and if it is correct, uses the connection. If the authentication response is not correct, the RAC terminates the connection.

Step 5: If a user authenticates by using MS-CHAP v2 and attempts to use an expired password, MS-CHAP prompts the user to change the password while connecting to the server. Other authentication protocols do not support this feature, effectively locking out the user who used the expired password.

If you configure your connection to use only MS-CHAP v2 and the server you're dialing into does not support MS-CHAP v2, the connection will fail. This behavior is different from Windows NT where the RAS servers negotiate a lower-level authentication if possible. In addition, MS-CHAP v2 passwords are stored more securely at the server but have the same vulnerabilities to dictionary and brute force attacks as CHAP. When using MS-CHAP v2, it is important to ensure that passwords are well chosen and long enough that they cannot be easily calculated. Many large customers require passwords to be at least six characters long with upper and lower case characters and at least one numeral.

The **unauthenticated access method (UAM)** allows remote access users to log on without checking their credentials. It does not verify the user's name and password. The only user validation performed in the UAM is authorization. Enabling UAM presents security risks that must be carefully considered when deciding whether or not to use it.

Leased point-to-point links do not typically use authentication because the ends of the link are known in advance and are fixed. Authentication (typically PAP or CHAP) is needed only when endpoints are not constant or are only intermittently connected, such as with ISDN.

SUMMARY

1. The most commonly used numbering system is the decimal number system.
2. The binary system is less complicated than the decimal system because it has only two digits: a zero (0) and a one (1).
3. The hexadecimal number system has sixteen digits. One hexadecimal digit is equivalent to a four digit binary number (4 bits, or a *nibble*) and two hexadecimal digits are used to represent a byte (8 bits).
4. To represent data on the network, you will need to use some form of signaling.
5. Signaling is the method for using electrical, light energy, or radio waves to communicate.
6. The process of changing a signal to represent data is often called modulation or encoding.
7. Digital signaling (the language of computers) is a system that is based on a binary signal system produced by pulses of light or electric voltages. The

site of the pulse is either ON/high or OFF/low to represent 1s and 0s.

8. The current state method periodically measures the digital signal for the specific state.
9. The second method is the transition state, which represents data by how the signal transitions from high to low or low to high.
10. An analog signal is the opposite of a digital signal. Instead of having a finite number of states, it has infinite number values that change constantly. Analog signals typically are sinusoidal waveforms, which are characterized by amplitude and frequency.
11. The amplitude represents the peak voltage of the sine wave.
12. The frequency indicates the number of times that a single wave will repeat over any period. It is measured in hertz (Hz) or cycles per second.

13. Another term used when talking about modulation is *time reference* or *phase*. A phase is measured in degrees.

14. The earliest form of encoding data over telephone lines is FSK, which is very similar to frequency modulation used with FM radios. FSK sends a logical 1 at one particular frequency (usually 1750 Hz) and a logical 0 at another frequency (often 1080 Hz).

15. PM is a process where two sinusoidal waveforms are compared with each other. The case where the two waveforms are going in the same direction at the same time is known as zero phase shift.

16. QAM allows the transmission of data using both the phase shift of PM and the signal magnitude of AM at the same time. The more phase shifts and magnitude levels used, the more data the technique can transmit.

17. Synchronous devices use a timing or clock signal to coordinate communications between the two devices.

18. Asynchronous signals are intermittent signals; they can occur at any time and at irregular intervals.

19. *Bandwidth* refers to the amount of data that can be carried on a given transmission medium.

20. Baseband systems use the transmission medium's entire capacity for a single channel. Baseband networks can use either analog or digital signals, but digital signaling is much more common.

21. A broadband system uses the transmission medium's capacity to provide multiple channels by using FDM. Each channel uses a carrier signal, which runs at a different frequency than the carrier signals used by the other channels. The data is embedded within the carrier channel.

22. A mux sends and receives the several data signals at different frequencies. When the various signals reach the end of the transmission media, another mux separates the frequencies so that the data can be read.

23. TDM divides the single channel into short time slots, allowing multiple devices to be assigned a time slot.

24. STDM analyzes the amount of data that each device needs to transmit and determines (on the fly) how much time each device should be allocated for data transmission on the cable or line.

25. Circuit switching is a technique that connects the sender and the receiver by a single path for the duration of a conversation. Once a connection is es-

tablished, a dedicated path exists between both ends.

26. In packet switching methods, messages are broken into packets and are sent to their destinations.

27. Cell relay is a data transmission technology based on transmitting data in relatively small, fixed-size packets (cells). Each cell contains only basic path information that allows switching devices to route the cell quickly.

28. Connections between two hosts in a packet switching network are often described as virtual circuits. A virtual circuit is a logical circuit created to ensure reliable communications between two network devices.

29. Sound is produced by vibrations of compressed air.

30. Sound is characterized by amplitude and frequency.

31. To carry a voice signal on a digital carrier, an analog voice signal must be converted to a digital signal.

32. Nyquist's theorem states that to ensure accuracy, a signal should be sampled at least twice the rate of its frequency.

33. PCM is the method used to digitize analog voice signals.

34. Digitizing is done by taking samples of the electrical signal and assigning a binary value to the amplitude of the signal. This process is also known as *sampling*.

35. When voice is transmitted over a network, losing or altering a few bits does not cause a problem. Minor data loss is not even noticed. What is more important is to deliver voice content promptly and in order.

36. Because data does not have to be delivered in real time, data networks are more concerned about reliable transport of information during which the data is neither lost nor corrupted.

37. Latency, which plays a role in the cause of jitter, can be simply defined as the time it takes for a packet to cross the network. Varied latency will cause jitter.

38. QoS refers to the capability of a network to provide better service to selected network traffic over various LAN and WAN technologies. The primary goal of QoS is to provide priority including dedicated bandwidth, controlled jitter and latency, and improved loss characteristics.

39. A modem is a device that enables a computer to transmit data over telephone lines.

40. *Baud rate* refers to the modulation rate or the number of times per second that a line changes state.

41. *Fax* is short for *facsimile transmission.* A fax machine takes a piece of paper, digitizes the text and pictures, and sends the data over a telephone line.

42. *Handshaking* is the process by which two devices initiate communications. Handshaking begins when one device sends a message to another device, thus indicating that it wants to establish a communications channel. The two devices then send several messages back and forth that enable them to agree on a communications protocol.

43. Flow control is the ability to slow down or speed up the flow of bytes in a wire.

44. Serial line protocols are used for a computer to connect to a server (such as those used by an ISP), via a serial line such as a modem to become an actual node on the Internet. Serial line protocols include SLIP, CSLIP, and PPP.

QUESTIONS

1. How many bits are in a byte?
   a. 1   b. 2
   c. 4   d. 8
   e. 16   f. 32

2. How many bits does a hexadecimal number represent?
   a. 1   b. 2
   c. 4   d. 8
   e. 16   f. 32

3. Convert the decimal value 6 to binary.
   a. 00000101   b. 00001111
   c. 00000111   d. 01010101
   e. 00000110

4. Convert the decimal value 68 to binary.
   a. 10101010   b. 00001111
   c. 01000010   d. 11110000
   e. 01010101   f. 01000100

5. Convert the binary value 10101010 to decimal.
   a. 170   b. 165
   c. 224   d. 128

6. Convert the hexadecimal number FH to binary.
   a. 1000   b. 1110
   c. 1111   d. 1010
   e. 0001

7. The ASCII character (standard + extended) set contains _____ characters.
   a. 8   b. 256
   c. 64   d. 512
   e. 128   f. 1024

8. The most basic format in which data and programs are stored in a computer is the _____ format.
   a. ASCII   b. octal
   c. binary   d. hexadecimal

9. What is the binary code for the *P* character?
   a. 01010001   b. 01010000
   c. 10100000   d. 00100000
   e. 01110000

10. What is the decimal code for the $ symbol?
   a. 100100   b. 5A
   c. 36   d. 44

11. You have a file that is 2.2 Mb in size. How many bytes is 2.2 Mb?
   a. 22000000.0   b. 2252.8
   c. 2252800.0   d. 2306867
   e. none of the above

12. What is the process of changing a signal to represent data?
   a. signaling
   b. modulation
   c. capping
   d. synchronous conversion

13. Which method is used to measure the digital signal at a particular time?
   a. current state   b. transition state
   c. differential state   d. statistical state

14. Which method is used to determine data by measuring the changes of a signal?
   a. current state   b. transition state
   c. differential state   d. statistical state

15. Which signal has an infinite number of values?
   a. analog signal
   b. digital signal
   c. infinity signal
   d. generating signal

16. When you have an analog signal, what is the peak voltage called?
   a. frequency   b. phase
   c. amplitude   d. ratio

17. When a device uses a timing or clock signal to coordinate communications, the device is known to be a _____ device.
   a. modulating   b. phasing
   c. synchronous   d. asynchronous

18. When a communication channel carries several signals at the same time, it is known as _____.
    a. bandwidth
    b. baseband
    c. circuit switching
    d. broadband

19. What switching method is used when data is broken into smaller parts and each part is sent out independently on the network to its destination?
    a. circuit switching
    b. packet switching
    c. statistical time switching
    d. frequency division switching

20. Sound is measured in (choose two):
    a. amplitude
    b. frequency
    c. phase
    d. distortion
    e. distance

21. Name one method used to convert an analog signal to a digital signal.
    a. Nyquist
    b. antialiasing
    c. PSTN
    d. PCM

22. In serial asynchronous transmissions, the _____ bit is used to signal the beginning of a new data frame.
    a. start
    b. stop
    c. parity
    d. data

23. Which of the following is the number of changes per second?
    a. baud
    b. bits per second
    c. raw transfer speed
    d. bit speed

24. The central part of the serial port is the _____.
    a. microprocessor
    b. ADC
    c. DAC
    d. UART

25. If you transmit the 8-bit binary number 11011000 and use even parity, the parity bit would be _____.
    a. 0
    b. 1

26. Which of the following signals must be present for a modem to receive data?
    a. high speed (HS)
    b. carrier detect (CD)
    c. transmit data (TxD)
    d. receive data (RxD)

27. In modem technology, CD stands for:
    a. change directory
    b. call data
    c. change dial
    d. carrier detect
    e. comm detect
    f. cease deliver

28. _____ is the term used to refer to the process of two modems establishing communications with each other.
    a. interacting
    b. connecting
    c. handshaking
    d. linking
    e. pinging

29. Which of the following asynchronous lines does the terminal activate when it wants to send data to a modem?
    a. CTS
    b. DSR
    c. RTS
    d. DTR

30. Modems use _____ transmission.
    a. synchronous
    b. asynchronous
    c. linking
    d. pinging

31. Which of the following is not a method used to encode data?
    a. PSK
    b. FSK
    c. QAM
    d. WRE

32. A modem that follows the AT Command set is known as:
    a. an AT follower
    b. a Hayes compatible modem
    c. a modem that can work only on a 286
    d. a modem that can work only on a 286 and above

33. What is the small plastic connector used on the end of UTP wires (such as telephone wires) called?
    a. RJ-5
    b. RJ-11
    c. RJ-45
    d. RJ-62

34. A customer complains that the modem they are using is bad. When they try to connect to another computer, it connects but it transmits and receives garbage. What do you do?
    a. Check the version of the software used.
    b. Check the version of the operating system used.
    c. Check the data bits, parity, and stop bits set for both modems.
    d. All of the above.

35. What are the three main components of PPP?
    a. NCPs
    b. SDLC
    c. SMDS
    d. HDLC
    e. HSSI for DTE/DCE connection
    f. LCP to establish, configure, and test the data link connection

36. Which of the following are dial-up communication protocols (select all that apply)?
a. FTP
b. TCP
c. PPP
d. SLIP

37. The 1948 theorem that is the basis for understanding the relationship of channel capacity, bandwidth, and SNR is known as _____.
a. the Peter Principle
b. Shannon's Law
c. the Heisenberg Uncertainty Principle
d. Boyle's Law

38. What appears to be the practical limit for analog modems over the standard telephone network?
a. 33 Kbps
b. 24 Kbps
c. 28.8 Kbps
d. 19.2 Kbps

39. Analog signals can be _____ by combining them with a carrier frequency.
a. carried
b. multiplexed
c. transported
d. mixed

40. In an AM wave, which of the following remains constant?
a. framing
b. frequency
c. amplitude
d. voltage

41. How is a statistical multiplexer similar to TDM?
a. Statistical multiplexing is used only for analog transmission, whereas TDM is used for digital transmission.
b. Statistical multiplexing relies on fiber optic cable, whereas TDM can be used on wire media.
c. Statistical multiplexing requires more bandwidth to process signals than TDM does.
d. Statistical multiplexing makes more efficient use of time slots than TDM does.

CHAPTER 4

Network Technology and Protocol Review

Topics Covered in this Chapter

Introduction

In Chapter 1, 2, and 3, we discussed the physical part of the network, but we haven't yet talked about the software, particularly the protocols that make the network run. It is essential that administrators understand these protocols so that they can configure and troubleshoot the network. This chapter is an overview of the TCP/IP and IPX protocol suites.

Objectives

- Given a RFC number, find the RFC document on the web.
- Explain TCP/IP protocols in terms of routing, addressing schemes, interoperability, and naming conventions.
- Define the purpose, function, and/or use of IP, TCP, UDP, ARP and ICMP protocols within TCP/IP.
- Define the function of TCP/UDP ports.
- Identify well known ports.
- Given a troubleshooting scenario, select the appropriate TCP/IP utility (tracert, ping, arp, netstat, nbtstat, ipconfig, ifconfig, winipcfg, or nslookup).
- Given output from a diagnostic utlity (e.g., tracert, ping, or ipconfig), identify the utility and interpret the output.
- List the protocols that can connect to a TCP/IP network.
- List and describe the ways to translate from a NetBIOS name to IP addresses and from host names to IP address.
- Explain the difference between IPX and SPX.
- Diagnose and troubleshoot a given IPX problem.

4.1 TCP/IP AND THE INTERNET

The Internet that you know today began as a U.S. Department of Defense (DoD) experiment to interconnect DoD-funded research sites in the United States. In December of 1968, the Advanced Research Projects Agency (ARPA) awarded a grant to design and deploy a packet switching network (messages divided into packets, transmitted individually, and recompiled into the original message). In September of 1969, the first node of the ARPANET was installed at UCLA. By 1971, the ARPANET spanned the continental U.S. and had connected with Europe by 1973.

Over time, the initial protocols used to connect the hosts together proved incapable of keeping up with the growing network traffic load. Therefore, a new TCP/IP protocol suite was proposed and implemented. By 1983, the popularity of the new TCP/IP protocol grew as it was included in the communications kernel for the University of California's UNIX implementation; 4.2BSD (Berkeley Software Distribution) UNIX. Today, the TCP/IP protocol is the primary protocol used on the Internet and is supported by Microsoft Windows, Novell NetWare, UNIX, Linux, and Apple Macintosh.

The standards for TCP/IP are published in a series of documents called **Requests for Comments (RFC).** A RFC can be submitted by anyone. Eventually, if it gains enough interest, it may evolve into an Internet standard. Each RFC is designated by a RFC number. Once published, a RFC never changes. Modifications to an original RFC are assigned a new RFC number.

RFCs are classified as one of the following: (1) approved Internet standards, (2) proposed Internet standards (circulated in draft form for review), (3) Internet best practices, or (4) for your information (FYI) documents. You should always follow approved Internet standards.

For more information on RFCs, visit the following websites:
http://www.rfc-editor.org/
http://www.cis.ohio-state.edu/hypertext/information/rfc.html

4.1.1   TCP/IP Protocols

TCP/IP does not worry about how the hosts (computers or any other network connection) connect to the network. Instead, TCP/IP was designed to operate over almost any underlying LAN or WAN (see Figure 4.1). This would include:

- **LAN Protocols**—Ethernet, Token Ring, and ARCnet networks
- **WAN Protocols**—ATM, Frame Relay, and X.25
- **Serial Line Protocols**—SLIP and PPP

When you send or receive data, the data is divided into little chunks called packets. Each of these packets contains both the sender's TCP/IP address and the receiver's TCP/IP address. When the packet needs to go to another computer on another network, the packet is directly sent to a gateway computer (usually a router). The gateway understands the networks that it is directly connected to.

The gateway computer reads the destination address to determine which direction the packet needs to be sent. It then forwards the packet to an adjacent gateway. The packet is

Figure 4.1 TCP/IP Protocol Suite

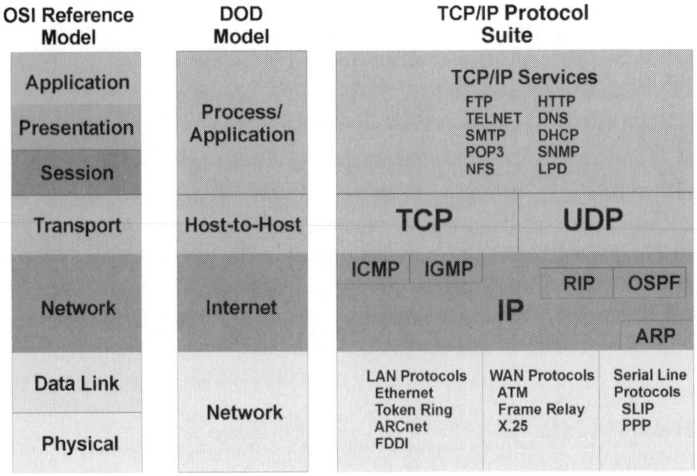

Figure 4.1 Continued

Internet Protocols

Routes data packets between different hosts or networks.

- **Internet Protocol (IP)**—Connectionless protocol primarily responsible for addressing and routing packets between hosts (RFC 791).

- **Address Resolution Protocol (ARP)**—Used to obtain hardware addresses (MAC addresses) of hosts located on the same physical network (RFC 826).

- **Internet Control Message Protocol (ICMP)**—Sends messages and reports errors regarding the delivery of a packet (RFC 792).

- **Internet Group Management Protocol (IGMP)**—Used by IP hosts to report host group membership to local multicast routers (RFC 1112).

- **Router Information Protocol (RIP)**—Distance vector route discovery protocol where the entire routing table is periodically sent to the other routers (RFC 1723).

- **Open Shortest Path First (OSPF)**—Link state route discovery protocol where each router periodically advertises itself to other routers (RFC 1245, 1246, 1247 and 1253).

Host-to-Host Protocols

Maintains data integrity and sets up reliable, end-to-end communication between hosts.

- **Transmission Control Protocol (TCP)**—Provides connection-oriented, reliable communications for applications that typically transfer large amounts of data at one time or that require an acknowledgement for data received (RFC 793).

- **User Datagram Protocol (UDP)**—Provides connectionless-oriented communications and does not guarantee that packets will be delivered. Applications that use UDP typically transfer small amounts of data at once. Reliable delivery is the responsibility of the application (RFC 768).

Process/Application Protocols

Acts as the interface for the user. Provides applications that transfer data between hosts.

- **File Transfer Protocol (FTP)**—Allows a user to transfer files between local and remote host computers (RFC 959).

- **Telecommunication Network (TELNET)**—a virtual terminal protocol (terminal emulation) allowing a user to log onto another TCP/IP host to access network resources (RFC 854).

- **Simple Mail Transfer Protocol (SMTP)**—The standard protocol for the exchange of e-mail over the Internet. It is used between e-mail servers on the Internet or to allow an e-mail client to send mail to a server (RFC 821 and 822).

- **Post Office Protocol (POP)**—Defines a simple interface between a user's mail client software and e-mail server. It is used to download mail from the server to the client and allows the user to manage their mailboxes (RFC 1460).

- **Network File System (NFS)**—Provides transparent remote access to shared files across networks (RFC 1094).

- **Hypertext Transfer Protocol (HTTP)**—The basis for exchange over the World Wide Web (WWW). WWW pages are written in the Hypertext Markup Language (HTML), an ASCII based, platform-independent formatting language (RFC 1945 and 1866).

- **Domain Name System (DNS)**—Defines the structure of Internet names and their association with IP addresses (RFC 1034 and 1035).

- **Dynamic Host Configuration Protocol (DHCP)**—Used to automatically assign TCP/IP addresses and other related information to clients (RFC 2131).

- **Simple Network Management Protocol (SNMP)**—Defines procedures and management information databases for managing TCP/IP-based network devices (RFC 1157 and 1441).

- **Line Printer Daemon (LPD)**—Provides printing on a TCP/IP network.

- **Network Time Protocol (NTP)**—An Internet standard protocol that assures accurate synchronization (to the millisecond) of computer clock times in a network of computers (RFC 1305).

Figure 4.2 TCP/IP Packet

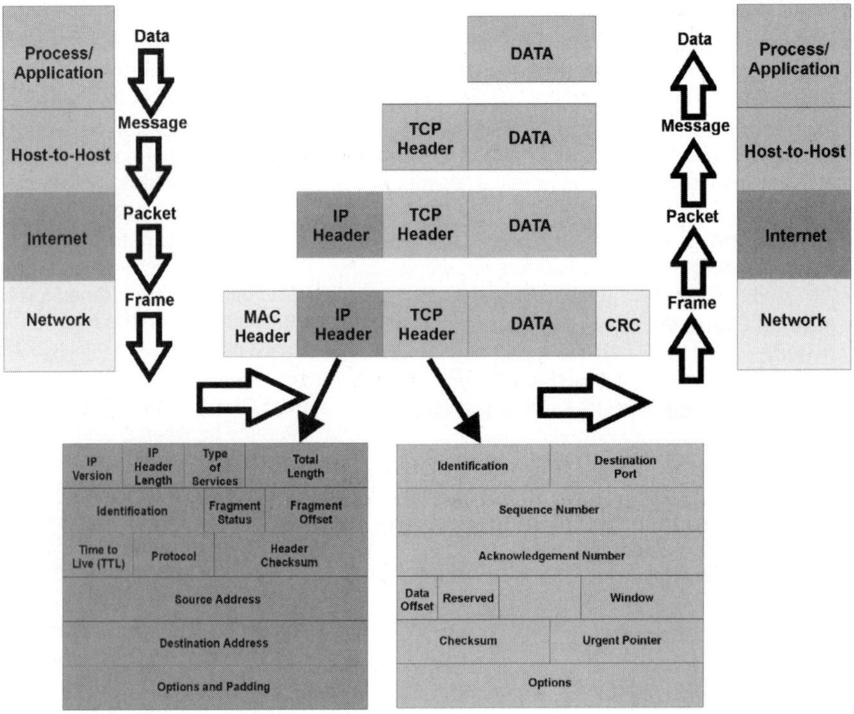

then forwarded from gateway to gateway until it gets to the network that the destination host belongs to. The last gateway then forwards the packet directly to the computer whose address is specified (see Figure 4.2).

The lowest protocol within the TCP/IP suite is the **Internet Protocol (IP).** IP is a connectionless protocol, which means that there is no established communications connection between the end points. Each packet (also known as a datagram) that travels through the Internet is treated as an independent datum. Therefore, each datum is not affected by other data packets. In addition, IP does not guarantee delivery. Therefore, packets can get lost, delivered out of sequence, or delayed. Instead, IP must rely on TCP to determine that the data arrived successfully at its destination and to retransmit the data if it did not.

When a packet is received from the TCP protocol, it inserts its own header in the datagram. The main content of the IP header are the source and destination addresses, the protocol numbers, and a checksum.

The protocols that work on top of the IP protocol are TCP and UDP. **Transmission Control Protocol (TCP)** is a reliable, connection-oriented delivery service that breaks the data into manageable packets, wraps them with the information needed to route them to their destinations, and then reassembles the pieces at the receiving end of the communication link. It establishes a virtual connection between the two hosts or computers so that they can send messages back and forth for a period of time. A virtual connection appears to be always connected, but in reality it is made of many packets being sent back and forth independently.

The most important information in the header includes the source and destination port numbers, a sequence number for the datagram, and a checksum. The source port number and destination port number ensure that the data is sent back and forth to the correct process (or program) running on each computer. The sequence number allows the datagram to be rebuilt in the correct order in the receiving computer, and the checksum allows the protocol to check whether the data sent is the same as the data received.

The TCP protocol has two other important functions: (1) TCP uses acknowledgements to verify that the data was received by the other host. If an acknowledgement is not sent, the data is resent. (2) Because the data packets can be delivered out of order, the TCP protocol must put the packets back in the correct order.

Another transport layer protocol is the **User Datagram Protocol (UDP).** Unlike TCP, which uses acknowledgements to ensure data delivery, UDP does not. Therefore, UDP is considered unreliable, "best effort" delivery. Because it is considered unreliable, UDP is used for protocols that transmit small amounts of data at one time or for broadcasts (packets sent to everyone).

> *NOTE:* Unreliability doesn't mean that the packets will not get delivered; it just means that there is no guarantee or check to make sure that they get to their destinations.

When TCP/IP is used, data is encapsulated in five steps:

Step 1: The user application creates the data and a variety of parameters is established. The data is then passed to the transport layer.

Step 2: The transport layer adds a TCP or UPD header and establishes the flow control parameters. The data is then passed to the network layer.

Step 3: The network layer places the destination network address in a header, puts the data behind it, and passes it to the data link layer.

Step 4: The data is converted to frames. A data link header and a trailer, including a frame sequence check, are added.

Step 5: The physical layer transmits the bits.

4.1.2   IP Addressing

Each connection on a TCP/IP address (logical address) is called a **host** (a computer or other network device that is connected to a TCP/IP network) and is assigned a unique **IP address.** A host can be any network interface, including NICs or a printer that connects directly onto the network. The format of the IP address is four 8-bit numbers (octets) divided by a period (.). The numbers used can be 0–255. For example, a TCP/IP address could be 131.107.3.1 or 2.0.0.1. Because the address is used to identify the computer, no two connections can use the same IP address. If there are repetitions, one or both of the computers will not be able to communicate.

IP v4 is based on 32-bit wide addresses which allow a little over 4 billion hosts. IP v6 uses 128 bits for its addresses. IP v6 can have up to 3.4×10^{38} hosts, which can handle all of today's IP-based machines without using network address translation to allow for future growth and to handle IP addresses for mobile devices such as PDAs and cell phones.

IP v6 addresses are usually divided into groups of 16 bits written as four hex digits, and the groups are separated by colons. An example is:

`FE80:0000:0000:0000:02A0:D2FF:FEA5:E9F5`

When configuring a host with an IP address, you must also include its subnet mask. The subnet masks identify which bits of an address identify the network address and which bits identify the host address. Examples of subnet masks may be `255.0.0.0`, `255.255.0.0`, `255.255.255.0` or `255.255.224.0`.

Lastly, if you need to communicate with other networks, you just specify the default gateway. The default gateway is usually the address of the nearest router. For more information on IP addressing, see Chapter 5.

4.1.3   Internet Control Message Protocol

The **Internet Control Message Protocol (ICMP)** works at the network layer and is used by IP for many different services. ICMP manages IP by reporting on IP status information. It transmits "destination unreachable" messages to the source device if the target device cannot be located. It can also provide notification that a router's buffer has become full, indicating that the router is congested and has been forced to drop packets. Additionally, the ICMP protocol notifies a transmitting device that a better route to a destination exists. Both the ping and traceroute utilities use ICMP messaging to identify whether a destination device is reachable and to track a packet as it is routed from a source to a destination device. As the IP processes the datagrams generated by ICMP, ICMP is not directly apparent to the application user.

4.1.4   TCP/IP Ports and Sockets

Every time one TCP/IP host communicates with another TCP/IP host, it will use the IP address and port number to identify the host and service/program running on the host. A TCP/IP port number is a logical connection placed by client programs to specify a particular server program running on a computer on the network defined at the transport layer. The source port number identifies the application that sent the data, and the destination port number identifies the application that receives the data. Port numbers are from 0–65536. Additionally, there are two types of ports that are based on their respective protocols: (1) TCP and (2) UDP.

Today, the very existence of ports and their numbers is transparent to the users of the network, as many ports are standardized. Thus, a remote computer will know which port it should connect to for a specific service. Ports 0–1024 are reserved for use by certain privileged services and popular higher-level applications. These are known as "well known ports," which have been assigned by the Internet Assigned Numbers Authority (IANA). Some of the well known protocols are shown in Table 4.1. For example, when using your browser to view a website, the default port to indicate the HTTP service is identified as port 80 and the FTP service is identified as port 21 (see Figure 4.3). Other application processes are given port numbers for each connection so that a single computer can run several services.

Table 4.1 Popular TCP/IP Services and Their Default Assigned Port Numbers

Network program or service	Default assigned port number
DHCP client	UDP port 68
DHCP server	UDP port 67
DNS	UDP port 53
FTP—Control	TCP port 21
FTP—Data	TCP port 20
HTTP	TCP/UDP port 80
NetBIOS session service	UDP port 139
Network news transport protocol (NNTP)	TCP port 119
POP3	TCP port 110
RPC	UDP port 111
Secure HTTP	TCP/UDP port 443
SMTP	TCP port 25
Telnet	TCP port 23
TFTP	UDP port 69

For a complete list of registered, well known port numbers, go to the following website:
http://www.isi.edu/in-notes/rfc1700.txt

Figure 4.3 Ports Used in TCP/IP

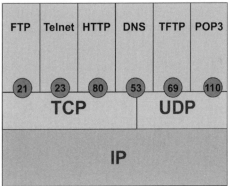

NOTE: In multiple user systems, a program can define a port "on the fly" if more than one user requires access to the same service at the same time. Such a port is known as a dynamically allocated port and it is assigned only when needed.

When a packet is delivered and processed, the TCP protocol (connection-based services) or UDP protocol (connectionless-based services) will read the port number and forward the request to the appropriate program.

A socket identifies a single network process in terms of the entire Internet. An application creates a socket by specifying three items: (1) the IP address of the host, (2) the type of service, and (3) the port that the application is using.

NOTE: For Windows, it is the WinSock that provides the interface between the network program or service and the Windows environment.

4.1.5   ARP and MAC Address Resolution

Early IP implementations ran on hosts commonly interconnected by Ethernet LANs. Every transmission on these LANs contained the MAC address of the source and destination nodes. Because there was no structure to identify different networks, routing could not be performed.

When a host needs to send a data packet to another host on the same network, the sender application must know both the IP address and the MAC address of the intended receiver. This is because the destination IP address is placed in the IP packet and the destination MAC address is placed in the LAN's protocol frame (such as Ethernet or Token Ring). If the destination host is on another network, the sender will look instead for the MAC address of the default gateway or router (see Figure 4.4).

Unfortunately, the sender's IP process may not know the MAC address of the intended receiver on the same network. Therefore, the **Address Resolution Protocol (ARP)** (RFC 826) provides a mechanism so that a host can learn a receiver's MAC address when knowing only the IP address (see Figure 4.5).

Any time a computer needs to communicate with a local computer, it will first look in the ARP cache in memory to see if it already knows the MAC address of a computer with the specified IP address. If the MAC address isn't in the ARP cache, it will try to discover the MAC address by broadcasting an ARP request packet. The station on the LAN recognizes its own IP address, which then sends an ARP response with its own MAC address.

Figure 4.4   IP Addresses (Logical Addresses) that are Mapped to MAC Addresses (Physical Addresses)

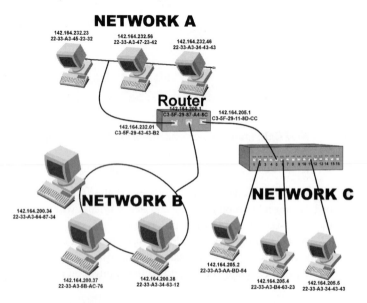

Figure 4.5   Name and Address Resolution Done on an IP Network

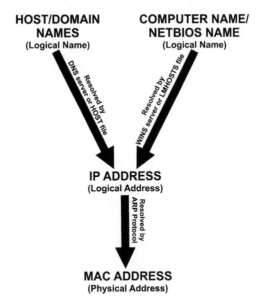

Then both the sender of the ARP reply and the original ARP requester record each other's IP address and MAC address as an entry in their ARP caches for future reference.

If a computer needs to communicate with another computer that is located on another network, it will do the same except that it will send the packet to the local router. Therefore, it will search for the MAC address of the local port of the router or it will send a broadcast looking for the address of the local port of the router.

When an IP machine happens to be a diskless machine, it has no way of initially knowing its IP address, but it does know its MAC address. The **Reverse Address Resolution Protocol (RARP)** discovers the identity of the IP address for diskless machines by sending out a packet that includes its MAC address and a request for the IP address assigned to that MAC address. A designated machine, called a RARP server, responds with the answer. RARP uses the information it does know about the machine's MAC address to learn its IP address and complete the machine's ID portrait.

4.1.6   Navigating a TCP/IP Network

Fully Qualified Domain Names (FQDN), sometimes just referred to as *domain names,* are used to identify computers on a TCP/IP network. Examples include Microsoft.com and Education.Novell.com.

While IP addresses are 32 bits (or 128 bits for IP v6) in length, most users do not memorize the numeric addresses of the hosts to which they attach. Instead, people are more comfortable with host names. Most IP hosts have both a numeric IP address and a host name. While this is convenient for people, the name must be translated back to a numeric address for routing purposes. This is done with either a HOSTS file or by using a DNS server.

Figure 4.6   Sample Host File

```
102.54.94.97          rhino.acme.com          # source server
38.25.63.10           x.acme.com              # x client host
127.0.0.1             localhost
```

The HOSTS file is a text file that lists the IP address followed by the host name. Each entry should be kept on an individual line. In addition, the IP address should be placed in the first column followed by the corresponding host name. A # symbol is used as a comment or REM statement. This means that anything after the # symbol is ignored (see Figure 4.6.)

If a computer uses the host table shown above, if rhino.acme.com is entered into a browser such as Internet Explorer or Netscape Navigator, it will find the equivalent address of 102.54.94.97 to connect to it.

NOTE: The HOSTS file is kept in the /ETC directory on most UNIX/Linux machines, in the WINDOWS directory in Windows 9X machines, and in the *%systemroot%*\SYSTEM32\DRIVERS\ETC directory in Windows NT, Windows 2000, Windows XP, and Windows Server 2003.

Another way to translate the FQDN to the IP address is to use a DNS server. DNS is a distributed database (the database is contained in multiple servers) containing host name and IP address information for all domains on the Internet. For every domain, there is a single authoritative name server that contains all DNS related information about the domain.

For example, if you type in a web address of Microsoft.com in your browser, your computer will then communicate with your LAN's DNS server. If the DNS server does not know the Microsoft.com address, another DNS server will be asked. This will continue until it finds the Microsoft.com address or it determines that the host name is not listed and replies back with *No DNS Entry*.

When you share a directory, drive, or printer on PCs running Microsoft Windows or on Linux machines running Samba, you would access these resources by using the uniform naming convention (UNC), to specify the location of the resources. UNC is also known as the universal naming convention. UNC uses the following format:

```
\\computer_name\shared-resource-pathname
```

To access the shared directory called data on the server1 computer, you would type the following:

```
\\server1\data
```

The computer name can be the IP address of the PC or the NetBIOS name. If you use the NetBIOS name, something will be needed to translate the NetBIOS name to the IP address. It could broadcast onto the network asking for the IP address of the computer. Therefore, you would have to connect the TCP/IP address with the computer name (NetBIOS name). Microsoft networks can use a LMHOSTS file (see Figure 4.7) or a WINS server.

A **Windows Internet Naming Service (WINS) server** contains a database of IP addresses and NetBIOS that update dynamically. For clients to access the WINS server, the

Figure 4.7   Sample LMHOSTS File

```
102.54.94.97      rhino        #PRE      #DOM:networking   #File Server
182.102.93.122    MISSERVER    #PRE                        #MIS Server
122.107.9.10      SalesServer                              #Sales Server
131.107.7.29      DBServer                                 #Database Server
191.131.54.73     TrainServ                                #Training Server
```

clients must know the address of the WINS server. Therefore, the WINS server needs to have a static address that does not change. When the client accesses the WINS server, the client doesn't do a broadcast but instead sends a message directly to the WINS server. When the WINS server gets the requests, it knows which computer it was that sent the request and can reply directly to the originating IP address. The WINS database stores the information and makes it available to other WINS clients.

When a WINS client starts up, it registers its name, IP address, and type of services within the WINS server's database. Because WINS was only made for Windows operating systems, other network devices and services (such as a network printer and UNIX machines) cannot register with a WINS service. Therefore, these addresses would have to be added manually.

4.2   TROUBLESHOOTING A TCP/IP NETWORK

For a TCP/IP network, several utilities can be used to test and troubleshoot the network. When you troubleshoot these types of problems, you should use the following systematic approach:

Step 1: check configuration
Step 2: ping 127.0.0.1 (Loopback address)
Step 3: ping IP address of the computer
Step 4: ping IP address of default gateway (router)
Step 5: ping IP address of remote host

The first thing that you need to do when troubleshooting an apparent TCP/IP problem is to check your TCP/IP configuration; specifically, your IP address, subnet mask, default gateway, DNS server, and WINS server. If the subnet mask is wrong, you may not be able to communicate with machines on the same subnet or remote subnets. If the default gateway is wrong, you will not be able to connect to any computer on a remote subnet. If the DNS server is wrong, you will not perform name resolution and you will not be able to surf the Internet. Having the wrong WINS server will stop your computer from using BIOS names when using UNC names.

To verify the TCP/IP configuration in Microsoft Windows, you would use either the IP configuration program command (WINIPCFG.EXE, available in Windows 9X) or the IPCONFIG.EXE (available in Windows 98, Windows NT, Windows 2000, Windows XP, and Windows 2002). To verify your `TCP/IP` in Linux, you can use the ifconfig and route commands.

4.2.1   The Ping Command

The ping command sends packets to a host computer and receives a report on their round trip time (see Figure 4.8). For example, you can ping an IP address by typing the following command at a command prompt:

```
ping 127.0.0.1
ping 137.23.34.112
```

The ping command can also be used to ping a host/computer by NetBIOS name or host/DNS name. Some examples would include:

```
ping FS1
ping WWW.MICROSOFT.COM
```

If you ping by address but not by name and the reply tells you that the TCP/IP is running fine but the name resolution is not working properly, you must check the LMHOSTS file and the WINS server to resolve computer names and HOSTS file and the DNS server to resolve domain names.

   If the time takes up to 200 milliseconds, the time is considered very good. If the time is between 200 and 500 milliseconds, the time is considered marginal. If the time is over 500 milliseconds, the time is unacceptable. A request timed out indicates total failure, as shown in Figure 4.9.

   Viewing the current configuration, pinging the loopback address (ping 127.0.0.1), and pinging the IP address of your computer will verify that the TCP/IP protocol is properly functioning on your PC. By pinging the IP address of the default gateway or router as well as other local IP computers, you determine if the computer is able to communi-

Figure 4.8   The Ping Command

```
C:\.ping 132.233.150.4

Pinging 132.233.150.4 with 32 bytes of data:

Reply from 132.233.150.4: bytes=32 time<10ms TTL=128
Reply from 132.233.150.4: bytes=32 time<10ms TTL=128
Reply from 132.233.150.4: bytes=32 time<10ms TTL=128
Reply from 132.233.150.4: bytes=32 time<10ms TTL=128

Ping statistics for 132.233.150.4:
  Packets: Sent = 4, Received = 4, Lost = 0 (0% loss),
Approximate round trip times in milli-seconds:
  Minimum = 0ms, Maximum = 0ms, Average = 0ms
```

Figure 4.9   The Ping Command Showing Total Failure

```
C:\.ping 132.233.150.2

Pinging 132.233.150.2 with 32 bytes of data:
Request timed out.
Request timed out.
Request timed out.
Request timed out.

Ping statistics for 132.233.150.2:
  Packets: Sent = 4, Received = 0, Lost = 4 (100% loss),
Approximate round trip times in milli-seconds:
  Minimum = 0ms, Maximum = 0ms, Average = 0ms
```

cate on the LAN. If it cannot connect to the gateway or any other local computer, either you are not connected properly or the IP protocol is misconfigured (IP address, IP subnet mask, or gateway address). If you cannot connect to the gateway but you can connect to other local computers, check your IP address, IP subnet mask, and gateway address, and check to see if the gateway is functioning. You can do this by using the ping command at the gateway to connect to your computer and other local computers on your network, as well as pinging the other network connections on the gateway/router or pinging computers on other networks. If you cannot ping another local computer, but you can ping the gateway, most likely the other computer is having problems and you need to restart this procedure at that computer. If you can ping the gateway but you cannot ping a computer on another gateway, you need to check the routers and pathways between the two computers by using the ping or tracert commands. The tracert command is shown next.

4.2.2   The Tracert Command

Another useful command is the traceroute command (Microsoft uses the tracert command), which sends out a packet of information to each hop (gateway/router) individually. Therefore, the `traceroute` command can help determine where the break is in a network (see Figure 4.10 and Table 4.2).

4.2.3   The ARP Utility

The ARP utility is useful for resolving duplicate IP addresses. For example, your work station receives its IP address from a DHCP server, but it accidentally receives the same address as another work station. When you try to ping it, you get no response. Your work station is trying to determine the MAC address, and it cannot do so because two machines are reporting that they have the same IP address. To solve this problem, you can use the ARP utility to view your local ARP table to see which TCP/IP address is resolved to which

Figure 4.10 The Tracert Command

```
C:\.tracert www.novell.com

Tracing route to www.novell.com [137.65.2.11]
over a maximum of 30 hops:

 1     97 ms     92 ms    107 ms     tnt3-e1.scrm01.pbi.net [206.171.130.74]
 2     96 ms     98 ms    118 ms     core1-e3-3.scrm01.pbi.net [206.171.130.77]
 3     96 ms     95 ms    120 ms     edge1-fa0-0-0.scrm01.pbi.net [206.13.31.8]
 4     96 ms    102 ms     96 ms     sfra1sr1-5-0.ca.us.ibm.net [165.87.225.10]
 5    105 ms    108 ms    114 ms     f1-0-0.sjc-bb1.cerf.net [134.24.88.55]
 6    107 ms    112 ms    106 ms     atm8-0-155M.sjc-bb3.cerf.net [134.24.29.38]
 7    106 ms    110 ms    120 ms     pos1-1-155M.sfo-bb3.cerf.net [134.24.32.89]
 8    109 ms    108 ms    110 ms     pos3-0-0-155M.sfo-bb1.cerf.net [134.24.29.202]
 9    122 ms    105 ms    115 ms     atm8-0.sac-bb1.cerf.net [134.24.29.86]
10    121 ms    120 ms    117 ms     atm3-0.slc-bb1.cerf.net [134.24.29.90]
11    123 ms    131 ms    130 ms     novell-gw-slc-bb1.cerf.net [134.24.116.54]
12      *         *         *        Request timed out.
13    133 ms    139 ms    855 ms     www.novell.com [137.65.2.11]

Trace complete.
```

Table 4.2 Tracert Options

-d	In the event that a name resolution method is not available for remote hosts, you can specify the -d option to prohibit the utility from trying to resolve host names as it runs. If you don't use this option, tracert will still function, but it will run very slowly as it tries to resolve these names.
-h	By specifying the -h option, you can specify the maximum number of hops to trace a route to.
Timeout_value	The timeout_value is used to adjust the timeout value, the value determines the amount of time (in milliseconds) the program will wait for a response before moving on. If you raise this value and the remote devices are responding whereas they were not responding before, it may indicate a bandwidth problem.
-j	Known as lose source routing, tracert -j <router name> <local computer> allows tracert to follow the path to the router specified and return to your computer.

Figure 4.11   Using the ARP Command

```
C:\.arp -a

Interface: 192.168.1.100 - - - 0×2
   Internet Address                 Physical Address          Type
   192.168.1.254                    00-00-89-2d-40-da         dynamic
   192.168.1.223                    00-a0-b1-2d-32-45         dynamic
   199.233.164.5                    00-a2-c0-c3-c2-14         static
```

MAC address. To display the entire current ARP table, use the arp command with the -a switch (see Figure 4.11).

> *NOTE:* You can also use the IPCONFIG/ALL (Windows) or ifconfig (Linux) commands if you need to identify the MAC address or network interface on your current machine.

In addition to displaying the ARP table, you can use the ARP utility to manipulate it. To add static entries to the ARP table, use the ARP command with the -s switch. These entries stay in the ARP table until the machine is rebooted. A static entry hard-wires a specific IP address to a specific MAC address so that when a packet needs to be sent to that IP address, it is sent automatically to the MAC address. The syntax for this command would be:

```
arp -s IP_Address MAC_Address
```

An example of using this command would be:

```
arp -s 199.223.164.5 00-a2-c0-c3-c2-14
```

If you want to delete entries from the ARP table, you can either wait until the dynamic entries time out, or you can use the -d switch with the IP address of the static entry you would like to delete. An example would be:

```
arp -d 199.223.164.5
```

4.2.4   The Netstat Utility

The netstat command is a great way to see the TCP/IP connections, both inbound and outbound, on your machine. You can also use netstat to view packet statistics, such as how many packets have been sent and received and the number of errors. Novell NetWare uses the MONITOR.NLM utility.

When netstat is used without any options, it produces output similar to that which shows all the outbound TCP/IP connections. The netstat utility, used without any options, is particularly useful in determining the status of outbound web connections.

Figure 4.12   The Netstat Command without Any Parameters

```
C:\Documents and Settings\Pat.netstat
Active Connections

  Proto    Local Address          Foreign Address                            State
  TCP      pregan:3001            pregan:3497                                ESTABLISHED
  TCP      pregan:3497            ftp.redhat.com:ftp                         ESTABLISHED
  TCP      pregan:3499            ftp.redhat.com:ftp                         ESTABLISHED
  TCP      pregan:4275            ftp.redhat.com:ftp-data                    ESTABLISHED
  TCP      pregan:4445            200-207-217-21.ds1.telesp.net.br:1214      TIME_WAIT
  TCP      pregan:4446            ads.web.aol.com:http                       TIME_WAIT
  TCP      pregan:4447            ads.web.aol.com:http                       TIME_WAIT
  TCP      pregan:4448            ads.web.aol.com:http                       TIME_WAIT
  TCP      pregan:4449            ads.web.aol.com:http                       TIME_WAIT
  TCP      pregan:4450            192.168.124.101:1214                       SYN_SENT
  TCP      pregan:4451            192.168.150.102:1214                       SYN_SENT
  TCP      pregan:4649            cs34.msg.sc5.yahoo.com:telnet              ESTABLISHED
  TCP      pregan:4669            64.12.29.24:5190                           ESTABLISHED
  TCP      pregan:4715            msgr-ns42.msgr.hotmail.com:1863            ESTABLISHED
  TCP      pregan:4889            24.244.138.36:1214                         ESTABLISHED
  TCP      pregan:4925            64.12.25.7:5190                            ESTABLISHED
  TCP      pregan:4926            61.12.27.196:5190                          ESTABLISHED

C:\Documents and Settings\Pat.netstat -n

Active Connections

  Proto    Local Address          Foreign Address                            State
  TCP      127.0.0.1:3001         192.168.1.100:3497                         ESTABLISHED
  TCP      192.168.1.100:3497     63.240.14.62:21                            ESTABLISHED
  TCP      192.168.1.100:3499     63.240.14.62:21                            ESTABLISHED
  TCP      192.168.1.100:4275     63.240.14.62:20                            ESTABLISHED
  TCP      192.168.1.100:4445     200.207.217.21:1214                        TIME-WAIT
  TCP      192.168.1.100:4446     205.188.165.57:80                          TIME-WAIT
  TCP      192.168.1.100:4447     205.188.165.57:80                          TIME-WAIT
  TCP      192.168.1.100:4448     205.188.165.89:80                          TIME-WAIT
  TCP      192.168.1.100:4449     205.188.165.89:80                          TIME-WAIT
  TCP      192.168.1.100:4452     192.168.150.102:1214                       SYN_SENT
  TCP      192.168.1.100:4453     4.62.189.73:1214                           TIME_WAIT
  TCP      192.168.1.100:4454     152.163.226.121:80                         TIME_WAIT
  TCP      192.168.1.100:4455     152.163.226.121:80                         TIME_WAIT
  TCP      192.168.1.100:4456     152.163.226.153:80                         TIME_WAIT
  TCP      192.168.1.100:4457     152.163.226.153:80                         TIME_WAIT
  TCP      192.168.1.100:4458     192.168.1.2:1214                           SYN_SENT
  TCP      192.168.1.100:4459     4.62.189.73:1214                           TIME_WAIT
  TCP      192.168.1.100:4649     216.136.227.168:23                         ESTABLISHED
  TCP      192.168.1.100:4669     64.12.29.24:5190                           ESTABLISHED
  TCP      192.168.1.100:4715     64.4.13.71:1863                            ESTABLISHED
  TCP      192.168.1.100:4889     24.244.138.36:1214                         ESTABLISHED
  TCP      192.168.1.100:4925     64.12.25.7:5190                            ESTABLISHED
  TCP      192.168.1.100:4926     64.12.27.196:5190                          ESTABLISHED
```

NOTE: If you use -N, addresses and port numbers are converted to names (see Figure 4.12).

The netstat -a command displays all connections, and netstat -r displays the route table plus active connections. Netstat -e command displays Ethernet statistics, and netstat -s displays per-protocol statistics (see Figure 4.13).

On occasion, you may need to have netstat occur every few seconds. Try placing a number after the netstat -e command, like so:

```
netstat -e 15
```

The command executes, waits the number of seconds specified by the number (in this example, 15), and then repeats until you press the Ctrl+C command.

Figure 4.13 The Netstat Command with the -s and -e Options

```
C:\Documents and Settings\Pat>netstat -s
Ipv4 Statistics

     Packets Received                       = 605088
     Received Header Errors                 = 0
     Received Address Errors                = 7
     Datagrams Forwarded                    = 0
     Unknown Protocols Received             = 0
     Received Packets Discarded             = 0
     Received Packets Delivered             = 605087
     Output Requests                        = 479600
     Routing Discards                       = 0
     Discarded Output Packets               = 0
     Output Packet No Route                 = 0
     Reassembly Required                    = 0
     Reassembly Successful                  = 0
     Reassembly Failures                    = 0
     Datagrams Successfully Fragmented      = 0
     Datagrams Failing Fragmentation        = 0
     Fragments Created                      = 0

ICMPv4 Statistics

                                   Received          Sent
     Messages                      14521             93
     Errors                        48                0
     Destination Unreachable       14452             3
     Time Exceeded                 14                0
     Parameter Problems            0                 0
     Source Quenchers              0                 0
     Redirects                     0                 0
     Echos                         0                 90
     Echo Replies                  7                 0
     Timestamps                    0                 0
     Timestamp Replies             0                 0
     Address Masks                 0                 0
     Address Mask Replies          0                 0

TCP Statistics for IPv4

     Active Opens                           = 12118
     Passive Opens                          = 184
     Failed Connection Attempts             = 2407
     Reset Connections                      = 679
     Current Connections                    = 10
     Segments Received                      = 559137
     Segments Sent                          = 430956
     Segments Retransmitted                 = 5832

UDP Statistics for IPv4

    Datagrams Received            = 26898
    No Ports                      = 18986
    Receive Errors                = 0
    Datagrams Sent                = 41690

C:\Documents and Settings/Pat>netstat -e
Interface Statistics

                               Received          Sent
Bytes                          713625649         35830464
Unicast packets                600782            476491
Non-unicast packets            7997              4129
Discards                       0                 0
Errors                         0                 30
Unknown protocols              0
```

4.3 THE IPX PROTOCOL SUITE

When Novell NetWare was introduced, it was designed to be a server platform for LANs and WANs. To that end, they designed a protocol stack that was very efficient over LANs and that would also work on WANs. The protocol stack was called Internetwork Packet eXchange/Sequenced Packet eXchange, or IPX/SPX (sometimes referred to as the NetWare Protocol). IPX is the fastest routable network protocol suite available (see Figure 4.14).

Similar to the TCP/IP network, you connect to an IPX network by using one of several interfaces, including Ethernet, Token Ring, or ARCnet. For a Novell NetWare network the software used to connect to an IPX network includes a Multiple Link Interface Driver (MLID), which is the driver used to control the NIC. Different from previous software interfaces used by early versions of IPX and other protocols, the MLID complies with the Novell Open Data Link Interface (ODI) architecture that allows a network driver to communicate with multiple protocol stacks such as TCP/IP and IPX.

Because the MLID supports multiple protocols, software is needed to identify the packets that come through the network card and route them to the proper protocol stack. This is known as the Link Support Layer (LSL).

NWLink is Microsoft's NDIS-compliant, 32-bit implementation of IPX, SPX, and NetBIOS protocols used in Novell networks. NWLink is a standard network protocol that supports routing and can support NetWare client/server applications, where NetWare-aware socket-based applications communicate with IPX/SPX sockets-based applications.

NOTE: You must use this protocol on Microsoft Windows if you want to use Gateway Service for NetWare or Client Service for NetWare to connect to NetWare servers.

Figure 4.14 IPX Protocol

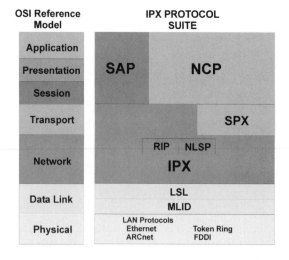

4.3.1   IPX and SPX

IPX is a networking protocol used to interconnect networks. It is a connectionless proto-col, and therefore it does not require a connection to set up before packets are sent to a destination.

Another protocol that works with the IPX protocol is SPX. Different from IPX, SPX uses packet acknowledgements to guarantee delivery of packets. SPX provides segmen-tation, reassembly, and segment sequencing of data streams that are too large to fit into the frame size. SPX uses virtual circuits referred to as *connections.* These connections are assigned specific connection identifiers as defined in the SPX header. Multiple connec-tion IDs can be attached to a single socket.

4.3.2   SAP and NCP Protocols

The **Service Advertising Protocol (SAP)** is used to advertise the services of all known servers on the network, including file servers, print servers and others. Servers periodi-cally broadcast their service information while listening for SAPs on the network and stor-ing the service information. Clients then access the service information table when they need to access a network service.

The NetWare Core Protocol consists of the majority of network services offered by a Novell NetWare server. This would include file services, print services, Novell Directory Services (NDS), and message services.

4.3.3   IPX Addressing

When assigning addresses within the IPX network, there are two types of addresses: (1) external and (2) internal IPX network numbers. When assigning both internal and exter-nal network numbers, the numbers must be different from each other for your entire net-work (see Figure 4.15).

- External IPX addresses are used to identify the network. Therefore, all servers and router interfaces on the same physical network must be assigned the same external IPX number. The external IPX address has a fixed length of thirty-two bits and is rep-resented as eight hexadecimal digits.
- Internal IPX addresses are assigned to and are used to identify servers and routers. Like external IPX addresses, internal IPX addresses are also thirty-two bits in length and are represented as eight hexadecimal digits.

Unlike TCP/IP, clients are not assigned internal network numbers. Instead, they use the ex-ternal IPX address and the MAC address to form an 80-bit IPX address. For example, if your NIC has a MAC address of 00:50:AD:73:0D:FE, which resides on the IPX network number (external IPX network number) 1E0, the IPX address of the computer would be:

```
1E0.0050.AD73.0DFE
```

Much like TCP/IP protocols, IPX also uses socket numbers to identify which network software the packet is sent to. Some examples of these are shown in Table 4.3.

Figure 4.15 An IPX Network

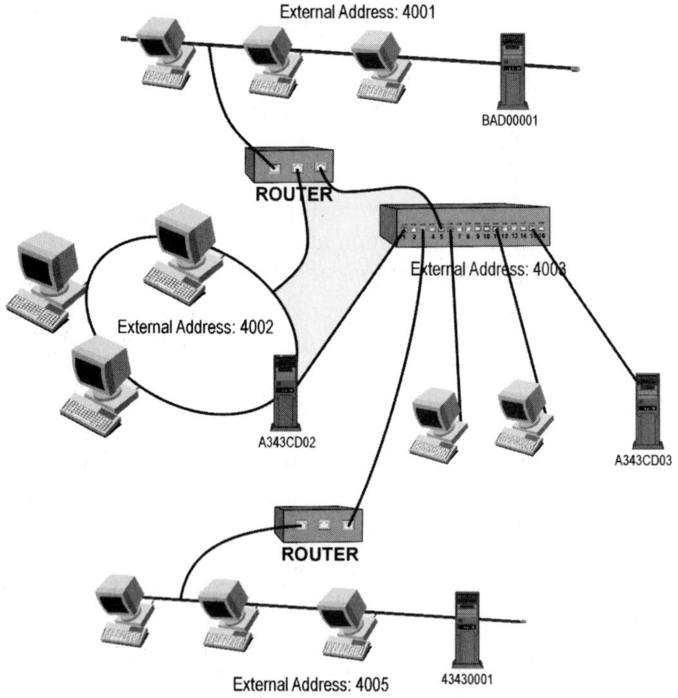

Table 4.3 Common IPX Network Services

Port number	Network service
0x0451	NetWare core protocol (NCP)
0x0452	Service advertising protocol (SAP)
0x0453	Routing information protocol (RIP)
0x0455	Novell NetBIOS
0x9001	NetWare link services protocol (NLSP)

4.3.4 Frame Types

There have been several versions of the IPX packet. On Ethernet networks, the standard frame type for NetWare 2.2 and NetWare 3.11 is 802.3. Starting with NetWare 3.12, the default frame type was changed to 802.2 (see Table 4.4). One of the biggest problems when connected to an IPX network is using the wrong frame type. For example, if one machine is using 802.2 and the other machine is using 802.3, the two machines cannot communicate with each other using IPX. Fortunately, most of these machines can support multiple frame types if necessary.

NOTE: Each subnet must use the same external addresses and frame type.

Table 4.4 Frame Types

Topology	Supported frame type
Ethernet	Ethernet II, 802.3, 802.2, and Subnetwork access protocol (SNAP)
Token Ring	802.5 and SNAP
FDDI	802.2 and 802.3

Figure 4.16 The Ipxroute Config Command

```
NWLink IPX Routing and Source Routing Control Program v2.00

Num    Name                    Network    Node          Frame
========================================================================
1.     IpxLoopbackAdapter      1234cdef   000000000002  [802.2]
2.     Local Area Connection   00000000   00c0f056bb98  [802.2]
3.     Local Area Connection 2 00000000   00a0c9e73b65  [802.2]
4.     NDISWANIPX              00000000   7ab920524153  [EthII] -

Legend
======
- down wan line
```

4.3.5   Troubleshooting IPX Networks

To help troubleshoot the IPX protocol in Windows 2000 and Windows XP we have the IPXROUTE command, which can be used to determine computer settings and perform diagnostic tests to resolve communication problems. If you type IPXROUTE CONFIG at the prompt, it will display the current IPX status, including the network number, MAC address, interface name, and frame type. If you use the IPXROUTE RIPOUT *network_number*, it will use RIP to determine if there is connectivity to a specific network. *network_number* is the external IPX number representing the network (see Figure 4.16).

SUMMARY

1. Today, the TCP/IP protocol is the primary protocol used on the Internet. It is supported by Microsoft Windows, Novell NetWare, UNIX, Linux, and Apple Macintosh.

2. The standards for TCP/IP are published in a series of documents called RFCs.

3. TCP/IP was designed to operate over nearly any underlying LAN or WAN.

4. IP is a connectionless-oriented protocol, which means that there is no established connection between the end points that are communicating. Each packet (also known as a *datagram*) that travels through the Internet is treated as an independent datum.

5. TCP is a reliable, connection-oriented delivery service that breaks data into manageable packets, wraps

them with the information needed to route them to their destinations, and then reassembles the pieces at the receiving end of the communication link.

6. UDP does not use acknowledgements to ensure data delivery. Therefore, the UDP is considered unreliable, "best effort" delivery.

7. Each connection on a TCP/IP address (logical address) is called a host (a computer or other network device that is connected to a TCP/IP network) and is assigned a unique IP address.

8. The format of the IP address is four 8-bit numbers (octets) divided by a period (.). Each number can be 0–255.

9. IP v6 addresses are 128 bits. They are usually divided into groups of sixteen bits written as four hex digits, and the groups are separated by colons.

10. ICMP works at the network layer and is used by IP for many different services. ICMP manages IP by reporting on IP status information.

11. Every time a TCP/IP host communicates with another TCP/IP host, it will use the IP address and port number to identify the host and service/program running on the host.

12. A TCP/IP port number is a logical connection placed by client programs to specify a particular server program running on a computer on the network defined at the transport layer.

13. Every transmission on LANs contains the MAC addresses of the source and destination nodes.

14. ARP provides a mechanism so that a host can learn a receiver's MAC address when knowing only the IP address.

15. FQDNs are used to identify computers on a TCP/IP network.

16. Domain names and host names are translated to IP addresses by a HOSTS file or by using a DNS server.

17. When you share a directory, drive, or printer on PCs running Microsoft Windows or on Linux machines running Samba, you would access these resources by using the UNC to specify the location of the resources.

18. UNCs are translated to IP addresses by a LMHOSTS file or a WINS server.

19. The first thing that you need to do when troubleshooting an apparent TCP/IP problem is to check your TCP/IP configuration, specifically your IP address, subnet mask, default gateway, DNS server, and WINS server.

20. Ping, a common TCP/IP troubleshooting command, sends packets to a host computer and receives a report on their round trip time.

21. The traceroute command (Microsoft uses the tracert command) sends out a packet of information to each hop (gateway/router) individually.

22. The protocol stack designed by NetWare protocol is IPX/SPX. IPX is the fastest routable network protocol suite available.

23. IPX is a networking protocol used to interconnect networks. It is a connectionless-oriented protocol, and therefore it doesn't require a connection to setup before packets are sent to a destination.

24. SAP is used to advertise the services of all known servers on the network, including file servers, print serves, and others.

25. The NetWare Core Protocol consists of the majority of network services offered by a Novell NetWare server. This would include file services, print services, NDSs, and message services.

26. When assigning addresses within the IPX network, there are two types of addresses: (1) external and (2) internal IPX network numbers. When assigning both the internal and external network numbers, the numbers must be different from each other for your entire network.

27. On Ethernet networks, the standard frame type for NetWare 2.2 and NetWare 3.11 is 802.3. Starting with NetWare 3.12, the default frame type was changed to 802.2.

QUESTIONS

1. The protocol used by the Internet is _____.
   a. TCP/IP
   b. NetBEUI
   c. IPX
   d. Appletalk

2. Which of the following DoD TCP/IP model layers use TCP and UDP?
   a. process/application   b. host-to-host
   c. Internet   d. network access

3. At which layer of the OSI model does the ICMP function?
   a. data link   b. network
   c. transport   d. session

4. Which of the following choices best describe TCP? (Select the best choice.)
   a. reliable, connectionless
   b. reliable, connection-oriented
   c. unreliable, connectionless
   d. unreliable, connection-oriented

5. Which of the following are transport layer protocols that provide acknowledgement of received segments? (Select 2 choices.)
   a. TCP   b. IP
   c. IPX   d. SPX
   e. UDP

6. What is the function of the RARP? (Select the best choice.)
   a. It maps a MAC address to a given IP address.
   b. It maps an IP address to a given MAC address.
   c. It maps an IP address to a NetBIOS name.
   d. It maps a NetBIOS name to an IP address.

7. Which of the following choices best describe UDP? (Select the best choice.)
   a. reliable, connectionless
   b. reliable, connection-oriented
   c. unreliable, connectionless
   d. unreliable, connection-oriented

8. Your computer resides on a network segment on which both TCP/IP and IPX/SPX are used. Your computer has a MAC address of 00:50:AD: 73:0D:FE and an IP address of 192.168.25.89/27. The IPX network number of the segment is 1E0. What is the IPX address of your computer?
   a. 1E0.0050.AD73.0DFE
   b. 0050.AD73.0DFE.01E0
   c. 192.168.25.64
   d. 25

9. What are the functions of the ICMP? (Select all choices that are correct.)
   a. notifies the source device if the destination device is unreachable
   b. resolves an IP address to a MAC address
   c. notifies a source device that a router is congested
   d. notifies a source device that a better route exists for packets to reach their destination
   e. resolves a MAC address to an IP address

10. What is the function of the ARP?
    a. maps a MAC address to a given IP address
    b. maps an IP address to a given MAC address
    c. maps an IP address to a NetBIOS name
    d. maps a NetBIOS name to an IP address

11. Several computers are simultaneously transmitting data to a host. Which mechanism is used by TCP and UDP to communicate with the upper layers? (Select the best choice.)
    a. ports   b. DLCI addresses
    c. NetBIOS names   d. IP addresses

12. Your company has a small network that uses Novell NetWare 4.11 servers and IPX. Which of the following protocols provides layer 4 (Transport layer) services that are connection-oriented to the upper layers? (Select the best choice.)
    a. SAP   b. RIP
    c. SPX   d. NLSP

13. Your computer has an IPX address of EFE.1DFA.0105.C01E.30B1 and an IP address of 10.99.201.45/24. What is the MAC address of your computer? (Select the best choice.)
    a. 45
    b. 10.99.201.0
    c. 0105C01E30B1
    d. EFE1DFA0105C

14. To connect to a TCP/IP network, you must configure which of the following? (Choose two answers.)
    a. the TCP/IP address
    b. the IPX address
    c. the DNS server address
    d. the gateway
    e. the subnet mask

15. To connect to a TCP/IP network that contains several subnets, which of the following must be configured? (Select all that apply.)
    a. the TCP/IP address
    b. the IPX address
    c. the DNS server address
    d. the gateway
    e. the subnet mask

16. All IP addresses are eventually resolved to NIC addresses. Which of the following is used to map an IP address to a NIC address?
    a. WINS   b. DNS
    c. DHCP   d. ARP

17. The enhanced version of the IP protocol (IP v4) is:
    a. IP v6   b. IP v5
    c. IPX   d. IPING

18. There are several UNIX computers and main-frames on your Windows NT network. You want to standardize the network protocol used on all computers and provide access to the Internet. Which protocol would you choose for your network?
    a. TCP/IP
    b. NetBEUI
    c. NWLink
    d. IPX/SPX

19. What is the default assigned ports for a web server browser?
    a. 21
    b. 119
    c. 80
    d. 139

20. What two types of names can be resolved in a Windows TCP/IP platform?
    a. host
    b. network name
    c. IPX Computer
    d. NetBIOS name

21. What is used to resolve host names such as MICROSOFT.COM? (Select two answers.)
    a. a DNS server
    b. LMHOSTS files
    c. HOSTS files
    d. a WINS server

22. You are troubleshooting a work station and you find the following information:

IP address:	131.123.140.14
subnet mask:	255.255.255.0
default gateway:	131.123.140.200
DNS servers:	130.13.18.3, 140.1.14.240
router's IP address:	131.123.140.1

    The work station cannot get to the Internet. Why is this? (Choose two answers.)
    a. The subnet mask is invalid for this network.
    b. There can only be one IP address for each DNS server.
    c. The IP address of the DNS should match the default gateway address.
    d. The IP address of the work station is wrong.
    e. The default gateway should match the router's address.

23. You have static IP addresses assigned to your work station. If two work stations are assigned the same IP address, what would happen as far as communication with these two work stations?
    a. The second work station will take over communication when it boots.
    b. The first work station to boot and log in will communicate.
    c. Both work stations will be OK.
    d. Neither work station will be able to communicate on the network.

24. Which of the following uses 15-character names to identify computers on a network?
    a. TCP/IP
    b. NetBIOS
    c. IPX/SPX
    d. AppleTalk

25. What file is used to resolve a host name to an IP address?
    a. LMHOSTS
    b. HOSTS.SAM
    c. HOSTS
    d. LMHOSTS.SAM

26. What is a WINS server's purpose in a network?
    a. To keep a database of host names and corresponding IP addresses.
    b. To keep communication flowing on a TCP/IP network by assigning IP addresses dynamically to each work station as it logs in.
    c. To keep a database of NetBIOS names and corresponding IP addresses.
    d. To authenticate each work station as it logs in and determine the MAC address and corresponding IP address of each work station.

27. Several users are complaining that they cannot access one of your Windows NT file servers, which has an IP address that is accessible from the Internet. When you get paged, you are not in the server room but at another company, in a friend's office that only has a UNIX work station available, which also has Internet access. What can you do to see if the file server is still functioning on the network?
    a. Use ping from the UNIX work station.
    b. Use ARP from the UNIX work station.
    c. Use WINS from the UNIX work station.
    d. Use DNS from the UNIX work station.

28. What tool can you use to see the path taken from a Windows NT system to another network host?
    a. ping
    b. WINIPCFG
    c. tracert
    d. IPCONFIG
    e. SNMP

29. What does the 127.0.0.1 address represent?
    a. a broadcast address
    b. a loopback address
    c. a network address
    d. a subnet address

30. You are troubleshooting the network connectivity for one of the client systems at your company, but you do not know the IP address for the system. You are at the client system and you want to make sure that the system can communicate with itself by using TCP/IP. How can you accomplish this?
    a. ping 127.0.0.1
    b. ping 255.255.0.0

c. ping 255.255.255.255
d. ping 0.0.0.0

31. A Windows 2000 server computer named SERVER1 resides on a remote subnet. Pat cannot ping SERVER1 using its IP address. He can successfully ping his default gateway address and the addresses of other computers on the remote subnet. What is the most likely cause of the problem?
a. Pat's computer is set up with an incorrect default gateway address.
b. Pat's computer is set up with an incorrect subnet mask.
c. SERVER1 is not WINS enabled.
d. The IP configuration on SERVER1 is incorrect.
e. The LMHOSTS file on Pat's computer has no entry for SERVER1.

32. Pat is planning to set up an intranet web server at his company. Employees will be able to access the web server using the server's host name. Which of the following services should Pat install on his intranet to provide name resolution?
a. DHCP   b. DNS
c. FTP   d. WINS

33. Pat fails repeatedly to access a Windows 2000 server computer on a remote subnet. Using Network Monitor to troubleshoot the problem, he finds that every time he tries to connect to the server, his work station broadcasts an ARP request for the IP address of the remote address of the remote Windows 2000 server computer. No other users on the TCP/IP network have trouble accessing the server. What is the most likely cause of Pat's problem?
a. The work station is not set up to use DNS.
b. The work station is not set up to use WINS.
c. The work station is set up with a duplicate IP address.
d. The work station is set up with an incorrect subnet mask.

34. Pat connects to a remote UNIX computer using its IP address. He knows TCP/IP is properly installed on this computer. How should he check to see if the router is working correctly?
a. ping 127.0.0.1
b. ping the local server
c. ping the far side of the router
d. ping the near side of the router

35. A Windows 2000 Professional user complains that he cannot connect to any other computers on his network. The network uses both a DHCP server and a DNS server. Seated at his work station, you

ping 127.0.0.1 and fail to get a response. What is the most likely cause of the problem?
a. TCP/IP is not properly installed on the work station.
b. The default gateway address on the work station is incorrect.
c. The subnet mask on the work station is incorrect.
d. The work station is not set up for DHCP.
e. The work station is not set up for DNS.

36. Which switch would you use if you want to prohibit the tracert utility from resolving names as it runs?
a. -r   b. -h
c. -n   d. -d

37. What value determines the amount of time (in milliseconds) the program will wait for a response before moving on?
a. hops   b. wait
c. time out   d. time to live

38. Which of the following entries in a HOSTS file residing on a Windows 2000 server computer will connect to the UNIX server SERVER1?
a. 132.132.11.53 #SERVER1 #corporate server
b. 132.132.11.53 SRV1 #corporate server
c. 132.132.11.53 SERVER1 #corporate server
d. 132.132.11 #SERVER1 #corporate server

39. IP version 6 (IP v6) uses how many bits in its addressing scheme?
a. 16   b. 32
c. 64   d. 128

40. HTTP usually connects to a web server on port number _____.
a. 21   b. 25
c. 80   d. 121

41. Which protocol is considered connection-oriented?
a. DLC   b. NetBEUI
c. TCP   d. UDP

42. FQDN is an acronym for _____.
a. fully qualified division name
b. fully qualified DNS name
c. fully qualified dynamic name
d. fully qualified domain name

43. What delimiter separates domain spaces when using a FQDN?
a. : (colon)
b. # (pound)
c. . (period)
d. / (forward slash)
e. \ (backward slash)

44. Which Windows 9X or Windows NT utility can display NetBIOS over TCP/IP statistics?
    a. nbtstat   b. netstat
    c. tracert   d. ARP
    e. ipconfig   f. wins

45. Which nbtstat utility switch will purge and reload the remote NetBIOS name table cache?
    a. -r   b. /r
    c. -p   d. -R
    e. /R   f. -P

46. You are a network administrator. A user calls you complaining that the performance of the intranet web server is sluggish. When you try to ping the server, it takes several seconds for the server to respond. You suspect that the problem is related to a router. Which work station utility could you use to find out which router is causing the problem?
    a. netstat   b. nbtstat
    c. ping   d. tracert
    e. ipconfig   f. arp

47. Which ARP command can you use to display the current ARP entries?
    a. ARP   b. ARP -A
    c. ARP -a   d. ARP /A
    e. ARP /a   f. ARP -C

48. Which netstat switch will enable you to view the ICMP packets your work station has sent and received?
    a. -a   b. -r
    c. -s   d. -I

49. How does a UNIX computer use port numbers?
    a. to determine which users have access to resources on the network
    b. to locate hosts on the network
    c. to establish communications between NICs
    d. to determine which TCP/IP service receives data packets

50. What character or character combination would you place at the beginning of a line in a HOSTS file to comment out the line?
    a. ;   b. /*
    c. #   d. //

51. Which of the following are characteristics of a HOSTS file?
    a. It is static.
    b. It resolves TCP/IP host names to IP addresses.
    c. It resolves NetBIOS names to IP addresses.
    d. It resolves IP addresses to MAC addresses.

52. You administer a network with four subnets connected with three routers. Subnet A is connected to Subnet B, Subnet B is connected to Subnet C, and Subnet C is connected to Subnet D. You use the tracert utility on COMPUTER_A on Subnet A to trace the route of a packet as it travels to COMPUTER_D on Subnet D. If the packet travels from COMPUTER_A to COMPUTER_D successfully, then how many hops will be reported by the tracert utility?
    a. 1   b. 3
    c. 2   d. 4

53. You are using a Windows NT 4.0 work station computer on a Novell NetWare 5.0 network. You attempt to contact a computer with the TCP/IP host name Rover, but you cannot contact this computer by using its TCP/IP host name. You know that Rover's IP address is 192.168.0.1, and you use it to successfully ping Rover. What is the most likely cause of this problem?
    a. DNS is incorrectly configured.
    b. The LMHOSTS file is incorrectly configured.
    c. WINS is incorrectly configured.
    d. The IP address of the remote computer is incorrectly configured.

54. Packets sent via UDP are considered to be what type of communication?
    a. connection-oriented
    b. connectionless-oriented
    c. session-oriented
    d. application-oriented

55. In configuring a TCP/IP client, which of the following is not an entry option?
    a. default gateway   b. subnet mask
    c. MAC address   d. IP address

56. Which TCP port does SMTP use?
    a. 21   b. 25
    c. 23   d. 53

57. Which TCP port does Telnet use?
    a. 25   b. 23
    c. 119   d. 21

58. Pat, one of your users, can't log onto the network. You go to his computer and after checking the cable connection, you obtain his IP address using the IPConfig utility. You then use the Nbtstat utility to see what MAC address is mapped to the IP address. You then look at the label on his NIC and see that a different MAC address is listed. What is the most likely cause of the problem?
    a. IP port conflict
    b. MAC address conflict
    c. ARP conflict
    d. IP address conflict

HANDS-ON EXERCISES

Exercise 1: Building a Network with a Router

For the initial exercises, classroom computers will be divided into three parts. The first set of computers will be connected to the first router port and will belong to the 192.168.1.0 network with a subnet mask of 255.255.255.0. The other two sets will be connected to the other two router ports and assigned the network numbers 192.168.2.0 and 192.168.3.0. The connections that connect the switches are Ethernet connections while the two ports that connect the two routers are serial connections.

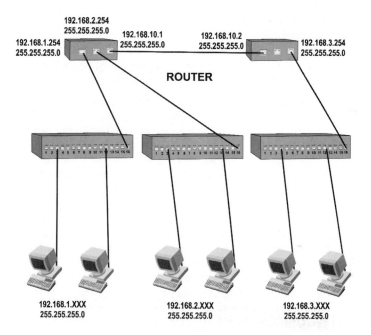

Exercise 2: Installing a Windows 2000 Server

NOTE: You can also install Windows 2000 Advanced Server or Windows Server 2003.

1. Reboot the computer with the proper DOS CD-ROM drivers. You can also boot with a bootable network disk and connect to a network drive to load the Windows 2000 files.
2. Load the Windows 2000 Server CD or go to the network drive/directory where the Windows 2000 installation files are.
3. Change into the I386 directory by using the CD I386 command.
4. Type in WINNT and press the Enter key.
5. When Windows 2000 Setup needs to know where the Windows 2000 files are located, press the Enter key. Windows 2000 will copy the installation files over the C drive. Be patient, this will take a few minutes.
6. When the MS-DOS-based portion of Setup is complete, remove any floppy disks from the A drive and press the Enter key to restart the computer.

7. Windows 2000 will welcome you to Setup. To set up Windows now, press the Enter key.

8. When the license agreement appears, press the F8 key to continue.

9. When Windows shows the partitions, select the C drive. This way, the system partition will be the C drive and the boot partition for the Windows 2000 Server will be the C drive. Press the Enter key to install.

10. If needed, convert or format the partition to NTFS option and press the Enter key. Windows 2000 will copy some more files. The system will reboot again.

11. When the system reboots and starts a graphical interface, it will automatically detect and install the hardware devices. It will then ask for the regional settings. Select the appropriate regional settings and click on the Next button.

12. To personalize your software, enter the name and the company that you work for. Click on the next button.

13. In the next screen, select the Per Server licensing mode and enter 50 connections. Click on the next button.
    NOTE:— To get the most out of this book, you will need to be working with a partner or a second computer. The computer on the left will be designated as computer A and the computer on the right will be designated as computer B.

14. The next screen shows a random computer name. Change the computer name to Server2000-xx where xx represents your two-digit student number in the class. Lastly, enter the password of `password` in the administrator password and confirm password text boxes. Click the Next button.

15. The installation wizard will ask you to add or remove components of Windows 2000. Because there is nothing that we want to add at this time, click the OK button.

16. If your computer has a modem, a modem dialing information box will appear. Enter your area code and type in the appropriate options for your computer. Click the Next button.

17. For the date and time settings, enter the proper information and click on the Next button.

18. Windows 2000 will configure the networking settings. Select custom settings and click the Next button.

19. The network components chosen by default are client for Microsoft networks, file and printer sharing for Microsoft networks, and Internet protocol (TCP/IP). Click the Internet protocol and click on the Properties button.

20. In the Internet Protocol (TCP/IP) properties dialog box, click on the Use the following IP address option and input the following:

    IP address: 192.168.XXX.1YY
    subnet mask: 255.255.255.0

    where XXX (1–255) is your subnet number and YY is the student number assigned.

21. The next window asks if you want to be a member of a workgroup or a computer domain. For now, select No and click on the Next button. It will then copy some files and perform final tasks.

22. When the Windows 2000 setup wizard is complete, click on the Finish button and the computer will reboot.

23. If the boot menu appears, select the Windows 2000 server.

24. Log on as the administrator.

25. Open the device manager. Either right-click the My Computer or click the Start button, select settings, select Control Panel, and double-click the System applet, then click on the hardware tab and the device manager button. Make sure that all drivers loaded properly. If not, load the appropriate drivers.

26. Right-click the desktop and create a Data folder.

27. Open the Data folder. Right click the empty space of the Data folder and select New to create a text file. In the Text file, type your name in the document.

28. Right-click the Data folder and select Sharing. Click Share this Folder and click the OK button.

29. Open the My Network Places and browse to your computer to see the Data share. You may need to click on *Computers Near Me* or *Entire Network.*

30. Browse to your partner's computer to see the Data share.

Exercise 3: Using the TCP/IP Network

1. Execute the IPCONFIG command and record the following settings:

IP Address
subnet mask
default gateway

2. Use the IPCONFIG /ALL command and record the following settings:

MAC address
WINS server (if any)
DNS server (if any)
If it is DHCP enabled or not

3. Ping the loopback address of 127.0.0.1.

4. Ping your IP address.

5. Ping a computer on your subnet.

6. Ping the router port that is on your subnet.

7. Ping another router port.

8. Ping a computer on another subnet.

9. Ping your partner's computer.

10. Use the tracert command to your instructor's computer.

11. If you are connected to the Internet, use the tracert command to Novell.com.

12. If you have router on your network, ping your gateway or local router connection.

13. Your network has a DHCP network, right-click My Network Places and select the Properties option.

14. Click on Internet Protocol (TCP/IP) and then click on the Properties button.

15. In the Internet Protocol (TCP/IP) Properties dialog box, select Obtain an IP address automatically. Click on the OK button.

16. Execute the IPCONFIG command at the command prompt and record the following settings:

IP Address
subnet mask
default gateway
WINS server (if any)
DNS server (if any)
If it is DHCP enabled or not

17. Ping the loopback address of 127.0.0.1.

18. Ping your IP address.

19. Ping a computer on your subnet.

20. Ping the router port that is on your subnet.

21. Ping another router port.

22. Ping a computer on another subnet.

23. Ping your partner's computer.

24. At the command prompt, execute IPCONFIG /RELEASE to remove your values specified by a DHCP server.

25. At the command prompt, execute IPCONFIG and compare the recorded values from Questions 1 and 2.
26. At the command prompt, execute IPCONFIG /RENEW.
27. At the command prompt, execute IPCONFIG and compare the recorded values from Questions 1 and 2.
28. Have your instructor stop the DHCP server (or DCHP service).
29. At the command prompt, execute IPCONFIG /RELEASE followed by the IPCONFIG/ RENEW. There will be a pause while Windows 2000 attempts to locate a DHCP server.
30. At the command prompt, execute IPCONFIG. Record the address and try to determine where this address came from.
31. Try to ping your instructor's computer and the local gateway. You should not be able to ping the IP addresses (and subnet mask) indicate that the two computers are on two different networks.
32. After your partner has acquired an Automatic Private IP address, try to ping each other. Because these addresses are on the same network (physically and logically), it should work.
33. Go back into the TCP/IP dialog box and enter the static addresses that you recorded in Questions 1 and 2.
34. Test your network by pinging your partner, your instructor's computer, and the gateway.
35. Disconnect the network cable from the back of the computer.
36. Look at the taskbar in the notification area (near the clock) and notice the red X.
37. From the command prompt, type in IPCONFIG.
38. Go into the Network and Dial-up Connection dialog box by right-clicking My Network Places and selecting properties. Notice the red X.
39. Connect the cable back into the network card. Notice that the red X in both places go away. In addition, notice that the icon disappears altogether from the notification area.
40. Right-click Local Area Connection and select properties.
41. Select the Show icon in taskbar when connected. Click on the OK button. Close the Local Area Connection dialog box.
42. Go to the notification area and notice the new icon representing the network connection.
43. Without clicking on the new icon, move the mouse pointer onto the icon. Without moving the mouse, notice the information given.
44. Double-click the icon to bring up the Local Area Connection dialog box.
45. From the command prompt, execute ARP -a.
46. Close all windows.

Exercise 4: Using IPX

For this exercise, you will be using the following internal and external IPX addresses:

1. Bring up the Network and Dial-up Connection window again.
2. Double-click on Local Area Connection and click on the Properties button.
3. Click on the Install button. In the Select Network Component Type dialog box, click the Protocol option and click the Add button. In the Select Network Protocol dialog box, click NWLink IPX/SPX/NetBIOS Compatible Transport Protocol, then click OK.
4. In the Local Area Connection Properties dialog box, click the NWLink IPX/SPX/NetBIOS Compatible Transport Protocol and then click Properties. Notice which type of frame detection is selected by default.
5. For the internal IPX address, specify your address. If you are connected to the first network and you are the first computer, you will assign 00001001. For the external IPX address, if you are connected to the first network, specify 10. For the second and third network, specify 20 and 30 respectively.

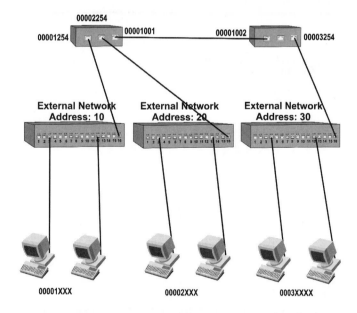

6. Close the Local Area Connection Properties dialog box.
7. In the Network and Dial-up Connections window, open the Advanced menu and select the Advanced Settings option.
8. In the Advanced Settings dialog box, under Client for Microsoft Networks, unbind TCP/IP by clearing the Internet Protocol (TCP/IP) check box. Click the OK button and close the Network and Dial-up Connections window.
9. Restart the computer.
10. Open a command prompt window.
11. At the prompt, type in IPXROUTE CONFIG and press the Enter key. Notice the frame type, network address, and MAC address.
12. Close the command prompt window.
13. Use My Network Places to access your partner's share that you created in the last exercise.
14. Open the Network and Dial-up Connections window.
15. Double-click the Local Area Connection and click on the Properties button.
16. Open the Network and Dial-up Connections window, open the Advanced menu, and select the Advanced Settings option. In the Advanced Settings dialog box, under Client for Microsoft Networks, bind TCP/IP by selecting the Internet Protocol (TCP/IP) check box. Click the OK button and close the Network and Dial-up Connections window.

CHAPTER 5

IP Addressing

Topics Covered in this Chapter

Introduction

In Chapters 1, 2, 3, and 4, we discussed the physical part of the network, but we haven't yet entered a discussion of software, in particular, the protocols that make the network run. It is essential that the administrator understands these protocols so that he or she can configure and troubleshoot the network.

Objectives

- Identify IP addresses (IPv4 and IPv6) and their default subnet masks.
- Identify the differences between public and private networks.
- Identify the purpose of subnetting and default gateways.
- Given an IP address and subnet mask, determine the network address and host address.
- Given a network situation, determine a subnet mask that can be used for the network.

- Explain how Classless InterDomain Routing (CIDR) differs from Classful IP.
- Explain variable length subnet masks (VLSMs) and CIDR.
- Identify the purpose of NAT network services and compare it to the purposes of a proxy service.
- Identify the purpose of subnetting and default gateways.
- Given a range of networks, aggregate them to the highest degree possible.

5.1   IPV4 ADDRESSING

Each connection on a TCP/IP address (logical address) is called a **host** (a computer or other network device that is connected to a TCP/IP network) and is assigned a unique **IP address.** A host is any network interface, including each NIC or a network printer that connects directly onto the network. The format of the IP address is four 8-bit numbers (octets) divided by a period (.). Each number can be between 0 and 255. For example, a TCP/IP address could be 131.107.3.1 or 2.0.0.1. Because the address is used to identify the computer, no two connections can use the same IP address. If there is repetition, one or both of the computers will not be able to communicate.

IP Addresses can be either manually assigned and configured (**static IP addresses**) or dynamically assigned and configured by a DHCP server (**dynamic IP addresses**). Because the address is used to identify the computer, no two connections can use the same IP address. Otherwise, one or both of the computers would not be able to communicate, and you will usually see a message stating "IP address conflict."

When communication occurs on a TCP/IP network, it can be classified as unicast, multicast, anycast, or broadcast. **Unicast** is when a single sender communicates with a single receiver over the network. The opposite of unicast is **multicast,** which is communication between a single sender and multiple receivers; **Anycast** communication occurs between any sender and the nearest of a group of receivers in a network. A **broadcast** is a packet that is sent to every computer on the network or a subnet.

NOTE: Broadcast packets are normally not forwarded by routers.

When connecting to the Internet, network numbers are assigned to a corporation or business. If the first number is between 1 and 126 (first bit is a 0), the network is a class A network. If the first number is between 128 and 191 (first two bits are 1 0), the network is a class B network. If the first number is between 192 and 223 (first three bits are 1 1 0), the network is a class C network (see Table 5.1).

Because Internet addresses must be unique and because address space on the Internet is limited, there is a need for some organization to control and allocate address number blocks. IP number management was formerly a responsibility of the Internet Assigned Numbers Authority (IANA), which contracted with Network Solutions Inc. for the actual services. In December 1997, IANA turned this responsibility over to the following organizations to manage the world's Internet address assignment and allocation:

■ **American Registry for Internet Numbers (ARIN)**—North and South America, the Caribbean, and subSaharan Africa
■ **Réseaux IP Européens Network Coordination Centre (RIPE NCC)**—Europe, the Middle East, and parts of Africa and Asia
■ **Asia Pacific Network Information Centre (APNIC)**—Asia Pacific region

Domain name management is still the separate responsibility of Network Solutions Inc. and a number of other registrars accredited by the Internet Corporation for Assigned Names and Numbers (ICANN).

There are two additional classes that should be mentioned. These are used for special functions only and are not commonly assigned to individual hosts. Class D addresses may begin with a value between 224 and 239, and are used for IP multicasting. Multicasting is

Table 5.1   Standard IP Classes for the IP Address of w.x.y.z

Class type	First octet — (decimal number and bits)	Network number	Host number	Default subnet mask	Comments
A	1–126 (01xxxxxx)	w	x.y.z	255.0.0.0	Supports 16 million hosts on each of 126 networks.
B	128–191 (10xxxxxx)	w.x	y.z	255.255.0.0	Supports 65,000 hosts on each of 16,000 networks.
C	192–223 (110xxxxx)	w.x.y	z	255.255.255.0	Supports 254 hosts on each of 2 million networks.

sending a single data packet to multiple hosts. Class E addresses begin with a value between 240 and 255, and are reserved for experimental use.

Many corporations will connect their corporate network (private network) to the Internet (public network). A **private network** is a network where only authorized users have access to the data while in a **public network,** everyone connected has access to the data. In a public network, because the IP hosts are directly accessible from the Internet, the network addresses must be registered with IANA. In a private network, the IP addresses are assigned by the administrator. It is recommended that you use the addresses reserved for private addresses. If you connect a private network to a public network, you increase the possibility for breaches in security. Firewalls can be implemented to protect a private network from unauthorized users on a public network.

Because TCP/IP addresses for the Internet are scarce, a series of addresses have been reserved to be used by private networks (networks not connected to the Internet). They are:

Class A—10.x.x.x (1 class A address)
Class B—Between 172.16.x.x and 172.31.x.x (16 class B addresses)
Class C—192.168.0.x and 192.168.255.x (256 class C addresses)

If you are not connected to the Internet or are using a proxy server, it is recommended that you use private addresses to prevent automatic renumbering of your internetwork when you eventually connect to the Internet.

The TCP/IP address is broken down into a network number (sometimes referred to as **network prefix**) and a host number. The network number identifies the entire network while the host number identifies the computer or connection on the specified network. If it is a class A network, the first octet describes the network number while the last three octets describe the host address. If it is a class B network, the first two octets describe the network number while the last two octets describe the host address. If it is a class C, the first three octets describe the network number while the last octet describes the host number (see Figure 5.1).

Example 1:

You have the following network address:
   131.107.20.4
   The 131 is between 128 and 191, identifying the address as a class B network. Therefore, the 131.107 identifies the network and the 20.4 identifies the host or computer on the 131.107 network.

Example 2:

You have the following network address:
   208.234.23.4
   The 208 is between 192 and 223, identifying the address as a class C network. Therefore, the 208.234.23 identifies the network and the 4 identifies the host or computer on the 208.234.23 network.

Figure 5.1   IP Network with Addresses and Subnet Masks. Notice the Multihomed Computer (Computer with Two Network Cards Connected to Two Subnets)

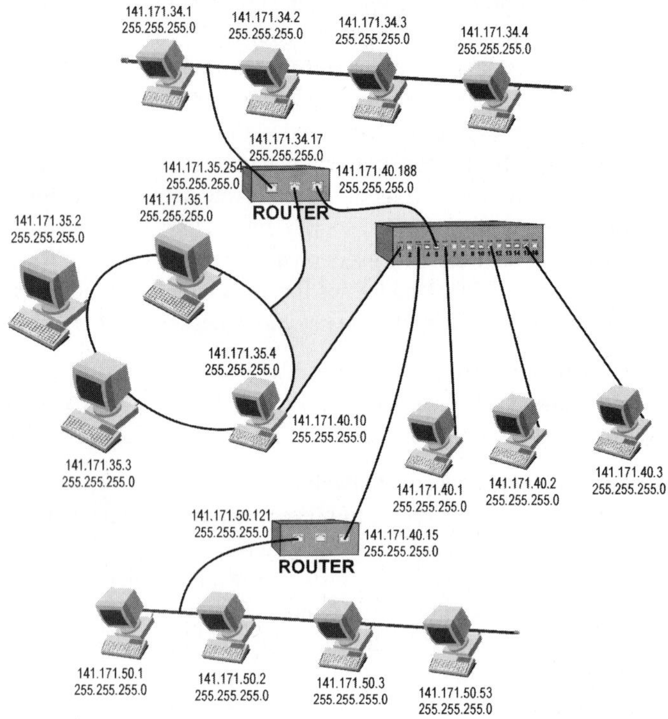

NOTE: Several address values are reserved and/or have special meaning. The network number 127 is used for loopback testing and the specific host address 127.0.0.1 refers to the local host or the actual host or computer that you are currently using.

NOTE: The 0.0.0.0 address is reserved for use as the default route.

Usually when you define the TCP/IP for a network connection, you would also specify a subnet mask. The subnet mask is used to define which bits describe the network number and which bits describe the host address. The default subnet mask for a class A network is 255.0.0.0. If you convert this to a binary equivalent, you would have 11111111.00000000.00000000.00000000, showing that the first octet (8 bits), marked with 1s, is used to define the network address. The last 24 bits (marked with 0s), are used to define the host address. The default subnet mask for a class B network is 255.255.0.0 (11111111.11111111.00000000.00000000 while the default subnet mask for a class C network is 255.255.255.0 (11111111.11111111.11111111.00000000).

If an individual network is connected to another network, and you must communicate with any computer on the other network, you must also define the **default gateway,** which specifies the local address of a router. If the default gateway is not specified, you will not be able to communicate with computers on other networks.

Figure 5.2   IP Addresses with Default Gateways (GW) that Point to the Router.

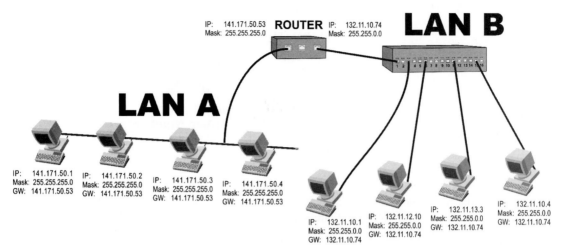

NOTE: If the LAN is connected to more than two or more networks, you only have to specify one gateway. This is because when a data packet is sent, it will first determine if the data packet needs to go to a local computer or a computer that is on another network. If it is meant to be sent to a computer on another network, it will forward the data packet to the router. The router will then determine the best route that the data packet must go to get to its destination. Occasionally, it will have to go back through the network to get to another gateway (see Figure 5.2).

Broadcasts are used to reach all devices on a network or subnetwork. The broadcast address is used when a machine wants to send the same packet to all devices on the network. There are two types of broadcasts: (1) an all-nets broadcast and (2) a subnet broadcast. While broadcasts are not forwarded by most routers, broadcasts can take up valuable bandwidth and processing power in the receiving devices. All-nets broadcasts packets are addressed to 255.255.255.255 in the IP header. Literally, the packets are addressed to all networks. Subnet broadcasts contain the subnet address in the broadcast packet and all 1s for the host address, and are aimed at all computers within the subnet. To get your broadcast address, you set the device or host portion of the IP address to 255. Therefore, if you have the IP address 129.23.123.2 (a class C network address of 129.23.123.0 with a mask of 255.255.255.0), your broadcast address will be 129.23.123.255. Your network address will be 129.23.123.0.

5.2   SUBNETTING THE NETWORK

The subnet mask can be changed to take a large network and break it into several small networks called subnets. This allows a corporation or organization to be free to assign a distinct subnetwork number for each of its internal networks. This allows the organization to deploy additional subnets without needing to obtain a new network number from the Internet.

Figure 5.3   The Host Number Can Be Split into a Subnet Number and a Host Number Address

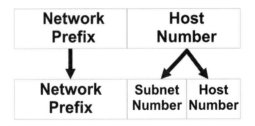

The subnet mask is used to define which bits represent the network prefix (including the subnet number) and which bits represent the host address. The network prefix and the subnet number (combined) are sometimes referred to as the **extended network prefix.** For a subnet, the network prefix, subnet number, and the subnet mask must be the same for all computers (see Figure 5.3).

Example 3:

Your network is assigned a network number of 161.13.0.0. Because it is a class B network, it already has a default subnet mask of 255.255.0.0. Therefore, any NIC that belongs to this network must have a TCP/IP address beginning with 161.13. Because it is a class B network, it uses 16 bits to define the host address. This allows the network to have up to 65,534 computers. I don't know of any single LAN that has 65,534 computers.

The network administrator could take this large network and divide it into several smaller subnets. For example, if 161.13 defines the entire corporation network (network prefix), the third octet could be used to define a site network or individual LAN (subnet number) while the last octet could be used to define the host address (host number).

Therefore, if you have three individual LANs, you can use the third octet to define the three LANs. The first building would have a network address of 161.13.1.0, the second building would have a network address of 161.13.2.0, and the third building would have a network address of 161.13.3.0. Because the last octet is used to define the host number, and there are eight bits to define the host number, there can be 254 hosts for each LAN. To let the network know that the 161.13 network is subnetted, the mask would have to be changed from 255.255.0.0 to 255.255.255.0 (11111111.11111111.11111111.00000000) to indicate that the first 24 bits indicate the network address.

To calculate the maximum number of subnets, you can use the following equation:

Number of subnets $= 2^{\text{number of masked bits}} - 2$

To calculate the maximum number of hosts, you can use the following equation:

Number of hosts$=2^{\text{number unmasked bits}}-2$

The -2 is used because you cannot use a network number, subnet number, or host number of all 0s or all 1s. For example if you had an address of 131.107.3.4, 131.107.0.0 is the network address and 0.0.3.4 is the host address. If you send a packet to the 131.107.0.0 (host address is all zeros), you are sending the packet to the network itself, not to the individual computer on the network. If you send it to 131.107.255.255 (host address is all ones), you are doing a broadcast to all of the computers on network 131.107.0.0. If you use the address of 0.0.3.4 (network number is all zeros), it assumes 3.4 is on the current LAN.

Example 4:

If you look at Example 3, you have eight bits to define the subnet/site number and eight bits to define the host number. Therefore,

Number of subnets$=2^{\text{number of masked bits}}-2=2^8-2=254$ subnets or sites
Number of hosts$=2^{\text{number unmasked bits}}-2=2^8-2=254$ hosts for each subnet

Example 5:

Your network is assigned an address of 207.182.15. You choose to subnet your network into several smaller networks. The largest network that you have will have 25 computers. Therefore, how many bits can you mask so that you can have the largest number of subnets or sites?

To start with, you only have the eight bits used for the host address to play with. The easiest way is to use the formula that calculates the number of hosts. To determine how many unmasked bits allow 25 or more computers, you would use the following calculations.

Number of hosts$=2^{\text{number unmasked bits}}-2=2^1-2=0$
Number of hosts$=2^{\text{number unmasked bits}}-2=2^2-2=2$
Number of hosts$=2^{\text{number unmasked bits}}-2=2^3-2=6$
Number of hosts$=2^{\text{number unmasked bits}}-2=2^4-2=14$
Number of hosts$=2^{\text{number unmasked bits}}-2=2^5-2=30$

Because you use 5 of the eight bits for the host number, it leaves 3 bits that are masked, which gives:

Number of subnets$=2^{\text{number masked bits}}-2=2^3-2=6$ subnets

Because 24 bits were previously masked, and you added three more bits to define the subnets, the subnet mask would be 11111111.11111111.11111111.11100000000, which is equivalent to 255.255.255.224.

Example 6:

Using the network discussed in Example 5, what is the range of TCP/IP addresses for the second subnet?

The network number is 207.182.15, with a subnet mask of 255.255.255.224, which describes the first three bits of the forth octet (used for the subnet number). The possible subnet numbers (in binary):

~~0 0 0~~
0 0 1
0 1 0
0 1 1
1 0 0
1 0 1
1 1 0
~~1 1 1~~

You can't use 0 0 0 or 1 1 1, which leaves 6 possible subnets.

Using binary counting, the second subnet is defined by 0 1 0. Because there are five bits left, the five bits can range from 0 0 0 0 1 (can't be all 0s) to 1 1 1 1 0 (can't be all 1s). Therefore, the last octet will be 0 1 0 0 0 0 0 1 to 0 1 0 1 1 1 1 0. If you translate these to decimal numbers, the last octet will be between 65 and 94. Therefore, the address range is 207.182.15.65 to 207.182.15.94 with a subnet mask of 255.255.255.224.

Subnetting reduces the number of routers on the Internet by ensuring that the subnet structure of a network is never visible outside of the organization's private network. The route from the Internet to any subnet of a given IP address is the same, no matter which subnet the destination host is on. This is because all subnets of a given network number use the same network prefix but different subnet numbers. The routers within the private organization need to differentiate between the individual subnets, but as far as the Internet routers are concerned, all of the subnets in the organization are collected into a single routing table entry. This allows the local administrator to divide his or her network as he or she sees fit, without affecting the size of the Internet's routing tables.

NOTE: Modern routing protocols still carry the subnet mask so that it knows which bits make up the extended network prefix.

Example 7:

If your organization has a network prefix of 161.13.0.0, and you have subnetted your network into 161.13.1.0, 161.13.2.0, and 161.13.3.0 subnets, the router table on the Internet would include an entry for the 161.13.0.0 network. The routers for the private network would have entries for the 161.13.1, 161.13.2, and 161.13.3 networks. When a packet needs to arrive at the 161.13.3 network from the Internet, it will first be sent to 161.13.0.0, as found in the Internet routing tables. Then that router will then route it to the 161.13.3.0 network.

Example 8:

You are the IT administrator for the Acme Corporation. Your main project is the design and production of widgets (your main product). It is your responsibility to plan and implement the IP addresses for your company. You currently have 35 sites throughout the country with plans to add 5 more sites within the next three years. The largest site (the corporate site) currently has 275 people, but it may add another 25 to 75 employees at that site over the next two years, depending on the market. In addition, the corporate building has 10 web servers, 15 corporate servers, and 5 routers that also need IP addresses. ARIN has assigned 182.24.0.0 to your corporation. Consider the following questions:

1. How would you subnet your network so that you can get the maximum number of people per site?
2. What is the number of sites that your network can have with this configuration?
3. What is the maximum number of people that your network can have with this configuration?
4. What would the subnet mask be for your corporation?
5. The primary site (which is also the largest site) is the corporate office. If you assign this site as your first subnet, what would the extended network prefix be for the corporate office site?
6. What would the range of addresses be for this site?
7. What is the broadcast address for this site?

Lets take the first question and determine how you would subnet your network to get the maximum number of people per site.

We know that we have a 182.24 (10110110.00011000) assigned by ARIN. Because it starts with 182, we know that it is a class B network with a default subnet mask of 255.255.0.0 (11111111.11111111.00000000.00000000). This tells us that the first 16 bits are locked for us and the last 16 bits are ours to assign. We know that we will have 40 (35 + 5) sites to plan for with the maximum number of 380 (275 + 75 + 10 + 15 + 5) hosts. Because we want to maximize the number of hosts, let's figure out how many bits it would take to assign the 40 sites.

$$\text{Number of subnets} = 2^{\text{number masked bits}} - 2 = 2^1 - 2 = 0$$
$$\text{Number of subnets} = 2^{\text{number masked bits}} - 2 = 2^2 - 2 = 2$$
$$\text{Number of subnets} = 2^{\text{number masked bits}} - 2 = 2^3 - 2 = 6$$
$$\text{Number of subnets} = 2^{\text{number masked bits}} - 2 = 2^4 - 2 = 14$$
$$\text{Number of subnets} = 2^{\text{number masked bits}} - 2 = 2^5 - 2 = 30$$
$$\text{Number of subnets} = 2^{\text{number masked bits}} - 2 = 2^6 - 2 = 62$$

Therefore, it would take 6 bits to define the subnets. As you can see, if we use six bits, we can actually grow to 62 sites (Question 2). This leaves 10 bits (16−6) left to define our hosts. Use the following equation:

$$\text{Number of hosts} = 2^{\text{number masked bits}} - 2 = 2^{10} - 2 = 1022$$

You can have up to 1022 hosts per site (Question 3).

NOTE: If this number was smaller than what you needed, you would have to come up with another solution so that you could get enough addresses for each site. Your options would be:

- You would have to assign multiple subnets per site
- Acquire a class A network from ARIN (highly unlikely)
- You would use a proxy server or a network address translation solution so that you can use one set of IP addresses for internal traffic (private network) and second set of addresses for external traffic (IP addresses assigned by ARIN)

Because we are going to use 6 bits to define the subnets, the new subnet mask (Question 4) would be:

11111111.11111111.**111111**00.00000000

This is equivalent to:
255.255.252.0
which would have to be assigned to every host on every subnet.
Looking at the 6 bits that define our subnets, you will number your subnets as follows:

Site number (decimal)	Site number (binary)	Extended network number (binary)	Extended network number (decimal)[2]
0[1]	000000	10110110.00011000.000000XX.XXXXXXXX	182.24.0.0
1	000001	**10110110.00011000.000001**XX.XXXXXXXX	182.24.4.0
2	000010	**10110110.00011000.000010**XX.XXXXXXXX	182.24.8.0
3	000011	**10110110.00011000.000011**XX.XXXXXXXX	182.24.12.0
4	000100	**10110110.00011000.000100**XX.XXXXXXXX	182.24.16.0
5	000101	**10110110.00011000.000101**XX.XXXXXXXX	182.24.20.0
6	000110	**10110110.00011000.000110**XX.XXXXXXXX	182.24.24.0
7	000111	**10110110.00011000.000111**XX.XXXXXXXX	182.24.28.0
8	001000	**10110110.00011000.001000**XX.XXXXXXXX	182.24.32.0
.	.	.	.
.	.	.	.
.	.	.	.
62	111110	**10110110.00011000.111110**XX.XXXXXXXX	182.24.248.0
63[1]	111111	10110110.00011000.111111XX.XXXXXXXX	182.24.252.0

[1]Remember that the subnet bits cannot be all 0s or all 1s.
[2]To calculate the extended network number in decimal, assign 0s to the host bits.

Every host on our first site (the corporate site) will start with the following bits:

10110110.00011000.000001XX.XXXXXXXX

which gives an extended network number of 182.24.4.0 (questions).

The Xs define the hosts on that site. If you remember, you have 10 bits to assign to the host. So the first host at this site would be:

10110110.00011000.000001**00.00000001**

which is equivalent to:

182.24.4.1

The last host at this site would be:

10110110.00011000.000001**11.11111110**

which is equivalent to:

182.24.7.254

So as you can see, the range of address for the first subnet is 182.24.4.1 to 182.24.7.254 (Question 6).

Host number (binary)	Host number (decimal)	IP address (binary)	IP address (decimal)
~~00.00000000~~[1]	~~0.0~~	~~10110110.00011000.00000100.00000000~~	~~182.24.4.0~~
00.00000001	0.1	10110110.00011000.00000100.00000001	182.24.4.1
00.00000010	0.2	10110110.00011000.00000100.00000010	182.24.4.2
00.00000011	0.3	10110110.00011000.00000100.00000011	182.24.4.3
00.00000100	0.4	10110110.00011000.00000100.00000100	182.24.4.4
00.00000101	0.5	10110110.00011000.00000100.00000101	182.24.4.5
00.00000110	0.6	10110110.00011000.00000100.00000110	182.24.4.6
00.00000111	0.7	10110110.00011000.00000100.00000111	182.24.4.7
00.00001000	0.8	10110110.00011000.00000100.00001000	182.24.4.8
00.00001001	0.9	10110110.00011000.00000100.00001001	182.24.4.9
.	.	.	.
.	.	.	.
.	.	.	.
11.11111110	3.254	10110110.00011000.00000111.11111110	182.24.7.254
~~11.11111111~~[1]	~~3.255~~	~~10110110.00011000.00000111.11111111~~	~~182.24.7.255~~

[1]Remember that the subnet bits cannot be all 0s or all 1s.

The broadcast address (Question 7) for the entire network would be:

10110110.00011000.1**1111111.11111111**

which is equivalent to 182.24.255.255
The broadcast address for the corporate subnet (site 1) would be:

10110110.00011000.000001**11.11111111**

which is equivalent to 182.24.7.255

5.3   VARIABLE LENGTH SUBNET MASKS (VLSM)

In 1987, TCP/IP was modified with RFC 1009, which specified how a subnetted network could use more than one subnet mask. When an IP network is assigned more than one subnet mask, it is considered a network with **variable length subnet masks (VLSM)** because the extended network prefixes have different lengths. The advantages of having more than one subnet mask assigned to a given IP network number are:

- Multiple subnet masks permit more efficient use of an organization's assigned IP address space.
- Multiple subnet masks permit route aggregation, which can significantly reduce the amount of routing information at the "backbone" level of an organization's routing domain.

When subnetting was first defined in RFC 950, it prohibited the use of all 0s and all 1s for the use of subnet. This is the reason that we use the "–2" when we calculate the number of subnets. This was done so that it would not confuse a classful router. Today, a router can be both classless and classful at the same time. But a classless router requires that each routing table update include the *route/<prefix-length>* pair to differentiate between a route to the all 0s subnet and a route to the entire network. The same can be said for the all 1s subnet. Because it indicates the number of bits for the network and for the host, you can use all 0s and all 1s for the subnet mask.

One of the major problems with the earlier limitations of IP addresses is that once the mask was selected across a given network prefix, it locked the organization into a fixed number of fixed-size subnets. For example, assume that a network administrator decided to configure the 130.5.0.0 network (default mask of 255.255.0.0) with a subnet mask of 255.255.252.0 (6 bits used for the subnet number). This permits 62 subnets ($2^{number\ masked\ bits}-2=2^5-2=30$), each of which supports a maximum of 1,022 hosts ($2^{number\ unmasked\ bits}-2=2^{10}-2$). Unfortunately, if you have some subnets that are small (maybe 20 or 30 hosts), you would waste approximately 1000 IP host addresses for each small subnet deployed.

By varying the number of network bits, VLSM supports more efficient use of an organization's IP address space. VLSM will allow you to assign your corporate network the 130.5.0.0 (10000010.00000101.00000000.00000000) with the subnet mask of 255.255.252.0 (11111111.11111111.11111100.00000000). The subnets would be divided into the following:

Site number (decimal)	Site number (binary)	Extended network number (binary)	Extended network number (decimal)
0	000000	10000010.00000101.**000000**XX.XXXXXXXX	130.5.0.0
1	000001	10000010.00000101.**000001**XX.XXXXXXXX	130.5.4.0
2	000010	10000010.00000101.**000010**XX.XXXXXXXX	130.5.8.0
3	000011	10000010.00000101.**000011**XX.XXXXXXXX	130.5.12.0
4	000100	10000010.00000101.**000100**XX.XXXXXXXX	130.5.16.0
5	000101	10000010.00000101.**000101**XX.XXXXXXXX	130.5.20.0
6	000110	10000010.00000101.**000110**XX.XXXXXXXX	130.5.24.0
7	000111	10000010.00000101.**000111**XX.XXXXXXXX	130.5.28.0
8	001000	10000010.00000101.**001000**XX.XXXXXXXX	130.5.32.0
.	.	.	.
.	.	.	.
.	.	.	.
62	111110	10000010.00000101.**111110**XX.XXXXXXXX	130.5.248.0
63	111111	10000010.00000101.**111111**XX.XXXXXXXX	130.5.252.0

You could then take one of these subnets and divide it into smaller subnets. Let's take the first subnet. While the other subnets would still have the 255.255.252.0 subnet mask, you would use routers to connect several subnets to the 130.5.4.0 subnet. The routers would have a subnet mask of 255.255.255.192. Because you are using an additional 4 bits to define the subnet, it would give you 16 ($2^{\text{number masked bits}} = 2^4$) smaller subnets connected to the 130.5.4.0 subnet. Each of these smaller subnets could accommodate 62 ($2^{\text{number unmasked bits}} - 2 = 2^6 - 2$) hosts.

Subsite number (decimal)	Subsite number (binary)	Extended network number (binary)	Extended network number (decimal)
1	0001	10000010.00000101.00000100.01XXXXXX	130.5.4.64
2	0010	10000010.00000101.00000100.10XXXXXX	130.5.4.128
3	0011	10000010.00000101.00000100.11XXXXXX	130.5.4.192
4	0100	10000010.00000101.00000101.00XXXXXX	130.5.5.0
5	0101	10000010.00000101.00000101.01XXXXXX	130.5.5.64
6	0110	10000010.00000101.00000101.10XXXXXX	130.5.5.128
7	0111	10000010.00000101.00000101.11XXXXXX	130.5.5.192
8	1000	10000010.00000101.00000110.00XXXXXX	130.5.6.64
.	.	.	.
.	.	.	.
.	.	.	.
14	1110	10000010.00000101.00000111.10XXXXXX	130.5.7.128

To help reduce the number of entries in the routers at the top level, the entire network would be expressed in as 130.5.0.0 on the Internet. The first internal router would have the entries for all of the 6 bit subnet numbers. The router assigned to the first subnet would have the entries for the smaller subnets (see Figure 5.4).

If you desired, you could even take one of the smaller subnets and divide it into even smaller subnets, or you take one of the other larger subnets and divide it into subnets with different subnets masks. The only real requirement is that the hosts within a specific subnet must all use the same subnet mask.

To successfully deploy VLSM, you must follow these three prerequisites:

- The routing protocols must carry extended network prefix information with each route advertisement because it is needed to determine the network bits and the host bits.
- All routers must implement a consistent forwarding algorithm based on the longest match. Therefore, when a packet arrives at a router, it will look for entries in its routing tables. Because the number of network bits varies from subnet to subnet, it will look through its routing tables for a match of the longest network number so that it can be sure to get to the correct subnet quickly.
- For route aggregation to occur, addresses must be assigned so that they have topological significance.

Modern routing protocols such as OSPF and RIP-II enable the deployment of VLSM by providing the extended prefix length or mask value along with each route advertisement. This permits each subnetwork to be advertised with its corresponding prefix length or mask.

Figure 5.4 Using VLSM to Divide an Assigned Network

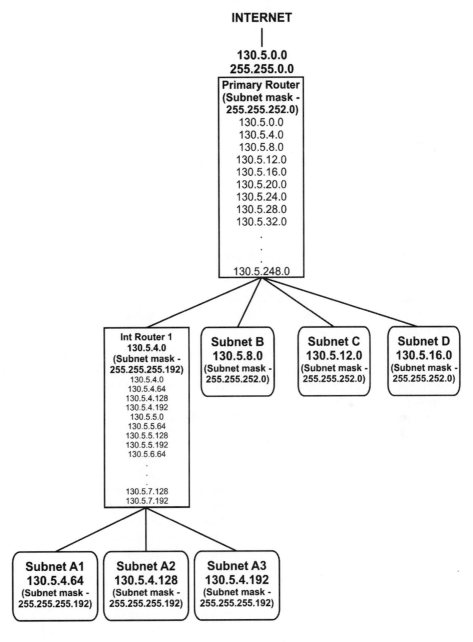

Figure 5.5 Address Strategy for VLSM Example

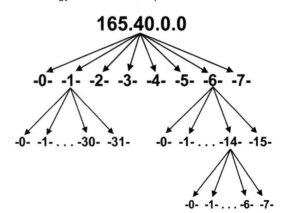

Example 9:

An organization that plans to deploy VLSM has been assigned the network number 165.40.0.0/16. Figure 5.5 provides a graphic display of the VLSM design for the organization.

NOTE: The /16 represents the number of bits that are masked. Therefore, the /16 is equivalent to an 11111111.11111111.00000000.00000000 or a 255.255.0.0 subnet mask. See the next section for more information on the /*x* notation.

To arrive at this design, the first step of the subnetting process divides the base network address into 14 equal-sized address blocks. Then Subnet #13 is divided it into 30 equal-sized address blocks and Subnet #14 is divided into 62 equal-sized address blocks. Finally, Subnet #14-62 is divided into 6 equal-sized address blocks.

To specify the sixteen subnets of 165.40.0.0/16:

```
Base Network: 10100101.00101000.00000000.00000000 = 165.40.0.0/16
Subnet #0:  10100101.00101000.00000000.00000000 = 165.40.0.0/20
Subnet #1:  10100101.00101000.00010000.00000000 = 165.40.16.0/20
Subnet #2:  10100101.00101000.00100000.00000000 = 165.40.32.0/20
Subnet #3:  10100101.00101000.00110000.00000000 = 165.40.48.0/20
Subnet #4:  10100101.00101000.01000000.00000000 = 165.40.64.0/20
Subnet #5:  10100101.00101000.01010000.00000000 = 165.40.80.0/20
Subnet #6:  10100101.00101000.01100000.00000000 = 165.40.96.0/20
Subnet #7:  10100101.00101000.01110000.00000000 = 165.40.112.0/20
Subnet #8:  10100101.00101000.10000000.00000000 = 165.40.128.0/20
Subnet #9:  10100101.00101000.10010000.00000000 = 165.40.144.0/20
Subnet #10: 10100101.00101000.10100000.00000000 = 165.40.160.0/20
Subnet #11: 10100101.00101000.10110000.00000000 = 165.40.176.0/20
Subnet #12: 10100101.00101000.11000000.00000000 = 165.40.192.0/20
Subnet #13: 10100101.00101000.11010000.00000000 = 165.40.208.0/20
Subnet #14: 10100101.00101000.11100000.00000000 = 165.40.224.0/20
Subnet #15: 10100101.00101000.11110000.00000000 = 165.40.240.0/20
```

NOTE: The /20 shows that the first 20 bits are the network bits.

Then list the host addresses that can be assigned to Subnet #1 (165.40.16.0)

```
Subnet #1: 10100101.00101000.00010000.00000000 = 165.40.16.0/20
Host #0: 10100101.00101000.00010000.00000000 = 165.40.16.1/20
Host #1: 10100101.00101000.00010000.00000001 = 165.40.16.1/20
Host #2: 10100101.00101000.00010000.00000010 = 165.40.16.2/20
Host #3: 10100101.00101000.00010000.00000011 = 165.40.16.3/20
        .
        .
        .
Host #4093: 10100101.00101000.00011111.11111101 = 165.40.31.253/20
Host #4094: 10100101.00101000.00011111.11111110 = 165.40.31.254/20
Host #4095: 10100101.00101000.00011111.11111111 = 165.40.31.254/20
```

The broadcast address for Subnet #1 (165.40.32.0) is:

```
10100101.00101000.00011111.11111111 = 165.40.32.255
```

To specify the 32 subnets of Subnet #13 (165.40.208.0/20):

```
Subnet #13: 10100101.00101000.11010000.00000000 = 165.40.208.0/20
Subnet #13-0: 10100101.00101000.11010000.00000000 = 165.40.208.0 /25
Subnet #13-1: 10100101.00101000.11010000.10000000 = 165.40.208.128/25
Subnet #13-2: 10100101.00101000.11010001.00000000 = 165.40.209.0 /25
        .
        .
        .
Subnet #13-30: 10100101.00101000.11011111.00000000 = 165.40.223.0 /25
Subnet #13-31: 10100101.00101000.11011111.10000000 = 165.40.223.128/25
```

NOTE: The /25 shows that the first 25 bits are the network bits.

To list the host addresses that can be assigned to Subnet #13-1 (165.40.208.0/25):

```
Subnet #13-1: 10100101.00101000.11010000.10000000 = 165.40.208.0/25
Host #0 10100101.00101000.11010000.10000000 = 165.40.208.128/25
Host #1 10100101.00101000.11010000.10000001 = 165.40.208.129/25
Host #2 10100101.00101000.11010000.10000010 = 165.40.208.130/25
Host #3 10100101.00101000.11010000.10000011 = 165.40.208.131/25
Host #4 10100101.00101000.11010000.10000100 = 165.40.208.132/25
Host #5 10100101.00101000.11010000.10000101 = 165.40.208.133/25
        .
        .
        .
Host #125 10100101.00101000.11010000.11111101 = 165.40.208.253/25
Host #126 10100101.00101000.11010000.11111110 = 165.40.208.254/25
Host #127 10100101.00101000.11010000.11111111 = 165.40.208.255/25
```

The broadcast address for Subnet #13-1 (165.40.208.0/25) is:

```
10100101.00101000.11010000.11111111 = 165.40.208.255
```

To specify the 64 subnets of Subnet #14 (165.40.224.0/20):

```
Subnet #14:   10100101.00101000.11100000.00000000 = 165.40.224.0/20
Subnet #14-0: 10100101.00101000.11100000.00000000 = 165.40.224.0 /26
Subnet #14-1: 10100101.00101000.11100000.01000000 = 165.40.224.64 /26
Subnet #14-2: 10100101.00101000.11100000.10000000 = 165.40.224.128/26
Subnet #14-3: 10100101.00101000.11100000.11000000 = 165.40.224.192/26
Subnet #14-4: 10100101.00101000.11100001.00000000 = 165.40.225.0 /26
  .
  .
  .
Subnet #14-62: 10100101.00101000.11101111.10000000 = 165.40.239.128/26
Subnet #14-63: 10100101.00101000.11101111.11000000 = 165.40.239.192/26
```

The host addresses that can be assigned to Subnet #14-1 (165.40.224.64/26):

```
Subnet #14-1: 10100101.00101000.11100000.01000000 = 165.40.224.64/26
Host #0 10100101.00101000.11100000.01000000 = 165.40.224.64/26
Host #1 10100101.00101000.11100000.01000001 = 165.40.224.65/26
Host #2 10100101.00101000.11100000.01000010 = 165.40.224.66/26
Host #3 10100101.00101000.11100000.01000011 = 165.40.224.67/26
Host #4 10100101.00101000.11100000.01000100 = 165.40.224.68/26
  .
  .
  .
Host #60 10100101.00101000.11100000.01111110 = 165.40.224.126/26
Host #61 10100101.00101000.11100000.01111111 = 165.40.224.127/26
```

The broadcast address for Subnet #14-1 (165.40.224.64/26):

```
10100101.00101000.11100000.01111111 = 165.40.224.127
```

To specify the eight subnets of subnet 14-62 (165.40.239.128/26):

```
Subnet #14-62:   10100101.00101000.11101111.10000000 = 165.40.239.128/26
Subnet #14-62-0: 10100101.00101000.11101111.10000000 = 165.40.239.128/29
Subnet #14-62-1: 10100101.00101000.11101111.10001000 = 165.40.239.136/29
Subnet #14-62-2: 10100101.00101000.11101111.10010000 = 165.40.239.144/29
Subnet #14-62-3: 10100101.00101000.11101111.10011000 = 165.40.239.152/29
Subnet #14-62-4: 10100101.00101000.11101111.10100000 = 165.40.239.160/29
Subnet #14-62-5: 10100101.00101000.11101111.10101000 = 165.40.239.168/29
Subnet #14-62-6: 10100101.00101000.11101111.10110000 = 165.40.239.176/29
Subnet #14-62-7: 10100101.00101000.11101111.10111000 = 165.40.239.184/29
```

To specify the hosts within subnet 14-62-4:

```
Subnet #14-62-4: 10100101.00101000.11101111.10100000 = 165.40.239.160/29
Host #0 10100101.00101000.11101111.10100000 = 165.40.239.160/29
Host #1 10100101.00101000.11101111.10100001 = 165.40.239.161/29
Host #2 10100101.00101000.11101111.10100010 = 165.40.239.162/29
Host #3 10100101.00101000.11101111.10100011 = 165.40.239.163/29
Host #4 10100101.00101000.11101111.10100100 = 165.40.239.164/29
Host #5 10100101.00101000.11101111.10100101 = 165.40.239.165/29
Host #6 10100101.00101000.11101111.10100110 = 165.40.239.166/29
Host #7 10100101.00101000.11101111.10100111 = 165.40.239.167/29
```

5.4　CLASSLESS INTERDOMAIN ROUTING (CIDR)

As the class B network IDs would be depleted in most organizations and a class C network does not contain enough host IDs to provide a flexible subnetting scheme for an organization, IP addresses are no longer given out under Class A, B or C designations. Instead, a method called **Classless Internetwork Domain Routing** (**CIDR,** pronounced "cider") is used.

Routers that support CIDR do not make assumptions about the first 3-bits of the address to determine if it is a class A, B, or C network. Instead, they rely on the prefix length information. The prefix length is described as slash x (/x) where x represents the number of network bits.

NOTE: Allocation can also be specified by using the traditional dotted-decimal mask notation.

Under the IPv4 addressing, a class C address (example 198.23.27.32) uses a subnet mask of 255.255.255.0 (equivalent to 11111111.11111111.11111111.00000000), which represented the first 24 bits as the network bits. The last 8 bits are the host bits. In CIDR addressing, the same address would be indicated as 198.23.27.32/24. The first 24 bits indicate the network bits.

Because CIDR eliminates the traditional concept of class A, B, and C network addresses, CIDR supports the deployment of arbitrarily sized networks rather than the standard 8-bit, 16-bit or 24-bit network numbers associated with classful addressing. Therefore, with CIDR, the addresses that were wasted for the class A and B networks were reclaimed and redistributed.

Prefixes are viewed as bitwise contiguous blocks of IP address space. For example, all prefixes with a /20 prefix represent the same amount of address spaces ($2^{12}-2$ or 4094 host addresses). Examples for traditional class A, B, and C are:

Traditional class A	10.23.64.0/20	**00001010.00010111.0100**0000.00000000
Traditional class B	140.5.0.0/20	**10001100.00000101.0000**0000.00000000
Traditional class C	200.7.128.0/20	**11001000.00000111.1000**0000.00000000

Table 5.2 provides information about the most commonly deployed CIDR address blocks.

Table 5.2 CIDR Address Blocks

CIDR prefix length	Dotted decimal	# of individual addresses	# of classful networks
/13	255.248.0.0	512 K	8 Bs or 2048 Cs
/14	255.252.0.0	256 K	4 Bs or 1024 Cs
/15	255.254.0.0	128 K	2 Bs or 512 Cs
/16	255.255.0.0	64 K	1 B or 256 Cs
/17	255.255.128.0	32 K	128 Cs
/18	255.255.192.0	16 K	64 Cs
/19	255.255.224.0	8 K	32 Cs
/20	255.255.240.0	4 K	16 Cs
/21	255.255.248.0	2 K	8 Cs
/22	255.255.252.0	1 K	4 Cs
/23	255.255.254.0	510	2 Cs
/24	255.255.255.0	254	1 C
/25	255.255.255.128	126	1/2 C
/26	255.255.255.192	62	1/4 C
/27	255.255.255.224	30	1/8 C

Example 10:

Let's say that you need to isolate a group of computers because they generate a lot of traffic amongst themselves compared to the other computers on the network, and you don't have another IP subnet to add to the network. So what you can do is to take one of your current subnets and divide them into various subnets. If you have class C subnet, you would first divide that subnet into two subnets (A1 and A2), each of which can handle 128 hosts, each of which have a /25 prefix length. Then you can divide the A2 subnet into two smaller subnets (B1 and B2), each of which can handle 64 hosts, each of which have a /26 prefix length. You can then divide the B2 subnet into two smaller subnets (C1 and C2), each of which can handle 32 hosts.

A1 128 hosts	/25 255.255.255.128
B1 64 hosts	/26 255.255.255.192
C1 32 hosts	/27 255.255.255.224
C2 32 hosts	/27 255.255.255.224

The A1, B1, and C1 can be combined as one physical subnet connected to one router link. C2 would be on its own router link.

Much like VLSM, CIDR allows you to take a single network ID and subdivide its network into smaller segments, depending upon its requirements. While VLSM divides the addresses on the private network, the CIDR divides the addresses by the Internet Registry, a high-level ISP, a mid-level ISP, a low-level ISP, or the private organization.

Like VLSM, another important benefit of CIDR is that it plays an important role in controlling the growth of the Internet's routing tables. The reduction of routing information requires that the Internet be divided into addressing domains. Within a domain, detailed information is available about all of the networks that reside in the domain. Outside of an addressing domain, only the common network prefix is advertised. This allows a single routing table entry to specify a route to many individual network addresses.

Supernetting is the process of combining multiple IP address ranges into a single IP network, such as combining several class C networks. For example, rather than allocating a class B network ID to an organization that has up to 2000 hosts, the InterNIC allocates a range of eight class C network IDs. Each class C network ID accommodates 254 hosts, for a total of 2032 host IDs.

Although this technique helps conserve class B network IDs, it creates a new problem. Using conventional routing techniques, the routers on the Internet now must have eight class C network ID entries in their routing tables to route IP packets to the organization. To prevent Internet routers from becoming overwhelmed with routes, CIDR is used to collapse multiple network ID entries into a single entry corresponding to all of the class C network IDs allocated to that organization.

Example 11:

Consider the following block of contiguous 32-bit addresses (192.32.0.0 through 192.32.7.0 in decimal notation). The supernet address (network address) for this block is 192.32.0.0 (11000000.00100000.00000000.00000000)—the 21 upper bits (/21) shared by the 32-bit addresses. The mask for the supernet address in this example is 255.255.248.0 (11111111.11111111.11111000.00000000).

192.32.0.0
192.32.1.0
192.32.2.0
192.32.3.0   /24   ⟹   192.32.0.0   /21
192.32.4.0
192.32.5.0
192.32.6.0
192.32.7.0

Example 12:

List the individual network numbers defined by the CIDR block 198.35.64.0/20.
First, express the CIDR block in binary format:

198.35.64.0/20 **11000110.00100011.0100**0000.00000000

The /20 mask is 4 bits shorter than the natural mask for a traditional /24. This means that the CIDR block identifies a block of 16 (or 2^4) consecutive /24 network numbers.

The range of /24 network numbers defined by the CIDR block 198.35.68.0/24 includes:

```
Net #0:  11000110.00100011.01000000.xxxxxxxx 198.35.64.0/20
Net #1:  11001000.00111000.01000001.xxxxxxxx 198.35.65.0/20
Net #2:  11001000.00111000.01000010.xxxxxxxx 198.35.66.0/20
Net #3:  11001000.00111000.01000011.xxxxxxxx 198.35.67.0/20
Net #4:  11001000.00111000.01000100.xxxxxxxx 198.35.68.0/20
Net #5:  11001000.00111000.01000101.xxxxxxxx 198.35.69.0/20
Net #6:  11001000.00111000.01000110.xxxxxxxx 198.35.70.0/20
Net #7:  11001000.00111000.01000111.xxxxxxxx 198.35.71.0/20
Net #8:  11001000.00111000.01001000.xxxxxxxx 198.35.72.0/20
Net #9:  11001000.00111000.01001001.xxxxxxxx 198.35.73.0/20
Net #10: 11001000.00111000.01001010.xxxxxxxx 198.35.74.0/20
Net #11: 11001000.00111000.01001011.xxxxxxxx 198.35.75.0/20
Net #12: 11001000.00111000.01001100.xxxxxxxx 198.35.76.0/20
Net #13: 11001000.00111000.01001101.xxxxxxxx 198.35.77.0/20
Net #14: 11001000.00111000.01001110.xxxxxxxx 198.35.78.0/20
Net #15: 11001000.00111000.01001111.xxxxxxxx 198.35.79.0/20
```

To aggregate the 16 IP /24 network addresses to the highest degree would give us

```
198.35.68.0.
```

Example 13:

Aggregate the following set of (4) IP /24 network addresses to the highest degree possible.

```
100.76.76.0/24
100.76.77.0/24
100.76.78.0/24
100.76.79.0/24
```

List each address in binary format and determine the common prefix for all of the addresses:

```
100.76.76.0/24 01100100.01001100.01001100.00000000
100.76.77.0/24 01100100.01001100.01001101.00000000
100.76.78.0/24 01100100.01001100.01001110.00000000
100.76.79.0/24 01100100.01001100.01001111.00000000
Common Prefix: 01100100.01001100.010011 00.00000000 =
100.76.76.0/22
```

Therefore, the CIDR aggregation is:

```
100.76.76.0/22
```

Example 14:

Aggregate the following set of 6 IP /24 network addresses to the highest degree possible.

```
199.76.110.0/24
199.76.111.0/24
199.76.112.0/24
199.76.113.0/24
199.76.114.0/24
199.76.115.0/24
```

First, list each address in binary format and determine the common prefix for all of the addresses:

```
199.76.110.0/24  11000111.01001100.01101110.00000000
199.76.111.0/24  11000111.01001100.01101111.00000000
199.76.112.0/24  11000111.01001100.01110000.00000000
199.76.113.0/24  11000111.01001100.01110001.00000000
199.76.114.0/24  11000111.01001100.01110010.00000000
199.76.115.0/24  11000111.01001100.01110011.00000000
```

As you can see, this cannot be summarized as a single /23 or single /22. Instead, it can be expressed as:

```
11000111.01001100.01101110.00000000 = 199.76.110.0/23
11000111.01001100.01110000.00000000 = 199.76.112.0/22
```

Example 15:

Aggregate the following set of (64) IP /24 network addresses to the highest degree possible.

```
202.1.96.0/24
202.1.97.0/24
202.1.98.0/24

    .
    .
    .

202.1.126.0/24
202.1.127.0/24
202.1.128.0/24
202.1.129.0/24

    .
    .
    .

202.1.158.0/24
202.1.159.0/24
```

List each address in binary format and determine the common prefix for all of the addresses:

```
202.1.96.0/24   11001010.00000001.01100000.00000000
202.1.97.0/24   11001010.00000001.01100001.00000000
202.1.98.0/24   11001010.00000001.01100010.00000000
   .
   .
   .
202.1.126.0/24  11001010.00000001.01111110.00000000
202.1.127.0/24  11001010.00000001.01111111.00000000
202.1.128.0/24  11001010.00000001.10000000.00000000
202.1.129.0/24  11001010.00000001.10000001.00000000
   .
   .
   .
202.1.158.0/24  11001010.00000001.10011110.00000000
202.1.159.0/24  11001010.00000001.10011111.00000000
```

As you can see, these networks cannot be summarized as a single /19. Instead, the CIDR aggregation is:

```
202.1.96.0/19   11001010.00000001.01100000.00000000
202.1.128.0/19  11001010.00000001.10000000.00000000
```

Similar to the previous example, if two /19s are to be aggregated into a /18, the /19s must fall within a single /18 block. Because each of these two /19s is a member of a different /18 block, they cannot be aggregated into a single /18. They could be aggregated into 202.1/16, but this aggregation would include 192 network numbers that were not part of the original allocation. Thus, the smallest possible aggregate is two /19s.

5.5   IPv6

Because the TCP/IP protocol and the Internet became popular, the growth of the Internet has grown and still continues to grow at an exponential rate. At this rate, it is easy to see that the Internet will eventually run out of network numbers. Therefore, a new IP protocol was developed called IPv6, previously known as IP Next Generation (IPng).

The IPv6 header includes a simplified header format that reduces the processing requirements and includes fields so that the packets can be identified for real-time traffic used in multimedia presentations so that routers can handle real-time traffic differently (Quality of Service). See Figure 5.6.

In addition, IPv6 introduces the Extension Header which is described by a value in the IPv6 Next Header field. Routers can view the Next Header value and then independently and quickly decide if the Extension Header holds useful information. Extension Headers carry much of the information that contributes to the large size of the IPv4 Header. This in-

Figure 5.6   IPv6 IP Header

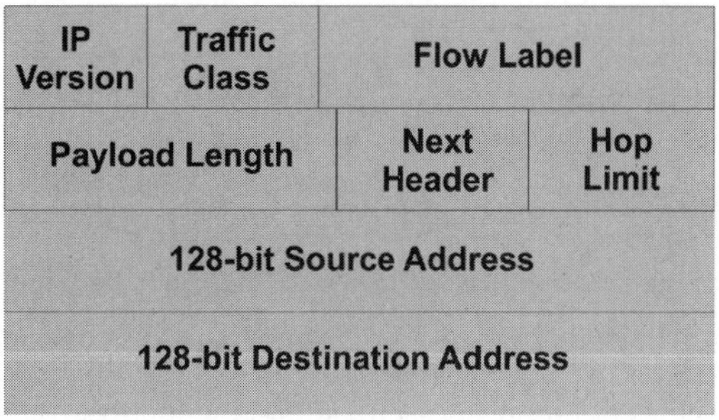

IP Version	Traffic Class	Flow Label	
Payload Length		Next Header	Hop Limit
128-bit Source Address			
128-bit Destination Address			

formation supports authentication, data integrity, and confidentiality, and should eliminate a significant class of network attacks including host masquerading attacks.

IPv6 has security built into it. While it is not bullet-proof security, it is enough to resist many of the common crippling problems that plagued IPv4. In IPv4, IPSec was optional; in IPv6, it is mandatory.

IPv4 is based on 32-bit addresses that allow a little over 4 billion hosts. IPv6 uses 128-bit addresses that allow up to 3.4×10^{38} hosts (can handle all of today's IP-based machines without using Network Address Translation), to allow for future growth and to handle IP addresses for upcoming mobile devices like PDAs and cell phones.

When writing IPv6 addresses, they are usually divided into groups of 16 bits written as four hex digits, and the groups are separated by colons. An example is:

```
FE80:0000:0000:0000:02A0:D2FF:FEA5:E9F5
```

Leading zeros within a group can be omitted. Therefore, the above address can be abbreviated as:

```
FE80:0:2A0:D2FF:FEA5:E9F5
```

You can also drop any single grouping of zero octets (as in the number above) between numbers as long as you replace them with a double colon (::) and they are complete octets. You cannot use the zero compression rule to drop more than one grouping of numbers between colons. For example, the above can be further abbreviated as:

```
FE80::2A0:D2FF:FEA5:E9F5
```

Because there must always be a certain number of bytes in the address, IPv6 can use this scheme to determine where the zeros are.

To make addresses manageable they are split in two parts: (1) the bits identifying the network a machine is on and (2) the bits that identify a machine on a network or subnetwork. The bits are known as netbits and hostbits, and in both IPv4 and IPv6, the netbits are the left (most significant bits of an IP number) and the host bits are the right (least significant bits).

In IPv4, the border is drawn with the aid of the netmask, which can be used to mask all net/host bits. In CIDR routing, the borders between net and host bits stopped being 8-bit boundaries, and started to use the /*x* designation (such as /64 to indicate 64 bits as network bits). The same scheme is used in IPv6.

IPv6 addresses can come with prefixes, which replace the "subnet mask" convention from IPv4. Prefixes are shown with a slash:

2180:FC::/48

In this example, the /48 is a routing prefix. A /64 would be a subnet prefix.

Usually though, you would have an address such as:

`FE80:0000:0000:0000:02A0:D2FF:FEA5:E9F5/64`

which tells us that the address used here has the first (left-most) 64 bits used as the network address, and the last (right-most) 64 bits are used to identify the machine on the network.

With 128 bits available for addressing in IPv6, the scheme commonly used is the same, only the fields are wider. Providers usually assign /48 networks, which leaves 16 bits for a subnetting and 64 host bits. This means that for your corporation or organization you can have up to 65,536 subnets. Each subnet could have 18,446,744,073,709,551,616.

The idea behind having fixed-width, 64-bit host identifiers is that they aren't assigned manually as in IPv4. Instead, IPv6 host addresses are recommended to be built from **EUI64 addresses.** The EUI64 addresses are built on 64-bits and are derived from the MAC address of the NIC. If the MAC address is

`01:23:45:67:89:AB`

a FF:FE is inserted in the middle of the MAC to become:

`01:23:45:FF:FE:67:89:AB`

The FF:FE was added because the MAC address is only 48 bits long.

Therefore, the host bits of the IPv6 address would be:

`:0123:45FF:FE67:89AB`

These host bits can now be used to automatically assign IPv6 addresses to hosts, which supports autoconfiguration of v6 hosts. All that is needed to get a complete IPv6 number are the net and subnet bits, which can be assigned automatically.

An IPv4-mapped IPv6 address is the address of an IPv4-only node represented as an IPv6 address. The IPv4 address is stored in the low-order 32-bits. The high-order 96 bits bear the prefix 0:0:0:0:0:0. The address of any IPv4-only node may be mapped into the IPv6 address space by prepending the prefix 0:0:0:0:0:0 to its IPv4 address.

An IPv4-compatible IPv6 address is an address, assigned to an IPv6 node, that can be used in both IPv6 and IPv4 packets. An IPv4-compatible IPv6 address holds an IPv4 address in the low-order 32-bits. The high-order 96 bits bear the prefix 0:0:0:0:0:FFFF. The entire 128-bit address can be used when sending IPv6 packets. The low-order 32-bits can be used when sending IPv4 packets.

NOTE: They never identify IPv4-only nodes.

As with IPv4, there are several addresses reserved for special uses. The IPv6 address ::/0 is the default address for a host (like 0.0.0.0 in IPv4). The address ::1/128 (0:0:0:0:0:0:0:1) is reserved for the local loopback (like 127.0.0.1 in IPv4).

To support autoconfiguration, the Neighbor Discovery protocol (NDP) is used to discover local nodes, routers, and link-layer addresses, and to maintain reachability information based on them. The aim of autoconfiguration is to make connecting machines to the network as easy as possible. In many cases it actually allows you to plug your machine into the network and start using it right away.

Each interface will have at least one globally unique unicast address and one link-local address. The link-local address will be used to provide addressing on a single link for the purpose of address auto-configuration, neighbor discovery, and internal routing. The unicast address will be used to establish hierarchical boundaries for the operation of routing protocols.

The long-term plans for IPv6 are probably going to stretch for the next 10 to 15 years. While Windows XP and Linux has support for it, for instance, this support is nowhere near complete. The stacks for OSes are still being tested and revised. Getting IPv6 to the average person on the desktop is going to be a long and involved procedure.

5.6   NETWORKING ADDRESS TRANSLATION AND PROXY SERVERS

Because IP addresses are a scarce resource, most ISPs will only allocate one address to a single customer. In majority of cases, this address is assigned dynamically, so every time a client connects to the ISP, a different address will be provided. Big companies can buy more addresses, but for small businesses and home users, the cost of doing so is prohibitive. Because such users are given only one IP address, they can have only one computer connected to the Internet at one time. Network Address Translation (NAT) is a method of connecting multiple computers to the Internet (or any other IP network) using just one IP address. With a NAT gateway running on this single computer, it is possible to share that single address between multiple local computers and connect them all at the same time. The outside world is unaware of this division and thinks that only one computer is connected.

To combat certain types of security problems, a number of firewall products are available. These are placed between the user and the Internet to verify all traffic before allowing it to pass through. This means, for example, that no unauthorized user would be allowed to access the company's file or e-mail server. The problem with firewall solutions is that they are expensive and difficult to set up and maintain, putting them out of reach for home and small business users.

NAT automatically provides firewall style protection without any special setup. The basic purpose of NAT is to multiplex traffic from the internal network and present it to the Internet as if it was coming from a single computer having only one IP address. The TCP/IP protocols include a multiplexing facility so that any computer can maintain multiple simultaneous connections with a remote computer. For example, an internal client can connect to an outside FTP server, but an outside client will not be able to connect to an internal FTP server because it would have to originate the connection and NAT will not allow that. It is still possible to make some internal servers available to the outside world via inbound mapping, which maps certain well-known TCP ports (e.g. 21 for FTP) to specific internal addresses, thus making services such as FTP or web available in a controlled way.

To multiplex several connections to a single destination, client computers label all packets with unique port numbers. Each IP packet starts with a header containing the source and destination addresses and port numbers. This combination of numbers completely defines a single TCP/IP connection. The addresses specify the two machines at each end, and the two port numbers ensure that each connection between this pair of machines can be uniquely identified.

Each separate connection is originated from a unique source port number in the client, and all reply packets from the remote server for this connection contain the same number as their destination port, so that the client can relate them back to the correct connection. In this way it is possible for a web browser to ask a web server for several images at once and to know how to put all the parts of all the responses back together.

A modern NAT gateway must change the source address on every outgoing packet to be its single public address. It therefore also renumbers the source ports to be unique, so that it can keep track of each client connection. The NAT gateway uses a port mapping table to remember how it renumbered the ports for each client's outgoing packets. The port mapping table relates the client's real local IP address and source port plus its translated source port number to a destination address and port. The NAT gateway can therefore reverse the process for returning packets and route them back to the correct clients.

When any remote server responds to a NAT client, incoming packets arriving at the NAT gateway will all have the same destination address, but the destination port number will be the unique source port number that was assigned by the NAT. The NAT gateway looks in its port mapping table to determine which "real" client address and port number a packet is destined for, and replaces these numbers before passing the packet on to the local client.

This process is completely dynamic. When a packet is received from an internal client, NAT looks for the matching source address and port in the port mapping table. If the entry is not found, a new one is created, and a new mapping port is allocated to the client:

- Incoming packet received on a non-NAT port
- Look for source address and port address in the mapping table
- If found, replace source port with previously allocated mapping port
- If not found, allocate a new mapping port
- Replace the source address with NAT address and replace the source port with mapping port

Packets received on the NAT port undergo a reverse translation process:

- Incoming packet received on NAT port
- Look up destination port number in the port mapping table
- If found, replace destination address and port address with entries from the mapping table
- If not found, the packet is not for us and should be rejected

Many higher-level TCP/IP protocols embed client addressing information in the packets. For example, during an "active" FTP transfer, the client informs the server of its IP address and port number, and then waits for the server to open a connection to that address. NAT must monitor these packets and modify them "on the fly" to replace the client's IP address (which is on the internal network) with the NAT address. Because this changes the length of the packet, the TCP sequence/acknowledge numbers must be modified as well.

A proxy is any device that acts on behalf of another. The term is most often used to denote a web proxy. A web proxy acts as a "half-way" web server. Network clients make requests to the proxy, which then makes requests on their behalf to the appropriate web server. Proxy technology is often seen as an alternative way to provide shared access to a single Internet connection.

> *NOTE:* Proxy servers also use a cache to store recently accessed web pages. Therefore, when the same page is accessed, the proxy server can provide the page without going out to the Internet.

Unlike NAT, web proxying is not a transparent operation. It must be explicitly supported by its clients. Due to early adoption of web proxying, most browsers, including Internet Explorer and Netscape Communicator, have built-in support for proxies. However, this must normally be configured on each client machine, and it may be changed by naive or malicious users.

A proxy server operates above the TCP level and uses the machine's built-in protocol stack. For each web request from a client, a TCP connection must be established between the client and the proxy machine, and another connection must be established between the proxy machine and the remote web server. This puts a lot of strain on the proxy server machine. Because web pages are becoming more and more complicated, the proxy itself may be a "bottleneck" on the network. This contrasts with a NAT, which operates on packet level and requires much less processing for each connection.

SUMMARY

1. Each connection on a TCP/IP address (logical address) is called a host (a computer or other network device that is connected to a TCP/IP network) and is assigned a unique IP address.

2. IP addresses will be manually assigned and configured (static IP addresses) or dynamically assigned and configured by a DHCP server (dynamic IP addresses).

3. When communication occurs on a TCP/IP network, communication can be classified as unicast, multicast, anycast, or broadcast.

4. Unicast is when a single sender communicates with a single receiver over the network.

5. The opposite of unicast is multicast, which is communication between a single sender and multiple receivers.

6. Anycast is communication between any sender and the nearest of a group of receivers in a network.

7. A broadcast is a packet that is sent to every computer on the network or subnet.

8. A private network is a network where only authorized users have access to the data. In a public network, everyone connected has access to the data.

9. The TCP/IP address is broken down into a network number (sometimes referred to as a network prefix) and a host number. The network number identifies the entire network while the host number identifies the computer or connection on the specified network.

10. If an individual network is connected to another network and you must communicate with any computers on the other network, you must also define the default gateway, which specifies the local address of a router. If the default gateway is not specified, you will not be able to communicate with computers on other networks.

11. The subnet mask is used to define which bits represent the network prefix (including the subnet number) and which bits represent the host address.

12. The network prefix and the subnet number (combined) are sometimes referred to as the extended network prefix.

13. When an IP network is assigned more than one subnet mask, it is considered a network with VLSM because the extended network prefixes have different lengths.

14. Because class B network IDs would be depleted in most organizations and a class C network does not contain enough host IDs to provide a flexible subnetting scheme, IP addresses are no longer given out under the class A, B, or C designations. Instead, a method called CIDR is used.

15. The prefix length is described as slash x (/x) where x represents the number of network bits.

16. Supernetting is the process of combining multiple IP address ranges into a single IP network, such as combining several class C networks.

17. A new IP protocol was developed called IPv6, previously known as IP Next Generation (IPng).

18. The IPv6 header includes a simplified header format that reduces the processing requirements and includes fields so that the packets can be identified for real-time traffic used in multimedia presentations so that routers can handle real-time traffic differently (Quality of Service).

19. IPv6 uses 128 bits for its addresses, which can have up to 3.4×10^{38} hosts, which can handle all of today's IP-based machines without using Network Address Translation, to allow for future growth and to handle IP addresses for upcoming mobile devices like PDAs and cell phones.

20. Network Address Translation (NAT) is a method of connecting multiple computers to the Internet (or any other IP network) using one IP address.

21. NAT automatically provides firewall-style protection without any special set-up. The basic purpose of NAT is to multiplex traffic from the internal network and present it to the Internet as if it was coming from a single computer having only one IP address.

22. A proxy is any device that acts on behalf of another.

23. A Web proxy acts as a "half-way" Web server; network clients make requests to the proxy, which then makes requests on their behalf to the appropriate Web server.

24. Proxy technology is often seen as an alternative way to provide shared access to a single Internet connection.

25. These proxy servers also use a cache to store recently accessed web pages. Therefore, when the same page is accessed, the proxy server can provide the page without going out to the Internet.

QUESTIONS

1. What is the default subnet mask for a class B network?
   a. 255.0.0.0
   b. 255.255.255.0
   c. 127.0.0.1
   d. 255.255.0.0
   e. 255.255.255.255

2. _____ is when you take a large network and divide it into smaller networks.
   a. Subnetting
   b. Gatewaying
   c. Broadcasting
   d. Hosting

3. Which of the following must you consider when deciding which subnet mask you should apply to a TCP/IP network? (Choose all that apply.)
   a. the IP address class
   b. the types of computers used on the network
   c. the number of subnets
   d. the potential for network growth

4. Your company is assigned the network address 150.50.0.0. You need to create seven subnets on the network. A router on one of the subnets will connect the network to the Internet. All computers on the network will need access to the Internet. What is the correct subnet mask for the network?
   a. 0.0.0.0
   b. 255.255.0.0
   c. 255.255.240.0
   d. the subnet mask assigned by InterNIC

5. A company with the network ID 209.168.19.0 occupies four floors of a building. You create a subnet for each floor. You want to allow for the largest possible number of host IDs on each subnet. Which subnet mask should you choose?
   a. 255.255.255.192
   b. 255.255.255.240
   c. 255.255.255.224
   d. 255.255.255.248

6. The Acme Corporation has been assigned the network ID 134.114.0.0. The corporation's eight departments require one subnet each. However, each department may grow to over 2500 hosts. Which subnet mask should you apply?

   a. 255.255.192.0.   b. 255.255.240.0.
   c. 255.255.224.0.   d. 255.255.248.0.

7. How are the network and host IDs for an IP address determined?

   a. subnet mask   b. range mask
   c. unicast mask   d. multicast mask

8. What are the TCP/IP addresses available for multicast transmissions?

   a. 128.0.0.0 to 191.255.0.0
   b. 224.0.0.0 to 239.255.255.255
   c. 192.0.0.0 to 223.255.255.0
   d. 240.0.0.0 to 247.255.255.255

9. At one of your company's remote locations, you have decided to segment your class B address down, because the location has three buildings and each building contains no more than 175 unique hosts. You want to make each building its own subnet and utilize your address space the best way possible. Which subnet masks meets your needs in this situation?

   a. 255.0.0.0
   b. 255.255.255.0
   c. 255.255.0.0
   d. 255.255.255.240

10. You have successfully obtained a class C subnet for your company. What is the default subnet mask?

   a. 255.255.255.0   b. 255.0.0.0
   c. 255.255.0.0   d. 255.255.240.0

11. IPv6 uses how many bits in its addressing scheme?

   a. 16   b. 32
   c. 64   d. 128

12. When you are using CIDR, how do you specify 26 network bits?

   a. 255.255.255.192   b. /26
   c. /25   d. –N 25

13. The class B address range for the first octet is _____.

   a. 1–127   b. 1–128
   c. 128–191   d. 129–223
   e. 224–255

14. What does a subnet mask separate?

   a. network ID and host ID
   b. host IDs
   c. workgroups and domains
   d. all of the above

15. NAT is found in _____.

   a. Windows 95
   b. the NIC protocol driver
   c. Windows NT
   d. routers

16. Which of the following is not a feature of a proxy server?

   a. It can reduce Internet traffic requests.
   b. It can assist with security.
   c. It can reduce user wait time for a request.
   d. It can convert a nonroutable protocol to a routable protocol.

17. What is the address range of valid hosts that exist on the same subnet as the IP address 192.168.55.68/27?

   a. 192.168.55.65 through 192.168.55.70
   b. 192.168.55.65 through 192.168.55.78
   c. 192.168.55.65 through 192.168.55.94
   d. 192.168.55.1 through 192.168.55.254

18. You are planning to divide your network address: (214.174.84.0) into multiple subnets. Each subnet must provide for 16 host IDs. Which subnet mask can you assign to your network to allow for the greatest number of additional subnets in the future?

   a. 255.255.255.192   b. 255.255.255.240
   c. 255.255.255.224   d. 255.255.255.248

19. What is the network ID portion of the IP address 191.154.25.66 if the default subnet mask is used?

   a. 191.0.0.0   b. 191.154.25.0
   c. 25.66.0.0   d. 191.154.0.0
   e. 154.25.66.0   f. 66.0.0.0

20. Pat has acquired a class C IP address for his company. After determining the physical requirements of his TCP/IP network, Pat realizes that he must create 5 subnets. If each subnet contains a maximum of 25 hosts, then which subnet mask should Pat choose for his network?

   a. 255.255.255.224   b. 255.255.255.248
   c. 255.255.255.240   d. 255.255.255.254

21. Your company has the network ID 165.121.0.0. You are responsible for creating subnets on the network, and each subnet must provide at least 900 host IDs. Which of the following subnet masks meets this minimum number of host IDs and provides the greatest number of subnets?

   a. 255.255.248.0   b. 255.255.254.0
   c. 255.255.252.0   d. 255.255.255.0

22. You have been contracted to design a TCP/IP network for a company that has been assigned the network ID 210.150.88.0. Each department in the

company will form its own subnet. Each department will require between 20 and 25 IP hosts. Which subnet mask will create the most subnets with the required number of hosts per subnet?
   a. 255.255.255.192   b. 255.255.255.240
   c. 255.255.255.224   d. 255.255.255.248

23. The Acme Corporation uses the network ID 200.11.5.0. It leases five floors of office space in its building. You are the network administrator for Acme and you want to create a subnet on each floor that contains the largest number of hosts possible. How many hosts can each floor contain?
   a. 2   b. 30
   c. 14   d. 64

24. The Acme Corporation has been assigned three class C network addresses: 196.56.12.0, 196.56.13.0, and 196.56.14.0. You want to combine these addresses into one logical network to increase the number of host IDs you can have on the Acme Corporation network. Which subnet mask must you use?
   a. 255.255.252.0   b. 255.255.254.0
   c. 255.255.255.254   d. 255.255.255.252

25. What is the broadcast address on subnet 32 given a prefix notation of 12.1.0.0/12?
   a. 12.32.0.1   b. 12.23.255.255
   c. 12.32.0.255   d. 12.47.255.255

26. Which subnet includes the IP addresses denoted by 188.25.63.88/22?
   a. 188.25.60.0   b. 188.25.62.0
   c. 188.25.63.0   d. 188.25.64.0

27. Which of the following is a valid IP host address given a network ID of 191.254.0.0 while using 11 bits for subnetting?
   a. 191.254.0.32   b. 191.254.0.96
   c. 191.254.1.29   d. 191.254.1.64

28. The Acme Corporation has been assigned the network address 165.87.0.0. You need to divide the network into eight subnets. What subnet mask should be applied to the network to provide the most hosts per subnet?
   a. 255.255.192.0   b. 255.255.240.0
   c. 255.255.224.0   d. 255.255.248.0

29. You work for Acme, which has been assigned a class A network address. Currently, the company has 1000 subnets in offices around the world. You want to add 100 new subnets over the next three years, and you want to allow for the largest possi-

ble number of host addresses per subnet. Which subnet mask should you choose?
   a. 255.192.0.0   b. 255.240.0.0
   c. 255.255.224.0   d. 255.224.0.0
   e. 255.255.192.0   f. 255.255.240.0

30. Which of the following IP addresses is appropriate for multicasting?
   a. 192.168.20.255   b. 235.168.255.20
   c. 223.168.255.20   d. 245.168.255.20

31. What is the default subnet mask for a class C network?
   a. 0.0.0.255
   b. 0.255.255.255
   c. 255.255.0.0
   d. 255.255.255.255
   e. 0.0.255.255
   f. 255.0.0.0
   g. 255.255.255.0

32. To which IP network class does the binary address 11000000.10101000.00000000.00000001 belong?
   a. class A   b. class C
   c. class E   d. class B
   e. class D

33. Which of the following statements is true regarding the IP address 192.255.254.255, assuming that no subnetting has taken place? (Select 2 choices.)
   a. This is a class B IP address.
   b. This is a directed broadcast address.
   c. This is a class C IP address.
   d. This is a local broadcast address.

34. To which IP network class does the address 188.25.25.32 belong?
   a. class A   b. class B
   c. class C   d. class D
   e. class E

35. You are the network administrator for your company's network. Every Monday morning, your company's CEO wants to transmit a live video feed over the company's intranet to a group of senior executives. You want to configure a multicast group that includes each of the senior executive's computers so that they can receive the video feed from the CEO. Which of the following IP network addresses should you configure for the multicast group?
   a. 172.255.0.0   b. 210.255.255.0
   c. 245.255.255.0   d. 192.168.50.0
   e. 225.192.10.0

36. Which of the following classes of network IP addresses provides the greatest number of host addresses?

a. class A
b. class B
c. class C
d. class D
e. class E

37. Which of the following classes of network IP addresses provides the fewest host addresses?

a. class A
b. class C
c. class B
d. class E

38. With the hierarchical number of IP addresses, what determines the portion that will identify the network number?

a. subnet mask
b. class of first octet
c. ARP
d. dots between octets
e. assignments of DHCP

39. The number of bits used in IPv6 are _____.

a. 32 bits, usually expressed in decimal format
b. 32 bits, usually expressed in hexadecimal format
c. 64 bits, usually expressed in decimal format
d. 64 bits, usually expressed in hexadecimal format
e. 128 bits, usually expressed in decimal format
f. 128 bits, usually expressed in hexadecimal format

40. Of the IPv6 address, the host bits are the _____.

a. left-most 32 bits
b. left-most 64 bits
c. right-most 32 bits
d. right-most 64 bits

41. You are the administrator of your company's network. The network consists of about 400 computers that are equally distributed between two subnets. You have been assigned the network addresses 208.199.32.0 and 208.199.33.0, which you have used on Subnet A and Subnet B, respectively. Your router supports BOOTP forwarding, CIDR, and VLSM.

The client computers on both subnets receive their IP configurations from a single DHCP server on Subnet A. The users in the digital publishing department routinely transfer very large graphics files between the computers in their department. Although the department has only eight computers, network analysis shows that they are using al-

most 50 percent of the bandwidth on Subnet B. To alleviate the network congestion being caused on Subnet B, you have decided to create a separate segment, named Subnet C, for the digital publishing department.

You do not have another Class C address to add to your network, so you have decided to segment a portion of the 208.199.33.0 address space for Subnet C and use logical subnets to assign the remaining address space to the physical segment for Subnet B. You have verified that your router will support assigning several secondary addresses to a network interface. The network address for Subnet C will be 208.199.33.240/28.

In order to provide the greatest number of available host addresses, which of the following network addresses should be assigned to the physical segment for Subnet B? (Select all choices that are correct.)

a. 208.199.33.0/24
b. 208.199.33.0/26
c. 208.199.33.192/26
d. 208.199.33.224/28
e. 208.199.33.0/25
f. 208.199.33.128/26
g. 208.199.33.192/27

42. If you have a MAC address of 01:45:45:67:89:34, and a network address of 1234.2345.2345.2345, what would the EUI64 address be?

a. 1234.2345.2345.2345.0145.45ff.fe67.8934
b. 01:45:45:67:89:34.1234.2345.2345.2345
c. 1234.2345.2345.2345.0145.45ff.fe67.8934
d. 01:45:45:67:89:34.1234.2345.2345.2345

43. You are a network administrator for a large corporation. You are responsible for the networks in the company's branch office in Sacramento, California. The corporate IT group has assigned you the network address 182.28.0.0/21 to use as you see fit for your network. CIDR and VLSM are supported on all routers throughout the organization. Your network consists of four subnets. Each network consists of between 35 and 50 computers. You have assigned the network addresses 182.28.0.0/24, 182.28.1.0/24, 182.28.2.0/24, and 182.28.3.0/24 to Subnet A, Subnet B, Subnet C, and Subnet D, respectively. You need to add two additional subnets: (1) Subnet E and (2) Subnet F. Subnet E will consist of 100 computers and Subnet F will consist of 180 computers. You do not anticipate the need to add any more computers or subnets in the future. Which of the following network addressing plans should you choose to allow you to deploy Subnet E and Subnet F while having the least impact on the existing addressing scheme? (Select the best choice.)

a. **Subnet A**—182.28.0.0/24
   Subnet B—182.28.1.0/24
   Subnet C—182.28.2.0/24
   Subnet D—182.28.3.0/24
   Subnet E—182.28.4.0/24
   Subnet F—182.28.5.0/24
b. **Subnet A**—182.28.0.0/25
   Subnet B—182.28.0.128/25
   Subnet C—182.28.1.0/25
   Subnet D—182.28.1.128/25
   Subnet E—182.28.2.0/25
   Subnet F—182.28.2.128/25

c. **Subnet A**—182.28.0.0/23
   Subnet B—182.28.2.0/23
   Subnet C—182.28.4.0/23
   Subnet D—182.28.6.0/23
   Subnet E—182.28.8.0/23
   Subnet F—182.28.10.0/23
d. **Subnet A**—182.28.0.0/26
   Subnet B—182.28.0.64/26
   Subnet C—182.28.0.128/26
   Subnet D—182.28.0.192/26
   Subnet E—182.28.2.0/25
   Subnet F—182.28.1.0/24

44. Look at the figure. The first number of each host is the IP address, the second number is the subnet mask, and the last number is the default gateway. What is the problem with the TCP/IP network?

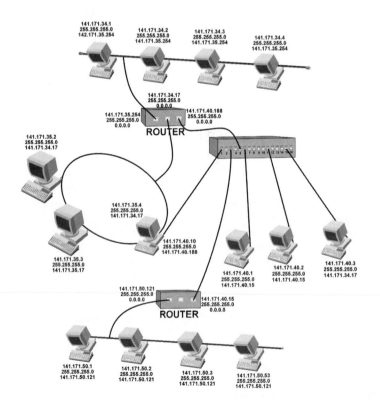

45. Look at the figure. The first number of each host is the IP address, the second number is the subnet mask, and the last number is the default gateway. What is the problem with the TCP/IP network? Note: there are two problems.

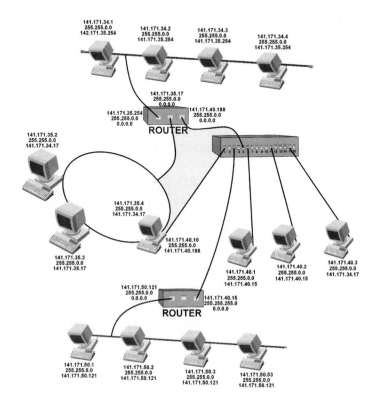

HANDS-ON EXERCISES

Exercise 1: Subnetting #1

Assume that you have been assigned the 132.45.0.0/16 network block. You need to establish eight subnets.

1. How many binary digits are required to define five subnets?
2. Specify the subnet mask that allows the creation of 8 subnets.
3. Specify the /x value for the subnet in Question 2 mask.
4. Express the subnets in binary format and dotted decimal notation.
5. List the range of host addresses that can be assigned to Subnet #3 (132.45.96.0/19).
6. What is the broadcast address for Subnet #3 (132.45.96.0/19).

Exercise 2: Subnetting #2

1. Assume that you have been assigned the 200.35.1.0/24 network block. Define an extended network prefix that allows the creation of 20 hosts on each subnet.
2. What is the maximum number of hosts that can be assigned to each subnet?
3. What is the maximum number of subnets that can be defined?
4. Specify the subnets of 200.35.1.0/24 in binary format and dotted decimal notation.
5. List the range of host addresses that can be assigned to Subnet #6 (200.35.1.192/27).
6. What is the broadcast address for subnet 200.35.1.192/27?

Exercise 3: VLSM

An organization has been assigned the network number 140.25.0.0/16 and it plans to deploy VLSM. The figure provides a graphic display of the VLSM design for the organization.

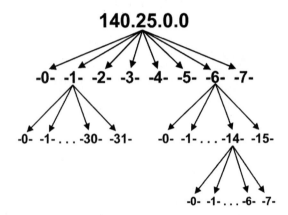

To arrive at this design, the first step of the subnetting process divides the base network address into 8 equal-sized address blocks. Then Subnet #1 is divided it into 32 equal-sized address blocks and Subnet #6 is divided into 16 equal-sized address blocks. Finally, Subnet #6-14 is divided into 8 equal-sized address blocks.

1. Specify the eight subnets of 140.25.0.0/16.
2. List the host addresses that can be assigned to Subnet #3 (140.25.96.0).
3. Identify the broadcast address for Subnet #3 (140.25.96.0).
4. Specify the 16 subnets of Subnet #6 (140.25.192.0/19).
5. List the host addresses that can be assigned to Subnet #6-3 (140.25.198.0/23).
6. Identify the broadcast address for Subnet #6-3 (140.25.198.0/23).
7. Specify the eight subnets of Subnet #6-14 (140.25.220.0/23).
8. List the host addresses that can be assigned to Subnet #6-14-2 (140.25.220.128/26).
9. Identify the broadcast address for Subnet #6-14-2 (140.25.220.128/26).

Exercise 4: CIDR

1. List the individual networks numbers defined by the CIDR block 200.56.168.0/21.
2. List the individual networks numbers defined by the CIDR block 195.24/13.

3. Aggregate the following set of 4 IP /24 network addresses to the highest degree possible.

   212.56.132.0/24
   212.56.133.0/24
   212.56.134.0/24
   212.56.135.0/24

4. Aggregate the following set of 4 IP /24 network addresses to the highest degree possible.

   212.56.146.0/24
   212.56.147.0/24
   212.56.148.0/24
   212.56.149.0/24

CHAPTER 6

Ethernet, Token Ring, and FDDI

Topics Covered in this Chapter

Introduction

As mentioned in Chapter 1, one of the primary components of a network is the common media used to connect the individual computers into a network by using a NIC. To allow the computers to communicate with each other, you have many cable type, cable layout, and protocol options. This chapter is an overview of Ethernet, Token Ring, and FDDI.

Objectives

- Specify the main features (speed, access, method, topology, and media) of 802.3 (Ethernet), 802.5 (Token Ring), and FDDI.
- Specify the speed, length, topology, and cable type characteristics for 802.3 (Ethernet) standards, 10Base-T, 100Base-TX, 10Base2, 10Base5, 100Base-FX, and Gigabit Ethernet.

- Given a troubleshooting scenario involving a network failure, identify the cause of the failure.
- Build an Ethernet network.
- Explain how to build a Token Ring network.

6.1   ETHERNET

LAN technology defines topologies, packet structures, and access methods that can be used together on a segment. This includes Ethernet, Token Ring, and ARCnet. Out of these, **Ethernet** is the most widely used LAN technology today. It offers good balance between speed, price, reliability, and ease of installation. Approximately 99 percent of all LAN connections installed are Ethernet. All popular operating systems and applications are Ethernet compatible, as are upper layer protocol stacks such as TCP/IP, IPX, and NetBEUI.

The original Ethernet network developed by Digital, Intel, and Xerox in the early 1970s is currently referred to as Ethernet II. Today, the Ethernet standard is defined by the IEEE in a specification commonly known as **IEEE 802.3.** The 802.3 specification covers rules for configuring Ethernet LANs, the types of media that can be used, and how the elements of the network should interact (see Table 6.1).

Ethernet was traditionally used on light to medium traffic networks, and performs best when a network's data traffic is sent in short bursts. Recently, newer and faster Ethernet standards combined with switches have significantly increased the performances of networks.

Ethernet networks can be configured in either a star topology using UTP connected to a hub or a bus topology using a coaxial cable acting as a backbone. Of these two, UTP

Table 6.1   Forms of Ethernet

Ethernet name	Cable type	Maximum speed	Maximum transmission distance	Notes
10Base5	Coax	10 Mbps	500 meters	Also called Thicknet
10Base2	Coax	10 Mbps	185 meters	Also called Thinnet
10BaseT	UTP	10 Mbps	100 meters	
100BaseT	UTP	100 Mbps	100 meters	
100BaseVG	UTP	100 Mbps	213 meters (cat 5) or 100 meters (cat 3)	100VG-AnyLAN
100BaseT4	UTP	100 Mbps	100 meters	Requires four pairs of Cat 3, 4, or 5 UTP cable
100BaseTX	UTP or STP	100 Mbps	100 meters	Two pairs of Category 5 UTP or Type 1 STP
10BaseFL	Fiber (multimode)	10 Mbps	2000 meters	Ethernet over fiber optic implementation; connectivity between NIC and fiber optic hub
100BaseFX	Fiber (multimode)	100 Mbps	2000 meters	100 Mbps Ethernet over fiber optic implementation
1000BaseTX (Gigabit Ethernet)	UTP	1000 Mbps	100 meters	Uses same connectors as 10BaseT; requires Category 5 or better
1000BaseSX	Fiber (multimode)	1000 Mbps	260 meters	Uses SC fiber connectors; designed for work station to hub implementation
1000BaseLX	Fiber (single mode)	1000 Mbps	550 meters	Uses longer wavelength laser than 1000BaseSX; typically used for backbone implementation
1000BaseCX	STP Type 1	1000 Mbps	25 meters	Typically used for equipment interconnection such as clusters
1000BaseT	UTP	1000 Mbps	100 meters	Requires category 5 or better

cabling is by far the most commonly used. Ethernet cards can have one, two, or possibly all three of the following connectors:

- **DIX (Digital Intel Xerox)/AUI connectors**—support 10Base5 external transceivers
- **BNC connectors**—support 10Base2 coax cabling
- **RJ-45 connectors**—support 10Base-T/100Base-TX (UTP) cabling

When a network device wants to access the network, the access method used is CSMA/CD. When a computer wants to send data over the network, it will listen to see if there is any traffic on the network. If the network is clear, it will then broadcast. Unfortunately, it is possible for two network devices to listen and try to send data at the same time.

As a result, a collision occurs where both data packets are corrupted. When a collision is detected by a sending device, it sends out a jamming signal that lasts long enough for all nodes to recognize it and stop broadcasting. While this is normal for an Ethernet network, both network devices will wait a different random amount of time and try again. If the network is heavily congested, more collisions will occur. This results in more traffic, which slows the entire network even more.

Within an Ethernet network, you are limited to a 1024 nodes identified by their MAC/physical addresses, which are burned into the ROM chip on the NIC. IEEE assigns the first three bytes of the 6-byte address to NIC vendors. The vendor is then responsible for assigning the rest of the address to make sure that the MAC address is unique.

6.1.1 The Ethernet Encoding Method

Although many methods are used for encoding a signal on an Ethernet, **Manchester Signal Encoding** is the most common. When a device driver receives a data packet from the higher-layer protocols, such as an IP or IPX packet, the device driver constructs a frame (much like an envelope) with the appropriate Ethernet header information and a frame check sequence at the end for error control. The circuitry on the adapter card then takes the frame and converts it into an electrical signal.

The data is measured as a transition state that occurs in the middle of each bit-time. To represent a binary one, the first half of the bit-time is a low voltage and the second half is high. To represent a binary zero, the first half of the bit-time is a high voltage and the second half is low (see Figure 6.1).

6.1.2 Ethernet Frame Types

When a packet is transmitted, information about the sender, receiver, and upper layer protocols is attached to the data. The format for the completed packet is called the frame type (which can also be referred to as the encapsulation method). There are four Ethernet frame

Figure 6.1 Ethernet Using Manchester Signal Encoding that Uses Transition State to Encode Data

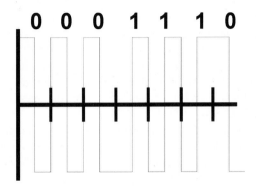

Table 6.2 Ethernet Frame Types

Novell name	Cisco name	Ethernet type
Novell Ethernet 802.3	Novell-ether	IEEE 802.3 frames without an LLC PDU. Also known as Ethernet Raw. Default Ethernet frame type of Novell NetWare 3.11 or earlier. Supports IPX.
Novell Ethernet II	ARPA	Used for IPX and TCP/IP. The default encapsulation used on Cisco Routers.
IEEE 802.2	SAP	Default Ethernet frame type of Novell NetWare 3.12 or later and Windows. Used for IPX.
IEEE 802.2 SNAP	SNAP	Used for IPX, TCP/IP, and AppleTalk.

types (see Table 6.2). You can think of frame types as Ethernet being the language and the four different frame types are the four dialects that exist for the language. Just as a person can know several dialects, a system or router can use several frame types at the same time.

They are all similar, yet there are some differences. The four frame types started with Novell Ethernet 802.3, when they decided they could not wait for the emerging Ethernet standard to be ratified by IEEE. The Ethernet packet starts with the preamble, which consists of 8 bytes of alternating ones and zeros, ending in 11. A station on an Ethernet network detects the change in voltage that occurs when another station begins to transmit, and uses the preamble to "lock on" to the sending station's clock signal. When it reads the 11 at the end, it then knows the preamble has ended. Because Ethernet 802.3 was an incomplete implementation of the IEEE 802.3 specification, Ethernet 802.3 is sometimes referred to as Ethernet Raw. Novell implemented the 802.3 header but not the fields defined in the 802.2 specification. Instead, the IPX packet begins immediately after the 802.3 fields.

Next, the MAC address of the target (destination) computer, followed by the MAC address of the source computer is sent.

> *NOTE:* The address could be represented in a multicast message. Most Ethernet adapters are set into **promiscuous** mode where they receive all frames that appear on the LAN, whether addressed to them or not. If this poses a security problem, a new generation of smart hub devices can filter out all frames with private destination addresses belonging to another station.

Depending on the Ethernet frame type, a Type field or a Length field is sent. For Ethernet 802.2, the length field describes the length of the data field including the LLC and SNAP headers. The data field can be between 64 and 1500 bytes. The LLC header is used to identify the process/protocol that generated the packet and the process/protocol that the packet is intended for. The data field is between 43 bytes and 1497 bytes, which include the TCP/IP or IPX packet. The last 4 bytes that the adapter reads is the Frame Check Sequence or CRC for error control (see Figure 6.2).

The Novell frame type Ethernet 802.2 is a complete implementation. It includes the 802.3 and 802.2 fields. Ethernet II, the standard frametype for TCP/IP networks, follows the addresses with a two-octet field that specifies the upper layer protocol. Ethernet SNAP includes 802.3, 802.2, and SNAP (sub-network access protocol) fields (see Figure 6.3).

Figure 6.7   The 5-4-3 Rule for an Ethernet Coaxial Network

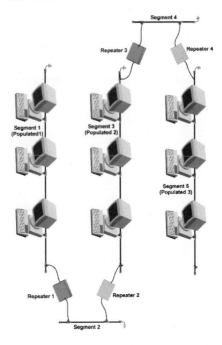

Figure 6.8   The 5-4-3 Rule for an Ethernet UTP Network

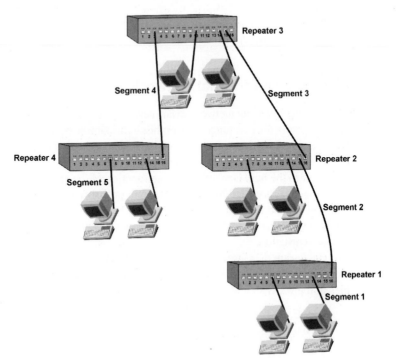

Figure 6.9   The 5-4-3 Rule for an Ethernet UTP/Coaxial Network

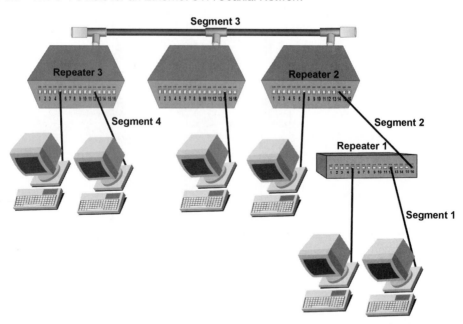

NOTE: You can reduce the collisions by using switches instead of hubs because those data packets will be sent only on cables on which the computer exists.

6.1.10   Planning an Ethernet Network

Let's take a look at two network examples. The first example would consist of a room with approximately ten computers. Assembling this simple network would include purchasing NICs for each computer, one or more hubs, and enough UTP cabling to connect all of the NICs. The hub is located somewhere within the room, and cables are stretched from each computer to the hub. Depending on the function of the network, standard 10 Mbps Ethernet using category 3 cabling (or better) will probably suffice.

If you need a larger network, it would be a lot more complicated. First, you would place your server or servers in a server room where the server can be secured and have proper ventilation.

Cables are then stretched from wall jacks throughout the building and lead to a patch panel located in the server room or in a wiring closet along with the hub or hubs. The cables in the walls should be eight-wire/four-pair category 5 or better solid wire cabling.

NOTE: Depending on the fire code for your area, some or all of the cabling will need to be Plenum cabling.

Patch cables are then made by using eight-wire/four-pair category 5 stranded cabling. They are used to connect the individual computers to the wall jacks. The port of the patch panel that connects to the wall jack is connected with another patch cable to the hub. The patch panel is a convenient way to connect the network together. In addition, it allows for easy reconfiguration. Again, depending on the function and load of the network, you could do one of two options:

■ The entire network could be 1 Gbps or 100 Mbps.
■ You could install a backbone of 1 Gbps connected to 100 Mbps switches, then use the 1 Gbps backbone to connect the computers.

When designing an Ethernet network or considering upgrading a current Ethernet network, you should make sure that no shared Ethernet segments are saturated (no more than 40 percent utilized). If so, you should then consider installing a faster network or breaking up the shared segments by either creating additional segments and dividing the computers among the links or by using switches.

6.2   TOKEN RING

Another major LAN technology in use today is **Token Ring.** Token Ring rules are defined in the IEEE 802.5 specification. As mentioned earlier in the chapter, the physical topology of token ring is a star, but the logical topology is a ring. Therefore, it is actually implemented in what can best be described as a collapsed ring. In Token Ring LANs, each station is connected to a Token Ring wiring concentrator called a **multistation access unit (MAU)** using STP or UTP. Like Ethernet hubs, MAUs are usually located in a wiring closet.

   Figure 6.10 depicts a typical Token Ring frame. Some of its characteristics are similar to those of the Ethernet frame, but significant differences arise in how the control information is handled. The following list describes the components of the typical Token Ring frame:

■ **Start Delimiter (SD)**—Signifies the beginning of the packet.
■ **Access Control (AC)**—Contains information about the priority of the frame.
■ **Frame Control (FC)**—Defines the type of frame used in the FCS.
■ **Destination Address**—Contains the destination node address.
■ **Source Address**—Contains the address of the originating node.
■ **Data**—Contains the data transmitted from the originating node. May also contain routing and management information.

Figure 6.10   A Token Ring Frame

Start Delimiter	Access Control	Frame Control	Destination Address	Source Address	Data	Frame Check Sequence	End Delimiter	Frame Status

- **Frame Check Sequence (FCS)**—Used to check the integrity of the frame.
- **End Delimiter (ED)**—Indicates the end of the frame.
- **Frame Status (FS)**—Indicates whether the destination node recognized and correctly copied the frame, or whether the destination node was not available.

The token frame consists of the SD, AC, and ED.

The access method used on Token Ring networks is called **token passing.** In token passing, a network device only communicates over the network when it has the token (a special data packet that is generated by the first computer that comes online in a Token Ring network. The token is passed from one station to another around a ring. When a station gets a free token and transmits a packet, it travels in one direction around the ring, passing all of the other stations along the way.

Each node acts as a repeater that receives token and data frames from its nearest active upstream neighbor (NAUN). After a frame is processed by the node, the frame is passed or rebroadcast downstream to the next attached node. Each token makes at least one trip around the entire ring. It then returns to the originating node. Work stations that indicate problems send a beacon to identify an address of the potential failure.

If a station has not heard from its upstream neighbor in seven seconds, it sends a packet down the ring that contains its address and the address of its NAUN. The Token Ring can then reconfigure itself to avoid the problem area.

Token Ring NICs can run at 4 Mbps or 16 Mbps. The 4 Mbps cards can run only at that data rate. However, 16 Mbps cards can be configured to run at 4 or 16 Mbps. All cards on a given network ring must run at the same rate. To run at 4 Mbps, you should use category 3 UTP or better while 16 Mbps requires category 4 cable or higher or type 4 STP cable or higher.

Like Ethernet cards, the unique node address on each NIC is burned in at the manufacturer on a ROM chip. For fault tolerance, a maximum of two Token Ring cards can be installed in any node, with each card being defined as either the primary or alternate Token Ring card in the machine. The Token Ring card will use two types of connectors, one is equipped with a female (DB-9) nine-pin connector (only four pins are used) while the second is a RJ-45 connector. MAU's repeaters, and most other equipment, use a special IBM Type-1 unisex data connector.

> *NOTE:* To connect multiple MAUs, the ring out (RO) port of each MAU must be connected to the ring in (RI) port of the next MAU so that it can complete a larger ring (see Figure 6.11). In a Token Ring network, you can have up to 33 MAUs chained together.

When building a Token Ring network, you must follow these rules:

- The maximum cable length between a node and a MAU is 330 feet (100 meters) for type 1 and 2 cables, 220 feet (66 meters) for types 6 and 9 cable, and 150 feet (45 meters) for a category 3 UTP cable.
- Nodes must be separated by a minimum of 8 feet (2.5 meters).
- The maximum ring length is 660 feet (200 meters) for types 1 and 2 cable, 400 feet (120 meters) for a type 3 cable, 140 feet (45 meters) for a type 6 cable, and 0.6 miles (1km) for a fiber optic segment.

Figure 6.11 MAUs Connected Together. Notice the Cables Attached to RI and RO are Connected to Form a Larger Ring

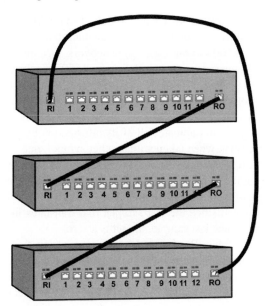

- While IEEE 802.5 specifies a maximum of 250 nodes, if using a small movable Token Ring cable system, IBM STP specifies a maximum of 96 nodes and 12 MAUs (IBM Model 8228) using IBM type 6 cable.
- While IEEE 802.5 specifies a maximum of 250 nodes, if using a large nonmovable Token Ring cable system, you are limited to a maximum of 260 nodes and 33 MAUs (using IBM type 1 and type 2 cable).
- While IEEE 802.5 specifies a maximum of 250 nodes, IBM UTP specifies 72 nodes.
- To run at 4 Mbps, you should use category 3 UTP or better while 16 Mbps requires category 4 cable or higher or type 4 STP cable or higher.

When designing a Token Ring network or considering upgrading a current Token Ring network, you should make sure that no shared Ethernet segments are saturated (no more than 70 percent utilized). Token based networks can have a higher utilization as compared to Ethernet networks. Because Ethernet networks are based on CSMA, an Ethernet becomes less efficient with higher utilization because of the collisions. When a collision occurs, the two nodes on the network have to rebroadcast, which causes even more network traffic. Token based networks are a little bit more orderly because each node on the network waits its turn to get the token so that it can use the network. There is no such thing as a collision in Token Ring. If the Token Ring network is saturated, you should, consider changing the network to fast Ethernet or breaking up the shared segments by either creating additional segments and dividing the computers among the links or by using switches.

6.3   FDDI

Fiber Distributed Data Interface (FDDI) is a MAN protocol that provides data transport at 100 Mbps (a much higher data rate than standard Ethernet or Token Ring) and can support up to 500 stations on a single network. Originally, FDDI networks required fiber optic cable, but today they can also run on UTP. Of course, fiber offers much greater distances than UTP cable. FDDI was used primarily as a backbone to connect several department LANs together within a single building or to link several building LANs together in a campus environment.

FDDI communicates all of its information by using symbols. Symbols are 5 bit sequences that, when taken with another symbol, make one byte. A bit can have one of two values. It is either a zero or a one. In FDDI, this is expressed by the change of state of the light on the other side. Approximately every eight nanoseconds, the station will take a sample of the light coming from the other machine. The light will either be on or off. If it has changed since the last sample, that translates into a bit of one. If the light has not changed since last sample, the bit is a zero.

Like Token Ring, FDDI is a token passing ring that uses a physical star topology. FDDI can be implemented in two basic ways: (1) as a dual-attached ring and (2) as a concentrator-based ring.

In the dual-attached scenario, stations are directly connected from one to another. FDDI's dual counter-rotating ring design provides a fail-safe mechanism in case a node goes down. If any node fails, the ring wraps around the failed node. However, one limitation of the dual counter-rotating ring design is that if two nodes fail, the ring is broken in two places, effectively creating two separate rings. Nodes on one ring are then isolated from nodes on the other ring. External optical bypass devices can solve this problem, but their use is limited because of FDDI optical power requirements.

Another way around this problem is to use concentrators to build networks. Concentrators are devices with multiple ports into which FDDI nodes connect. FDDI concentrators function like Ethernet hubs or token ring MAUs. Nodes are single-attached to the concentrator, which isolates failures occurring at those end stations. With a concentrator, nodes can be powered on and off without disrupting ring integrity. Because concentrators make FDDI networks more reliable, most FDDI networks are now built with concentrators.

An extension to FDDI, called **FDDI-2,** supports the transmission of voice and video information as well as data. Another variation of FDDI, called **FDDI Full Duplex Technology (FFDT),** uses the same network infrastructure but has the potential to support data rates up to 200 Mbps.

When designing an FDDI network, you should make sure that no shared FDDI segments are saturated (no more than 70 percent utilized). Like Token Ring, FDDI uses tokens for its access method. If the Token Ring network is saturated, you should consider upgrading the network to Gigabit Ethernet or faster or breaking up the shared segments by both creating additional segments and dividing the computers among the links or by using switches.

6.4   THE EIA 568-A WIRING STANDARD

With a physical star topology used in Ethernet networks, all of the cables lead and connect to a hub or a set of hubs. While a small network will only use one or two hubs, a network consisting of a few hundred computers will use a few hundred cables. In these situations, it is important to use some form of cable management.

In a large network, you would establish a horizontal wiring and/or backbone wiring system. The **horizontal wiring system** has cables that extend from wall outlets throughout the building to the wiring closet or server room. **Backbone wiring,** which is often designed to handle a higher bandwidth, consists of cables used to interconnect wiring closets, server rooms, and entrance facilities (telephone systems and WAN links from the outside world). The backbone wiring is sometimes referred to as the **vertical cabling system.** Vertical connections between floors are known as **risers.** For example, the horizontal wiring system could be category 5 UTP (or better) while the backbone wiring system could be category 5 UTP (or better), coax, or fiber optics.

NOTE: Horizontal wiring and backbone wiring is usually done by a wiring contractor.

In 1991, TIA/EIA released their joint 568 Commercial Building Wiring Standard, also known as structured cabling, for uniform, enterprise-wide, multivendor cabling systems. Structured cabling suggests how networking media can best be installed to maximize performance and minimize upkeep. The cabling infrastructure is described as follows (see Figure 6.12):

Figure 6.12   EIA/TIA 568-A Wiring Summary

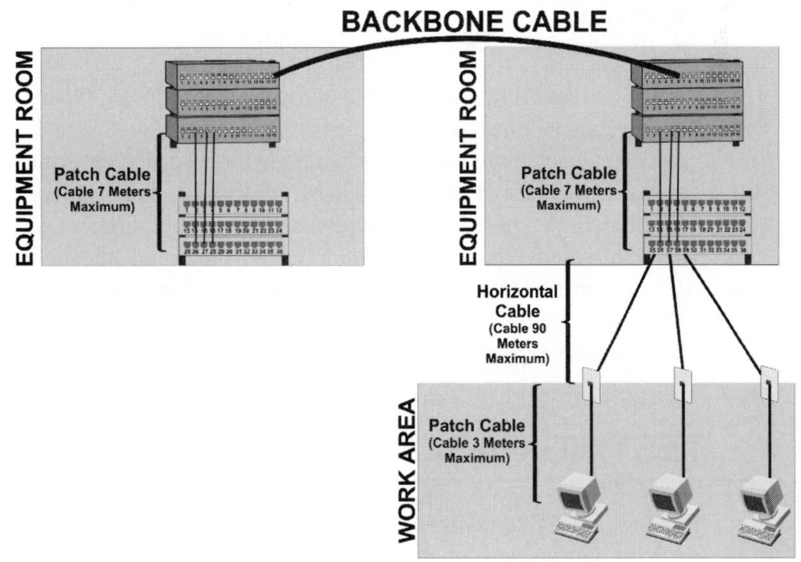

- **Work area**—The work area includes the station equipment, patch cable, and adapters (such as a media filter). The maximum recommended patch cable is 3 meters.
- **Telecommunications Closet**—The telecommunications closet is considered to be the floor serving facilities for horizontal cable distribution and can be used for intermediate and main cross-connects. The closet must be designed with minimal cable stress from bends, cable ties, and tensions (as defined in the ANSI/EIA/TIA-569A standard).
- **Equipment Room**—The equipment room is the area in a building where telecommunications equipment is located and the cabling system terminates.
- **Horizontal Cabling**—Horizontal cabling covers the work area receptacle to the horizontal cross-connect in the telecommunications closet. It includes the receptacle and optional transition connector (such as undercarpet cable connecting to round cable). The maximum of length of a horizontal cable should be 90 meters.
- **Backbone Cabling**—Backbone cabling provides interconnections between telecommunications closets, equipment rooms, and entrance facilities, and includes the backbone cables, intermediate and main cross-connects, terminations, and patch cords for backbone-to-backbone cross-connections. Cabling should be 30 meters or less for connection equipment to the backbone. If there are no intermediate cross-connects, a maximum of 90 meters is allowed. Hierarchical cross-connects cannot exceed two levels.
- **Entrance Facility**—The entrance facility is where the outside telecommunications service enters the building and interconnects with the building's telecommunications systems. In a campus or multi-building environment, it may also contain the building's backbone cross-connections.

Two outlets are required at the work area:

- 100-ohm UTP
- 100-ohm STP-A or 62.5/125 μm multimode fiber.

The two outlets allow for both data and voice connections. Grounding needs to conform to applicable building codes.

The characteristic impedance is 100 ohms ±15 percent from 1 MHz to the highest referenced frequency (16, 20, or 100 MHz) of a particular category. The recognized STP cables are IBM type 1A for backbone and horizontal distribution and IBM type 6A for patch cables with 2-pair, 22 AWG solid wire with a characteristic impedance of 150 ohms ±10 percent (3 MHz–300 MHz). The optical fiber medium for horizontal cabling is 62.5/125 μm multimode optical cable with a minimum of two fibers, and for backbone cabling it is 62.5/125 μm multimode and single mode optical fiber.

6.5 TESTING CABLE SYSTEMS

The best method for addressing a faulty cable installation is to avoid problems in the first place by purchasing high quality components and installing them carefully. No matter how careful you are, problems do arise.

Troubleshooting your network's cable requires the use of common sense skills. You try to isolate the cause of the problem by asking questions like the following:

- Has the cable ever worked properly?
- When did the malfunctions start?
- Do the malfunctions occur at specific times?
- Is the cable new or has it been in use for a while?
- What has changed since the cable functioned properly?

Once you have gathered all the information you can, the general troubleshooting process consists of steps like the following:

Step 1. Split the system into its logical elements.
Step 2. Locate the element that is most likely the cause of the problem.
Step 3. Test the element or install a substitute to verify it as the cause of the problem.
Step 4. If the suspected element is not the cause, move on to the next likely element.
Step 5. After locating the cause of the problem, repair or replace it.

Thus, you might begin troubleshooting by determining whether the cable is the source of the problem. You can do this by connecting different devices to both ends of the cable to see if the problem continues to occur. Once you verify that the cable is at fault, you can logically break it down into its component elements. For example, a typical cable run might consist of two patch cables, a wall plate, a punch-down block or patch panel, and the permanently installed cable itself.

In this type of installation, the easiest thing to do is to test the patch cables, either by replacing them or by testing them with a cable scanner. Replacing components can be a good troubleshooting method, as long as you know that the replacements are good. The most accurate method is to test the individual components with some form of cable tester.

The type of problems that can occur with cables include:

- **open**—A conductor with a break in it or wires that are unconnected, preventing electricity to flow.
- **short**—When a circuit has zero or abnormally low resistance between two points, resulting in excessive current. In Networking cables, a short is an unintentional connection made between two conductors (such as wires) or pins/contacts.
- **crossed pairs**—When two wires are connected improperly, causing the two wires to be crossed.
- **split pair**—Incorrect pinouts that cause data-carrying wires to be twisted together, resulting in additional crosstalk. Split pairs can be the result of mistakes during the installation. The solution is to reattach the connectors at both ends using either the T568-A or T568-B pinouts.
- **excessive length**—Cables that are longer than the recommended maximum for the network protocol you plan to use. Don't be overly concerned if the maximum length for a cable segment is 100 meters and you have a run that is 101 meters long. Most protocols have some leeway built into them, permitting a little excess.
- **excessive attenuation**—Excessive losses of signal typically caused by excessive length or use a cable that is inferior or not designed for a particular network standard

or speed. They can also be caused by faulty or substandard connectors, punch-down blocks, or patch panels.

- **excessive NEXT**—Excessive near-end crosstalk typically caused by inferior cable, inferior components, improper patch cables, split pairs, loose twisting, or sharing cables for other signals such as voice communications.
- **excessive noise**—Excessive noise can be caused by AC power lines, light fixtures, electric motors, and other sources of electromagnetic interference (EMI) and radio frequency interference (RFI). Therefore, cabling should be routed away from these items.

As you will see, there are many tools and devices that can test cables. Some are simple and inexpensive while others are elaborate and expensive. Some are easy to use as they supply easy-to-read pass/fail test results or simple numeric values while others need to be analyzed. Of course, these tools can be used during installation to verify the installation and components used, as well as for troubleshooting future problems.

6.5.1   Voltmeters and Ohm Meters

Because computers are sophisticated electronic devices, voltmeters and ohm meters can be used to test certain aspects of the computer. A **voltmeter** can be used to see if a device is generating the correct voltage output or signal. An **ohm meter** can be used to check wires and connectors and measure the resistance of an electronic device. A **digital multimeter (DMM)** combines several measuring devices, including a voltmeter and an ohm meter.

Ohm meters can be used to test wires. Because a wire or fuse is essentially a conductor, you should measure no resistance (0 ohms), showing that there is no break in the wire or fuse. This is known as a **continuity check.**

6.5.2   Cable Testers

Before looking at cable testers, remember that most cables will have only two conductors, such as those found in a coaxial cable or a cable that contains several pairs of wires (such as UTP). Unfortunately, because the pinouts of the UTP vary depending on its implementation, it becomes more complicated to test it.

Of all of the cable testers, the simplest type of tester performs continuity testing. Continuity testing is designed to check a copper cable connection for basic installation problems such as opens, shorts, and crossed pairs. A continuity tester consists of two separate units that you connect to each end of the cable to be tested. In many cases, the two units can snap together for storage and easy testing of patch cables. While these devices usually cannot detect more complicated STP/UTP wiring faults such as split pairs, they are sufficient for basic cable (coax) testing (see Figure 6.13).

A more sophisticated form of a cable tester is a wire map tester. A wire map tester is a device that transmits signals through each wire in a copper twisted pair cable to determine if it is connected to the correct pin at the other end. Wire mapping is the most basic

Figure 6.13 A Cable Tester

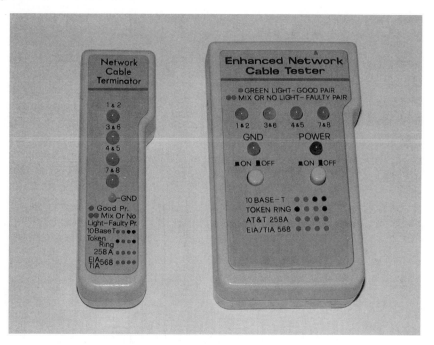

test for twisted pair cables because the eight separate wire connections involved in each cable run are a common source of installation errors. Wire map testers detect transposed wires, opens, and shorts.

A wire map tester consists of a remote unit that you attach to the far end of a connection and the battery-operated, hand-held main unit that displays the results. Typically, the tester displays various codes to describe the type of faults it finds. In some cases, you can purchase a tester with multiple remote units that are numbered so that one person can test several connections without constantly traveling back and forth from one end of the connection to the other to move the remote unit.

The one wiring fault that is not detectable by a dedicated wire map tester is split pairs, because even though the pinouts are incorrect, the cable is still wired straight through. To detect split pairs, you must use a device that tests the cable for the near-end crosstalk that split pairs cause.

6.5.3   Tone Generators

The simplest type of copper cable tester is also a two-piece unit. It is called a tone generator and probe (fox and hound) wire tracer. This type of device consists of a unit that you connect to a cable with a standard jack, or an individual wire with alligator clips. The unit transmits a signal over the cable or wire. The other unit is a penlike probe that emits an

Figure 6.14 A Tone Generator

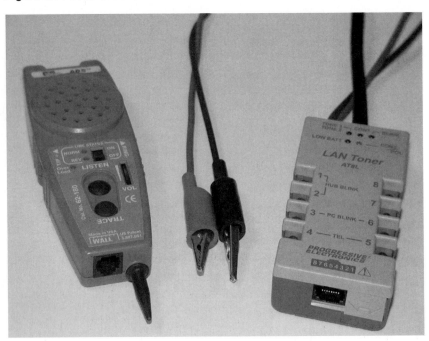

audible tone when touched to the other end of the cable or wire or even its insulating sheath (see Figure 6.14).

This type of device is most often used to locate a specific connection in a punch-down block. For example, some installers prefer to run all network cables to the central punch-down block without labeling them, then to use a tone generator to identify which block is connected to which wall plate, and then label the punch-down block accordingly. You can also use the device to identify a particular cable at any point between the two ends. Because the probe can detect the cable containing the tone signal through its sheath, you can locate one specific cable out of a bundle in a ceiling conduit or other type of raceway by connecting the tone generator to one end and touching the probe to each cable in the bundle until you hear the tone.

In addition, by testing the continuity of individual wires using alligator clips, you can use a tone generator and probe to locate opens, shorts, and miswires. An open wire will produce no tone at the other end, a short will produce a tone on two or more wires at the other end, and an improperly connected wire will produce a tone on the wrong pin at the other end.

This process is extremely time-consuming, however, and it's nearly as prone to errors as the cable installation itself. You either have to continually travel from one end of the cable to the other to move the tone generator unit or use a partner to test each connection, keeping in close contact using phones, radios, or some other means of communication in order to avoid confusion. When you consider the time and effort involved, you will properly find that investing in a wire map tester is a more practical solution.

6.5.4   Time Domain Reflectometers

A **time domain reflectometer (TDR)** is the primary tool used to determine the length of a copper cable and to locate the impedance variations that are caused by opens, shorts, damaged cables, and interference with other systems. The TDR works much like radar, by transmitting a signal on a cable with the opposite end left open and measuring the amount of time that it takes for the signal's reflection to return to the transmitter. When you have this elapsed time measure, called the nominal velocity of propagation (NVP), and you know the speed at which electrons move through the cable, you can then determine the length of the cable.

The NVP (measured as a percentage of light) for a particular cable is usually provided by its manufacturer along with other specifications. Some manufacturers provide the NVP as a percentage, such as 75 percent, while others express it as a decimal value multiplied by the speed of light (c), such as $0.75c$. Many cable testers compute the length internally, based on the results of the TDR test and an NVP value that is either preprogrammed or specified for the cable you are testing. Because the NVP values for various cables can range from 60 to 90 percent, you can have a margin of error for the cable length results of up to 30 percent if you are using the wrong value.

There are two basic types of TDRs available, those that display their results as a waveform on an LCD or CRT screen and those that use a numeric readout to indicate the distance to a source of impedance. The numeric readout provides less detail but is easy to use and relatively inexpensive. Waveform TDRs are not often used for field testing these days, because they are much more expensive than the numeric type and require a great deal more expertise to use effectively.

You can use a TDR to test any kind of cable that uses metallic conductors, including the coaxial and twisted-pair cables used to construct LANs. A high quality TDR can detect a large variety of cable faults, including open conductors, shorted conductors, loose connectors, sheath faults, water damage, crimped cables, cut cables, or smashed cables, and many other conditions. In addition, the TDR can measure the length of the cable and the distance to any of these faults.

6.5.5   Visual Fault Locators

The light that carries signals over fiber optic cable is invisible to the naked eye, making it difficult to ensure that installers have made the proper connections without a formal test. A visual fault locator (sometimes called a cable tracer) is a quick and easy way to test the continuity of a fiber cable connection by sending visible light over a fiber optic cable. A typical fault locator is essentially a flashlight that applies its LED or incandescent light source to one end of a cable. The light is then visible from the other end. This enables you to locate a specific cable out of a bundle and ensure that a connection has been established.

More powerful units that use laser light sources can actually show points of high loss in the cable, such as breaks, kinks, and bad splices, as long as the cable sheath is not completely opaque. For example, the yellow or orange colored sheaths commonly used on single mode or multimode cables respectively usually admit enough of the light energy lost by major cable faults to make them detectable from the outside.

6.5.6   Fiber Optic Power Meters

A fiber optic power meter is a device that measures the intensity of the signal being transmitted over a fiber optic cable. The meter is similar in principle to a multimeter that measures electrical current, except that it works with light instead of electricity. The meter uses a solid state detector to measure the signal intensity. There are different meters for different fiber optic cables and applications such as those used for short wavelength systems and those for long wavelength systems. More expensive units can measure both long and short wavelength signals.

In order to measure the strength of an optical signal, there must be a signal source at the other end of the cable. While you can use a fiber optic power meter to measure the signal generated by your actual network equipment, accurately measuring the signal loss or a cable requires a consistent signal generated by a fiber optic test source. A companion to the power meter in a fiber optic tool kit, the test source is also designed for use with a particular type of network. Sources typically use LEDs for multimode fiber or lasers for single mode fiber to generate a signal at a specific wavelength, and you should choose a unit that simulates the type of signals used by your network equipment.

6.5.7   Optical Time Domain Reflectometers

An **optical time domain reflectometer (OTDR)** is the fiber optic equivalent of the TDR used to test copper cables. The OTDR transmits a calibrated signal pulse over the cable to be tested and monitors the signal that returns back to the unit. Instead of measuring signal reflections caused by electrical impedance, the OTDR measures the signal returned by backscatter; a phenomenon that affects all fiber optic cables.

As with a TDR, the condition of the cable causes variances in the amount of backscatter returned to the OTDR, which is displayed on an LCD or CRT screen as a waveform. By interpreting the signal returned, it is possible to identify cable faults of specific types and other conditions. An OTDR can locate splices and connectors and measure their performance; identify stress problems caused by improper cable installation; and locate cable breaks, manufacturing faults, and other weaknesses. Knowing the speed of the pulse as it travels down the cable, the OTDR can also use the elapsed time between the pulse's transmission and reception to pinpoint the location of specific condition of the cable.

The two primary tasks that OTDRs should not be used for are measuring a cable's signal loss and locating faults on LANs. Measuring loss is the job of the power meter and light source, which are designed to simulate the actual conditions of the network. Using an OTDR, it is possible to compute a cable's length based on the backscatter returned to the unit, but the results are almost certain to be far less accurate. The only possible advantage to using an OTDR for this purpose is that you can test the cable from one end, while the traditional method requires that the light source be connected to one end and the power meter to the other.

OTDRs also have limited distance resolution capabilities, making them quite difficult to use effectively in a LAN environment where the cables are only a few hundred feet long. OTDRs are used primarily on long distance connections, such as those used by telephone and cable television networks. Of course, OTDRs waveforms require a good deal of training and experience to interpret them. Lastly, full-featured OTDR units are quite expensive.

6.5.8   Fiber Optic Inspection Microscopes

Splicing and attaching connectors to fiber optic cables are tasks that require great precision, and the best way to inspect cleaved fiber ends and polished connection ferrules is with a microscope. Fiber optic inspection microscopes are designed to hold cables and connectors in precisely the correct position for examination, enabling you to detect dirty, scratched, or cracked connectors. This ensures that cables are cleaved correctly in preparation for splicing. Good microscopes typically provide at least 100 power magnification, have a built-in light source (not a fiber optic light source, but a source of illumination for the object under the scope), and are able to support various types of connectors using additional stages, which may or may not be included.

6.5.9   Multifunction Cable Scanners

Multifunction cable scanners (certification tools) are devices that are available for both copper and fiber optic networks and perform a series of tests on a cable run, compare the results against either preprogrammed standards or parameters that you supply, and display the outcome as a series of pass or fail ratings. Most of these units perform the basic tests called for by the most commonly used standards; such as wire mapping, length, attenuation, and NEXT for copper cables; and optical power and signal loss for fiber optic. Many of the copper cable scanners also go beyond the basics to perform a comprehensive battery of tests, including propagation delay, delay skew, various versions of crosstalk, and return loss.

The primary advantage of this type of device is that anyone can use it. You simply connect the unit to a cable, press a button, and read off the results after a few seconds. Many units can store the results of many individual tests in memory, download them to a PC, or output them directly to a printer.

6.5.10   Protocol Analyzers

Sometimes when you have to troubleshoot network problems, you need to take a good look at what is being sent through your network to determine the cause. This is where **protocol analyzers** come in. A protocol analyzer, also known as a network analyzer and sniffer, is software or a hardware/software device that allows you to capture or receive every packet on your media, store it in a trace buffer, and then show a breakdown of each of the packets by protocol in the order that they appeared. Therefore, it can help you analyze all levels of the

OSI model to determine the cause of the problem. Network analysis is the art of listening in on the network communications to examine how devices communicate and determine the health of that network. An example of a protocol analyzer is Microsoft's Network Monitor.

The operation of a protocol analyzer is actually quite simple:

- Receive a copy of every packet on a piece of wire by operating in a promiscuous capture mode (a mode that captures all packets on the wire, not just broadcast packets and packets addressed to the analyzer's adapter).
- Timestamp the packets.
- Filter out the stuff you're not interested in.
- Show a breakdown of the various layers of protocols, bit by bit.

These packet traces can be saved and retrieved for further analysis. Once a packet is captured from the wire, the analyzer breaks down the headers and describes each bit of every header in detail.

While it is easy to capture and timestamp the packets, people often have a tendency to capture every packet on a segment when trying to troubleshoot a specific problem. The only problem with that is that you will be amazed at how much traffic is sent through a wire. Therefore, when you analyze the packets, you can easily become overwhelmed. By setting up filters to do some basic statistical analysis, you can isolate the problem with more ease and less time.

For example, if the problem only affects users communicating with a certain server, put an analyzer on that segment and filter traffic to and from the server. If the problem only affects users who go through a router, start by putting an analyzer on one of the routed segments and filter traffic to and from the router's MAC addresses. If you are troubleshooting a slow login process, you should start by analyzing the client's segment and putting a filter on the client's MAC address.

Protocol analyzers can be used for more than just troubleshooting. You can use them to monitor your network performance and head off problems before they occur, and you can determine when your network is becoming too congested. This way, you can update your network hardware or subdivide your network so that your network performance does not become a problem. In addition, you can find out what is using the bandwidth of your network so that you can optimize or tweak your network.

In addition, you can baseline the throughput of a particular application. Therefore, you can determine how much traffic the application is causing. This is particularly important if you can actually test the application before purchasing it to see if your current network can handle the additional generated traffic. This would include looking at how much traffic is generated when you log onto the new application or server, querying and updating a database, and the transfer of files.

Of course, if you analyze your network when everything is working properly, it will be easier to identify packet anomalies and you can compare the difference in performance when you update or replace drivers, network interfaces, platform upgrades, and so forth. This will even give you concrete numbers that you can use in reports to management so that you can justify equipment costs and upgrades.

A good analyzer should have some alerts/alarms that notify you of unusual or faulty traffic patterns. Some useful alarms should include:

- **Utilization percentage**—Shown as a percentage of the bandwidth that is used. On Ethernet networks especially, the performance degrades significantly when the utilization gets above 40 percent. Watch the collision/fragment error count in relationship to utilization.
- **Packets per second**—Shown in number of packets per second seen on the network. This number can give you an idea of how many packets an interconnecting device (such as a router or switch) will need to process per second.
- **Broadcasts per second**—This number tells you how much broadcast (packets processed by all devices regardless of their operating system or protocol) is on your network. Excessive broadcast will slow your network dramatically.
- **Server/router down**—When the server and/or router goes down.
- **MAC layer errors**—Shown in "per second" increments. These MAC layer errors are defined as layer 1 and 2 errors that corrupt packet formats or make access to the network impossible.

The analyzer should also be able to build trend graphs to illustrate the current and long-term traffic patterns (such as utilization and packets per second). In order to make the communications information useful to you, the analyzer decodes (interprets) the actual packet information received.

While ICMP messages are invaluable for troubleshooting TCP/IP networks, you should be aware that hackers find ICMP messages equally useful. For example, excessive port unreachable messages may be the first sign that a hacker is trying to discover what network services are running on a network. Port scanning utilities often use the simplistic approach of sending packets to a device and incrementing the destination port number by 1 in each packet. Port unreachable messages help determine which ports are not active, thereby identifying the ports or processes that are available on a system. Because hackers sometimes use port unreachable messages in this way, you should carefully examine these types of messages on your company's network. You should also examine the echo request and echo reply messages being transmitted on the network. Hackers sometimes use echo requests to "discover" IP addresses of live devices on the network. If echo requests are being used in this way, the destination IP address is typically incremented by one in each message. For example, you will see an echo request sent to 10.0.0.1, an echo request sent to 10.0.0.2, an echo request sent to 10.0.0.3, and so on.

These types of requests may also be sent by a management product that is building a map of your company's network (and, therefore, has a legitimate reason for discovering devices). However, if an unknown or suspect device is performing this type of discovery, it can be the first sign that a hacker is attempting to get information about your company's network.

In addition, hackers use ICMP messages to cripple network devices. For example, if you find an excessive number of ICMP echo packets on a network, you may have cause for concern. An excessive number of ICMP echo packets may indicate a denial of service attack. A denial of service attack focuses on overloading or crippling a device to the point that it cannot provide services to other devices.

Lastly, protocol analyzers can be used to capture packets that include passwords. This is particularly dangerous when passwords are sent in clear text (in such a format, the password can be read without being cracked).

SUMMARY

1. LAN technology defines topologies, packet structures, and access methods that can be used together on a segment. This includes Ethernet, Token Ring, and ARCnet.

2. Ethernet is the most widely used LAN technology today. It offers good balance between speed, price, reliability, and ease of installation.

3. Ethernet networks can be configured in either a star topology using UTP connected to a hub or as a bus topology using a coax acting as a backbone. Of these two, UTP cabling is by far the most commonly used.

4. Although many methods are used for encoding the signal on an Ethernet medium, Manchester Signal Encoding is the most common.

5. When a packet is transmitted, information about the sender, receiver, and upper layer protocols is attached to the data. The format for the completed packet is called the frame type (which can also be referred to as the encapsulation method).

6. The original Ethernet was called 10Base5 or ThickNet. The name is derived because 10Base5 is a 10 Mbps baseband network that can have a cable segment up to 500 meters long.

7. 10Base2 (Thinnet) is a simplified version of the 10Base5 network. The name describes a 10 Mbps baseband network with a maximum cable segment length of approximately 200 meters (actually 185 meters).

8. 10BaseT uses UTP, which costs less, is smaller, and is easier to work with than coax.

9. While Ethernet is a logical bus topology, 10BaseT is a physical star topology, which has the network devices connected to a hub.

10. In Ethernet, when a network device wants to access the network, the access method used is CSMA/CD.

11. Fast Ethernet is an extension of the 10BaseT Ethernet standard that transports data at 100 Mbps yet still keeps using the CSMA/CD protocol used by 10 Mbps Ethernet.

12. When creating and expanding an Ethernet network, you must always follow the 5-4-3 Rule. An Ethernet network must not exceed 5 segments connected by four repeaters. Of these segments, only three of them can be populated by computers.

13. Propagation delay is the amount of time that passes between the time a signal is transmitted and the time it is received at the opposite end of the copper or optical cable.

14. Token Ring rules are defined in the IEEE 802.5 specification. The physical topology of Token Ring is a star but the logical topology is a ring.

15. In Token Ring LANs, each station is connected to a Token Ring wiring concentrator called a MAU with a STP or UTP.

16. The access method used on Token Ring networks is called token passing.

17. FDDI is a MAN protocol that provides data transport at 100 Mbps (a much higher data rate than standard Ethernet or Token Ring) and can support up to 500 stations on a single network.

18. In a LAN, you would establish a horizontal wiring and/or backbone wiring system.

19. TIA/EIA released their joint 568 Commercial Building Wiring Standard, also known as structured cabling, for uniform, enterprise-wide, multivendor cabling systems.

20. The best method for addressing a faulty cable installation is to avoid the problems in the first place by purchasing high quality components and installing them carefully.

21. The simplest type of cable tester performs continuity testing, which is designed to check a copper cable connection for basic installation problems such as opens, shorts, and crossed pairs.

22. A more sophisticated form of cable tester is the wire map tester.

23. The simplest type of copper cable tester is a two-piece unit called a tone generator and probe (fox and hound) wire tracer.

24. A TDR is the primary tool used to determine the length of a copper cable and locate the impedance variations that are caused by opens, shorts, damaged cables, and interference with other systems.

25. A visual fault locator (sometimes called a cable tracer) is a quick and easy tool used to test the continuity of a fiber cable connection by sending visible light over a fiber optic cable.

26. A fiber optic power meter is a device that measures the intensity of the signal being transmitted over a fiber optic cable.

27. An OTDR is the fiber optic equivalent of the TDR, and is used to test copper cables.

28. Fiber optic inspection microscopes are designed to hold cables and connectors in precisely the correct position for examination, enabling you to detect dirty, scratched, or cracked connectors. The microscope helps to ensure that cables are cleaved correctly in preparation for splicing.

29. Multifunction cable scanners (certification tools) are devices that are available for both copper and fiber optic networks. They perform a series of tests on a cable run, compare the results against either preprogrammed standards or parameters that you supply, and display the outcome as a series of pass or fail ratings.

30. A protocol analyzer (network analyzer or sniffer) is software or a hardware/software device that allows you to capture or receive every packet on your media, store it in a trace buffer, and then show a breakdown of each of the packets by protocol in the order that they appeared. Therefore, it can help you analyze all levels of the OSI model to determine the cause of the problem.

QUESTIONS

1. Twisted pair cables use different connection hardware than coax. Which type of connector is commonly used by twisted pair cables?
   a. BNC
   b. DIX
   c. AUI
   d. RJ-45

2. Ethernet uses which of the following access methods?
   a. CSMA/CD
   b. token passing
   c. CSMA/CA
   d. polling

3. How does token passing prevent data collisions on a Token Ring network?
   a. by having multiple tokens take alternate paths
   b. by broadcasting the intent to transmit before actually sending data
   c. by assigning a priority to each token and transmitting the highest priority token first
   d. by allowing only one computer at a time to use the token

4. You want to have a 10BaseT segment that is greater than 300 meters. Which device will be required?
   a. a repeater
   b. a multiplexer
   c. an amplifier
   d. a RJ-45 connector

5. Which of the following network standards is known as Fast Ethernet?
   a. 10Base2
   b. 100BaseTX
   c. 10Base5
   d. 100BaseVG-AnyLAN

6. What is the maximum cable segment length for ThinNet Ethernet?
   a. 100 meters
   b. 215 meters
   c. 185 meters
   d. 285 meters

7. What is the distance limitation of a 10BaseT network?
   a. 100 meters
   b. 500 meters
   c. 185 meters
   d. 1 km

8. You have a ThinNet bus network that has been in use for about a year. You have just added three new client computers to the network. When you test the network after installation, none of the computers on the network can access the server. Which of the following can be preventing the network from functioning?
   a. The bus network is not properly terminated.
   b. A client computer on the network has failed.
   c. The new cables added to service the new computers are not compatible with the existing cable type.
   d. The NICs in the new computers are not compatible with the NICs in other computers.

9. A client machine cannot connect to the network, but all other computers can access network resources. Which of the following is the most likely cause of the problem?
   a. a faulty cable terminator
   b. a faulty NIC on the domain controller
   c. a faulty NIC on the client computer
   d. excessive media collisions

10. You have been given the task of installing cables for an Ethernet network in your office building. The network cable will have to share the existing

conduit with telephone cables. Cable segments will be up to 95 meters in length. Which cable is best suited for this installation?

   a. fiber optic
   b. category 3 UTP
   c. category 1 UTP
   d. ThickNet coaxial

11. Which of the following networks is also known as Standard Ethernet?

   a. 10Base2   b. 10BaseT
   c. 10Base5   d. 100BaseX

12. Which of the following is a characteristic of 10BaseT topology?

   a. RJ-11 connectors
   b. UTP cabling
   c. BNC T connectors
   d. 50-ohm BNC terminators

13. What type of connector is normally used by a ThickNet cable for connection to the NIC?

   a. a BNC T connector
   b. a RJ-45 connector
   c. an AUI connector
   d. a BNC barrel connector

14. There are two types of coaxial cable: ThinNet and ThickNet. Both types are good choices for data transmission over long distances. Which of the following is true of ThinNet and ThickNet?

   a. ThinNet and ThickNet are specified in IEEE Standard 802.5.
   b. The maximum cable segment length is 100 meters for ThinNet and 500 meters for ThickNet.
   c. ThickNet is generally associated with 10Base5 topology, while ThinNet is associated with the 10Base2 topology.
   d. Because of their different sizes and construction, ThickNet and ThinNet should not be used in the same network.

15. You need to terminate a 10Base2 network. What should the value for the terminating resistors be?

   a. 25 ohms   b. 75 ohms
   c. 100 ohms   d. 50 ohms
   e. 93 ohms   f. none of the above

16. When using 10Base2 and 10Base5 Ethernet, which of the following statements are true?

   a. You should terminate one end and ground the other end.
   b. You should terminate both ends and ground one end.

   c. You should terminate one end and ground both ends.
   d. You should terminate both ends and ground one end.
   e. You should terminate both ends of the cable and ground both ends.

17. You are installing a 100 Mbps Ethernet LAN where there is existing category 2 UTP cabling. Which of the following types of cable will satisfy the installation requirement?

   a. the existing cable
   b. category 3 UTP
   c. ThickNet
   d. category 5 UTP

18. What type of connector is used by ThinNet for connection to the NIC?

   a. an AUI connector
   b. a BNC T connector
   c. a RJ-45 connector
   d. a BNC barrel connector

19. Ethernet uses a special type of data format called frames. Which of the following statements is true of Ethernet frames?

   a. All Ethernet frames are 1518 bytes long.
   b. All Ethernet frames contain preambles that mark the start of the frame.
   c. All Ethernet frames contain starting and ending delimiters.
   d. All Ethernet frames contain CRC fields that store the source and destination addresses.

20. 10Base5 is one of the topologies defined in the IEEE 802.3 specifications. Which of the following is another name for 10Base5 cabling?

   a. category 5 UTP   b. ThinNet
   c. STP   d. ThickNet

21. Which type of media access method is used by IBM-based LANs with MAUs?

   a. token passing   b. CSMA/CD
   c. demand priority   d. CDMS/CA

22. Which 100-Megabit Ethernet standard is designed to use two pairs of wires in a UTP cable?

   a. 100BaseVG   b. 100Base T4
   c. 10BaseF   d. 100BaseTX

23. A RJ-45 connector should be wired with _____ pairs when used on a category 5 UTP cable.

   a. 1   b. 2
   c. 4   d. 8

24. ThickNet can be extended to _____ meters per segment.

  a. 100   b. 200

  c. 500   d. 1000

25. The best cable choice for linking a few computers in a small office using a bus Ethernet network is a cable with a _____ designation.

  a. RG-49   b. RG-58

  c. RG-59   d. RG-62

26. A network that uses 10Base2 requires _____ terminator(s) for each network segment in order to function correctly.

  a. 0   b. 1

  c. 2   d. 3

27. You are a network technician for a network consulting firm. One of your firm's clients is opening a new location, and you are responsible for installing the network for that location. The client's new location will contain two buildings located 50 meters apart. Each building will contain 25 network hosts, and data should be transmittable at speeds up to 100 Mbps between the two buildings. Which of the following Ethernet LAN standards should you use in the installation of the client's network?

  a. 10Base5   b. 100BaseTX

  c. 10BaseT   d. 1000BaseCX

28. Which of the following statements are associated with the use of CSMA/CD by a half duplex NIC to detect a collision on a 10BaseT network? (Select 3 choices.)

  a. The hub detects collisions.

  b. The original frame that is sent is looped back onto the NIC receive pair.

  c. The hub forwards the frame to all other devices.

  d. The NIC compares the transmitted frame to the frame that is looped back to its receive pair.

  e. The hub compares the frame that it received to the frame it sent out.

29. Which of the following accurately describes half duplex transmissions on Ethernet 10BaseT topologies?

  a. Half duplex transmissions avoid collisions by using CSMA/CD.

  b. Half duplex transmissions occur at half the normal speed.

  c. Half duplex transmissions can occur in only one direction at a time.

  d. Half duplex transmissions must use switches rather than hubs.

30. Which of the following statements is true regarding full duplex? (Select the best choice.)

  a. Full duplex Ethernet transmits and receives data simultaneously.

  b. Full duplex Ethernet works with any Ethernet hardware.

  c. Full duplex Ethernet requires only one circuit.

  d. Full duplex Ethernet uses hubs.

31. What are the effects of sustained, heavy collisions in CSMA/CD LANs? (Choose three answers.)

  a. increased broadcast traffic

  b. delay

  c. low throughput

  d. high throughput

  e. congestion

  f. high bandwidth

32. Modern networks are often described as using 100Base-TX components. What is meant by the term 'Base' in this definition?

  a. It describes the signaling method for communication on the network.

  b. It refers to the type of media used in the network.

  c. It relates to the speed of transmission of network signals.

  d. It defines the allowable length of media that can be used.

  e. It defines half duplex or full duplex operation.

33. How efficiently does full duplex Ethernet utilize its theoretical 20 Mbps bandwidth?

  a. 100 percent   b. 70 to 80 percent

  c. 80 to 90 percent   d. 60 to 70 percent

34. In theory, standard Ethernet (half duplex) provides 10 Mbps bandwidth. What efficiency is typically achieved on real world networks?

  a. 90 to 100 percent   b. 60 to 70 percent

  c. 70 to 80 percent   d. 50 to 60 percent

35. CSMA/CD was created to help detect collisions. In regards to CSMA/CD, what is the backoff algorithm used for on an 802.3 network?

  a. It is latency in store and forward switching.

  b. It is the time used for token passing from machine to machine.

  c. It is the retransmission delay that is reinforced when a collision occurs.

  d. It is the result of two nodes transmitting at a same time. The frames from each transmitting device collide and are damaged.

36. Look at the figure and determine the problem with this Ethernet network.

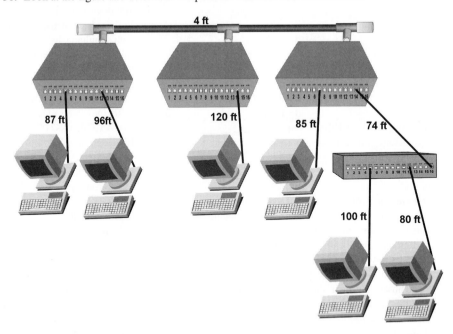

37. Look at the figure and determine the problem with this Ethernet network.

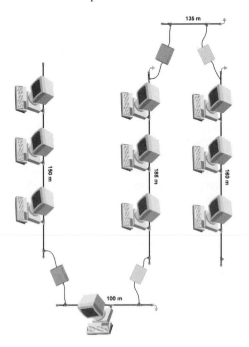

CHAPTER 7

Using Bridges
and Switches

Topics Covered in this Chapter

Introduction

Now that you have the basics of how a LAN works, you are ready to move on to making your LAN run more efficiently. This is typically done with bridges and switches.

Objectives

- Given a scenario, use a bridge or switch to segment the network.
- Explain the differences among layer 2, 3, and 4 switches.
- Explain how the spanning tree algorithm (STA) can provide fault tolerance without creating a network loop.

- Differentiate between STA and source-route bridging.
- Compare and contrast store-and-forward, cut-through, and FragmentFree processing.
- Explain how a virtual LAN can make a network more secure.

7.1   SEGMENTATION

When a network device wants to access an Ethernet network, the access method used is CSMA/CD. When a computer wants to send data over the network, it will listen to see if there is any traffic on the network. If the network is clear, it will then broadcast on to the network segment. Unfortunately, it is possible for two network devices to listen and try to send data at the same time. As a result, a collision occurs where both data packets are corrupted. When a collision is detected by a sending device, it sends out a jamming signal that lasts long enough for all nodes to recognize it and stop broadcasting. While this is normal for an Ethernet network, both network devices will wait a different random amount of time and try again. If the network is heavily congested it will have more collisions, which results in more traffic. This slows the entire network even more.

A **collision domain** is a network segment in which all devices share the same bandwidth. It is a set of NICs for which a frame sent by one NIC could result in a collision with a frame sent by any other NIC in the collision domain. The more devices you have on a segment, the more likely it is that you will experience collisions. With too many devices on a segment network, performance is considerably less than optimal. Increasing bandwidth is one way to deal with the problem, but a better way to deal with this problem is by using the available bandwidth more efficiently.

Microsegmentation is the process of creating smaller collision domains by segmenting a LAN rather than creating additional subnets. This makes a network run more efficiently because you can divide a network into smaller parts known as segments. Because this reduces the number of devices on a segment, it will increase the amount of available bandwidth by keeping local traffic local. Because it decreases congestion, it also decreases the number of collisions. Both bridges and LAN switches create LAN segments without creating additional subnets, while routers create LAN segments by creating additional subnets (see Figures 7.1, 7.2, 7.3, and 7.4).

Figure 7.1   A Hub Defines One Collision Domain

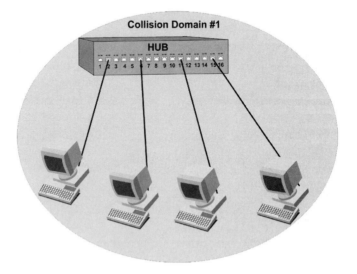

Figure 7.2   A Bridge Breaks Up a Collision Domain

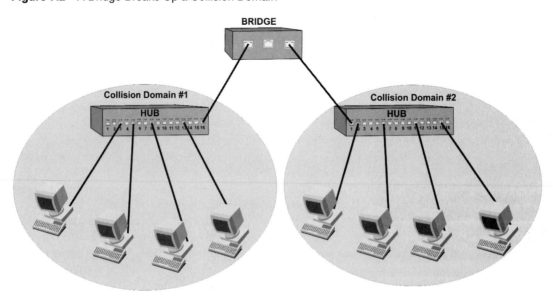

Figure 7.3 Like a Bridge, a Switch Breaks Up a Collision Domain without Creating Additional Subnets

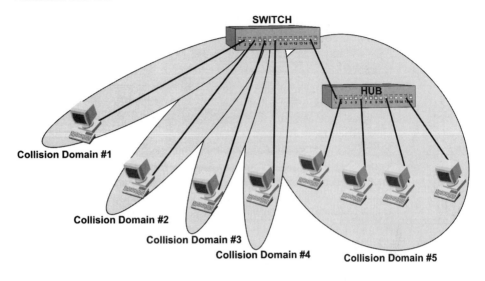

Figure 7.4 A Router Breaks Up a Collision Domain by Creating Additional Subnets

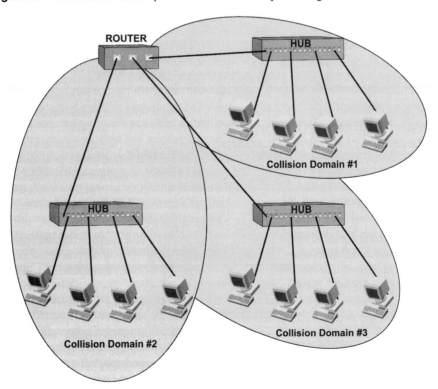

7.2   BRIDGES

A bridge, which is a layer 2 device, is used to break larger network segments into smaller network segments. It works much like a repeater but because a bridge works only with layer 2 protocols and layer 2 MAC sublayer addresses, it operates at the data link layer.

Some bridges can also connect dissimilar network types (for example, Token Ring and Ethernet) as long as the bridge operates at the LLC sublayer of the data link layer. If the bridge operates only at the lower sublayer (the MAC sublayer), bridges can connect only similar network types (Token Ring to Token Ring and Ethernet to Ethernet).

Several kinds of bridging have proven to be as important as internetworking devices. Transparent bridging is found primarily in Ethernet environments, while source-route bridging occurs primarily in Token Ring environments. **Translational bridging** provides translation between the formats and transit principles of different media types (usually Ethernet and Token Ring). Finally, source-route transparent bridging combines the algorithms of transparent bridging and source-route bridging to enable communication in mixed Ethernet/Token Ring environments.

7.2.1   Basic Bridges

There are two kinds of bridges: (1) basic and (2) learning. A basic bridge is used to interconnect LANs using one (or more) of the IEEE 802 standards. Packets received on one port may be retransmitted on another port. Unlike a repeater, a bridge will not start retransmission until it has received the complete packet. As a consequence, stations on both sides of a bridge can transmit simultaneously without causing collisions. Bridges, like repeaters, do not modify the contents of a packet in any way.

7.2.2   Transparent Bridges

Transparent bridging, used in Ethernet and documented in IEEE 802.1, is based on the concept of a spanning tree. A transparent bridge (also referred to as a learning bridge) is called transparent because the endpoint devices do not need to know that the bridge(s) exist(s). In other words, computers attached to the LAN do not behave any differently in the presence or absence of transparent bridges.

Transparent bridges build up their routing tables by cataloging the network nodes that send out messages. A bridge examines the MAC address of a message's source or sending node. If this address is new to the bridge, it adds it to the routing table along with the network segment from which it originated. The bridge's routing table is stored in its RAM. Just like a PC's RAM, it is dynamic. Therefore, if the power goes off, it goes away. When the power is restored, the bridge rebuilds the table. Because most network nodes send and receive packets continuously, it doesn't take long to completely rebuild the routing table.

The bridge operates with its Ethernet interfaces in promiscuous mode where it receives all frames sent on the network segments. The bridge "learns" by looking at the source and destination addresses of the frames sent on each network segment. It then builds a Forwarding Database (FDB) from the addresses as follows:

- which port the frame came from (source)
- which port to send the frame to (destination)

The bridge then applies three simple rules to an incoming frame:

- If its source and destination addresses are the same, then ignore the frame.
- Find the destination address of the incoming frame in the FDB and send the frame to the port listed in the FDB for that destination address.
- If destination address is not in the FDB (it is unknown) send frame to all ports (flood) except the port it came in on.

NOTE: Broadcasts and multicast frames are forwarded by a bridge.

Store-and-forward operation is typical in transparent bridging devices and is Cisco's primary LAN switching method. When in store-and-forward mode, the LAN switch copies the entire frame onto its onboard buffers and then computes the CRC. Because an entire frame is received before being forwarded, additional latency is introduced (as compared to a single LAN segment). The frame is discarded if it contains a CRC error, if it's too small (known as *runts*—less than 64 bytes including the CRC), and if it is too large (known as *giants*—over 1518 bytes including the CRC).

If the frame doesn't contain any errors, the LAN switch looks up the destination hardware address in its forwarding or switching table to find the correct outgoing interface. If a given address has not been heard from in a specified period of time, the address is then deleted from the address table. Lastly, to create a loop-free environment with other bridges, the Spanning Tree Algorithm is used.

7.2.3　The Spanning Tree Algorithm

Complex topology can cause multiple loops to occur. For example, to make your network more fault tolerant, you may have multiple bridge (or switch) connections from one segment to another. When a computer sends a message and the bridge does not know the destination computer, it will forward the messages to all of the ports except for the port that the message came from. The only problem is that when it gets to the other segment and the bridge does not know where the computer is, it will forward the message to all of the ports except for the port that the message came from, including the other connections to the other segment. In reality, the message looped back to the other segment and will keep on looping. Because the layer 2 has no mechanism to stop the loop, the spanning tree protocol was created (see Figure 7.5).

The **spanning tree algorithm (STA),** developed by Digital Equipment Corporation, was revised by the IEEE 802 committee and published in the IEEE 802.1d specification.

NOTE: The Digital algorithm and the IEEE 802.1d algorithm are not compatible. The STA analyzes the network and places the bridges into standby mode (blocking condition) if it would result in a loop when active. To provide fault tolerance, the blocking bridge ports can be activated if the primary link fails.

Figure 7.5 The Problem with Complex Topology is that a Nonstop Loop Can Occur for Packets Destined for Unknown Computers

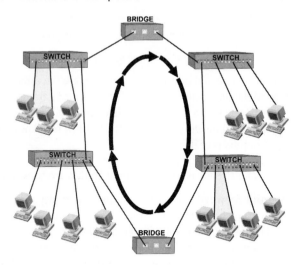

Table 7.1 STP Cost Values for STA

Bandwidth	STP cost value
4 Mbps	250
10 Mbps	100
16 Mbps	62
45 Mbps	39
100 Mbps	19
155 Mbps	14
622 Mbps	6
1 Gbps	4
10 Gbps	2

The STA assigns each bridge a unique identifier. Typically, this identifier is one of the bridge's MAC addresses plus a priority. In addition, each port in every bridge is assigned a unique identifier within that bridge. Again, this is typically its own MAC address. Lastly, each bridge port is associated with a path cost, which represents the cost of transmitting a frame onto a LAN through that port (see Table 7.1). By default, 10 Gbps links have a lower cost than 1 Gbps links, which have a lower cost than 100 Mbps, which have a lower cost than 10 Mbps links. Path costs are usually defaulted but can be assigned manually by network administrators.

When bridges (and switches) are added to the network, the bridges (and switches) will first send out a Bridge Protocol Data Unit (BPDU) to determine the spanning tree topology. The first activity in spanning tree computation is the selection of the **root bridge,** which will act as the default pathway from one segment to another, based on the lowest cost assigned to each link. If two or more bridges can have the same root path cost, the bridge identifiers are used to determine the designated bridges.

>*NOTE:* When a bridge or switch first initializes, the bridge or switch assumes that it is the root device. When the bridge or switch starts transmitting BPDUs to exchange information, the bridges and switches will create only one path between any two LAN segments.

Convergence occurs when bridges and switches have transitioned to either the forwarding or blocking modes and no data is forwarded. Of course, it is important to make sure all devices have the same database, which takes some time to accomplish.

The ports on a bridge running STP can transition through four different modes:

1. **Blocking**—A blocked port won't forward frames. It just listens to BPDUs. All ports are in blocking state (the default) when the switch is powered up.
2. **Listening**—The port listens to BPDUs to make sure no loops occur on the network before passing data frames.
3. **Learning**—The port learns MAC addresses and builds a filter table but does not forward frames.
4. **Forwarding**—The port sends and receives all data on the bridged port.

Bridge and switch ports are most often in either the blocking or forwarding state. The forwarding port is one that has been determined to have the lowest cost to the root bridge.

>*NOTE:* The only ports that should be in forwarding state are the ports in the root bridge, which places all of its ports in the forwarding state. All bridges and switches have one port that is considered the root port (see Figure 7.6). It usually takes 50 seconds to go from blocking mode to forwarding mode. It is not recommended that you change the default STP timers, but they can be adjusted if necessary.

Bridges exchange configuration messages at regular intervals (typically one to four seconds). If a bridge fails and the neighboring bridges do not receive a configuration message, the neighbors will initiate spanning tree recalculation.

7.2.4   Troubleshooting STA

A failure in the STA will generally lead to a bridging loop, which means either that a port should be blocked but instead is forwarding traffic or that a port is blocked, not allowing any traffic to flow through it. Most of these failures are related to a massive loss of BPDUs, either causing blocked ports to transition to forwarding mode or a reelection of the root bridge.

When troubleshooting a STA problem, you will need to know a few things. First, you should have a diagram of your network so that you know the topology of the bridged network. This should also include where the root bridge is located and where the blocked ports or redundant links are located. Of course, most of the switches will have some kind of method to view the status of all ports and any errors that they may have.

In addition, you should also look to see if there have been any changes to your network. If you have brought a new bridge or switch online, it would have said it was the root

Figure 7.6 The Spanning Tree Algorithm Prevents Looping of Packets Destined to Unknown Computers

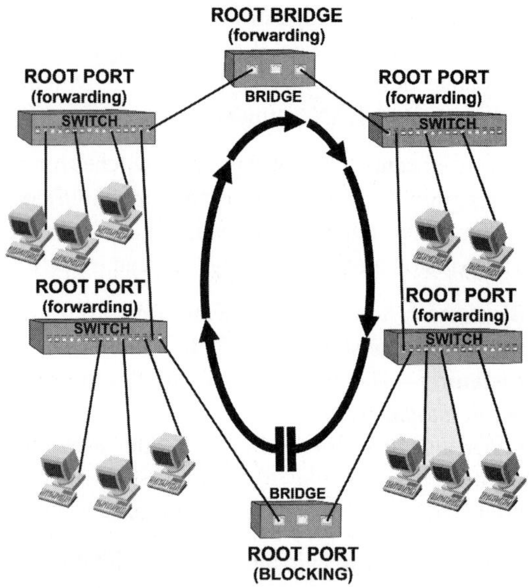

bridge and it would have forced a new election. During this time, all ports are put in blocking mode, which would result in a temporary network outage. This reelection could be avoided if you use a bridge priority parameter to override the MAC ID. You should choose the root switch that is nearest to the center of your network and has adequate processing power to handle the traffic because it will act as the backbone of your network.

One indication of a bridging loop is if all users in a certain domain have connectivity issues at the same time. In addition, you would see high port utilization. You can then verify a bridging loop either by checking status of all ports that make up the bridged network or by using a protocol analyzer to capture the traffic on a saturated link and check that similar packets are seen multiple times.

If a bridging loop occurs, most administrators generally don't have time to look for loops and would prefer restoring connectivity as soon as possible. The easiest way to accomplish this is to manually disable every single port that is providing redundancy in the network. If one area of the network is exhibiting the problem, this would be the best area to start. Of course, you should be a little systematic about it. Therefore, each time you disable a port, check if connectivity is restored in the network. If you know the port that you disabled stopped the loop, you are sure that the failure was located on a redundant path where this port was located. If this port should have been blocking, you have probably found the link on which the failure appeared.

Another cause for a bridging loop could be packet corruption. If a link is experiencing a high rate of physical errors, a certain number of consecutive BPDUs could be lost, leading a blocking port to transition to forwarding. Packet corruption is most likely caused by bad cables, incorrect cable lengths, or EMI but can also be caused by a bad port.

Lastly, another cause of a bridging loop is a bridge or switch that is so over-utilized that it lacks resources to send out BPDUs. For this to occur, the bridge or switch would have to be heavily overused because STA is generally not very processor intensive and has priority over other processes.

7.2.5   Source Route Bridging

Token Ring networks use source route bridging (SRB). In SRB, the responsibility of determining the path to the destination node is placed on the sending node, not on the bridge. In an SRB environment, these steps are taken:

Step 1: Token Ring devices send out a test frame to determine whether the destination node is on the local ring.

Step 2: If no answer is forthcoming, which means the destination node is not on the local ring, the sending node sends out a broadcast message called an *explorer frame.*

Step 3: The bridge forwards the explorer frame across the network through the network's bridges. Each bridge adds its ring number and bridge number to the frame's routing information field (RIF), so it can retrace its route later.

Step 4: The destination device, if it exists, receives and responds to the explorer frame. The sending node gets this response.

Step 5: The sending node initiates communication between the two devices with each intermediate bridge using the RIF value to determine the path between the two nodes.

Because SRB uses RIF information to determine its routes, no bridging table is created.

7.3   SWITCHES

In the most basic type of network found today, nodes are simply connected together using hubs. As a network grows, there are some potential problems with this configuration:

■ **Scalability**—In a hub network, limited shared bandwidth makes it difficult to accommodate significant growth without sacrificing performance.

■ **Latency**—The amount of time that it takes a packet to get to its destination. Because each node in a hub-based network has to wait for an opportunity to transmit (CSMA) in order to avoid collisions, the latency can increase significantly if you add more nodes. In addition, if someone is transmitting a large file across the network, then all of the other nodes must wait for an opportunity to send their own packets.

■ **Collisions**—A network with a large number of nodes on the same segment will often have a lot of collisions (a large collision domain). More collisions cause more traffic as these packets must be retransmitted.

■ **Network failure**—In a typical network, one device on a hub can cause problems for other devices attached to the hub due to wrong speed settings (100 Mbps on a 10 Mbps hub) or excessive broadcasts (remember that each hub forms a broadcast domain).

A **switching hub** (sometimes referred to as switch or a layer 2 switch) is a fast multiported bridge. Like a transparent bridge, a switch builds a table of the MAC addresses of all the connected stations. It then reads the destination address of each packet and forwards the packet to the correct port.

Switches can be used to segment a large network into several smaller, less congested segments (breaking up collision domains) while providing necessary interconnectivity between them. Switches increase network performance by providing each port with dedicated bandwidth without requiring users to change any existing equipment such as NICs, hubs, wiring, or any routers or bridges that are currently in place.

A major advantage of using a switch is that it allows one computer (or LAN segment) to open a connection to another computer (or LAN segment). While those two computers communicate, other connections between the other computers (or LAN segments) can be opened at the same time. Therefore, several computers can communicate at the same time through the switching hub. In addition, if the Ethernet connections that connect to the switch are full-duplex, a computer can send data to one computer and receive data from another computer at the same time.

> *NOTE:* Remember that to transmit and receive simultaneously, full duplex Ethernet requires a switch port, not a hub. This sets up a point-to-point connection, which eliminates collisions.

LAN switches rely on packet switching. The switch establishes a connection between two segments just long enough to send the current packet. Incoming packets are saved to a temporary memory area known as a buffer, the MAC address contained in the frame's header is read and then compared to a list of addresses maintained in the switch's lookup table. In an Ethernet LAN, an Ethernet frame contains a normal packet: the payload of the frame with a special header that includes the MAC address information for the source and destination of the packet.

LAN switches vary in their physical design. Currently, there are three popular configurations in use:

- **Shared-memory**—Stores all incoming packets in a common memory buffer shared by all the switch ports and then sends them to the correct port for the destination node.
- **Matrix**—An internal grid with the input port and the output port crossing each other. When a packet is detected on an input port, the MAC address is compared to the lookup table to find the appropriate output port. The switch then makes a connection from one port to the other port at their point of intersection.
- **Bus architecture**—A common bus or internal transmission path shared by all of the ports using TDMA. A switch based on this configuration has a dedicated memory buffer for each port and an application specific integrated circuit (ASIC) to control the internal bus access.

While switches work like bridges do, there are some important differences that you should always keep in mind:

- Layer-2 switching is hardware based, which means it uses the MAC addresses from the host's NIC cards to filter the network. Unlike bridges that use software to create and manage a filter table, switches use ASICs to build and maintain their filter tables. As a result, switches are faster than bridges.

■ Bridges can only have one Spanning Tree instance per bridge, while switches can have many.

■ Bridges can have up to 16 ports. A switch can have hundreds.

Unfortunately, because LAN switches review the MAC addresses of a frame, there is a small amount of latency added before the frame can be forwarded to the correct port. Therefore, one disadvantage of a switch would be the latency that is added.

Transparent bridges use store-and-forward processing, meaning that the entire frame is received before the first bit of the frame is forwarded. Switches can also use cut-through processing or FragmentFree processing. With **cut-through processing,** the first bits of the frame are sent out on the outbound port before the last bit of the incoming frame is received instead of waiting for the entire frame to be received. In other words, as soon as the switching port receives enough of the frame to see the destination MAC address, the frame is transmitted out the appropriate outgoing port to the destination device. This reduces the latency as compared to store-and-forward processing. The unfortunate side effect is that because the FCS is in the Ethernet trailer, the forwarded frame may have bit errors that the switch would have noticed with store-and-forward logic. If the outbound port is busy, the switch will store the frame until the port is available. Very few switches use cut-through processing.

With some switches, you configure the switch to perform cut-through switching on a per-port basis until a user defined error threshold is reached. At the point that the threshold is attained, the ports automatically change over to store-and-forward mode so they will stop forwarding the errors. When the error rate on the port falls back below the threshold, the port automatically changes back to cut-through mode.

The other method that can be used by switches is called FragmentFree processing. **FragmentFree processing** performs like cut-through processing, but the switch waits for 64 bytes to be received before forwarding the first bytes of the outgoing frame. According to Ethernet specifications, collisions should be detected during the first 64 bytes of the frame. Frames in error due to collision will not be forwarded. Like cut-through processing, the FCS still cannot be checked.

7.4   LAYER 3 SWITCHES

In this chapter, most of the discussion has been based on layer 2 switches. They are known as layer 2 switches because they switch packets from one port to another by looking at the MAC addresses (layer 2) within the packet. A newer type of switch, the layer 3 switch switches packets (such as IP addresses) based on the logical (layer 3) addresses, much like a router does. A layer 3 switch does everything to a packet that a traditional router does:

■ Determines forwarding path based on layer 3 information
■ Validates the integrity of the layer 3 header via checksum
■ Verifies packet expiration and updates accordingly
■ Processes and responds to any option information

Table 7.2   Layer 3 Switches *v.* Legacy Routers

Characteristic	Layer 3 switch	Legacy router
Routes core LAN protocols: IP, IPX, AppleTalk	Yes	Yes
Subnet definition	Layer 2 switch domain	Port
Forwarding architecture	Hardware	Software
Price	Low	High
Forwarding performance	High	Low
WAN support	No	Yes

- Updates forwarding statistics in the Management Information Base (MIB)
- Applies security controls if required

In many respects, the switching of packets is the simplest part of the operation of a layer 3 switch. The only major difference between the packet switching operation of a router and a layer 3 switch is the physical implementation. In general purpose routers, packet switching takes place using microprocessor-based engines, whereas a layer 3 switch performs this using ASIC hardware. As a result, the layer 3 switch can switch packets much faster than a router. Layer 3 switches tend to have packet switching throughputs in the millions of packets per second, while traditional general purpose routers have evolved from the hundreds of thousands of packets per second range to over a million packets per second.

One of the advantages of the layer 2 switch was its implementation and operational simplicity, especially over routers. Deployment was often as easy as powering on the switch, enabling the routing protocols, assigning it an IP address, and making the physical network connections.

The layer 3 switch has been optimized for high-performance LAN support and is not meant to service wide area connections (although it could easily satisfy the requirements for high-performance MAN connectivity, such as SONET). Because it is designed to handle high-performance LAN traffic, a layer 3 switch can be placed anywhere within a network core or backbone, thus easily and cost-effectively replacing the traditional collapsed backbone router. The layer 3 switch communicates with the WAN router using industry standard routing protocols like RIP and OSPF. Therefore, if you need a router to segment your network, you can use a high-performance layer 3 switch. If you need to connect through a WAN connection, you would use a router. For your campus or large building, you can use level 3 switches to connect your segments and then link the level 3 switches to the router to connect to the WAN. See Table 7.2 to compare layer 3 switches and legacy routers.

7.5   LAYER 4 SWITCHES

As networks have evolved and new technologies have emerged, multilayer-capable switches have become a popular alternative to the traditional hub, bridge, or layer 2 switch. Layer 4 switching refers to an added feature and capability of layer 3 switches. It enhances their ability to control and forward network traffic based on the information that can be derived from protocols that operate at layer 4 of the OSI model.

Because a layer 4 switch can identify the layer 4 protocol information together with the IP address that is identified on layer 3, it not only knows where the data needs to go, but also knows what application will use it. This information can be used to enhance the features of a layer 3 switch, which essentially performs packet routing at high speeds by means of hardware, by allowing it to filter network traffic and perform switching based on the application the data is intended for. Therefore, a layer 4 switch not only has the ability to examine the IP address, but also to control the traffic based on the port numbers located at layer 4 of the OSI model.

This gives layer 4 switches the ability to implement a variety of services that take advantage of this application-specific information. For example, routers are often used as a network firewall. They filter packets and provide security features by either allowing or blocking certain connections. A layer 4 switch can offer this same service but implement it by means of hardware. Thus, offering the same service with a much higher speed of data throughput.

Layer 4 switches can also use this information to prioritize traffic flow. Because they can see both the port number and IP address of a data packet, they can give priority to data intended for mission critical applications. For example, data intended for the HTTP (port 80) application on a web server can be given higher priority than data intended for another application that may be running on that same server. This provides that application a higher class of service. This can be used to ensure QoS, which basically refers to a guaranteed throughput level.

Another service that can be made possible by a layer 4 switch is load balancing. Load balancing can be implemented to more efficiently control the amount of information that a particular server, among a group of servers supporting the same application, may receive.

For example, a group of physical servers that are being used as a web server farm can all be grouped together into one virtual (logical) server. The new virtual server, made up of these physical servers, would be assigned just one IP address. Traffic intended for these servers would be directed towards this IP address. A layer 4 switch can then manage load balancing among the group that makes up the virtual server. The data can be balanced among the servers based on a number of factors. For instance, by keeping track of how many sessions each individual server is supporting, traffic can be forwarded to the server with the least number of sessions. Or, traffic can be distributed based on a percentage. Faster servers can be assigned a higher percentage, and slower servers can be assigned a smaller percentage of the overall network traffic. These are just a couple of ways that load balancing can be implemented. But in any case, this provides a more efficient means of handling traffic on the network by avoiding the overloading of any one physical server.

7.6   VIRTUAL LANS

As networks have grown in size and complexity, many companies use **Virtual LANs (VLANs)** to provide a way to logically structure their network. A VLAN is a collection of nodes that are grouped together in a single broadcast domain that is based on something other than physical location. It is a switched network that is logically segmented on an organizational basis; either by functions, project teams, or applications rather than on a physical or geographical basis. Members who belong to the same VLAN can communicate as if they were attached to the same wire, while they may be located on different physical LANs. In addition, because a VLANs form broadcast domains, members of a VLAN enjoy the connectivity, shared services, and security associated with physical LANs. Changing a member from one VLAN to another is done through software rather than physically unplugging and moving devices or wires.

7.6.1 Segmentation, Broadcast Control, and Security

In a traditional network that uses a hub connected to a router, you often might have your network divided by function. For example, let's say that you are responsible for a network in a five story building and each floor is assigned to a function group. For example, the 2nd floor contains all of the salespeople and their computers and the 3rd floor contains all of the engineers and their computers. The computers on the 2nd floor are connected to a hub or hubs while the 3rd floor is connected to a different hub or hubs. Both sets of hubs are then connected to a router.

If you run out of space on the 2nd floor and you need to add another salesperson, you could set him or her up on the 3rd floor and connect him or her to the 3rd floor hub. Unfortunately, if you connect them into the hubs used by the 3rd floor, the person has to go through a slower router to get to the resources that have been assigned to the 2nd floor. The system will see all of the broadcasts meant for the salespeople. The router will give that person slower performance and the broadcast could be a security issue.

While some older applications have been rewritten to reduce their bandwidth needs, today's new generation of multimedia applications consume more bandwidth than ever before. In addition, these applications use broadcast (packets sent to everyone) and multicasts (packets meant for multiple hosts) extensively, which also consumes bandwidth. Faulty equipment, inadequate segmentation, and poorly designed firewalls can also compound the problem. Therefore, it has become more important to properly segment your network to isolate one segment's problems and keep those problems from propagating throughout the internetwork. This can be done effectively with strategic switching and routing.

A broadcast domain is a set of NICs for which a broadcast frame sent by one NIC will be received by all other NICs in the broadcast domain. While a bridge and switch isolate collision domains on the same subnet, a VLAN (defined using a manageable switch) will isolate broadcast domains.

> *NOTE:* Because routers typically do not allow broadcasts, they also define broadcast domains (see Figures 7.7 and 7.8).

Just as switches isolate collision domains for attached hosts and only forward appropriate traffic out a particular port, VLANs provide complete isolation between VLANs. A VLAN is a bridging domain that has all broadcast and multicast traffic contained within it. Therefore, a VLAN can be thought of as a broadcast domain that exists within a defined set of switches. Because switches recently became more cost effective, many companies are replacing their flat hub networks with a pure switched network and VLAN environment (see Figure 7.9).

Figure 7.7 A Broadcast Domain

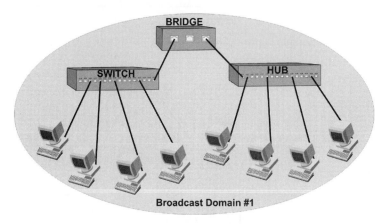

Broadcast Domain #1

Figure 7.8 A Broadcast Domain is Defined by Routers

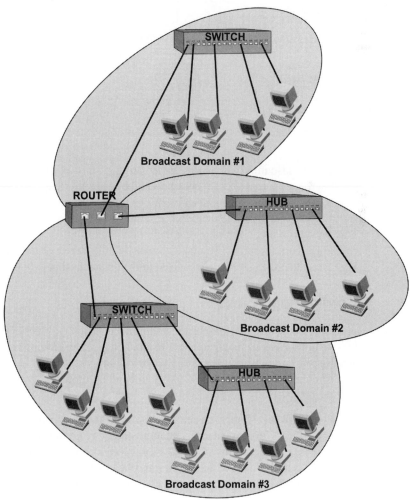

Figure 7.9 A Sample Network Using a VLAN

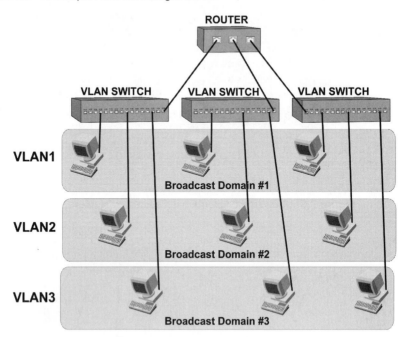

VLANs also improve security by isolating groups. If you desire high security, users can be grouped into a VLAN, possibly on the same physical segment, and no users outside that VLAN can communicate with them. Administrators can then control each port and they can specify which network resources (such as servers) that port could access. This prevents a user from plugging their work station into a switch port and gaining access to network resources. To make it more flexible, servers can be members of multiple VLANs so that the users can get access to the resources that they need.

7.6.2   Configuring VLANs

As mentioned earlier, because users are grouped logically, it is not necessary to pull cables to move a user from one network to another. Adding, moving, and changing users are achieved by configuring a port into the appropriate VLAN.

Assigning computers to a VLAN can be done on a switch in one of the following four ways:

■ **Port address**—Port assigned VLANs are the most commonly implemented. The ports of a switch can be assigned individually, in groups, in rows, or even across two or more switches, if the switches are properly connected through a trunking protocol. Port based VLANs are the simplest to implement and typically are used in situations where DHCP is used to assign IP addresses to network hosts.

- **MAC address**—MAC address assigned VLANs are rare, primarily due to the increased popularity and use of DHCP on networks. MAC based VLANs enable a user to belong to the same VLAN at all times, even when connecting through a different port on the switch. MAC addresses in a MAC based VLAN must be entered into the switch and configured as a part of a specific VLAN. Although this is great for users who may move around the office or who may travel, this type of VLAN can be very complex and difficult for the administrator to manage and troubleshoot.
- **User ID**—User ID assigned VLANs are also quite rare because they are complex to set up, administer, and troubleshoot. All VLAN users must be identified and entered into the switch and configured as a part of a specific VLAN. On a user ID based VLAN, users remain a part of the same VLAN regardless of where they are on the network or from which host they log onto the network.
- **Network address**—Network address assigned VLANs are configured much like MAC based VLANs, with the exception that nodes are registered using their logical or IP addresses. Network address based VLANs are uncommon primarily because of the use of DHCP to assign work station IP addresses. Like MAC based VLANs, this type of VLAN allows users to remain part of the same VLAN even when they relocate to a different physical port connection on the network, if they keep the same IP addresses.

7.6.3   VLAN Identifiers

To keep the network traffic local within a VLAN, the traffic carries a unique VLAN identifier (VLAN ID), which uniquely identifies the VLAN. The switch that receives the frame from the source station inserts the VLAN ID and the packet is switched onto the shared backbone network. When the frame exits the switched LAN, a switch strips the header and forwards the frame to interfaces that match the VLAN color. Depending on how your switches are programmed, the switches and routers can then make intelligent decisions on how to forward the packets by using the VLAN IDs.

7.6.4   VLAN Trunking

Normally, segmenting a LAN with switches involves the creation of at least two VLANs across two or more switches. After the VLANs are created, any information that needs to be shared is done by using a trunking protocol, so that all the switches involved in a VLAN are fully aware of the VLAN, its hosts, and the locations of the hosts so that each switch is ready to support it.

By default, trunking protocols used to pass information between switches are disabled on all ports. Therefore, before a VLAN can be configured between two switches, trunking must be enabled on the ports to be used to connect the switches together. A trunk line would then carry the combined traffic of one or more VLANs to another switch or router. The two most commonly used trunking methods are:

- **Inter-Switch Link (ISL)**—ISL is a proprietary Cisco protocol that is supported only by Cisco devices. ISL supports transportation across Ethernet, FDDI, or Token Ring environments. A physical router interface to each VLAN is unnecessary with a Cisco router running ISL.

■ **IEEE 802.1Q**—The 802.1 subcommittee defines this as an industry standard protocol that allows VLAN information to be exchanged between equipment from various, dissimilar manufacturers.

Two other trunking methods used on Cisco networks are IEEE 802.10 (FDDI) and an ATM-based protocol called LANE (LAN Emulation). If you are only using Cisco devices, it is recommended that you use ISL. If you need to use a nonproprietary VLAN protocol, it is recommended that you use 802.1Q.

7.6.5   The VLAN Trunk Protocol

Using VLAN trunking works well for a small number of switches with a limited number of VLANs. In a large network environment that has a large number of switches and requires several VLANs, it can be difficult to maintain the configuration on each switch. To centralize the administration of VLANs in a large switched network, you would use the VLAN Trunking Protocol (VTP) and VTP Domains.

Created by Cisco, VTP is a layer 2 messaging protocol that maintains VLAN configuration consistency throughout a common administration domain. VTP manages the additions, deletions, and name changes of VLANs across multiple switches. It minimizes misconfigurations and configuration inconsistencies that can cause problems, such as duplicate VLAN names or incorrect VLAN-type specifications.

Lastly, VTP provides a way for you to preserve bandwidth by configuring it to reduce the amount of broadcasts, multicasts, and other unicast packets. This is called pruning. VTP pruning only sends broadcasts to trunk links that truly must have the information. For example, if a switch doesn't have any ports configured for a particular VLAN, and a broadcast is sent throughout that VLAN, that broadcast would not traverse the trunk link to this switch. By default, VTP pruning is disabled on all switches.

NOTE: When you enable pruning on a VTP server, you enable it for the entire domain.

The core principle of VTP is that interconnected switches are configured to belong to the same VTP domain (sometimes referred to as a VLAN management domain). The VTP domain is a logical group of switches that share VLAN information. Each switch can only belong to a single VTP domain. The switches in a VTP domain must be adjacent, and the links connecting the switches must be configured for trunk mode.

Switches that are members of a VTP domain can be set up in one of three possible modes:

■ **VTP Server**—Maintains the VLAN database. VLAN information is stored in NVRAM (flash). VLANs can be created, deleted, and edited on the server. You need at least one server in your VTP domain to propagate VLAN information through the domain. The switch must be in server mode to be able to create, add, or delete VLANs in a VTP domain. Changing VTP information must also be done in server mode, and any change made to a switch in server mode will be advertised to the entire VTP domain.

- **VTP Client**—Switches receive information from VTP servers, and they also send and receive updates but cannot make any changes to the VLAN. If you want to make a switch a server; first make it a client so it receives all the correct VLAN information then change it to a server.
- **Transparent**—Does not participate in the VTP domain. VTP advertisements are forwarded. VLANs can be created, deleted, and edited, but are local to the switch only. They are not shared with other switches.

Switches are configured to be VTP servers without a VTP domain by default. To join a VTP domain, the switch must be manually configured, or connected to a VTP domain by a trunk port (the switch will receive domain information via a VTP advertisement). When changes are made to a VLAN configuration on a VTP server, VTP advertisements are sent out to all trunk ports to propagate the changes to the rest of the domain. VTP advertisements can be sent over ISL, 802.1q, 802.10, and LANE trunks. VTP traffic is sent over the management VLAN (VLAN1), so all trunks must be configured to pass VLAN1.

To start using VTP, you must first create a VTP server. All servers that need to share VLAN information must use the same domain name, and a switch can only be in one domain at a time. This means that a switch can only share VTP domain information with other switches if they're configured into the same VTP domain. You can use a VTP domain if you have more than one switch connected in a network, but if you've got all your switches in only one VLAN, you don't need to use VTP. VTP information is sent between switches through a trunk port.

To track changes to the VLAN configuration, VTP relies on a revision number. When a VTP domain is initially configured, the revision number is 0. Each time the VLAN database is edited, the revision number is incremented by 1. If a switch receives a VTP advertisement with a higher revision number, the information in the advertisement overwrites the previous information. Before a switch is added to a VTP domain, the VTP revision number should be cleared for this very reason.

To secure your network from users adding switches to your VTP domain, you can use passwords. Every switch must be set up with the same password.

7.6.6   Routing between VLANs

Network devices in different VLANs cannot communicate with one another without a router to forward traffic between them. In most network environments, VLANs are associated with individual networks or subnetworks.

When communicating from one computer in one subnet to another computer in another subnet, the source computer will send a packet to the default gateway (typically a router). The gateway will then determine which is the best way to go to get the packet to its destination and will send the packet toward the direction. If the two subnets are connected to the same router, the router will forward that packet to the client on the destination subnet.

Because VLANs are logically isolated networks, you must use a router (or a level 3 switch) to communicate from one computer in one VLAN to another computer in another VLAN. For this to work, the router (or level 3 switch) must be able to forward the frame from one interface to another while maintaining the VLAN header. If you often need to send packets between VLANs, the efficiency of VLANs is greatly decreased.

> *NOTE:* If you use a layer 3 switch instead of a layer 2 switch, packet forwarding is performed as close as possible to the work stations involved. When a layer 2 or layer 3 switch is used, the packets concerned are sent directly to the switch port where the destination work station is connected.

7.7   DESIGNING LANS

Now that you have looked at all of the parts of a LAN, you are ready to look at designing a LAN. In a small office networks, the best design is a simple design. Therefore, unless you have a large number of stations or heavy traffic needs, creating one segment containing all users is the easiest and usually the best way to go. When the number of stations increases or the traffic level reaches a point where the network starts slowing down, adding a simple bridge or a switch is usually all that is needed. Considering the low price of switches today, you should consider starting with one.

In larger corporate or campus LANs the network is based on the centralization of resources. These networks typically strive for a lower cost of ownership, reduced cost of maintenance, and fault tolerance. They usually use a high-speed backbone to connect buildings and floors within the building. Often, these floors and buildings will be connected together with high-speed switches or routers.

When figuring out which components to use and how you want to break up your network, you should estimate on the amount and type of traffic that your network needs to carry. You should also look at how the traffic needs to be distributed. Remember that shared Ethernet segments are considered saturated at 40 percent network utilization and collisions should be kept to a minimum. Shared Token Ring segments are saturated at 70 percent. In addition, no segment should have more than 20 percent broadcasts and multicasts.

SUMMARY

1. A collision domain is a network segment in which all devices share the same bandwidth.

2. Microsegmentation is the process of creating smaller collision domains by segmenting a LAN rather than creating additional subnets. This makes a network run more efficiently because you can divide a network into smaller parts known as segments.

3. A bridge, which is a layer 2 device, is used to break larger network segments into smaller network segments.

4. Some bridges can also connect dissimilar network types as long as the bridge operates at the LLC sublayer of the data link layer. If the bridge operates only at the lower sublayer (the MAC sublayer), the bridge can connect only similar network types.

5. Transparent bridging is found primarily in Ethernet environments, while source-route bridging occurs primarily in Token Ring environments.

6. Translational bridging provides translation between the formats and transit principles of different media types (usually Ethernet and Token Ring).

7. When using bridges and switches, complex topology can cause multiple loops to occur. To avoid a looping of a packet to an uknown computer, transparent bridging uses the STA.

8. A switching hub (a *switch* or a *layer 2 switch*) is a fast, multiported bridge. Each port on the switching hub creates a collision domain.

9. A major advantage of using a switch is that it allows one computer (or LAN segment) to open a connection to another computer (or LAN segment). While those two computers (or LAN segments) communicate, other connections between the other computers (or LAN segments) can be opened at the same time.

10. When in store-and-forward mode, the LAN switch copies the entire frame onto its onboard buffers and then computes the CRC. If the frame doesn't contain any errors, the LAN switch looks up the destination hardware address in its forwarding or switching table to find the correct outgoing interface.

11. With cut-through processing, the first bits of the frame are sent out on the outbound port before the last bit of the incoming frame is received instead of waiting for the entire frame to be received.

12. FragmentFree processing performs like cut-through processing, but the switch waits for 64 bytes to be received before forwarding the first bytes of the outgoing frame.

13. Like a router, a layer 3 switch switches packets based on the logical (layer 3) addresses such as IP addresses. While a layer 3 switch will switch packets faster than a router, it will not connect directly to a router.

14. Layer 4 switching refers to an added feature and capability of layer 3 switches. It enhances their ability to control and forward network traffic based on the information that can be derived from protocols that operate at layer 4 of the OSI model.

15. A VLAN is a collection of nodes that are grouped together in a single broadcast domain that is based on something other than physical location. A VLAN is a switched network that is logically segmented on an organizational basis by functions, project teams, or applications rather than on a physical or geographical basis.

16. A broadcast domain is a set of NICs for which a broadcast frame sent by one NIC will be received by all other NICs in the broadcast domain.

17. Normally, segmenting a LAN with switches involves the creation of at least two VLANs across two or more switches. After the VLANs are created, any information about them is shared between the switches by using a trunking protocol.

18. The two most commonly used trunking methods are ISL and IEEE 802.1Q.

19. Created by Cisco, VTP is a layer 2 messaging protocol that maintains VLAN configuration consistency throughout a common administration domain.

20. Network devices in different VLANs cannot communicate with one another without a router to forward traffic between them.

QUESTIONS

1. Which of the following devices examine the MAC address of a packet before forwarding the packet?
   a. repeaters   b. gateways
   c. bridges   d. switches

2. You are the network administrator for the Acme Corporation. The network contains 250 host computers connected together by 10BaseT hubs. Packet collisions on the network have caused an increase in the amount of time that it takes to access network resources. Consequently, you want to reduce the number of packet collisions on Acme's network. Which of the following can you do to accomplish this? (Choose all answers that apply.)
   a. Add a 100BaseT hub to the network.
   b. Add a bridge to the network.

c. Add a router to the network.

d. Add a repeater to the network.

e. Add a switch to the network.

3. Why do half duplex Ethernet 10BaseT topologies have a slower data transmission rate than full duplex Ethernet 10BaseT topologies?

a. Half duplex transmissions have more frequent collisions.

b. Half duplex transmissions can travel in only one direction at a time.

c. Half duplex transmissions are sent at half the normal speed of the transmission media.

d. Full duplex uses faster hubs.

4. Which of the following is a disadvantage of a LAN switch? (Select the best choice.)

a. additional collision domains

b. concurrent frame forwarding

c. decreased bandwidth per user

d. latency

5. Which of the following are advantages of VLANs?

a. Separate VLANs use layer 3 addressing, which is faster than layer 2 addressing.

b. Multiple VLANs reduce bandwidth utilization.

c. Separate VLANs do not require routers.

d. Multiple VLAN devices are easily changed.

6. Which of the following are internal LAN switching methods? (Choose all that apply.)

a. filtering

b. store-and-forward

c. routing tables

d. cut-through

7. Which of the following actions relate to detecting collisions on a 10BaseT network using CSMA/CD by a half duplex NIC? (Select three choices.)

a. The hub detects collisions.

b. The receive pair on the NIC captures the frame as the frame is being transmitted.

c. The NIC transmits a frame across the media.

d. The NIC receives the frame transmitted by the hub and compares the frame to the original frame.

e. The NIC compares the transmitted and received frames internally.

8. Cisco Catalyst 3000 and 5000 series switches use frame tagging to identify each frame that passes through a VLAN switch. Which of the following are features of frame tagging?

a. It functions at layer 3 of the OSI model.

b. A unique user defined identification is placed in the frame header as the frame enters the switch.

c. The user defined identification is removed from the frame as the frame leaves the switch.

d. The user defined identification becomes the destination address as the frame leaves the switch.

9. Why does store-and-forward switching have the highest latency of the different switching methods? (Select 2 choices.)

a. The store-and-forward method receives the complete frame before forwarding it.

b. The store-and-forward method checks the MAC address in the frame before forwarding it.

c. Latency is a function of the length of the frame.

d. The store-and-forward method does not block broadcasts.

10. Which of the following are advantages of full duplex Ethernet? (Select 2 choices.)

a. point-to-point connections

b. uses only one pair of wires

c. eliminates collisions

d. uses switches or hubs

11. At which OSI layer does a switch operate? (Select the best choice.)

a. physical   b. data link

c. application   d. network

12. Which of the following are reasons that a port on a bridge would be placed in the forwarding state when STP is used? (Select 2 choices.)

a. The designated bridge in a LAN places all of its ports in the forwarding state.

b. The hello time expires. Therefore, the bridge places all of its ports in the forwarding state.

c. The root bridge places all of its ports in the forwarding state.

d. All bridges have one port that is considered the root port. The root port is placed in the forwarding state.

13. Which of the following devices increase the effective bandwidth within a single broadcast do-

main, increase the number of collision domains, and use MAC addresses to determine if packets should be forwarded or dropped? (Select all correct choices.)

a. bridges
b. routers
c. hubs
d. switches

14. Your network consists of ten computers on a single network segment. Each computer contains a NIC that supports both 10BaseT and 100BaseTX. The hub supports only 10BaseT and all of the physical cabling is category 5 UTP. Because of the increasing demand for network services, you determine that you need to increase the effective bandwidth of the network. Which of the following steps is the least expensive way to increase the effective bandwidth of your network? (Select the best choice.)

a. Install a bridge to divide the network into two or more collision domains.
b. Install a router to divide the network into two or more logical subnets.
c. Install a switch to divide the network into two or more broadcast domains.
d. Replace the 10BaseT hub with a 100BaseTX hub.

15. When referring to LAN switches, what does the term *microsegmentation* denote?

a. limiting all traffic to the same LAN segment
b. creating more segments with more users on each segment
c. creating more segments with fewer users on each segment
d. forwarding packets more quickly by using the cut-through switching method

16. Your company has several bridges and switches in its internetwork, which uses STP. A new switch is added to the internetwork. Which bridge or switch does the new switch believe to be the root device when the new switch first initializes?

a. the first device to transmit a CBPDU
b. itself
c. the device with the lowest MAC address
d. the device with the highest MAC address

17. Which of the following are benefits of installing a switch to segment a LAN?

a. additional broadcast domains
b. increased bandwidth
c. additional collision domains
d. reduced latency

18. Which of the following can use STP. (Select all correct choices.)

a. bridges
b. routers
c. hubs
d. switches

19. Which of the following devices provide microsegmentation to reduce Ethernet collision domains? (Select all correct choices.)

a. repeaters
b. routers
c. bridges
d. LAN switches

20. Which of the following are modes of VTP? (Select all correct choices.)

a. client
b. flooding
c. server
d. configuration
e. pruning
f. transparent

21. Which switching method discards giants and runts?

a. cut-through
b. store-and-forward

22. What is the function of VTP pruning?

a. eliminates all broadcasts
b. reduces unnecessary flooded traffic
c. converts flooded multicast traffic to directed broadcasts
d. restricts flooded multicast traffic to a single VTP domain

23. Which protocol do bridges and switches use to prevent loops in a network?

a. STP
b. RARP
c. ARP
d. DLOOP

24. Which bridge does the spanning tree algorithm select as the root bridge?

a. the bridge with the least number of ports
b. the bridge with the greatest number of ports
c. the bridge with the lowest-value bridge identifier
d. the bridge with the highest-value bridge identifier
e. a bridge selected at random by the STP

25. Which phrase best describes the VLAN Trunking Protocol?

a. a network layer protocol that functions to associate VLAN membership with IP addresses
b. a layer 3 messaging protocol used to associate VLAN identifiers with switch port assignments
c. a layer 2 messaging protocol used to distribute and synchronize information about VLANs throughout a switched network

d. a physical layer protocol that associates distributed device MAC addresses to the appropriate LAN cable virtual segments

26. What does a bridge do with a packet if the bridge does not have information about the destination address?
    a. The packet is dropped.
    b. The packet is resent on the receiving port.
    c. The packet is forwarded to all ports except the receiving port.
    d. The time-to-live count is decremented and the packet is resent on the receiving port.

27. What is the primary benefit of implementing VLANs?
    a. VLANs provide switchless networking using virtual addresses.
    b. Users in a single geographical location can be microsegmented.
    c. Subnets are configured based on location rather than network addresses.
    d. Users can share a common broadcast domain regardless of their physical location in the internetwork.

28. What are the benefits of STP? (Choose two answers.)
    a. Bridge loops are eliminated
    b. Multiple paths can be used for load balancing.
    c. Blocking bridge ports can be activated in case the primary link fails.
    d. Network bandwidth is conserved due to the elimination of BPDU packets.

29. Which statements about LAN switches are true?
    a. A LAN switch is a high-speed multiport bridge.
    b. LAN switches use source addresses to make switching decisions.
    c. A switch reduces or eliminates device contention for media access.
    d. Use of network layer information for transmitting packets enable a LAN switch to be protocol independent.

30. What is the primary benefit of implementing VLANs?
    a. VLANs provide switchless networking using virtual addresses.
    b. Users in a single geographical location can be microsegmented.

c. Subnets are configured based on location rather than network addresses.
    d. Users can be grouped by their work functions, shared applications or protocols, or departments.

31. In which three modes does VTP operate? (Choose three answers.)
    a. host   b. server
    c. transparent   d. client
    e. forwarding   f. management

32. What is shared by users on a VLAN?
    a. cable segments
    b. collision domains
    c. TCP/IP subnets
    d. broadcast domains

33. What is the purpose of the ISL protocol?
    a. allows a single ISL capable device to control VLAN trunking between noncapable devices
    b. provides a mechanism to allow non-Cisco devices to fully participate in a Cisco VLAN environment
    c. provides a mechanism for multiplexing multiple VLANs on a single path between switches, routers, and servers
    d. Strips VLAN information from packets transmitted by Cisco switches to avoid protocol errors in non-ISL devices.

34. On a LAN segmented with bridges, what happens to a packet with a source and destination address on the same segment?
    a. The packet is returned to the source device.
    b. The packet will be dropped by all bridges it encounters.
    c. Each bridge decrements the FCS number by one.
    d. The packet will be forwarded only by a bridge directly connected to the segment.

35. What are characteristics of the store-and-forward switching method? (Choose three.)
    a. Erroneous frames are discarded.
    b. The frame is discarded if it is a runt or a giant.
    c. It has less latency than the cut-through method.
    d. The CRC is computed after the frame is copied to the router's buffer.
    e. Only the destination address is copied into the router's buffer before the frame is forwarded to its destination.

36. Which of the following are unique characteristics of half duplex Ethernet as compared to full duplex Ethernet? (Choose two answers.)
  a. shared collision domain
  b. private collision domain
  c. higher effective throughput
  d. lower effective throughput
  e. private broadcast domain

37. Switches have three primary modes to handle frame switching. Which one of these modes looks at the destination address and then immediately forwards the frame to the destination?
  a. CSMA/CD
  b. cut-through
  c. fragmentation
  d. full duplex
  e. half duplex
  f. store-and-forward

38. STP was originally developed by DEC. What is the reason STP is used in a switched LAN?
  a. to provide a mechanism for network monitoring in switched environments
  b. to prevent routing loops in networks with redundant paths
  c. to prevent routing switching loops in networks with redundant switched paths
  d. to manage the addition, deletion, and naming of VLANs across multiple switches
  e. to segment a network into multiple collision domains

39. Switches have three primary modes to handle frame switching. Which two statements about store-and-forward switching are true? (Choose two.)
  a. Latency remains constant regardless of frame size.
  b. Latency through the switch varies with frame length.
  c. The switch receives the complete frame before beginning to forward it.
  d. The switch checks the destination address as soon as it receives the header and immediately begins forwarding the frame.

40. What are good reasons for using layer 2 switches? (Choose two.)
  a. to reduce collisions
  b. to increase collisions
  c. to increase the number of collision domains

  d. to decrease the number of collision domains
  e. to decrease the number of broadcast domains

41. Which of the following devices support full duplex Ethernet ? (Choose two.)
  a. switch to host   b. hub to hub
  c. hub to host   d. switch to switch
  e. switch to hub

42. How does a layer 2 device such as a bridge or switch function?
  a. It maintains a table of the IP address of the host connected to its internet segment
  b. It passes packets outside of its network segment if its IP address cannot be found on its table.
  c. It looks up the frames destination in its address table and sends the frame towards the destination.
  d. It maintains the table of the data link layer and network layer addresses for the host connected to its network segment.

43. Which of the following are reasons to use VLANs? (Choose three.)
  a. They increase the size of collision domains.
  b. They allow logical grouping of users by function.
  c. They enhance network security.
  d. They increase the size of broadcast domains while decreasing the number of broadcast domains.
  e. They increase the number of broadcast domains while decreasing their size.
  f. They simplify switch administration.

44. You need to segment your network. Which of the following hardware devices can you use to do so? (Choose three.)
  a. hubs   b. switches
  c. routers   d. repeaters
  e. bridges   f. media converters

45. Which of the following correctly defines switched and routed data flow?
  a. Switches create a single collision domain and a single broadcast domain. Routers provide separate broadcast domains.
  b. Switches create separate collision domains but a single broadcast domain. Routers provide separate broadcast domains.

c. Switches create a single collision domain and a separate broadcast domain. Routers provide a separate broadcast domain.

d. Switches create separate collision domains and separate broadcast domains. Routers provide separate collision domains.

46. What is an advantage of segmenting your LAN with a switch?

a. smaller collision domains

b. elimination of broadcast

c. decreased cost of implementation

d. larger number of users within the same domain

47. Which of the following statements about layer 2 bridges and switches are true? (Choose three.)

a. Switches are primarily software based while bridges are hardware based.

b. Both bridges and switches forward layer 2 broadcasts.

c. Bridges are frequently faster than switches.

d. Switches have a higher number of ports than most bridges.

e. Bridges define broadcast domains while switches define collision domains.

f. Both bridges and switches make forwarding decisions based on layer 2 addresses.

48. The ABC Company has hired you as a consultant to add a new VLAN named SALES to their existing switched network. Which of the following are true regarding configuration of this VLAN? (Choose three.)

a. The VLAN must be created.

b. The VLAN must be named.

c. An IP address must be configured for the SALES VLAN.

d. The desired ports must be added to the new VLAN.

e. The VLAN must be added to the STP domain.

49. Which of the following devices operate at the data link layer of the OSI model? (Choose two.)

a. routers   b. transceivers

c. bridges   d. SMTP servers

e. switches   f. hubs

50. Which one of the following characteristics of Ethernet switches is true?

a. Symmetric switching allows connection between ports of unlike bandwidth and does not require memory buffering.

b. Memory buffering is used to prevent a bottleneck when ports of different bandwidths are connected on a symmetric switch.

c. Latency can be reduced if the switch utilizes the store-and-forward method of switching. Store-and-forward is better for error detection.

d. The cut-through method of switching is faster because the switch forwards the packet to the destination as soon as it reads the destination address.

51. Using your protocol analyzer, you have determined that your network is very congested. All the devices are connected through a hub. Which solution would best decrease congestion on the network?

a. Add a second hub.

b. Replace the hub with a switch.

c. Replace the hub with a router.

d. Replace the hub with a repeater.

52. Which of the following are methods that can be used to simplify network management by implementing VLANs? (Choose four.)

a. VLANs allow you to implement multiple layer switching.

b. VLANs can group several broadcast domains into multiple logical subnets.

c. It is no longer necessary to install cables to move a user from one network to another.

d. Network adds, moves, and changes are achieved by configuring a port into a VLAN.

e. A group of users who need high security can be put into a VLAN so that no users outside the VLAN can communicate with them.

f. As a logical grouping of users, VLANs can be considered independent from their physical or geographic locations.

53. Ethernet switches operate at the data link layer of the OSI model. These layer 2 devices have three major functions. Which of the following describe these functions? (Choose three.)

a. loop avoidance

b. hop count limiting

c. packet forward/filtering

d. address learning

e. broadcast filtering

54. Which one of the following is not a characteristic of a network segment on a transparent switch?
   a. The segment has its own collision domain.
   b. The segment can translate from one media to a different media.
   c. All devices in the segment are part of the same broadcast domain.
   d. One device per segment can currently send frames to the switch.

55. What are the characteristics of the cut-through switching method? (Choose two answers.)
   a. Erroneous frames are discarded.
   b. The frame is discarded if it is a runt or a giant.
   c. It has less latency than the store-and-forward method.
   d. The CRC is computed after the frame is copied to the router's buffer.
   e. Only the destination address is copied into the router's buffer before the frame is forwarded to its destination.

56. What advantages do routers have over bridges for network segmentation? (Choose three answers.)
   a. multiple paths
   b. greater throughput
   c. increased management control
   d. less overhead
   e. greater functionality

CHAPTER **8**

Using Cisco Switches

Topics Covered in this Chapter

Introduction

In Chapter 7 you learned about bridges and switches and how you can use them to improve your network performance. In this chapter you will learn more about switches, use the knowledge from the last chapter, and apply it by installing and configuring Cisco switches.

Objectives

- Install and configure a Cisco switch.
- Change among the various operating modes of Cisco switches.
- Enable and configure a VLAN on a Cisco switch.

- Access a Cisco switch and clear all configuration settings from the switch.
- Configure a Cisco switch to provide more security for your network.

8.1   AN OVERVIEW OF CISCO SWITCHES

As you probably already know, Cisco is one of the leading manufacturers of network equipment. Their primary business is in internetworking products such as routers, bridges, and switches.

Cisco has many different series of switches available to accommodate any situation for any network. These switches can be divided into two groups: (1) Micro Switches and (2) Catalyst switches. Because Ethernet is the most popular LAN technology, most Cisco LAN switches are Ethernet products. The Catalyst line of switched backbone products incorporates a wide range of technology to support Fast Ethernet, Gigabit Ethernet, FDDI, and ATM.

Cisco's most basic switches are the Micro Switches, which are eight-port 10/100 devices. To keep these switches low cost, they are nonintelligent and nonmanagement switches (see Table 8.1).

The main line of Cisco switches is the Catalyst Switches, which come in many series and models. They included fixed-configuration desktop models, configurable plug-and-play modular chassis models and huge packages with high-speed buses into which many cards can be inserted.

To configure a Cisco Catalyst switch, you would use either the Visual Switch Manager (VSM), an IOS command line interface, or the management console. The VSM is tool operated through a web browser interface. The IOS command line interface is a command-driven interface and the management console is a simple, menu based interface.

The Cisco Catalyst 1900 and 2820 switches, as well as other switches, come in two different versions. The Standard Edition provides an aggressive price per port while providing Ethernet workgroups and individual users with increased performance. The Enterprise Edition would be used when a customer needs end-to-end VLANs, Fast EtherChannel

Table 8.1   Cisco Switches

Micro Switches	Cisco basic unmanaged switches.
Catalyst 1900 Series	These switches provide both 10 Mbps and 100 Mbps, powering both desktop and workgroup connectivity over UTP wire or fiber optic.[1]
Catalyst 2820 Series	The Cisco Catalyst 1900 and 2820 series switches provide industry leading performance and Cisco end-to-end network integration. The modular Catalyst 2820 Series Switch is the ideal solution for Ethernet workgroups and individual users who need increased flexibility and performance at an affordable price. It supports Cisco Switch Clustering technology, twenty-four switched 10BaseT ports, two high-speed expansion slots, bandwidth aggregation with Fast EtherChannel technology, and collision-free operation for full duplex 100BaseT (providing up to 200-Mbps bandwidth and extended distances using fiber cabling).[1]
Catalyst 2900 Series	The Cisco Catalyst 2900 series is Cisco's industry-leading, 10/100 autosensing Ethernet switch solution for workgroup and wiring closets. The Catalyst 2926 is a single configuration 10 Mbps/100 Mbps autosensing switch that uses the same architecture and software as the larger Catalyst 5000. It can deliver more than one million packets per second (pps) throughput across a 1.2-Gbps media independent backplane. The Catalyst 2948G is similar to the Catalyst 2926 but includes dedicated 48 port 10/100 Mbps Ethernet and two port 1000BaseX Gigabit Ethernet with flexible media interfaces.
Catalyst 2950	The Cisco Catalyst 2950 Series Intelligent Ethernet Switch is a line of fixed-configuration, stackable and standalone devices that provide wire speed Fast Ethernet and Gigabit Ethernet connectivity. This is the most affordable Cisco switching product line, providing intelligent services for midsized networks and metro access applications.
Catalyst 3500 Series	The 12, 24, and 48 port switches in this series are 10/100 and gigabit Ethernet switches that offer very fast switching. They are an excellent choice for high performance LANs including such features as Cisco Switch Clustering multi-device management architecture and VoIP (Voice over IP).
Catalyst 3900 Series	Offers a stackable, flexible switching solution for Token Ring networks.
Catalyst 5000/5500 Series	The switch series provides large intranets and high-performance switched LANs with media independent support for all LAN switching technologies over Ethernet, Fast Ethernet, FDDI, ATM, Token Ring, and Gigabit Ethernet so that it can allow voice and other mission critical traffic to be prioritized at the network edge. This switch group is capable of handling more than 10 million packets per second.
Catalyst 6000 Family	This high-performance multilayer switch for enterprise campus backbone or server family supports up to 284 10/100 ports, 192 100BaseFX ports, or 130 1000 BaseX ports. It has a 150 Mbps throughput and 32 Gbps backplane scalable up to 256 Gpbs.
Catalyst 8500 Series	A high-performance, modular, multimedia layer 3 switch that supports multiserver ATM switching and is optimized for aggregating multiprotocol traffic.

[1] Cisco has announced that they are phasing out the Catalyst 1900 and Catalyst 2820 switches.

bandwidth optimization (including bandwidth aggregation), and enhanced security. Enterprise Edition software is preinstalled in Enterprise Edition switches, and available as an optional Upgrade Kit for Standard Edition switches.

For more information on Cisco switches, see the following websites:

Catalyst 1900 Series Installation and Configuration Guide

http://www.cisco.com/univercd/cc/td/doc/product/lan/28201900/1928v9x/19icg9x/

Catalyst 2820 Series Installation and Configuration Guide

http://www.cisco.com/univercd/cc/td/doc/product/lan/28201900/1928v9x/28icg9x/index.htm

Catalyst 1900/2820 Enterprise Edition SW Config Guide

http://www.cisco.com/univercd/cc/td/doc/product/lan/28201900/1928v9x/ee_scg/index.htm

Catalyst 1900 Series and Catalyst 2820 Series Command Reference

http://www.cisco.com/univercd/cc/td/doc/product/lan/28201900/1928v9x/cli/index.htm

Catalyst 2900 User Guide

http://www.cisco.com/univercd/cc/td/doc/product/lan/cat2900/c2900/index.htm

Catalyst 2900 Series Configuration Guide and Command Ref

http://www.cisco.com/univercd/cc/td/doc/product/lan/cat2900/cgcr29k/index.htm

8.2   SETTING UP CISCO SWITCHES

Figure 8.1 shows a Cisco Catalyst 1900 switch. The front panel of a Catalyst 1900 switch provides twelve or twenty-four 10-Mbps and two 100-Mbps switched ports to connect to other network devices, a set of LEDs, and a Mode button for monitoring the switch and its ports. The 10BaseT network ports (indicated as 1x through 12x or 1x through 24x) use standard RJ-45 connectors. These ports can connect to 10BaseT compatible devices, such as individual work stations and hubs, with category 3, 4, or 5 cabling. Using this type of cabling,

Figure 8.1   The Front Panel of a Cisco Catalyst 1900 Switch

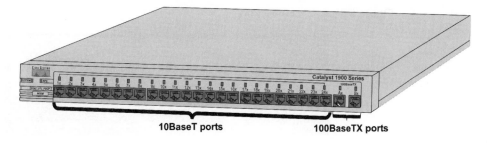

10BaseT ports   100BaseTX ports

the distance between the switch and the attached device can be up to 100 meters. A Cisco Catalyst 2820 switch is very similar except that it offers up to 48 10/100 Ethernet connectors and the Cisco 2900 can offer up to 10/100 48 Ethernet connectors and 2 Gigabit Ethernet.

The rear panel of a Catalyst 1900 switch has an AC power connector, a console port, a redundant power system (RPS) connector, and a switched AUI port. You can provide power to the switch either by using the switch internal AC power supply or by connecting the optional Cisco 600W AC RPS to the RPS connector on the switch (see Figure 8.2).

8.2.1 Ports

Ethernet is widely used in Cisco devices. There are two main types of cabling supported: (1) UTP and (2) 10Base5. UTP cabling is attached to RJ-45 connectors and 10Base5 is connected via a transceiver attached to the 15-pin AUI port (see Figure 8.3). In addition, you can connect 10Base2, fiber optic, and UTP to the AUI port with the appropriate AUI adapter. Most current Ethernet implementations use UTP cabling with RJ-45 connectors.

NOTE: The Ethernet AUI transceivers and cable are not supplied with the switch.

When connecting computers to a switch, you would typically use a straight-through cable. However, as reviewed in Chapter 6, a straight-through cable has each pin on one connector connected directly to the same pin position on the connector at the other end of the cable.

Figure 8.2   The Back Panel of a Cisco Catalyst 1900 Switch

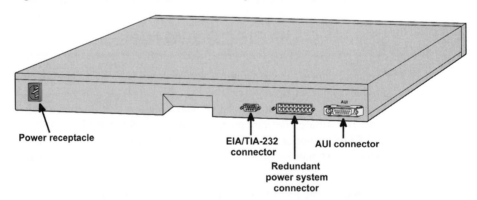

Figure 8.3   A 15-pin AUI Port

Figure 8.4 The Rule for Cabling Cisco Devices Is That You Should Use a Straight-Through Cable When One and Only One of the Jacks Is Marked with an x. Use a Crossover Cable When Both or Neither of the End Jacks Is Marked with an x

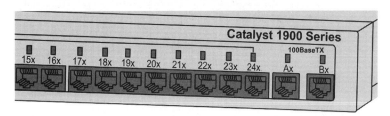

A crossover cable can be used to connect from one NIC to another NIC or a hub or switch to another hub or switch without using a hub or switch uplink port. Different from the straight-through cable, crossover cables reverse the transmit and receive wires.

As an aid to correct cabling, Cisco marks the RJ-45 Ethernet jacks on their hubs and switches with an x (for example 1x, 2x, 3x, Ax, or Bx). The rule for cabling Cisco devices is that you should use a straight-through cable when **one and only one** of the jacks is marked with an x. Use a crossover cable when **both or neither** of the end jacks is marked with an x (see Figure 8.4).

8.2.2   LEDs

You can use LEDs to monitor switch activity and performance by using the Mode button to select the modes in which the port LEDs operate. The colors of the system status (SYSTEM) LED show that the switch is receiving power and functioning properly. If the system LED is off, the switch is not powered up. If it is off, be sure the power cable is attached to the rear of the switch and that it is connected to a working AC outlet. If the system LED is solid green, the switch is operating normally.

To power up the switch, connect one end of the AC power cord to the AC power connector on the switch and the other end of the power cord to a power outlet. If the system LED is solid amber, this tells you that the switch is receiving power. Of course, the switch may not be functioning properly or may not be configured properly.

The switch power up and all port LEDs are green. When turned on, it begins the **power-on self-test (POST)**—a series of tests. As each test is executed, a port LED turns off. For example, if the LED for port 4x is off, the console port test (test 4) is being executed. On a switch with 12 10BaseT ports, the port LED for port Ax (or port A) turns off first, followed by ports 12x, 11x, 10x, and so on. On a switch with 24 10BaseT ports, the port LED for port 16x turns off first, followed by ports 12x, 11x, 10x, and so on. The LEDs for ports 15x, 14x, 13x and Bx are not used during POST. The thirteen tests are shown in Table 8.2.

When a fatal failure(s) is detected and the POST has completed all tests, the test that failed will be indicated by the system LED and one or more of the port LEDs glowing amber. Again, refer to Table 8.2 to see which test(s) failed.

NOTE: While Cisco switches are very similar and boot in a similar manner, you may need to check the documentation for the switch for error codes.

Table 8.2   Catalyst 1900 POST

Port LEDs	Test
16x	Fatal—ECU DRAM test. Switch is not operational.
15x	Not used during POST.
14x	Not used during POST.
13x	Not used during POST.
12x	Fatal—Forwarding engine test. Switch is not operational.
11x	Fatal—Forwarding engine SRAM test. Switch is not operational.
10x	Fatal—Packet DRAM test. Switch is not operational.
9x	Fatal—ISLT ASIC test. Switch is not operational.
8x	Fatal—Port control/status test. Switch is not operational.
7x	Fatal—System timer interrupt test. Switch is not operational.
6x	Fatal—CAM SRAM test. Switch is not operational.
5x	Nonfatal—Real-time clock test. If this test failed, the switch forwards packets. However, if the switch unexpectedly shuts down, it cannot automatically restart itself.
4x	Nonfatal—Console port test. If this test failed, you cannot access the management console through the console port. You can still Telnet to the management console.
3x	Fatal—Content addressable memory test. Switch is not operational.
2x	Nonfatal—Built-in address test. If this test failed, the switch uses the default Ethernet address of the switch and begins forwarding packets.
1x	Nonfatal—Port loopback test. If this test failed, some functionality to one or more ports is lost. The switch disables any port(s) that failed this test, and the failure message on the Management Console Logon Screen indicates which port(s) did not pass this test. Connect only to ports that passed this test.

While the switch is operating, the LEDs on the switch can give you information about the switch. The Ports LEDs (consisting of the STAT, UTL, and FDUP) indicate what the LEDs above the ports indicate. If the Port status LED (STAT) is on, the LEDs above the ports indicate the status of the individual ports. If the Bandwidth Utilization (UTL) LED is on, the LEDs above the ports indicate the percentage of the switched total bandwidth being used at any one time. If the Full duplex operation (FDUP) LED is on, the LEDs above the ports show which ports are operating in half (off) or full duplex mode (solid green) (see Figure 8.5).

To change the mode, press the Mode button on the front panel. The default is Port Status mode. The Select mode remains on for approximately 30 seconds before returning to the default mode (Port Status). You can change the default mode from the console settings menu, which will be discussed later. When the switch is in Port Status mode, the colors of the LEDs above the ports show the status of the corresponding ports (see Table 8.3).

In the UTL mode, the port LEDs as a group show the switch bandwidth being used at any one time. The more LEDs that are lit, the higher the bandwidth being used (see Table 8.4).

8.2.3   Setting up Consoles

To configure and manage the switch using the command-line interface (CLI) or management console, you can connect the console port (located at the back of the switch) to a

Figure 8.5   LEDs on a Cisco Switch

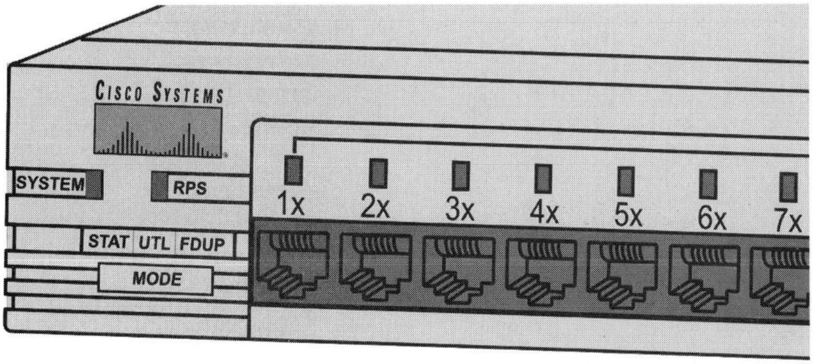

Table 8.3   Port LEDs in Port Status Mode

Port Status mode LED description (color)	Port status
Off	No link.
Solid green	Link operational (with no link activity).
Flashing green	Link operational (with activity).
Alternating green and amber	Link fault. Error frames can affect connectivity. Excessive collisions and CRC, alignment, and jabber errors are monitored for a link-fault indication.
Solid amber	Port is not forwarding. This could be because the port was disabled by management, suspended because of an address violation, or suspended by STP because of network loops.

Table 8.4   Port LEDs in Bandwidth Utilization Mode

12-port	Ports 1–4 lit Bandwidth is 0.1 Mbps to <1.5 Mbps	Ports 5–8 lit Bandwidth is 1.5 Mbps to 20 Mbps	Ports 9–12 lit Bandwdith is 20 Mbps to <140 Mbps
24-port	Ports 1–9 lit Bandwidth is 0.1 Mbps to <6 Mbps	Ports 9–16 lit Bandwith is 6 Mbps to <120 Mbps	Ports 17–24 lit Bandwith is 120 Mbps to 280 Mbps

management station (typically a PC) or modem with the supplied RJ-45 to RJ-45 rollover console cable and an appropriate adapter. The rollover console cable and a RJ-45 to DB-9 female DTE adapter are supplied with the switch, which allows you to connect to a 9-pin serial port. You then run a terminal emulation program, such as HyperTerminal which comes with Windows, where you can specify the port to communicate with. Table 8.5 lists the pin assignments for the RJ-45 to RJ-45 rollover cable and the RJ-45 to DB-9 female DTE adapter. Table 8.6 lists the pins for the RJ-45 to RJ-45 rollover cable and the RJ-45 to DB-25 female DTE adapter. Table 8.7 lists the pins for the RJ-45 to RJ-45 rollover cable, and the RJ-45 to DB-25 male DCE adapter (modem), both of which are not provided with the switch.

Table 8.5   Console Port Signaling and Cabling Using a DB-9 Adapter Console Port (DTE)

	RJ-45 to RJ-45 rollover cable		RJ-45 to DB-9 terminal adapter	Console device
Signal	RJ-45 Pin	RJ-45 Pin	DB-9 Pin	Signal
RTS	1[1]	8	8	CTS
DTR	2	7	6	DSR
TxD	3	6	2	RxD
GND	4	5	5	GND
GND	5	4	5	GND
RxD	6	3	3	TxD
DSR	7	2	4	DTR
CTS	8[1]	1	7	RTS

[1]Pin 1 is connected (inside the terminal adapter) to Pin 8.

Table 8.6   Console Port Signaling and Cabling Using a DB-25 Adapter Console Port (DTE)

	RJ-45 to RJ-45 rollover cable		RJ-45 to DB-25 terminal adapter	Console device
Signal	RJ-45 Pin	RJ-45 Pin	DB-25 Pin	Signal
RTS	1[1]	8	5	CTS
DTR	2	7	6	DSR
TxD	3	6	3	RxD
GND	4	5	7	GND
GND	5	4	7	GND
RxD	6	3	2	TxD
DSR	7	2	20	DTR
CTS	8[1]	1	4	RTS

[1]Pin 1 is connected (inside the terminal adapter) to Pin 8.

Table 8.7   Console Port Signaling and Cabling Using a DB-25 Adapter Console Port (DTE)

	RJ-45 to RJ-45 rollover cable		RJ-45 to DB-25 modem adapter	Modem
Signal	RJ-45 Pin	RJ-45 Pin	DB-25 Pin	Signal
RTS	1[1]	8	4	RTS
DTR	2	7	20	DTR
TxD	3	6	3	TxD
GND	4	5	7	GND
GND	5	4	7	GND
RxD	6	3	2	RxD
DSR	7	2	8	DCD
CTS	8[1]	1	5	CTS

[1]Pin 1 is connected (inside the terminal adapter) to Pin 8.

Figure 8.6   A Rollover Cable

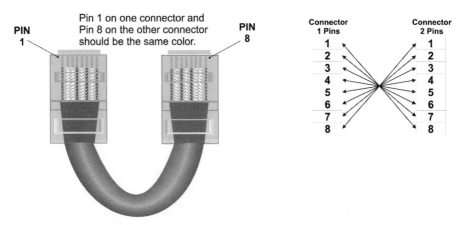

A rollover cable can be identified by comparing the two modular ends of the cable. If you hold the cable ends side-by-side, with the tab at the back, the wire connected to the pin on the outside of the left plug should be the same color as the wire connected to the pin on the outside of the right plug (see Figure 8.6.)

Regardless of which cable you use, start your terminal emulation program and specify the port that you are connecting to. Make sure the settings of the switch console port and the management station or the modem match. These are the default settings of the switch console port:

9600 baud
8 data bits
1 stop bit
No parity
No flow control

Assuming that you have a cable connected and a terminal emulation program running, you will be shown a User Interface Menu similar to what is shown in Figure 8.7. To move into the CLI, you press the [K] key. To configure the switch using menus, you would press the [M] key.

8.2.4   Configuring Passwords

When the switch is shipped, no password is assigned to it. A privileged-level password (encrypted or unencrypted) is required to access the switch management interfaces (switch manager, management console through a Telnet session, or CLI). If you do not assign a password, this access will not be available until the switch joins a cluster or until you assign the switch a privileged-level password from the management console through a direct connection to the switch console port.

From the initial Console Settings menu, you can change the passwords by pressing the [P] key to enter the Password Configuration option. From the next screen, you can

Figure 8.7 User Interface Console

```
Catalyst 2820 Management Console
Copyright (c) Cisco Systems, Inc. 1993-1999
All rights reserved.
Enterprise Edition Software
Ethernet address: 00-E0-1E-7E-B4-40
PCA Number: 73-2239-01
PCA Serial Number: SAD01200001
Model Number: WS-C2822-A
System Serial Number: FAA01200001
- - - - - - - - - - - - - - - - - - - - - - - - - - - - - -
     User Interface Menu
     [M]  Menus
     [K]  Command Line
     [I]  IP Configuration
     [P]  Password Configuration
Enter Selection:
```

press the [M] key to use the Modify password option to assign an unencrypted password or press the [E] key to use the Modify secret password option to assign an encrypted (secret) privileged-level password. The encrypted password provides higher security and supersedes any existing unencrypted privileged-level password, including the unencrypted privileged-level passwords options.

If you press the [K] key to use the Command option to enter the command line interface, you must first move into the Global Configuration mode to change passwords. To get into the Global Configuration mode, you must first use the `enable` command to enter Enable mode followed by using the `config t` command to enter the Global Configuration command. To exit the Global Configuration mode, press the [Ctrl+Z] keys or use the `exit` command. To enable the user mode password, type `enable password level 1 password` and to enable the privileged mode password type in `enable password level 15 password`.

NOTE: The password must be at least four characters but not longer than eight characters. It is not case sensitive (see Figure 8.8).

8.2.5   Configuring TCP/IP

Now you are probably wondering why a switch would need an IP address. First, a switch does not need an IP configuration for a switch to work. You can just plug in devices and they should start working, just like they would on a hub. The IP address and default gateway is used so that you can manage the switch via Telnet or other management software or configure the switch with different VLANs and other network functions. In addition, if

Figure 8.8   Setting Passwords on the Cisco IOS of the Cisco Catalyst 1900 Switch

```
- - - - - - - - - - - - - - - - - - - - - - - - - - - - - - - -

      User Interface Menu
      [M]  Menus
      [K]  Command Line
      [I]  IP Configuration
      [P]  Password Configuration


Enter Selection:  K

>enable
#config t
Enter configuration commands, one per line. End with CNTL/Z.
(config)#enable password level 1 pw111111
(config)#enable password level 15 pw222222
```

you want to use the ping command from the switch to help you troubleshoot connectivity problems, the device needs to have an IP address and a default gateway.

To change the IP configuration, you would press the [I] key to select the IP address option from the initial management console logon screen. To input the IP address, you would use the IP address option. If the switch does not have an IP address, the Current setting appears as 0.0.0.0, and you can enter the IP address of the switch as the New setting. If the switch is connected to a network that has a Dynamic Host Configuration Protocol (DHCP)/Bootstrap Protocol (BOOTP) server, the server might automatically assign an IP address. You would then have to use the Subnet mask and Default gateway options to set the subnet masks and default gateway (see Figure 8.9).

To show the IP configuration of a Cisco switch from the command prompt, you would execute the `show ip` command from Enable mode (# prompt). To set or change the IP address of a switch, you would use the `ip address` command from the Global Configuration mode. For example, to set the IP address to 168.1.1.2 with a subnet mask to 255.255.255.0:

```
ip address 168.1.1.2 255.255.255.0
```

To configure the default gateway, you would use the `ip default-gateway` command. For example, to set the default-gateway to 168.1.1.254, you would use the following command:

```
ip default-gateway 168.1.1.254
```

To verify the IP connectivity, you can use the ping command within the Enable mode. Different from the ping command that you use with Windows, a successful ping will be denoted by an exclamation point (!) and a timeout will be denoted by a period (.) (see Figure 8.10).

Figure 8.9 IP Configuration

```
Catalyst 1900 - IP Configuration

Ethernet Address:00-E0-1E-7E-B4-40

- - - - - - - Settings - - - - - - -
[I]  IP address
[S]  Subnet mask
[G]  Default gateway
[B]  Management Bridge Group
[M]  IP address of DNS server 1
[N]  IP address of DNS server 2
[D]  Domain name
[R]  Use Routing Information Protocol
- - - - - - - Actions - - - - - - -
[P]  Ping
[C]  Clear cached DNS entries
[X]  Exit to previous menu

Enter Selection: I
```

Figure 8.10 Using the Ping Command on a Cisco Switch

```
#ping 192.168.1.5

Type escape sequence to abort.
Sending 5, 100-byte ICMP Echos to 192.168.1.2, timeout is 2 seconds:
!!!!!
Success rate is 100 percent (5/5), round-trip min/avg/max
0/2/10/ ms
#
#ping 192.168.1.2

Type escape sequence to abort.
Sending 5, 100-byte ICMP Echos to 192.168.1.2, timeout is 2 seconds:
.....
Success rate is 0 percent (0/5)
#
```

8.3   IOS COMMAND LINE INTERFACE

The **command line interface (CLI)** is an Enterprise Edition software feature that supports all configuration and management options. While many of these switches will have the management/menu console available for basic configuration and for configuring VLANs, you cannot access all features from using the menus. Therefore, it is best that you know how to use the CLI.

For those who are familiar with running commands from a command prompt in DOS or UNIX, the CLI is not as foreign. For those who are not accustomed to a command-driven operating system, you must type in the command to configure or monitor the switch. When typing the commands, you must know the spelling and syntax of the commands. If you misspell the command or you do not specify the parameters in a certain way, the switch will give you a somewhat cryptic looking error message. Tables 8.8 and 8.9 show a summary of the common commands used at the command prompt.

8.3.1   Changing Modes

The working name of the CLI is the Exec command interpreter. As mentioned when discussing passwords, the Exec command interpreter has two Exec modes, or command groups, that can be used to perform a variety of functions: (1) User Exec mode and (2) Privileged Exec mode.

If you have the user mode password enabled and you select the command line option, you would then be asked for the user mode password. You will know that you are in User Exec mode if the prompt displayed on your screen looks like this:

```
SwitchHostName>
```

If you have not named your switch, the enable mode prompt will only be the > symbol. The enable mode will be mostly used to view the configuration and status information of the switch.

To change to Privileged Exec mode, you will use the enable command at the User Exec mode prompt. If you enable the privilege mode password and you enter the enable mode (by using the enable command at the command prompt), you will then be asked for the privileged mode password. If the Enable Exec mode password has not been set, this mode can be accessed only from the router console port. It is from the enable mode that you can change the configuration of the switch. You will know that you are in Privileged Exec mode because the prompt will end with a pound or number sign (#):

```
SwitchHostName#
```

If you have not named your switch, Privileged Exec mode will only be the # symbol.

To change the running-config (the current configuration running in Dynamic RAM), you would use the `configure terminal` command (or just `config t` for short) executed from Privileged Exec mode. This is also known as the Global Configuration mode.

`[Ctrl+Z]` can be used in any of the IOS configuration modes, including Global Configuration mode and the Interface Configuration mode. You can use the exit command

Table 8.8   Changing Modes on Cisco Switches

CLI prompt	Resultant prompt	Purpose
Name>**enable**	Name#	Moves to Privileged Exec mode from User Exec mode
Name#**configure terminal (or config t)**	Name(config)#	Moves to Global Configuration mode from Privileged Exec mode
Name(config)#**interface ethernet0**	Name(config-if)#	Opens the configuration of the ethernet0 interface port from Global Configuration mode
Name(config)#**end**	Name#	Saves changes and returns the user to Privileged Exec mode from any configuration mode or submode
Name(config-if)#**exit**	Name(config)#	Exits to Global Configuration mode from Interface mode
Name(config)#**exit**	Name#	Exits to Privileged Exec mode from Global Configuration mode
Name#**exit**	Name>	Returns to User Exec mode from Privileged Exec mode
Name#**disable**	Name>	Returns to User Exec mode while in Privileged Exec mode

from Global Configuration mode to return to Privileged Exec mode. Using the exit command from submodes of Global Configuration mode, for example Interface Configuration mode, will back up one level toward Global Configuration mode. The end command saves changes and returns the user to Privileged Exec mode from any configuration mode or submode. To return to User Exec mode while in Privileged Exec mode, you would use the disable command.

8.3.2   General Settings

While in Global Configuration mode, you can use the hostname command to set the system name or the no hostname command to clear the name.

```
>hostname name
name>no hostname
>
```

Table 8.9   Common Commands Used on Cisco Switches

Command	Description
`ip address` *address subnet-mask*	Sets the IP address for in-band management of the switch
`ip default-gateway`	Sets the default gateway so that the management interface can be reached from a remote network
`show ip`	Displays IP address configuration
`show interfaces`	Displays interface information
`mac-address-table permanent` *mac address type module/port*	Sets a permanent MAC address
`mac-address-table restricted static` *mac address type module/port src-if-list*	Sets a restricted static MAC address
`port secure` [`max-mac-count` *count*]	Sets port security
`show mac-address-table security`	Displays the MAC address table. The security option displays information about the restricted or static settings.
`address-violation {suspend | disable | ignore}`	Sets the action to be taken by the switch if there is a security address violation
`show version`	Displays version information
`copy tftp://10.1.1.1/config. cfg nvram`	Copies a configuration file from the TFTP server at IP address 10.1.1.1.
`copy nvram tftp://10.1.1.1/ config.cfg`	Saves a configuration file to the TFTP server at IP address 10.1.1.1.
`delete nvram`	Removes all configuration parameters and returns the switch to factory default settings

The Catalyst 1900 switch has some default settings already configured on the switch from the factory. The default settings on the switch are as follows:

IP address and default gateway: 0.0.0.0
CDP: Enabled
Switching mode: FragmentFree
100BaseT ports: Auto-negotiate duplex mode
10BaseT ports: Half duplex
Spanning Tree: Enabled
Console password: Not set

To view the current configuration, change into Enable mode and execute the `show running-config` (`show run`) command from the # prompt (see Figure 8.11). To show the IOS version on the switch, execute the `show version` command (see Figure 8.12).

8.3.3   Configuring Switch Interfaces

The 1900 switch uses the type slot/port command. For example, Ethernet 0/3 is 10BaseT port 3. The 0 indicates slot 0 and the 3 indicates port 3 on that slot. For the Catalyst 1900,

Figure 8.11 The Show Run Command

```
>enable
#show run
Building configuration...Current configuration:
!
!
!
!
!


ip default-gateway 172.16.10.1
ip name-server 144.4.1.100
!
!
!
!


enable password level 15 'PASSWORD'


!
interface Ethernet 0/1
!
interface Ethernet 0/2
!
interface Ethernet 0/3
!
interface Ethernet 0/4
!
interface Ethernet 0/5
!
interface Ethernet 0/6
!
--More--
```

it only has one slot and it will have either 12 or 24 ports depending on the model that you have. Some of the larger, modular switches will have additional slots and a larger number of ports.

For the Catalyst 1900 switch, Port 25 is designated as the AUI on your switch (if available). In addition, you have two additional FastEthernet ports designated as ports 26 and 27. So the first FastEthernet port will be designated as FastEthernet 0/26.

Figure 8.12   The Show Version Command

```
#show version
1900A uptime is 0day(s) 06hour(s) 55minute(s) 41second(s)
Cisco Catalyst 1900 (486sxl) processor with 2048K/1024K bytes of memory
Hardware board revision is 5
Upgrade Status: No upgrade currently in progress.
Config File Status: No configuration upload/download is in progress
15 Fixed Ethernet/IEEE 802.3 interface(s)
Base Ethernet Address: 00-30-80-C7-01-80

#
```

To display your interfaces, you can use the show int command. If you want to show the port 5 interface, you would use the show int e0/5. To show the fastEthernet ports, you would use the show int f0/26 command. This shows you the duplex mode, if it is set to forwarding mode, and vital statistics for that interface that may be used for troubleshooting (see Figure 8.13).

To change the configuration of a port, you must enter the interface configuration mode by executing the int ethernet command for ports 1–24 and int fastethernet for ports 26 and 27 from Global Configuration mode (see Figure 8.14).

To configure the duplex mode, you would then use the Interface Configuration mode. To force the port into full duplex mode, you would type duplex full. To put the port into half duplex mode, you would use the duplex half command. To put the port into auto mode, you would type duplex auto.

8.3.4   Managing the MAC Address Table

As you recall from Chapter 7, bridges and switches switch packets based on MAC addresses. The switches create a MAC table that includes dynamic, permanent, and static addresses. This filter table is used to determine which port or ports a packet will be forwarded and is created by learning and remember the MAC addresses, port and segment that a packet comes from.

The switch keeps adding new MAC addresses sent on the network into the MAC filter table. As hosts are added or removed, the switch dynamically updates the MAC filter table. If a device is removed, or it is not connected to the switch for a period of time, the switch will drop the entry.

To view the switch's MAC filter table, you would use the show mac-address-table command (or sh mac-address-table command) (see Figure 8.15).

The Catalyst 1900 switch can store up to 1024 MAC addresses. Other switches will vary. If the MAC filter table gets full, the switch will flood all new addresses until one of the existing entries gets aged out. To clear the MAC filter table, you would use the clear mac-address-table command.

Figure 8.13 Using the Show Interface Command

```
>enable
#sh int
Ethernet e0/1 is Suspended-no-linkbeat
Hardware is Built-in 10Base-T
Address is 0030.80C7.0181
MTU 1500 bytes, BW 10000 Kbits
802.1d STP State:  Forwarding Forward Transitions:  1
Port monitoring:  Disabled
Unknown unicast flooding:  Enabled
Unregistered multicast flooding:  Enabled
Description:
Duplex setting:  half duplex
Back pressure:  Disabled

   Receive Statistics                     Transmit Statistics
- - - - - - - - - - - - - - - - -    - - - - - - - - - - - - - - - - -
Total good frames           0        Total frames              0
Total octets                0        Total octets              0
Broadcast/multicast frames  0        Broadcast/multicast frames 0
Broadcast/multicast octets  0        Broadcast/multicast octets 0
Good frames forwarded       0        Deferrals                 0
Frames filtered             0        Single collisions         0
Runt frames                 0        Multiple collisions       0
No buffer discards          0        Excessive collisions      0
                                     Queue full discards       0

Errors:                              Errors:
  FCS errors                0          Late collisions          0
  Alignment errors          0          Excessive deferrals      0
  Giant frames              0          Jabber errors            0
  Address violations        0          Other transmit errors    0
Ethernet e0/2 is Suspended-no-linkbeat
Hardware is Built-in 10Base-T
Address is 0030.80C7.0181
MTU 1500 bytes, BW 10000 Kbits
802.1d STP State:  Forwarding Forward Transitions:  1
Port monitoring:  Disabled
Unknown unicast flooding:  Enabled
Unregistered multicast flooding:  Enabled
Description:
Duplex setting:  half duplex
Back pressure:  Disabled
```

Continued

Figure 8.13 Continued

```
     Receive Statistics                  Transmit Statistics
- - - - - - - - - - - - - - - - -    - - - - - - - - - - - - - - - - -
Total good frames           0        Total frames                0
Total octets                0        Total octets                0
Broadcast/multicast frames  0        Broadcast/multicast frames  0
Broadcast/multicast octets  0        Broadcast/multicast octets  0
Good frames forwarded       0        Deferrals                   0
Frames filtered             0        Single collisions           0
Runt frames                 0        Multiple collisions         0
No buffer discards          0        Excessive collisions        0
                                     Queue full discards         0
Errors:                              Errors:
  FCS errors                0          Late collisions           0
  Alignment errors          0          Excessive deferrals       0
  Giant frames              0          Jabber errors             0
  Address violations        0          Other transmit errors     0
--More-
```

Figure 8.14 Changing First into Global Configuration Mode Then to Interface
Configuration Mode

```
>enable
#config t
Enter configuration commands, one per line.  End with CNTL/Z.
 (config)#int ethernet 0/1
(config-if)#
```

Figure 8.15 The Show Mac-Address-Table Command

```
#sh mac-address-table
Number of permanent addresses:  0
Number of restricted static addresses:  0
Number of dynamic addresses:  4

Address            Dest Interface   Type        Source Interface List
00A0.246E.0FA8     Ethernet 0/2     Dynamic     All
0000.8147.4E11     Ethernet 0/5     Dynamic     All
0000.8610.C16F     Ethernet 0/1     Dynamic     All
00A0.2448.60A5     Ethernet 0/4     Dynamic     All
```

To have more control over the MAC addresses allowed by the switch, administrators can also create permanent and static entries. To configure a permanent MAC address to a switch port, change into Global Configuration mode and execute the `mac-address-table permanent` *mac-address interface* command. To add the permanent entry for the 00:A2:24:48:82:A5 to the port 5, you would execute the following command:

```
mac-address-table permanent 00A2.2448.82A5 e0/4
```

The static MAC addresses go one step further, and tell a source interface that it is only allowed to send frames out of a defined interface. To specify that packets can only go from port 2 to port 5 with the MAC address of 00A2.2448.82A5, you would use the following command:

```
mac-address-table restricted static 00A2.2448.82A5 e0/2
e0/5
```

8.3.5   Configuring Port Security

To provide a more secure environment that stops users from connecting a hub into their network jack in their office or cubicle and connecting several hubs without your knowledge, you would use port security. By default, a Cisco switch allows up to 132 hardware addresses on a single switch interface. To change this number, you should use the `port secure max-mac-count` command within interface mode. For example, to specify that only one address can be connected to the switch, you would specify:

```
port secure max-mac-count 1
```

The secured port or ports you create can use either static or sticky-learned hardware addresses. Sticky-learned hardware addresses are source addresses of incoming frames that are automatically assigned as permanent addresses. Therefore, if someone connects another computer beyond the max-mac-count value, they will not be allowed to transfer any data.

8.3.6   Changing LAN Switch Types

As you recall from Chapter 7, there are three modes available for switches. The Catalyst 1900 switch only supports fragment-free and store-and-forward. To view the type of switching set for your switch, use the `show port system` command from the Enable mode. To change the switching mode, you use the switching-mode command from the Global Configuration mode. To change to the fragment-free mode, type in `switching-mode fragment-free`. To change to the store-and-forward mode, type in `switching-mode store-and-forward`.

8.4   CONFIGURING VLANS ON CISCO SWITCHES

On a 1900 switch, you can create up to 64 VLANs. A separate Spanning Tree instance can be configured per VLAN (see Table 8.10).

Table 8.10 VLAN Commands

Command	Description
`delete vtp`	Resets all VTP parameters to defaults and resets the configuration revision number to 1
`vtp [server	transparent	client]` `[domain domain-name] [trap {enable |` `disable}] [password password]` `[pruning {enable	disable}]`	Defines VTP parameters
`vtp trunk pruning-disable vlan-list`	Disables pruning for specified VLANs on a particular trunk interface (interface subcommand)
`show vtp`	Displays VTP status
`trunk [on	off	desirable |` `auto	nonegotiate]`	Configures a trunk interface
`show trunk`	Displays trunk status
`vlan vlan# name vlanname`	Defines a VLAN and its name
`show vlan`	Displays VLAN information
`vlan-membership static vlan#`	Assigns a port to a VLAN
`show vlan-membership`	Displays VLAN membership
`show spantree vlan#`	Displays Spanning Tree information for a VLAN

8.4.1   Creating a VLAN

To create a VLAN, switch to Global Configuration mode and use the following command:

```
vlan vlan# name name_of_vlan
```

Then to add ports to the VLAN, change to the Interface Configuration mode and use the `vlan-membership static vlan#` command. When done, you can view the VLANs by typing the `show vlan` command. To a specific VLAN, you would use the `show vlan vlan#` command. You can also use the `show vlan-membership` command to list all of the ports and the VLAN that they are in (see Figures 8.16 and 8.17).

8.4.2   Configuring VLAN Trunking

The Catalyst 1900 switch only runs the Dynamic Inter-Switch Link (DISL) trunking. To configure trunking on a Fast Ethernet port, use the trunk command with the appropriate parameter shown in Table 8.11. For example, to enable the trunk, execute the `trunk on` command.

To verify your trunk ports, use the `show trunk` command. If you have more than one port trunking and want to see statistics on only one trunk port, you can use the `show trunk port_number` command. For the Catalyst 1900 switch, the FastEthernet port 0/26 is identified by trunk A, and port 0/27 is identified by trunk B. Therefore, to view the trunk port on interface 26, use the `show trunk A` command. To see which VLANs are allowed on a trunked line, use the `show trunk A allowed-vlans` or `show trunk B allowed-vlans` command.

Figure 8.16 Working with VLANs on Cisco Switches

```
#config t
(config) #vlan 2 name sales
(config) #vlan 3 name marketing
(config) #vlan 4 name mis
(config) #int e0/2
(config-if) #vlan-membership static 2
(config) #int e0/4
(config-if) #vlan-membership static 2
(config-if) #int e0/5
(config-if) #vlan-membership static 2
(config-if) #^Z
```

Figure 8.17 Showing VLANs on Cisco Switches

```
#sh vlan
LAN Name                Status          Ports
- - - - - - - - - - - - - - - - - - - - - - - - - - - - - - - - - - - -
1    default            Enabled         1, 3, 6-12, AUI, A, B
2    sales              Enabled         2, 4, 5
3    marketing          Enabled
4    mis                Enabled
1002 fddi-default       Suspended
1003 token-ring-defau   Suspended
1004 fddinet-default    Suspended
1005 trnet-default      Suspended
- - - - - - - - - - - - - - - - - - - - - - - - - - - - - - - - - - - -

VLAN Type           SAID   MTU   Parent RingNo BridgeNo Stp  Trans1 Trans2
- - - - - - - - - - - - - - - - - - - - - - - - - - - - - - - - - - - -
1    Ethernet       100001 1500  0      0      0        Unkn 1002   1003
2    Ethernet       100002 1500  0      1      1        Unkn 0      0
1002 FDDI           101002 1500  0      0      0        Unkn 1      1003
1003 Token-Ring     101003 1500  1005   1      0        Unkn 1      1002
1004 FDDI-Net       101004 1500  0      0      1        IEEE 0      0
1005 Token-Ring-Net 101005 1500  0      0      1        IEEE 0      0
- - - - - - - - - - - - - - - - - - - - - - - - - - - - - - - - - - - -

#sh vlan 2
VLAN Name                Status          Ports
- - - - - - - - - - - - - - - - - - - - - - - - - - - - - - - - - - - -
2    sales              Enabled         2, 4, 5
- - - - - - - - - - - - - - - - - - - - - - - - - - - - - - - - - - - -

VLAN Type           SAID   MTU   Parent RingNo BridgeNo Stp  Trans1 Trans2
- - - - - - - - - - - - - - - - - - - - - - - - - - - - - - - - - - - -
2    Ethernet       100002 1500  0      1      1        Unkn 0      0
- - - - - - - - - - - - - - - - - - - - - - - - - - - - - - - - - - - -
```

Continued

Figure 8.17 Continued

```
#sh vlan-membership
Port  VLAN   Membership Type      Port  VLAN   Membership Type
- - - - - - - - - - - - - --      - - - - - - - - - - - - - -
1     1        Static
2     2        Static
3     1        Static
4     2        Static
5     2        Static
6     1        Static
7     1        Static
8     1        Static
9     1        Static
10    1        Static
11    1        Static
12    1        Static
AUI   1        Static
A     1        Static
B     1        Static


#
```

Table 8.11 VLAN Trunk Parameters

Parameter	Description
Auto	The interface will become trunked only if the connected device is set to ON or desirable.
Desirable	If a connected device is either ON, desirable, or auto, it will negotiate to become a trunk port.
Nonegotiate	The interface becomes a permanent ISL trunk port and will not negotiate with any attached device.
OFF	The interface is disabled from running trunking and tries to convert any attached device to be ON-trunk as well.
ON	The interface is a permanent ISL trunk port. It can negotiate with a connected device to convert the link to trunk mode.

To stop broadcasts on a certain VLAN from using a trunk link or because you want to stop topology-change information from being sent across a link where a VLAN is not supported, you would use the `clear trunk` command. To delete a VLAN from a trunk port, use the `no trunk-vlan vlan#` from the Interface Configuration mode.

8.4.3   Configuring a VTP

A Catalyst switch is configured by default to be a VTP server. To further configure VTP, you must first configure the domain name you want to use. To set the switch as a VTP

Figure 8.18   Using the Show VTP Command

```
#sh vtp

 VTP version:  1
 Configuration revision:  0
 Maximum VLANs supported locally:  1005
 Number of existing VLANs :  3
 VTP domain name          :  vtpdomain
 VTP password             :  pw444444
 VTP operating mode       :  Server
 VTP pruning mode         :  Disable
 VTP traps generation     :  Enabled
Configuration last modified by:  0.0.0.0 at 00-00-000000:00:00
```

server, the VTP domain to vtpdomain and the VTP password to pw111111, you would use the following commands from the Global Configuration mode:

```
vtp server
vtp domain vtpdomain
vtp password pw111111
```

After you configure the VTP information, you can verify it with the `show vtp` command from the Enable mode (see Figure 8.18).

When adding a switch into a domain, you need to be careful that the switch does not have incorrect VLAN information. If the switch does have incorrect information, the information could be propagated throughout the internetwork. Therefore, Cisco recommends that you delete the VTP database before adding a switch to a VTP domain. This is done by using the `delete vtp` command. When it asks to reset the system with VTP parameters set to factory defaults, just type yes.

The last command concerns VTP pruning. If you need to enable VTP pruning, you would execute the `vtp pruning enable` command from the Global Configuration mode.

8.5   NAVIGATING THE MANAGEMENT CONSOLE

You have already been introduced to the menu interface when this chapter discussed passwords and configuring IP parameters. When using menus on a Cisco switch, the management console menu-driven system uses the following conventions:

- Select a menu by entering the letter in square brackets that precedes the selection. The selected menu appears.
- Press [Return] after entering any parameters. When pressed at the beginning of a parameter entry, [Return] cancels the attempt and the menu reappears.
- Use [Backspace] to erase the character previously entered. Press [Backspace] at the beginning of a parameter to clear the entry.

Figure 8.19   Management Console Main Menu

```
Catalyst 1900 - Main Menu

[C]  Console Settings
[S]  System
[N]  Network Management
[P]  Port Configuration
[A]  Port Addressing
[D]  Port Statistics Detail
[M]  Monitoring
[B]  Bridge Group
[R]  Multicast Registration
[F]  Firmware
[I]  RS-232 Interface
[U]  Usage Summaries
[H]  Help


[X]  Exit Management Console

Enter Selection:
```

■ Enter [x] to return to the previous menu. Enter [x] on the Main Menu to exit the management console and return to the command prompt.

When you enter the management console, the main menu will appear as shown in Figure 8.19. To display the System Configuration Menu, enter the [S] System option from the Management Console Main Menu (see Figure 8.20). From here, you can configure the host name for the switch and the switching mode.

NOTE: If your switch is running the Cisco Catalyst 1900/2820 Enterprise Edition Software, the System Configuration Menu provides the options to enable and disable bridge groups and VLANs.

You can also reset the system or reset the factory defaults. If you reset the system, all configured system parameters and static addresses are retained while all dynamic addresses are removed. If you reset to factory defaults, all static and dynamic addresses, IP addresses, and all other configuration information is removed.

To display the Network Management Menu, enter the [N] Network Management option from the Management Console Main Menu (see Figure 8.21). To display the Spanning Tree Configuration Menu, enter the [B] Bridge - Spanning Tree option from the Network Management Menu (see Figure 8.22).

Figure 8.20 System Configuration Menu

```
Catalyst 1900 - System Configuration
System Revision: 0    Address Capacity: 1024
System UpTime:     0day(s) 00hour(s) 11minute(s) 29second(s)


- - - - - - - - - - - - - Settings - - - - - - - - - - - - - - - - -
[N]  Name of system
[C]  Contact name
[L]  Location
[S]  Switching mode                                      FragmentFree
[U]  Use of store-and-forward for multicast              Disabled
[A]  Action upon address violation                       Suspend
[G]  Generate alert on address violation                 Enabled
[I]  Address aging time                                  300 second(s)
[P]  Network Port                                        None
[H]  Half duplex back pressure       (10-mbps ports)     Disabled
[E]  Enhanced Congestion Control     (10 Mbps Ports)     Disabled


- - - - - - - - - - - - - Actions - - - - - - - - - - - - - - - - - -
[R]  Reset system                 [F]  Reset to factory defaults
- - - - - - - - - - - - - Related Menus - - - - - - - - - - - - -
[B]  Broadcast storm control      [X]  Exit to Main Menu


Enter Selection
```

Figure 8.21 Network Management Menu

```
Catalyst 1900 - Network Management

[I]  IP Configuration
[S]  SNMP Management
[B]  Bridge - Spanning Tree
[C]  Cisco Discovery Protocol
[G]  Cisco Group Management Protocol
[H]  HTTP Server Configuration
[R]  Cluster Management


[X]  Exit to Main Menu


Enter Selection:
```

Figure 8.22   Configuring STA from the Management Console

```
Catalyst 1900 - Bridge Group 1 - Spanning Tree Configuration
Bridge ID: 8000 00-E0-1E-81-1E-40


- - - - - - - - - - Information - - - - - - - - - -
Designated root 8000 00-E0-1E-81-1E-40
Number of member ports   27      Root port                N/A
Max age (sec)            20      Root path cost             0
Forward Delay (sec)      15      Hello time (sec)           2
Topology changes          0      Last TopChange     0d00h00m00s


- - - - - - - - - - - Settings - - - - - - - - - -
[S] Spanning Tree Algorithm & Protocol        Enabled
[B] Bridge priority                           32768 (8000 hex)
[M] Max age when operating as root            20 second(s)
[H] Hello time when operating as root         2 second(s)
[F] Forward delay when operating as root      15 second(s)


- - - - - - - - - - - Actions - - - - - - - - - - -
[N] Next bridge group [G]  Goto bridge group
[P] Previous bridge group [X]  Exit to previous menu

Enter Selection:
```

When you enter the [P] Port Configuration option from the Management Console Main Menu, the following prompt is displayed:

```
Identify Port: 1 to 24[1-24], [AUI], [A], [B]:
Select [1 - 24, AUI, A, B]:
```

At the prompt, enter the specific port that you want to configure.

- If you select a 10BaseT port (ports 1x through 12x or 24x or AUI), the Port Configuration Menu (10BaseT Ports) in Figure 8.23 is displayed.
- If you select a 100BaseT port (ports Ax or Bx), the Port Configuration Menu (100BaseT Ports) in Figure 8.24 is displayed.

The STP State field displays the STP state of the port. A port can be in one of the following states as shown in Table 8.12.

The status of port option is used change the status of the port. You would use [E] to enable the port to transmit and receive data and [D] to disable the port.

Figure 8.23   Port Configuration Shown for a 10BaseT Port

```
Catalyst 1900 - Port 1 Configuration

Built-in 10Base-T
802.1d STP State: Blocking        Forward Transitions: 0

- - - - - - - - - - - - - - Settings - - - - - - - - - - - - -
[D]  Description/name of port
[S]  Status of port                      Suspended-no-linkbeat
[F]  Full duplex                         Disabled
[I]  Port priority (spanning tree)       128 (80 hex)
[C]  Path cost (spanning tree)           100
[H]  Port fast mode (spanning tree)      Enabled

- - - - - - - - - - - - - Related Menus - - - - - - - - - - -
[A]  Port addressing          [V]  View port statistics
[N]  Next port                [G]  Goto port
[P]  Previous port            [X]  Exit to Main Menu

Enter Selection:
```

Figure 8.24   Port Configuration Shown for a 100BaseT Port

```
Catalyst 1900 - Port A Configuration

Built-in: 100Base-TX
802.1d STP State: Blocking        Forward Transitions: 0

- - - - - - - - - - - - - - Settings  - - - - - - - - - - - - - - - - -
[D]  Description/name of port
[S]  Status of port
[I]  Port priority (spanning tree)       128 (80 hex)
[C]  Path cost (spanning tree)           10
[H]  Port fast mode (spanning tree)      Disabled
[E]  Enhanced congestion control         Disabled
[F]  Full duplex / Flow control          Half duplex

- - - - - - - - - - - - - Related Menus - - - - - - - - - - - - - -
[A]  Port addressing          [V]  View port statistics
[N]  Next port                [G]  Goto port
[P]  Previous port            [X]  Exit to Main Menu

Enter Selection:
```

Table 8.12   STP States

Blocking	The port is not forwarding frames and is not learning new addresses.
Listening	The port is not forwarding frames but is progressing toward a forwarding state. The port is not learning addresses.
Learning	The port is not forwarding frames but is learning addresses.
Forwarding	The port is forwarding frames and learning addresses.
Disabled	The port has been removed from STP operation. You need to reenable the port.

Table 8.13   Port States

Status	Description
Enabled	Port can transmit and receive data.
Disabled-mgmt	Port is disabled by management action. Port must be manually reenabled.
Suspended-no-linkbeat	Port is suspended because of no linkbeat. This is usually because the attached station is disconnected or powered down. Port automatically returns to enabled state when the condition causing the suspension is removed.
Suspended-jabber	Port is suspended because attached station is jabbering. Port automatically returns to enabled state when the condition causing the suspension is removed.
Suspended-violation	Port is suspended because of an address violation. Port automatically returns to enabled state when the condition causing the suspension is removed.
Disabled-self-test	Port is disabled because it failed a self-test.
Disabled-violation	Port is disabled because of an address violation. Port must be manually enabled.
Reset	Port is in the reset state.

NOTE: Security violations, management intervention, or STP actions can change the port status. No packets are forwarded to or from a disabled or suspended port. However, suspended ports do monitor incoming packets to look for an activating condition. For example, when a linkbeat returns, a port suspended for no linkbeat returns to the enabled state. Each port is always in one of the states listed in Table 8.13.

If it is a 10 Mbps port, you can then use the [F] option to enable full duplex or the [E] key to select half duplex. If it is a 100 Mbps port, you can set it as one of the following options:

[1] Full duplex
[2] Half duplex
[3] Full duplex with flow control
[4] Autonegotiate

The default of the 100BaseTX ports is [4] Autonegotiate. The default of the 100-Mbps fiber-optic ports is [2] Half duplex.

To configure STP options, you would use the port priority and path cost. The port priority is a number from 0 to 255 for each port. The default is 128. The lower the number, the higher the priority. The higher priority port remains enabled by STP if two ports form a loop. The path cost is a number from 1 to 65535 for each port. The default for 10 Mbps ports is 100, while the default for the 100 Mbps ports is 10.

When you enter the [A] Port Addressing option from the Management Console Main Menu, the following prompt is displayed:

```
Identify Port:1 to 24[1-24], [AUI], [A], [B]:
Select [1 - 24, AUI, A, B]:
```

At the prompt, enter the specific port that you want to configure. The Port Addressing Menu is displayed (see Figure 8.25). The top of the menu displays the current addressing situation:

■ **Dynamic addresses**—The current number of unicast addresses that have been automatically learned on this port. If this is a secured port, the dynamic addresses field is set to 0. The switch provides dynamic addressing by learning the source

Figure 8.25 Port Addressing

```
Catalyst 1900 - Port 1 Addressing

Address: Unaddressed

- - - - - - - - - - - - - - - Settings - - - - - - - - - - - - - - - -
[T] Address table size            Unrestricted
[S] Addressing security           Disabled
[K] Clear addresses on link down  Disabled
[U] Flood unknown unicasts        Enabled
[M] Flood unregistered multicasts Enabled


- - - - - - - - - - - - - - - Actions - - - - - - - - - - - - - - - -
[A] Add a static address
[D] Define restricted static address
[L] List addresses
[E] Erase an address
[R] Remove all addresses

[C] Configure port            [V] View port statistics
[N] Next port                 [G] Goto port
[P] Previous port             [X] Exit to Main Menu

Enter Selection:
```

MAC address of each packet received on each switch port and then adding the address and its associated forwarding switch port number to the Dynamic Address Table. As end stations are added or removed from the network, the switch updates the table by adding new entries and removing unused ones. If you have a new switch, the switch will not have learned any addresses. Therefore, it will show Unaddressed.

■ **Static addresses**—The current number of unicast addresses that have been assigned to this port. The entries in the Permanent Unicast Address Table allow MAC addresses to be permanently associated with a switch port. Unlike the Dynamic Address Table, the entries in the Permanent Unicast Address Table are manually assigned (static) or sticky-learned (see the [D] Define a Restricted Static Address option on this menu). If the address table is full, an error message is generated. You can change the size of the address table by using the [T] Address Table Size option on this menu.

The Detailed Port Statistics Report displays the receive and transmit statistics for the port you select. You can use this page to help identify performance or connectivity problems, which are listed under the Errors area of the menu. For example, FCS and alignment errors could be the result of cabling problems such as the following:

■ Cabling distance exceeded
■ Split pairs
■ Defective patch-panel ports
■ Wrong cable type
■ Misconfigured full duplex connection

> *NOTE:* If you are using VT100 terminal emulation, the statistics on this menu are refreshed every five seconds. If you are connected to the management console through a modem running at less than 2400 baud, the statistics displays are refreshed every eight seconds. Press [Return] or the space bar to refresh these reports at any time.

When you enter the [D] Port Statistics Detail option from the Management Console Main Menu, the following prompt is displayed:

```
Identify Port:1 to 24[1-24], [AUI], [A], [B]:
Select [1 - 24, AUI, A, B]:
```

At the prompt, enter the specific port for which you want to display the statistics and errors. The Detailed Port Statistics Report is displayed. The errors are described in Table 8.14. Figure 8.26 is an example statistics report for a 10BaseT port. It is similar to the report for the 100BaseT ports.

For more information on the Management Console, see the following website:

Configuring and Monitoring from the Management Console

> http://www.cisco.com/univercd/cc/td/doc/product/lan/28201900/1928v9x/
> 19icg9x/19icoutb.htm

Table 8.14 Errors Found on a Switch

Heading error	Description
FCS errors	Number of frames received on a particular interface that are an integral number of octets in length but do not pass the FCS test.
Alignment errors	Number of frames received on a particular interface that are not an integral number of octets in length and do not pass the FCS check.
Giant frames	Number of frames received on a particular interface that exceed the maximum permitted frame size.
Address violations	Number of times a source address was seen on this secured port that duplicates a static address configured on another port plus the number of times a source address was seen on this port that does not match any addresses secured for the port.
Late collisions	Number of times that a collision is detected on a particular interface later than 512 bit-times into the transmission of a packet.
Excessive deferrals	Number of frames for which transmission is deferred for an excessive period of time.
Jabber errors	Number of times the jabber function was invoked because a frame received from this port exceeded a certain time duration.

Figure 8.26 Detailed Port Statistics Report

```
Catalyst 1900 - Port 1 Statistics Report

Receive Statistics                    Transmit Statistics
- - - - - - - - - - - - - - - -       - - - - - - - - - - - - - - - - - -
Total good frames         0           Total frames              0
Total octets              0           Total octets              0
Broadcast/multicast frames 0          Broadcast/multicast frames 0
Broadcast/multicast octets 0          Broadcast/multicast octets 0
Good frames forwarded     0           Deferrals                 0
Frames filtered           0           Single collisions         0
Runt frames               0           Multiple collisions       0
No buffer discards        0           Excessive collisions      0
                                      Queue full discards       0


Errors:                               Errors:
  FCS errors              0             Late collisions          0
  Alignment errors        0             Excessive deferrals      0
  Giant frames            0             Jabber errors            0
  Address violations      0             Other transmit errors    0

Select [A] Port addressing, [C] Configure port,
       [N] Next port, [P] Previous port, [G] Goto port,
       [R] Reset port statistics, or [X] Exit to Main Menu:
```

8.6 VISUAL SWITCH MANAGERS

The VSM has six configuration management areas that lead to a combined total of eighteen browser screens: (1) Port, (2) System, (3) Security, (4) Device, (5) VLAN, and (6) Fault One feature of the VSM is that the device's status can be viewed by looking at the live image of it on the switch's home page. If a port is colored green, its status is Link Up, blue means No Link Status, and red indicates Link Faulty or Port Disabled (see Figure 8.27).

The VSM makes the distinction between a port and a link. A port is the physical connection where the cable is plugged in. A link is a logical connection taken place over that port to a port on some other device, which could be another switch, hub, router, server, or other device. A port could be operating fine, and at the same time the link running through it could be malfunctioning.

When you make changes to the switch, you can change the switch settings by entering information into fields, adding and removing list items, or selecting and deselecting check boxes. You must then click the Apply button to save your changes or click the Cancel button to discard all your unsaved changes and to return the previous settings to the page.

For more information on the VSM, see the following website:

Configuring and Monitoring from the VSM

> http://www.cisco.com/univercd/cc/td/doc/product/lan/28201900/1928v9x/19icg9x/19icweb.htm

Figure 8.27 A Visual Switch Manager

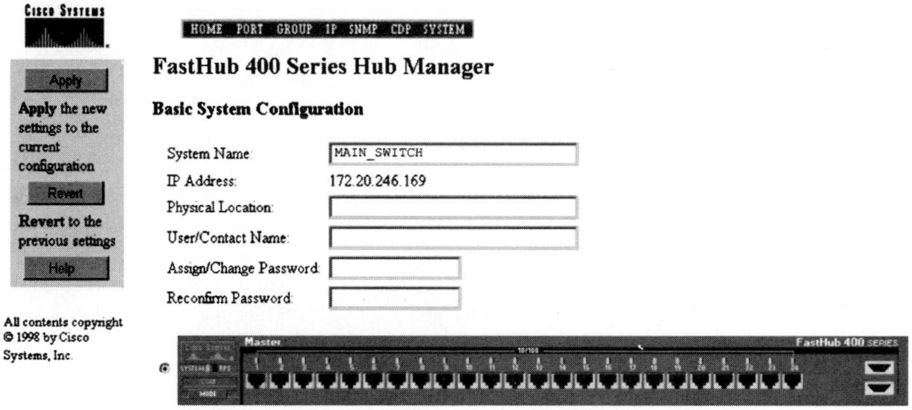

8.7 RESTORING OR UPGRADING THE CATALYST 1900 IOS

You can upgrade or restore the IOS on the Catalyst 1900 switches. The command to upgrade or restore the IOS to a 1900 switch is:

```
copy tftp://tftp_host_address/IOS_filename opcode
```

The configuration file for the Cisco Catalyst 1900 switch is called *nvram*. Therefore, the command to copy the file to a TFTP host is:

```
copy nvram tftp://tftp_host_address/configfile_name
```

To restore the copy of the nvram, you would use the following command:

```
copy tftp://tftp_host_address/configfile_name nvram
```

To delete the configuration file from the switch, execute the following command:

```
delete nvram
```

8.8 SWITCH CLUSTERING TECHNOLOGY

For some switches, Cisco includes its Cluster Management Suite (CMS), an embedded web application that lets enterprises use a single IP address to manage a cluster of switches (up to 16 switches). The new version of CMS offers wizards that automatically configure voice, video, and high-priority data ports; enhanced control over network adds, moves, and changes; improved LAN troubleshooting tools; and automated software upgrades without having to learn the CLI. In addition, it simplifies deployment of intelligent services such as IP routing, QoS, multicast, and security access control lists offered on Cisco Catalyst 3550 and 2950 Intelligent Ethernet Switches.

SUMMARY

1. Cisco has many different series of switches available, one of which will provide an appropriate type of switching to any network.
2. Micro Switches are low cost and simple to operate package switches that are not intelligent and do not have management features.
3. The Catalyst Switches are Cisco's main line of switched network solutions. They come in many series and models.
4. The rule for cabling Cisco devices is that you should use a straight-through cable when one and only one of the jacks is marked with an x. Use a crossover cable when both or neither of the end jacks is marked with an x.
5. The 15-pin AUI port is used for making connections to a Thick Wire (10Base5) Ethernet cable via a transceiver.
6. To configure and manage the switch using the CLI, you can connect the console port (located at the back of the switch) to a management station or modem with the supplied RJ-45 to RJ-45 rollover console cable and an appropriate adapter.
7. There are two levels of security available in accessing the switch, User Exec mode and Privileged Exec Mode.
8. Enter the Enable mode by using the `enable` command and then enter Global Configuration mode by using the `config t` command.

9. The Global Configuration mode allows you to configure most options of the Cisco router.
10. To view the current configuration, change into Enable mode and execute the `show running-config` (or `show run`) command from the # prompt. To show the IOS version on the switch, execute the `show version` command.
11. To show the IP configuration, execute the `show ip` command from the # prompt.
12. Port security is a way of stopping users from plugging a hub into their jack in their office or cubicle and adding a bunch of hosts without your knowledge.
13. The Catalyst 1900 switch only supports fragment-free and store-and-forward. To create a VLAN, switch to Global Configuration mode and use the following command: `vlan` `vlan#` `name` `name_of_vlan`.
14. The Catalyst 1900 switch only runs DISL trunking.
15. A Catalyst 1900 switch is configured by default to be a VTP sever, as are all switches.
16. You can upgrade or restore the IOS on the Catalyst 1900 switches.

QUESTIONS

1. Which of the following will be displayed if you issue the de? command while in Privileged Exec mode on a Cisco Catalyst 1900 switch? (Select the best choice.)
   a. common help
   b. all commands starting with "de"
   c. the parameters of the debug command
   d. the parameters of the delete command
2. To connect through the console port of the switch, you would use which type of cable?
   a. crossover cable
   b. straight-through cable
   c. rollover cable
   d. null-modem cable
3. Which command do you use on a Cisco switch to show the current configuration of the switch?
   a. show start   b. show int
   c. show version   d. show run
4. To show the interfaces available on a Cisco switch, you would use what command?
   a. show start   b. show int
   c. show run   d. show version
5. To change into Global Configuration mode, you would use what command?
   a. Execute the `enable` command followed by executing the `config t` command.
   b. Execute the `g config` command.
   c. Execute the `exit` command.
   d. Execute the `enable` command.
6. Which show command displays the DISL state and encapsulation type for Fast Ethernet ports?
   a. show vtp
   b. show vlan [vlan_ID]
   c. show trunk
   d. show vlan_membership
7. Which command can be used from the Privileged Exec mode to reset the VTP configuration revision number on a Cisco switch?
   a. Reset vtp
   b. reset vtp revision
   c. delete vtp
   d. set vtp revision 1
8. Which show command displays the VLAN name, status, and the member ports for a specific VLAN?
   a. show vtp
   b. show vlan [vlan_ID]
   c. show trunk
   d. show vlan-membership
9. Which command will create a VLAN with the ID number 0004 and assign the name HQLAN to this VLAN?
   a. SwitchName#vlan vlan0004 HQLAN
   b. SwitchName(config)#vlan0005 HQLAN
   c. SwitchName#(config-vlan)#vlan 0005 HQLAN
   d. Switch(config)#vlan 0005 name HQLAN
10. Which show command displays the VLAN assignment for all switch ports?
    a. show vtp
    b. show vlan [vlan_ID]
    c. show trunk
    d. show vlan-membership
11. When you execute a command at the prompt on a Cisco switch, you are using which interface?
    a. visual manager   b. CLI
    c. management console   d. DOS prompt

HANDS-ON EXERCISES

In Chapters 8, 13, and 15, you will build the network shown in the figure.

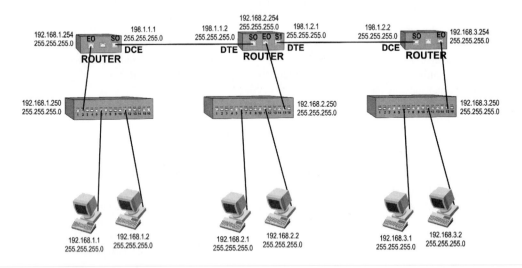

Exercise 1: Starting a Cisco Switch

1. Turn OFF your computer.
2. Make sure that the Cisco switch is OFF. There may be no ON/OFF button on the switch so you may need to disconnect the power.
3. Connect one end of the rollover cable to the console port on the switch. Connect the other end of the cable to the COM1 port on your PC. If you need to, you can connect to the COM2 port.
4. Turn on your computer.
5. Turn on the switch and watch the port lights blink as the switch powers up.
6. On the PC, click the Start button. Then select the Programs option, select the Accessories option, select the Communications option, and select the HyperTerminal program.
7. If it asks you to make HyperTerminal your default telnet program, click the Yes button.
8. When it asks you to enter a name for your Switch console connection, type Switch Console in the text box and click the OK button.
9. In the Connect To dialog box, select the appropriate COM port and click the OK button.
10. In the COM properties dialog box, set the following options and click the OK button:

    Bits per Second=9600
    Data Bits=8
    Parity=None
    Stop Bits=1
    Flow Control=Xon/Xoff

11. The Management Console should now be displayed.

    What is the model number for the switch?
    What is the Ethernet Address (layer 2 MAC address) of the switch?
    Is the switch running standard software or enterprise software?

12. Before beginning, enter the CLI and execute the following command to reset the switch:

    ```
    delete nvram
    ```

    Click Yes if it asks to reset the system with the factory defaults.
13. Unplug the power cable from the switch and plug it back in.
14. If necessary, reconnect with the HyperTerminal program.
15. Next, set the password. Depending on the switch, you will either enter the password option from the Main menu or you will have to enter the Console Settings option and modify the password. Set the Enable password to password and the privilege password to testword.
16. Next, specify the IP address, subnet mask, and default gateway. Depending on the switch, you will either enter IP configuration from the User Interface Menu or you would enter the User Interface Menu if you are not already there. Select the Network Management option and then the IP Configuration from the menus. Assign an IP address and subnet mask to the switch.
17. Connect the work station Ethernet cable (straight-through) to a port on the switch. Then from your Windows computer, use the ping command from the work station command prompt to test connectivity and IP configuration between the work station and switch by pinging the switch.
18. On the Windows computer, telnet to the switch. You should see the same menu as when you are connected via the console.
19. Start Internet Explorer. Type the http://*IP_address* you just assigned to the switch in the browser address area where you would normally type in the URL of a website. The Switch Management GUI should be displayed by the HTTP server in the switch.
20. Using the Switch Manager, enter a name for the switch.
21. Select the port where your work station is connected and click on it with the mouse. Scroll down the port table until you get to port 0/1. What is the current actual duplex mode?
22. Change the mode from half duplex to full duplex. The NIC in your work station may not support full duplex operation.
23. Check the port statistics for frames received and transmitted by clicking on the "Stats" button. Enter the number of packets below:

    Good Frames Received:
    Packets Transmitted:

24. Go back to the Main menu and select the System option. Change the switching mode to store-and-forward.

Exercise 2: Changing Operating Modes

1. Enter the command prompt of the switch.
2. To change to the privileged exec mode, execute the `enable` command.
3. To change to the global configuration mode, execute the `config t` command.
4. Use the `exit` command to return to the privileged exec mode.
5. Run the `show ip` command to display the IP configuration.
6. Execute the `show ver` command to display the version of the IOS.
7. Execute the `show run` command to display the current configuration commands. Use the space bar to browse to the next screen.
8. Execute the `sh int` command to show the interface statistics. Press the space bar to browse through the various interfaces on your switch. You can use [Ctrl-Z] to break out of this command.
9. Change back to Global Configuration mode.

10. Change to Interface mode for port 1 by executing the following command: `int ethernet 0/1`
11. Execute the `end` command.
12. Execute the `exit` command.

Exercise 3: Comparing a Switch and a Hub

Copying files from one computer to another by using a hub

1. Connect two computers to a single hub. Make sure that the link lights are ON and that two computers can ping each other.
2. On computer 1, you will need 200 MB of data files in a folder called Data. Share the Data folder so that the other computers can access it.
3. From the Network Neighborhood, have computer 2 access the Data share files on computer 1.
4. Time the copying to see how long it takes the files to copy to computer 2. While the files copy, notice the collision lights.
5. How long did it take to copy all of the files?
6. Delete the files on computer 2.

Copying files with several computers using a hub

7. Connect six computers to a single hub. Make sure that the link lights are ON and that all computers can ping all other computers.
8. On computers 1, 3, and 5, you will need 200 MB of data files in a folder called Data. Share the Data folder so that the other computers can access it.
9. From the Network Neighborhood, have computer 2 access the Data share files on computer 1, have computer 4 access the Data share files on computer 3, and have computer 6 access the Data share files on computer 5.
10. Time the copying to see how long it takes to copy the files to computers 2, 4 and 6. Be sure to start the copying at the same time. While the files copy, notice the collision lights.
11. How long did it take to copy all of the files?
12. Disconnect the six computers from the switch. Make sure that the link lights are ON and that all computers can ping all other computers.
13. Delete the files that you just copied onto computers 2, 4 and 6.

Copying files with several computers using a switch

14. Disconnect the computers from the hub and connect them to the switch. Make sure that the link lights are ON and that all computers can ping all other computers.
15. On computers 1, 3, and 5, you will need 200 MB of data files in a folder called Data. Share the Data folder so that the other computers can access it.
16. From the Network Neighborhood, have computer 2 access the Data share files on computer 1, have computer 4 access the Data share files on computer 3, and have computer 6 access the Data share files on computer 5.
17. Time the copying to see how long it takes the files to copy to computers 2, 4, and 6. Be sure to start the copying at the same time. While the files copy, notice the collision lights.
18. How long did it take to copy all of the files?
19. Disconnect the six computers from the switch. Make sure that the link lights are ON and that all computers can ping all other computers.
20. Delete the files that you just copied onto computers 2, 4, and 6.

Exercise 4: Configuring a VLAN

1. Have Windows computers connected to ports 1, 4, 5, 8, 9, and 12. Make sure that the computers can ping each other.
2. Enter the management console and select the VLAN menu.
3. Press [C] to configure a VLAN. How many VLANs can be configured on the switch?
4. Type [1] and then press [Enter] to choose VLAN 1.
5. Type [V] for VLAN name, type Engineering when prompted for the VLAN name, and then press [Enter]. Type [x] to exit. Which ports are assigned to the Engineering VLAN?
6. Type [C] to configure another VLAN. Type [2], and then press [Enter] to configure the second VLAN. Then create a Finance VLAN.
7. Type [M] to move ports away from the Engineering VLAN and into the Finance VLAN.
8. Type [4–8], press [Enter] to move ports 4 through 8, and then type [x] to exit.
9. Create a third VLAN with a name called Marketing and move ports 9–12 to it.
10. Exit to the previous menu and you should see all three configured VLANs.
11. Exit to the main menu.
12. Have the computer connected to port 1 ping the computer connected to port 4, have the computer connected to port 5 ping the computer connected to port 8, and have the computer connected to port 9 ping the computer connected to port 12.
13. Now have the computers try to ping the computers in the other VLANs.
14. Go back to the Main menu. Use the System menu to reset the factory defaults of the switch.

CHAPTER 9

WAN Technology

Topics Covered in this Chapter

Introduction

In Chapters 1 and 2, we briefly described a WAN and described routers. In this chapter, we look at Wide Area Network (WAN) technology used to link individual computers or entire networks. These connections are usually through telephone companies or some other common carrier. While LANs typically are multipoint connections, WANs typically are made of multiple point-to-point connections.

Objectives

- Identify the purpose, features, and functions of CSU/DSUs, modems, and ISDN adapters.
- Compare and contrast packet switching and circuit switching.
- List the characteristics, requirements, and appropriate situations for ISDN connection services.

- Identify the basic characteristics (speed, capacity, and media) for ISDN, Sonet, SDH, T1/E1, T3/E3, OCx, DSL, and cable modems.
- Given a scenario, troubleshoot the serial line.

9.1   WAN DEVICES

Typically, when talking about the various WAN connection devices, the devices can be divided into the following categories:

- Data terminal equipment
- Data circuit-terminating equipment

Data terminal equipment (DTE) devices are end systems that communicate across WANs. They are usually terminals, PCs, or network hosts that are located on the premises of individual subscribers.

Data circuit-terminating equipment (DCE) devices are special communication devices that provide the interface between the DTE and the network. Examples include modems and adapters. The purpose of the DCE is to provide clocking and switching services in a network and they actually transmit data through the WAN. The DCE controls data flowing to or from a computer. Therefore, the DCE device supplies the clock signal that paces the communications on the bus. Examples of DCEs are modems and multiplexers (see Figure 9.1).

Another term that is used often when discussing WAN connections is the **channel service unit/data service unit (CSU/DSU).** The DSU is a device that performs protective and diagnostic functions for a telecommunications line. The CSU is a device that connects a terminal to a digital line. Typically, the two devices are packaged as a single unit. You can think of it as a very high-powered and expensive modem.

Figure 9.1   An Example of DTEs and DCEs.

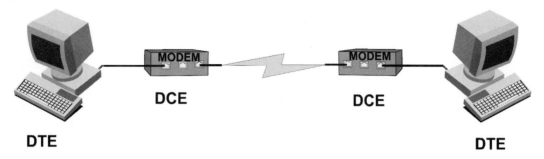

There are four types of WAN connections. They are:

- **Dedicated links**—Dedicated links are point-to-point connections, which are pre-established WAN communications paths from the customer premises equipment (CPE), through the DCE switch, to the CPE of the remote site. The advantage of dedicated links is that they are always available to communicate at any time with no set up procedures before transmitting data. Examples include T1 and T3 lines.
- **Circuit switching**—Circuit switching sets up a line like a phone call. No data transfers before the end-to-end connection is established. Examples include dial-up modems and ISDN lines.
- **Packet switching**—A WAN switching method that allows you to share bandwidth with other companies to save money. It operates by taking messages and dividing them into packets before they are sent. Each packet is then transmitted individually and can even follow different routes to its destination. Packet switching is good for bursty data transfers but is not as good for constant data transfer. Examples include Frame Relay and X.25.
- **Cell Relay**—A data transmission technology based on transmitting data in relatively small, fixed-size packets or cells. Each cell contains only basic path information that allows switching devices to route the cell quickly. An example is ATM.

See Table 9.1 for various WAN carrier technologies.

If you recall from Chapter 2, a **virtual circuit** is a logical circuit created to ensure reliable communications between two network devices. To provide this, it provides a bidirectional communication path from one device to another and it is uniquely identified by some type of identifier. A number of virtual circuits can be multiplexed into a single physical circuit for transmission across the network. This capability often can reduce the equipment and network complexity required for multiple device connections.

A virtual circuit can pass through any number of intermediate devices or switches located within the virtual circuit. In this case, the two hosts can communicate as though they have a dedicated connection even though the packets might actually travel very different routes before arriving at their destinations. While the path may vary, the computers neither know this nor do they need to.

Virtual networks are sometimes depicted as a cloud because the user does not worry about the path taken through the cloud. They are only worried about entering the cloud

Table 9.1 WAN Carrier Technologies

Carrier technology	Speed	Physical medium	Connection type	Comment
Plain Old Telephone Service (POTS)	Up to 56 Kbps	Twisted pair	Circuit switch	Used by home and small businesses
Asymmetrical Digital Subscriber Line Lite (ADSL Lite)	Up to 1.544 Mbps downstream Up to 512 Kbps upstream	2 twisted pair	Circuit switch	Used by home and small businesses
Asymmetrical Digital Subscriber Line (ADSL)	1.5–8 Mbps downstream Up to 1.544 Mbps upstream	2 twisted pair	Circuit switch	Used by small to medium businesses
High Bit-Rate Digital Subscriber Line (HDSL)	1.544 Mbps full duplex (T1) 2.048 Mbps full duplex (E1)	2 pair of twisted pair	Circuit switch	Used by small to medium businesses
DS0 Leased Line	64 Kbps	1 or 2 pair of twisted pair	Dedicated point-to-point	The base signal on a channel in the set of digital signal levels
Switched 56	56 Kbps	1 or 2 pair of UTP	Circuit switch	Used by home and small businesses
Switched 64	64 Kbps	1 or 2 pair of UTP	Circuit switch	Used by home and small businesses
Fractional T-1 Leased Line	64 Kbps–1.536 Mbps in 64 Kbps increments	1 or 2 pair of twisted pair	Dedicated point-to-point	Used by small to medium businesses
T-1 Leased Line (DS-1)	1.544 Mbps (24–64 Kbps channels)	2 pair UTP or UTP or optical fiber	Dedicated point-to-point	Used by medium to large businesses, ISP to connect to the Internet
T-3 Leased Line (DS-3)	44.736 Mbps	2 pair of UTP or optical fiber	Dedicated point-to-point	Used by large businesses, large ISP to connect to the Internet or as the backbone of the Internet
E-1	2.048 Mbps	Twisted pair, coaxial cable, or optical fiber		32-channel European equivalent of T-1
ISDN—BRI	64–128 Kbps	1 or 2 pair of UTP	Circuit switch	Used by home and small businesses

Continued

Table 9.1   Continued

Carrier technology	Speed	Physical medium	Connection type	Comment
ISDN—PRI	23–64 Kbps channels plus control channel up to 1.544 Mbps (T-1) or 2.048 (E-1)	2 pair of UTP	Circuit switch	Used by medium to large businesses
X.25	Up to 64 Kbps	1 or 2 twisted pair	Packet switch	Older technology still used in areas where newer technology is still not available.
Frame Relay	56 Kbps to 1.536 Mbps (using T-1) or 2.048 Mbps using E-1	1 or 2 twisted pair	Packet switch	Popular technology used mostly to connect LANs together.
FDDI/FDDI-2	100 Mbps/200 Mbps	Optical fiber	Packet switch	Large, wide-range LAN usually in a large company or a larger ISP
SDH/Sonet	51.84 Mbps and up	Optical fiber	Dedicated point-to-point	Used by ATM
SMDS	1.544 to 34 Mbps using T-1 and T-3 lines	1 or 2 twisted pair	Cell relay	Popular growing technology used mostly to connect LANs together. SMDS is the connectionless component of ATM.
ATM	Up to 622 Mbps	T-1, T-3, E-1, E-3, SDH and SONET	Cell relay	The fastest network connection to date
Cable Modems	500 Kbps to 1.5 Mbps or more	Coaxial cable	Leased point-to-point	Used by home and small businesses

and exiting the cloud. It acts as a direct connection even though it may not be directly connected (see Figure 9.2).

Virtual circuits can be either **permanent virtual circuits (PVCs)** or **temporary virtual circuits (TVCs)** (also known as **switched virtual circuits (SVCs)**). A PVC is a permanently-established virtual circuit that consists of one mode: data transfer mode. PVCs are used in situations in which data transfer between devices is constant. PVCs decrease the bandwidth use associated with the establishment and termination of virtual circuits, but increase costs due to constant virtual circuit availability. Of course, PVCs are

Figure 9.2   A Virtual Circuit Depicted as a Cloud

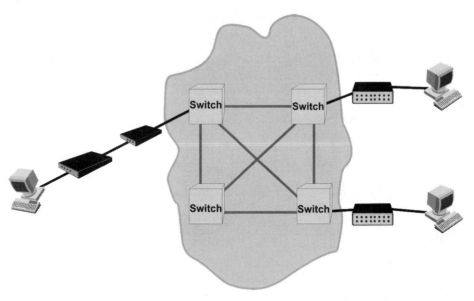

more efficient for connections between hosts that communicate frequently. PVCs play a central role in Frame Relay and X.25 networks.

SVCs are virtual circuits that are dynamically established on demand and terminated when transmission is complete. Communication over an SVC consists of three phases: (1) circuit establishment, (2) data transfer, and (3) circuit termination. The establishment phase involves creating the SVC between the source and destination devices. Data transfer involves transmitting data between the devices over the virtual circuit, and the circuit-termination phase involves tearing down the virtual circuit between the source and destination devices. SVCs are used in situations in which data transmission between devices is sporadic, largely because SVCs increase bandwidth used due to the circuit establishment and termination phases, but decrease the cost associated with constant virtual circuit availability.

When leasing a PVC or SVC end-to-end circuit, you will have to pay monthly whether you send data or not. If you choose not to lease the line but sign up with a network provider, the provider then bills you only for the amount of data packets you send and the distance that the packets travel. The cost will also be based on the technology used.

NOTE: There is often a minimum charge per call.

Two types of interfaces defined in packet switching and cell relay networks are (1) **user-network interfaces (UNI)** and (2) **network-node interfaces (NNI).** UNI describes the user's interface to the network, while NNI describes how different types of networks can be interconnected. Such interconnection may involve networks run by different operators, installed in different countries, or one private and one public frame-relay network (see Figure 9.3).

Figure 9.3 UNI and NNI Interfaces

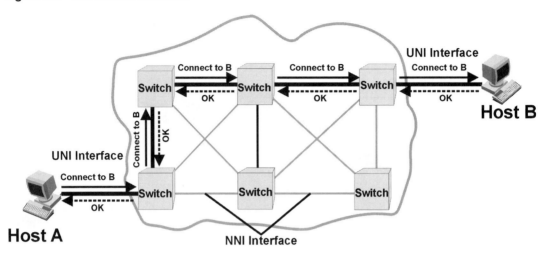

9.2 PSTNS

A **PSTN** is the international telephone system based on copper wires (UTP cabling) carrying analog voice data. The PSTN, also known as **POTS,** is the standard telephone service that most homes use. The PSTN is a huge network with multiple paths that link source and destination devices. PSTN uses circuit switching when you make a call. Therefore, the data is switched to a dedicated path throughout the conversation.

The original concept of the Bell system was a series of PSTN trunks connecting major U.S. cities. The PSTN network originally began with human operators sitting at a switchboard manually routing calls. Today, PSTN systems still use analog signals from the end node (phone) to the first switch. The switch then converts the analog signal to a digital signal and routes the call on to its destination. Because digital signals travel on fiber optic cabling, the signals are switched at high speeds. Once the call is received on the other end, the last switch in the loop converts the signal back to analog, and the call is initiated. The connection will stay active until the call is terminated (user hangs up). The active circuit enables you to hear the other person almost instantaneously.

The **subscriber loop** or **local loop** is the telephone line that runs from your home or office to the telephone company's CO or neighborhood switching station (often a small building with no windows). While its cable length can be as long as twenty miles, it is referred to as the **last mile**—not because of its length, but because it is the slow link in the telecommunications infrastructure as it carries analog signals on twisted pair cables. The point where the local loop ends at the customer's premises is called the **demarcation point (demarc).**

NOTE: Unless you have an agreement with the phone company, the phone company is only responsible from the CO to the demarc (see Figure 9.4).

Figure 9.4   A PSTN

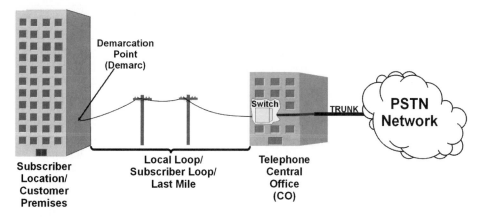

The standard home phone communicates over the local loop using analog signals. Therefore, when a PC needs to communicate over the local loop, it must use a modem to convert the PC's digital data to analog signals. Unfortunately, analog lines can only reach a maximum speed of 53 Kbps due to FCC regulations that restrict the power output. Unfortunately the speed is not guaranteed and is often not reached.

9.3   LEASED DIGITAL LINES

The **T-carrier system** was introduced by the Bell System in the US in the 1960s as the first successful system that converted analog voice signals to digital bit streams. While the T-carrier system was originally designed to carry voice calls between telephone company COs, today it is used to transfer voice, data, and video signals between different sites and to connect to the Internet.

9.3.1   T- and E-Carrier Systems

T-carrier and E-carrier systems are entire digital systems that consist of permanent dedicated point-to-point connections. These digital systems are based on 64-Kbps channels (DS0 channels), whereas each voice transmission is assigned a channel.

NOTE: DS stands for digital signal.

Once digitized, voice and/or data signals from many sources can be combined (i.e., multiplexed) and transmitted over a single link. This process is made possible by TDM. TDM divides the link into discrete 64 Kbps timeslots. An identical number of DS0 signals (representing separate voice and/or data calls) is assigned to each timeslot for transmission within the link.

In North America and Japan, you would typically find a T-1 line that has twenty-four 64 Kbps-channels for a bandwidth of 1.544 Mbps and T-3 line that has 672 64 Kbps-channels

Table 9.2 Digital Carrier Systems

Digital signal designator	T-Carrier	E-Carrier	J-Carrier	Data Rate	DS0 multiple
DS0	T-0	E-0	J-0	64 Kbps	1
DS1	T-1	—	J-1	1.544 Mbps	24
—	—	E-1	—	2.048 Mbps	32
DS1C	—	—	J-1C	3.152 Mbps	48
DS2	T-2	—	J-2	6.312 Mbps	96
—	—	E-2	—	8.448 Mbps	128
—	—	—	J-3	32.064 Mbps	480
-	—	E-3	—	34.368 Mbps	512
DS3	T-3	—	—	44.736 Mbps	672
—	—	—	J-3C	97.728 Mbps	1,440
—	—	E-4	—	139.264 Mbps	2,048
DS4/NA	—	—	—	139.264 Mbps	2,176
DS4	—	—	—	274.176 Mbps	4,032
—	—	—	J-4	397.200 Mbps	5,760
—	—	E-5	—	565.148 Mbps	8,192

for a bandwidth of 44.736 Mbps. In Europe, you will find E-1 lines with thirty-two 64-Kbps channels for a bandwidth of 2.048 Mbps and an E-3 line with 512 64-Kbps channels for a bandwidth of 34.368 Mbps. T-1 lines are a popular leased line option for businesses connecting to the Internet and for ISPs connecting to the Internet backbone. T-3 connections make up the Internet backbone and are used by larger ISPs to connect to the backbone (see Table 9.2).

If your company is not ready for a full T-1 line, your company can lease a fractional T-1 line where your company uses only a portion of the twenty-four channels. Because the hardware already exists to use a full T-1 line, you just have to call the carrier to increase the number of channels. Therefore, a fractional T-1 line leaves room for growth.

The T-carrier system is a bipolar, framed format, time division digital communication system. T-1 lines will usually use one of two encoding methods, Alternate Mark Inversion (AMI) and bipolar 8-zero substitution (B8ZS).

AMI bipolar encoding uses no voltage to indicate a digital 0 and uses alternating positive and negative voltages to represent a digital 1. The reason that unipolar encoding (a positive voltage indicates a digital 1 and no voltage indicates a digital 0) wasn't used is because there is no "return to 0," which can lead to a loss of synchronization of the signal as the system loses track of the number of many sequential digital 1s. Therefore, the bipolar signal alternates between positive voltage and negative voltage and adds redundancy to the timing of the circuit (see Figure 9.5).

The trouble with this scheme is that when a device receives a long string of 0s, it loses bit time synchronization. The solution originally used to solve this problem was to convert some 0s to 1s, following a set of rules that require:

- no more than 15 consecutive 0s
- At least N 1s in every time window of 8 $N + A$ bit time slots, where N can equal 1 through 23. (For example, if $N = 1$, then there must be a 1 bit in every window of 16 bits.)

Figure 9.5 AMI Bipolar Encoding

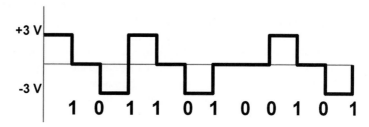

Figure 9.6 B8ZS Encoding Used by T-1 Lines

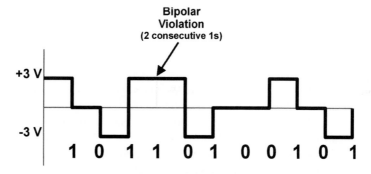

No harm is done by inserting an occasional 1 into a string of 0s in a voice call. However, it is not acceptable to change payload 0s to 1s on a leased line used for data communications. Network service providers solve this problem by restricting the user data payload to the first 7 bits of each time slot byte and coding a 1 in the last bit. This reduces the capacity of a 64 Kbps channel to 56 Kbps. For a full T-1 line, this means that you lose 192 Kbps of throughput. By using B8ZS coding instead of AMI coding, you would reclaim the lost data throughput.

Today, American T-1 lines use B8ZS. B8ZS is like AMI, but to avoid the loss of synchronization with a large number of sequential zeros, B8ZS replaces eight consecutive zeros with a fictional word. To differentiate between a real word and a fictional one, the hardware creates a bipolar violation where it will send two consecutive positive pulses or two consecutive negative pulses (see Figure 9.6).

A T-3 system uses B3ZS, which works the same as B8ZS but modifies any group of three zeros instead of eight. E-carrier systems use High Density Bipolar 3 (HDB3), which replaces a 4 Zero bit pattern with two zeros followed by a bipolar violation.

A T-1 line uses a D4 framing format, where a frame bit prefixes 24 bytes of data, each from one of the 24 channels. The framing bit follows a special 12-bit pattern, called the frame alignment signal. After every 12 frames, the signal repeats, allowing the hardware on either side of the connection to signal changes in line status. This group of 12 D4 frames is called a superframe.

When connecting multiple remote locations to a central site through a T-1 line, each line would have its own dedicated CSU/DSU device and physical router port. Another method is to use a channelized T-1 line, which would have one CSU/DSU (typically built into the router) to supply each of the 24 individual channels with one connection at the CO. These connections are terminated in individual circuits in different geographic locations.

If the T-1 connects directly to the router, the T-1 controller in the router must be configured for ESF framing and B8ZS line code. Once this is done, there should be twenty-four 64-Kbps channels that the telephone company can spread out to up to twenty-four locations, typically using a piece of equipment called a Digital Access Cross Connect (DACC). At the central site router, the twenty-four channels appear as virtual interfaces on the one physical line; each virtual interface can receive its own configuration as if it were a separate physical connection.

The T-3 uses a framing called M13, which uses a 4760-bit frame, compared with a 193-bit D4 frame. Of this, fifty-six bits are used for frame alignment, error correction, and network monitoring.

9.3.2   T-Carrier Hardware

The CO buildings contain the computerized telephone switching equipment (sometimes referred to as nodes) for a predesignated geographical area and they will be cross-linked and redundantly connected with other CO buildings. Depending on your location in the world, a telephone system node may contain one or more of the following telephone switching systems as shown in Table 9.3.

While analog signals can travel up to 18,000 feet from the subscriber to the CO or switching station, T-1 lines require cleaner lines for the faster speeds. Therefore, repeaters are placed about every 6000 feet. In addition, repeaters are located within 3000 feet of the central office and the customer premises to avoid crosstalk problems when the signal is carried into the building wiring.

Traditionally, T-1 systems use two UTP copper wires to provide full duplex capability (one pair to receive and one pair to send). Today, the T-carrier system can also use coaxial cable, optical fiber, digital microwave, and other media (see Table 9.4). Of these, the twisted pair (normal telephone wire) is the most widely spread form of transmission.

Cable runs from the service provider switch to the demarc. You are responsible for repairing problems on your side of the demarc, and the service provider is responsible for

Table 9.3   Telephone System Switches

Switch	Description
Basic-NET3	Basic rate switches for Great Britain and Europe
Basic-5ESS	AT&T basic rate switches
Basic DMS100	NT DMS-100 basic rate switches
VN2	French VN2 ISDN switches
VN3	French VN3 ISDN switches
NTT	Japanese NTT ISDN switches
Basic-1TR6	German 1TR6 ISDN switches
Basic-NI1	National ISDN-1 switches
Basic-TS013	Australian TS013 switches

Table 9.4   Different Media Used in T-carrier Systems

Media	T-carrier capacity
Twisted pair	Up to 1 T-1 circuit
Coaxial cable	Up to 4 T-1 circuits
Microwave	Up to 8 T-3 circuits
Fiber optics	Up to 24 T-3 circuits

Table 9.5   RJ-48X Pinout

Pin number	Usage
1	RX ring
2	RX tip
3	Grounding
4	TX ring
5	TX tip
6	Grounding
7	Unused
8	Unused

anything beyond the demarc. Frequently, the demarc is the service provider's Network Interface Unit (NIU), nicknamed a smart jack, which performs a variety of network maintenance functions and makes it much easier for the service provider to manage the network remotely.

The smart jack is located with other telephone equipment at your building and is placed where it is convenient for the architect and the service provider. Unfortunately, its placement may be far away from the server room or network wiring room that contains your CSU/DSU. In these situations, you may need to add additional wiring from the demarc to the CSU/DSU location. This is called an extended demarc.

To combat crosstalk, the lines from the demarc to the extended demarc often use individually shielded twisted pair (ISTP) cable, which wraps each pair of wires in a foil shield, especially if the distance is over 1000 feet. It also adds drain wires to help terminate the shields. The shielding and drain wires will make the cable cost more than standard UTP cabling and it is more complicated to work with because the shield foil must be peeled back and the drain wires must be terminated properly.

The NIC that you connect the CSU/DSU to follows the RJ-48X standard in which the RJ-48X jack contains shorting bars (see Table 9.5). The shorting bars automatically loop the line back if the cable is unplugged from the jack. The cable that attaches from the CSU/DSU is done with a V.35 DTE cable.

The CSU/DSU does the following:

- Terminates the line from the telecommunications networks
- Places signals on the line and controls the strengths of the transmission signal
- Supports loopback tests

- Provides timing or synchronizes with timing received on the line
- Frames the signal for T-1
- Optionally applies an algorithm that scrambles a signal. A signal is scrambled to improve the density of 0s and 1s.

By law, all T-1s require that a CSU be connected between your DTE and the T-1 line to act as a surge protector and to monitor the line. Some routers have built-in CSU/DSUs.

In some situations, you may need a multiplexer. A multiplexer is used to split the circuit into the various channels and some can also provide PCM encoding for analog devices such as an analog phone.

> *NOTE:* Remember that most business systems use digital phone systems. The router can connect one or more Ethernet LANs to a WAN by providing one or more RJ-45 connections. In addition, it will include one or more serial connections for CSU/DSUs or will include a built-in CSU/DSU (see Figure 9.7).

A variety of equipment is found at the ends of T-1 lines. D4 channel banks are a traditional form of a multiplexer that converts ordinary telephone wires to 64 Kbps channels for multiplexing onto a DS1. Newer D4 banks offer a wide variety of channel plug-ins to handle DDS style circuits, private line circuits, and even ISDN. M13 multiplexes are a traditional higher-order multiplexer for T-1s. These units take up to 28 DS1s and multiplex them into a T-3.

9.3.3   CSU/DSU Lights

The CSU/DSU has a series of lights and a switch that is used to control the loopback test mode (see Table 9.6). When the incoming signal is lost, a CSU/DSU transmits the

Figure 9.7   A Multiplexer on a T-1 Line

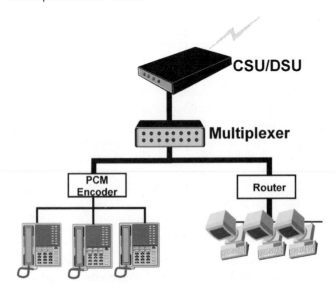

Table 9.6   CSU/DSU Indicator Lights

Indicator	Common labels	Meaning
Clear to send	CTS, CS	The CSU/DSU is ready to receive data
Request to send	RTS, RS	The DTE is ready to send data
Carrier detect	DCD, CD	The CSU/DSU is generating a carrier signal
Send data	TX, TXD, SD	The CSU/DSU is transmitting pulses to the service provider network
Receive data	RX, RXD, RD	The CSU/DSU is receiving pulses from the service provider network
Loss of signal	LOS	When no pulses arrive within 100 to 250 bit times, LOS is declared. Under normal conditions, at least a few pulses would be present in that interval.
Out of frame	OOF	The CSU/DSU triggers this when framing bits are in error and clears it when frame synchronization is regained.
Loss of frame (red alarm)	LOF	The CSU/DSU asserts this when OOF has persisted continuously for 2.5 seconds. This alarm is usually cleared when frame synchronization has been obtained for at least one second, but some CO hardware may not clear the alarm for much longer (15 seconds or more).
Keepalive transmission	KA	When framing is lost, the CSU/DSU transmits a KA signal to other network components.
Remote alarm indication (yellow alarm)	RAI	The remote end is reporting a loss of signal.

RAI/yellow alarm signal in the opposite direction. If equipped, the local CSU/DSU may then light up the appropriate indicator to show that it is receiving the RAI/yellow alarm signal.

Transmission of the RAI/yellow alarm signal depends on having a signal that is correctly in-frame in the outbound direction. To the receiver, RAI/yellow indicates a potential problem with the outgoing path, but its reception indicates that the incoming path is functioning normally. In simple terms, it is a report from the remote end that nothing appears to be transmitted on the circuit.

When some condition prevents a T-1 component from transmitting data, it transmits an unframed all-ones keepalive (KA) signal, which is also called the alarm indication signal (AIS). Using all 1s helps to keep the timing in the network synchronized. A T-1 generates AISs for two main reasons. The first is to inform other network equipment of the fault. For example, if one of the repeaters detect a fault or is placed in loopback mode, it transmits a KA signal in the other direction. If the CSU/DSU is receiving a KA signal, call the service provider to report the problem. When an AIS is coming in from the service provider, it typically means that some piece of equipment along the circuit has not been configured, connected, or turned on. It may also mean the local smart jack is in loopback.

9.3.4   Point-to-Point Leased Lines

WAN protocols used on point-to-point serial links provide the basic function of delivery of data across that one link. When configuring these types of links, you will need to understand and configure a variety of protocols used on point-to-point links, including Link Access Protocol Balanced (LAPB), High-Level Data Link Control (HDLC), and Point-to-Point Protocol (PPP). Each of these WAN protocols has the following functions in common:

- LAPB, HDLC, and PPP provide for delivery of data across a single point-to-point serial link.
- LAPB, HDLC, and PPP deliver data on synchronous serial links. PPP supports asynchronous functions as well.

When a signal is synchronous, it means that a signal occurs at regular intervals. The opposite of synchronous is asynchronous. When one device communicates with another device via a synchronous signal, the two devices must agree on a certain speed. Because it is very expensive to build devices that can truly operate at exactly the same speed, the devices adjust their rates to match a clock source. Synchronous links, rather than asynchronous links, are typically used between routers.

Unlike asynchronous links, in which no bits are sent during idle times, synchronous data links define idle frames so that clocks can be adjusted on the receiving end. In other words, they indirectly maintain synchronization. Protocols used between routers typically are synchronous signals

9.4   CIRCUIT SWITCHED LINES

As you see from the previous information, digital lines are much faster than analog lines. The disadvantages of leased digital lines is that they come with a higher price tag and they are limiting as point-to-point connections. If you had multiple sites, you would have to put several lines connecting one site to all the other sites.

The advantage of POTS is its circuit switching ability, it has multiple paths linking many devices together. When one device needs to communicate with another device, a circuit consisting of a dedicated path is established. When the conversation is done, the connection is terminated. This circuit is established on demand. Circuit switch technology can be referred to as **dial-up technology.**

If you can combine the best features of both systems, you would basically have a switched digital technology. Examples of switched digital technology is switched 56, switched 64, and ISDN.

9.4.1   Switched 56 and 64 Technology

While T-Carrier system lines are permanent leased lines, switched 56 and **switched 64** lines are digitally switched or dial-up lines that provide a single digital channel for dependable data connectivity. While it supports sporadic high-speed applications, it is typically cheaper than having a dedicated DS0 line and the cost of the termination equipment is cheaper.

The 56 Kbps value is because the **switched 56** technology is based on the DS0 64 Kbps technology. To avoid a loss of synchronization with many consecutive 0s, it uses pulse stuffing where every eighth bit is taken out of the signal and forced to be a pulse.

9.4.2   Integrated Services Digital Networks

Integrated Services Digital Networks (ISDNs) are the planned replacement for POTS so that they can provide voice and data communications worldwide using circuit switching while using the same wiring that is currently being used in homes and businesses. Because ISDN is a digital signal from end to end, it is faster and much more dependable and has no line noise. ISDN has the ability to deliver multiple simultaneous connections in any combination of data, voice, video, or fax, over a single line and allows for multiple devices to be attached to the line.

The ISDN network uses two types of channels: (1) a B channel and (2) a D channel. The **bearer channels (B channels)** transfer data at a bandwidth of 64 Kbps for each channel. The **Data channels (D channels)** use a communications language called DSS1 for administrative signaling, such as to instruct the carrier to set up or terminate a B-channel call, to ensure that a B-channel is available to receive a call, or to provide signaling information for features such as caller identification. Because the D channel is always connected to the ISDN network, the call set up time is greatly reduced to 1 to 2 seconds (versus 10 to 40 using an analog modem) as it establishes a circuit.

> *NOTE:* The bandwidths listed here are the uncompressed speeds of the ISDN connections. The compressed bandwidth has a current maximum transmission speed of four times the uncompressed speed. You will probably see a much lower speed, as much of the data flowing across the network is already compressed.

Today, there are several well-defined standards used, including the **Basic Rate Interface (BRI)** and **Primary Rate Interface (PRI).** BRI defines digital communication lines consisting of three independent channels: two Bearer (or B) channels, each carrying 64 Kilobytes per second; and one Data (or D) channel carrying 16 Kilobits per second. For this reason, the ISDN BRI is often referred to as **2B+D.** BRIs were designed to enable customers to use the existing wiring in homes or businesses. This provides a low-cost solution for customers and is why it is the most basic type of service today intended for small business or home use.

H channels are used to specify a number of B channels. The following list shows the implementations:

- **H0**—384 Kbps (6 B channels)
- **H10**—1472 Kbps (23 B channels)
- **H11**—1536 Kbps (24 B channels)
- **H12**—1920 Kbps (30 B channels)—Europe

In BRI, ISDN devices use two binary, one quaternary (2B1Q) encoding along with TDM to create the 2B+D basic ISDN channels. The 2B1Q means that the input voltage level can be one of 4 distinct levels. Each level is called a quaternary (see Figure 9.8). Each quaternary represents two data bits, because there are four possible ways to represent two bits. Therefore two bits are carried per baud (see Table 9.7).

PRI is a higher-level network interface that operates across a leased T-1 or E-1 line in North America and Japan. It is defined at the rate of 1.544 Mbps per second on a T-1 line, which consists of twenty-three B channels, each at 64 Kbps, and one 64 Kbps D channel for signaling. These B channels can interconnect with the BRI, or when carrying services

Figure 9.8 TB1Q Used by BRI ISDN

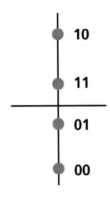

Table 9.7 Quaternaries

Bits	Quaternary symbol	Voltage level
1 1	+1	+0.833
1 0	+3	+2.5
0 1	−1	−0.833
0 0	−3	−2.5

to any POTS line. Therefore, it can provide Remote Access Service (RAS) to your network, which would enable twenty-three dial-up access lines that can be used by remote works to dial into the local network.

NOTE: Some switches limit the B channels to 56 Kbps.

European countries support a different kind of ISDN standard for PRI that consists of thirty B channels and one 64 Kbps D channel for a total of 1984 Kbps.

NOTE: A technology known as Non-Facility Associated Signaling (NFAS) is available to enable you to support multiple PRI lines with one 64 Kbps D channel.

An ISDN PRI line can have separate phone numbers assigned to each of the twenty-three B channels, or it can be terminated in a RJ-45 connector and directly connected to an ISDN PRI interface on a router. Together, these two features simplify the deployment of dial-up RAS connections by eliminating multiple phone lines, modems, and connecting cables.

NOTE: Generally, ISDN PRI is priced so that if more than eight BRIs are required, a single PRI is more cost-effective.

9.4.3   HDLC and PPP

As introduced in Chapter 3, as part of the PPP protocol, HDLC is a popular ISO-standard, bit-oriented data link layer protocol that encapsulates data during transmission. It specifies an encapsulation method for data on synchronous serial data links using frame characters and checksums.

NOTE: Remember that the HDLC does not perform authentication.

HDLC is the basis of a family of related protocols including:

- **Link Access procedure on the D-channel (LAPD)**—Used with ISDN.
- **Link Access Protocol Balanced (LAPB)**—Used with X.25.
- **Link Access Procedures to Frame-Mode Bearer (LAPF)**—Used with frame relay.
- **Point-to-Point Protocol (PPP)**—Used for general data communications across WANs.

HDLC is the default encapsulation used by Cisco routers over synchronous serial links. Unfortunately, vendors' HDLC implementations, including Cisco's implementation, is proprietary. Therefore, if you have a Cisco router that needs to communicate with another type of router such as a Bay router, you cannot use the Cisco HDLC. Instead, you will have to use PPP. PPP protocol is a data link protocol that can be used over either asynchronous serial (dial-up) or synchronous (ISDN) media.

HDLC supports four different transfer modes:

- **Normal Response Mode (NRM)**—Allows a secondary device to communicate with a primary device, but only when the primary device initiates the request.
- **Asynchronous Response Mode (ARM)**—Allows either the primary or the secondary devices to initiate communications.
- **Asynchronous Balance Mode (ABM)**—Allows a device to work in what is called combined mode, which means it can work as either a primary or secondary device.
- **Link Access Procedure, Balance (LAPB)**—Is an extension of the ABM transfer mode, but allows circuit establishment with both DTE and DCE.

9.4.4 ISDN Protocols

ISDN protocols can be divided into three groups, which are designated by the letters E, I, and Q in their first letter (see Tables 9.8 and 9.9). A tool to help you remember the specifications and layers is that the second digit in the Q-series matches the OSI layer. For example, in ITU-T Q.920, the second digit, 2, corresponds to OSI layer 2. In the I-series, the second digit of the specification numbers is two more than the corresponding OSI layer. For example, I.430, with the second digit of value 3, defines OSI layer 1 equivalent functions.

Table 9.8 ISDN Protocol Groups

Issue	Protocols	Key examples
Supports ISDN on the PSTN	E-series	E.163: international telephone numbering plan E.164: international ISDN addressing
ISDN concepts, aspects, and Interfaces	I-series	I.100 series: concepts, structures, terminology I.400 series: UNI
Switching and signaling	Q-series	Q.921: LAPD Q.931: ISDN network layer

Table 9.9   Some ISDN I-Series and Q-Series with an OSI Layer Comparison

Layer, as compared with OSI	I-series equivalent	Q-series specification	General purpose
1	ITU-T I.430 ITU-T I.431		Defines connectors, encoding, framing, and reference points
2	ITU-T I.440 ITU-T I.4411	ITU-T Q.920 ITU-T Q.921	Defines the LAPD protocol used on the D channel to encapsulate signaling requests
3	ITU-T I.450 ITU-T I.451	ITU-T Q.930 ITU-T Q.931	Defines signaling messages—for example, call setup and takedown messages

9.4.5   ISDN Equipment

To use BRI services, you must subscribe to ISDN services through a local telephone company or provider. By default, you must be within 18,000 feet (about 3.4 miles) of the telephone company CO. Repeater devices are available for ISDN service to extend this distance, but these devices can be very expensive. The various ISDN equipment and interfaces are shown in Table 9.10 (see Figure 9.9).

Accessing ISDN with routers means that you will need to purchase either a router with a built-in NT1 or an ISDN modem (called a TA). So either your router will need to have a BRI interface or you can use one of your router's serial interfaces connected with an ISDN modem. A router with a BRI interface is called a TE1 (terminal equipment type 1), and one that requires a TA is called a TE2 (terminal equipment type 2).

The **Directory number (DN)** is the ten-digit phone number that the telephone company assigns to any analog line. A **Service Profile Identifier (SPID)** includes the DN and additional identifier used to identify the ISDN device to the telephone network. However, depending on which kind of switch you are served from and how you are going to use the ISDN service, you may not need a SPID or you may need a SPID for each B-channel (each device). Unlike an analog line, a single DN can be used for multiple channels or devices or up to eight DNs can be assigned to one device. Therefore, a BRI can support up to 64 SPIDs. Most standard BRI installations include only two directory numbers, one for each B channel.

> *NOTE:* The second part of the SPID configuration is the local dial number for that SPID. The SPID is optional, but some switches need to have those set on the router in order to use both B channels simultaneously.

9.4.6   Combining Channels

Several B channels can be combined into a higher bandwidth channel so that it can be used for videoconferencing or some other high bandwidth application. The combining of channels can be done with H-channels or inverse multiplexing.

Table 9.10   ISDN Equipment and Interfaces

Equipment and interface types	Descriptions:
U interface	The U interface is the two-wire interface between the customer premise and the CO. In North America, the customer is responsible for supplying all the equipment from the U interface forward.
NT1	At the customer premise, the ISDN line is terminated by an NT1 at the demarcation (boundary between the customer premise and the phone company's network). It converts the physical wiring interface delivered by the telephone company to the wiring interface needed by your ISDN equipment and provides a testing point for troubleshooting. The NT1 interface combines the B channels and the D channel into a single bit stream at the physical level and is also capable of supporting more than one device attached to an ISDN line, sometimes referred to as a multidrop configuration.
S/T interface	The S/T interface is the interface between the NT1 and the ISDN networking equipment, which can support up to seven devices. To allow full duplex interface, the S/T interface uses two pairs of wires. One pair is to receive data and the other pair is to transmit data.
TE1	Terminal Equipment Type 1 (TE1) devices are those that are manufactured from the outset to be completely ISDN compatible. These are ISDN phones, integrated video devices, etc.
R interface	The R reference point provides a non-ISDN interface between equipment that is not ISDN compatible with the rest of the ISDN network.
TA	Terminal adapters allow nonnative ISDN devices (TE2) such as PCs to connect to the S interface so that they may communicate over the ISDN network.
TE2	Terminal Equipment Type 2 (TE2) are non-ISDN compatible equipment. Therefore they require a terminal adapter (TA) to provide ISDN functionality to the rest of the network. Examples of TE2 are personal computers or 3270 terminals.

An H channel is a special, high-speed clear channel. H channels, designed primarily for full-motion color video, are not yet in common use. There are currently three kinds of H channels:

- **H0**—384 Kbps, made up of six 64 Kbps channels
- **H11**—1536 Kbps, made up of twenty-four 64 Kbps channels
- **H12**—1920 Kbps, made up of thirty 64 Kbps channels

Not all telecommunications providers support H0 channels. Therefore, a user can obtain aggregated bandwidth by using devices called inverse multiplexers. While multiplexers combine several channels into a single high-bandwidth channel, inverse multiplexers enable several low-speed channels to be given the appearance of a single high-bandwidth channel. To do this, a pair of inverse multiplexers has to coordinate their actions to deliver data in the same order in which it was sent. The multiplexer may be a separate device, or it might be implemented by a communications card installed in a router, PBX, or computer.

NOTE: An inverse multiplexer may combine multiple ISDN channels that traverse a single line, or may combine transmissions that are carried across several separate lines.

Figure 9.9 ISDN Network

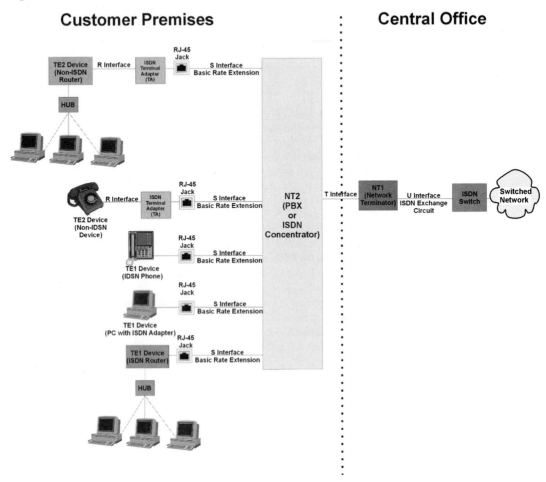

Until recently, there were no standards for inverse multiplexing. Vendors built proprietary products, and the only way to be sure that a pair of inverse multiplexers could work together was to buy compatible models from the same vendor. However, two inverse multiplexing standards recently have been proposed.

The first standard is called BONDING, which stands for Bandwidth ON Demand Interoperability Group. BONDING is a solution designed for a digital dial-up environment. It enables communicating devices to turn multiple digital calls into a single, high-bandwidth communications link.

BONDING does have some drawbacks. A subscriber must invest in conforming inverse multiplexer devices or add special interface cards to endpoint devices. Once a bandwidth level has been selected for a connection, it cannot be changed during the lifetime of a connection. All of the channels must be maintained.

But for some customers, this is exactly what they want. BONDING can provide constant bandwidth that is needed for a videoconference. It is a simple hardware-based solution. A BONDING inverse multiplexer is configured with the telephone number of an inverse multiplexer at a remote site. When a call is made to the remote device, it sends back a list of other numbers that can be called. The originating multiplexer calls as many members as are needed. If the circuits are set up with different bandwidths and different delay characteristics, the pair of multiplexers performs a training procedure that discovers the channel delays and establishes the order of transmission.

The other standard is the PPP Multilink Protocol, which comes from the Internet Engineering Task Force (IETF) committee. PPP Multilink Protocol is designed for PPP based data transmissions. The IETF solution consists of a set of extensions to PPP, including the:

- **PPP multilink protocol (MP)**—Supports dynamic bandwidth allocation, which means that physical links can be added or removed from the bundle as needed.
- **Bandwidth allocation protocol (BAP)**—A PPP control protocol that is used on an MP connection to dynamically manage links so that it can adapt to changing conditions by adding extra links when needed or terminating extra links when unneeded.
- **Bandwidth allocation control protocol (BACP)**—A PPP NCP that negotiates a single option: the election of a favored peer. If both peers of an MP and BAP-enabled connection send BAP Call-Request or BAP Link-Drop-Query-Request messages at the same time, the favored peer is the peer whose requests are implemented.

IETF protocols have several advantages. They are free, and can be implemented via software upgrade to a computer or router. They can be used across any kind of WAN, and can combine different types of wide area connections. For example, ISDN channels could be combined with one or more analog dial-ups, or an overloaded frame relay circuit could be enhanced with ISDN channels. On the negative side, the solution is fairly complicated to configure and troubleshoot.

9.4.7   Dial-On-Demand Routing

Dial-On-Demand Routing (DDR) is used to allow two or more routers to dial an ISDN dial-up connection on an as-needed basis. This makes a remote site appear to an internetwork as if it had a direct full-time router connection. DDR brings significant phone-line savings for small offices by letting them connect through dial-up lines instead of costly lines. It's important to get a DDR router's configuration right so that network overhead traffic doesn't tie up phone lines.

9.4.8   Always On/Dynamic ISDN

Always On/Dynamic ISDN (AO/DI) is a networking application that uses the 16 Kbps ISDN D-channel X-25 packet service to maintain an "always on" connection between an ISDN end-user and an ISP. Low bandwidth requirements, such as sending and receiving simple e-mail, news feeds, automated data collection, credit card verification, etc., can be met by using this constant virtual connection, which accommodates speeds up to 9.6 Kbps. The rest of the 16 Kbps D-channel continues to be used for call set up and tear-down signaling.

When additional bandwidth is necessary, for example to download a graphics intensive file from the Internet, AO/DI automatically adds circuit-switched B channels of 64 Kbps each, for a total of 128 Kbps speed when both B-channels are in use. When the additional bandwidth is no longer required, one or both B channels are dropped, leaving the D-channel connection in place. Adding and tearing down the B channels is determined by the BACP. Because the D-Channel is an always-available, connectionless, packet-oriented link between the subscriber and the central office, it is possible to offer an always-available service based on it.

9.5   DIGITAL SUBSCRIBER LINE

Digital Subscriber Line (DSL) is a special communication line that uses sophisticated modulation technology to maximize the amount of data that can be sent over plain twisted pair copper wiring, which already carries phone service to subscriber homes. It was originally aimed to transmit video signals to compete against the cable companies, but soon found use as a high-speed data connection with the explosion of the Internet. DSL is sometimes expressed as xDSL, because there are various kinds of DSL technologies including ADSL, R-DSL, HDSL, SDSL, and VDSL (see Table 9.11).

9.5.1   DSL Technology

The best thing about DSL technologies is their ability to transport large amounts of information across existing copper telephone lines. This is possible because DSL modems leverage signal processing techniques that insert and extract more digital data onto analog lines. The key is modulation, a process in which one signal modifies the property of another.

In the case of digital subscriber lines, the modulating message signal from a sending modem alters the high-frequency carrier signal so that a composite wave, called a modulated wave, is formed. Because this high-frequency carrier signal can be modified, a large digital data payload can be carried in the modulated wave over greater distances than on ordinary copper pairs. When the transmission reaches its destination, the modulating message signal is recovered, or demodulated, by the receiving modem.

There are many ways to alter the high-frequency carrier signal that results in a modulated wave. For ADSL, there are two competing modulation schemes: (1) carrierless amplitude phase (CAP) modulation and (2) discrete multitone (DMT) modulation. CAP and DMT use the same fundamental modulation technique–QAM—but apply it in different ways.

QAM, a bandwidth conservation process routinely used in modems, enables two digital carrier signals to occupy the same transmission bandwidth. With QAM, two independent message signals are used to modulate two carrier signals that have identical frequencies but differ in amplitude and phase. QAM receivers are able to discern whether to use lower or higher numbers of amplitude and phase states to overcome noise and interference on the wire pair.

CAP modulation is a proprietary modulation of AT&T Paradyne. CAP uses two ranges of frequencies. The larger range is used for the downstream path and the smaller

Table 9.11   Various xDSL Technologies

Technology	Speed	Distance limitation (24-gauge wire)	Applications
Asymmetrical Digital Subscriber Line Lite (ADSL Lite)	Up to 1 Mbps downstream Up to 512 Kbps upstream	18,000 feet	Internet/intranet access, web browsing, IP telephony, video telephony
Asymmetrical Digital Subscriber Line (ADSL)	1.5–8 Mbps downstream Up to 1.544 Mbps upstream	18,000 feet (12,000 feet for fastest speeds)	Internet/intranet access, video-on-demand, remote LAN access, VPNs, VoIP
Rate Adaptive Digital Subscriber Line (R-ADSL)	1.5–8 Mbps downstream Up to 1.544 Mbps upstream	18,000 feet (12,000 feet for fastest speeds)	Internet/intranet access, video-on-demand, remote LAN access, VPNs, VoIP
ISDN Digital Subscriber Line (IDSL)	Up to 144 Kbps full duplex	18,000 feet (additional equipment can extend the distance)	Internet/intranet access, web browsing, IP telephony, video telephony
High Bit-Rate Digital Subscriber Line (HDSL)	1.544 Mbps full duplex (T-1) 2.048 Mbps full duplex (E-1) (uses 2–3 wire pairs)	12,000–15,000 feet	Local, repeatered T-1/E-1 trunk replacement, PBX interconnection, Frame Relay traffic aggregator, LAN interconnect
Single-Line Digital Subscriber Line (SDSL)	1.544 Mbps full duplex (T-1) 2.048 Mbps full duplex (E-1) (uses 1 wire pair)	10,000 feet	Local, repeatered T-1/E-1 trunk replacement, collaborative computing, LAN interconnect
Very High Bit-Rate Digital Subscriber Line (VDSL)	13–52 Mbps downstream 1.5–2.3 Mbps upstream (up to 34 Mbps if symmetric)	1,000–4,500 feet (depending on speed)	Multimedia Internet access, high-definition television program delivery

range is used for the upstream path. Income data modulates a single carrier channel that is sent down a telephone line. The carrier is suppressed before transmission and is reconstructed at the receiving end. Generating a modulated wave that carries amplitude and phase state changes is not easy. To overcome this challenge, the CAP version of QAM stores parts of a modulated message signal in memory and then reassembles the parts in the modulated wave. The carrier signal is suppressed before transmission because it contains no information and is reassembled at the receiving modem (hence the word "carrierless" in CAP). At start-up, CAP also tests the quality of the access line and implements the most efficient version of QAM to ensure satisfactory performance for individual signal transmissions. CAP is normally FDM based.

While there are still a lot of CAP used, the current DSL standard is DMT. DMT is actually a form of FDM. Because high-frequency signals on copper lines suffer more loss in the presence of noise, DMT discretely divides the available frequencies into 256 subchannels, or tones. As with CAP, a test occurs at start up to determine the carrying capacity of each subchannel. Incoming data is then broken down into a variety of bits and distributed to a specific combination of subchannels based on their ability to carry the transmission. To rise above noise, more data resides in the lower frequencies and less in the upper ones.

To create upstream and downstream channels, ADSL modems divide the phone line's available bandwidth using either FDM or echo cancellation. FDM assigns one band or frequency for upstream data and another band or frequency for downstream data. The downstream path is further divided by TDM into one or more high-speed channels for data and one or more low-speed channels, one of which is for voice. The upstream path is multiplexed into several low-speed channels.

Echo cancellation, the same technique used by V.32 and V.34 modems, means that the upstream and the downstream signals are sent on the wire at the same frequencies. The advantage of echo cancellation is that the signals are both kept at the lowest possible frequencies (because cable loss and crosstalk noise both increase with frequency) and therefore achieves greater cable distance for a given data rate. An ADSL receiver will see an incoming signal that is both the incoming signal from the far end and the outgoing signal from the local transmitter. These are mixed together at the same frequency range. In other words, the received signal is composed not only of the signal to be recovered from the far end but also of a local echo due to the local transmitter. The local echo must be accurately modeled by DSP circuitry and then this replica echo is electronically subtracted from the composite incoming signal. If done properly, all that is left behind is the incoming data from the far end ADSL system. While echo cancellation uses bandwidth more efficiently, the process of modeling the echo is quite complicated and is more costly. Therefore, only a few vendors have implemented them.

9.5.2   ADSL

Currently, existing POTS data is transmitted over a frequency spectrum that ranges from 0 to 4 kHz. Copper phone lines can actually support frequency ranges much greater than those, and ADSL takes advantage of these ranges by transmitting data in the ranges between 4 kHz and 2.2 MHz. Therefore, ADSL relies on advanced DSP and complex algorithms to compress all the information into the phone line. In addition, ADSL modems correct errors caused by line conditions and attenuation. With this technology, any computer or network can easily become connected to the Internet at speeds comparable to T-1 access for a fraction of the cost, and it can serve as a suitable medium for video streaming and conferencing.

As its name implies, **Asymmetrical DSL (ADSL)** transmits an asymmetric data stream, with much more going downstream to the subscriber and much less coming back. The reason for this has less to do with transmission technology than with the cable plant itself. Twisted pair telephone wires are bundled together in large cables. Fifty pairs to a cable is a typical configuration towards the subscriber, but cables coming out of a CO may have hundreds or even thousands of pairs bundled together. An individual line from a CO to a subscriber is spliced together from many cable sections as they fan out from the CO (Bellcore claims that the average U.S. subscriber line has twenty-two splices). Alexander

Bell invented twisted pair wiring to minimize crosstalk. Because a small amount of crosstalk does occur, the amount of crosstalk increases as the frequencies and the length of line increases. Therefore, if you have symmetric signals in many pairs within the same cable, the crosstalk significantly limits the data rate and the length of the line.

Because most people download information as they view web pages and download files, the amount of information downloaded is far greater than the amount of information that a user uploads or transfers to the other computers. This asymmetry, combined with "always on" access (which eliminates call set up), makes ADSL ideal for Internet/intranet surfing, video-on-demand, and remote LAN access.

ADSL modems usually include a POTS splitter, which enables simultaneous access to voice telephony and high-speed data access. Some vendors provide active POTS splitters, which enable simultaneous telephone and data access. However, if the power fails or the modem fails with an active POTS splitter, then the telephone service fails. A passive POTS splitter, on the other hand, maintains lifeline telephone access even if the modem fails (due to a power outage), because the telephone is not powered by external electricity. Telephone access in the case of a passive POTS splitter is a regular analog voice channel, the same that customers currently receive to their homes.

Downstream, ADSL supports speeds between 1.5 and 8 Mbps, while upstream, the rate is between 640 Kbps and 1.544 Mbps. ADSL can provide 1.544 Mbps transmission rates at distances of up to 18,000 feet over one wire pair. Optimal speeds of 6 to 8 Mbps can be achieved at distances of 10,000 to 12,000 feet using standard 24-gauge wire.

Currently, the ADSL Lite specification, also known as g.lite, is a low-cost, easy-to-install version of ADSL specifically designed for the consumer marketplace. ADSL Lite is a lower-speed version of ADSL that will eliminate the need for the telephone company to install and maintain a premises-based POTS splitter. ADSL Lite is also supposed to work over longer distances than full-rate ADSL, making it more widely available to mass market consumers. It will support both data and voice and provide an evolution path to full-rate ADSL.

9.5.3   HDSL

High-bit-rate Digital Subscriber Line (HDSL) derives its name from the high bandwidth that is transmitted in both directions over two copper loops. HDSL has proven to be a reliable and cost-effective means for providing repeater less T-1 and E-1 services over two twisted pair loops. HDSL transceivers can reliably transmit a 1.544 and 2.048 Mbps data signal over two nonloaded, 24 gauge (0.5mm), unconditioned twisted wire pair loops at a distance of up to 13,100 ft (4.2 km) without the need for repeaters. Different from ADSL, HDSL does not provide standard voice telephone service on the same wire pair.

Eliminating the need for repeater equipment and removal of bridged taps significantly simplifies the labor and engineering effort to provision the service. This attribute eliminates the need to identify, modify, and verify a controlled environment, with power, secured access, and other factors needed to support repeater equipment. It also reduces the time, cost, and effort of isolating faults and taking corrective action when a failure does occur. Studies by some ISPs have indicated that troubleshooting and replacing defective repeater equipment often costs significantly more than the cost of the equipment itself.

These attributes translate into increased network up time and reduced engineering time, making T-1 provisioning possible in a matter of days, as opposed to weeks. Faster service provisioning and greater up time leads to increased customer satisfaction and increased service revenues. To provision a 12,000 ft (3.6 km) local loop with traditional T-1 transmission equipment requires two transceivers and two repeaters. To provision the same loop with HDSL requires only two HDSL transceivers, one at each end of a line.

HDSL2 is the next generation of HDSL. HDSL2 was designed to accomplish three primary goals. The first being full T-1 rates (1.544 Mb/s) on a single pair of copper wires with the same spectral compatibility as traditional HDSL; the second being vendor interoperability, meaning that service providers are no longer tied to proprietary solutions; and the third being that it must extend to full CSA reach (12,000 feet). HDSL2 can be thought of as offering everything traditional HDSL offers, but it can be done on a single pair of copper wires. HDSL2 has become the DSL of choice for corporations.

9.5.4   ADSL2, ADSL2+ and eXtremeDSLMAX

The ADSL2 G.992.3 and G.992.4 standards, recently approved by the International Telecommunication Union, improve data rate and reach performance, dynamic rate adaptation and diagnostics, as well as include a power-saving standby mode. Another forthcoming standard, ADSL2+ (G.992.5), more than doubles the downstream data rate of ADSL to 25M bit/sec.

ADSL2 addresses the growing demand for bandwidth to support services such as video. Forthcoming ADSL2 and ADSL2+ gear will interoperate with existing ADSL equipment, allowing carriers to roll out new high-speed services while gradually upgrading their legacy infrastructure.

Some of the enhancements ADSL2 and ADSL2+ offer include:

- **Better rate and reach**—Improved modulation efficiency reduces framing overhead, achieves higher coding gain, improves the initialization state machine, and provides enhanced signal processing algorithms. ADSL2 increases downstream data rates to more than 12M bit/sec, as compared with between 8M and 10M bit/sec for original ADSL. ADSL2 extends reach by approximately 600 feet.
- **Diagnostics**—Real-time performance-monitoring capabilities provide information regarding line quality and noise conditions at both ends of the line. Service providers can use the data to monitor the quality of the ADSL connection and prevent service failures. Carriers also can use the data to determine if a customer qualifies for higher data-rate services.
- **Channelization**—ADSL2's channelization capability provides support for Channelized Voice over DSL (CVoDSL), a method to transport derived lines of TDM voice traffic transparently over DSL. CVoDSL transports voice within the physical layer, letting derived voice channels ride over DSL bandwidth while maintaining both plain old telephone service (POTS) and high-speed Internet access.
- **Power enhancements**—Two power management modes help reduce power consumption while maintaining ADSL's always-on functionality for users.
- **Bonding for higher data rates**—The new standards support the ATM Forum's inverse multiplexing over ATM (IMA) standard developed for traditional ATM architectures.

Through IMA, ADSL2 chipsets can bind two or more copper pairs in an ADSL link. The result is fiber-like data rates over existing copper lines.

- **Improved interoperability**—Modem initialization procedures are clarified, which improves interoperability and provides better performance when connecting ADSL transceivers from different chip suppliers.
- **Fast startup**—A fast start-up mode reduces initialization time from about 10 seconds to less than 3 seconds.
- **All-digital mode**—An optional mode allows for transmission of data in the POTS portion of the phone line. This adds 256K bit/sec to the upstream data rate, which can be an attractive option for businesses that have voice services on different phone lines and value the additional upstream bandwidth.
- **Packet-based services**—Packet-based services such as Ethernet can be transported over ADSL2.
- **ADSL2+**—The ADSL2+ standard doubles the maximum frequency used for downstream data transmission from 1.1 MHz to 2.2 MHz. This effectively provides downstream data rates of 25M bit/sec on phone lines as long as 5,000 feet.

Equipment supporting ADSL2 and ADSL2+ is expected to become available this year, driving the growth of ADSL and enabling new services.

The most recent improvement in DSL is by Centillium Communications, Inc. with their eXtremeDSLMAX technology. eXtremeDSLMAX can deliver up to 50 Megabits per second (Mbps) in downstream and 3 Mbps in upstream data rates using existing ADSL copper network infrastructure. It enhances capabilities and increases performance of ADSL for residential markets, accelerating the introduction of new premium services such as High Definition Television (HDTV), Video on Demand (VoD), Voice over Packet (VoP), and video and audio streaming for consumers. In addition, eXtremeDSLMAX can reach far more customers by extending the reach of ADSL services to ranges up to 22,000 feet (7,000 meters).

9.5.5   Connecting to a DSL Line

To connect to an ADSL line, you install an ADSL modem via an expansion card or a USB port or external standalone device connected to a NIC. If you are using the expansion card or USB device, you would assign and configure the TCP/IP protocol. If you are using the external standalone device, you assign and configure the TCP/IP protocol for the NIC. Today, some DSL lines may use PPPoE.

9.6   CABLE MODEMS

Cable systems were originally designed to deliver broadcast television signals efficiently to subscribers' homes. To ensure that consumers could obtain cable service with the same TV sets they use to receive over-the-air broadcast TV signals, cable operators recreate a portion of the over-the-air radio frequency (RF) spectrum within a sealed coaxial cable line.

Traditional coax cable systems typically operate with 330 MHz or 450 MHz of capacity, whereas modern hybrid fiber/coax (HFC) systems are expanded to 750 MHz or more. Logically, downstream video programming signals begin around 50 MHz, the equivalent of channel 2 for over-the-air television signals. Each standard television channel occupies 6 MHz of the RF spectrum. Thus, a traditional cable system with 400 MHz of downstream bandwidth can carry the equivalent of 60 analog TV channels. A modern HFC system with 700 MHz of downstream bandwidth has the capacity for about 110 channels.

While regular cable is analog, digital cable uses digital signals. Digital signals can be compressed much more than analog signals. Digital cable can give you 200 to 300 channels of the same bandwidth as analog cable.

To deliver data services over a cable network, one television channel in the 50 to 750 MHz range is typically allocated for downstream traffic to homes and another channel in the 5 to 42 MHz band is used to carry upstream signals. A cable modem termination system (CMTS) communicates through these channels with **cable modems** located in subscriber homes to create a VLAN connection. Most cable modems are external devices that connect to a PC through a standard 10Base-T Ethernet card and twisted-pair wiring or through external Universal Serial Bus (USB) modems and internal PCI modem cards.

A single downstream 6 MHz television channel may support up to 27 Mbps of downstream data throughput from the cable using 64 QAM transmission technology. Speeds can be boosted to 36 Mbps using 256 QAM. Upstream channels may deliver 500 Kbps to 10 Mbps from homes using 16 QAM or QPSK modulation techniques, depending on the amount of spectrum allocated for service. This upstream and downstream bandwidth is shared by the active data subscribers connected to a given cable network segment, typically 500 to 2000 homes exist on a modern HFC network.

An individual cable modem subscriber may experience access speeds from 500 Kbps to 1.5 Mbps or more, depending on the network architecture and traffic load, blazing performance compared with dial-up alternatives. However, when surfing the web, performance can be affected by Internet backbone congestion. In addition to speed, cable modems offer another key benefit: constant connectivity. Because cable modems use connectionless technology, much like in an office LAN, a subscriber's PC is always online with the network. That means that there is no need to dial-in to begin a session, so users do not have to worry about receiving busy signals. Additionally, going online does not tie up their telephone line.

NOTE: Like DSL lines, some cable lines may use PPPoE.

9.7   SYNCHRONOUS DIGITAL HIERARCHY AND SYNCHRONOUS OPTICAL NETWORKS

Synchronous Digital Hierarchy (SDH) and **Synchronous Optical Networks (Sonet)** are transmission technology standards for synchronous data transmission over fiber optic cables. They provide a high-speed transfer of data, video, and other types of information across great distances without regard to the specific services and applications they support. ISPs that have to aggregate (combine) multiple T-1s to provide connections across the country or around the world typically use them. SDH is an international standard. The ITU coordinates the development of SDH standards. Sonet is the North American equivalent of SDH, which is published by ANSI.

When referring to Sonet or SDH, Sonet and SDH do not apply directly to switches. Instead, they specify the interfaces between switches that are linked by fiber optic cable. There is no such thing as a Sonet or SDH switch. Instead, an ATM switch, or similar switch (such as FDDI, ISDN, or SMDS) is used. SDH and Sonet map the physical layer of the OSI model.

9.7.1   Building Blocks of SDH and Sonet

The basic foundation of Sonet consists of groups of DS-0 signals (64 Kbits/sec) that are multiplexed to create a 51.84 Mbps signal, which is also known as STS-1 (Synchronous Transport Signal). STS-1 is an electrical signal rate that corresponds to the Optical Carrier line rate of OC-1, Sonet's building block.

> *NOTE:* OC-1 has enough bandwidth to support twenty-eight T-1 links or one T-3 link. Higher rates of transmission are a multiple of this basic rate. For example, STS-3 is three times the basic rate, or 155.52 Mbps. OC-12 is twelve times the basic rate, giving a rate of 622 Mbps, and OC-192 is 9.95 Gbps. The SDH standard is based on STM-1, which is equivalent to OC-3. Therefore, SDH uses multipliers of 155.52 Mbps (see Table 9.12).

In essence, Sonet and SDH are the same technology. There are minor differences in header information, payload size, and framing. But at 155 Mbps and above, the two are completely interoperable.

Just because the basic level of Sonet starts at approximately 51 Mbps doesn't mean lower bit rate asynchronous signals are ignored. The basic STS-1 frame contains 810 DS-0s, 783 of which are used for sending data (including slower asynchronous signals) and 27 of which are overhead. The overhead in this case is information concerning framing, errors, operations, and format identification.

Signals with speeds below STS-1, such as DS-1 and the European E-1 (2.048Mbits/sec) can be accommodated by dividing the STS-1 payload into smaller segments that are

Table 9.12   The Sonet/SDH Digital Hierarchy

Optical level	SDH equivalent	Electrical level	Line rate (Mbps)	Payload rate (Mbps)	Overhead rate (Mbps)
OC-1	-	STS-1	51.840	50.112	1.728
OC-3	STM-1	STS-3	155.520	150.336	5.184
OC-9	STM-3	STS-9	466.560	451.008	15.552
OC-12	STM-4	STS-12	622.080	601.344	20.736
OC-18	STM-6	STS-18	933.120	902.016	31.104
OC-24	STM-8	STS-24	1,244.160	1,202.688	41.472
OC-36	STM-13	STS-36	1,866.240	1,804.032	62.208
OC-48	STM-16	STS-48	2,488.320	2,405.376	82.944
OC-96	STM-32	STS-96	4,976.640	4,810.752	165.888
OC-192	STM-64	STS-192	9,953.280	9,621.504	331.776
OC-768	STM-256	STS-768	39,813.12	38,486.01	1,327.10

Figure 9.10   SDH/Sonet Networks Use Dual Rings to Provide Redundant Pathways

Carrier SDH/SONET Network

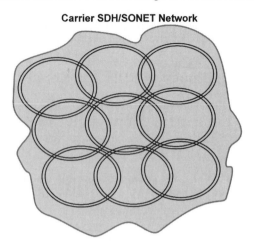

known as Virtual Tributaries (VTs). The lower data rate signals are combined with over-head information, which leads to the creation of Synchronous Payload Envelopes (SPEs). SPEs allow these signals to be transported at high speeds without compromising integrity. Each VT on an STS-1 signal includes its own overhead information and exists as a distinct segment within the signal.

9.7.2   SDH and Sonet Lines and Rings

Local SDH and SONET services are sold in two forms: (1) point-to-point dedicated lines and (2) dual fiber rings. Both deliver high speed, but only dual fiber rings guarantee automatic rerouting around outages. Long distance SDH and Sonet connections employ multiple rings within the public network. Some are even using dual ring-pairs (four redundant rings on one circuit) (see Figure 9.10).

When using dual rings, if one circuit is broken, the traffic reverses and flows in the opposite direction on the same ring—avoiding the cut altogether. If the ring is broken in two places, the traffic is automatically rerouted onto the second circuit. This takes a few milliseconds longer than merely reversing direction, but it still happens nearly instantaneously.

Long-distance point-to-point SDH and Sonet services are similar to standard leased lines. A company buys a connection between two points, but its traffic is sent over multiple rings within the public network. Although the customer doesn't buy rings, the customer gets all the benefits associated with rings within a long-distance portion of the carrier network. Customers who need high-reliability end to end should use local access rings.

9.7.3   Sonet Network Devices

Sonet can be used for a single point-to-point circuit or as the basis of a large, multisite network. Sonet devices are being used today to rebuild the public telecommunications infrastructure.

A variety of equipment is available to meet the needs of the Sonet user:

- **Terminal devices**—Devices that define the boundaries of a Sonet network. They gather bytes to be sent out onto the Sonet network and deliver bytes arriving from the Sonet network.
- **Regenerators**—Devices that recreate a signal so that it can be sent across great distances.
- **Add/drop multiplexers**—Devices that combine and split signals.
- **Digital cross-connect switches**—Devices that route traffic and enable complex and robust networks with a lot of redundancy and backup capacity to be constructed.

9.7.4   Sonet Frames

Sonet is a synchronous system. Therefore, timing may be provided by an internal clock of a Sonet terminal or it may derive its timing signal from a building integrated timing supply (BITS) used by switching systems and other equipment. Other Sonet nodes will operate in a slave mode called loop timing with their internal clocks timed by the incoming OC–N signal. Current standards specify that a Sonet network must be able to derive its timing from a Stratum 3 or higher clock.

> *NOTE:* The number of steps that a particular system lie from a primary time source is known as its "stratum." A radio clock has stratum-0. The computer directly linked to it has stratum-1. Intermediate servers and the majority of end-user systems will run at stratum-3, -4, or -5.

The frame format of the STS-1 can be divided into two main areas: (1) the transport overhead and (2) the SPE. The SPE can also be divided into two parts: (1) the STS path overhead (POH) and (2) the payload. The payload is the revenue-producing traffic being transported and routed over the Sonet network. Once the payload is multiplexed into the synchronous payload envelope, it can be transported and switched through Sonet without having to be examined and possibly demultiplexed at intermediate nodes. Thus, Sonet is said to be service-independent or transparent.

STS-1 is a specific sequence of 810 bytes (6480 bits), which includes various overhead bytes and an envelope capacity for transporting payloads. It can be depicted as a 90-column by 9-row structure. With a frame length of 125 µs (8000 frames per second), STS-1 has a bit rate of 51.840 Mbps. The order of transmission of bytes is row-by-row from top to bottom and from left to right (most significant bit first).

The first three columns of the STS-1 frame are for the transport overhead. The three columns contain twenty-seven bytes. Of these, 9 bytes are overhead for the section layer (for example, each section overhead), and 18 bytes are overhead for the line layer (for example, line overhead). The remaining 87 columns constitute the STS-1 envelope capacity (payload and POH).

A SPE matches the size of the STS-1 payload area perfectly. However, an SPE is not aligned with the boundaries of the payload areas. Instead, it is dropped into the payload area at a convenient point. This allows electrical signals (DS1, E1, DS3, E3, and so on) arriving at terminal multiplexers that do not have tight synchronization like the Sonet signals have in order to be placed in the Sonet signal with ease.

9.8   NETWORKING WITH WAN LINKS

Typically, when you connect your network to a WAN link, you will often have a switch or router that connects your LAN within a site. That switch or router is then connected to your WAN connection using a router and/or DSU/CSU (see Figure 9.11).

9.9   TROUBLESHOOTING SERIAL LINES

Before involving others, it helps to pinpoint the problem as accurately as possible. To do this, trace the signal from the origin to its intended destination and make a note of where it fails to propagate. Your main tools are the CSU/DSU's loopback features, though you may wish to involve vendors and service providers.

9.9.1   Basic Troubleshooting

When you start troubleshooting a serial line problem, you should always start with checking the obvious. First check to see if the router and/or CSU/DSUs power cables are connected properly and that the router and/or CSU/DSUs are turned on.

> *NOTE:* Typically, these devices should have some lights, which indicate that you have power.

Make sure that all cables are connected properly and that you are using the correct cables. Remember that 10Base-T, 10Base-100, crossover cables, and rollover cables all look alike but are wired differently. In addition, you should remember that cabling is also one of the most common problems in networking. So make sure that the cable is not bad and if you decide to extend the demarc, make sure that you hire an experienced installer who has tested the line.

Next, make sure that your CSU/DSU and/or routers are configured properly. Check the following:

- Line framing and line code
- Line speed (channel speed and the number of DS0s)
- Transmit clocking and DTE clocking settings
- Link layer information such as frame relay DLCI or ATM virtual path and virtual circuit IDs
- IP addressing and routing information from the service provider
- If you require CHAP or PAP, make sure that you have the correct username and passwords. Remember that both of these are case sensitive.
- Check the lights on your CSU/DSU and routers to determine the status of the devices
- Make sure the CSU/DSU and routers are administratively enabled

In addition, don't forget your network troubleshooting commands such as arp, ping, and traceroute to determine where the failure is occurring.

9.9.2   Loopback Testing

Loopback testing is used to verify that a link is good by looping received data back onto the transmit path. Two main types of loopback exist, remote loopback and local loopback.

Figure 9.11   LANs connected to ISDN WAN links

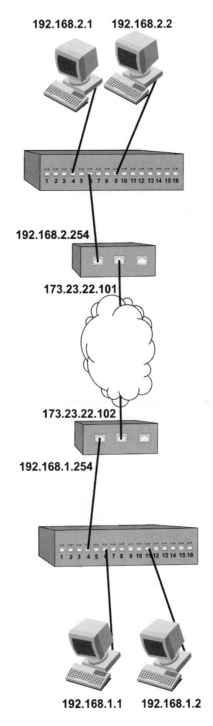

192.168.2.1   192.168.2.2

192.168.2.254

173.23.22.101

173.23.22.102

192.168.1.254

192.168.1.1   192.168.1.2

Remote loopback sends the data received on the ISP network interface back out toward the ISP to verify the line between two locations. If data is transmitted across the line, sent back across the line due to a loopback setting, and received intact at the sender, then the main link is good. Local loopback verifies the CSU/DSU-to-router connection in exactly the same way.

The service providers can activate and deactivate the loopback capabilities of each repeater along a line's path to verify its operation. In addition, if certain conditions occur on the network, the circuit equipment may trigger loopback tests. Lastly, loopback can also be triggered by a smart jack. Removing a plug from a smart jack will connect the input side so that it can become a path from the end span repeater to the customer location, then back to the repeater. Using the built-in loopback capability of a jack lets you determine whether the problem lies in the service provider or the customer's wiring.

Local loopback tests can isolate the problem in the cable or the timing in the serial circuits between the router and CSU/DSU. Local loopback tests need to be run at both the local and remote ends. In a local loopback test, any data sent by the DTE should be looped back from the CSU/DSU to the DTE. When local loopback tests fail, contact the DTE vendor and the CSU/DSU vendor after checking the configuration on the timing of the router-to-CSU/DSU serial link.

Remote loopback tests isolate problems in the carrier's network. In a remote loopback test, the CSU/DSU is configured to take any data received from the network and transmit it back through the network to its source. If all goes correctly, data flows from one router through the router's CSU/DSU and through the carrier's network. When it reaches the remote end, the remote CSU/DSU in loopback mode transmits that data back through the carrier's network, testing the circuit in both directions.

To use loopback testing effectively for problem isolation, follow these three steps:

Step 1: Run a local loopback test at the side of the T-1 having problems and make sure that any bits the local DTE transmits are received on the DTE's serial port.

Step 2: Remove the local loopback setting on the local CSU/DSU. Call the remote end and have them put the remote CSU/DSU into loopback mode. Alternatively, the remote end may call you and ask you to put your CSU/DSU into loopback mode. The two tests are equivalent because they test the same four wires. The sender should receive anything that is sent out. If this test fails, call the service provider.

Step 3: Run a local loopback test on the remote side of the T-1 to verify its DTE-to-CSU/DSU connection.

9.9.3   Red and Yellow Alarms

When an alarm signal occurs, it indicates a severe error condition. Alarms initially had color names because of the corresponding color of the indicator lights on the channel banks (see Table 9.13).

A red alarm indicates a downed link. Either no incoming signal is being received (LOS—loss of signal) or no framing synchronization is possible (LOF—loss of framing).

NOTE: Do not be concerned if the red alarm is not cleared for several seconds after you plug in the cable. If you do not have an incoming signal, the cable that

Table 9.13   Serial Line Alarms

Name	Cause
Red alarm (receive alarm)	This is declared when the local CSU/DSU is not able to detect an incoming framing signal.
Yellow alarm (remote alarm) also known as remote alarm indicator (RAI)	This is sent as the outbound signal when a CSU/DSU enters the red alarm state to inform the remote end of a potential failure. The most important thing about the yellow alarm is that, in most cases, the span from the remote end to the local end must be functional to send the yellow alarm signal. On superframe-framed links, a yellow alarm is indicated by setting the second bit of each channel to zero.
Blue alarm (alarm indication signal (AIS))	When no incoming signal is detected, a CSU/DSU transmits an unframed all-1s pattern. AIS signals serve two purposes: the continuous transitions may help resynchronize the network, and they indicate a problem to the network.

leads to the service provider may not be connected, the cable may be bad, the incorrect cable may be used, or the T-1 circuit is bad. Of course, if the T-1 circuit is bad, you can run the loopback test and call the ISP with the results.

If you are unable to synchronize the frame, the cable may be bad or the CSU/DSU is misconfigured. You need to check the frame format and line code. If there are still problems, use the loopback tests to help you further isolate the problem.

A yellow alarm is sent by the remote end to indicate that it is not receiving the signal. The problem exists somewhere in the local transmit to remote receive path. The most significant thing about a yellow alarm is that framing is received correctly, so the remote transmit to local receive path is good. Besides checking for bad cables, you should also check to see if the CSU/DSU is not bad.

The CSU/DSU usually offer counters so that you can have more insight into physical difficulties. Controlled slips, seconds in which the physical layer framing is lost, and bipolar violations can be caused by incorrect configuration or crosstalk. In theory, a functioning line on a well-maintained network should have no errors, and any positive error count can indicate a potentially serious condition.

Clock slips occur due to mismatched timing between the two ends of the T-1. Timing can drift for a variety of reasons, but links with multiple service providers are especially susceptible to timing problems because the different service providers may employ different primary reference source clocks.

Excessive bipolar violations are the result of one of two problems. An AMI line receiving B8ZS code words will record bipolar violations, and a high bipolar count can indicate a device that should be set for AMI and is instead set for B8ZS. B8ZS devices receiving AMI-encoded data, however, will not record line code violations due to excessive zeros.

If the line coding inserts intentional bipolar violations and the local CSU/DSU has an incorrect line code setting, all of the inserted intentional bipolar violations will be flagged. On the other hand, the violations could be caused by a noisy line with crosstalk. After verifying that the line code is set correctly and the cable is good, report the problem to the ISP.

Bipolar violations accompanied by clock slips indicate near-end crosstalk (NEXT). When cable pairs run close together, the magnetic fields resulting from a strong signal on one pair may induce a current in a nearby pair. Twisting cable pairs tightly both reduces the emissions and improves immunity to crosstalk. Near-end crosstalk is most often seen at the customer end of a T-1 because the transmit power is the strongest there, while the received signal is at its weakest point and is susceptible to being drowned out by the crosstalk signal. Standards limit the acceptable crosstalk levels at various points on the T-1 line, but staying below the limits imposed by the standards may require the use of high-quality prefabricated cabling. Extended demarcs and the attendant wiring problems are the most common cause of near-end crosstalk.

When the link layer fails to come up, a common problem is an incorrect clocking setting. One common scenario is that the line has physical connectivity, but no link layer protocol is able to initiate. This usually occurs because the clocking between the CSU/DSU and the router is not configured correctly. Incoming link layer negotiation requests are received by the CSU/DSU and passed out the serial interface to the router. At the router, the requests are processed correctly and responses are sent. If the transmit clocking on the data port is configured incorrectly, however, the response to the incoming configuration request is not received by the CSU/DSU and cannot be sent out the NIC. At the remote end, the line appears to be quiet. No physical problems exist and no alarms are present, but no data comes in either.

Not all routers can supply a transmit clock with the data. If the CSU/DSU is looking for an external transmit clock from the router, it will not read any incoming data, even if that data is supplied according to the transmit clock from the CSU/DSU. Some routers also have significant internal phase delays and must supply an external transmit clock to avoid frequent corrupted bits when the clock trigger falls on the edge of a voltage transition. To be safe, use external (router supplied) clocking on the data port if it is supported.

SUMMARY

1. DTE devices are end systems that communicate across WANs.

2. DCE devices are special communication devices that provide the interface between the DTE and the network.

3. A DSU is a device that performs protective and diagnostic functions for a telecommunications line. A CSU is a device that connects a terminal to a digital line. Typically, the two devices are packaged as a single unit.

4. The dedicated lines are point-to-point connections, which are preestablished WAN communications paths from the CPE through the DCE switch, to the CPE of the remote site.

5. Circuit switching sets up on a line like a phone call. No data transfers before the end-to-end connection is established. Examples include dial-up modems and ISDN lines.

6. Packet switching is a WAN switching method that allows you to share bandwidth with other companies to save money, which takes messages and divides them into packets before they are sent. Each packet is then transmitted individually and can even follow different routes to its destination.

7. Cell relay is a data transmission technology based on transmitting data in relatively small, fixed-size packets or cells. Each cell contains only basic path information that allows switching devices to route the cell quickly. An example includes ATM.

8. A virtual circuit is a logical circuit created to ensure reliable communications between two network devices.

9. Virtual networks are sometimes depicted as a cloud because the user does not worry about the path taken through the cloud.

10. The method of digitizing analog voice signals is PCM.
11. Telephone systems use a single pair of twisted pair copper wiring. Telephones are connected to the cable using a RJ-11 jack.
12. PSTN is the international telephone system based on copper wires (UTP cabling) carrying analog voice data.
13. The PSTN, also known as POTS, is the standard telephone service that most homes use.
14. The subscriber loop or local loop is the telephone line that runs from your home or office to the telephone company's CO or neighborhood switching station (often a small building with no windows).
15. While its cable length can be as long as twenty miles, it is referred to as the last mile, not because of its length, but because it is the slow link in the telecommunications infrastructure as it carries analog signals on a twisted pair cable.
16. The point where the local loop ends at the customer's premises is called the demarcation point (demarc).
17. A modem (modulator-demodulator) is a device that enables a computer to transmit data over telephone lines.
18. T-carrier and E-carrier systems are entire digital systems that consist of permanent dedicated point-to-point connections.
19. T-carrier and E-carrier systems are based on 64-Kbps channels (DS0 channel), whereas each voice transmission is assigned a channel.
20. In North America and Japan, you would typically find a T-1 line that has twenty-four 64-Kbps channels for a bandwidth of 1.544 Mbps and T-3 lines that have 672 64-Kbps channels for a bandwidth of 44.736 Mbps.
21. In Europe, you will find E-1 lines with thirty-two 64-Kbps channels for a bandwidth of 2.048 Mbps. E-3 lines have 512 64-Kbps channels for a bandwidth of 34.368 Mbps.
22. The CSU/DSU has a series of lights to help you troubleshoot line problems.

23. Circuit switch technology can be referred to as dial-up technology.
24. ISDN is the planned replacement for POTS so that it can provide voice and data communications worldwide using circuit switching while using the same wiring that is currently being used in homes and businesses.
25. BRI defines a digital communications line consisting of three independent channels, two Bearer (or B) channels, each carrying 64 Kbps and one Data (or D) channel at 16 Kbps.
26. PRI is a higher-level network interface defined at the rate of 1.544 Mbps for North America and Japan. PRI, used on T-1 digital lines (which uses T-1 framing and line coding), consists of twenty-three B channels, each at 64 Kbps, and one 64 Kbps D channel for signaling.
27. DDR is used to allow two or more routers to dial an ISDN dial-up connection on an as-needed basis.
28. AO/DI is a networking application that uses the 16 Kbps ISDN D-channel X-25 packet service to maintain an "always on" connection between an ISDN end-user and an ISP.
29. A DSL is a special communication line that uses sophisticated modulation technology to maximize the amount of data that can be sent over plain twisted pair copper wiring, which is already carrying phone service to subscriber homes.
30. Cable systems were originally designed to deliver broadcast television signals efficiently to subscribers' homes, but can also be used to connect to the Internet.
31. SDH and Sonet are transmission technology standards for synchronous data transmission over fiber optic cables.
32. OC-1 has enough bandwidth to support twenty-eight T-1 links or one T-3 link.
33. Loopback testing is used to verify that a span is good by looping received data back onto the transmit path.
34. Alarm signals indicate severe error conditions.

QUESTIONS

1. PSTN is an acronym for what?
   a. partial switched telephone network
   b. public switched transmission network
   c. partial switched transmission network
   d. public switched telephone network

2. Which of the following technologies is intended to replace analog phone lines?
   a. PSTN/POTS   b. ATM
   c. Frame Relay   d. ISDN

3. T-1 is a widely used type of digital communication line. What does T-1 technology offer?
   a. transmission speed of up to 1.544 Mbps
   b. transmission speed of up to 45 Mbps
   c. point-to-point, full duplex transmission
   d. two 64-Kbps B channels and one 16-Kbps D channel per line

4. T-1 lines take advantage of technology that combines signals from different sources onto one cable for transmission. Which of the following devices can be used to combine multiple data signals onto a single transmission line?
   a. data assemblers   b. transceivers
   c. multiplexers   d. redirectors

5. How many separate devices can be connected to a BRI?
   a. 1
   b. 8
   c. 16
   d. 64
   e. there is no physical limitation

6. What is the maximum number of individual phone numbers that could be assigned to an ISDN BRI?
   a. 1   b. 8
   c. 16   d. 64

7. What is another representation for a standard BRI ISDN line?
   a. 64B2+16D   b. B2+D
   c. 2B+D   d. 2B64+D16

8. You decide to implement PPP Multilink over multiple ISDN BRI lines. How many BRIs without compression will you need to achieve your minimum required rate of 384 Kbps?
   a. 1
   b. 2
   c. 3
   d. 4
   e. you cannot use PPP Multilink with ISDN

9. What is the compressed theoretical maximum transmission speed you could achieve with compression if you implemented three BRIs to achieve a minimum uncompressed transmission speed of 384 Kbps?
   a. 512 Kbps   b. 768 Kbps
   c. 1536 Kbps   d. 2048 Kbps

10. One of your offices is 2 miles from a local telephone CO. The other is approximately five miles away from the local telephone CO. What will you need to be able to use an ISDN BRI?
    a. You will need one repeater between the telephone CO and your first office and two repeaters between the telephone CO and your second office.
    b. You will need one repeater between the telephone CO and your second office.
    c. You will need two repeaters between the telephone CO and your second office.
    d. You will not need any repeaters.

11. Suppose the following situation exists: Your company is based in Sacramento. It has branch offices in Los Angeles and New York City. Each of the three offices has a 10Base-T network. Users need to access resources in all three offices.

    Required result: You must implement a networking solution, which will offer WAN communications between the three sites.

    Optional desired results: The WAN connection needs to support about 256 Kbps of data and several analog telephone conversations between sites. The WAN connection needs to be able to continue operations even if one of the WAN links should fail.

    Proposed solution: Use three T-1 connections: one between Sacramento and Los Angeles, one between Los Angeles and New York, and one between New York and Sacramento.

    Which results do the proposed solution produce?
    a. The proposed solution produces the required result and produces both of the optional desired results.
    b. The proposed solution produces the required result and produces only one of the optional desired results.
    c. The proposed solution produces the required result but does not produce any of the optional desired results.
    d. The proposed solution does not produce the required result.

12. Suppose the following situation exists: Your company is based in Atlanta, and has branch offices in Los Angeles and New York City. Each of the three

offices has a 10Base-T network. Users need to access resources in all three offices.

> **Required result:** You must implement a networking solution that would offer WAN communications between sites.
>
> **Optional desired results:** The WAN connection needs to support about 1.5 Mbps of data.
>
> The WAN connection needs to be able to continue operations at 1.5 Mbps even if one of the WAN links should fail.
>
> **Proposed solution:** Use two T-1 connection lines: one between Atlanta and Los Angeles and one between Los Angeles and New York.

Which results does the proposed solution produce?

a. The proposed solution produces the required result and produces both of the optional desired results.

b. The proposed solution produces the required result and produces only one of the optional desired results.

c. The proposed solution produces the required result but does not produce any of the optional desired results.

d. The proposed solution does not produce the required result.

13. Sonet systems are _____ technology.
    a. twisted pair, copper based
    b. ThinNet cabling
    c. fiber optic
    d. wireless

14. Sonet's base signal (STS-1) operates at a bit rate of _____.
    a. 64 Kbps   b. 1.544 Mbps
    c. 51.840 Mbps   d. 155.520 Mbps

15. _____ is the standard for North America, while _____ is the standard for the rest of the world.
    a. Sonet; SDH   b. SDH; Sonet
    c. ATM; Sonet   d. ATM; SDH

16. ADSL increases existing twisted pair access capacity by _____.
    a. twofold   b. threefold
    c. thirtyfold   d. fiftyfold

17. A modem translates _____.
    a. analog signals into digital signals
    b. digital signals into analog signals

c. both of the above
d. none of the above

18. DSL refers to _____.
    a. a specific gauge of wire used in modem communications
    b. a modem enabling high-speed communications
    c. a connection created by a modem pair enabling high-speed communications
    d. a specific length of wire

19. True or false: T-1/E-1 and HDSL are essentially equivalent technologies.
    a. true   b. false

20. The practical upper limit of length of ADSL is _____.
    a. 6000 ft   b. 12,000 ft
    c. 18,000 ft   d. 36,000 ft

21. What is the major roadblock to providing full digital service over POTS?
    a. The "last mile" of telephone cable is still copper.
    b. Competition isn't strong enough to warrant full digital service.
    c. Fiber optic lines can be brought out to rural areas.
    d. It is too expensive for the telephone companies to implement.

22. Name two advantages of xDSL technology.
    a. it runs on fiber optic cables and increased bandwidth
    b. it is inexpensive and uses commonly available modems
    c. provides high speed digital access and is inexpensive
    d. provides fast analog service and "always on" Internet access
    e. widely available in rural areas for a modest cost

23. Which ISDN protocol series defines telephone network standards? (Select the best choice.)
    a. E   b. Q
    c. I   d. S

24. Which ISDN protocol series specifies concepts, terminology, and general techniques? (Select the best choice.)
    a. E   b. Q
    c. I   d. T

25. Which of the following ISDN terminal equipment types requires the use of a terminal adapter in order to connect to an ISDN service provider? (Select the best choice.)

a. TE1   b. TE2
c. NT1   d. NT2

26. Which statement best describes the configuration of bearer (B) channels and delta (D) channels in a standard ISDN BRI? (Select the best choice.)

a. two 64-Kbps B channels and one 16-Kbps D channel
b. two 16-Kbps D channels and one 64-Kbps B channel
c. twenty-three 64-Kbps B channels and one 16-Kbps D channel
d. twenty-three 64-Kbps B channels and one 64-Kbps D channel

27. Which of the following WAN protocols provides both voice and data capabilities over regular telephone lines? (Select the best choice.)

a. SDLC   b. ISDN
c. HDLC   d. DDR

28. In the standard North American configuration, which of the following types of communication lines provides bandwidth of 1.544 Mbps that consists of twenty-three 64-Kbps bearer channels and one 64-Kbps delta channel? (Select the best choice.)

a. ISDN BRI   b. T1
c. ISDN PRI   d. OC-3

29. Which of the following specifically describes equipment located at a customer's site? (Select the best choice.)

a. DTE   b. DCE
c. CPE   d. CO

30. CBR is used for _____.

a. multimedia e-mail
b. videoconferencing
c. Internet messenging
d. web pages

31. Which of the following is an advantage that packet-based voice provides over circuit-switched voice?

a. bandwidth can be significantly reduced through VAD
b. faster time to market for new services
c. capital investment for packet-based platforms is significantly less than circuit-switched equivalent
d. all of the above

32. Transmission systems that are designed according to North American rules work with groups of _____ calls.

a. 24   b. 26
c. 30   d. 32

33. The _____ is a particular set of standards that allows the internetworking of products from different vendors. It usually embodies a fiber optic ring that will permit transmission in both directions.

a. LAN
b. WAN
c. Sonet
d. common channel signaling network

34. Sonet's base signal (STS-1) operates at a bit rate of _____.

a. 64 Kbps   b. 51.840 Mbps
c. 1.544 Mbps   d. 155.520 Mbps

35. DMT, CAP, and QAM are all methods of which the following?

a. packetizing voice onto data networks
b. compression
c. line coding
d. all of the above

36. Pat is an employee who is able to work from home to provide technical support for the company during the evening hours. Part of Pat's responsibility is to make sure that the company's SQL database is working at all times for the company's customers. Pat runs big client-server applications and also transfers large files. These changes must happen quickly. The company is concerned about cost for these connections and also would like a practical solution. What connection would you suggest for this organization?

a. an ISDN BRI connection to the user's home
b. a dedicated T-1 connection to the user's home
c. a dedicated frame relay connection to the user's home
d. a standard 28.8 analogue dial up connection to the user's home

37. You have a leased line configured at a small office that connects to the corporate office. Your company would also like to have a backup in case the leased line goes down. Which WAN service would you most likely choose to back up the leased line?

a. frame relay with SVC
b. ISDN with DDR
c. dedicated serial line
d. ATM

38. Which WAN technology was designed to use high-performance digital lines and is packet switched?

    a. FDDI   b. ISDN

    c. ATM   d. frame relay

39. What is the total bandwidth of an ISDN BRI circuit?

    a. 54 Kbps   b. 112 Kbps

    c. 144 Kbps   d. 64 Kbps

    e. 128 Kbps

40. Your company has decided to pay for one ISDN B channel to your house so that you can do some technical support from home. What is the bandwidth capacity of a single ISDN B channel?

    a. 16 Kbps   b. 128 Kbps

    c. 64 Kbps   d. 512 Kbps

    e. 1.54 Mbps

41. You have just configured DDR and would like to test the link. What can you use to bring up the connection?

    a. Increase the idle timeout parameter.

    b. Send interesting traffic across the link.

    c. Reboot one of the ISDN routers.

    d. Reset the DDR ISDN router statistics to zero.

42. Which two are facts about ISDN? (Choose two.)

    a. ISDN provides only data-only capability.

    b. ISDN provides an integrated voice/data capability.

    c. The ISDN standards define the hardware and call set up schemes for end-to-end digital connectivity.

    d. Users receive more bandwidth on WANs with a leased line of 56 Kbps than with multiple B channels.

43. ISDN is sometimes used in locations that do not offer support for DSL or cable modem connections. Your choices may be analog modems or an ISDN connection in those remote locations. ISDN has benefits over regular dial-up modem connections. Which of the following are examples of these benefits? (Choose three.)

    a. PVCs are faster and more reliable.

    b. No specialized equipment is required.

    c. Data transfer is faster than typical modems.

    d. Call set-up is faster than with standard telephone service.

    e. It carries many types of data traffic such as voice, video, and data.

44. In today's networks which encapsulation methods are most commonly used (ISDN)?

    a. IP and IPX   b. PPP and SDLC

    c. IP and PPP   d. PPP and HDLC

45. Which of the following WAN encapsulations support multiple upper-layer protocols? (Choose Two.)

    a. PPP   b. LAPD

    c. ISDN   d. HDLC

CHAPTER 10

Packet Switching Networks

Topics Covered in this Chapter

Introduction

In Chapter 9, permanent and leased lines were discussed. After Chapter 10 reviews what a packet switching network is, common types of packet switching networks, including X.25 and Frame Relay, are discussed.

Objectives

- Compare and contrast X.25 and Frame Relay networks.
- Explain the need for SLAs and list and define SLA criteria.
- For Frame Relay networks, define DLCI and explain how they can be used.
- For Frame Relay networks, explain why and how to use subinterfaces.
- Given a scenario, troubleshoot a Frame Relay problem.

10.1   PACKET SWITCHING

Because large internetworks can have multiple paths linking source and destination devices, information is switched as it travels through the various communication channels. A common technique used in data networks is packet switching.

In **packet switching** methods, messages are broken into small parts called packets. Each packet is tagged with source, destination, and intermediary node addresses as appropriate. Packets can have a defined maximum length and can be stored in RAM instead of on a hard disk. Packets can take a variety of possible paths through the network in an attempt to keep the network connections filled at time. However, because the message is broken into multiple parts, sending packets via different paths adds to the possibility that packet order could get scrambled. Therefore, a sequencing number is added to each packet. Packets are sent over the most appropriate path. Each device chooses the best path at that time for every packet. Therefore, if one path is too busy, it can send the packet through another path. Because some packets may be delayed, which cause the packets to arrive out of order, the device will reorder them by sequence number to reconstruct the original message (see Figure 10.1). The Internet is based on a packet switching protocol. Other examples include ATM, Frame Relay, switched multimegabit data service (SMDS), and X.25. Message switching is typically used to support services such as e-mail, web pages, calendaring, or workflow information. Two well-known examples of packet switched networks are X.25 and Frame Relay.

When a subscriber accesses a WAN network, such as X.25, Frame Relay, or ATM, the leased network is sometimes referred to as a cloud. The **cloud** represents a logical network with multiple pathways and is depicted as a black box in illustrations. Subscribers

Figure 10.1 Packet Switching

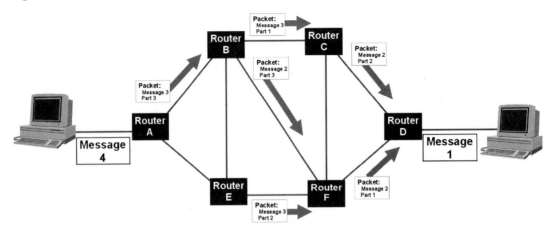

Table 10.1 Comparisons between X.25 and Frame Relay

X.25	Frame Relay
X.25 has link and packet protocol levels. The link level of X.25 consists of a reliable data link protocol called LAPB. X.25 LAPB information frames are numbered and acknowledged. Circuits are defined at the packet layer, which runs on top of the LAPB data link layer. Packets are numbered and acknowledged. There are complex rules that govern the flow of data across a X.25 interface. These rules often interrupt and impede the flow of data.	Frame Relay is a simple data link layer protocol. Frame Relay provides a basic data transfer service that does not guarantee reliable delivery of data. Frame Relay frames are neither numbered nor acknowledged. Circuits are identified by an address field in the frame header. Data is packaged into simple Frame Relay frames and transmitted toward their destinations. Data can be sent across a Frame Relay network whenever there is bandwidth available to carry it.

who connect to the cloud don't worry about the details inside the cloud. Instead, the only thing that subscribers need to know is that they connect at one edge of the cloud and the data is received at the other edge of the cloud.

The next few sections describe X.25 and Frame Relay. The major differences between Frame Relay and X.25 data networks are summarized in Table 10.1.

10.2   X.25

In the 1970s, many public data networks were actually owned by private companies and government agencies. In most cases, the WAN of one company or agency was unique and often incompatible with the WAN of another company or agency. Of course, when these companies need to interconnect these networks, some form of common network interface protocol was needed.

In 1976, the CCITT, which is now called the ITU, recommended. X.25. **X.25** is a packet switched network that allows remote devices to communicate with each other across digital links without the expense of individual leased lines. ISO standards view the X.25 packet layer as a layer 3 network protocol and X.121 addresses would be used to identify the endpoints of every network communication. It typically is used in packet switched networks of common carriers, such as the telephone companies, implemented at speeds below 64 Kbps.

While Frame Relay has replaced many X.25 networks, X.25 is still used in IBM networks and interconnects LANs in areas where Frame Relay service is not available. X.25 also continues to be popular for applications such as bank ATM connections and credit card validations. A version of X.25 operating across an ISDN Basic Rate Interface D channel is very cost effective for intermittent, low-bandwidth, data communications.

10.2.1   Establishing Virtual Circuits

The user end of the network contains DTE and the carrier's equipment contains DCE. Connections occur on logical channels using either switched virtual circuits or permanent virtual circuits.

ITU-T standard X.121 defines the global addressing scheme for X.25 DTEs. X.121 addresses are also called international data numbers (IDNs). The length of an X.121 address is not fixed; however, the length is limited to a maximum of 14 decimal digits. The first three digits of the address identify a country. The fourth digit identifies a specific packet switched data network (PSN). When combined, the first four digits are called the data network identification code (DNIC).

The remaining address digits identify a specific DTE attached to the network and is known as the network terminal number (NTN). It is up 10 decimal digits, including the country code and a provider number that is assigned by the ITU. Because there is no Address Resolution Protocol (ARP) incorporated into an X.25 network, X.25 addresses must be manually mapped to layer 3 (IP) addresses in a router.

You can directly access the X.25 data network by using a X.25 smart card or by using a modem, which would dial into a packet assembler/disassembler (PAD). A PAD is used when a DTE device such as a character-mode terminal is too simple to implement the full X.25 functionality. The PAD is located between a DTE device and a DCE device, and it performs three primary functions: (1) buffering, (2) packet assembly, and (3) packet disassembly (see Figure 10.2).

Switched virtual circuits (SVCs) are temporary connections used for sporadic data transfers. They require that two DTE devices to establish, maintain, and terminate a session each time the devices need to communicate. To establish a connection on a SVC, the calling DTE sends a call request packet to its local packet switching equipment (usually the phone company), which includes the address of the remote DTE to be contacted. The destination for each packet is identified by its logical channel identifier (LCI) or logical channel number (LCN).

As packets are being sent, the calling DCE device examines the packet headers to determine which virtual circuit to use and then sends the packets to the closest switch in the path of that virtual circuit. The X.25 switches pass the traffic to the next intermediate node

Figure 10.2   A X.25 Network

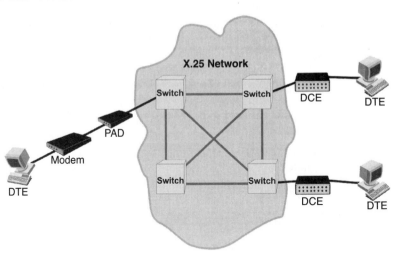

in the path, which may be another switch or the remote DCE device. This continues until the packets reach their destinations.

At the destination DCE, a second VCI is assigned to the request and it is forwarded to the destination DTE. The destination DTE decides whether or not to accept the call (the call request packet includes the sender's DTE address as well as other information that the called DTE can use to decide whether or not to accept the call). A call is accepted by issuing a call accepted packet (CAP),or cleared by issuing a clear request packet (CRP). Once the originating DTE receives the call accepted packet, the virtual circuit is established and data transfer may take place.

After the SVC is created, the information transfer phase assigns each packet the same VCI numbers that were used to create the circuit. This enables the DTEs to differentiate packets from multiple sessions arriving on the same link. Because error and flow control are provided at the packet level, data reliability is very high. When either DTE wishes to terminate the call, a clear request packet is sent to the remote DTE, which responds with a clear confirmation packet.

PVCs are permanently established connections used for frequent and consistent data transfer. PVCs do not require that sessions be established and terminated. Therefore, DTEs can begin transferring data whenever necessary because the session is always active.

A single X.25 interface on a router can be configured to support up to 4095 SVCs. By combining multiple SVCs for a single specific protocol, the throughput can be increased—provided that the protocol provides its own packet resequencing. A maximum of eight SVCs may be combined into one path for a protocol.

10.2.2   X.25 Protocols

X.21bis is a physical-layer protocol used in X.25 that defines the electrical and mechanical procedures for using the physical medium. X.21bis handles the activation and deactivation of the physical medium that connects DTE and DCE devices. It supports point-to-point connections, speeds up to 19.2 Kbps, and synchronous, full duplex transmission over four-wire media.

The most commonly used X.25 link level protocol is the link access procedure, balanced (LAPB), a derivative of HDLC. It is a data link layer protocol that manages communication and packet framing between DTE and DCE devices. LAPB is a bit oriented protocol, which ensures that frames are correctly ordered and error free by using a sequence of frames that contain address, control, and data fields. It is also responsible for link synchronization (see Figure 10.3).

> *NOTE:* PLPs also can run over logical link control 2 (LLC2) implementations on LANs and over ISDN interfaces running link access procedure on the D channel (LAPD).

There are three types of LAPB frames: (1) information, (2) supervisory, and (3) unnumbered. The information frame (I-frame) carries upper-layer information and some control information. I-frame functions include sequencing, flow control, and error detection and recovery. I-frames carry send and receive sequence numbers. The supervisory frame (S-frame) carries control information. S-frame functions include requesting and suspending transmissions, reporting on status, and acknowledging the receipt of I-frames. S-frames carry only receive sequence numbers. The unnumbered frame (U-frame) carries control information. U-frame functions include link setup and disconnection, as well as error reporting. U-frames carry no sequence numbers.

Packet layer protocol (PLP) is the X.25 network layer protocol. PLP manages packet exchanges between DTE devices across virtual circuits. It also is responsible for defining the datagrams, which are self-contained units that include the information needed to route the unit to its destination. PLP operates in five distinct modes: (1) call setup, (2) data transfer, (3) idle, (4) call clearing, and (5) restarting.

Figure 10.3   The X.25 Protocol Suite

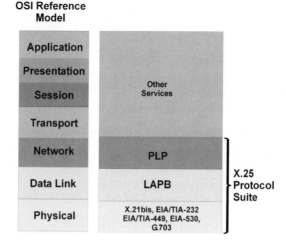

10.3   FRAME RELAY

It is now clear to many organizations that Frame Relay is a far more efficient and cost effective WAN solution than a private, leased line network for data applications. Estimates state that the average enterprise network customer will save at least 40 percent by migrating their WAN from leased lines to Frame Relay. In some cases the savings can be as much as 60 percent. Much of the efficiency and cost effectiveness of Frame Relay is based on the concept of statistical multiplexing, where instead of a fixed circuit of permanent bandwidth, bandwidth is allocated on demand. Frame Relay's flexible bandwidth allocation scheme fits well with the "bursty" nature of data traffic; the growth of IP traffic is surpassing that of all other protocols across the WAN.

Frame Relay is a direct descendant of X.25 and is defined by ITU Q.922 and Q.933 standards. **Frame Relay** is a connection-oriented, packet switching protocol designed to use high-speed digital backbone links to support modern protocols. Instead of providing error handling and flow control like X.25 does, it depends on the upper-layer protocols to provide error handling and flow control for connecting devices on a WAN. It only defines the physical and data link layers of the OSI model, which allows for greater flexibility of upper-layer protocols to be run across Frame Relay. It operates at the physical and data link layer of the OSI reference mode.

Frame Relay is a multi-access network, which means that more than two devices can attach to the medium. Multi-access is the most obvious difference between Frame Relay and leased lines. However, leased lines are used as the access the link component of Frame Relay networks. Therefore, while Frame Relay originally was designed for use across ISDN interfaces, it can also be found on any serial interface including switched 56 line, a fractional T-1 line, full T-1 line, fractional-T-3 line and full T-3 line. In countries supporting the E-carrier hierarchy, connectivity is available at the E-1 and E-3 speed, where demand is strong and the network infrastructure supports it.

10.3.1   Accessing a Frame Relay Network

The equipment at a point of presence is either a full-fledged switch that connects to subscribers and also is part of the provider's core network, or a multiplexer that combines traffic from several low-speed subscriber lines onto a high-speed line connecting back to the core network.

The cost of a circuit that crosses the Frame Relay provider's network normally does not depend on distance, although there might be a surcharge for a circuit that spans thousands of miles or crosses national boundaries. A circuit fee is calculated according to:

- The bandwidth in each direction of each virtual circuit
- The degree to which you can burst extra traffic onto the circuit
- Special features such as a high level of reliability or high-priority delivery

The most common use of a Frame Relay network is to connect individual LANs together. DTE is user terminal equipment that creates information for transmissions such as PCs and routers. Using a Frame Relay network, it typically costs less than using dedicated point-to-point circuits because customers can use multiple virtual circuits on a single

Figure 10.4 Dedicated Point-to-Point *v.* Frame Relay

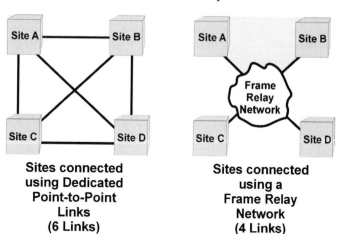

physical circuit. For example, if you look at Figure 10.4, it would take six dedicated point-to-point links to connect four sites. With a Frame Relay network, it would only take four links to connect the same sites. If you have five sites, it would take ten links using dedicated point-to-point links versus five links to a Frame Relay network.

To connect the DTEs to a Frame Relay network, you use a **Frame Relay Access Device (FRAD),** sometimes referred to as a Frame Relay assembler/disassembler. It multiplexes and formats traffic for entering a Frame Relay network. A FRAD is a device that allows non-Frame Relay devices to connect to a Frame Relay network. FRADs can be included in routers and bridges, or can stand alone.

> *NOTE:* You may also need a CSU/DSU to connect to common links such as a T-1 line. The CSU/DSU may be included with the FRAD.

Frame Relay routers are the most versatile of the three because they can handle traffic from other WAN protocols, reroute traffic if a connection goes down, and provide flow and congestion control. Frame Relay bridges, which are used to connect a branch office to a hub, are low cost, unintelligent routers. Stand-alone FRADs are designed to aggregate (gather) and convert data, but have no routing capabilities. They typically are used on sites that already have bridges and routers or for sending mainframe traffic.

> *NOTE:* The distinctions between these devices are blurring as vendors combine their functions into a single device.

Initially, Frame Relay gained acceptance as a means to provide end users with a solution for LAN-to-LAN connections and other data connectivity requirements. Due to advances in areas such as digital signal processing and faster backbone links within the Frame Relay network, vendors are beginning to develop viable methods that incorporate non-data traffic such as voice or video over the Frame Relay network.

If you have a common private Frame Relay network and you are using both Frame Relay and non-Frame Relay interfaces (such as a phone system), you will need a special multiplexer. The multiplexer will forward the Frame Relay traffic to the Frame Relay interface and onto the data network while non-Frame Relay traffic would be forwarded to the appropriate application or service (such as private branch exchange (PBX) for telephone service or a video-teleconferencing application) (see Figure 10.5).

To get to a Frame Relay network, you must first get a Frame Relay Bearer Service (FRBS), which is offered by common carriers such as telephone companies. If you use SVC as provided by a public carrier, the Frame Relay switching equipment is located in the CO of a telecommunications carrier. Of course, administering and maintaining Frame Relay network equipment and service is provided by the carrier, which relieves the customer of such duties. The majority of today's Frame Relay networks are public, carrier-provided networks.

Today, many worldwide organizations are using PVCs to deploy private Frame Relay networks. In these cases, the administration and maintenance of the network is the responsibility of the customer. The customer owns all the equipment, including the switching equipment.

When a packet is being sent on a Frame Relay network, it first reaches the switch. Using PVCs or SVCs, the packet is then switched or forwarded to the next switch toward its final destination. The network is connection-oriented because the originating and terminating ends are programmed into network switches. Frame Relay networks use **data-link connec-**

Figure 10.5 A Frame Relay Network

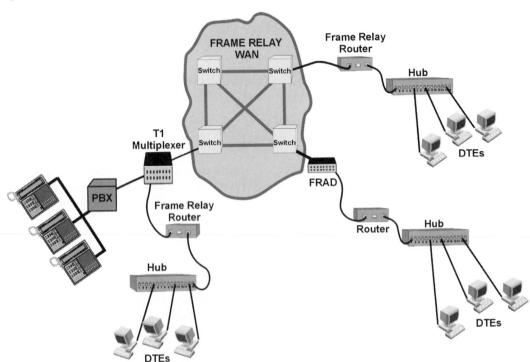

Figure 10.6 A Single Frame Relay Virtual Circuit Can be Assigned Different DLCIs on Each End of a Virtual Circuit

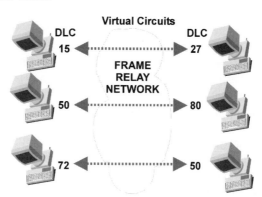

tion identifiers (DLCIs) for addressing to identify the originating and terminating ends. A DLCI is a 10-bit address (with 1024 different combinations) that identifies a particular PVC.

In most Frame Relay networks, each end of a connection assigns its own DLCIs from a pool of locally unused numbers—a scheme called "local addressing" or "locally significant DLCIs." The service provider's frame relay network then maps one DLCI to the other by using a look-up table. Locally significant DLCIs have become the primary method of addressing because the same address can be used in several different locations while still referring to different connections. Thus, local addressing prevents a customer from running out of DLCIs as the network grows (see Figure 10.6).

An alternative to addressing DLCIs locally is to use global addressing, where each endpoint is assigned its own unique DLCI. In global addressing, DLCI numbers cannot be reused. When global addressing is used, a DLCI can be thought of as the MAC address of the destination. The advantage of global addressing is that you can look at a DLCI value in a frame and immediately know its destination (or source) without having to consult translation tables. You can think of a DLCI in global addressing as being similar to the MAC address of the destination. One benefit of global addressing is that it is quite convenient to add new sites.

Using the same DLCI at both ends of a connection would require some sort of global management of DLCI values, which could add operational complexity—particularly in large networks. In addition, this scheme would require many more DLCI values, which translates into a larger DLCI field and a larger frame relay header. A larger header would decrease network efficiency and could pose interoperability problems with standard header implementations of Frame Relay. However, use of global addressing does impose a limit on the size of your network; if you go beyond 1024 sites, you run out of unique DLCIs.

While local addressing is how Frame Relay works, if you follow the convention of global addressing, planning is easier because the addressing appears similar to LAN addressing. A global address for one DTE simply means that all other DTEs with a VC to this one DTE use its global address on their local access links. While local addressing is customer port unique, global addressing is customer network unique. Local addressing is more scalable (and more confusing), while global addressing is simpler.

Routers can be configured to perform Frame Relay switching. Doing so involves a series of things in pairs. There are two parts to Frame Relay switching, the Frame Relay DTE (router) and the Frame Relay DCE (switch).

There are two types of switching that a router can be configured for, Local Frame Relay switching and Remote Frame Relay switching. Configuring a router for Local Frame Relay switching enables it to forward frames based on the DLCI number found in the frame header. Configuring a router for Remote Frame Relay switching enables it to encapsulate frames into an IP packet and tunnel them across an IP backbone. For IP devices to communicate with each other over a Frame Relay network, their IP addresses must be mapped to their DLCIs. This mapping can function as a multipoint device; one that can identify to the Frame Relay network the appropriate destination virtual circuit for each packet that is sent over the single physical interface to the Frame Relay network. The mapping can be done dynamically through Inverse ARP (IARP) or manually through Frame Relay map commands.

When a user connects using a Frame Relay network, he or she should not see the difference between connecting to and gathering resources from a local server and a server at a remote site connected with Frame Relay. Chances are that the Frame Relay connection will be slower than a 10 Mbps Ethernet LAN, but the physical difference in the connection should be transparent to the user.

When two DTE devices communicate, they use the following process:

Step 1: The user's network device sends a frame out of the local network. The hardware address of the router (default gateway) will be in the header of the frame.

Step 2: The router picks up the frame, extracts the packet, and discards the frame. It then looks at the destination IP address within the packet and checks to see whether it knows how to get to the destination network by looking in the routing table.

Step 3: The router then forwards the data out the interface that may be able to find the remote network. If it cannot find the network in its routing table, it will discard the packet. Because this will be a serial interface encapsulated with Frame Relay, the router puts the packet onto the Frame Relay network encapsulated within a Frame Relay frame. It will add the DLCI number associated with the serial interface. DLCIs identify the virtual circuit (PVC or SVC) to the routers and provider's switches participating in the Frame Relay network.

Step 4: The CSU/DSU receives the digital signal and encodes it into the type of digital signaling that the switch at the Packet Switch Exchange (PSE) can understand. The PSE receives the digital signal and extracts the 1s and 0s from the line.

Step 5: The CSU/DCU is connected to a demarcation installed by the service provider, and its location is the service provider's first point of responsibility (last point on the receiving end). The demark typically is just a RJ-45 jack installed close to the router and CSU/DSU.

Step 6: The demark typically is a twisted-pair cable that connects to the local loop. The local loop connects to the closest CO, sometimes called a point of presence (POP). The local loop can connect using various physical mediums, but twisted-pair or fiber is very common.

Step 7: The CO receives the frame and sends it through the Frame Relay cloud to its destination. This cloud can be many switching offices. It looks for the destination IP address and DLCI number. It typically can find the DLCI number of the remote device or router by looking up the IP-to-DLCI mapping. Frame Relay mapping is usually done statically by the service provider, but it can be done dynamically by using the IARP protocol. Remember that before data is sent through the cloud, the virtual circuit is created from end to end.

Step 8: Once the frame reaches the switching office closest to the destination office, it is sent through the local loop. The frame is received at the demarc and then it is sent to the CSU/DSU. Finally, the router extracts the packet, or datagram, from the frame and puts the packet in a new LAN frame to be delivered to the destination host. The frame on the LAN will have the final destination hardware address in the header. This was found in the router's ARP cache, or an ARP broadcast may have been performed.

The destination DLCI address is placed in the header initially, but it is replaced with the source DLCI address before the frame arrives at the destination. The destination DLCI address initially is placed in the LAPF header that is used by Frame Relay. Before going into the Frame Relay cloud, the value in this field is replaced so that the receiving router knows the frame's origin. The LAPF header contains only one DLCI address.

10.3.2   Service Level Agreements

When you use Frame Relay, you will share with many customers. Traffic that belongs to other customers might pile up at switches internal to the Frame Relay network and cause unpredictable delays. A customer pays a fixed monthly fee for the access line that attaches a customer device to the service provider's network. The cost of this line depends on the distance between the subscriber's site and the provider's network. A provider helps its customers keep this cost down by installing equipment at dozens, or even hundreds, of POPs.

A service level agreement (SLA) is a contract between a provider of WAN services and a buyer of those services. SLAs differ from ordinary, generic service agreements in that they obligate service providers to maintain a certain grade or level of service that is contractually guaranteed. The overall level of service is defined by a set of measurable parameters, each having thresholds that are negotiated by the service provider and customer. Usually there is a provision for some degree of compensation if thresholds are not met. In some cases, multiple tiered thresholds with corresponding degrees of compensation are negotiated between service provider and customer.

Often, the parameters and thresholds in a SLA are specific to each virtual circuit purchased by the customer. Many times, some VCs are more important than others due to the sites they connect or the traffic they carry. Therefore, it often makes sense to have different parameters or thresholds for different VCs. However, monitoring and maintaining different service levels for different VCs sharing the same physical connection can be a difficult and labor-intensive task. In addition, many customers are beginning to take a look at SLA parameters that are defined on a network protocol basis and even on an application basis.

Vendors and providers that participate in the Frame Relay industry have recognized the need to define standard measurements that can be used as the basis of SLAs. SLA parameters are defined in Frame Relay document FRF.13. It includes the following four parameters:

- **Frame transfer delay**—The time required to transport a frame between the first bits of the entry and the last bits of the exit points, measured in milliseconds. FRF.13 states that measurements should be made relative to frames containing a 128-byte payload (although a different size could be specified in the SLA).
- **Frame delivery ratio**—The proportion of frames successfully delivered.
- **Data delivery ratio**—Measures the quotient for delivered payload bytes (total payload bytes delivered/total payload bytes offered). This gives a customer a measure of the proportion or ratio of its data that is getting through. This ratio should be close to the frame delivery ratio.
- **Service availability**—Measures that are applied to individual virtual circuits. There are three criteria of service availability.
  - The percentage of time a virtual circuit is available.
  - The average time to repair a broken virtual circuit.
  - The average time between fault outages for a virtual circuit.

After contracting to meet specified service levels, a provider should issue periodic reports that describe the measurement results to the customer with each monthly bill.

10.3.3   Frame Relay Frames and Local Management Interface

A standard Frame Relay frame consists of the following fields (see Figure 10.7):

- **Flags**—Delimits the beginning and end of the frame. The value of this field is always the same and is represented either as the hexadecimal number 7E or as the binary number 01111110.
- **Address**—Contains the following information:
  - **DLCI**—The 10-bit DLCI is the essence of the Frame Relay header. This value represents the virtual connection between the DTE device and the switch. Each virtual connection that is multiplexed onto the physical channel will be represented by a unique DLCI. DLCI values have local significance only, which means that they are unique only to the physical channel on which they reside. Therefore, devices at opposite ends of a connection can use different DLCI values to refer to the same virtual connection.

Figure 10.7   A Frame Relay Packet

Field Length in bytes	8	16	Variable	16	8
	Flags	Address	Data	FCS	Flags

- **Extended Address (EA)**—The EA is used to indicate whether the byte in which the EA value is 1 is the last addressing field. If the value is 1, then the current byte is determined to be the last DLCI octet. Although current Frame Relay implementations all use a two-octet DLCI, this capability does allow longer DLCIs to be used in the future. The eighth bit of each byte of the address field is used to indicate the EA.
- **C/R**—The C/R is the bit that follows the most significant DLCI byte in the address field. The C/R bit is not currently defined.
- **Congestion Control**—This consists of the 3 bits that control the Frame Relay congestion-notification mechanisms. These are the FECN, BECN, and DE bits, which are the last 3 bits in the address field.
- **Data**—Contains encapsulated upper-layer data. Each frame in this variable length field includes a user data or payload field that will vary in length up to 16,000 octets. This field serves to transport the higher-layer PDU through a Frame Relay network.
- **FCS**—Ensures the integrity of transmitted data. This value is computed by the source device and verified by the receiver to ensure integrity of transmission.

At the physical layer, all signals in Frame Relay networks are binary and are represented by either a one or a zero. The FRAD is responsible for receiving these binary signals from the telephone carrier. To transmit binary signals on electronic media, voltage is either raised or lowered. Most encoding methods are bipolar.

Frame Relay networks are statistically time-division multiplexed to combine multiple virtual circuits and transmit them over a single transmission circuit, assigning each set of DTEs (source and destination) a data link connection identifier. Because it uses STDM, it assigns time slots dynamically, to make better use of the link by not using empty time slots. As a result, it uses the bandwidth more efficiently, particularly for bursty data traffic among clients and servers and for inter-LAN links. Lastly, it uses variable length packets to make efficient and flexible transfers.

Frame Relay networks do not provide error handling or control. When an error occurs in a frame, typically caused by noise on the line, it is detected upon receipt of the frame by using the FCS, a form of CRC, and the frame is simply thrown away. Instead, the error handling is left to destination devices such as the router and upper protocols such as TCP/IP or IPX. Because the Frame Relay is built on top of an all digital network, the network discards very few frames, particularly when the networks are operating at well below design capacity.

Because a Frame Relay network does not have to perform any error handling, and because the network automatically preserves the order of data; there are no frame retransmissions, sequence numbers, or acknowledgements. Therefore, the Frame Relay network has low overhead, which results in a faster network.

Much like NICs, Frame Relay cards have a buffer (temporary memory) that holds the incoming frames until they are processed or holds the outgoing frames until they are sent. Like any other network connection, a Frame Relay network may experience network congestion, such as when a network node or switch receives more frames than it can process or when a network node or switch needs to send more frames across a given line than the speed of the line permits. As a result, the buffer fills up and the node is forced to discard frames. Because LAN traffic is extremely bursty, the probability of occasional congestion is high. Therefore, it is very important that the Frame Relay network have excellent congestion management features—both to minimize the occurrence and severity of congestion and to minimize the effects of discards when they are required.

When you subscribe for a 56 Kbps, fractal T-1 or full T-1 line, you will be asked to specify a **Committed Information Rate (CIR)** for each DLCI. This value specifies the maximum average data rate that the network undertakes to deliver under "normal conditions". If you send faster than the CIR on a given DLCI, the network will flag some frames with a discard eligibility (DE) bit. The network will do its best to deliver all packets but will discard any DE packets first if there is congestion.

> *NOTE:* Many inexpensive Frame Relay services are based on a CIR of zero. This means that every frame is a DE frame, and the network will throw any frame away when it needs to.

To help, Frame Relay provides indications that the network is becoming congested by means of the forward explicit congestion notification (FECN) bit and the backward explicit congestion notification (BECN) bit, which are embedded within data frames. These are used to tell the application to slow down, hopefully before packets start to be discarded. For these bits to be used, the router or bridge would have to recognize and process the bits.

Frame Relay offers bursting, a unique advantage over leased lines. Because the leased line bandwidth is fixed, if a device attempts to send data at a rate higher than the line bandwidth, the packets will not get through and performance will be degraded. Frame Relay, however, allows a device to transmit data at a higher rate than the CIR for a few seconds if the excess data does not encounter a congested switch.

Devices using the extra free bandwidth available do run a risk: Any data beyond the CIR is eligible for discard depending on network congestion. The greater the network congestion, the greater the risk that frames transmitted above the CIR will be lost. While the risk typically is very low up to the CIR, if a frame is discarded it will have to be resent. Data can even be transmitted at rates higher than the CIR, but doing this has the greatest risk of lost packets. If you find that you consistently need long bursts, you should consider purchasing a higher CIR.

The **Local Management Interface (LMI),** a signaling standard between a CPE device (router) and a frame switch, adds extensions onto the Frame Relay protocol that manage complex internetworks. Key Frame Relay LMI extensions include global addressing, virtual circuit status messages, and multicasting.

> *NOTE:* There are actually three LMI standards. In addition to the one already mentioned, which is referred to as the Cisco LMI (developed in 1990 by Cisco Systems, StrataCom, Northern Telecom, and Digital Equipment Corporation), there are also the ANSI and Q.933A standards.

The LMI global addressing extension gives a Frame Relay DLCI values global rather than local significance. DLCI values become DTE addresses that are unique in the Frame Relay WAN. The global addressing extension adds functionality and manageability to Frame Relay internetworks. Individual network interfaces and the end nodes attached to them, for example, can be identified by using standard address resolution and discovery techniques. In addition, the entire Frame Relay network appears (to routers) to be a typical LAN.

LMI virtual circuit status messages provide communication and synchronization between Frame Relay DTE and DCE devices. These messages are periodically used to report on the status of PVCs, which prevents data from being sent into black holes (that is, over PVCs that no longer exist).

The LMI multicasting extension allows multicast groups to be assigned. Multicasting saves bandwidth by allowing routing updates and address resolution messages to be sent only to specific groups of routers. The extension also transmits reports on the status of multicast groups in update messages.

There are several versions of the Cisco LMI, Q.933A, and ANSI. The Cisco LMI, Q.933A, and ANSI all provide information regarding the ISDN configuration and the status of the virtual circuits. The LMI type you configure on your router must match the type that your service provider uses. In addition, the LMI type must be the same on both ends of the connection.

10.3.4   IETF Encapsulation

Today's enterprise networks carry a diverse array of protocols including IP, NetWare IPX, DECnet, shared LAN, and wide area links. Incoming LAN and PPP frames are not a problem. The headers of Ethernet, Token Ring, FDDI, and PPP frames include a field that identifies the protocol being carried. This enables a router (or other networking device) to process each frame appropriately.

Unfortunately, Frame Relay standards did not define a header field that identifies the type of protocol data that is carried in a Frame Relay payload. This is not a problem when a virtual circuit carries only a single protocol. In this case, the protocol type is identified when the circuit is configured.

However, using separate circuits for each protocol usually is more costly than combining traffic on a shared circuit. In addition, a subscriber might be able to use throughput more effectively by merging bursty traffic onto a shared circuit. For example, if IP and NetWare traffic is sent between two sites on separate 128 Kbps circuits, many of the frames in a short IP burst of 256 Kbps are likely to be discarded. If both types of traffic share a 256 Kbps circuit, and there is a lull in the NetWare transmission, the IP burst would be within the CIR.

An IETF work group defined Frame Relay encapsulation formats that include a field identifying the protocol being carried. By supporting IETF encapsulations, providers give their customers the opportunity to decide if they want to merge traffic for multiple protocols on one circuit.

The first byte is a control field with the value X'03, which means unnumbered information. The next byte is a Network Layer Protocol Identifier (NLPID) code. NLPIDs are administered by the ISO and the ITU-T. For example, IP version 4 has been assigned the NLPID value X'CC, and the ISO Connectionless Network Protocol (CLNP) has been assigned X'81 (see Table 10.2).

10.3.5   Broadcast Handling

Broadcasts are not supported over a Frame Relay network. In other words, no capability exists for a DTE to send a frame that is replicated and delivered across more than one VC. However, routers need to send broadcasts for several features, such as routing protocol updates and SAP updates, to work.

Table 10.2   IETF Protocol Header Information. NLPID Code Used in IETF Protocol Header

NLPID	Protocol
X'81	ISO connectionless network protocol (CLNP)
X'82	ISO end system to end system (ES-IES)
X'83	ISO intermediate system to intermediate system (IS-IS)
X'8E	IP version 6
X'B0	FRF.9 data compression protocol frames
X'B1	FRF.12 fragmented frames
X'CC	IP version 4
X'CF	PPP in Frame Relay

Figure 10.8   A Fully Meshed Frame Relay Network Does Not Require Subinterfaces

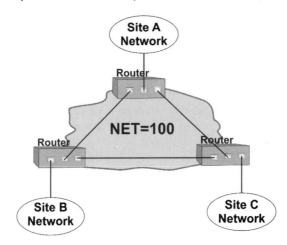

To get around this problem, routers can send copies of the broadcast each to VC that you instruct it to. If hundreds of VCs terminate in one router, then hundreds of copies could be sent for each broadcast. Some routers can be configured to limit the amount of bandwidth that is used for these replicated broadcasts.

10.3.6   Subinterfaces

Frame Relay configuration can be accomplished with or without the use of subinterfaces. Early implementation of Frame Relay technology required that a router (DTE device) must have a WAN serial interface for every PVC (see Figure 10.8). If subinterfaces are not used, then all router interfaces attached to this same Frame Relay cloud should be configured with IP addresses in the same subnet (or the same external IPX address). In other words, treat the Frame Relay cloud as any other multiaccess medium (such as a LAN). However, Frame Relay configuration without subinterfaces introduces some rout-

Figure 10.9   Split-Horizon Does Not Allow Remote Sites to Send Routing Updates to Each Other

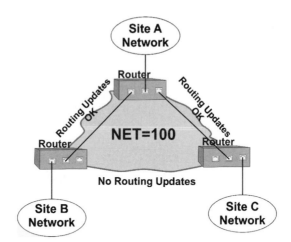

ing protocol issues when there is not a full mesh of virtual circuits (VCs) between each pair of routers.

The concept of subinterfaces was originally created to better handle issues caused by split-horizon over Non-Broadcast Multiple Access (NBMA) networks (such as Frame Relay and X.25) and distance-vector based routing protocols (such as IPX RIP/SAP or AppleTalk).

Split-horizon dictates that a routing update received on an interface cannot be retransmitted out onto the same interface. This rule holds even if the routing update was received on one Frame Relay PVC and destined to retransmit out onto another Frame Relay PVC. Referring to Figure 10.9, this would mean that Sites B and C can exchange routing information with Site A, but would not be able to exchange routing information with each other. Split-horizon does not allow Site A to send routing updates received from Site B on to Site C, and vice versa.

If you have a partially-meshed Frame Relay network and you divide it into a number of virtual, point-to-point networks by using subinterfaces, you can overcome the problem when using split-horizon.

Subinterfaces provide a flexible solution for routing various protocols over partially-meshed Frame Relay networks. A single, physical interface can be logically divided into multiple, virtual subinterfaces. With subinterfaces, each new point-to-point subnetwork is assigned its own network number. To the routed protocol, each subnetwork now appears to be located on separate interfaces (see Figure 10.10). Routing updates received from Site B on one logical point-to-point subinterface can be forwarded to Site C on a separate logical interface without violating split-horizon.

The subinterface may be defined as either a point-to-point connection or a multipoint connection. Multipoint interfaces/subinterfaces are still subject to split-horizon limitations. All nodes attached to a multipoint subinterface belong to the same network number. Typically, multipoint subinterfaces are used in conjunction with point-to-point interfaces

Figure 10.10   Subinterfaces Allow Remote Sites to Exchange Routing Updates with Each Other

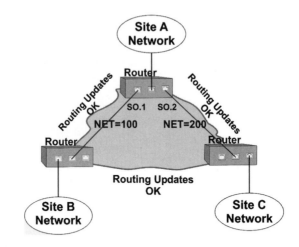

Figure 10.11   Multipoint and PPP Subinterfaces Can Coexist

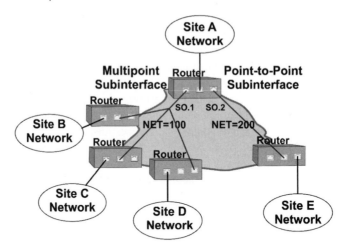

in cases where an existing multipoint Frame Relay cloud is migrating to a subinterfaced point-to-point network design. A multipoint subinterface is used to keep remote sites on a single network number while slowly migrating remote sites to their own point-to-point subinterface network. Figure 10.11 shows serial 0.1 as a multipoint subinterface connecting to three different locations. All devices on the multipoint subinterface belong to the same network number (100). Site E has migrated off of the multipoint network to its own point-to-point subinterface network (200). Eventually, all remote sites can be moved to their own point-to-point subinterface networks, and the multipoint subinterface will not be necessary.

Subinterfaces are identified by their subinterface number, which can range from 0 to 4,292,967,295. Typically, the DLCI number is assigned to an interface as the subinterface number. Correlating the DLCI(s) to its/their subinterface(s) is required when using either type of subinterface. LMI enquiry messages notify the router that PVCs are active; the router then needs to know which subinterface uses the DLCI. An individual DLCI is used by only one subinterface. For a point-to-point subinterface, only one DLCI is used; for multipoint, many DLCIs are used.

Subinterfaces are never required; they can be used in any Frame Relay configuration, and most sites tend to use them. Some general guidelines when using subinterfaces include the following:

- When the network is partially meshed, using point-to-point subinterfaces overcomes split-horizon issues by treating each subinterface as a separate interface.
- When the network is partially meshed, using a multipoint subinterface will work.
- When the network is fully meshed, a multipoint subinterface can be used to reduce the number of network-layer groups (for example, IP subnets) that are used.
- When the network is fully meshed, point-to-point subinterfaces can be used. This is typically chosen to maintain consistency with other Frame Relay networks elsewhere in the network that are not fully meshed. This choice requires a larger number of IP subnets to be used.
- When the network contains some fully meshed portions (for example, when three sites have VCs between each other but the other ten do not), a multipoint subinterface can be used for the fully meshed portion and point-to-point subinterfaces can be used for the rest.
- When the network contains some fully meshed portions (for example, when three sites have VCs between each other but the other ten do not), using only point-to-point subinterfaces is another option. This requires more IP subnets and IPX networks than when using a multipoint subinterface for the fully meshed portion of the network.
- Many sites avoid confusion by always using point-to-point subinterfaces to maintain consistency.

10.3.7   Troubleshooting Frame Relay

Frame Relay is a link layer protocol service that depends on a physical connection, a physical layer access port, the data link layer, in-channel signaling procedures, and proper VC configuration. Given this information, troubleshooting Frame Relay networks can be summarized as:

- Check the connections and cabling.
- Check the clocking and line rate.
- Check the interface encapsulation.
- Check the LMI type.
- Verify the DLCI-to-IP address mapping.
- Verify the Frame Relay PVCs.

- Verify the Frame Relay LMI.
- Verify the Frame Relay Map.
- Verify the loopback tests, as described in the CSU/DSU Loopback Tests section.
- Check the integrity of the link itself, making sure that there are no unacceptable error indications.

You should also make note of reliability problems, protocol problems, and other error or congestion indications.

SUMMARY

1. In packet switching, messages are broken into small parts called packets. Each packet is tagged with source, destination, and intermediary node addresses as appropriate. Packets are sent over the most appropriate path.

2. X.25 is a packet switched network that allows remote devices to communicate with each other across digital links without the expense of individual leased lines.

3. The X.25 addressing scheme consists of a four-decimal-digit number called the DNIC and an eleven-decimal-digit number known as a NTN.

4. You can directly access the X.25 data network by using a X.25 smart card or by using a modem, which would dial into a PAD.

5. A single X.25 interface on a router can be configured to support up to 4095 SVCs.

6. The most commonly used X.25 link level protocol is the LAPB, a derivative of HDLC.

7. Frame Relay is a direct descendant of X.25. It is a connection-oriented, packet switching protocol designed to use high-speed digital backbone links to support modern protocols.

8. The most common use of a Frame Relay network is to connect individual LANs together.

9. To connect DTEs to a Frame Relay network, you use a FRAD.

10. Frame Relay networks use DLCIs for addressing to identify the originating and terminating ends.

11. A DLCI is a 10-bit address (with 1024 different combinations) that identifies a particular PVC.

12. While local addressing is how Frame Relay works, if you follow the convention of global addressing, planning is easier because the addressing appears similar to LAN addressing.

13. Frame Relay networks are statistically time-division multiplexed to combine multiple VCs and transmit them over a single transmission circuit, assigning each set of DTEs (source and destination) a data link connection identifier.

14. Because Frame Relay uses STDM, it assigns time slots dynamically to make better use by not using empty time slots. As a result, it uses the bandwidth more efficiently, particularly for bursty data traffic among clients and servers and for inter-LAN links.

15. Because Frame Relay networks do not have to perform any error handling, and because they automatically preserve the order of data, there are no frame retransmissions, sequence numbers, or acknowledgements. Therefore, the Frame Relay network has low overhead, which results in a faster network.

16. A LMI is a signaling standard between a CPE device (router) and a frame switch. It adds extensions onto the Frame Relay protocol that manage complex internetworks. Key Frame Relay LMI extensions include global addressing, virtual circuit status messages, and multicasting.

17. Early implementation of Frame Relay technology required that a router (DTE device) have a WAN serial interface for every PVC.

18. If you have a partially-meshed Frame Relay network and you divide it into a number of virtual, point-to-point networks by using subinterfaces, you can overcome the problem when using split-horizon.

19. Subinterfaces are identified by their subinterface number, which can range from 0 to 4,292,967,295.

QUESTIONS

1. A WAN requires complex and expensive packet switching equipment. Which of the following WAN technologies is actually a protocol suite that uses packet assemblers and disassemblers?
   a. X.25
   b. ATM
   c. ISDN
   d. Frame Relay

2. Frame Relay is a form of packet switching technology that evolved from X.25. Which of the following best describes Frame Relay?
   a. It transmits fixed-length packets at the physical layer through the most cost-effective path.
   b. It transmits variable-length packets at the physical layer through the most cost-effective path.
   c. It transmits fixed-length frames at the data link layer through the most cost-effective path.
   d. It transmits variable-length frames at the data link layer through the most cost-effective path.

3. Why is CRC needed in Frame Relay?
   a. It helps detect connection failures.
   b. It helps prevent congestion.
   c. It ensures transmission speed.
   d. It ensures frame accuracy.

4. Your manager has given you the task of connecting Cisco routers in several branch offices to a Frame Relay service provider. Your service provider uses StarNet routers. Which LMI type should your Cisco routers use?
   a. Cisco
   b. Q.933A
   c. ANSI
   d. IETF
   e. the LMI type used by your service provider's StarNet routers

5. At which layer of the OSI model does Frame Relay operate?
   a. transport
   b. network
   c. data link
   d. application
   e. physical

6. Which of the following WAN protocols uses a packet switched network, provides bandwidth on demand, functions at the physical and data link layers, and does not provide error recovery?
   a. X.25
   b. ISDN
   c. PPP
   d. Frame Relay

7. Your company uses the Frame Relay protocol to connect multiple WAN sites. As part of the configuration process, you have established DLCI addresses; the LCI addresses are used in the LAPF header. What happens to the value in the DLCI field as the frame travels between the source and destination routers?
   a. The destination DLCI address is placed in the header and it remains in the header.
   b. The destination DLCI address is placed in the header initially, but it is replaced with the source DLCI address before the frame arrives at the destination.
   c. The source DLCI address is placed in the header and it remains in the header.
   d. The source DLCI address and the destination DLCI address are placed in the header and they remain in the header.

8. Frame Relay has a feature that prevents PVCs from shutting down from lack of activity. What is the name of this feature?
   a. DLCI
   b. FECN
   c. CIR
   d. BECN
   e. LMI
   f. De

9. To distinguish between each PVC, what does a Frame Relay switch use?
   a. DLCIs
   b. CNs
   c. FECNs
   d. LMI

10. When using Frame Relay, which statement about the CIR is true?
    a. It is the rate, in bits per second, at which the Frame Relay switch agrees to transfer data.
    b. It is the clock speed (port speed) of the connection (local loop) to the Frame Relay cloud.
    c. It is the maximum number of bits that the switch can transfer during any committed rate measurement interval.
    d. None of the above.

11. For what purpose does Frame Relay use DLCIs?
  a. They determine the Frame Relay encapsulation type.
  b. They identify the logical circuit between a local router and a Frame Relay WAN switch.
  c. They represent the keepalives used to maintain the PVC in an active state.
  d. They represent the physical address of the router attached to a Frame Relay network.

12. When configuring a Frame Relay network your provider assigns you a DLCI number between 16 and 1007. Which one of the following statements about this DLCI is true?
  a. It is a number that identifies a local VC in a Frame Relay network.
  b. It is a signaling standard between the CPE device and the Frame Relay switch.
  c. It is the port speed of the connection (local loop) to the Frame Relay cloud.
  d. It is the maximum number of uncommitted bits that the Frame Relay switch will attempt to transfer beyond the CIR.

13. Which type of switching method takes the data, breaks it up into smaller packets, and sends each packet individually over the network to its destination?
  a. circuit switching
  b. both circuit and packet switching
  b. packet switching
  d. None of the above.

14. The _____ is a logical network with multiple pathways, and is represented as a black box in illustrations.
  a. pond   b. pipe
  c. VC   d. cloud

15. Which packet switched network is fine for low-bandwidth data communications and allows remote devices to communicate with each other across digital links without the expense of individual leased lines?
  a. X.25   b. Frame Relay
  c. ATM   d. ISDN

16. To connect a DTE to a Frame Relay network, you would use a _____.
  a. FRAD   b. ATM multiplexer
  c. router   d. receiver

CHAPTER 11

Cell Relay Networks

Topics Covered in this Chapter

Introduction

Cell relay networks similar to packet switching networks. However, unlike packet switching networks, cell relay networks are ideal for large networks that need fast WAN connections. Common cell relay networks include SMDS and ATM.

Objectives

- Compare and contrast packet switching and cell relay networks.

- Compare and contrast ATM and SMDM networks.
- Compare and contrast CIP and LANE.

11.1   CELL RELAY

Cell relay is a data transmission technology based on transmitting data in relatively small, fixed size packets or **cells.** Each cell contains only basic path information that allows switching devices to route the cell quickly. Cell relay systems can reliably carry live video and audio because cells of fixed size arrive in a more predictable way than systems with packets or frames of varying size. Examples of cell relay are SMDS and ATM.

11.1.1   An Introduction to ATM

Asynchronous Transfer Mode (ATM) for both LANs and WANs, is generally implemented as a backbone technology. It is a cell switching and multiplexing technology that combines the benefits of circuit switching and packet switching. The small, constant cell size allows ATM equipment to transmit video, audio, and computer data. Current implementations of ATM support data transfer rates of from 25 to 622 Mbps. ATM standards allow it to operate in virtually every transmission medium including T-1, T-3, E-1, E-3, SDH, and Sonet.

Because of its asynchronous nature, ATM is more efficient than synchronous technologies such as TDM. With TDM, users are assigned to time slots, and no other station can be sent in that time slot. If a station has a lot of data to send, it can send only when its time slot comes up, even if all other time slots are empty. However, if a station has nothing to transmit when its time slot comes up, the time slot gets sent empty and is wasted. Because ATM is asynchronous, time slots are available on demand.

11.1.2   The ATM Overlay Model

The protocol reference model used for ATM is taken from a model that was developed by the ITU for **Broadband-Integrated Services Digital Network (B-ISDN).** Because ATM is the transport mode used for B-ISDN, this model applies directly to ATM and is often used as the protocol to describe it.

The ATM overlay model is a three-dimensional model consisting of three planes and four layers. The three planes span all layers. The planes are:

- **Control**—Responsible for generating and managing signaling requests to perform connection administration, such as call setup and call teardown.
- **User**—Responsible for managing the transfer of data across the network.
- **Management**—Maintains the network and carries out operational functions. This plane is further subdivided into layer management and plane management to manage the different layers and planes.
  - **Layer Management**—Manages layer specific functions such as the detection of failures and protocol problems.
  - **Plane management**—Manages and coordinates functions related to the complete system.

The ATM reference mode is composed of the following ATM layers:

- **Physical layer**—Analogous to the physical layer of the OSI reference model, the ATM physical layer manages the medium-dependent transmission.
- **ATM layer**—Combined with the ATM adaptation layer, the ATM layer is roughly analogous to the data link layer of the OSI reference model. The ATM layer is responsible for establishing connection and passing cells through the ATM network. To do this, it uses information in the header of each ATM cell.
- **ATM adaptation layer (AAL)**—Combined with the ATM layer, the AAL is roughly analogous to the data link layer of the OSI model. The AAL is responsible for isolating higher-layer protocols from the details of the ATM processes.

The ATM physical layer has four functions: (1) bits are converted into cells, (2) the transmission and receipt of bits on the physical medium are controlled, (3) ATM cell boundaries are tracked, and (4) cells are packaged into the appropriate type of frame for the physical medium. The ATM physical layer is divided into two parts: (1) the physical medium-dependent (PMD) sublayer and (2) the transmission-convergence (TC) sublayer. The PMD sublayer synchronizes transmission and reception by sending and receiving a continuous flow of bits with associated timing information and it specifies the physical details for the physical medium used, such as cable and connector types. The TC sublayer performs cell delineation, header error control (HEC) sequence generation and verification, cell-rate decoupling and transmission-frame adaptation (see Figure 11.1).

The ATM layer describes how cells are transported through the network and how quality of service is enforced so that connections provide the necessary bandwidth for the specified service. The ATM layer provides creation of cells, multiplexing and demultiplexing of cells, management of cell flow and sequencing, handling of dropped cells, and switched-based routing using virtual paths and virtual circuits (see Table 11.1).

The AAL is where user information is created and received as 48-byte payloads. The adaptation layer resolves any disparity between services provided by the cell-based technology of the ATM layer to the bit-stream technology of digital services (such as tele-

Figure 11.1   The ATM Model

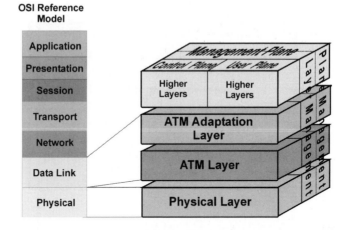

Table 11.1   ATM Model Layers

Layer	Description
AAL1	Supports circuit emulation using ATM cells for traditional voice, T-1, and T-3 carrier services. AAL1 uses two methods: (1) structured data transfer (SDT) and (2) synchronous residual time stamp (SRTS). Requirements include a constant bit rate and connection-oriented, isochronous (time-dependent) service.
AAL2	Supports packet-based video and other time-dependent applications that can use variable bit rate. AAL2 is not currently defined by ATM standards.
AAL3/4	Supports multiplexing of data streams, including connection-oriented and connectionless services. AAL3/4 was used in early ATM implementations but is no longer favored because of additional overhead cost resulting from the SAR sublayer. The SAR header and SAR trailer are each 2 bytes long, effectively reducing available cell payload for data to 44 bytes.
AAL5	Designed to support efficient transport of LAN traffic. Widely implemented today in most ATM products. AAL5 is the adaptation layer used most often, offering the best performance when compared to other AALs for LAN traffic.

phones and video cameras) and the packet-stream technology of traditional data networks (such as Frame Relay and X.25 used in WANs and LAN protocols such as Ethernet and TCP/IP).

The ITU first determined the need to provide several standard AALs (classes of service) to satisfy the requirements of encapsulating different information types into ATM layer cells.

The upper layers of the ATM protocol reference model include optional protocol layers that are used to further encapsulate ATM service for use with TCP/IP and other protocols. Some examples of upper-layer protocols include those specified by RFC 1483 (multiprotocol encapsulation over AAL5) and RFC 1577 (classical IP over ATM).

Figure 11.2 ATM Cell Content

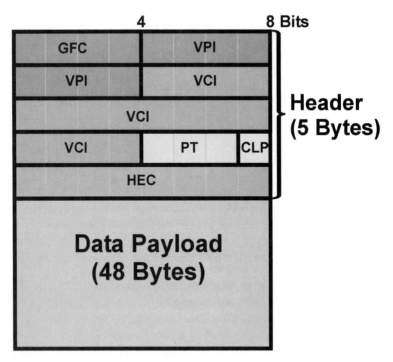

GFC - Generic flow control (000=uncontrolled access) — 4 bits
VPI - Virtual path identifier — 8 bits
VCI - Virtual channel identifier — 16 bits
PT - Payload type — 3 bits
CLP - Cell loss priority — 1 bit
HEC - Header error control — 8 bits

11.1.3 The ATM Cell

The ATM cell has a size of 53 bytes. This cell contains 48 bytes of payload or data and 5 bytes to hold the control and routing information. A fixed cell was chosen for two reasons: (1) The switching devices necessary to build the ATM network need to use very fast silicon chips to perform the cell switching at such high speeds. These chips can run much faster if these cells do not vary, but remains a fixed, known value. By using a payload length of 48 bytes for data, ATM offers a compromise between a larger cell size (such as 64 bytes) optimized for data and a smaller cell size (such as 32 bytes) optimized for voice (see Figure 11.2). (2) ATM is designed to carry multimedia communications composed of data, voice, and video. Unlike data, however, voice and video require a highly predictable cell arrival time in order for sound and video to appear natural. These cells need to arrive one after the other in a steady stream, with no late cells. If the cells varied in size, a very long cell might block the timely arrival of a shorter cell. Therefore, a constant cell size was chosen.

NOTE: The ISDN data communication discussed earlier in this chapter is known as narrowband ISDN, which was designed to operate over the current communications infrastructure based on twisted pair copper cable. In B-ISDN, the end-user gets true bandwidth on demand, only paying for the bandwidth used. Bandwidth of B-ISDN is faster than a T-1 (1.544 Mbps), which generally is found on fiber optic cables running ATM or SMDS.

11.1.4   ATM Network Operation

An ATM network is made up of ATM switches (sometimes referred to as NNIs) and ATM endpoints (sometimes referred to as UNI), consisting of PCs with ATM adapter cards, routers, bridges, CSU/DSUs, and video coder-decoders. When a packet initially enters the ATM network, the packet is segmented into ATM cells. This process is known as cell segmentation.

An ATM switch is responsible for moving cells through an ATM network. It accepts the incoming cell from an ATM endpoint or another ATM switch. It then reads and updates the cell-header information and quickly switches the cell to an output interface near its destination. An ATM endpoint (or end system) contains an ATM network interface adapter. Examples of ATM endpoints are workstations, routers, data service units, LAN switches, and video coder-decoders.

NOTE: ATM cells used by UNI and NNI have a slightly different cell format. NNI cells have no GFC field. Instead, the first four bits of the cell are used by an expanded 12-bit VPI space.

On an ATM network, each attached device (work stations, servers, routers, and bridges) has immediate, exclusive access to the switch. Because each device has access to its own switch port, devices can send cells to the switch simultaneously. Latency becomes an issue only when multiple streams of traffic reach the switch at the same time. To reduce latency at the switch, the cell size must be small enough so the time it takes to transmit a cell has little effect on the cells waiting to be transmitted. Because each ATM device has immediate, exclusive access to a switch port, devices connected to an ATM switch do not need to use complete media access schemes to determine which device has access to the switch.

On an ATM network, each attached device (work stations, servers, routers, and bridges) is attached directly to a switch. When an ATM-attached device requests a connection with a destination device, the switches to which the two devices are attached set up the connection. While setting up the connection, the switches determine the best route to take. Therefore, the ATM switch is a routing switch.

Connection setup standards for the ATM layer define VCs and virtual paths (VPs). An ATM VC is the connection between two ATM end stations for the duration of the connection. The VC is bidirectional, which means that once a connection is established, each end station can send to or receive from the other end station.

Whereas a VC is a connection that is established between two end stations for the duration of a connection, a VP is a path between two switches that exists all the time, regardless of whether a connection is being made. In other words, a VP is a remembered path that all traffic from a single switch can take to reach another switch.

When a user requests a VC, the switches determine which VP to use in order to reach the end stations. Traffic for more than one VC may travel the same VP at the same time.

For example, a VP with 120 Mbps of bandwidth can be divided into four simultaneous connections of 30 Mbps each.

After the connection is established, the switches between the end stations receive translation tables, which specify where to forward cells based on the port where the cells enter and the special values in the cell headers that identify the VCIs and VPIs. The translation table also specifies which VCIs and VPIs the switch should include in the cell headers before the switch sends the cells.

ATM can use three types of VCs, including PVCs, SVCs, and **smart permanent virtual circuits (SPVCs).** The PVCs and the SVCs are the same as discussed earlier in this chapter. The PVCs are manually established pathways between two end stations that don't require setting up or tearing down the connection. Most early ATM devices supported only PVCs, while today's devices support all three.

SVCs are established dynamically whenever an end station needs to send data. First, the end station requests a connection with another end station. An SVC is established between two end stations on an as-needed basis and expires after an arbitrary amount of time. In ATM, the process of determining whether or not to establish a connection is called connection admission control (CAC). SVCs are often the preferred mode of operation because they can be dynamically established, thus minimizing reconfiguration complexity (see Figure 11.3).

SPVCs are a hybrid of a PVC and a SVC. Like a PVC, a SPVC is established manually when the network is configured. However, the ATM service provider or network administrator sets up only the end stations. For each transmission, the network determines which switches the cells will pass through.

When VCs are established, the application or service specifies the average and peak traffic rates, peak traffic duration, and burstiness of the traffic. By setting these parameters, network designers can ensure that voice, video, and data traffic get the required QoS. For example, the network can respond to a traffic burst by automatically allocating additional bandwidth to a particular VC. Certain types of traffic or calls can be prioritized ac-

Figure 11.3 An ATM Virtual Circuit

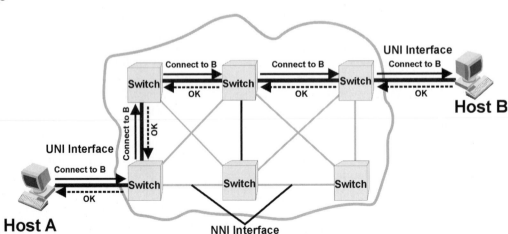

cording to their importance or sensitivity to time delay. The AAL defines the following service categories:

- **Constant Bit Rate (CBR)**—Specifies a fixed bit rate so that data is sent in a steady stream for applications and services that require a small amount of bandwidth at all times and are sensitive to delay and cell loss. Some typical CBR applications are circuit emulation, voice, video, and any type of data that is time-defined. CBR applications do not burst. One example would include supporting voice traffic connected to a PBX.
- **Real time Variable Bit Rate (rt-VBR)**—Provides a specified throughput capacity when services and applications require high bandwidth but data is not sent evenly. This is a popular choice for voice and videoconferencing data.
- **Non-real time Variable Bit Rate (nrt-VBR)**—Similar to rt-VBR except that there is no latency requirement. Applications that might use this category are routers connecting LANs together.
- **Unspecified Bit Rate (UBR)**—Does not guarantee any throughput levels. It is for non-real time ones with no required service guarantees. UBR gives no guarantee that the cells will even be delivered. Therefore, ATM provides the carrier with the option of dropping certain cells if the network gets congested. This is used for applications such as file transfer and e-mail, which can tolerate delays.
- **Available Bit Rate (ABR)**—Provides a guaranteed minimum capacity but allows data to be bursted at higher capacities when the network is free. This is used for applications such as file transfer and e-mail, which can tolerate delays.

NOTE: While ATM is connection-oriented, there are many applications such as mail services and other data services that are characterized by small amounts of data sent sporadically. To save time and expense, no connection is established (connectionless service). User information is sent in a message containing all necessary addressing and routing information, such as those used in LANs. SMDS provides the connectionless service for ATM networks.

11.1.5   Classical IP over ATM

Classical IP Over ATM (CIP) is a mature standard that enables you to route IP packets over an ATM network or cloud by using ATM as either a backbone technology or a workgroup technology. CIP maps IP network layer addresses to ATM addresses and enables ATM-attached devices to send IP packets over an ATM network.

The CIP client is an end station (computer, router, or bridge) with an ATM adapter installed and connected to the ATM network. These end stations may be physically located in separate LANs, but because they are both connected to the ATM network, they are part of the same logical subnetwork or virtual subnetwork. ATM networks are partitioned into Logical IP Subnets (LIS) that communicate with each other via routers. Because there is no native broadcast capability in ATM, the traditional broadcast ARP is replaced by a client-server based ATMARP protocol.

The ATMARP server maintains a database of IP and ATM addresses of all clients on the network, resolving multicast and broadcast IP addresses to ATM addresses. ATMARP only supports unicast traffic, allowing the client to set up point-to-point connections with other end stations.

The multicast address resolution server (MARS) maintains a database of the broadcast and multicast addresses of all members of the network. The MARS can pass a list of addresses directly to a client so that the client can set up a point-to-point call. If a multicast server is available, the MARS can pass the address of a multicast server to the client. In this case, the client contacts the MARS and the MARS creates a point-to-multipoint connection and distributes the packets to the end stations.

An end station can use either PVC or SVC connections. If an end station is using a PVC, the ATM service provider or network administrator manually maps the IP addresses of reachable destination end stations to ATM VCs. To establish a connection using CIP, a sending station sends an ATMARP request to the ATMARP server on the logical IP subnet. The server reconciles the IP address of the receiving station with its ATM address and returns the ATM address to the sending client. The sending client then uses the address to establish an ATM link. When the receiving computer receives the first packet, it also sends an ATMARP request to the server to find the location of the sender. Once the server returns the appropriate address, the link is established and the two clients can communicate directly without further involvement by the server. After the PVC or SVC has been established, the sending end station converts its packets into AAL 5 cells and sends them over the VC to the destination end station. The destination end station then converts the AAL 5 cells into IP packets.

A station can have more than one VC active at any time. A file server or e-mail server may have hundreds of connections within a short period of time, depending on how many client systems it serves. Connections that go unused for a specified amount of time (the default is 15 to 20 minutes) are automatically cleared to recover adapter and ATM network resources.

NOTE: To use CIP as a backbone to connect physically separate LANs, you can route IP packets over ATM by using routers as end stations.

CIP has several disadvantages: (1) Because the ATMARP server can reach only one IP subnetwork, IP hosts can communicate directly only with destination IP hosts in that subnetwork. (2) To send packets to a destination IP host in another virtual subnetwork, a sending IP host must send the packets through a router. The sending IP host uses a virtual circuit to connect to the router, and the router uses another virtual circuit to connect to the destination IP host. (3) Routers create a bottleneck because they are slower than switches. (4) CIP can route only IP. If you want to route other protocols, such as IPX, you cannot use CIP. Furthermore, CIP does not solve delay or congestion problems because CIP cannot take advantage of ATM's QoS.

11.1.6   ATM LAN Emulation

LAN Emulation (LANE), as defined by the ATM Forum, is an ATM standard that emulates an Ethernet or Token Ring LAN on top of an ATM network. In other words, the LANE protocol makes an ATM network look and behave like an Ethernet or Token Ring LAN. Because the LANE emulates the MAC sublayer of the OSI model, LANE enables any network layer protocol that works with the OSI model (including IPX, IP, and Net-BIOS) to travel over an ATM network without modification. Users can then run applications over the ATM network just as they would over an Ethernet or Token-Ring LAN; the ATM network is invisible to LAN users.

An **emulated LAN (ELAN)** consists of a set of LAN emulation clients that reside as ATM endpoints. The ELAN is equivalent to a VLAN. The end systems (ATM NICs and internetworking and LAN switching equipment) have LAN emulation service that is implemented as device drivers that will resolve MAC addresses to ATM addresses, set up direct connections between the clients, and forward the data. The LANE protocol operates transparently over and through the ATM switches and does not directly impact ATM switches.

NOTE: End stations on the same physical segment can be part of different ELANs, and end stations can be members of more than one ELAN.

Each ELAN supports connectivity only between an ATM network and a single traditional (Ethernet or Token Ring) LAN environment. LANE cannot serve as a gateway between Ethernet and Token Ring LANs. LANE clients are implemented in work stations, servers, ATM switches, routers, and ATM LAN switches. An ELAN consists of the following components:

- **LAN Emulation Client (LEC)**—The LEC is implemented in ATM end system computers so that the end system computers can forward data between the ATM and LAN environments, process LAN broadcasts and registration of MAC addresses with the LAN Emulation Server (LES). The LEC also provides a standard LAN interface to a high-level protocol on legacy LANs. The LEC is jointly identified by two addresses: (1) Its ATM address when communicating to the ATM network, and (2) a MAC address when communicating with the Ethernet or Token Ring LAN. ELANs will have one LEC per ELAN.
- **LAN Emulation Server (LES)**—The LES provides a central control point for LECs to include registration of MAC addresses for new LECs, resolution of MAC addresses to ATM addresses for existing LECs, and maintenance of a mapped pairing of ATM addresses-to-MAC addresses for all ELAN member devices.
- **LAN Emulation Configuration Server (LECS)**—The LECS is responsible for assigning LAN emulation clients to specific ELANs. When a client requests configuration information for joining an ELAN, the LECS supplies the ATM address of the LES for the ELAN. Clients are directed to an appropriate LES based on either their physical location (as interpreted by analyzing the client ATM address) or on the identity of a particular destination LAN. The configuration server can, as an option, allow a client to configure and directly assign itself to a specific LES and emulated LAN. There is only one LECS for each internetwork and it serves all LECs within it.
- **Broadcast and Unknown Server (BUS)**—A BUS is a multicast server that is used to flood unknown destination address traffic and to forward multicast and broadcast traffic to clients within a particular ELAN. Each client is associated with a single BUS, identified by a unique ATM address, and located within a particular ELAN.

Suppose that you were working on an emulated LAN and you wanted to access a file stored on a server that was located on a physically separate LAN. First, you would send the file request and your LANE client would determine if it knew the ATM address of its LANE server. If your LANE client did not know this address, the client would query the LANE configuration server and ask for the ATM address of the LANE server.

After your LANE client received the correct address, your client would query the LANE server for the ATM address of the LANE server on which the file was stored. If the LANE server knew this address, the LANE server would send the address to your LANE client. If the LANE server did not know this address, the server would query the LANE BUS. The LANE BUS, in turn, would ask all of the LANE clients on the ELAN for their ATM addresses. The LANE BUS would then return the correct address to the LANE server, which would return the address to your LANE client.

Finally, your LANE client would establish a VC to the server on which the file was stored. Then the LANE client would convert its Ethernet or Token Ring frames into cells and send these cells over the VC to the server.

With LANE, you can also send cells to other LANE clients without establishing a VC. Every LANE client that joins the ELAN establishes a permanent SVC with the LANE BUS. As a result, all LANE clients are connected to the LANE BUS via SVCs. If you want to send cells to another LANE client, your LANE client would forward cells to the BUS via an existing SVC, and the BUS would forward the cells to the destination LANE client. In this way, LANE enables the connection-oriented ATM network to mimic a connectionless network. LANE also allows you to broadcast cells to the entire ELAN. Your LANE client sends the cells to the LANE BUS, and the BUS forwards these cells to all of the other LANE clients.

Because existing LANs mainly support connectionless services, LANE uses Available Bit Rate (ABR) service. ABR service is important not only for LANE, but also for applications involving bursty data traffic where the bandwidth requirements cannot be predicted.

Because the LANE 1.0 standard does not specify a standard way for servers to communicate, each ELAN can have only one LANE server. Therefore, you cannot have redundant LANE servers, and the LANE server may become a bottleneck in large ELANs. In addition, because the LANE server must use VCs to route traffic, and because ATM switches can support only a limited number of VCs (depending on your switch's capacity), using only one LANE server can overburden the switches.

> *NOTE:* The LANE 2.0 standard will solve this problem by defining a way for the components of the LANE services to be distributed and defining the interface between these components. As a result, you can have up to 20 LANE BUS servers.

LANE does have its limitations. As with IP hosts on CIP subnetworks, an end station in one ELAN must use a router to communicate with an end station in another ELAN. The sending end station must establish a VLAN with a router, which establishes a VC with the destination end station. Routers can create bottlenecks because routers are slower than switches.

Because LANE is a bridging technology, LANE limits you to a maximum of 2000 end stations per ELAN. Of course, the more end stations you have, the worse your network will perform. More end stations mean more broadcasts and more VCs, which could be a problem because an ATM network can support only a certain number of VCs at any one time.

Because LANE is an OSI data link layer technology, it is transparent to the higher layers of the OSI model. As a result, LANE cannot take advantage of ATM's QoS. In addition, the LANE 1.0 standard supports only unspecified bit rate. LANE 2.0 enables you to specify the type of traffic your ELAN will carry, constant bit rate (CBR), variable bit rate (VBR), UBR, or ABR. Unfortunately, the LANE 2.0 standard requires all of the VCs on your ELAN to use the type of traffic you specify.

For more information on how to configure LAN emulation, see the following website: http://www.cisco.com/univercd/cc/td/doc/product/software/ios120/12cgcr/switch_c/xcprt7/xclane.htm.

11.1.7   Multiprotocol over ATM

Multiprotocol over ATM (MPOA) was developed by the ATM Forum to route protocols such as IP, IPX and NetBIOS from traditional LANs over a switched ATM backbone. MPOA incorporates LANE to provide bridging capabilities while allowing the MPOA to route between virtual subnetworks without using traditional routers. Using routers in an ATM network significantly slows packet throughput because each router has to reassemble cells of the OSI network layer packets for routing, then segment the packets into cells again for forwarding.

MPOA consists of route servers and edge devices. Route servers, also known as MPOA servers, maintain routing tables and calculate routes on behalf of edge devices. Route servers also communicate with traditional routers and with other route servers. Route servers can either be one piece of hardware or can be built into routers and switches.

Edge devices, also known as MPOA clients, can be intelligent switches that forward packets and cells between LANs and ATM networks or network interface boards that forward packets and cells between ATM-attached devices and ATM networks. Together, route servers and edge devices act as distributed routes. Separately, route servers determine where to send packets and edge devices forward these packets.

If an end station on a LAN wanted to communicate with an ATM-attached device, the end station would send a packet to the edge device. This device would check the destination MAC address or the network layer address of the packet. The device would then check its cache to see if it knew the corresponding ATM address. If the edge device did not know the ATM address, this device would query the route server. If the route server knew the ATM address, this server would simply respond with the address. If the route server did not know the ATM address, this server could use one of several routing protocols to communicate with other routers (both traditional routers and other route servers) to determine this address.

When the edge device knows the ATM address, the device would establish a VC with the appropriate destination end station, convert its LAN packets into ATM cells, and send these cells to the destination end station. The edge device can establish a VC even if the destination end station is on a different subnetwork; the edge device bypasses the route server when sending cells, which sends them directly to the destination end station. This process is called cut-through routing or one-hop routing.

For short transmissions, however, cut-through routing may not be the best approach because connection setup takes a long time relative to the size of the transmission. Using a process called hop-by-hop routing, MPOA can eliminate connection setup. With hop-by-hop routing, edge devices can forward packets to the route server just as LANE clients can forward packets to the LANE BUS. Edge devices can also perform flow detection.

They can forward packets to the route server, but if they detect a flow (a long transmission), they can set up a VC to the destination end station.

MPOA's biggest disadvantage is its relative newness. The ATM Forum has not yet finalized the standard. Depending on the implementation, MPOA can also add complexity to your network.

However, MPOA does provide many capabilities that neither CIP nor LANE provides. Because MPOA is an OSI network layer technology, it has access to important network layer information such as traffic characteristics and ATM's QoS. When establishing a connection, the edge device can use this network layer information to chart the best path to a destination end station based on the QoS the sending end station requests.

MPOA also provides routing capabilities, which no other ATM interoperability architecture provides. With MPOA, you can route between traditional LANs connected by a high-speed ATM backbone, thus creating a high-speed internetwork without the bottleneck of a traditional router. You can also use cut-through and hop-by-hop routing to optimize both short and long transmissions.

11.2   SWITCHED MULTIMEGABIT DATA SERVICE

Switched Multimegabit Data Service (SMDS) is a high-speed, cell-relay, WAN service designed for LAN interconnection through the public telephone network. SMDS can use fiber- or copper-based media. While it mostly supports speeds between 1.544 Mbps and 34 Mbps, it has been extended to support lower and higher bandwidth to broaden its target market. While SMDS and Frame Relay are both very desirable ways of gaining Internet access for your business, Frame Relay is popular for speeds of T-1 and below and SMDS is popular for speeds above T-1 and up to T-3. An SMDS circuit is committed at its specified speed. Bursting of the circuit to full bandwidth is never required.

Different from Frame Relay and ATM, SMDS is a connectionless service. Connectionless service means that there is no predefined path or VC setup between devices. Instead, SMDS simply sends the traffic into the network for delivery to any destination on the network. With no need for a predefined path between devices, data can travel over the least congested routes in an SMDS network. As a result, it provides faster transmission for the networks "bursty" data transmissions and greater flexibility to add or drop network sites. SMDS currently supports only data, and is being positioned as the connectionless part of ATM services.

A SMDS DSU or CSU takes frames that can be up to 7168 bytes long (large enough to encapsulate entire IEEE 802.3, IEEE 802.5, and Fiber-FDDI frames) from a router and breaks it up into fifty-three-byte cells. The cell is then passed to a carrier switch. Each cell has forty-four bytes of payload or data and nine bytes for addressing, error correction, reassembly of cells, and other control features. The switch then reads addresses and forwards cells one-by-one over any available path to the desired endpoint. SMDS addresses ensure that the cells arrive in the right order.

Each destination is assigned from one to sixteen unique SMDS addresses (ten digit numbers similar to telephone numbers) depending on needs. This feature gives the subscribers of SMDS so those individual users within a business can be reached. This will allow you to create the illusion that you have dedicated access for specific customers when in fact you are using a single SMDS connection.

Another feature is called Group Addressing. With group addressing, files or information can be sent to multiple users at one time. This means that files can be sent to all members of a group and allows one member to make last minute changes. That member can then send all the members of the group (via computer) the updated copy in minutes.

SMDS implements two security features: (1) source address validation and (2) address screening. Source address validation ensures that the source address is legitimately assigned to the device from which it originated. This helps prevent address spoofing, in which illegal traffic assumes the source address of a legitimate device. Address screening allows a subscriber to establish a PVN that excludes unwanted traffic. If an address is disallowed, the data unit is not delivered.

To connect to a SMDS network, you will need to communicate with a common carrier to provide a T-1 connection. To connect to SMDS, you would use a CSU/DSU (or some other connection device) and router. Often, the CSU/DSU and router can be found packaged together.

SUMMARY

1. Cell Relay is a data transmission technology which is based on transmitting data in relatively small, fixed-size packets or cells.

2. Each cell contains only basic path information that allows switching devices to route the cell quickly.

3. ATM is both a LAN and a WAN technology, and is generally implemented as a backbone technology.

4. The ATM overlay model is a three-dimensional model consisting of three planes and four layers.

5. The ATM cell has a size of fifty-three bytes. This cell contains forty-eight bytes of payload or data and five bytes to hold the control and routing information.

6. The chips in ATM switches run much faster if these cells do not vary but it remains a fixed, known value.

7. An ATM network is made up of ATM switches (sometimes referred to as NNI) and ATM endpoints (sometimes referred to as UNI), consisting of PCs with ATM adapter cards, routers, bridges, CSU/DSUs, and video coder-decoders.

8. When a packet initially enters the ATM network, the packet is segmented into ATM cells. This process is known as cell segmentation.

9. An ATM switch is responsible for moving cells through an ATM network. It accepts the incoming cell from an ATM endpoint or another ATM switch. It then reads and updates the cell-header information and quickly switches the cell to an output interface towards its destination.

10. ATM can use three types of VCs, including PVCs, SVCs, and SPVCs.

11. CIP is a mature standard that enables you to route IP packets over an ATM network or cloud using ATM as either a backbone technology or a work group technology.

12. Because there is no native broadcast capability in ATM, the traditional broadcast ARP is replaced by a client-server based ATMARP protocol.

13. LANE, as defined by the ATM Forum, is an ATM standard that emulates an Ethernet or Token Ring LAN on top of an ATM network.

14. An ELAN consists of a set of LANE clients that reside as ATM endpoints. The ELAN is equivalent to a VLAN.

15. MPOA was developed by the ATM Forum to route protocols such as IP, IPX, and NetBIOS from traditional LANs over a switched ATM backbone.

16. SMDS is a high-speed, cell-relay, WAN service designed for LAN interconnection through the public telephone network.

17. Different from Frame Relay and ATM, SMDS is a connectionless service.

QUESTIONS

1. In ATM networks, all information is formatted into fixed-length cells consisting of _____ bytes.
   - a. 32
   - b. 48
   - c. 64
   - d. 128

2. Packet-switching networks divide data into packets and send them over a common transmission line using VCs. Which of the following is an implementation of a packet switching technology?
   - a. T1
   - b. ISDN
   - c. Switched 56
   - d. ATM

3. The basic connection unit in an ATM network is known as the _____.
   - a. VC connection
   - b. VP connection
   - c. DSL connection
   - d. DS-0 connection

4. CBR is used primarily for _____.
   - a. multimedia e-mail
   - b. videoconferencing
   - c. data transport
   - d. simple e-mail

5. Which service category is most likely to suffer cell loss due to bandwidth constraints?
   - a. CBR
   - b. ABR
   - c. UBR
   - d. VBRnrt

6. _____ is a high-performance switching and multiplexing technology that utilizes fixed-length packets to carry different types of traffic.
   - a. ATM
   - b. ADSL
   - c. Sonet
   - d. None of the above.

7. In ATM networks, all information is formatted into fixed-length cells consisting of a payload of _____ bytes.
   - a. 32
   - b. 48
   - c. 64
   - d. 128

8. The basic connection unit in an ATM network is known as the _____.
   - a. VC connection
   - b. VP connection
   - c. NTU
   - d. ATM pipe

9. In ATM LANE, most unicast LAN traffic moves directly between clients over _____.
   - a. servers
   - b. direct ATM SVCs
   - c. indirect ATM PVCs
   - d. dial-up connections

CHAPTER 12

Introduction to Routers and Routing

Topics Covered in this Chapter

Introduction

As LANs become more popular and more vital to the daily operation of an organization, the need to connect multiple LANs together has become as crucial as it once was to link individual PCs into a work group. While segmenting the network can solve all kinds of problems, including increasing available bandwidth on LANs, linking distant networks, and breaking a large network into smaller, more manageable subnets; you must have a mechanism for the different segments to communicate with each other. To connect those networks, you should use routers.

Objectives

- Differentiate between static and dynamic routes.
- Explain how metrics are used with routing algorithms.
- Given two IP addresses, show how a host would determine if the addresses are local or remote to each other.
- Compare and contrast distance vectors and link-state algorithms.
- Differentiate between routed and routing protocols.
- Given a routing protocol, determine if it is a distance vector or a link-state algorithm.
- Differentiate between an interior gateway protocol and a gateway protocol.

12.1   ROUTERS: AN OVERVIEW

A **router,** which works at the network ISO layer, is a device that connects two or more LANs. As multiple LANs are connected together, multiple routes are created to get from one LAN to another. The primary role of a router is to transmit similar types of data packets from one LAN or wide area communications link (such as a T-1 or fiber link) to another. The second role of a router is to select the best path between the source and the destination.

When you send a packet from one computer to another computer, it first determines if the packet should be sent locally to another computer on the same LAN or if the packet should be sent to a router so that it can be routed to the destination LAN. If the packet is meant to go to a computer on another LAN, it is sent to the router (or gateway). The router will then determine the best route to take and will forward the packets to that route. The packet will then go to the next router and the entire process will repeat itself until it gets to the destination LAN. The destination router will then forward the packets to the destination computer.

To determine the best route, the router uses complex routing algorithms that take into account a variety of factors, including the number of fastest sets of transmission media, the number of network segments, and the network segment that carries the least amount of traffic. Routers then share status and routing information with other routers so that they can provide better traffic management and bypass slow connections. In addition, routers provide additional functionality, such as the ability to filter messages and forward them to different places based on various criteria. Most routers are multiprotocol routers because they can route data packets by using many different protocols.

A **metric** is a standard of measurement, such as a hop count, that is used by routing algorithms to determine the optimal path to a destination. A hop is the trip a data packet takes from one router to another router or a router to another intermediate point on the network. On a large network, the number of hops a packet has taken toward its destination is called the hop count. When a computer communicates with another computer, and the computer has to go through four routers, it would have a hop count of four. With no other factors taken into account, a metric of four would be assigned. If a router had a choice between a route with four metrics and a route with six metrics, it would choose the route with four metrics over the route with six metrics. If you want the router to choose the route with six metrics, you can overwrite the metric for the route with four hops in the routing table to a higher value.

To keep track of the various routes in a network, routers will create and maintain routing tables. The routers communicate with one another to maintain their routing tables through a routing update message. The routing update message can consist of all or a portion of a routing table. By analyzing routing updates from all other routers, a router can build a detailed picture of the network topology.

Routed protocols are transported by routing protocols across an internetwork. In general, routed protocols in this context also are referred to as network protocols. These network protocols perform a variety of functions required for communication between user applications in source and destination devices, and these functions can differ widely among protocol suites. Network protocols occur at the upper five layers of the OSI reference model: (1) the network layer, (2) the transport layer, (3) the session layer, (4) the presentation layer, and (5) the application layer. Examples of network protocols are the TCP/IP protocol suite and the IPX protocol suite.

Confusion about the terms *routed protocol* and *routing protocol* is common. Routed protocols are protocols that are routed over an internetwork. Routing protocols, on the other hand, are protocols that implement routing algorithms. In other words, routing protocols are used by intermediate systems to build tables used in determining path selection of routed protocols. Examples of these protocols include Routing Information Protocol (RIP), Open Shortest Path First (OSPF), Interior Gateway Routing Protocol (IGRP), Enhanced Interior Gateway Routing Protocol (Enhanced IGRP), Exterior Gateway Protocol (EGP) and Border Gateway Protocol (BGP).

12.2   CHARACTERISTICS OF ROUTING PROTOCOLS

There are various types of routing algorithms. Each algorithm has a different impact on network and router resources. Routing algorithms use a variety of metrics that affect calculation of optimal routes.

Routing algorithms can be differentiated based on several key characteristics: (1) The capability of the routing algorithm to optimally choose the best route is very important. One routing algorithm may use the number of hops and the length of delays, but may weigh the length of delay more heavily in the calculation. To maintain consistency and predictability, routing protocols use strict metric calculations. (2) Routing algorithms are designed to be as simple as possible. In other words, the routing algorithm must offer efficiency with a minimum of software and utilization overhead. But while being efficient, the routing algorithm must be robust so that it can quickly change routes when a route goes down because of hardware failure or high load (high amount of traffic). When this is happening, the routing algorithm must be stable. (3) Routing algorithms must converge rapidly. Convergence is the process of agreement (by all routers) about which routes are the optimal routes. When a route goes down, routers distribute the new routes by sending routing update messages. The time that it takes for all routers to get new routes on which they all agree should be quick. If not, routing loops or network outages can occur. A routing loop is when a packet is forwarded back and forth between several routers without ever getting to its final destination (see Table 12.1).

Count to infinity, which typically happens when a network has slow convergence, is a loop that happens when a link in a network goes down and routers on the network update their routing tables with incorrect hop counts. For example, a loop can occur if the link to Router C goes down. Router B then advertises that the link is down and that it has no route to C. Because Router A has a route to C with a metric of 2, it responds to Router B and sends its link to C. Because two hops is a better route than 16 hops, Router B then updates its table to include a link with metric 3, and the routers continue to announce between the two routers and update their routing entries to C until they reach the number 16, a count to infinity (see Table 12.2).

To handle the count to infinity problem, networks use either split-horizon or poison reverse. Split-horizon is a route advertising algorithm that prevents the advertising of routes in the same direction in which they were learned. In other words, the routing protocol differentiates which interface a network route was learned on and then will not advertise that route back out that same interface. This would prevent Router B from sending the updated information it received from Router C back to Router C.

Table 12.1   Distance (Number of Hops) to Network 1

Network 1	Router A	Network 2	Router B	Network 3	Router C	Network 4

	Network 2	Network 3	Network 4
Initially	∞	∞	∞
After 1 Exchange	1	∞	∞
After 2 Exchanges	1	2	∞
After 3 Exchanges*	1	2	3

*Convergence in 3 exchanges

Table 12.2   Distance (Number of Hops) to Network 1 When the Link Between Network A and B Goes Down

	Network 1 — Router A — Network 2 — Router B — Network 3 — Router C — Network 4		
	Network 2	**Network 3**	**Network 4**
Initially	1	2	3
After 1 Exchange	3	2	3
After 2 Exchanges	3	4	3
After 3 Exchanges	5	4	5
After 5 Exchanges	5	6	5
After 6 Exchanges	7	6	7
After 7 Exchanges	7	8	7
After 8 Exchanges	9	8	9
After 9 Exchanges	9	10	9
After 10 Exchanges	11	10	11
After 11 Exchanges	11	12	11
After 12 Exchanges	13	12	13
After 13 Exchanges	13	14	13
After 14 Exchanges	15	14	15
After 15 Exchanges	15	∞	15
After 16 Exchanges*	∞	∞	∞

*Convergence to infinity has occurred.

Poison reverse is a process that, when used with split-horizon, improves RIP convergence over simple split-horizon by advertising all network IDs. A poison reverse is a way in which a gateway node tells its neighbor gateways that one of the gateways is no longer connected. To do this, the notifying gateway sets the number of hops to the unconnected gateway to a number that indicates "infinite." Because RIP allows up to 15 hops to another gateway, setting the hop count to 16 would mean "infinite."

Two other techniques to avoid routing loops are either to perform a holddown or to set up triggered update. A **holddown** is basically a set time limit during which a router should not change its routing tables because of turmoil over the network. If a router receives a message that a particular route has gone down it will start a holddown timer, during which time it will not transmit any info about that route. Instead, it will listen to the network for other reports. This will prevent flapping when a connection seems to be flaky and the link goes up and down.

Triggered updates allow a router to announce changes in metric values almost immediately rather than waiting for the next periodic announcement. The trigger is a change to a metric in an entry in the routing table. For example, networks that become unavailable can be announced with a hop count of 16 through a triggered update. The update is sent almost immediately, where a time interval to wait is typically specified on the router. If triggered updates were sent by all routers immediately, each triggered update could cause a cascade of broadcast traffic across the IP internetwork. Triggered updates improve the convergence time for internetworks but at the expense of additional broadcast traffic as the triggered updates are propagated.

12.2.1   Static *v.* Dynamic Routes

Static routing algorithms are hardly algorithms at all, but are table mappings established by the network administrator prior to the beginning of routing. These mappings do not change unless the network administrator alters them. Algorithms that use static routes are simple to design and work well in environments where network traffic is relatively predictable and network design is relatively simple.

Because static routing systems cannot react to network changes, they generally are considered unsuitable for today's large, changeable networks. Most of the dominant routing algorithms in the 1990s were **dynamic routing** algorithms, which adjust to changing network circumstances by analyzing incoming routing update messages. If the message indicates that a network change has occurred, the routing software recalculates routes and sends out new routing update messages. These messages flow through the network, stimulating routers to rerun their algorithms and change their routing tables accordingly.

Dynamic routing algorithms can be supplemented with static routes where appropriate. A router of last resort (a router to which all unroutable packets are sent), for example, can be designated to act as a repository for all unroutable packets, ensuring that all messages are at least handled in some way.

12.2.2   Single Path *v.* Multipath Algorithms

Some sophisticated routing protocols support multiple paths to the same destination. Unlike single path algorithms, multipath algorithms permit traffic multiplexing over multiple lines where the traffic can be split among the different routes. In addition, they provide redundancy in case one of the routes fails. Networks connected with redundant routes can also be referred to as spanning tree algorithms.

12.2.3   Flat *v.* Hierarchical Algorithms

In a flat routing system, routers are peers of all other routers. In a hierarchical routing system, some routers form what amounts to a routing backbone. Packets from non-backbone routers travel to backbone routers, where they are sent through the backbone until they reach the general area of the destination. At this point, they travel from the last backbone router, through one or more non-backbone routers, to the final destination.

Routing systems often designate logical groups of nodes called domains, autonomous systems, or areas. In hierarchical systems, some routers in a domain can communicate with routers in other domains, while others can communicate only with routers within their domain. In very large networks, additional hierarchical levels may exist where routers at the highest hierarchical level form the routing backbone.

The primary advantage of hierarchical routing is that it mimics the organization of most companies and therefore supports their traffic patterns well. Most network communication occurs within small company groups (domains). Because an intradomain router needs to know only about other routers within its domain, its routing algorithm can be simplified. Depending on the routing algorithm used, routing update traffic can be reduced accordingly.

12.2.4   Distance Vector *v.* Link State Algorithms

Routers use **distance vector-based routing** protocols to periodically advertise or broadcast the routes in their routing tables, but they only send the routes to their neighboring routers. Routing information exchanged between typical distance vector-based routers is unsynchronized and unacknowledged. Distance vector-based routing protocols are simple and easy to understand and easy to configure. The disadvantage is that multiple routes to a given network can reflect multiple entries in the routing table, which leads to a large routing table. In addition, if you have a large routing table, network traffic increases as it periodically advertises the routing table to other routers, even after the network has converged. Lastly, for distance vector protocols, convergence of large internetworks can take several minutes.

Link-state algorithms are also known as shortest path first algorithms. Instead of using broadcast, link-state routers send updates directly (or by using multicast traffic) to all routers within the network. Each router, however, sends only the portion of the routing table that describes the state of its own links. In essence, link-state algorithms send small updates everywhere. Because they converge more quickly, link-state algorithms are somewhat less prone to routing loops than distance-vector algorithms. In addition, link-state algorithms do not exchange any routing information when the internetwork has converged. They have small routing tables because they store a single optimal route for each network ID. On the other hand, link-state algorithms require more CPU power and memory than distance-vector algorithms. Link-state algorithms, therefore, can be more expensive to implement and support and are considered harder to understand.

There are some protocols that are a hybrid of both distance-vector algorithms and link-state algorithms. An example of a hybrid protocol is EIGRP.

12.2.5   Metrics

Various routing protocols use different metrics, such as path length, hop counts, routing delay, bandwidth, load, reliability, and cost. Path length is the most common routing metric. Some routing protocols allow network administrators to assign arbitrary costs to each network link. In this case, path length is the sum of the costs associated with each link traversed. Other routing protocols define hop counts, which has been described.

Routing delay refers to the length of time required to move a packet from its source to its destination through the internetwork. Delay depends on many factors, such as the bandwidth of intermediate network links, the port queues at each router along the way, network congestion on all intermediate network links, and the physical distance to be traveled. Because delay is a conglomeration of several important variables, it is a common and useful metric.

Bandwidth refers to the available traffic capacity of a link. All other things being equal, a 10-Mbps Ethernet link would be preferable to a 64-Kbps leased line. Although bandwidth is a rating of the maximum attainable throughput on a link, routes through links with greater bandwidth do not necessarily provide better routes than routes through slower links. For example, if a faster link is busier than a slower link, then the actual time required to send a packet to the destination could be greater.

Load refers to the degree to which a network resource, such as a router, is busy. Load can be calculated in a variety of ways, including CPU utilization and packets processed per second. Monitoring these parameters on a continual basis can be resource-intensive.

Reliability, in the context of routing algorithms, refers to the dependability (usually described in terms of the bit-error rate) of each network link. Some network links might go down more often than others. After a network fails, certain network links might be repaired more easily or more quickly than other links. Any reliability factors can be taken into account for assignment of reliability ratings, which are arbitrary numeric values usually assigned to network links by network administrators.

Communication cost is another important metric, especially because some companies may not care about performance as much as they care about operating expenditures. Even though line delay may be longer, they will send packets over their own lines rather than through the public lines that cost money for usage time.

12.2.6   Administrative Distances

Administrative distances (ADs) are used to rate the trustworthiness of routing information received on a router from a neighbor router. An administrator distance is an integer from 0 to 255, where 0 is the most trusted and 255 means no traffic will be passed via this route (see Table 12.3).

If a router receives two updates listing the same remote network, the first thing a router checks is the AD. If one of the two advertised routes has a lower AD than the other, the route with the lowest AD will be placed in the routing table.

If both advertised routes to the same network have the same AD, then routing protocol metrics such as hop count or bandwidth will be used to find the best path to the remote network. The advertised route with the lower metric will be placed in the routing table. However, if both advertised routes have the same AD, as well as the same metrics, then the routing protocol will load balance to the remote network.

Table 12.3   Administrative Distances for Common Routing Protocols

Route source	Default AD
Connected interface	0
Static route	1
EIGRP	90
IGRP	100
OSPF	110
RIP	120
External EIGRP	170
Unknown	255 (this route will never be used)

If a network is directly connected, it will always use the interface connected to a network. If an administrator configures a static route, the router will believe that route over any other learned. You can change the administrative distance of static routes, but they have a default AD of 1.

12.3   THE IP ROUTING PROTOCOL

IP protocol is a connectionless, unreliable protocol responsible for addressing and routing between hosts. Connectionless means that a session is not established before exchanging data. Each packet that travels through the Internet is treated as an independent unit of data that is not affected by other data packets. Unreliable means that the delivery is not guaranteed. IP always makes a best effort attempt to deliver a packet. An IP packet might be lost, delivered out of sequence, duplicated, or delayed. IP does not attempt to recover from these types of errors. Instead, the acknowledgment of packets delivered and the recovery of lost packets is the responsibility of a higher-layer protocol, such as TCP.

12.3.1   IP Packets

The IP protocol specifies the format of packets (also called datagrams). An IP packet consists of an IP header and an IP payload. The IP header consists of (see Figure 12.1):

- **The IP Version**—Indicates the version of IP currently being used.
- **The IP Header Length (IHL)**—Indicates the datagram header length in 32-bit words.
- **The Type-of-Services**—specifies how an upper-layer protocol would like a current datagram, and assigns datagrams various levels of importance.
- **The Total Length**—Specifies the length, in bytes, of the entire IP packet (including the data and header).
- **The Identification**—Contains an integer that identifies the current datagram. This field is used to help piece together datagram fragments.

Figure 12.1   An IP Packet

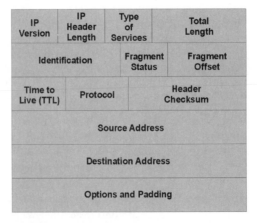

- **The Flags**—Consist of a 3-bit field, the two least-significant bits control fragmentation. The low-order bit specifies whether the packet can be fragmented. The middle bit specifies whether the packet is the last fragment in a series of fragmented packets. The third is not used.
- **The Fragment Offset**—Indicates the position of the fragment's data relative to the beginning of the data in the original datagram. This allows the destination IP process to properly reconstruct the original datagram.
- **The Time-to-Live (TTL)**—Designates the number of network segments on which the datagram is allowed to travel before being discarded by a router. The TTL is set by the sending host and is used to prevent packets from endlessly circulating on an IP internetwork. When forwarding an IP packet, routers are required to decrease the TTL by at least 1.
- **The Protocol**—Indicates which upper-layer protocol receives incoming packets after IP processing is complete.
- **The Header Checksum**—Helps ensure IP header integrity.
- **The Source Address**—The IP address of the original source of the IP datagram.
- **The Destination Address**—The IP address of the final destination of the IP datagram.
- **The Options**—Allows IP to support various options, such as security while padding to help make the datagram in the correct format and to have a minimum size.

12.3.2   IP Addresses and Routing

TCP/IP hosts use a routing table to maintain knowledge about other IP networks and hosts. As discussed in Chapter 4, networks and hosts are identified with an IP address and corresponding subnet mask specify which bits of the address are the network address and which bits are the host address.

When a computer prepares to send an IP datagram, it inserts its own source IP address and the destination IP address of the recipient into the IP header. The computer then examines the destination IP address, compares it to a locally maintained IP routing table, and takes appropriate action based on what it finds. The computer does one of three things:

1. It passes the datagram up to a protocol layer above IP on the local host.
2. It forwards the datagram through one of its attached network interfaces.
3. It discards the datagram.

IP searches the routing table for the route that is the closest match to the destination IP address (a route that matches the IP address of the destination host followed by the route that matches the IP address of the destination network). If a matching route is not found, IP discards the datagram.

To determine if a packet must be sent to a host on the local network or if the packet must be sent to a remote network via the router, the TCP/IP protocol will complete a couple of calculations. When TCP/IP is initialized on a host, the host's IP address is ANDed (logical bit-wise AND) with its subnet mask at a bit-by-bit level. Before a packet is sent, the destination IP address is ANDed with the same subnet mask. If both results match, IP knows that the packet belongs to a host on the local network. If the results don't match, the packet is sent to the IP address of an IP router so that it can be forwarded to the host.

When ANDing an IP address and subnet mask, each bit in the IP address is compared to the corresponding bit in the subnet mask. If both bits are 1s, the resulting bit is a 1. If there is any other combination, the resulting bit is a 0.

NOTE: By ANDing the address and subnet mask, you essentially isolate the network addresses.

Example 1:

You have a host 145.17.202.56 with a subnet mask of 255.255.224.0 with data that needs to be delivered to 145.17.198.75 with a subnet mask of 255.255.224.0. Are the two hosts on one local network or are they located on two remote networks?

To figure this out, we need to first convert the addresses and subnet masks to binary.

145.17.202.56	10010001.00010001.11001010.00111000
145.17.198.75	10010001.00010001.11000110.01001011
255.255.224.0	11111111.11111111.11100000.00000000

Next, AND the source address and the subnet mask.

145.17.202.56	10010001.00010001.11001010.00111000
255.255.224.0	<u>11111111.11111111.11100000.00000000</u>
	10010001.00010001.11000000.00000000

Finally, AND the destination address and the subnet mask.

145.17.198.75	10010001.00010001.11000110.01001011
255.255.224.0	<u>11111111.11111111.11100000.00000000</u>
	10010001.00010001.11000000.00000000

If you compare the two results, you will find that they are the same. Therefore, the packet will be sent directly to the host and not the router. If they were different, it would send the packet directly to the router.

12.3.3   Internet Control Message Protocol

IP does not provide reliable communication. It does not provide acknowledgments either end-to-end or hop-by-hop. There is no error control for data, other than a header check-sum. IP does not provide error control or flow control. There are no retransmissions. Instead, all of these are left to higher protocols such as TCP.

To report errors and other information regarding IP packet processing, the Internet control-Message Protocol (ICMP) sends notices back to the source. ICMP messages are usually sent automatically in one of the following situations:

- An IP datagram cannot reach its destination.
- An IP router (gateway) cannot forward datagrams at the current rate of transmission.
- An IP router redirects the sending host to use a better route to the destination.

Table 12.4   ICMP Messages

ICMP message	Description
Echo request	Determines whether an IP node (a host or a router) is available on the network.
Echo reply	Replies to an ICMP echo request.
Destination unreachable	Informs the host that a datagram cannot be delivered.
Source quench	Informs the host to lower the rate at which it sends datagrams because of congestion.
Redirect	Informs the host of a preferred route.
Time exceeded	Indicates that the TTL of an IP datagram has expired.

NOTE: ICMP is documented in RFC 792 (see Table 12.4).

When you use the *ping* command, an ICMP echo request message is sent and the receipt of an ICMP echo replay message is recorded. This allows you to detect network or host communication failures and troubleshoot common TCP/IP connectivity problems.

By using ICMP messages, the ICPM protocol can be used by local routers to provide a way for hosts to sense routers that are down and to perform router solicitation and advertisement. Router solicitations are sent by hosts to discover routers on their networks. Router advertisements are sent by routers in response to router solicitation and periodically to notify hosts on the network that the router is still available. ICMP router discovery is documented in RFC 1256, "ICMP Router Discovery Messages."

12.4   INTERIOR GATEWAY PROTOCOLS

As IP provides addressing and connectionless services for packet forwarding, IP relies on other protocols for address resolution, dynamic route discovery, and prioritization. Because IP networks can be quite large and complex internetworks, TCP/IP allows the IP internetwork to be divided into logical groups called **autonomous systems (AS).** The routing protocols that manage routing information within an autonomous system are called **interior gateway protocols (IGPs).** Examples of an IGP would be RIP, OSPF, and IGRP. Autonomous systems are interconnected using an exterior gateway protocol such as BGP or EGP.

NOTE: RIP and OSPF protocols are standard TCP/IP routing protocols that can run either as a stand-alone autonomous systems or within an autonomous system that belongs to a larger network (see Figure 12.2).

12.4.1   The Routing Information Protocol

The **Routing Information Protocol (RIP),** a distance-vector protocol, is designed for exchanging routing information within a small- to medium-sized network. The biggest advantage of RIP is that it is extremely simple to configure and deploy.

Figure 12.2   Autonomous Systems Connected with an EGP

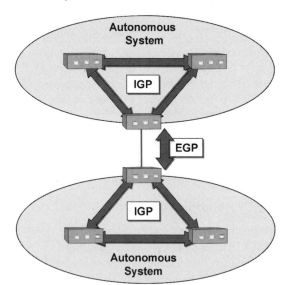

RIP uses a single routing metric of hop counts to measure the distance between the source and a destination network. Each hop in a path from source to destination is assigned a hop count value, which is typically 1. When a router receives a routing update that contains a new or changed destination network entry, the router adds 1 to the metric value indicated in the update and enters the network in the routing table. The IP address of the sender is used as the next hop.

RIP uses only hop count to determine the best path to an internetwork. If RIP finds more than one link to the same remote network with the same hop count, it will automatically perform a round-robin load balance. RIP can perform load balancing for up to six equal cost links.

However, a problem with using hops as the only metric occurs when two links to a remote network have different bandwidths. For example, if you have a 56 Kb switched link and a T-1 running at 1.544 Mbps, there would be some inefficiency when sending equal data through both pathways. This is known as pinhole congestion. To overcome pinhole congestion, you would have to design a network with equal bandwidth links or use a routing protocol that takes bandwidth into account.

RIP prevents routing loops from continuing indefinitely by implementing a limit on the number of hops allowed in a path from the source to a destination. The maximum number of hops in a path is fifteen. If a router receives a routing update that contains a new or changed entry, and if increasing the metric value by one causes the metric to be infinity (in this case, sixteen), the network destination is considered unreachable. Of course, this makes RIP have the inability to scale to large or very large internetworks.

NOTE: The count-to-infinity problem is the reason why the maximum hop count of RIP for IP internetworks is set to fifteen (sixteen for unreachable). Higher maximum hop count values would make the convergence time longer when count-to-infinity occurs.

Initially, the routing table for each router includes only the networks that are physically connected to it. A RIP router periodically (every thirty seconds) sends announcements that contain routing table entries so that the other routers can update their routing tables. RIP version 1 uses IP broadcast packets for its announcements. RIP version 2 uses multicast or broadcast packets for its announcements. All RIP messages are sent over UDP port 520.

Silent RIP processes RIP announcements but does not announce its own routes. Silent RIP could be enabled on non-router hosts to produce a routing table with as much detail as the RIP routers. With more detailed routes in the routing table, a silent RIP host can make better routing decisions.

RIP routers can also communicate routing information through triggered updates, which are triggered when the network topology changes. Different from scheduled announcements, triggered updates are sent immediately rather than waiting for the next periodic announcement. For example, when a router detects a link or router failure, it updates its own routing table and sends the updated routes. Each router that receives the triggered update modifies its own routing table and propagates the change to other routers.

RIP uses three different types of timers to regulate its performance:

■ **Route update timer**—Sets the interval (typically thirty seconds) between periodic routing updates, in which the router sends a complete copy of its routing table out to all neighbors.

■ **Route invalid timer**—Determines the length of time that must expire (180 seconds) before a router determines that a route has become invalid. It will come to this conclusion if it hasn't heard any updates about a particular route for that period. When that happens, the router will send out updates to all its neighbors letting them know that the route is invalid.

■ **Route flush timer**—Sets the time between a route becoming invalid and its removal from the routing table (120 seconds). Before it is removed from the table, the router notifies its neighbors of that route's impending doom. The value of the route invalid timer must be less than that of the route flush timer. This is to provide the router with enough time to tell its neighbors about the invalid route before the routing table is updated.

You can configure each RIP router with a list of routers (by IP address) from which RIP announcements are accepted. By configuring a list of RIP peers, RIP announcements from unauthorized RIP routers are discarded. In addition, to prevent RIP traffic from being received by any node except neighboring RIP routers, you can set up some routers to use unicast RIP announcements to neighboring RIP routers.

You can configure route filters on each RIP interface so that the only routes considered for addition to the routing table are those that reflect reachable network IDs within the internetwork. For example, if an organization is using subnets of the private network ID 10.0.0.0, route filtering can be used so that the RIP routers discard all routes except those within the 10.0.0.0 network ID.

Because the RIP is a distance vector protocol, as internetworks grow larger in size, the periodic announcements by each RIP router can cause excessive traffic. Another disadvantage of RIP is high convergence time. When the network topology changes, it may take several minutes before the RIP routers reconfigure themselves to the new network topology. While the network reconfigures itself, routing loops that result in lost or unde-liverable data may form. To help prevent routing loops, RIP implements split-horizon.

To overcome some RIP shortcomings, RIP Version 2 (RIP II) was introduced. RIP II provides the following features:

- You can use a password for authentication by specifying a key that is used to authen-ticate routing information to the router. Simple password authentication was defined in RFC 1723, but newer authentication mechanism such as Message Digest 5 (MD5) are available.
- RIP II includes the subnet mask in the routing information and supports variable-length subnets. Variable-length subnet masks can be associated with each destination, allow-ing an increase in the number of hosts or subnets that are possible on your network.
- The routing table can contain information about the IP address of the router that should be used to reach each destination. This helps prevent packets from being for-warded through extra routers on the system.
- Multicast packets only speak to RIP II routers and are used to reduce the load on hosts not listening to RIP II packets. The IP multicast address for RIP II packets is 224.0.0.9. Silent RIP nodes must also listen for multicast traffic sent to 224.0.0.9. If you are using silent RIP, verify that your silent RIP nodes can listen for multicasted RIP II announcements before deploying multicasted RIP II.

RIP I was designed with forward compatibility in mind. If a RIP I router receives a message and the RIP version in the RIP header is not 0x01, it does not discard the RIP announcement but processes only the RIP I defined fields. RIP II is supported on most routers and end nodes. Make sure that the mode you configure is compatible with all implementations of RIP on your network.

RIP II routers and RIP I routers should be used together with caution. Because RIP I routers do not interpret the subnet mask field in the route, RIP II routers must not an-nounce routes that can be misinterpreted by a RIP I router. Variable length subnet masks and disjointed subnets cannot be used in mixed environments.

For an interface using RIP II to make announcements such that RIP I routers can process the announced routes, the RIP II routers must summarize subnet routes when announcing outside a subnetted environment. A specific subnet route announced to a RIP I router can be misinterpreted as a host route. Also, RIP II routers cannot announce supernet routes. A RIP I router would misinterpret the route as a single network rather than as a range of networks.

If RIP II routers are on the same network as RIP I routers, the RIP II router interface must be configured to broadcast RIP I announcements. Multicasted RIP II announcements are not processed by the RIP I routers.

12.4.2 Troubleshooting RIP for IP

If a RIP environment is properly configured, RIP routers learn all the best routes from neighboring routers after convergence. The exact list of routes added by RIP to the IP rout-ing table depends, among other factors, on whether or not the router interfaces are inside a subnetted region, whether or not RIP II is being used, and whether or not host routes or default routes are being advertised.

Problems with RIP can occur in a mixed RIP I and RIP II environment, with the use of silent RIP hosts, or when all the appropriate RIP routes are not being received and added to the IP routing table. On networks containing RIP I routers, verify that RIP II is configured to broadcast its announcements on networks containing RIP I routers. On networks containing RIP I routers, verify that the RIP II router interfaces are configured to accept both RIP I and RIP II announcements.

If there are silent RIP hosts on a network that do not receive routes from the local RIP router, verify the version of RIP supported by silent RIP hosts. For example, if the silent RIP hosts only support listening for broadcasted, RIP I announcements, you cannot use RIP II multicasting.

If RIP routers are not receiving expected routes, check the following:

- Verify that you are not deploying variable length subnetting, disjointed subnets, or supernetting in a RIP I or mixed RIP I and RIP II environment.
- If authentication is enabled, verify that all interfaces on the same network are using the same case-sensitive password.
- If RIP peer filtering is being used, verify that the correct IP addresses for the neighboring peer RIP routers are configured.
- If RIP route filtering is being used, verify that the ranges of network IDs for your internetwork are included or are not being excluded.
- If RIP neighbors are configured, verify that the correct IP addresses are configured for the unicasted RIP announcements.
- Verify that IP packet filtering is not preventing the receiving (through input filters) or sending (through output filters) of RIP announcements on the router interfaces enabled for RIP. RIP traffic uses UDP port 520.
- Verify that TCP/IP filtering on router interfaces is not preventing the receiving of RIP traffic.
- For dial-up demand-dial interfaces using auto-static updates, configure the demand-dial interfaces to use RIP II multicast announcements. When a router calls another router, each router receives an IP address from the other router's IP address pool, which is on a different subnet. Because broadcasted RIP announcements are addressed to the subnet broadcast address, each router does not process the other router's broadcasted request for routes. Using multicasting, RIP requests and announcements are processed regardless of the subnet for the router interfaces.

12.4.3   Autonomous System Topology

For small or medium networks, distributing data throughout the network and maintaining a route table at each router is not a problem. When the network grows to a size that includes hundreds of routers, the routing table can be quite large (several megabytes) and may require significant time to recalculate routes as router interfaces go up or down.

Some protocols, such as OSPF, allow areas (groupings of contiguous networks) to be grouped together into an **autonomous system (AS).** Areas that make up the autonomous areas usually correspond to an administrative domain such as a department, a building, or a geographic site. An AS can be a single network or a group of networks owned and administered by a common network administrator or group of administrators.

The backbone (given an address of 0.0.0.0) of an AS is a high-bandwidth logical area (where all areas are connected) that acts as a hub for inter-area transit traffic and the distribution of routing information between areas. The routers that attach an area to the backbone are called **area border routers (ABRs)** (see Table 12.5). Because the ABR is supposed to be a high-bandwidth pathway connecting the areas and because the ABR knows the AS's overall topology, ABRs require additional memory and processing power compared to regular routers located within an area. Therefore, you should not use a low-end router as an ABR (see Figure 12.3).

Areas that are not backbone areas can be classified as either a stub area or a transit area. A **stub area** is an area with only one ABR. All routes to the destination outside the area must pass through the single router. Because the ABR is the only router that routes data in and out of the area, the ABR advertises itself as the default router to all external destinations, thus reducing traffic and the size of the routing database. A transit area is an area that contains more than one ABR.

AS routers within an area are not required to maintain a database of routers and networks located inside other areas. Because the topology of an area is invisible from outside the area and because routers internal to a given area know nothing of the detailed topology outside the area, the isolation reduces the network traffic because not all routing information has to be sent to routers in other areas.

Routing in an AS takes place on two levels, depending on whether the source and destination of a packet reside in the same area (intra-area routing is used) or different areas

Table 12.5 Routers Used in ASs

Router type	Description
Internal router	Internal routers route packets only within a single area. The internal router can also be a backbone router if they have no interfaces to other areas.
Area border router (ABR)	Area border routers have interfaces in multiple areas and they route packets between these areas. Area border routers condense topological information before passing it to the backbone. This reduces the amount of routing information passed across the backbone.
Backbone router	A backbone router has an interface on the backbone area. This includes all routers that interface to more than one area (area border routers). However, backbone routers do not have to be area border routers. Routers with all interfaces connected to the backbone are considered internal routers.
ASBR	A router that exchanges routing information with routers belonging to other ASs. Such a router has AS external routes that are advertised throughout the AS. The path to each AS boundary router is known by every router in the AS. This classification is completely independent of the previous classifications: AS boundary routers may be internal or area border routers, and may or may not participate in the backbone.

Figure 12.3   An Autonomous System

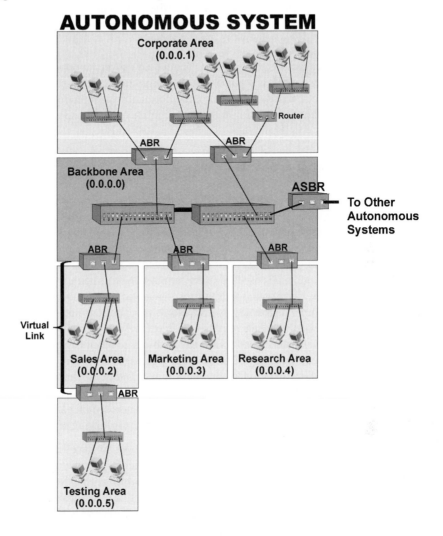

(inter-area routing is used). In intra-area routing, the packet is routed solely on information obtained within the area; no routing information obtained from outside the area needs to be used. This protects intra-area routing from the injection of bad routing information and helps to simplify the routing tables.

When routing a packet between two areas, the packet must travel on the backbone. The path that the packet will travel can be broken up into three contiguous pieces: (1) An intra-area path from the source to an area border router, (2) a backbone path between the source and destination areas, and (3) another intra-area path to the destination.

A **virtual link** is a logical link between a backbone area border router, an unspecified number of routers, and a second border router that is not connected to the backbone.

NOTE: Virtual links are not recommended because they can cause routing and other problems and they can be difficult to configure. Instead, always make an effort to connect new areas in your AS directly to the backbone by planning ahead before your AS is implemented.

To connect the ASs to other ASs, you would use an Autonomous System Border Router (ASBR). An ASBR is a router that exchanges routing information with routers belonging to other ASs. ASBRs access routing information from the Internet by using EGP and accesses routing information about the corporate network (AS) from OSPF. EGP will be explained later in this chapter.

12.4.4   Open Shortest Path First

Open Shortest Path First (OSPF) is a link-state routing protocol, used in medium-sized and large networks, that calculates routing table entries by constructing a shortest-path tree. It is designed to be run as an Interior Gateway Protocol (IGP) to a single AS. In a link-state routing protocol, each router maintains a database of router advertisements called link-state advertisements (LSAs). LSAs for routers within an AS consist of router, its attached networks, and their configured costs. An OSPF cost is a unitless metric that indicates the preference of using a link. There are also LSAs for summarized routes and routes outside the AS.

The router distributes its LSAs to its neighboring routers. LSAs are gathered into a database called the link state database (LSDB). By synchronizing LSDBs between all neighboring routers, each router has each other router's LSA in its database. Therefore, every router has the same LSDB. From the LSDB, entries for the router's routing table are calculated by using the Dijkstra algorithm to determine the least cost path (the path with the lowest accumulated cost) to each network in the internetwork. Different from RIP, that has its metric based on hop, the OSPF metric is based on bandwidth.

OSPF is considered superior to RIP for the following reasons:

- It is a more efficient protocol than RIP and does not have the restrictive sixteen hop-count problem, which causes data to be dropped after the sixteenth hop. An OSPF network can have an accumulated path cost of 65,535, which enables you to construct very large networks (within the maximum TTL value of 255) and assign a wide range of costs. An OSPF network is best suited for a large infrastructure with more than 50 networks.
- OSPF networks can detect changes to the network and calculate new routes quickly (rapid convergence). The period of convergence is brief and involves minimal overhead. The count-to-infinity problem does not occur in OSPF internetworks.
- Less network traffic is generated by OSPF than by RIP. RIP requires each router to broadcast its entire database every thirty seconds. OSPF routers only broadcast link-state information when it changes.
- LSAs include subnet mask information about networks. You can assign a different subnet mask for each segment of the network (variable-length subnetting). This increases the number of subnets and hosts that are possible for a single network address.

The shortest path first (SPF) routing algorithm is the basis for OSPF operations. When an SPF router is started, it initializes its routing protocol data structures and then waits for indications from lower-layer protocols that its interfaces are functional.

The main operation of the OSPF protocol occurs in the following consecutive stages and leads to the convergence of the internetwork:

Step 1: Compiling the LSDB.
Step 2: Calculating the Shortest Path First (SPF) Tree.
Step 3: Creating the routing table entries.

After a router is assured that its interfaces are functioning, it uses the OSPF Hello protocol to acquire neighbors, which are routers with interfaces to a common network. The router sends hello packets to its neighbors and receives their hello packets. In addition to helping acquire neighbors, hello packets also act as keep-alives to let routers know that other routers are still functional.

Adjacency is a relationship formed between selected neighboring routers for the purpose of exchanging routing information. When the link-state databases of two neighboring routers are synchronized, the routers are said to be adjacent. Not every pair of neighboring routers becomes adjacent. From the topological database generated from these hello packets, each router calculates a shortest-path tree, with itself as the root. The shortest-path tree, in turn, yields a routing table. To maintain the table, the established adjacencies are compared to the Hello messages sent out so that it can quickly detect failed routers and the network's topology can be altered appropriately.

An LSA from a given router is flooded across the AS so that each other router contains that router's LSA. While it appears that flooding LSAs across the AS causes a large amount of network traffic, OSPF is very efficient in the propagation of LSA information.

To keep track of LSAs in the LSDB, each router is assigned a router ID (a thirty-two-bit dotted decimal number that is unique to the AS). The router ID identifies the router in the AS, not the IP address of one of the router's interfaces. The router ID is not used as a destination IP address for sending information to the router. It is a common industry convention to use the largest or smallest IP address assigned to the router as the router ID. Because IP addresses are unique, this convention ensures that the OSPF Router IDs are also unique.

OSPF message addresses are determined by the type of network to which the OSPF interface is connected. One of the following OSPF network types must be selected when configuring an interface on an OSPF router.

- **Broadcast**—A network that can connect more than two routers with a hardware broadcast facility where a single packet sent by a router is received by all routers attached to that network. Ethernet, Token Ring, and FDDI are broadcast networks. OSPF messages sent on broadcast networks use IP multicast addresses (224.0.0.5 and 224.0.0.6).
- **Point-to-Point**—A network that can connect only two routers. Leased-line WAN links such as Dataphone Digital Service (DDS) and T-Carrier are point-to-point networks. OSPF messages sent on point-to-point networks use IP multicast addresses (224.0.0.5).
- **Non-Broadcast Multiple Access (NBMA)**—A network that can connect more than two routers but has no hardware broadcast facility. X.25, Frame Relay, and ATM are NBMA networks. Because multicasted OSPF messages do not reach all the OSPF routers on the network, OSPF must be configured to unicast to the IP addresses of the routers on the NBMA network.

12.4.5   Troubleshooting OSPF

If an OSPF environment is properly configured, OSPF routers learn all the least cost routes from adjacent OSPF routers after convergence. The exact list of routes added by OSPF to the IP routing table depends, among other factors, on whether or not areas are configured to summarize their routes, whether or not stub areas or totally stubby areas are being used, and whether or not ASBRs and route filtering are being used.

Most OSPF problems are related to the formation of adjacencies, either physical or logical (through virtual links). If adjacencies cannot form, the LSDBs cannot be synchronized and the OSPF routes will not accurately reflect the topology of the internetwork. Other OSPF problems are related either to the lack of routes or the existence of improper routes in the IP routing table.

If the adjacency is not forming, check the following:

Step 1: Before proceeding, verify that the two neighboring routers should form an adjacency. If the two routers are the only routers on the network, an adjacency should form. If there are more than two routers on the network, adjacencies should form only with the DR and BDR. If the two routers have already formed adjacencies with the DR and the BDR, they will not form adjacencies with each other. In this case, their neighbor should appear 2-way under neighbor state.

Step 2: Ping the neighboring router to ensure basic IP and network connectivity. Use the tracert command to trace the route to the neighboring router. There should not be any routers between the neighboring routers.

Step 3: Use OSPF logging to log errors and use warnings to record information about why the adjacency is not forming. To obtain additional information about OSPF processes, enable tracing for the OSPF component.

Step 4: Verify that the areas are enabled for authentication and the OSPF interfaces are using the same password. Change the authentication to match all neighboring OSPF routers on the same network. The password can vary from network to network.

Step 5: Verify that the routers are configured for the same Hello Interval and Dead Interval. By default, the Hello Interval is 10 seconds and the Dead Interval is 40 seconds.

Step 6: Verify that the routers agree on whether the area to which the common network belongs is a stub area or not.

Step 7: Verify that the interfaces of the neighboring routers are configured with the same Area ID.

Step 8: If the routers are on a NBMA network such as X.25 or Frame Relay, and the connection to the NBMA network appears as a single adapter (rather than separate adapters for each VC), their neighbors must be manually configured using the unicast IP address of the neighbor or neighbors to which the link-state information needs to be sent. Also verify that Router Priorities are configured so that one router can become the DR for the network.

Step 9: On broadcast networks (Ethernet, Token Ring, FDDI) or NBMA networks (X.25 or Frame Relay), verify that all routers do not have a Router Priority of 0. At least one router must have a Router Priority of 1 or greater so that it can become the DR for the network.

Step 10: Verify that IP packet filtering is not preventing the receiving (through input filters) or sending (through output filters) of OSPF messages on the router interfaces enabled for OSPF. OSPF uses the IP protocol number 89.

Step 11: Verify that TCP/IP packet filtering is not preventing the receiving of OSPF messages on the interfaces enabled for OSPF.

If the virtual link is not forming, check the following:

Step 1: Verify that the virtual link neighbor routers are configured for the same password, Hello Interval, and Dead Interval.

Step 2: For each router, verify that the virtual link neighbor's Router ID is correctly configured.

Step 3: Verify that both virtual link neighbors are configured for the correct transit area ID.

Step 4: For large internetworks with substantial round-trip delays across the transit area, verify that the retransmit interval is long enough.

If the OSPF routes do not appear or you experience improper OSPF routes, check the following:

Step 1: If you are not receiving summarized OSPF routes for an area, verify that all the ABRs for the area are configured with the proper {Destination, Network Mask} pairs summarizing that area's routes.

Step 2: If you are receiving both individual and summarized OSPF routes for an area, verify that all the ABRs for the area are configured with the proper Destination and Network Mask summarizing that area's routes.

Step 3: If you are not receiving external routes from the ASBR, verify that the source and route filtering configured on the ASBR are not too restrictive, preventing proper routes from being propagated to the OSPF AS.

Step 4: Verify that all ABRs are either physically connected to the backbone or logically connected to the backbone by using a virtual link. There should not be back door routers (routers connecting two areas without going through the backbone).

12.4.6 The Interior Gateway Routing Protocol

The **Interior Gateway Routing Protocol (IGRP)** is an extension of the open RIP standard developed in the mid-1980s by Cisco Systems, Inc. Cisco's principal goal in creating IGRP was to provide a robust protocol for routing within an AS that has arbitrarily complex topology and consists of media with diverse bandwidth and delay characteristics. Cisco developed EIGRP in the early 1990s to improve the operating efficiency of IGRP.

IGRP is a distance vector protocol that allows gateways to build up their routing table by exchanging information with other gateways. The metric used by IGRP includes the topological delay time, the bandwidth of the narrowest bandwidth segment of the path, the channel load of the path, and the reliability of the path. To get the most out of the network, it will split traffic between two or more paths proportional to its bandwidth. Therefore, if you have a 10 Mbps pathway and a 20 Mbps pathway, the 20 Mbps will get roughly twice as much traffic as the 10 Mbps pathway.

Periodically, each gateway broadcasts its entire routing table (with some censoring because of the split-horizon rule) to all adjacent gateways. While RIP's default update time is thirty seconds, IGRP broadcasts periodic updates every ninety seconds, whether it needs to or not. When a gateway gets this broadcast from another gateway, it compares the table with its existing table. Any new destinations and paths are added to the gateway's routing table. Paths in the broadcast are compared with existing paths. If a new path is better, it may replace the existing one. Information in the broadcast is also used to update channel occupancy and other information about existing paths.

IGRP uses the same routing loop control techniques found in RIP, including poison reverse, holddown timers, and split-horizon. However, IGRP has slightly different rules for the use of each technique:

- **Poison reverse**—IGRP sends out poison reverse updates when a route metric increases by a factor of 1.1.
- **Hold-down timer**—The IGRP hold-down timer is set to three times the periodic update interval, plus ten seconds. This means that because the default update interval is ninety seconds, the hold-down timer is 280 seconds.
- **Split-horizon**—Using the split-horizon technique increases the speed of convergence on an IGRP internetwork because route updates are not sent back across the same route. If a router does not receive an update about a route for three consecutive update periods, that route is marked as unreachable. If seven update periods pass without a route update, that route is removed from the routing table, which helps to reduce the size of routing tables stored in the router's memory.

In 1994, Cisco augmented IGRP with a product called **Enhanced Interior Gateway Routing Protocol (EIGRP).** EIGRP combines the advantages of link-state protocols with those of distance-vector protocols. The key features include the diffusing update algorithm (DUAL) finite state machine, variable length subnet masks, partial routing table updates rather than full updates, and bounded updates. DUAL allows routers to synchronize route changes and does not involve routers unaffected by the change. Different from IGRP, DUALs store all of their neighbors' routing tables so that they can more intelligently recalculate alternate paths in order to speed convergence. Bounded updates is a method whereby routing update messages are sent only to those routers affected by the topology change, which saves overhead and helps speed convergence.

EIGRP maintains separate routing tables for IP, IPX, and AppleTalk protocols but forwards routing update information by using a single protocol. Network traffic is reduced because three separate updates are not required when a change occurs. Without EIGRP, each network protocol would require its own routing protocol to transmit updates. For example, IP could transmit RIP updates, IPX could transmit its version of RIP updates, and AppleTalk could transmit Routing Table Maintenance Protocol (RTMP) updates. This conserves network bandwidth, router memory, and router CPU cycles.

12.5   GATEWAY PROTOCOLS

As mentioned earlier, autonomous systems are interconnected by using an exterior gateway protocol. Two common exterior gateway protocols are BGP and EGP. BGP is an enhancement of EGP and is one of several new interdomain routing protocols designed to give administrators more control. These newer protocols also scale better in large internetworks.

12.5.1   Exterior Gateway Protocols

While most companies and organizations group all their routers into one AS, large companies might use more than one AS. The local routing information of an autonomous area is gathered using an internal gateway protocol such as RIP or OSPF.

In these autonomous areas, one or more routers are chosen to use the exterior gateway protocol (EGP) to talk to other autonomous areas by providing a way for two neighboring routers located at the edges of their respective autonomous areas to exchange routing information. EGP routers only forward routing table information to routers on the edge of their autonomous areas.

The first step that EGP takes to establish communication between exterior routers is to perform neighbor acquisition. During neighbor acquisition, one exterior router makes a request to another exterior router to agree that they share router table information. After communications have been established, the router then continually tests to see if the EGP neighbors are responding. Routing table information is exchanged at intervals of 120 to 480 seconds between EGP neighbors using routing update messages. The neighbor responds by sending its complete routing table.

EGP restricts exterior gateways by allowing them to advertise only those destination networks reachable entirely within that gateway's autonomous system. Thus, an exterior gateway using EGP passes along information to its EGP neighbors but does not advertise itself to routers outside the autonomous system.

EGP has one major limitation: The distance indicated for a particular destination does not specify the cost to the destination. EGP only reports whether a destination is reachable. Because of this limitation, EGP can only be used in a tree-type network. All routing protocol domains must connect to the same central network.

Because all routing protocol domains must connect to the same central network, EGP cannot support a looped topology. EGP can advertise only one route to a given network. There can be no load sharing for traffic between any given pair of machines and packets can take nonoptimal paths when certain traffic conditions cause congestion in the selected route. As a result, it is difficult for EGP to switch to an alternate route if the primary route fails.

NOTE: EGP-2 is the latest version of EGP.

12.5.2   Border Gateway Protocols

Because of its limitations, EGP has been made obsolete by the Border Gateway Protocol (BGP). BGP version 4 (BGP-4), documented in RFC 1771, is the current exterior routing protocol used on the Internet. Other BGP-related documents are RFC 1772 (BGP Application), RFC 1773 (BGP Experience), RFC 1774 (BGP Protocol Analysis), and RFC 1657 (BGP MIB). BGP uses TCP as its transport protocol, on port 179.

BGP is a vector-distance protocol but, unlike traditional vector-distance protocols such as RIP where there is a single metric, BGP determines a preference order by applying a function mapping each path to a preference value and selects the path with the highest value. Where there are multiple viable paths to a destination, BGP maintains all of them but only advertises the one with the highest preference value. This approach allows a quick change to an alternate path if the primary path should fail. BGP-4 supports CIDR, IP prefixes, and path aggregation.

The internal Border Gateway Protocol (iBGP) is used by routers that all belong to the same autonomous system. These routers may use loopback interfaces to provide greater reachability in the AS. This is possible because an IGP can provide multiple routes to any given destination address if the network has redundant (multiple) links to each router. If one interface on a router goes down, the TCP connection to the loopback address can be maintained by using redundant interfaces.

Before any BGP route information can be exchanged between two routers, a TCP connection must be established. Another routing protocol, other than BGP, can then be used to establish the TCP connection. The TCP connection is made by a three-way handshake using a SYN, ACK, SYN sequence. Once a TCP connection has been established, route information can be exchanged.

Routing information is not advertised from one iBGP peer to another iBGP peer. This prevents inconsistent route information and routing loops in the network. To share route information among all iBGP routers, you must establish a logical mesh. Routing information is then exchanged only between routers that are members of this mesh. Router B can learn BGP networks only from Router A. When Router C sends its BGP information, only its own information is sent. Routing information learned from Router A is not included.

The external Border Gateway Protocol (eBGP) is used to exchange route information between different autonomous systems. When only one link connects two autonomous systems, the IP addresses of the connected interfaces are used to establish a BGP session between the two.

You can use any other IP address on the interfaces, but the address must be reachable without using an IGP. Static routes are OK. If multiple links are used to connect to the other autonomous systems, then using loopback addresses is your best option.

Outside of each AS, eBGP is used to inject routes owned by one AS through the enterprise network and into another AS. Two prerequisites need to be met for internal routes to be propagated via BGP:

- In order for a router to advertise routes to BGP, the route must exist in an IGP's routing table on the router.
- The BGP must be able to learn the route.

The router can place routes in its routing table by using an IGP to learn the network topology. It uses its own table and calculates its own routes. A default (static) route can be configured, or a directly connected network can advertise the route. BGP has a synchronization option that requires the BGP's learned routes and the IGP's learned routes to synchronize before BGP will advertise the IGP's learned network topologies.

12.6   IP MULTICAST

IP multicast allows a host to communicate simultaneously with several hosts by transmitting information using one data stream. Multicast can greatly reduce the network traffic that bandwidth-hungry applications such as videoconferencing, software distribution, and Webcast create. Network vendors widely support IP multicast in their routers. ISPs have started to offer multicast service in their backbones.

The purpose of IP multicast is to deliver a data stream from a source to a group of receivers. Receivers interested in a particular multicast application join the application's multicast group. A multicast group is dynamic and transient—receivers can join and leave the group at will, and the group disappears when no receivers remain. Group members listen to and receive data that the source delivers to the group's IP multicast address. Individual Class D IP addresses in the range from 224.0.0.0 to 239.255.255.255 represent all multicast groups. The multicast's source neither needs to join its group, nor knows who and where its receivers are. The source simply transmits multicast streams to the IP multicast address of its multicast group, then lets the network handle multicast data delivery. An IP multicast-enabled network can efficiently forward and route multicast data to receivers. Three key techniques manage multicast network delivery: (1) Scoping, (2) group management, and (3) distribution trees.

12.6.1   Multicast Scoping

Multicast scoping determines how far a multicast stream can travel from its source. Limiting the range of a multicast can prevent business data from traveling outside a network, thereby providing security. In multicast group management, multicast-enabled routers keep track of multicast group membership through subnets the routers directly attach to. The multicast-enabled routers forward multicast data only to the subnets that have group members, thereby saving network bandwidth. Multicast distribution trees define data delivery from a source to a multicast group, then build an optimized distribution tree that contains a set of routers and links to let group members receive data from the source. Let's take a close look at each of these network delivery technologies.

Traditionally, IP multicast uses a TTL parameter in an IP multicast application and multicast routers to control the multicast distribution. When you define the TTL value in an IP multicast application, contents don't transmit beyond the TTL value. For example, if you set Site Server's Active Channel Multicaster TTL value to 16, you ensure that Site Server's Web contents don't multicast beyond 16 router hops. Each multicast packet carries a TTL value in its IP header. Just as in unicast, every time a multicast router forwards a multicast packet, the router decreases the packet's TTL by 1. By default, a router won't forward packets with a value of TTL=1. You can modify the default TTL threshold to another value on each interface in a multicast router. For example, if you set the TTL threshold to 10 on a router interface, only packets with a TTL value that is greater than 10 can pass that router interface.

TTL-based multicast scoping has a couple of shortcomings. First, defining a proper TTL value in a multicast application can be difficult. If the value is too large, your multicast data might go out of your network. If the TTL value is too small, your multicast data might not reach interested receivers beyond the multicast scope. Second, if someone sets custom TTL thresholds in certain router interfaces, your multicast range can be unpredictable. For example, you wouldn't be able to divide your network into multicast regions to limit multicast applications to those regions, because if one router has an interface TTL threshold that is lower than a packet's TTL value, the router will forward the packet.

To overcome these limitations, the Internet Engineering Task Force (IETF) proposed Administratively Scoped IP Multicast as an Internet standard in RFC 2365 (July 1998). Administrative scoping lets you scope a multicast to a certain network boundary (within your organization) by using an administratively scoped address. IETF has designated IP multicast addresses between 239.0.0.0 and 239.255.255.255 as administratively scoped addresses for local use in intranets. You can configure routers that support administratively scoped addressing on the border of your network to confine your private multicast region. You can also define multiple isolated multicast regions in your network so that sensitive multicast data will travel only within a designated area. Figure 1 shows a network with three multicast regions: (1) Region 239.253.1.0 in Data Center 1, (2) region 239.253.2.0 in Data Center 2, and (3) region 239.253.3.0 in Data Center 3. When multicast data traverses Data Center 1, Router 1—which the boundary 239.253.1.0 defines—blocks any multicast packets with administratively scoped addresses of 239.253.1.x from transmitting to other data centers.

A multicast network forwards multicast data only to network subnets that have receivers in the corresponding multicast group in a scoped multicast region. (Selective forwarding is the biggest difference between multicast and broadcast. Broadcast floods data to all subnets.) To forward multicast data to receivers in a scoped multicast region, routers need information about group membership on their local subnets. One router on each subnet periodically multicasts membership query messages to all computers on the local subnet. Computers (group members) on the local subnet respond to the router's query message with a membership report about the group they belong to. The router keeps this membership information in its group database. Local subnet computers also multicast membership reports to the groups they belong to. When other group members receive a member computer's report, the group members postpone their membership reports and wait for a variable period of time. This waiting period reduces membership report traffic and router processing time. As long as a router knows one group member on the local subnet, the router forwards multicast data to that subnet, and other group members will receive the multicast data. When a new member joins a group, the member doesn't need to wait for the next membership query from the router. Instead, the new member immediately sends a membership report as if in response to a membership query. When the router receives this report, it immediately forwards multicast data to the subnet on which the new member resides if the new member is the first member of that subnet's multicast group.

12.6.2   Internet Group Membership Protocol

Routers and computers use the **Internet Group Membership Protocol (IGMP)** to exchange membership information. IGMP is an integral part of IP. The two standard versions of IGMP are IGMP v1 (RFC 1112) and IGMP v2 (RFC 2236). IETF released IGMP v2 as an enhanced version of IGMP v1 in November of 1997. Today, many routers and OSs support IGMP v2. Microsoft implements IGMP v2 in Windows 2000 (Win2K), in NT with Service Pack 4 (SP4), in Windows 98, and in Windows 95 with Winsock 2.

IGMP v2's biggest enhancement is a group notification feature. In IGMP v1, a receiver that leaves a multicast group doesn't automatically notify the router. Rather, the router assumes no group member is on the local subnet if the router doesn't receive a membership report after several queries and waiting intervals. Several minutes or more can then pass before the router stops forwarding data to that subnet. In IGMP v2, receivers leaving a group directly inform the router. The router then queries the subnet to see whether any other group members remain. If the router doesn't receive a response, it assumes that no other group members exist on that subnet and stops multicast forwarding to that subnet.

IETF is working on IGMP v3 to further improve IGMP v2. IGMP v3 will include several new features. One such feature will let a computer specify which sources in a specific group the computer will receive data from.

12.6.3   Multicast Routing Protocols

Five multicast routing protocols currently exist, and you can classify each into either the source-based tree (dense mode) or shared-tree (sparse mode) protocols. The three dense mode protocols are Distance Vector Multicast Routing Protocol (DVMRP), Multicast Open Shortest Path First (MOSPF), and Protocol Independent Multicast-Dense Mode (PIM-DM). The two sparse mode protocols are Protocol Independent Multicast-Sparse Mode (PIM-SM) and Core Based Trees (CBT).

DVMRP (RFC 1075) is the first multicast routing protocol researchers developed to implement MBone in the Internet, and DVMRP is still prevalent in MBone. DVMRP builds a source-based distribution tree based on broadcast-and-prune. The DVMRP tree includes a dedicated RIP—like the unicast routing protocol—and it depends on this protocol to determine the shortest path from the source to the multicast group when setting up the distribution tree. UNIX machines were among the first to implement DVMRP. DVMRP support is ubiquitous in almost all vendors' routers.

MOSPF (RFC 1584) is simply an extension of OSPF, a well-known unicast routing protocol in IP networks. OSPF divides a network into one or more OSPF areas and uses link-state information (i.e., information about router interfaces and network wires) to set up and maintain a unicast routing table. MOSPF uses OSPF as the native protocol to advertise IGMP group membership in each router as part of the link-state information within an OSPF area. MOSPF can easily construct a source-based distribution tree by using the link-state database in a router instead of the usual broadcast-and-prune procedure. MOSPF supports multicast between multiple OSPF areas and uses border routers that link OSPF areas to forward IGMP group membership information and multicast data between OSPF areas. MOSPF is a native choice if your network uses OSPF as its unicast routing protocol. 3Com and Nortel support MOSPF in their routers.

PIM-DM, an Internet draft, uses broadcast-and-prune to form a source-based tree, similar to DVMRP. However, PIM-DM uses the existing unicast routing protocol in your network, such as RIP or OSPF, to determine the shortest path from the source to the multicast group. The use of existing protocols is the reason behind PIM's name (*Protocol Independent Multicast*).

PIM-SM (RFC 2362) is another PIM protocol, but PIM-SM is suitable for use in sparse mode. PIM-SM uses shared trees to deliver data and refers to the root of a shared tree as a RP. However, a shared tree might not reflect the shortest path from source to multicast group. Thus, PIM-SM can let routers optionally switch to a source-based tree to receive source data after initial data delivery in the shared tree and is based on some triggered conditions (if the shared tree's data delivery rate is too low). Cisco is PIM's primary advocate and supports both PIM protocols in its routers.

CBT (RFC 2189) is similar to PIM-SM. However, CBT uses only shared trees for data delivery and can't switch from shared trees to source-based trees, as PIM-SM can. CBT calls the root of the shared tree a *core*. Vendors haven't widely implemented CBT.

12.7   IPX ROUTING PROTOCOLS

The two main routing protocols used in IPX are RIP (IPX's distance vector protocol) and NLSP (IPX's link state protocol). Any routing protocol that maintains IPX routes also maintains SAP lists so that it can keep track of services.

IPX RIP has many similarities to TCP/IP RIP. They both can use split-horizon or poison-reverse to help prevent routing loops and improve convergence time. They also each have a hop count limit of fifteen, and they both send out complete routing table updates at regular intervals. IPX RIP, however, uses sixty seconds as the update interval, not thirty, and IPX RIP sends out SAP information as well as routing information. The extra SAP information that is pushed by IPX RIP is the reason that the update interval is longer.

> *NOTE:* Don't confuse TCP/IP RIP and IPX RIP. While they have many similarities, they are two separate protocols.

Only in the last couple of years has Novell begun using NLSP as the default routing protocol, but also by default, NLSP is enabled on NetWare servers with RIP compatibility enabled. NLSP is a link state routing protocol that allows the construction of a hierarchy of areas within large networks, in much the same way that OSPF and BGP do. You can also use EIGRP to distribute IPX routing information, but because this is proprietary to Cisco, you can only use this between Cisco Routers, segments that support NetWare servers, or NetWare resources that have either RIP or NLSP enabled to work properly.

NLSP routers exchange information such as connectivity states, path costs, throughput, maximum packet size (MTU size), and networks learned through RIP (external network numbers). This information is carried in a Link-State Packet (LSP). By exchanging this information with its peer routers, each NLSP router builds and maintains a logical map of the entire internetwork. Because NLSP is a link-state routing protocol, NLSP transmits routing information only when a change occurs in a route or service, or every two hours, whichever occurs first.

SUMMARY

1. A router, which works at the network ISO layer, is a device that connects two or more LANs.
2. When you send a packet from one computer to another computer, it first determines if the packet should be sent locally to another computer on the same LAN or to a router so that it can be routed to the destination LAN. If the packet is meant to go to a computer on another LAN, it is sent to the router (gateway).

3. The router will then determine what is the best route to take and will forward the packets to that route.

4. A metric is a standard of measurement used by routing algorithms to determine the optimal path to a destination.

5. A hop is the trip a data packet takes from one router to another router or a router to another intermediate point to another in the network.

6. Routing algorithms must converge rapidly. Convergence is the process of agreement by all routers on which routes are the optimal routes.

7. Count to infinity, which typically happens when a network has slow convergence, is a loop that happens when a link in a network goes down and routers on the network update their routing tables with incorrect hop counts.

8. To handle the count to infinity problem, networks use either split-horizon or poison-reverse.

9. Static routing algorithms are hardly algorithms at all, but are table mappings established by the network administrator prior to the beginning of routing. These mappings do not change unless the network administrator alters them.

10. Because static routing systems cannot react to network changes, they generally are considered unsuitable for today's large, changing networks.

11. Dynamic routing algorithms can be supplemented with static routes where appropriate.

12. Routers use distance vector-based routing protocols to advertise or broadcast the routes in their routing tables periodically, but they only send them to their neighboring routers.

13. Link-state algorithms are also known as SPF algorithms. Instead of using broadcast, link-state routers send updates directly (or by using multicast traffic) to all routers within the network. Each router, however, sends only the portion of the routing table that describes the state of its own links.

14. ADs are used to rate the trustworthiness of routing information received on a router from a neighbor router.

15. By using ICMP messages, the ICMP protocol can be used by local routers to provide a way for hosts to sense routers that are down and to perform router solicitation and advertisement.

16. RIP, a distance-vector protocol, is designed for exchanging routing information within a small to medium-sized network. The biggest advantage of

RIP is that it is extremely simple to configure and deploy.

17. RIP uses a single routing metric of hop counts to measure the distance between the source and a destination network.

18. Some protocols, such as OSPF, allow areas (groupings of contiguous networks) to be grouped together into an AS.

19. The backbone (given an address of 0.0.0.0) of the AS is a high-bandwidth logical area where all areas are connected.

20. Routers that attach an area to the backbone are called ABRs.

21. AS routers within an area are not required to maintain a database of routers and networks located inside other areas.

22. A virtual link is a logical link between a backbone area border router, an unspecified number of routers, and a second border router that is not connected to the backbone.

23. To connect ASs to other ASs, you would use an ASBR.

24. OSPF is a link-state routing protocol, used in medium-sized and large networks, that calculates routing table entries by constructing a shortest-path tree.

25. IGRP is a distance vector protocol that allows gateways to build up their routing tables by exchanging information with other gateways.

26. In these autonomous areas, one or more routers are chosen to use EGP to talk to other autonomous areas by providing a way for two neighboring routers located at the edges of their respective autonomous areas to exchange routing information.

27. BGP-4 is the current exterior routing protocol used on the Internet.

28. IP multicast allows a host to communicate simultaneously with several hosts by transmitting information by using one data stream.

29. Five multicast routing protocols currently exist, and you can classify each into either the source-based tree (dense mode) or shared-tree (sparse mode) protocols.

30. The two main routing protocols used in IPX are RIP (IPX's distance-vector protocol) and NLSP (IPX's link-state protocol).

31. Any routing protocol that maintains IPX routes also maintains SAP lists so that it can keep track of services.

QUESTIONS

1. Which of the following communications devices would be used to transport packets between ASs that are over 1000 kilometers apart?
   a. concentrator
   b. router
   c. hub
   d. transparent bridge

2. What is the default update timer value and the default administrative distance for routers using IGRP on TCP/IP internetworks?
   a. 30 seconds and 120
   b. 60 seconds and 1
   c. 90 seconds and 100
   d. 100 seconds and 90

3. Which of the following routing protocols is a distance-vector routing protocol used on TCP/IP internetworks and supports multipath routing?
   a. NLSP
   b. OSPF
   c. EIGRP
   d. IGRP

4. Which of the following routing protocols maintains separate routing tables for IP, IPX, and AppleTalk but uses only one protocol to disseminate routing information?
   a. OSPF
   b. EIGRP
   c. IGRP
   d. IP RIP

5. You are the network administrator for a company that uses TCP/IP for its network. The routing protocol in use is OSPF. You are frequently adding routers to your internetwork. Which of the following best describes convergence time as it relates to adding new routers to your internetwork?
   a. the time it takes for a packet to travel from the source to the destination
   b. the time it takes for a new router to receive the first LSP
   c. the time it takes for the designated router to learn all of the new routes
   d. the time it takes for all of the routers in the internetwork to update their tables with the changes

6. Which of the following can you configure on a router to alleviate routing loops? (Select all choices that are correct.)
   a. route update timers
   b. hold-down timers
   c. split-horizon
   d. AD

7. What is the default routing update timer value if RIP is the routing protocol implemented on a Novell NetWare 3.11 IPX internetwork?
   a. 30 seconds
   b. 90 seconds
   c. 60 seconds
   d. 240 seconds

8. Which of the following are distance-vector routing protocols? (Select all choices that are correct.)
   a. RIP
   b. OSPF
   c. IGRP
   d. EIGRP

9. What is the default hold-down timer value for routers that use IGRP on TCP/IP internetworks?
   a. 60 seconds
   b. 270 seconds
   c. 90 seconds
   d. 280 seconds

10. As network administrator for a company, you want to configure a static IP route between two Cisco routers. Which of the following are syntactically correct? (Select all choices that are correct.)
    a. ip route *network subnet-mask next-hop-router-address*
    b. ip route *network subnet-mask interface-used-to-get-to-destination-network*
    c. ip route *network subnet-mask next-hop-router-address administrative-distance*
    d. ip route *network subnet-mask next-hop-router-address interface-used-to-get-to-destination-network*

11. The Acme Corporation uses TCP/IP for its internetwork. Pat, the network administrator, has installed OSPF for dynamic configuration of routing tables. Why would Pat have chosen to use OSPF rather than RIP?
    a. RIP requires more metrics.
    b. OSPF updates the routing tables more frequently.
    c. Link-state routing protocols converge faster than distance-vector routing protocols.
    d. Link-state routing protocols require less processing power than distance-vector routing protocols.

12. What is the default update interval on a TCP/IP internetwork if RIP is the routing protocol implemented on the internetwork?
    a. 30 seconds
    b. 90 seconds
    c. 60 seconds
    d. 240 seconds

13. Which of the following methods prevents routing loops by not allowing a packet to travel the same router interface twice on its way to a destination? (Select the best choice.)
    a. split-horizon
    b. route poisoning
    c. hold-downs
    d. STP

14. Which of the following methods prevents routing loops by preventing a router from advertising a

path to a recently downed router too quickly? (Select the best choice.)

a. split-horizon   b. route poisoning

c. hold-downs   d. balanced hybrid

15. You are suggesting that your company uses IP RIP as its routing protocol. Your boss would like you to list some facts about IP RIP before he approves your request. Which of the following statements about IP RIP are true? (Choose two.)

a. It limits hop counts to 31.

b. It is a link-state routing protocol.

c. It uses autonomous system numbers.

d. It is capable of load sharing over multiple paths.

e. It uses bandwidth as the metric for path selection.

f. It broadcasts updates every 30 seconds by default

16. The Acme Corporation uses TCP/IP for their internetwork. The network administrator for the Acme Corporation, Pat, wants to enable the dynamic configuration of routing tables for the internetwork. Consequently, he has installed RIP on Acme Corporation's routers. Why would Pat have chosen to use RIP rather than OSPF? (Select all choices that are correct.)

a. RIP requires fewer metrics than OSPF.

b. RIP updates the routing tables less frequently than OSPF.

c. RIP converges faster than OSPF.

d. RIP requires less processing power than OSPF.

17. Which of the following protocols is referred to as a hybrid routing protocol because it has features of both distance-vector and link-state?

a. RIP   b. EIGRP

c. OSPF   d. IGRP

18. You are the administrator of a Windows 2000 network. The network consists of 10 segments. These segments are connected by four Windows 2000 server-based routers named Router 1, Router 2, Router 3, and Router 4. Routing and remote access is enabled as a router on these four servers. To exchange routing information, the four servers use RIP II for IP. There are two other routers on the network that use RIP II to exchange routing information. These other routers might have been erroneously configured and, consequently, contain incorrect routing information. You want to ensure that Router 1, Router 2, Router 3, and Router 4 do

not process routes received from any router other than Router 1, Router 2, Router 3, or Router 4. How can you configure the four routers to accomplish this goal? (Choose all that apply.)

a. Configure the RIP routing protocol on the four routers to RIP peer filters. List the other three routers as RIP peers.

b. Configure each RIP interface on the four routers to unicast announcements to RIP neighbors. List the other three routers as RIP neighbors.

c. Configure each RIP interface on the four routers to use password authentication. Use the same password on all four routers.

d. On each RIP interface on the four routers, configure routes for outgoing routes. Announce only routes in the route ranges of the network IDs that are connected to the four routers.

19. You are the administrator for your company's Windows 2000 routed network. Your network has grown considerably over the last year and includes 15 subnets and routers connected in series. To accommodate new growth you install 2 new subnets and routers. You also install a RRAS server and configure it as a RIP II router on Subnet_17. All subnets are referred as Subnet_A through Subnet_Q, inclusive. All routers are referred to as Router_1 through Router_17, inclusive. However, users on Subnet_R report that they cannot access resources on Subnet_A. After further investigation you find that Subnet_R users cannot access resources on Subnet_A either. What's wrong?

a. RIP has a maximum hop count of 15.

b. RIP has a maximum TTL of 15.

c. The metric count for Router_1's and Router_17's routing tables is not set correctly.

d. Router_1 needs a static route configured for Router_17 and Router_17 needs a static route configured for Router_1.

20. Your boss is concerned about routing loops with the use of distance vector routing protocols such as RIP and IGRP in your network. You would like to ensure him that there are mechanisms used to prevent the possibility of a routing loop. Which of the following are examples of this mechanism? (Choose two.)

a. LSA

b. Shortest path first tree

c. Hold-down timers

d. STP

e. Split-horizon

CHAPTER 13

Introduction to Cisco Routers

Topics Covered in this Chapter

Introduction

Cisco Systems is a leading manufacturer of network equipment. When you discuss routers, you will have to mention Cisco routers. Cisco routers are able to build routing tables, execute commands, and route packets across network interfaces using routing protocols. This chapter is the first of three chapters that introduce you to Cisco routers. This chapter introduces you to the command line interface used on Cisco routers and is the first step in installing and configuring them.

Objectives

- List the main components of a Cisco router and explain how they relate to a server.
- Given a picture of a Cisco router port, identify the port and list its purpose.
- Install and enable a Cisco router.
- Explain how to configure a Cisco router.
- From the command line interface on a Cisco router, change from one operating mode to another.
- Enable and disable TCP/IP and IPX protocol on a Cisco router.

13.1 INTRODUCTION TO CISCO ROUTERS

For all intents and purposes, routers are purpose-built computers dedicated to internetwork processing. Because they have the capabilities of handling the traffic for hundreds, and maybe even thousands of uses, when a router goes down or slows down, it can be devastating to a company.

Just like the switches, routers don't come with a monitor, a keyboard, or a mouse (see Figure 13.1). Instead, you connect and manage the router using one of the following three methods:

- Using a terminal (usually a PC or work station running in terminal mode) connection through a cable to the back of the router.
- From a terminal that is in a different location and is connected to it via a modem that calls a modem connected to the router with a cable.
- Via the network on which the router sits.

Because routers on large networks are hidden away from the normal users, routers are often accessed through the network. Unfortunately, if the router is unreachable due to a network problem, or if there is a problem with the router itself, someone must go to the location of the router and use one of the terminals to reconfigure or troubleshoot the router.

Figure 13.1   A Cisco 1600 Router

13.1.1   Router Memory

Like a PC, routers use various kinds of memory to operate. The first type is **dynamic random access memory (DRAM),** which is the working storage that is used by the router's central processor. When a router is operating, its DRAM contains an image of the Cisco IOS software, the running configuration file, the routing table, other tables built by the router after startup, and the packet buffer.

NOTE: When the router is shut off, the contents of the DRAM is lost.

Cisco's smallest router, the 700 series, ships with 1.5 MB of DRAM and can be expanded to a maximum of 2.5 MB. The 12,000 gigabit switch router, one of Cisco's largest, ships with 32 MB minimum DRAM, which can be expanded to 256 MB maximum.

The RAM is logically divided into two sections: (1) Primary memory and (2) shared memory (see Table 13.1). **Primary memory** contains a running copy of the Cisco IOS, which is loaded into RAM from Flash at startup. It also contains a running copy of the configuration file, which is loaded into RAM from NVRAM at startup. In addition, primary memory stores the routing tables, ARP tables, and other IOS data structures. **Shared memory** (also called packet memory) is used for buffering. This is a temporary storage area where packets go when they are waiting to be processed.

Nonvolatile RAM (NVRAM) is memory that will retain information after losing power. Cisco routers store a copy of the router's configuration file in NVRAM. When the router is intentionally turned off, or if power is lost, NVRAM enables it to restart with its proper configuration.

Flash memory is also nonvolatile. It differs from NVRAM in that it can be erased and reprogrammed as needed. Originally developed by Intel, flash memory is in wide use in computers and other devices. This is an important feature because it enables network managers to stage new versions of IOS on routers throughout an internetwork and then upgrade them all at once to a new version.

Table 13.1 Memory Types Used in Router

Memory type	Volatile or Nonvolatile	Contents
RAM/DRAM	Volatile	Active program and operating system instructions, the running configuration file, routing tables
NVRAM	Nonvolatile	Startup configuration file
ROM	Nonvolatile	POST, bootstrap, and startup/power-up utilities, usually limited version of Cisco IOS
Flash	Nonvolatile	Cisco IOS

Read only memory (RDM) is another form of nonvolatile memory. Cisco routers use ROM to hold the bootstrap program, which is a file that can be used to boot to a minimum configuration state after catastrophe. ROM is also referred to as ROMMON. In fact, when you boot from ROM, the first thing you'll see is the rommon > > prompt. ROMMON is short for ROM monitor. During the early days of the UNIX operating system, UNIX relied on ROMMON to reboot a computer to the point at which commands could at least be typed into the system console monitor. In smaller Cisco routers, ROM holds a bare-bones subset of the Cisco IOS software. ROM in some high-end Cisco routers holds a full copy of IOS.

13.1.2   Internetwork Operating System

Like a PC, the router needs an operating system. The operating system used on routers is the **Internetwork Operating System (IOS).** Because a router is more specialized than a PC, the IOS is contained in a single file. Depending on the version, an IOS software image can be anywhere from 3 to 10 MB in size. System images of the IOS can be uploaded and downloaded in order to back up routers, upgrade their capabilities, and restart them after a failure. Cisco IOS software contains instructions for the router so that it can act as a traffic cop, directing activity inside the router. IOS manages internal router operations by telling the various hardware components what to do.

When you order IOS software for a Cisco router, it is different from buying a Windows 98 or Windows 2000 server. There is no single IOS software product. Instead, IOS is a common software platform on which a suite of IOS implementations are based, each packaged depending on specific missions. Cisco calls these IOS package feature sets (also called software images or feature packs). When you order a Cisco router, you choose an IOS feature set that contains the features and capabilities that you require. The versions and subsets of Cisco IOS software are defined by feature set and by release. Feature sets define the job or purpose of the IOS while releases are versions and subversions of the IOS.

Cisco IOS feature sets are made to be compatible with certain router platforms while enabling interoperability between various networking protocols such as TCP/IP, Novell NetWare, and AppleTalk. In addition, it specifies network services and applications such as network management and security provided by the IOS.

NOTE: Not all feature sets will run on all router platforms. See Tables 13.2 and 13.3.

Table 13.2 Available Features on Cisco Routers

Category	Examples of features
LAN support	IP, Novell IPX, AppleTalk, Banyan Vines, DECnet
WAN services	PPP, ATM LANE, Frame Relay, ISDN, X.25
WAN optimization	Dial-on-demand, snapshot routing, traffic shaping
IP routing	BGP, RIP, IGRP, EIGRP, OSPF, IS-IS, NAT
Other routing	IPX RIP, AURP, NLSP
Multimedia and QoS	Generic traffic shaping, random early detection, RSVP
Security	Access lists, extended access lists, lock and key, TACACS+
Switching	Fast-switched policy routing, AppleTalk Routing over ISL
IBM support	APPN, Bisync, Frame Relay for SNA, SDLC integration
Protocol translation	LAT, PPP, X.25
Remote node	PPP, SLIP, MacIP, IP pooling, CSLIP, NetBEUI over PPP
Terminal services	LAT, Xremote, Telnet, X.25 PAD

Table 13.3 IOS Feature Set Families

Feature set family	Target customer environments
IP	Basic IP routing
Desktop	IP, Novel IPX, AppleTalk, DECnet
Enterprise	High-end functionality for LANs, WANs, and management
Enterprise/APPN	Same as Enterprise, but with many IBM-specific features added

When you determine which part number to order, you first choose a feature set family. Feature set families are grouped by general characteristics into four groups based on the function of the router: (1) IP Routing, (2) Desktop, (3) Enterprise, and (4) Enterprise/APPN. Feature sets are further grouped into software product variants:

- **Basic**—The basic feature set for the hardware platform
- **Plus**—The basic set and additional features, which are dependent on the hardware platform selected
- **Encryption**—The addition of either a 40-bit (Plus 40) or a 56-bit (Plus 56) data encryption feature atop either the Basic or Plus feature set

You then choose the hardware that the IOS is to run on and finally you can choose the IOS release (see Figure 13.2). You can then look up the part number in the Cisco Catalog.

Cisco IOS software release numbers have four basic parts. The first part is a major release, which marks First Customer Shipments (FCSs) of an IOS version of stable, high-quality software for customers to use in their production networks. Major releases are further defined by the following:

- **Stage**—Marks FCSs of various major release stages. Stage releases are often referred to in the future tense, when they are still planned but have not yet taken place.

Figure 13.2   Ordering a Specific IOS Feature Set

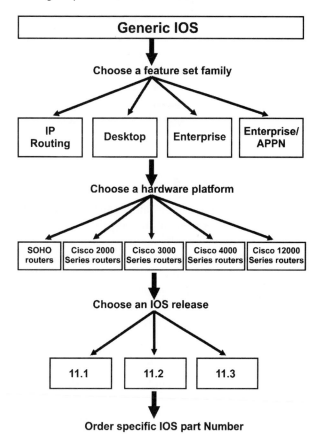

■ **Maintenance Update**—Denotes support for additional platforms of features beyond what was available in the major release's FCS.

The fourth part of the release number is the deployment. A general deployment (GD) release is available for customers. Early deployment (ED) releases are to deliver new functionality or technologies to customers to deploy in a limited manner in their networks. Limited deployment (LD) denotes a limited lifecycle between FCS and GD (see Figure 13.3).

Just like with Windows, at any given time, there can be several major releases in use at the same time. While most experienced administrators are content to stick with a release that works for them, an advanced IOS released may contain necessary features that were not previously available. Remember, when managing a network environment, reliability is usually more important than to have the newest version.

Figure 13.3   Cisco IOS Version

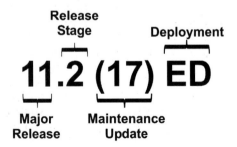

13.1.3   Configuration Files

Managing a router involves installing, upgrading, backing up, recovery, configuring and monitoring. Of course, one of the biggest parts of router management is installing and backing up the router's configuration file. The configuration file runs the router and specifies how all the traffic goes through it. It contains information describing the network environment in which the router will run and how the network manager wants it to behave. The configuration file tells the router what to do and the IOS tells the router how to do it.

13.1.4   Range of Cisco Routers

Table 13.4 provides a list of many different Cisco router series. Cisco is constantly updating and upgrading its series, by adding and discontinuing products all the time. You can always get an up-to-date list of Cisco routers at the following websites:

Product Catalog

> http://www.cisco.com/univercd/cc/td/doc/pcat/

Quick Reference Guide

> http://www.cisco.com/warp/public/752/qrg/

Cisco Products

> http://www.cisco.com/public/Product_root.shtml

Cisco Routers

> http://www.cisco.com/warp/public/44/jump/routers.shtml

For documentation of Cisco routers, refer to the following websites:

Cisco 1700 Series Routers

> http://www.cisco.com/univercd/cc/td/doc/product/access/acs_mod/1700/

Cisco 2500 Series Routers

> http://www.cisco.com/univercd/cc/td/doc/product/access/acs_fix/cis2500/

Cisco 2600 Series Routers

> http://www.cisco.com/univercd/cc/td/doc/product/access/acs_mod/cis2600/

Table 13.4 Cisco Router Series

Product series	Description	Applications
Cisco 12000	Gigabit switch routers	Accepts data from PSTN, ATM, Frame Relay, DSL, and PBX for high-speed transmission over the IP backbone
Cisco 10720	Internet-class metro edge access routers	High-performance router and a principle building block in the next-generation metro IP network. The Cisco 10720 Internet router is the industry's first router combining IP, resilient packet ring (RPR), and Ethernet technologies optimized for high-speed multitenant Internet services
Cisco 10000	Edge services routers	High-density T-1 aggregation IP edge routers
Cisco 7500	Data, voice, and video routers	Supports multiprotocol multimedia routing and bridging with a wide variety of protocols and LAN and WAN options
Cisco 7200	High-performance multifunction routers	Chassis-based, modular central site router that provides high performance and availability with serviceability and manageability features
Cisco 7100	VPN routers	Integrated solution that combines high-speed routing with VPN services
Cisco 4000	Modular, high-density routers	Modular access routers with a broad set of connectivity features and an internetworking software set. A good choice when protecting a legacy system investment is important
Cisco 3600	Modular, high-density access routers	Multi-service access routers for medium-sized and large offices and smaller ISPs
Cisco 2600	Modular access routers	Cost-effective, modular access router for branch offices that supports voice, data, and dial-up access
Cisco 2500	Fixed and modular access routers	Flexible branch office choice that features integrated hubs and access servers for either Ethernet or Token Ring
Cisco 1700	Modular access routers	For secure Internet, intranet, and extranet access with optional VPN and firewall service designed for small branch offices or small and medium-sized businesses
Cisco 1600	Modular desktop access routers	Small footprint routers that are excellent choices for small business or branch offices to connect an Ethernet LAN to the Internet or a corporate WAN
Cisco 1400	xDSL routers	Secure router that features both Ethernet and ATM interfaces that include VPN and firewall support
Cisco 1000	Fixed-configuration desktop access routers	For connecting small offices to ISDN or serial WAN connections
Cisco 900	Cable access routers	Provides telecommuters and small offices with high-speed secure connection and access
Cisco 800	ISDN, serial, and IDSL routers	Inexpensive router series that connects up to 20 users to the Internet or intranet over ISDN, IDSL, or a serial connection. Small office router for offices of up to 20 users and corporate telecommuters
Cisco 700	ISDN access routers	A series of affordable, fast routers that connect small office and home office workers to the Internet

13.2   ROUTER PORTS

Three major categories of modules can be configured into Cisco routers to support either LAN or WAN connectivity. LAN connectivity includes Ethernet and Token Ring; newer protocols such as ISDN, Frame Relay, and ATM; and legacy protocols such as SDLC and X.25.

Lower-end routers tend to have "fixed configuration" in that the modules are factory integrated only (preconfigured). Midrange routers, such as the Cisco 4500, are modular in that they can accept a variety of modules, often packaging different protocols in the same box. Interface modules are plugged into the motherboards for this class of routers. High-end routers such as the Cisco 7000 and Cisco 12000 series have buses (also called backplanes). Bus-based routers accept larger modules, usually referred to as blades or cards that are effectively self-contained routers that have their own CPUs, memory units, and so on.

An empty bus is simply an empty slot, in which you can plug any other type of interface that you purchase as an add-in card. Wide varieties of modular interfaces are available, such as ISDN, Frame Relay, and voice interface cards. You can also add additional serial or Ethernet interfaces like the ones already discussed. The modular interface cards for T-1 and ISDN lines come with built-in CSU/DSUs and NT1s, respectively. This eliminates the need for additional hardware between the router and the line. Modular routers make it easier to build a solution that suits individual needs.

13.2.1   LAN Ports

Ethernet is widely used in Cisco devices. There are two main types of cabling supported: (1) UTP and (2) 10Base5 (thick wire). UTP cabling is attached to RJ-45 connectors and 10Base5 is connected via a transceiver attached to the AUI port. It is worth noting that 10Base2 (thin wire) connections are not directly supported. However, a 10Base2 transceiver attached to the AUI port can provide access to thin wire Ethernet. The AUI port is included to support legacy Ethernet installations. Most current Ethernet implementations use UTP cabling with RJ-45 connectors.

There are two ways in which the wires are generally connected to the RJ-45 connectors at each end of a cable: (1) straight through and (2) crossover. The most common arrangement for Ethernet UTP cabling is straight through cabling. In straight through cabling, each pin on one connector is connected directly to the same pin position on the connector at the other end of the cable. Straight through connections are used to connect other devices, such as routers or PCs (which connect to an Ethernet LAN), to hubs and switches (which implement Ethernet functionality).

A crossover cable, which can be used to connect from one NIC to another NIC or one hub to another hub, reverses the transmit and receive wires. You would also use a crossover cable to connect a PC to a router. This can be useful when testing a router's configuration—a PC can be attached directly to a router's Ethernet port without the need for an intermediate hub or switch.

The 15-pin AUI port is used for making connections to a thick wire (10Base5) Ethernet cable via a transceiver. Transceivers for 10Base2 are also available. You will find a

Figure 13.4   A 10BaseT and 15-Pin AUI Port

fixed ·AUI interface on many Cisco devices. Their use is largely confined to supporting legacy Ethernet implementations (see Figure 13.4).

13.2.2   **WAN Serial Ports**

Cisco routers support a wide variety of WAN interfaces and associated data link layer protocols using three types of ports (see Table 13.5):

- **RJ-45**—BRI ISDN and auxiliary connections
- **DB-60**—High-speed synchronous serial port (see Figure 13.5)
- **DB-60**—Low-speed asynchronous/synchronous serial port

The RJ-45 connector appears exactly like an Ethernet connector (10BaseT or Fast Ethernet) but, it has different electrical specifications. Some routers will include two connectors (one for each D channel) or one connector for both channels. The ISDN RJ-45 ports will be marked with a S/T or a U. The S/T device means that it needs to connect to an external NT1 device while the U indicates that it has built-in NT1 functionality.

Low-speed asynchronous/synchronous ports connect terminals, printers, modems, microcomputers, and remote LANs over asynchronous serial lines to an internetwork, or to synchronous devices such as CSU/DSUs on the same ports. Low-speed asynchronous/synchronous serial ports support data transmission rates of up to 115.2 Kbps and high-speed synchronous serial ports support data transmission rates of up to 2.048 Mbps. To learn what your router supports, refer to the documentation that comes with your router.

Cisco serial cables are "smart" because they have on-board circuitry that informs the serial port to which the cable is attached whether it should function as a DTE or a DCE. Each cable is produced in a DTE or DCE version. The cable also informs the port which WAN standard is being used—X.21, V.35, etc. In some cases the router may need to provide the clocking and function as a DCE, which would be needed if you connect two routers back-to-back via a null modem cable.

Table 13.5   Common WAN Connector Types

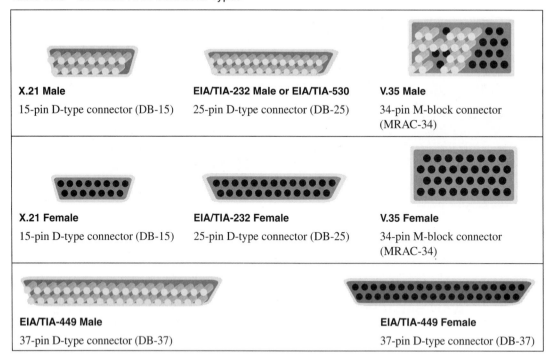

X.21 Male	**EIA/TIA-232 Male or EIA/TIA-530**	**V.35 Male**
15-pin D-type connector (DB-15)	25-pin D-type connector (DB-25)	34-pin M-block connector (MRAC-34)
X.21 Female	**EIA/TIA-232 Female**	**V.35 Female**
15-pin D-type connector (DB-15)	25-pin D-type connector (DB-25)	34-pin M-block connector (MRAC-34)
EIA/TIA-449 Male		**EIA/TIA-449 Female**
37-pin D-type connector (DB-37)		37-pin D-type connector (DB-37)

Figure 13.5   A DB-60 Serial Port

By default, synchronous serial lines use the HDLC serial encapsulation method, which provides the synchronous framing and error detection functions of HDLC without windowing or retransmission. Because non-Cisco routers cannot use HDLC, you can specify other encapsulation methods to support the following WAN links:

■ ATM
■ Frame Relay

- PPP
- SDLC
- SMDS
- X.25-based encapsulations

Synchronous ports can be set up to send SLIP or PPP packets.

RS-232C, short for recommended standard-232C, is the standard interface approved by the EIA for connecting serial devices. In 1987, the EIA released a new version of the standard and changed the name to EIA-232-D. In 1991, the EIA teamed up with Telecommunications Industry Association (TIA) and issued a new version of the standard: EIA/TIA-232-E. Many people, however, still refer to the standard as RS-232C, or just RS-232. Almost all modems conform to the EIA-232 standard, and most personal computers have an EIA-232 port (serial port) for connecting a modem or other device. In addition to modems, many display screens, mice, and serial printers are designed to connect to an EIA-232 port. The EIA-232 standard supports two types of connectors: (1) a 25-pin D-type connectors (DB-25) and (2) a 9-pin D-type connector (DB-9). The type of serial communication used by PCs requires only 9 pins. The length a data cable depends on speed of the data and the quality of the cable (see Table 13.6).

EIA/TIA-449, formerly called RS-449, is a popular physical layer interface developed by EIA and TIA. EIA DB37 is for higher-speed (up to 2 Mbps) serial binary data interchange using synchronous data link lines over 60 meters. Different from the RS-232 wiring, EIA/TIA-449 uses differential signaling, which looks for the difference between two wires. When stray noise is picked up, it will be picked up by both of the twisted pair wires. Because the same noise is on both wires, it is ignored leaving the data signal sent on the one wire.

Basically, V.35 is a high-speed serial interface designed to support both higher data rates and connectivity between DTEs or DCEs over digital lines. V.35 is an interface (V.35 is the ITU standard termed "Data Transmission at 48 Kbps Using 60 108 KHz Group-Band Circuits") commonly used on higher speed circuits of 56 Kbps and above. Recognizable by its blocky, 34-pin connector; V.35 combines the bandwidth of several telephone circuits to provide the high-speed interface between a DTE or DCE and a CSU/DSU. To achieve such high speeds and great distances, V.35 combines both balanced and unbalanced voltage signals on the same interface. Transmission is usually a synchronous protocol (note clocking pins

Table 13.6 Available Data Speeds

Data (bps)	Distance (meters) EIA/TIA-232	Distance (meters) EIA/TIA-449
2400	60	1250
4800	30	625
9600	15	312
19,200	15	156
38,400	15	78
115,200	3.7	N/A
TI (1,544,000 bps)	N/A	15

receive and transmit clock). Although V.35 is commonly used to support speeds ranging anywhere from 48 to 64 Kbps, much higher rates are possible (BRI ISDN, Fractional T-1, T-1, ATM, and Frame Relay). V.35 cable distances theoretically can range up to 4000 feet (1200 m) at speeds up to 100 Kbps. Actual distances will depend on your equipment and the quality of the cable. LAN routers often come equipped with a V.35 electrical interface but today many use a HSSI interface at speeds higher than T-1 (typically T-3 45 Mbps).

X.21 is an ITU standard for serial communications over synchronous digital lines. X.21 is similar to RS-422 except that it uses a DB-15 connector. It is primarily used in Europe and Japan. It can operate at data rates from 600 bps to 64 Kbps.

The EIA-530 standard, formerly RS-530, is just like RS-422, which uses differential signaling on a DB25-RS232 format. This interface is used for high-speed (up to 2 Mbps) synchronous protocols.

13.2.3   Console Ports

The console port is where you hook a PC or terminal up to the router in order to access the operating system. This is the most important port when initially connecting to a Cisco router because you must connect through the console port in order to configure the other interfaces. You can hook up an ASCII terminal to this port, or more commonly, a PC running terminal emulation software (such as HyperTerminal in Windows 98). This port gives you access to the command interpreter, which can be used to configure and monitor the router.

The console port is an asynchronous serial interface. It has a RJ-45 connector, which looks just like a phone jack but is slightly larger. To connect a PC or a laptop to the router, you need a RJ-45 rollover cable. Then, to plug into your PC's serial port, you need a RJ-45 to DB-9 female or RJ-45 to DB-25 female adapter, depending on the size of the serial port (see Figures 13.6, 13.7, and 13.8, see Tables 13.7, 13.8, and 13.9). The console port operates at 9600 baud, 8 data bits, no parity, and 2 stop bits. It does not support hardware flow control.

Figure 13.6   A Rollover Cable

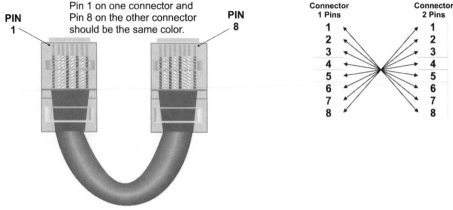

Figure 13.7 A Console Cable Used to Connect to a Serial Port

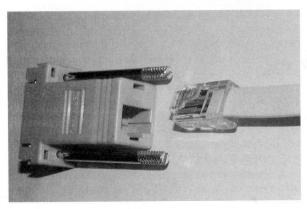

Figure 13.8 A Console Port Found on the Back of a Cisco Router

Table 13.7 Console Port Signaling and Cabling Using a DB-9 Adapter Console Port (DTE)

	RJ-45-to-RJ-45 rollover cable		RJ-45-to-DB-9 terminal adapter	Console device
Signal	RJ-45 Pin	RJ-45 Pin	DB-9 Pin	Signal
RTS	1[1]	8	8	CTS
DTR	2	7	6	DSR
TxD	3	6	2	RxD
GND	4	5	5	GND
GND	5	4	5	GND
RxD	6	3	3	TxD
DSR	7	2	4	DTR
CTS	8[1]	1	7	RTS

[1]Pin 1 is connected (inside the terminal adapter) to pin 8.

Table 13.8 Console Port Signaling and Cabling Using a DB-25 Adapter Console Port (DTE)

	RJ-45-to-RJ-45 rollover cable		RJ-45-to-DB-25 terminal adapter	Console device
Signal	RJ-45 Pin	RJ-45 Pin	DB-25 Pin	Signal
RTS	1[1]	8	5	CTS
DTR	2	7	6	DSR
TxD	3	6	3	RxD
GND	4	5	7	GND
GND	5	4	7	GND
RxD	6	3	2	TxD
DSR	7	2	20	DTR
CTS	8[1]	1	4	RTS

[1]Pin 1 is connected (inside the terminal adapter) to pin 8.

Table 13.9 Console Port Signaling and Cabling Using a DB-25 Adapter Console Port (DTE)

	RJ-45-to-RJ-45 rollover cable		RJ-45-to-DB-25 modem adapter	Modem
Signal	RJ-45 Pin	RJ-45 Pin	DB-25 Pin	Signal
RTS	1[1]	8	4	RTS
DTR	2	7	20	DTR
TxD	3	6	3	TxD
GND	4	5	7	GND
GND	5	4	7	GND
RxD	6	3	2	RxD
DSR	7	2	8	DCD
CTS	8[1]	1	5	CTS

[1]Pin 1 is connected (inside the terminal adapter) to pin 8.

13.2.4   Auxiliary Ports

An auxiliary port is another asynchronous serial port that looks just like the console port. It typically is used to connect a modem to the router. The difference between the console and the auxiliary port is that the auxiliary port supports flow control. Flow control synchronizes communication between two devices, ensuring that the receiving device has received data before the sending device sends more. When the buffers on the receiving device get full, they send a message to the sender, requesting that it suspended transmission until the data in the buffer has been processed. Because modems can use much higher transmission speeds than terminal devices, the auxiliary port is ideal for high-speed modem connections. Maximum speed on this interface is 38,400 bps.

This interface can also be set up as a backup for some other WAN interface. If a dedicated link goes down, the router can dial up its remote counterpart and continue routing over the public telephone network. Because the maximum speed on this interface is 38,400 bps, it is hardly a viable alternative to a T-1 line, but it is better than being down altogether.

To connect the auxiliary port to a modem, you need a RJ-45 crossover cable just like the one used for the console port. Then, you must use a RJ-45 to DB-25 male adapter, compatible with most external modems.

13.3   INSTALLING AND SETTING UP THE ROUTER

When installing a router, you should consider a number of environmental factors. Some of the recommended environmental considerations are obvious. To protect the investment you have made in a Cisco router, you should definitely include these things in your site preparations:

- **Temperature**—maintain an ambient temperature of from 32°F to 104°F (0°C through 40°C). Remember that when you add several computers and/or routers to a room, your room many need additional cooling capacity to keep the room at acceptable operating temperatures.
- **Power**—The router needs voltage between 100 and 240 VAC and 50 through 60 Hertz. Some routers also have options for DC power. Be sure to read the product specifications carefully for the power requirements of your specific router.
- **Wiring**—When setting up the router site, consider distance limitations, EMI, and connector compatibilities.
- **Airflow**—You must maintain two inches or more clearance between the sides of the chassis and the enclosure walls to allow air to properly flow through cooling ports on the router.
- **Dust**—Keep the area as dust-free as possible. In addition, don't place the router directly on the floor or in any other area that may collect dust.
- **Electrostatic discharge (ESD)**—When working on, in, or near the router, follow standard ESD-avoidance procedures to protect the router and its modules from damage.

After your Cisco router is installed and configured, you can use the *show environment* command to monitor the internal system environmental conditions. The router's environmental monitor continuously checks the interior chassis's environment, looking for marginal or alarm-level conditions such as high temperature and maximum and minimum voltages. Any out-of-range conditions are recorded and reported.

If your router ever displays warning messages like this:

```
WARNING: Fan has reached CRITICAL level
```

or this:

```
%ENVM-2-FAN: Fan array has failed, shutdown in 2 minutes
```

be sure that you take immediate action to identify and isolate the problem and then correct it. You will only see these messages if you maintain a console on the router. Otherwise, you should frequently check the router's log file.

Your Cisco router comes with rack-mounting hardware compatible with most 19-inch rack systems and Telco-style racks. When mounting the router, be sure to have free access to both the interface processor and the chassis cover panel. You can also set the router on a rack shelf as long as the router can be secured to the shelf.

13.3.1   Powering Up the Router the First Time

The first time a router is powered up, it automatically enters setup mode, and the router display should look something like this:

```
Router#setup
--- System Configuration Dialog ---
At any point you may enter a question mark '?' for help.
Use Ctrl-c to abort configuration dialog at any prompt.
Default settings are in square brackets '[]'.
Continue with configuration dialog? [yes]:
```

If you want to continue with the setup dialog, its default answer is in square brackets ([ ]). You need only press the Enter key to accept the default value or response. Beyond the first time you power on the router, you can access setup mode in two other ways and both are entered in the Enable Exec (Privileged) mode:

■ Enter the setup command at the # prompt to display the command sequence.
■ Enter the erase startup-config, or erase start command (with the network administrator's permission) and then power the router off and back on or begin again just like when the router was brand new.

Setup shows an initial interface summary that shows the default values assigned to the router interfaces and then prompts you to accept the current values (if any) for the hostname, Enable Secret, Enable, and Virtual Terminal passwords. Alternatively, you can change them. This sequence looks like this:

```
The enable secret is a one-way cryptographic secret used
          instead of the enable password when it exists.

Enter enable secret [<use current secret>]:

The enable password is used when there is no enable secret
          and when using older software and some boot
          images.

Enter enable password [pass11]:
Enter virtual terminal password [pass22]:
```

As the first line indicates, when the Enable Secret password is used, you don't need to set an Enable password for most of the newer Cisco routers. When in doubt, set it to a value that you can remember, just in case. The virtual terminal password is used to gain access to the router through a telnet session from a remote host.

After you finish the passwords, the setup process continues by configuring the router's interfaces. Notice that the setup process first asks you if you want to configure and enable the IP routing, and then this question repeats for each of the individual interfaces (see Figure 13.9).

IP routing is enabled as the default. If you wish to turn off IP routing for all interfaces, then you must enter the command no ip routing. To turn it back on again at some future point, enter the command ip routing. The "yes" is implied.

After you respond to all of setup's enable and configuration requests, the setup command displays a summary of the router's configuration as you just defined it and asks

Figure 13.9 Part of Cisco Router Setup

```
Configure IP? [yes]
    Configure IGRP routing? [no]:
      Your IGRP autonomous system number [1]:

Configuring interface parameters:

Configuring interface Ethernet0:
  Is this interface in use? [yes]:
  Configure IP on this interface? [yes]:
    IP address for this interface [192.168.1.254]:
```

where you want to accept the configuration shown. As a safety against a default value being accidentally entered, no default value appears and you must enter either Yes or No. If you answer yes, the router's configuration as defined is then built and stored in NVRAM, and the router is ready to be put into service.

If you answer no, the configuration you have just defined is discarded, the default configuration continues as the active configuration, and you will be returned to the router's default prompt. If you wish to rerun the configuration program, enter the setup command.

13.3.2 Router POST

After the router receives its initial configuration, the next time you power it on, the router goes through a four-step startup process:

Step 1: The router performs a POST. The POST tests the hardware to verify that all components of the device are operational and present. For example, the POST checks for the different interfaces on the router. The POST is stored in and run from ROM.

Step 2: The bootstrap looks for and loads the Cisco IOS software. The bootstrap is a program in ROM that is used to execute programs. It is responsible for finding where each IOS program is located and then loading the file. By default, the IOS software is loaded from flash memory in all Cisco routers.

Step 3: The IOS software looks for a valid configuration file stored in NVRAM. This file is called startup-config and is only there if an administrator copies the running-config file into NVRAM.

Step 4: If a startup-config file is in NVRAM, the router will load and run this file. The router is now operational. If a startup-config file is not in NVRAM, the router will start the setup mode configuration upon bootup.

The POST on a Cisco router is similar to the POST that runs at startup on a personal computer. The router's POST checks its CPU, memory, and all interface ports to make sure that they're present and operational. If all is well, the bootstrap (also called the boot) program is read from ROM and begins the process of locating and loading the IOS operating system.

The primary purpose of the bootstrap program is to find a valid Cisco IOS configuration image from a location specified by the router's configuration register. The configuration register contains the location from which the IOS software is to be loaded. The value representing the location of the IOS software can be changed using the config-register command from the Global Configuration mode.

Typically, the Cisco IOS is loaded from flash memory, the default value found in the configuration register. The router looks for the IOS software in the flash memory, ROM, or TFTP server. The router knows where to look based on the value in the configuration register. The configuration register holds a hexadecimal value that designates the location of the IOS software. The value in the configuration register actually supplies a bit pattern in the same pattern that can be configured with a hardware jumper block.

- **0x02 through 0x0Fh**—The router will look for boot system commands in startup configuration to tell it where to find IOS. If no boot system commands are in the startup configuration, the router searches in the default places: flash, then ROM, then a TFTP server
- **0x01h**—The router boots from ROM
- **0x00h**—The router will enter ROMMON mode

The configuration running in the router's RAM is the running configuration, and the configuration saved in the router's NVRAM is the startup configuration. Restarting the router loads the startup configuration into RAM, where it becomes the running configuration. Copying the running configuration to flash (NVRAM) overwrites the startup configuration previously stored there.

A Cisco router can boot from three locations: (1) flash memory, (2) a TFTP server, or (3) ROM. If flash memory does not contain an operating system and the TFTP server is unavailable, then ROM is the last resort. To cause the router to boot from ROM, you can type the `boot system ROM` command into the startup configuration file. Alternatively, you can set the boot field in the configuration register to 0x1. This setting causes the router to ignore any boot system commands and load the IOS from ROM. The `boot system flash` command loads the IOS from flash memory.

The `boot system ROM` command directs the Cisco router to boot IOS from ROM. The system can then be configured manually, or the configuration can be loaded when a TFTP server that stores a copy of the IOS becomes operational. Older Cisco routers stored only a subset of the IOS to allow disaster recovery. Newer Cisco routers store the complete IOS in ROM. After the system boots from ROM, it looks for a configuration file to load. If one is not present, then the router enters manual setup mode. Flash memory contains one or more versions of the IOS, but IOS is not loaded from flash memory during the boot sequence unless a `boot system flash` command is issued. The `boot system ROM` command cannot copy any configuration files.

The `boot system TFTP` command will boot the router from a TFTP server if the name of the file and the IP address of the server are listed on the command line. The `copy TFTP running config` command will copy a file from a TFTP server into the running configuration of a router.

13.3.3   Working with Configuration Files

FTP is a reliable, connection-oriented tool used to copy files from one computer to another over a TCP/IP network. Another flavor of FTP is the Trivial File Transfer Protocol (TFTP). Different from FTP, which uses TCP as the transport protocol, TFTP uses UDP—which makes it an unreliable file transfer protocol. In this case, unreliable means that delivery is not guaranteed because UDP does not use acknowledgements to verify delivery. TFTP works fine to transport small files over LANs because LANs tend to be stable and the TFTP has less overhead than FTP.

NOTE: If you need a TFTP host and you do not have any server software that provides a TFTP host, you can download a shareware version of TFTP from Cisco:

Using TFTP on a PC to Download WAN Switch Software and Firmware

http://www.cisco.com/warp/public/74/156.html

Cisco TFTP Server for Windows 95

http://www.cisco.com/pcgi-bin/tablebuild.pl/tftp

Two types of configuration files are stored on a router: (1) startup and (2) running. Both files can be copied to and from each other, as well as to and from the TFTP server.

If you make changes to the configuration of a running router, those changes are made to the running configuration file. If you wish to save these changes and make them permanent, the running configuration must be saved to the startup configuration file. Otherwise, the next time the router is booted, and the startup configuration is loaded, all of your changes would be lost. Remember that at boot time, the startup configuration is loaded to RAM to become the running configuration.

You would copy the startup configuration to the running configuration to reset any changes you have made and did not save by copying the running configuration to the startup configuration. These changes could be configuration tests or mistakes. Rebooting the router causes the stored version of the system's configuration to be loaded to RAM as the running configuration.

Configuration files can be copied and stored on computers using the TFTP protocol. In fact, as mentioned earlier in this chapter, the copy of the configuration file on the TFTP server can be used as the configuration source during the boot sequence.

The primary reason you would back up the configuration to an outside server is to ensure that the router has a source for its configuration, even in the event that the configuration file on the router gets corrupted or accidentally erased. If the router's configuration is corrupted or removed, the router's boot system can be directed via the configuration register to look for a TFTP server. The TFTP host must have the IP running, you must be able to ping the router from the TFTP host, and the TFTP host must have room for the downloaded configuration file.

As with IOS system image backups and updates, TFTP servers are used to back up and update configuration files. For example, if you run the *copy running-config tftp* command, you can back up the router's running configuration file to a TFTP server (see Figure 13.10).

Figure 13.10 Running the Copy Running-config tftp Command

```
RouterHostName#copy running-config tftp
Remote host []? 192.168.30.3
Name of the configuration file to write [router-confg]? router1
Write file server1 on host 192.168.30.3? [confirm]↵
Building configuration...

Writing router1 !! [OK]
RouterHostName#
```

Other commands that work with the startup-config and running-config commands are:

- `copy tftp running-config`—Configures the router by copying from the TFTP directly into the router's DRAM
- `copy startup-config tftp`—Backs up the startup configuration from the router's NVRAM to the TFTP server
- `copy tftp startup-config`—Updates the router's startup configuration file by downloading from the TFTP server and overwriting the one stored in the router's NVRAM
- `copy running-config startup-config`—Copies the running-config file to the startup-config file
- `copy startup-config running-config`—Copies the startup-config to the running-config file

In addition to the configuration files, you should have a backup copy of the router's flash memory on the TFTP server. The size of the flash can be determined ahead of time by using the `show flash` command. The command to copy the flash to the TFTP would be `copy flash tftp`.

If you need to restore IOS to flash memory to replace an original file that has been damaged or to upgrade the IOS, you can download the file from a TFTP host to flash memory by using the *copy tftp flash* command. After you enter the *copy tftp flash* command, you will see a message as shown in Figure 13.11 informing you that the router must reboot and run a ROM-based IOS image to perform this operation.

To view your running-config and startup-config files, you would use the `show running-config` (or `sh run` for short) and `show startup-config` (`sh start` for short) commands. To delete the startup-config file, you would use the `erase startup-config` command. If you delete the startup-config file and try to view it with the show startup-config command, you will get an error.

13.3.4   Managing Configuration Registers

All Cisco routers have a 16-bit software register written into NVRAM. By default, the configuration register is set to load the Cisco IOS from flash memory and to look for and load the startup-config file from NVRAM.

The sixteen bits of the configuration register are read 15–0, from left to right. The default configuration setting on Cisco routers is 0x2102h. If you convert this from hexadecimal to binary (0010 0001 0000 0010), you see that bits 13, 8, and 1 are ON (see Tables 13.10 and 13.11).

You can see the current value of the configuration register by using the `show version` (or `sh ver` for short), as in Figure 13.12.

You can change the configuration register value to modify how the router boots and runs as follows:

Step 1: Force the system into the ROM monitor mode

Step 2: Select a boot source and default boot filename

Step 3: Enable or disable the Break function

Figure 13.11   Using the *copy tftp flash* Command

```
RouterHostName>enable⏎
RouterHostName#copy tftp flash⏎
                        ****  NOTICE  ****
Flash load helper v1.0
This process will accept the copy options and then terminate
the current system image to use the ROM based image for the copy.
Routing functionality will not be available during that time.
If you are logged in via telnet, this connection will terminate.
Users with console access can see the results of the copy operation.
                    ____ ******** ____
Proceed? [confirm]
System flash directory:
File  Length    Name/status
  1   6078548   c2500-js56i-1.120-9.bin

[6078612 bytes used, 2309996 available, 8388608 total]
Address or name of remote host [255.255.255.255]?192.68.1.66⏎
Source file name? c2500-js56i-1.120-9.bin⏎
Destination file name [c2500-js56i-1.120-9.bin]?⏎
Accessing file 'c2500-js56i-1.120-9.bin' on 172.16.30.2...
Loading 'c2500-js56i-1.120-9.bin' from 172.16.30.2 (via Ethernet0): !
[OK]⏎

Erase flash device before writing? [confirm]⏎
Flash contains files. Are you sure you want to erase? [confirm]⏎

Copy 'c2500-js56i-1.120-9.bin' from server
as 'c2500-js56i-1.120-9.bin' into Flash WITH erase? [yes/no]yes⏎
```

Step 4:   Control broadcast addresses
Step 5:   Set the console terminal baud rate
Step 6:   Load operating software from ROM
Step 7:   Enable booting from a TFTP server

You can change the configuration register by using the config-register command from the Global Configuration mode. For example, the following commands tell the router to enter the ROMMON mode and then show the current configuration register value:

```
RouterHostName(config)#config-register 0x0101
```

Table 13.10 Configuration Register

Bit	Description
0–3	Boot field (see table 13.X)
6	Ignore NVRAM contents
7	OEM bit enabled
8	Break disabled
10	IP broadcast with all zeros
11–12	Console line speed
13	Boot default ROM software if network boot fails
14	IP broadcasts do not have net numbers
15	Enable diagnostic messages and ignore NVM contents

Table 13.11 Meaning of Configuration Register

00H	ROM monitor mode	To boot to ROM monitor mode, set the configuration register to 2100. You must manually boot the router with the *b* command. The router will show the *rommon>* prompt.
01H	Boot image from ROM	To boot an IOS image stored in ROM, set the configuration register to 2101. The router will show the *router (boot)>* prompt.
02-FH	Specifies a default boot filename	Any value from 2102 through 210F tells the router to use the boot commands specified in NVRAM.

Figure 13.12 Running the Show Version Command

```
RouterHostName#show ver
ROM: System Bootstrap, Version 12.0, RELEASE SOFTWARE
BOOTFLASH: 3000 Bootstrap Software (IGS-RXBOOT), Version 10.2(8a),
RELEASE SOFTWARE (fc1)

RouterA uptime is 11 minutes
System restarted by power-on
System image file is flash:c2500-d-l_113-5.bin, booted via flash

Bridging software.
X.25 software, Version 3.0.0.
1 Ethernet/IEEE 802.3 interface(s)
2 Serial network interface(s)
32K bytes of non-volatile configuration memory.
8192K bytes of processor board System flash (Read ONLY)

Configuration register is 0x2102
```

> *NOTE:* Any change to the configuration register will not take effect until the router is reloaded. The 0x0101 will load the IOS from ROM the next time the router is rebooted.

13.4   ROUTER COMMAND MODES

The working name of the CLI is the Exec command interpreter. The Exec command interpreter has two Exec modes (command groups) that can be used to perform a variety of functions.

13.4.1   User Exec Mode

After you successfully log into the router, meaning that you entered the appropriate password, you automatically enter User Exec mode. In this mode, you can connect to other devices (such as another router) to perform simple tests and display system information. You will know that you are in User Exec mode if the prompt display on your screen looks like this:

```
RouterHostName>
```

In this example, the RouterHostName represents the assigned name of the router. It's the greater than sign (>) that's significant here. When this symbol appears in the prompt, it means you are in User Exec mode.

13.4.2   Enable Exec Mode

The Enable Exec mode, also known as Privileged or Privileged Exec, is accessed from User Exec mode through the `enable` command and a password. If an Enable Exec mode password has not been set, this mode can be accessed only from the router console port. You can perform all User Exec mode functions from within the Enable Exec mode. In addition, you have access to higher-level testing and debugging, detailed probing of the router functions, and the ability to update or change configuration files. The prompt that indicates this mode is:

```
RouterHostname#
```

The pound or number sign (#) at the end of the prompt indicates Enable Exec mode.

13.4.3   ROMMON Mode

ROMMON mode is displayed during the boot process if no operating system is loaded in flash memory. From this mode, the router's configuration can be completed. After configuring the router so that it may complete the startup process, the continued command moves you into User Exec mode. The prompt that indicates this mode is either just a greater than sign or the prompt.

```
rommon>
```

13.4.4   Setup Mode

When a router is first configured from the console port, Setup mode is invoked. Setup mode can also be invoked from the Enable Exec mode prompt with the *setup* command or by rebooting the router after deleting its startup-config file through the *erase startup-config* command.

The setup command is a prompted dialog that guides you through the setup process to configure the router. This action has no special prompt. You should know that after you erase the startup-config file, which is stored in the flash memory, the router will be in Setup mode when it is restarted.

13.4.5   Configuration Mode

To change the running-config (the current configuration running in Dynamic RAM), you would use the `configure terminal` command (or just `config t` for short). To change startup-config (the configuration stored in NVRAM), you can use the `configure memory` command, or `configure mem` for short. If you want to change a router configuration stored on a TFTP host, you use the `configure network` command (or use `config net`).

However, you need to understand that for a router to actually make a change to a configuration, it needs to put that configuration in RAM. So, if you actually type *config mem* or *config net,* you will replace the current running-config with the configuration stored in NVRAM or a configuration stored on a TFTP host.

Of these, the most common that you will use is the configure terminal command executed at the Enable Exec prompt (the one with the # symbol), which changes you into what is called the Global Configuration mode:

`RouterHostName#`**config terminal**

After executing the `config terminal` or `config t` command, the configuration mode will be designated by the following prompt:

`RouterHostName#(config)#`

The Global Configuration mode allows you to manually configure the router or make changes to the router's status (see Table 13.12).

You may also move to another mode within the Global Configuration mode. The Configuration Interface mode is used to make changes to individual interfaces. The Configuration Interface Mode looks like this:

`RouterHostName#(config-if)#`

The config command can be used to configure network settings and memory with the `config net` and `config mem` commands, respectively.

Ctrl+Z can be used in any of the IOS configuration modes, including Global Configuration mode, Interface Configuration mode, Subinterface Configuration mode, and Line Configuration mode. You can use the *exit* command from Global Configuration mode to return to Privileged Exec mode. Using the *exit* command from submodes of

Table 13.12   Changing Modes on Cisco Routers

CLI prompt	Resultant prompt	Purpose
Name>**enable**	Name#	Moves to Privileged Exec mode
Name#**configure terminal** (or terminal t)	Name(config)#	Moves to Global Configuration mode
Name(config)#**interface ethernet0**	Name(config-if)#	Opens the configuration of the ethernet0 interface port
Name(config-if)#**exit**	Name(config)#	Exits to Global Configuration mode
Name#**copy running-config startup-config**	Name#	Saves the modified configuration to NVRAM for IOS version 11.0 and after
Name#**write memory**	Name#	Used on IOS versions prior to 11.0
Name#**disable**	Name>	Returns to User Exec mode
Name>**prompt**	Name>	Shows CLI is in User Exec mode

Global Configuration mode, for example, interface configuration mode, will back up one level toward Global Configuration mode. The end command saves changes and returns the user to Privileged Exec mode from any configuration mode or submode. To return to User Exec mode while in Privileged Exec mode, you would use the disable command.

13.4.6   Passwords

As explained earlier, Cisco routers and switches are administered through the command interpreter of the Cisco IOS. In order to perform administrative functions on the router, you must log into the Exec mode. The Exec mode has two levels: the User Exec mode and the Privileged Exec mode. The Exec mode provides access to commands to set and modify the general configuration of the router. The Privileged EXEC mode provides access to commands that are used to configure the operating parameters of the router. Because of its sensitive nature, a second and protected password is used to prevent unauthorized access to this level of authority.

Since Cisco IOS released 10.2(3), the *enable secret* command has been available to set a password for access to Priveleged Exec mode. The *enable password* command is still available for protecting access to User Exec mode. The *enable secret* command creates a secure password that is stored in an encrypted form. The enable password is much less secure and is stored in clear text form. If an enable secret password is configured an enable password is not required, but if one is configured it must be used. These passwords should be different. The IOS will accept them as the same, but it will warn you about using the same password for both.

Passwords play an important role in the security of your router, protecting its configuration and access lists. In the same way that passwords are used to protect data networking elements by verifying that someone logging on has authorization to do so, passwords protect your network's routers. A Cisco router can have up to five different passwords, each on a different level.

Cisco router passwords are case sensitive, which means that it does matter whether an alphabetic character is upper case or lower case in a password. The first step in the procedure used to change a password on a Cisco router is to be in Global Configuration mode. To get to Global Configuration mode, use the `config t` command.

Cisco router passwords are divided into two groups with different policies applied to the groups. The first group, Enable Secret and Enable passwords, are much more secure than the other group. User passwords include Virtual Terminal, Console, and Auxiliary Passwords.

The Enable Secret password adds a level of security over and above the Enable password. When set, this password (which is one-way encrypted) has precedence over the Enable password. One-way encryption is a hashing algorithm that converts the password into a 128-bit or 160-bit value, depending on the device. This encryption scheme is based on a security process called the Secure Hash Algorithm. Cisco claims that it is impossible to decode an Enable Secret password using the contents of a router's configuration file.

The following statement shows the commands used to set the Enable Secret password:

```
RouterHostName(config)#enable secret pass1111
```

Your best bet is to set the Enable Secret password and not use the Enable password. The only difference between these two passwords is the level of encryption. The Enable password uses a very lightweight encryption compared to the IPSec level encryption used for the Enable Secret password. The following statements are used to set the Enable password:

```
RouterHostName(config)#enable password pass1111
The enable password that you have chosen is the same as
your enable secret.
This is not recommended. Re-enter the enable password.
RouterHostName(config)#enable password pass2222
```

Cisco recommends that the Enable password command no longer be used, and recommends use of the Enable Secret command instead. They feel this provides for better router security. However, the one time that the Enable password command might be used is when the router is running in boot mode, which doesn't support the Enable Secret command.

The Virtual Terminal (vty) password is used to gain access to the router using a Telnet session. Unless the password is set, you cannot Telnet into the router from another computer through the network.

The following statements show the commands used to set the Virtual Terminal password:

```
RouterHostName(config)#line vty 0 4
RouterHostName(config-line)#login
RouterHostName(config-line)#password pass3333
```

The line command enters Line Configuration mode, which is used to configure physical access points, such as Telnet, and the console and aux ports. The vty 0 4 part of the command line specifies that the password entered will apply to vty 0 through 4. It is possible to set a different password for each vty line.

In order to set a password on the vty lines, you must first indicate the lines to be affected. In this case, the command line vty 0 4 is the first line of the commands and indicates that the actions that follow it should affect the login password for all five vty lines.

The Console password is used to gain access to the router through the console port. To set the Console password, use the following commands (changing the password):

```
RouterHostName(config)#line console 0
RouterHostName(config-line)#login
RouterHostName(config-line)#password pass4444
```

The Auxiliary password controls access to any auxiliary ports on the router. To set the password for this interface, use the following commands:

```
RouterHostName(config)#line aux 0
RouterHostName(config-line)#login
RouterHostName(config-line)#password pass5555
```

13.4.7   Recovering Passwords

If you are locked out of a router because you forgot the password, you can change the configuration register to help you recover. As noted earlier, bit 6 in the configuration register is used to tell the router whether or not to use the contents of NVRAM to load a router configuration.

The default configuration register value for bit 6 is 0x2102, which means that bit 6 is off. The router will then look for and load a router configuration stored in NVRAM (startup-config). To recover a password, you need to turn on bit 6, which will tell the router to ignore the NVRAM contents. The configuration register value to turn on bit 6 is 0x2142.

To recover a lost password, you would follow these steps:

Step 1: Boot the router and interrupt the boot sequence by performing a break.
Step 2: Change the configuration register to turn on bit 6 (with the value of 0x2142).
Step 3: Reload the router.
Step 4: Enter Privileged Exec mode.
Step 5: Copy the startup-config file to the running-config file.
Step 6: Change the password.
Step 7: Reset the configuration register to the default value.
Step 8: Reload the router.

The first step is to boot the router and perform a break. Typically, you perform a break by pressing the Ctrl+Break key combination when using a hyperterminal. Then, change the configuration register by using the *config-register* command. To turn on bit 6, use the configuration register value 0x2142. For Cisco 2600 Series routers, simply enter confreg 0x2142 at the prompt. For Cisco 2500 Series routers, type *o* to bring up a menu of configuration register option settings. To change the configuration register, enter the *o/r* command followed by the register value (for example: o/r 0x2142).

Next you need to reboot the router. If you are using the 2600 series router, you would use the reset command or if you have the 2500 series router, you would use the I command. Because the startup-config file is not being used, the router will ask if you want to use Setup mode. Answer *No* to entering Setup mode, press *Enter* to go into User Exec mode and then type the enable command to go into Privileged Exec mode.

Next, copy the startup-config file to the running-config file by using one of the following commands:

```
copy startup-config running-config
copy start run
```

The configuration is not running in RAM, and you are in Privileged Exec mode, which means that you can view and change the configuration. Although you cannot view the enable secret setting for the password, you can change the password as follows:

```
config t
enable secret pass1111
```

After you have finished changing passwords, set the configuration register back to the default value with the config-register command:

```
config-register 0x2102
```

Finally, save the new configuration with a `copy running-config startup-config` command and reload the router.

As you can see, it is relatively easy to recover passwords. You just have to know the steps to do it. This is the reason that your routers should be secured in a locked room to prevent anyone from tampering with them.

13.5   CISCO ROUTER BASICS

Before showing you how to configure your routers with the specific routing protocols and WAN technologies, you should learn some of the basics of Cisco routers. This includes using the help features of the Cisco routers, establishing host names, and establishing banners.

13.5.1   Using Help

Getting help on a Cisco router is fairly easy. Two levels of connect-sensitive help are available to assist you with IOS commands. In fact, Cisco IOS tries to guess what you are trying to do and provides you with help in both the User Exec and Enable Exec modes.

The two levels of context-sensitive help available on the command line from the IOS are:

- **Word help**—the IOS tries to recognize the command you are entering from as few keystrokes as possible, sometimes even from a single keystroke.
- **Command syntax help**—If you are unsure of a command's syntax or required or optional parameters, the IOS will provide you with the command structure and parameter list.

For example, if you know Cisco has a specific command to perform a task, but cannot remember its command word, you can just type its first letter or as many letters as you feel are needed and a question mark without a space in between. The router then displays a list of the available commands that begin with that letter. If multiple commands meet your criteria, they are all displayed. For example, entering *cl?* on the command line interface produces the following results:

```
RouterHostName#cl?
clear clock
```

The display indicates that two commands begin with *cl: clear* and *clock.*

The location of the question mark in the command line entry is very important. If you include no space before the question mark, as in *cl?,* the command line interface lists all the commands that being with *cl.* If you include a space before the question mark, as in *cl ?,* the command line interpreter attempts to display the next element of syntax for the command.

However, entering the letter *c* followed by a space and then a question mark (*c ?*) will not get you a list of all the commands that begin with *c.* Instead, you will get the response "Ambiguous Command Request." Remember that the space in the command line indicates that you wish the CLI to complete the command line for you, if it can. Because it cannot, it tells you that it doesn't know what command you want.

To see all the commands available for a command mode, simply enter a question mark at the command prompt. If the list being displayed requires more than one screen, only the first screen of information is displayed followed by the – – more – – prompt.

Another feature built into the user interface of the Cisco router is that if you type partial command and then press the Tab key, the command will be completed for you. For example, if you type in *disc* and then press the Tab key, the word "disconnect" is completed for you.

Another level of context-sensitive help available from the Cisco IOS is command syntax help that displays the remaining command elements for a partially entered command string. If you enter the command, or at least enough of the command so that it can be recognized, followed by a space and a question mark, the command line interpreter displays the next parameter of the command (see Figure 13.13).

Figure 13.13   Using the *?* with Commands

```
RouterHostName#show ?
access-expression  List access expression
access-lists       List access lists
accounting         Accounting data for active sessions
aliases            Display alias command
arp                Arp Table
async              Information on terminal lines used as router interfaces
.
.
.
```

13.5.2   Command History and Shortcuts

The user interface of the Cisco IOS include some features that allow you to review and reuse commands you have entered in the past, to move the cursor around the command line or its history, or both. They include:

- **Working with the command history**—The Cisco IOS allows you to scroll back through all previously entered commands to review what you have already entered.
- **Command line shortcuts**—The Cisco IOS includes a variety of keyboard commands, called enhanced editing, that allow you to control the cursor position and move it directly to certain points on the command line or its history.
- **Combining the editing features**—When used together (the ability to access the command history and the enhanced editing features), you can move back into the command history to edit and reuse long or complicated commands instead of reentering them.

The command history is a chronological listing of commands that have been entered or displayed on the router in the current session. Depending on the Cisco device, you may have by default 10 to 20 of the previous commands available for review or reuse. On most Cisco devices, you have the ability to set the size of the command history buffer through the terminal history command.

The command history is a very handy feature because during a logged in session you can recall previously entered commands, especially those long or complex commands. Any of the entries in the command history buffer can be edited, copied, or removed. This gives you flexibility and saves you time because you don't have to reenter a long command string that really only needs some minor editing or a new IP address to be used again. The ability to edit the IOS command history allows you to copy these long sequences for reuse, or to check back on an earlier action that may need correcting. Remember that the history is only the short-term past and it is only from the history from the current session. In addition, it is limited by the buffer size set for your device. After you save the running configuration and log off, the command history is gone.

The Cisco IOS uses a special set of keyboard commands that are included in the enhanced editing commands to recall the command history. Some devices, such as Catalyst switches and high-end routers, have their own set of commands called history substitution commands that can be used to access, retrieve, and replace entries in the command history. Table 13.13 lists a few of the history substitution commands available to some Cisco internetworking devices.

The show history command can be entered in any Exec mode to display the contents of a router's command history buffer. The history list will begin with the oldest command in the buffer and finish with the most recently executed command. The terminal history size command is used to adjust the number of recently used commands that can be stored in a router's command history buffer. The value for terminal history size can be any integer value between 0 and 256.

Enhanced editing mode is designed to make your life with routers easier. It provides you with such time savers as the ability to enter one or more commands quickly by repeating one or more entries. Enhanced editing is actually a series of keystroke combinations that move the command line cursor about, recall recent commands, or automatically complete entries for you.

Table 13.13   History Substitution Commands

Keyboard entries	Action
!!	Repeats the most recent command
!-nn	Repeat the nth most recent command (where n is the number of commands prior to the current command)
!n	Repeats command number n
!aaa	Repeats the command beginning with the string aaa (where aaa is a text string)
!?aaa	Repeats the command containing the string aaa anywhere in the command
^aaa^bbb	Replaces the string aaa with the string bbb in the most recent (immediately preceding) command
!!aaa	Adds string aaa to the end of the most recent command
!n aaa	Adds string aaa to the end of command n
!aaa bbb	Adds string bbb to the end of the command beginning with string aaa
!?aaa bbb	Adds string bbb to the end of the command containing the string aaa

Table 13.14   Editing Keyboard Commands

Key(s)	Action
Ctrl+A	Moves to the beginning of the current line
Ctrl+E	Moves to the end of the current line
Ctrl+B (or left arrow key)	Moves back one character without deleting the character. Use backspace to back one character and delete the character.
Ctrl+F (or right arrow key)	Moves forward one character
Ctrl+N (or down arrow key)	Recalls most recent command
Ctrl+K	Deletes all characters from the cursor to the end of the command line
Ctrl+U	Deletes all characters from the cursor to the beginning of the command line
Ctrl+W	Deletes the work to the left of the cursor
Ctrl+P (or up arrow key)	Recalls the previous command
Esc+B	Moves back to beginning of previous word (or beginning of current word)
Esc+F	Moves forward one word
Tab	Completes the current word

To use enhanced editing commands, you press the key combinations together to cause the associated action. For example to move to the end of the current command line, press Ctrl+E (uppercase or lowercase). The cursor moves to the end of the current command line.

To show how truly enhanced it is, enhanced editing is automatically enabled in either User Exec mode or Enable Exec mode. To disable it, enter the command `terminal no editing`. To turn it back on, enter `terminal editing`. Some of the other important editing keyboard commands that you will find handy are listed in Table 13.14.

13.5.3   Establishing Hostnames

By default, the router hostname is "Router," as displayed by the command line prompt. You can keep the name Router, but if you have more than one router on your network or you plan to interact with other nearby routers on the WAN, it would be good idea to give your router a meaningful hostname.

When assigning these hostnames, you must be in the Enable Exec (Privileged) mode. Then you use the hostname command:

```
Router#config t
Router(config)#hostname RouterHostName
```

Hostnames cannot be duplicated within a LAN. In addition, you should always assign a hostname that is somewhat meaningful. The hostnames must identify each specific router on the network uniquely. If your network has only one router, then the name is less important.

To enable your router to lookup host names by using a DNS name server, you need to perform the following commands:

- The `ip domain-lookup` command is used to enable hostname lookup. Because it is turned on by default, you will only need to enter this command if you previously turned it off with the *no ip domain-lookup* command.
- The `ip name-server ip_address` command sets the IP address of the DNS server. You can enter the IP addresses of up to six servers.
- The `ip domain-name domain_name` is an optional command that appends the domain name to the host name that you type in. Because DNS uses a Fully Qualified Domain Name (FQDN) system, you must have a full DNS name such as domain.com.

13.5.4   Using Banners

Each router can be configured with a banner message to be displayed whenever someone logs onto the router. The banner message is a text display that is sent to the display device of anyone logging onto the router. It can be virtually anything the administrator wishes to have displayed. The message part of the banner is called the message of the day (MOTD). The MOTD banner is displayed at login and is a good way to get the word out about scheduled network downtime or any other message that the administrator wants to share with fellow administrators.

To create a MOTD banner, put yourself in Global Configuration mode. Then use the *banner motd* command. Entering the delimiting character at this point declares to the IOS which character you will be using to delimit your message. The choice of the delimiting character that you will use to indicate the end of your message is totally up to you. The delimiting character is entered as part of the *banner motd* # command string, where # represents the character that you have chosen. Then enter the message followed by the delimiting character. Your message cannot contain the delimiting character.

For example:

```
RouterHostName#config t
RouterHostName(config)#banner motd $
Enter TEXT message. End with the character '$'.
IOS upgrade scheduled this weekend.
$
RouterHostName(config)#
```

The result of this would be that the next time anyone logs onto the router, the following would be displayed:

```
IOS upgrade scheduled this weekend.

User Access Verification

Password
```

13.6   CONFIGURING INTERFACES

To begin the process of building the router's configuration, you must first be in Global Configuration mode. With that out of the way, you can begin entering each of the specific interfaces that you want to configure. Remember that "interface" means the ports and connection points on the router.

13.6.1   Showing the Interfaces

With routers that have a fixed configuration (which means that when you buy that model of router, you cannot change its configuration), you always use the *interface mediatype port#*. With other routers that do not have fixed configuration, you have to specify the slot. Therefore, they follow the *interface mediatype slot#/port#* format. The common media types are Ethernet, fastethernet, tokenring, and serial. These slots are numbered on the router and the port number is left-to-right starting at 0 (not 1).

To show your interfaces, change to Enable Exec mode and execute the show interfaces command. Besides showing what interfaces you have, it also shows you if the port is active and if the protocol on the port is active (see Figure 13.14).

You can also use the show interface command to specify the information for an individual interface. For example, a Cisco 7206 is a 7200 series router with six slots. To refer to an interface that is the third port of an Ethernet module installed in the sixth slot, it would be interface ethernet 6/2. Therefore, to display the configuration of that interface you use the command:

```
RouterHostName#show interface ethernet 6/2
```

If your router does not have slots (such as a 1600) then the interface name consists only of:

```
RouterHostName#show interface serial 0
```

You could also have used sh int s0.

Cisco 7000 and 7500 series routers can use VIP cards. Each of the port adapters can have multiple ports. The correct syntax to configure a port on a Cisco 7000 or 7500 series router that contains a Versatile Interface Processor (VIP) card is *interface-type slot/port-adapter/port*.

Figure 13.14 Using the Show Interface Command

```
Router>enable
Router#show interface
FastEthernet0/0  is down, line protocol is down
Hardware is AmdFE, address is 00b0.6483.01c0 (bia 00b0.6483.01c0)
  MTU 1500 bytes, BW 100000 Kbit, DLY 100 usec,
      reliability 255/255, txload 1/255, rxload 1/255
  Encapsulation ARPA, loopback not set
  Keepalive set (10 sec)
 Half-duplex, 10Mb/s, 100BaseTX/FX
 ARP type: ARPA, ARP Timeout 04:00:00
 Last input 00:00:10, output 00:00:00, output hang never
 Last clearing of "show interface" counters never
 Queueing strategy: fifo
 Output queue 0/40, 0 drops; input queue 0/75, 0 drops
 5 minute input rate 0 bits/sec, 0 packets/sec
 5 minute output rate 1000 bits/sec, 0 packets/sec
    2705 packets input, 463756 bytes
    Received 2704 broadcasts, 0 runts, 0 giants, 0 throttles
    0 input errors, 0 CRC, 0 frame, 0 overrun, 0 ignored
    0 watchdog, 0 multicast
    0 input packets with dribble condition detected
    7582 packets output, 1007598 bytes, 0 underruns
    0 output errors, 0 collisions, 3 interface resets
    0 babbles, 0 late collision, 0 deferred
    0 lost carrier, 0 no carrier
    0 output buffer failures, 0 output buffers swapped out

FastEthernet0/1 is down, line protocol is down
Hardware is AmdFE, address is 00b0.6483.01c0 (bia 00b0.6483.01c0)
 Keepalive set (10 sec)
  Full-duplex, 100Mb/s, 100BaseTX/FX
  ARP type: ARPA, ARP Timeout 04:00:00
  Last input 00:00:01, output 00:00:02, output hang never
  Last clearing of "show interface" counters never
  Queueing strategy: fifo
  Output queue 0/40, 0 drops; input queue 0/75, 0 drops
  5 minute input rate 0 bits/sec, 0 packets/sec
  5 minute output rate 0 bits/sec, 0 packets/sec
     52845 packets input, 3778179 bytes
     Received 52845 broadcasts, 0 runts, 0 giants, 0 throttles
```

Continued

Figure 13.14 Continued

```
0 input errors, 0 CRC, 0 frame, 0 overrun, 0 ignored
0 watchdog, 0 multicast
0 input packets with dribble condition detected
9785 packets output, 1368297 bytes, 0 underruns
0 output errors, 0 collisions, 6 interface resets
0 babbles, 0 late collision, 0 deferred
0 lost carrier, 0 no carrier
0 output buffer failures, 0 output buffers swapped out
```

13.6.2   Changing into Interface Configuration Mode

To configure an interface, you must first change into Global Configuration mode. Then you have to change into Interface Configuration mode by typing interface or int followed by the port designation. Ethernet ports can be designated by *Ethernet* or *e*. For example, to modify the interface for Ethernet 0, you would type the following:

```
RouterHostName#config t
Enter configuration command. One per line. End with
CNTL/Z.
RouterHostHame(config)#int ethernet 0
RouterHostName(config-if)#
```

You will know that you are in Interface mode as the prompt changes to *RouterHostName (config-if)*. To exit Interface Configuration mode and return to the Global Configuration mode, use the exit command. To exit the interface configuration mode and return to Enable Exec mode, you would use Ctrl+Z.

Instead of using Ethernet 0, you could also have used e0. For Fast Ethernet connections, you would use int fastethernet 0 or int fa0. For a Token Ring interface, you would use int token 0. For serial interfaces, you would use int serial 0 or int s0. If these routers have slots, you would have to use *slot#/port#* instead of just *port#*.

While you are in Interface Configuration mode, you also establish a description. Setting descriptions on an interface is helpful to the administrator and, like the hostname, is only locally significant. That means that the description for a router can not be seen from other routers. This can be helpful because it can be used to keep track of what is connected to a particular interface or it can be used to track circuit numbers (see Figure 13.15). Then when you use the *show running-config* command or the *show interface* command, the router administrator can see the description.

13.6.3   Enabling and Configuring TCP/IP Protocols

After changing into the Interface Configuration mode, you can then use the IP address command to assign an IP address to the port. Don't forget to include both the IP address and its subnet mask.

Figure 13.15   Using Descriptions to Describe Your WAN Links on the Router

```
RouterHostName(config)#int e0
RouterHostName(config-if)#description Sales LAN
RouterHostName(config-if)#int s0
RouterHostName(config-if)desc WAN to New York circuit:3ddaa4242
RouterHostName(config-if)^Z
RouterHostName#sh run

.

.

.

interface ethernet0
description Sales LAN

.

.

.

interface Serial0
description WAN to New York circuit:3ddaa4242

.

.

.
```

RouterHostName(config-if)#**ip address 192.168.1.254 255.255.255.0**

NOTE: The IP address mask command starts the IP processing on the interface.

To activate the interface, you then use the no shutdown command (or no shut for short). To disable an interface, you can use the shutdown command. To see if an interface is administratively shut down or not, you would use the show running-config command (or show run for short) or the show interface port# command (sh int port# for short).

13.6.4   Enabling and Configuring IPX Protocols

To enable IPX support for a Cisco router, you must first change into Global Configuration mode and execute the IPX routing command:

RouterHostName#**config t**
RouterHostName(config)#**ipx routing**

Once you have enabled IPX routing on the router, RIP and SAP are automatically enabled as well. However, nothing happens until you configure the individual interfaces with IPX addresses.

To enable IPX on an interface, first enter Interface Configuration mode, and then issue the following command:

```
ipx network number [encapsulation encapsulation-type]
[secondary]
```

You should add the novell-ether encapsulation type to the routers. Novell NetWare 4.11 servers use the Ethernet_802.2 frame type by default. If another frame type is added on the network, then Cisco routers must add the corresponding encapsulation type to the appropriate interfaces. NetWare 3.11 servers use the Ethernet_802.3 frame type by default. You can use several frame types on a single medium. However, each frame type must have a different network number. Devices using different network numbers cannot communicate directly.

NOTE: The Cisco encapsulation name, not the Novell encapsulation name, must be specified.

The network_number is the external IPX number. The encapsulation type is optional. If you do not specify an encapsulation type by using the Cisco keyword, it will choose a default encapsulation type.

NOTE: You can use the encap command as a shortcut to encapsulation (see Table 13.15). Therefore, the following command:

```
HostRouterName(config)#ipx routing
HostRouterName(config)#int ethernet e0/0
HostRouterName(config-if)#ipx network 12341234
```

will assign the external IPX number of 12341234 to that interface and assign a default encapsulation of Ethernet 802.3 (novell-ether). If you want to use the Ethernet 802.2 instead, you would have used:

```
ipx network 12341234 sap
```

Table 13.15 Novell IPX Frame Types

Interface type	Frame type	Cisco keyword
Ethernet	Ethernet 802.3	novell-ether (default)
	Ethernet 802.2	sap
	Ethernet II	arpa
	Ethernet snap	snap
Token Ring	Token-Ring	sap (default)
	Token-Ring snap	snap
FDDI	Fddi snap	snap (default)
	Fddi 802.2	sap
	Fddi raw	novell-fddi

To configure a secondary address on an Ethernet LAN to support multiple frame types, use the `ipx network` command with the `secondary` parameter (or `sec` for short) at the end of the command.

> HostRouterName(config-if)#**ipx network 1234123A encap**
> **sap sec**

If you don't use the secondary command at the end of the line, the `ipx network` command will replace the existing entry. In addition, remember, that each frame type must have a different IPX network number.

To verify that the router is advertising all of the appropriate SAP services on your IPX network, you should first wait a sufficient time for the router tables across the internetwork to converge. Then you would use the `show ipx servers` command to display the SAP services advertised by the router and verify that your network services are listed in the table.

Figure 13.16   Using the Show Interface Port# Command

```
Router#sh int s0
Serial0 is down, line protocol is down
Hardware is HD64570
  MTU 1500 bytes, BW 1544 Kbit, DLY 20000 usec, rely 255/255, load 1/255
  Encapsulation HDLC, loopback not set, keepalive set (10 sec)
  Last input 00:00:09, output 00:00:12, output hang never
  Last clearing of "show interface" counters never
  Input queue: 0/75/0 (size/max/drops); Total output drops: 0
  Queueing strategy: weighted fair
  Output queue: 0/1000/64/0 (size/max total/threshold/drops)
    Conversations  0/1/256 (active/max active/max total)
    Reserved Conversations 0/0 (allocated/max allocated)
  5 minute input rate 0 bits/sec, 0 packets/sec
  5 minute output rate 0 bits/sec, 0 packets/sec
    1721 packets input, 106287 bytes, 0 no buffer
    Received 1301 broadcasts, 0 runts, 0 giants, 0 throttles
    0 input errors, 0 CRC, 0 frame, 0 overrun, 0 ignored, 0 abort
    2195 packets output, 100497 bytes, 0 underruns
    0 output errors, 0 collisions, 221 interface resets
    0 output buffer failures, 0 output buffers swapped out
    280 carrier transitions
    DCD=up  DSR=up  DTR=up  RTS=up  CTS=up

Router#
```

13.6.5   Determining the Status of the Interfaces

One tool that is very helpful in troubleshooting is the *show interface* (sh int) command (see Figure 13.16). The show interface command will give you the status of the line and data link protocol. For example, if you perform the following command:

```
RouterHostName#sh int e0
```

it might reply back with the following:

```
Ethernet0 is up, line protocol is up.
```

The first parameter refers to the physical layer, which is up when it receives carrier detect. The line protocol denotes both the cable into the router and the LAN protocol running over it. The second parameter, which is the line protocol, looks for keepalives from the connection end. Keepalives are used between devices to make sure connectivity has not been dropped.

If you see that the line is up but the protocol is down, you are experiencing a clocking (keepalive) or framing problem. Check the keepalives on both ends to make sure they match, the clock rate is set (if needed) and the encapsulation type is the same on both ends. A line protocol reported as down probably indicates that the LAN segment's shared

Table 13.16   Common Commands Used on Cisco Routers

Command	Action	When to use
show version	Displays the current software version	To verify the current software version and the name of the system image file
show config	Displays the startup configuration, which includes the current passwords assigned, information on the interfaces, and routing protocols configured	To verify the overall configuration
show startup-config	Displays the startup configuration	To verify the startup configuration
show running-config	Displays the running configuration, which is the configuration in use	To verify the running configuration
setup	Begins the manual configuration prompting sequence	To enter or modify all or part of the router's configuration
write mem	Used in IOS version 10.3 and earlier to save changes made to the running configuration	Saves the running configuration to the startup configuration; performs the same action as copying running-config startup-config
reload	Copies the startup configuration into RAM	To reset the running configuration to the startup configuration
erase startup-config	Deletes the startup configuration in NVRAM	Probably never, unless you want to reset the router back into its initial startup and configuration states

medium (a hub, an access switch, or a cable) is faulty. From there you would physically check the medium to identify the hardware problem.

If one end is administratively shut down, the physical end would be administratively down and the line protocol would be down, as shown here:

```
Ethernet0 is administratively down, line protocol is down
```

Besides the status of the interface, the `show interface` command also gives you some statistics of the interface. First, it gives you the Maximum Transmission Unit (MTU) and the default bandwidth for the interface. Another important configuration to notice is the keepalive time, which is ten seconds by default. Each router sends a keepalive message to its neighbor every ten seconds. If both routers aren't configured for the same keepalive time, it won't work.

Lastly, the `show interface` command gives you counters for the interface, which can be used for troubleshooting the reliability of the interface and link. You can clear the counters on the interface by typing the clear counters command:

```
RouterHostName#clear counters s0
```

SUMMARY

1. Routers are purpose-built computers dedicated to internetwork processing.
2. You connect and manage a router by using a terminal or through the network on which the router sits.
3. Like a PC, routers use various kinds of memory to operate.
4. The operating system used on routers is IOS.
5. Cisco IOS software release numbers have four basic parts.
6. One of the biggest parts of router management is installing and backing up the router's configuration file.
7. The configuration file runs the router and specifies how all the traffic goes through it.
8. The console port is where you hook a PC or terminal up to the router in order to access the operating system.
9. To connect a PC or a laptop to the router, you need a RJ-45 rollover cable.
10. The auxiliary port is another asynchronous serial port that looks just like the console port. It is typically used to connect a modem to a router.
11. A Cisco router can boot from three locations: (1) Flash memory, (2) a TFTP server, or (3) ROM.
12. All Cisco routers have a 16-bit software register written into NVRAM. By default, the configuration register is set to load the Cisco IOS from flash memory and to look for and load the startup-config file from NVRAM.
13. The working name of the command line interpreter (CLI) is the Exec command interpreter.
14. The first mode on a Cisco router after you successfully log into the router is the User Exec mode. In this mode, you can connect to other devices (such as another router) to perform simple tests and display system information.
15. ROMMON mode is displayed during the boot process if no operating system is loaded in flash memory. From this mode, the router's configuration can be completed.
16. When a router is first configured from the console port, Setup mode is invoked, which guides you through the setup process to configure the router.

QUESTIONS

1. Pat is making some configuration changes to a router. He issues the *shutdown* command for the serial 0 interface. He then issues the *show interface serial 0* command. What status is displayed?
   a. serial0 is up, line protocol is up
   b. serial0 is up, line protocol is down
   c. serial0 is down, line protocol is down
   d. serial0 is administratively down, line protocol is down

2. Pat is attempting to set passwords on a Cisco router. She has just typed the *config t* command. What command should Pat issue next to set "babylon" as the console password?
   a. line aux 0   b. enable
   c. line console 0   d. disable

3. Which of the following commands are valid methods for configuring the running configuration of a router? (Select all choices that are correct.)
   a. configure terminal
   b. configure network
   c. configure memory
   d. configure overwrite

4. How do you log onto a router from a console?
   a. by pressing the Enter key and then typing a password if required
   b. by typing login and then a password if required
   c. by typing Exec to enter User Exec mode
   d. by typing enable to enter Privileged Exec mode
   e. by typing console, aux or Telnet, depending on how you accessed the router

5. Which of the following commands will restrict access to Privileged Exec mode by establishing "babylon" as an encrypted password? (Select the best choice.)
   a. password omnipresence
   b. enable password omnipresence
   c. password secret omnipresence
   d. enable secret omnipresence

6. You are using a Cisco router that runs IOS Release 11. You want to make several changes to the running configuration, but you do not want to type all of the necessary configuration commands. Which of the following commands can you use to accomplish this task? (Select two answers.)
   a. config overwrite   b. config network
   c. config memory   d. config t

7. Pat is new to Cisco router configuration. She has made several changes, and she wants to verify the current mode. What prompt character is displayed if Pat is in Privileged mode?
   a. >   b. !
   c. #   d. :

8. What is the result of pressing the Tab key while typing a command parameter in the Cisco CLI?
   a. The cursor is returned to the beginning of the command line.
   b. The cursor is moved forward one character.
   c. The cursor is moved forward one word.
   d. The command parameter is automatically completed.
   e. The command parameter is deleted.

9. After you type in a long command, you realize that you typed the first letter of the command incorrectly. What key sequence returns the cursor to the beginning of the command?
   a. Ctrl+P   b. Ctrl+E
   c. Ctrl+A   d. Esc+B

10. While configuring an Ethernet interface on your Cisco router, you discover a spelling error earlier in the command line. Which of the following Cisco IOS commands will allow you to move the cursor back in the command line, one character at a time, without deleting characters?
    a. Ctrl+B   b. Esc+B
    c. Ctrl+F   d. Esc+F

11. You are assigning IP addresses to your router's Ethernet and Token Ring interfaces. To save time, you would like to reuse and edit previous IOS commands while completing this task. Which of the following Cisco IOS commands will allow you to display the previously executed command?
    a. down arrow
    b. show history
    c. Ctrl+P
    d. terminal history size 1

12. While in enable mode, you want to set the clock time, but you cannot remember the parameters required by the clock command. What can you type to see the first required parameter of the clock command?
    a. clock ?   b. help clock
    c. clock?   d. help clock ?

13. You want to copy the version of Cisco IOS running on your router to a TFTP server on your network. Which of the following commands will enable you to accomplish this task?
    a. copy run start
    b. copy flash tftp
    c. copy tftp flash
    d. copy tftp run

14. Pat is changing the configuration of the serial 0 interface on a router. He issues the *show interface serial* 0 command. The status that is displayed indicates that the serial interface is operational, but the line protocol is not operational. Which of the following choices could result in this problem? (Select all choices that are correct.)
    a. The physical connection is faulty.
    b. The serial 0 interface has been administratively shut down.
    c. Keepalive signals are not active.
    d. The clock rate has not been specified.

15. What command is used to configure the router to boot from the method of last resort?
    a. boot system TFTP
    b. copy TFTP running-config
    c. boot system flash
    d. boot system ROM

16. Where is the routing table stored on a Cisco router?
    a. flash memory   b. ROM
    c. NVRAM   d. RAM

17. Which of the following commands should you use while in Privileged Exec mode to return to User Exec mode?
    a. Ctrl+Z   b. enable
    c. resume   d. disable
    e. logout

18. Gary is logged in to a router and is in User Exec mode. He wants to enter Privileged Exec mode. Which of the following commands should Gary issue to accomplish this task?
    a. cdp enable   b. enable secret
    c. enable   d. login

19. What syntax is used to configure an Ethernet port on a Cisco 7000 series router that contains a VIP card?
    a. e slot/port
    b. e slot/port-adapter/port
    c. e port/slot
    d. e port-adapter/slot/port

20. An IOS image file named img302.bin is located on a TFTP server that has an IP address of 122.23.1.2. Which of the following commands boots a router from this TFTP server by using this file?
    a. boot run tftp
    b. copy tftp 122.23.1.2 img302.bin run
    c. boot system tftp 122.23.1.2 img302.bin
    d. copy tftp run

21. A junior network administrator in your organization has accidentally deleted your router's startup-config file, and has carried out the reload command. Into which mode will the router boot?
    a. Global Configuration mode
    b. Basic Management Setup mode
    c. Interface Configuration mode
    d. Setup mode

22. Which of the following will be displayed if you issue the *de?* command while in Privileged Exec mode on a Cisco Catalyst 1900 switch?
    a. common help
    b. all commands starting with "de"
    c. the parameters of the debug command
    d. the parameters of the delete command

23. A banner appears when users log onto the console port of your router. You want to change the banner that is displayed. Which of the following commands can you use to accomplish this task? (Select all choices that are correct.)
    a. banner This is a sample message.
    b. banner motd #
    c. banner motd #This is a sample message.#
    d. banner

24. What command can you type to create a banner that is displayed when an administrator logs in to the console port of your router?
    a. banner This is for authorized use only!
    b. banner #This is for authorized use only!#
    c. banner motd # This is for authorized use only!#
    d. banner ##motd.txt##

25. You want to configure the banner, so you must enter Config mode. What mode must you be in so that you can enter Config mode?
    a. Network Configuration mode
    b. User mode
    c. Interface Configuration mode
    d. Privileged Exec mode

26. What function does the boot system ROM command perform on a Cisco router?
    a. boots the system and loads the IOS into flash memory
    b. directs the system to boot by using the IOS stored in ROM
    c. copies the boot configuration into ROM
    d. copies the running configuration into ROM

27. You have issued a number of commands on your Cisco router in the last few minutes. You cannot remember a particular command that you issued several moments ago, but you want to issue it again. Which of the following allows you to see previous commands with a minimum amount of effort?
    a. Press Ctrl+N repeatedly until you see the command.
    b. Press Ctrl+P once.
    c. Issue the *show history* command.
    d. Issue the *terminal editing* command.

28. Pat has been experimenting with router configuration commands. She has not copied the running configuration into the startup configuration, and she has not erased the startup configuration. She wants to determine which configuration is used when she shuts down and restarts the router. Which of the following commands should Pat use to accomplish this task? (Select 2 choices.)
    a. show startup-config
    b. write term
    c. show running-config
    d. show config

29. Where is the startup-config file stored on a Cisco router? (Select the best choice.)
    a. RAM   b. ROM
    c. NVRAM   d. EEPROM

30. You have entered Configuration mode. You want to configure the first Ethernet port on your router to use an IPX subinterface and Ethernet_802.2 encapsulation. Which of the following commands should you use to accomplish your task?
    a. int e0.50
       ipx network 50 encapsulation Ethernet_802.2
    b. int e0.50
       ipx network 50 encapsulation sap
    c. int e0
       ipx network 50 encap Ethernet_802.2 sec
    d. int e1
       ipx network 50 encap sap sec

31. Which of the following IOS commands will allow you to configure the second Ethernet port on your organization's Cisco router? (Select the best choice.)
    a. show interface e1   b. in e1
    c. interface e1   d. show interface e2
    e. in e2   f. interface e2

32. Your network runs Novell NetWare 4.11 servers using the NetWare default frame type. All of the Cisco routers are properly configured, and they are operational. You add a NetWare 3.11 server to the network and use NetWare's default frame type on this server. What configuration change must you make to the Cisco routers?
    a. Change all of the encapsulation types to SAP.
    b. Add the novell-ether encapsulation type only.
    c. Add the Ethernet_802.2 encapsulation type only.
    d. Add the Ethernet_SNAP encapsulation type.

33. Which of the following prompt and command pairs best represents the mode and command that should be used to configure interface e0 on the router named ROUTER_B with the IP address 10.254.23.5/16? (Select 2 choices.)
    a. ROUTER_B(config)#ip address 10.254.23.5 255.0.0.0
    b. ROUTER_B(config)#ip address 10.254.23.5 255.255.0.0
    c. ROUTER_B(config-if)#ip address 10.254.23.5 255.0.0.0
    d. ROUTER_B(config-if)#ip address 10.254.23.5 255.255.0.0
    e. ROUTER_B(config)#no shutdown
    f. ROUTER_B(config)#open interface e0
    g. ROUTER_B(config-if)#no shutdown
    h. ROUTER_B(config-if)#open interface e0

34. You have entered Configuration mode on a Cisco router on your Novell NetWare 3.11 server internetwork. You want to configure the first Ethernet port to use an IPX subinterface, network number 200, and Ethernet_802.3 encapsulation. Which of the following commands accomplishes your task?
    a. int e0.200
       ipx network 200 encapsulation novell-ether
    b. int e0.200
       ipx network 200 encapsulation Ethernet_802.3
    c. int e0
       ipx network 200 encap Ethernet_802.3 sec
    d. int e0
       ipx network 200 encap novell-ether sec

35. Your company has an IPX network, numbered 341, with several Novell NetWare 3.11 servers. All of the NetWare servers run the default Novell Ethernet frame type and use the same network number. You are planning to install a NetWare 4.11 server on the same physical network, and you want to use the default Ethernet frame type for NetWare 4.11. You have already configured the Ethernet interface, E0, to support the Ethernet_802.3 frame type. You now want to enable the Ethernet_802.2 frame type without changing the configuration of the NetWare 3.11 servers. Which of the following commands can you type to allow both frame types to coexist on the same wire? (Select all choices that are correct.)

  a. int e0
    ipx network B341 encap sap sec
  b. int e0.341
    ipx network B341 encap sap
  c. int e0
    ipx network B341 encap novell-ether sec
  d. int e0.341
    ipx network B341 encap Ethernet_802.2

36. Your network runs Novell NetWare 3.11 servers using the NetWare default frame type. All of the Cisco routers are properly configured and are operational. You add a NetWare 4.11 server to the network, and you configure it to use NetWare's default frame type. What configuration change must you make to the Cisco routers?

  a. Change all of the encapsulation types to SAP.
  b. Add the Ethernet_802.2 encapsulation type only.
  c. Add the SAP encapsulation type only.
  d. Add the Ethernet_SNAP encapsulation type only.

37. IPX is enabled on your Cisco router. You now want to enable IPX on the Ethernet port E0 and assign a network number of FEEDF1D0. What commands should you use to enter Configuration mode and assign the required network number?

  a. config t
    ipx routing FEEDF1D0
  b. config t
    int e0 FEEDF1D0
  c. config t
    int e0
    ipx network FEEDF1D0
  d. FEEDF1D0 is not a valid IPX network address

38. You are planning to install a router on your network to combine two NetWare networks into a single LAN. You have decided to leave the client computers on the two Ethernet network segments and to create a third backbone segment for the servers. Currently, the servers on one of the networks run NetWare 3.11, and the servers on the other network run NetWare 4.11. Each server is configured to use its default Ethernet frame type. You are ready to create the backbone segment and have already configured the Ethernet interface for the new segment, E2, to support the Ethernet_802.3 frame type. Which of the following commands can you type to enable the Ethernet_802.2 frame type in addition to the Ethernet_802.3 frame type on the server segment? (Select all choices that are correct.)

  a. int e2
    ipx network B210 encap novell-ether sec
  b. int e2.999
    ipx network B210 encap Ethernet_802.2
  c. int e2
    ipx network B210 encap sap sec
  d. int e2.210
    ipx network B210 encap sap

39. You carry out the *show ipx int e0* command on your router and determine that the IPX address associated with Ethernet port 0 on the router is DABC.BBCD.1234.44FA. What is the IPX network address associated with E0?

  a. DABC
  b. DABC.BBCD.1234
  c. 1234.44FA
  d. DABC.BBCD
  e. BBCD.1234.44FA
  f. 44FA

40. You have configured IPX on Token Ring port 1 of the Dallas router by using the following commands on the Dallas router:

config t
int to1
ipx network B211

Then, you press the Ctrl+Z key combination. Which Cisco encapsulation type have you configured on the Token Ring interface? (Select the best choice.)

  a. arpa   b. novell-ether
  c. sap   d. snap

41. You have been making configuration changes on a Cisco router. You now want to verify that the router is advertising all of the appropriate SAP services on your IPX network. You wait a sufficient time for the router tables across the internetwork to converge. Which of the following commands should you issue to display the SAP services advertised by the router?

a. show ipx interface   b. debug ipx routing
c. debug ipx sap   d. show ipx servers

42. Which of the following displays the message of the day stored on a Cisco router?

a. using the show banner command
b. switching to enable mode

c. switching to configuration mode
d. logging in to a router

43. Your Cisco router has nothing in NVRAM, nothing in flash memory, and no currently-available TFTP servers. What command tells the router where to obtain the IOS? (Select the best choice.)

a. boot system flash
b. boot system ROM
c. boot system flash *filename*
d. boot system RAM

HANDS-ON EXERCISES

Exercise 1: Accessing a Cisco Router

1. Turn OFF your computer.
2. Make sure that the Cisco router is OFF. There may be no ON/OFF button for the switch so you may need to disconnect the power.
3. Connect one end of the rollover cable to the console port on the router. Connect the other end of the cable to the COM1 port on your PC. If you need to, you can connect to the COM2 port.
4. Turn ON your computer.
5. Turn ON the router.
6. On the PC, click the Start button. Then select the Programs option, select the Accessories option, select the Communications option, and select the HyperTerminal program.
7. If it asks you to make HyperTerminal your default telnet program, click on the Yes button.
8. When it asks you to enter a name for your router console connection, type Router Console in the text box and click on the OK button.

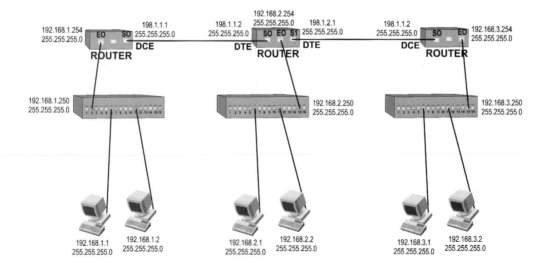

9. In the Connect To dialog box, select the appropriate COM port and click the OK button.
10. In the COM properties dialog box, set the following options and click on the OK button:

    Bits per Second=9600
    Data Bits=8
    Parity=None
    Stop Bits=1
    Flow Control=Xon/Xoff

11. Press the Enter key on the PC if you need to initiate a response from the router.
12. To change to Privileged Exec mode, execute the `enable` command. Login if necessary.
13. To change to Global Configuration mode, execute the `config t` command.
14. Use the `exit` command to return to Privileged Exec mode.
15. Execute the `show ver` command to display the version of the IOS.

    What version of the IOS is the router running?
    What is the value of the Configuration register?
    By analyzing the configuration register, where is the Router to boot from?
    Is the Break enabled or disabled?

16. Execute the `sh int` command to show the interface statistics. Press the space bar to browse through the various interfaces on your router. You can use Ctrl-Z to break out of this command.
17. Change back to Global Configuration mode.
18. Change into the interface mode for port 1 by executing the following command:
    `int ethernet 0`
19. If the `int ethernet 0` command does not work, try the `int fastethernet 0` command.
20. Execute the `end` command.
21. Type a ? and press the Enter key to list the commands that are available on the router. Use the space bar to browse to the next screen.
22. Execute the `show ?` command. Use the space bar to browse to the next screen.
23. Execute the `show run` command to display the current configuration commands. Use the space bar to browse to the next screen.
24. Execute the `show start` command to display the startup configuration file.
25. To erase the startup-config file and current configuration, execute the `erase start` and the `erase run` commands.
26. Display the current configuration.
27. Try to display the startup configuration file.
28. Change into Global Configuration mode.
29. Set the secret password to password by executing the `enable secret password` command.
30. Set the virtual terminal password to passtest by using the following commands:

    `line vty 0 4`
    `login`
    `password passtest`

31. Execute the `exit` command.
32. Change back into Global Configuration mode.
33. Execute the `show run` command and view your passwords.
34. To establish the host name of routerXX where XX is your student number, use the `hostname routerXX` command.
35. Change to the Ethernet.
36. Change to the first Ethernet interface.

37. Configure the IP address and subnet mask by using the `ip address` *IP_address sub-netmask* command.
38. Use the `ping` command to ping your PC.
39. Activate the interface by executing the `no shutdown` command.
40. Execute the `Exit` command.
41. Press the Enter key and log onto the router.
42. Ping your work station.

Exercise 2: Configuring the IPX Protocol

1. From your computer, ping the router.
2. From your computer, start a Telnet session with the router.
3. Log onto the router.
4. Change into Global Configuration mode.
5. Add the IPX protocol by executing the `ipx routing` command.
6. Change into the first Ethernet interface.
7. Assign 10XX (where XX is your student number) as the IPX network number by executing the `ipx network 10XX` command.
8. Execute the `show ipx` command.
9. Close your Telnet session.

CHAPTER 14

Configuring WAN Protocols on the Router

Topics Covered in this Chapter

Introduction

Now that you have learned the basics of Cisco routers and you are familiar with various WAN technologies, you are ready to connect the Cisco routers to your WAN connections such as ISDN, Frame Relay, and ATM. You will soon learn that Cisco routers can handle a wide range of interfaces.

Objectives

- Enable WAN protocols on a Cisco router including ISDN, Frame Relay, and ATM.
- Enable PPP on your Cisco router.

14.1 ESTABLISHING WAN PROTOCOLS

Cisco routers support a wide range of WAN protocols using the serial port. Some of the websites available from Cisco are:

Cisco IOS Wide-Area Networking Configuration Guide, Release 12.2

http://www.cisco.com/univercd/cc/td/doc/product/software/ios122/122cgcr/fwan_c/

Cisco IOS Wide-Area Networking Command Reference, Release 12.2

http://www.cisco.com/univercd/cc/td/doc/product/software/ios122/122cgcr/fwan_r/

Configuring ATM

http://www.cisco.com/univercd/cc/td/doc/product/software/ios122/122cgcr/fwan_c/wcfatm.htm

ATM Commands

http://www.cisco.com/univercd/cc/td/doc/product/software/ios122/122cgcr/fwan_r/atmcmds/index.htm

Configuring Broadband Access: PPP and Routed Bridge Encapsulation

http://www.cisco.com/univercd/cc/td/doc/product/software/ios122/122cgcr/fwan_c/wcfppp.htm

Broadband Access: PPP and Routed Bridge Encapsulation Commands

http://www.cisco.com/univercd/cc/td/doc/product/software/ios122/122cgcr/fwan_r/wrfbrda.htm

Configuring Frame Relay

http://www.cisco.com/univercd/cc/td/doc/product/software/ios122/122cgcr/fwan_c/wcffrely.htm

Frame Relay Commands

http://www.cisco.com/univercd/cc/td/doc/product/software/ios122/122cgcr/
fwan_r/frcmds/index.htm

Configuring Frame Relay-ATM Interworking

http://www.cisco.com/univercd/cc/td/doc/product/software/ios122/122cgcr/
fwan_c/wcffratm.htm

Frame Relay-ATM Interworking Commands

http://www.cisco.com/univercd/cc/td/doc/product/software/ios122/122cgcr/
fwan_r/wrffratm.htm

Configuring SMDS

http://www.cisco.com/univercd/cc/td/doc/product/software/ios122/122cgcr/
fwan_c/wcfsmds.htm

SMDS Commands

http://www.cisco.com/univercd/cc/td/doc/product/software/ios122/122cgcr/
fwan_r/wrfsmds.htm

Configuring X.25 and LAPB

http://www.cisco.com/univercd/cc/td/doc/product/software/ios122/122cgcr/
fwan_c/wcfx25.htm

X.25 and LAPB Commands

http://www.cisco.com/univercd/cc/td/doc/product/software/ios122/122cgcr/
fwan_r/x25cmds/index.htm

14.2   CONFIGURING SERIAL PORTS

The serial interface will usually be attached to a CSU/DSU type device that provides clocking for the line. But, if you want to connect two CSU/DSUs back-to-back so that you practice with it in a lab environment, one of the CSU/DSUs must act as a DCE. Because Cisco routers are all DTE devices, you must tell an interface to provide clocking if you need it to act like a DCE device. You configure a DCE serial interface with the clock rate command:

```
RouterHostName# config t
RouterHostName(config)# int s0
RouterHostName(config-if)# clock rate 64000
```

You can configure the bandwidth of the command by using the *bandwidth* command. However, the bandwidth is used by the routing protocol (such as IGRP, EIGRP, and OSPF) as a metric to determine the best route to take and not as the actual bandwidth of the link. If you are using RIP, then the bandwidth setting of a serial link is irrelevant because it only uses hop counts to determine the best route. Cisco routers ship with a default serial link bandwidth of a T-1 (1.544 Mbps). To configure the bandwidth, you would use the bandwidth command:

```
RouterHostName# config t
```

Figure 14.1   Using the *Show Controllers* Command

```
RouterHostName#sh controllers serial 0
HD unit 0, idb=0x1229E4, driver structure at 0x127E70
buffer size 1524 HD unit 0, V.35 DTE cable
cpb=0xE2, eda=0x4140, cda-0x4000

RouterHostName#sh controllers serial 1
HD unit 0, idb=0x12CC174, driver structure at 0x131600
buffer size 1524 HD unit 0, V.35 DCE cable
cpb=0xE3, eda=0x2940, cda-0x2800
```

```
RouterHostName(config)# int s0
RouterHostName(config-if)# bandwidth 64
```

NOTE: The bandwidth is expressed in kilobytes.

The `show controllers` command displays information about the physical interface itself. It will also give you the type of serial cable plugged into a serial port. Usually, this will only be a DTE cable that plugs into a type of DSU. If you look at Figure 14.1, you will notice that serial 0 has a DTE cable, whereas the serial 1 connection has a DCE cable. Therefore, serial 1 would have to provide clocking with the clock rate command while serial 0 would get its clocking from a DTE device.

14.3   CONFIGURING PPP ON CISCO ROUTERS

Configuring PPP encapsulation on an interface is a fairly straightforward process. To do so, follow these router commands:

```
RouterHostName#config t
RouterHostName(config)#int s0
RouterHostName(config-if)#encapsulation ppp
```

To configure authentication using PPP between routers, you must first set the hostname of the router if it is not already set and then set the username and password for the remote router connected to your router:

```
RouterHostName#config t
RouterHostName(config)#username RouterB password cisco
```

You must make sure that the name entered is identical to the remote peer's router hostname. Also make sure that both sides of the PPP peering connections use identical passwords. In addition, remember that both username entries and passwords are case sensitive. Therefore, on RouterB, you would execute the following command:

```
RouterB(config)#username RouterHostName password cisco
```

Figure 14.2   Using the *Show Interface* Command

```
RouterHostName#show int s0
Serial0 is up, line protocol is up
Hardware is HD64570
Internet address is 168.1.1.5/24
  MTU 1500 bytes, BW 1544 Kbit, DLY 20000 usec, rely 255/255, load 1/255
  Encapsulation PPP, loopback not set, keepalive set (10 sec)
  LCP Open
  Listen: IPXCP
  Open: IPCP, CDPCP, ATCP
  Last input 00:00:05, output 00:00:05, output hang never
  Last clearing of "show interface" counters never
  Input queue: 0/75/0 (size/max/drops); Total output drops: 0
  Queuing strategy: weighted fair
  Output queue: 0/1000/64/0 (size/max total/threshold/drops)
     Conversations 0/2/256 (active/max active/max total)
     Reserved Conservations 0/0 (allocated/max allocated)
  5 minute input rate 0 bits/sec, 0 packets//sec
  5 minute output rate 0 bits/sec, 0 packets/sec
     670 packets input, 31845 bytes, 0 no buffer
     Received 596 broadcasts, 0 runts, 0 giants, 0 throttles
     0 input errors, 0 CRC, 0 frame, 0 overrun, 0 ignored, 0 abort
     707 packets output, 31553 bytes, 0 underruns
     0 output errors, 0 collisions, 18 interface resets
     0 output buffers failures, 0 output buffers swapped out
     21 carrier transitions
     DCD=up DSR=up DTR=up RTS=up CTS=up
RouterHostName#
```

After you set the hostname, usernames, and passwords, choose the authentication type: either CHAP or PAP.

```
RouterHostName#config t
RouterHostName(config)#int s0
RouterHostName(config-if)#ppp authentication chap
RouterHostName(config-if)#ppp authentication pap
```

If both methods are configured, as shown in this example, then only the first method is used during link negotiation. If the first method fails, the second method will be used.

To show that PPP is up and running, use the *show interface* command (see Figure 14.2). Besides showing you the encapsulation is PPP as shown in the sixth line, it will also tell you that the LCP is open. If you recall, the LCP protocol builds and maintains connections. The eighth line reports that it is listening for IPXCP and the ninth line tells us that IPCP, CDPCP, and ATCP are open. IPCP is short for IP Control Program, CDPCP is short for Cisco Discovery Protocol Control program, ATCP is short for Apple Talk Control program and IPXCP is short for IPX Control Program, which shows that these protocols support NCP.

NOTE: You can verify the PPP authentication configuration by using the debug ppp authentication command.

14.4   CONFIGURING BRI ISDN

To access ISDN with a Cisco router, your router must have a built-in NT1 (U reference point) or an ISDN modem (called a TA). If your router has a BRI interface (RJ-45 connection specifically designated for a BRI ISDN), you just connect the ISDN cable to the router. If not, you can use the router's serial interface. Remember that a router with a BRI interface is called a TE1 (terminal equipment type 1) and one that requires a TA is called a TE2 (terminal equipment type 2).

As you recall from earlier chapters, an ISDN provider will have switches that connect the segments that link the ISDN connections. Because each switch manufacturer has a proprietary protocol for signaling, you need to know the type of switch that your service provider is using so that you can specify the switch type in the router's configuration. To get this information, you will have to contact your ISDN provider. See Table 14.1 for a list and a summary of ISDN configuration commands.

Table 14.1   ISDN Configuration Commands

Command	Configuration mode	Purpose
isdn switch-type *switch-type*	Global or Interface	Defines to the router the type of ISDN switch to which the ISDN line is connected at the CO
isdn spid1 *spid*	Interface	Defines the first SPID
isdn spid2 *spid*	Interface	Defines the second SPID
isdn caller *number*	Interface	Defines a valid number for incoming calls when using call screening
isdn answer1 [*called-partynumber*] [*:subaddress*]	Interface	Specifies the ISDN number or subaddress that must be used on incoming calls for this router to answer
isdn answer2 [*called-partynumber*] [*:subaddress*]	Interface	Specifies a second ISDN number or subaddress that must be used on incoming calls for this router to answer
dialer-list [*list nnn*] **protocol** [*protocol-type*] **permit** ¦ **deny**	Global	Defines types of traffic considered interesting
dialer-group *n*	Interface	Enables a dialer list on this interface
dialer in-band	Interface	Enables dial out and dial in on this interface. This command is used only for serial lines that connect to a TA, not for native ISDN interfaces that use the out-of-band D channel
dialer string *string*	Interface	A dial string used when dialing only one site
dialer map *protocol next-hop address* [**name** *hostname*] [**speed 56** ¦ **64**] [**broadcast**] *dial-string*	Interface	A dial string to reach the next hop. However, the **map** command is used when dialing more than one site. This also is the name used for authentication. Broadcast ensures that copies of broadcasts go to this next-hop address.

To see which switches your router supports, use the `isdn switch-type ?` command in Global Configuration mode or Interface Configuration mode. Table 14.2 lists the common switch types used on Cisco routers and their configuration keywords. If you configure the switch type while in Global Configuration mode, you set the switch type for all BRI interfaces in the router. If you only have one interface, it doesn't matter where you use the `isdn switch-type` command. If you configure it in Interface Configuration mode, you only configure that individual ISDN connection. Lastly, it is also important to note that any router configured for ISDN support must be connected to the same switch type on all of its ISDN interfaces.

The SPIDs are like phone numbers that identify your individual connection. To configure SPIDs for your router, you would use the `isdn spid1` and `isdn spid2` interface commands. Of course, your SPIDs are provided by your ISDN provider (see Figure 14.3).

> *NOTE:* Some providers no longer require SPIDs to be configured on the router. Check with your provider to be sure. The second part of the SPID configuration is the local dial number for that SPID. It is optional, but some switches need to have those set on the router in order to use both B channels simultaneously. Lastly, most ISDN connections use PPP encapsulation, typically CHAP.

BRI is usually configured on a Cisco router as a dial-on-demand router (DDR) link. DDR is a Cisco IOS interface configuration type that provides several functions, including creating the illusion that the router has full-time connectivity over dial-up interface.

Table 14.2 Common ISDN Switches

Switch type	Configuration keyword
AT&T 5ess	primary-5ess
AT&T 4ess	primary-4ess
AT&T basic rate	basic-5ess
ISDN PRI	primary-dms100
National ISDN-1	basic-ni1
Nortel DMS-100 basic rate	basic-dms100

Figure 14.3 Configuring the ISDN on a Cisco Router

```
RouterHostName#config t
RouterHostName(config)#isdn switch-type basic-ni
RouterHostName(config)#int bri0
RouterHostName(config-if)#encap ppp
RouterHostName(config-if)#ppp authentication chap
RouterHostName(config-if)#isdn spid1 086506610100 8650661
RouterHostName(config-if)#isdn spid2 086506620100 8650662
```

14.5 CONFIGURING PRI ISDN

The configuration of PRI service is quite simple. Although the command variations and options are very similar to that of its BRI counterpart, a PRI configuration has additional requirements.

To meet the needs of the PRI provisioning, the T-1 or E-1 (whichever is appropriate) must be configured to match the telephone company or other ISDN provider requirements of framing and line code. The T-1/E-1 controller is actually an internal CSU/DSU. It must be told which time slots are included in the PRI configuration. For purposes of controller configuration, the time slot numbering starts at 1 (1–24 for T-1, and 1–30 for E-1). Table 14.3 illustrates the options available for T-1 and E-1 configuration.

Figure 14.4 shows an example configuration of a PRI ISDN. Like the BRI ISDN, you must configure the switch type. The `controller t1 0/0` command specifies that the controller is in slot 0, port 0. In this example, because the PRI ISDN uses a full T-1, it is using all twenty-four timeslots in this configuration. In addition, you will need to specify the framing and line code.

In this example, the framing is ESF and the line code is B8ZS, which is the most commonly deployed in North America. For E-1 implementations, the most common implementations are CRC4 and HDB3. Again, this information is provided by your ISDN

Table 14.3   T-1/E-1 Framing and Line Code Options

Options	Framing	Line code
T-1	SF (D4)	AMI
	ESF	B8ZS
E-1	CRC4	AMI
	NO-CRC4	HDB3
	CRC4 Australia	
	NO-CRC4 Australia	

Figure 14.4   Configuring an ISDN Connection Based on a T-1 Connection

```
RouterHostName(config)#isdn switch-type primary-ni
RouterHostName(config)#controller t1 0/0
RouterHostName(config-controller)#pri-group timeslots 1-24
RouterHostName(config-controller)#framing esf
RouterHostName(config-controller)#linecode b8zs
RouterHostName(config-controller)#clock source line primary
RouterHostName(config)#interface serial 0/0:23
RouterHostName(config-if)#ip address 10.12.1.1 255.255.255.0
RouterHostName(config-if)#isdn incoming-voice modem
```

Figure 14.5 Configuring an ISDN Connection Based on an E-1 Connection

```
RouterHostName(config)#isdn switch-type primary-ni
RouterHostName(config)#controller e1 0/0
RouterHostName(config-controller)#pri-group timeslots 1-30
RouterHostName(config-controller)#framing crc4
RouterHostName(config-controller)#linecode hdb3
RouterHostName(config-controller)#clock source line primary
RouterHostName(config)#interface serial 0/0:15
RouterHostName(config-if)#ip address 10.12.1.1 255.255.255.0
RouterHostName(config-if)#isdn incoming-voice modem
```

provider. If your ISDN connection is not working, the line code and framing should be one of the things that you check.

After you configure the controller, you must define the characteristics of the D channel. Because the T-1 PRI has twenty-four slots (numbered 0 to 23), the last time slot (slot 23) is the D channel. The D channel in E-1 PRI is timeslot 15 (numbered 0 to 30) (see Figure 14.5). In this example, serial 0/0:15 carries the protocol specific configuration (such as the IP address and the IPX network) for protocols that need to traverse this link.

Since some ISDN providers charge more for ISDN data calls, you could save money by specifying ISDN calls as voice calls. This is done with the isdn incoming-voice modem command.

14.6   CONFIGURING DIAL-ON-DEMAND ROUTING

DDR is used to allow two or more Cisco routers to dial an ISDN dial-up connection on an as-needed basis. DDR is only used for low-volume, periodic network connections using either a PSTN or ISDN.

When an interface on the router receives a packet, it first determines which route it needs to take. If it is determined that the best route is to use the dial-up connection, the router looks up the dialer information, establishes the connection, and transmits the data. After the data has been transmitted, the call is terminated.

To configure DDR, you need to perform three tasks:

Step 1: Define static routes, which define how to get to the remote networks and what interface to use to get there.

Step 2: Specify the traffic that should be transmitted through the DDR link.

Step 3: Configure the dialer information that will be used to dial the interface to get to the remote network.

It is recommend to use static routes because DDR links are usually inactive. While you can configure dynamic routing protocols to run on your ISDN like, the link will never be dropped because of the routing information being passed back and forth. Of course, if you use static routes, you must define all routes of known networks. If the network is a stub network (the DDR ISDN connection is the only WAN connection for your network) you can establish default routing.

After setting the route tables in each router, you need to configure the router to determine what brings up the ISDN line. An administrator using the `dialer-list` `global configuration` command defines interesting packets. The command to turn on all IP traffic is as follows:

```
RouterHostName(config)#dialer-list 1 protocol ip permit
RouterHostName(config)#int bri0
RouterHostName(config-if)#dialer-group 1
```

The dialer-group command sets the access list on the BRI interface. Extended access lists can be used with the dialer-list command to define interesting traffic just to certain applications.

There are five steps in the configuration of the dialer information:

Step 1: Choose the interface.
Step 2: Set the IP address.
Step 3: Configure the encapsulation type.
Step 4: Link interesting traffic to the interface.
Step 5: Configure the number or numbers to dial.

Here is an example of how to configure the five steps:

```
RouterHostName#config t
RouterHostName(config)#int bri0
RouterHostName(config-if)#ip address 192.68.60.1
255.255.255.0
RouterHostName(config-if)#no shut
RouterHostName(config-if)#encapsulation ppp
RouterHostName(config-if)#dialer-group 1
RouterHostName(config-if)#dialer-string 8560231
```

Instead of the dialer-string command, you can use a dialer map, which provides more security.

```
RouterHostName(config-if)#dialer map ip 192.68.60.1 name
804B 8350661
```

The dialer map command can be used with the dialer-group command and its associated access list to initiate dialing. The dialer map command uses the IP address of the next hop router, the hostname of the remote router for authentication, and then the number to dial to get there.

If you execute the `show run` command to view the configuration of an 804 router, you will see something like what is shown in Figure 14.6. The BRI interface is running the PPP encapsulation and has a timeout value of 300 seconds. The load-threshold command makes both BRI interfaces come up immediately. The one thing you really want to notice is the `dialer-group 1` command. The number must match the dialer-list number. The

Figure 14.6   Using the *show run* Command

```
RouterHostName#sh run
Building configuration...
Current configuration:
!
version 12.0
no service pad
service timestamps debug uptime
service timestamps log uptime
no service password-encryption
!
hostname RouterHostName
!
ip subnet-zero
!
isdn switch-type basic-ni
!
interface Ethernet0
 ip address 192.68.3.4 255.255.255.0
 no ip directed broadcast
!
interface BRI0
 ip address 192.68.60.2 255.255.255.0
 no ip directed-broadcast
 encapsulation ppp
 dialer idle-timeout 3000
 dialer string 8358660
 dialer load-threshold 2 either
 dialer-group 1
 isdn switch-type basic-ni
 isdn spid1 0845822221 8560231
 isdn spid2 0845822221 8560232
hold-queue 80 in
!
ip classless
ip route 192.68.30.0 255.255.255.0 192.68.60.0
ip route 192.68.60.1 255.255.255.255 BRI0
!
dialer-list 1 protocol ip permit
!
```

hold-queue 80 in command tells the router that when it receives an interesting packet, it should queue up to 80 packets while it is waiting for the BRI to come up. If there are more than 80 packets queued before the link comes up, the packets will be dropped.

The dialer load-threshold command tells the BRI interface when to bring up the second B channel. The option is from 1–255, where 255 tells the BRI to bring up the second

B channel only when the first channel is 100 percent loaded. The second option for that command is in, out, or either. This calculates the actual load on the interface either on output traffic, inbound traffic, or combined. The default is outbound.

The dialer idle-timeout command specifies the number of seconds before a call is disconnected after the last of the data is sent. The default is 120 seconds.

```
RouterHostName(config-if)#dialer load-threshold 125
either
RouterHostName(config-if)#dialer idle-timeout 180
```

The `dialer load-threshold 125` tells the BRI interface to bring up the second B channel if either the inbound or outbound traffic load is 50 percent. The `dialer idle-timeout 180` changes the default disconnect time from 120 to 180 seconds.

14.7   CONFIGURING FRAME RELAY

You must perform the following tasks to enable Frame Relay (see Table 14.4):

■ Enable Frame Relay encapsulation
■ Establish mapping

When enabling Frame Relay on Cisco routers, you need to specify it as an encapsulation on serial interfaces. There are two encapsulation types: Cisco and IETF.

```
RouterHostName(config)#int s0
RouterHostName(config-if)#encapsulation frame-relay
```

NOTE: You can abbreviate the `encapsulation frame-relay` command as the `encap fr` command. If you don't specify an encapsulation type, the `encapsulation frame-relay` command will default to Cisco. This is typically used when connecting two Cisco devices together. If you are connecting your Cisco router to a non-Cisco device, you have to use the `encapsulation frame-relay ietf` command. So before choosing an encapsulation type, check with your Frame Relay provider and find out which one they use. Beginning with IOS version 11.2, the LMI type is auto-sensed. This enables the interface to determine the LMI type supported by the switch.

The correct syntax for creating a Frame Relay subinterface is as follows:

```
interface serial-interface.subinterface-number
subinterface-type
```

The subinterface number used can be any decimal digit between 1 and 4,294,967,295. For convenience, it is often desirable when configuring Frame Relay subinterfaces to use the DLCI used for that connection as the subinterface number. The point-to-point subinterface keyword is used when a Frame Relay PVC will exist between two routers. The multipoint subinterface keyword is used when the local router shares a PVC with multiple routers.

Table 14.4   Frame Relay Configuration Commands

Command	Configuration mode	Purpose
encapsulation frame-relay **[ietf ¦ cisco]**	Interface	Defines Frame Relay encapsulation that is used rather than HDLC, PPP, and so on
frame-relay lmi-type **{ansi ¦ q933a ¦ cisco}**	Interface	Defines the type of LMI messages sent to the switch
bandwidth *num*	Interface	Sets the route's perceived speed of the interface. Bandwidth is used by some routing protocols to influence the metric
frame-relay map *protocol* *protocol-address dlci* **[payloadcompress {packet-by-packet ¦ frf9 stac}]** **[broadcast] [ietf ¦ cisco]**	Interface	Statically defines a mapping between a network layer address and a DLCI
keepalive *sec*	Interface	Defines whether and how often LMI status enquiry messages are sent and expected
interface serial *num.sub* [*pointto-point ¦ multipoint*]	Global	Creates a subinterface or references a previously created subinterface
Frame-relay interface-dlci *dlci* **[ietf ¦ cisco]**	Interface	Defines a DLCI used for a VC to another DTE
Frame-relay payload-compress **{packet-by-packet ¦ frf9 stac}**	Interface subcommand	Defines payload compression on point-to-point subinterfaces
show interface	Exec	Shows physical interface status
show frame-relay {pvc ¦ map ¦ lmi}	Exec	Shows PVC status, mapping (dynamic and static), and LMI status
debug frame-relay {lmi ¦ events}	Exec	Lists messages describing LMI flows (LMI option). The events option lists inverse ARP information. Other options include lapf, information elements, ppp, and packet

The keyword ppp refers to the Point-to-Point Protocol, not the point-to-point subinterface type.

Example 1:

The first example of configuring Frame Relay discussed in this chapter does not use subinterfaces. See Figure 14.7 and Table 14.5. All default settings (IOS version 12.0) were used and are as follows:

- The LMI type is automatically sensed.
- The encapsulation is Cisco instead of IETF.
- PVC DLCIs are learned via LMI status messages.
- Inverse ARP is enabled (by default) and is triggered when the status message declaring that the VCs are up has been received.

Figure 14.7   A Full Mesh Frame Relay Network that Does Not Use Subinterfaces

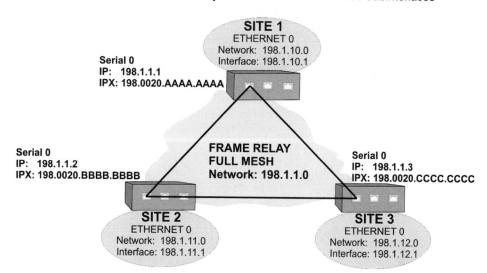

Table 14.5   Configuration of Routers Used in Figure 14.7

Site 1	Site 2	Site 3
ipx routing	ipx routing	ipx routing
0198.aaaa.aaaa	0198.bbbb.bbbb	0198.cccc.cccc
interface serial0	interface serial0	interface serial0
encapsulation frame-relay	encapsulation frame-relay	encapsulation frame-relay
ip address 198.1.1.1 255.255.255.0	ip address 198.1.1.2 255.255.255.0	ip address 198.1.1.3 255.255.255.0
ipx network 198	ipx network 198	ipx network 198
interface ethernet 0	interface ethernet 0	interface ethernet 0
ip address 198.1.10.1 255.255.255.0	ip address 198.1.11.2 255.255.255.0	ip address 198.1.12.3 255.255.255.0
ipx network 1	ipx network 2	ipx network 3
router igrp 1	router igrp 1	router igrp 1
network 198.1.1.0	network 198.1.1.0	network 198.1.1.0
network 198.1.10.0	network 198.1.11.0	network 198.1.12.0

In some cases, the default values will not be appropriate. For instance, if one router is not a Cisco router and does not support Cisco encapsulation, then IETF encapsulation would be required. Therefore, for the purpose of showing an alternate configuration, suppose that the following requirements were added:

- The Site 3 router requires IETF encapsulation on both VCs.
- Site 1's LMI type should be ANSI; LMI autosense should not be used.

Table 14.6 Modified Configuration of Routers Used in Figure 14.7

Site 1	Site 2	Site 3
ipx routing 0198.aaaa.aaaa interface serial0 encapsulation frame-relay frame-relay lmi-type ansi frame-relay interface-dlci 42 ietf ip address 198.1.1.1 255.255.255.0 ipx network 198 interface ethernet 0 ip address 198.1.10.1 255.255.255.0 ipx network 1 router igrp 1 network 198.1.1.0 network 198.1.10.0	*ipx routing* *0198.bbbb.bbbb* *interface serial0* *encapsulation frame-relay* *ip address 198.1.1.2 255.255.255.0* *ipx network 198* interface ethernet 0 ip address 198.1.11.2 255.255.255.0 ipx network 2 router igrp 1 network 198.1.1.0 network 198.1.11.0	ipx routing 0198.cccc.cccc interface serial0 encapsulation frame-relay ietf ip address 198.1.1.3 255.255.255.0 ipx network 198 interface ethernet 0 ip address 198.1.12.3 255.255.255.0 ipx network 3 router igrp 1 network 198.1.1.0 network 198.1.12.0

The encapsulation was changed in two different ways. Site 3 changed its encapsulation for both its PVCs with the `ietf` keyword on the encapsulation command. Site 1 could not change because only one of the two VCs to Site 1 was directed to use IETF encapsulation. In addition, Site 1 was forced to code the `frame-relay interface-dlci` command, coding the DLCI for the VC to Site 3. The `ietf` keyword was needed to change from the default encapsulation of Cisco (see Table 14.6).

The LMI configuration in Site 1 would have been fine without any changes because autosense would have recognized ANSI. However, by coding `frame-relay lmi-type ansi`, Site 1 is forced to use ANSI because this command disables autonegotiation of the LMI type. Site 1's `frame-relay interface-dlci` configuration would need to be modified like Site 1's for the VC from Site 2 to Site 3 so that the VC will use IETF encapsulation.

Example 2:

If you have a network that is not a fully meshed network, then you need to use point-to-point subinterfaces (see Figure 14.8 and Table 14.7). The `frame-relay interface-dlci` command is needed when using subinterfaces. This is because the status messages come into the physical interface stating that a VC with a particular DLCI is up; the IOS then needs to associate that VC with a subinterface.

Figure 14.8 Frame Relay on Cisco Routers Using Subinterfaces

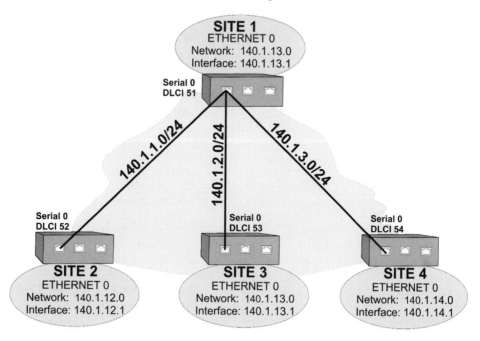

Table 14.7 IP and IPX Addresses for Figure 14.8

Router	DLCI	Subnet	IP address	IPX network	IPX address
Site 1	51	140.1.1.0/24	140.1.1.1	1	1.0200.aaaa.aaaa
Site 2	52	140.1.1.0/24	140.1.1.2	1	1.0200.bbbb.bbbb
Site 1	51	140.1.2.0/24	140.1.2.1	2	2.0200.aaaa.aaaa
Site 3	53	140.1.2.0/24	140.1.2.3	2	2.0200.cccc.cccc
Site 1	51	140.1.3.0/24	140.1.3.1	3	3.0200.aaaa.aaaa
Site 4	54	140.1.3.0/24	140.1.3.4	3	3.0200.dddd.dddd

The subinterface numbers in the configuration example happen to match on either end of the VCs. For example, Subinterface 2 was used in Site 1 for the PVC to Site 3. Site 3 also uses Subinterface 2. There is no requirement that the subinterface numbers be the same.

By using the `show frame-relay pvc` command, you can see useful management and troubleshooting information. The counters for each VC, including increments in the FECN and BECN counters, can be particularly useful. Likewise, comparing the packets/bytes sent with what is received on the other end of the VC is also quite useful because it reflects the number of packets/bytes lost inside the Frame Relay cloud. If the PVC shows as inactive instead of active, it would be a great place to start to troubleshoot a connection problem.

Table 14.8 Point-to-Point Configuration for Example 2

Site 1	Site 2	Site 3	Site 4
ipx routing	ipx routing	ipx routing	ipx routing
0200.aaaa.aaaa	0200.bbbb.bbbb	0200.cccc.cccc	0200.dddd.dddd
interface serial0	interface serial0	interface serial0	interface serial0
encapsulation	encapsulation	encapsulation	encapsulation
frame-relay	frame-relay	frame-relay	frame-relay
interface serial	interface serial	interface serial	interface serial
0.1 point-to-point	0.1 point-to-point	0.2 point-to-point	0.3 point-to-point
ip address	ip address	ip address	ip address
140.1.1.1	140.1.1.2	140.1.2.3	140.1.3.4
255.255.255.0	255.255.255.0	255.255.255.0	255.255.255.0
ipx network 1	ipx network 1	ipx network 2	ipx network 3
frame-relay	frame-relay	frame-relay	frame-relay
interface-dlci 52	interface-dlci 51	interface-dlci 51	interface-dlci 51
interface serial	interface	interface	interface
0.2 point-to-point	ethernet 0	ethernet 0	ethernet 0
ip address	140.1.12.2	140.1.13.2	140.1.14.2
140.1.2.1	255.255.255.0	255.255.255.0	255.255.255.0
255.255.255.0	ipx network 12	ipx network 13	ipx network 14
ipx network 2			
frame-relay			
interface-dlci 53			
interface serial			
0.3 point-to-point			
ip address			
140.1.3.1			
255.255.255.0			
ipx network 3			
frame-relay			
interface-dlci 54			
interface			
ethernet 0			
ip address			
140.1.11.1			
255.255.255.0			
ipx network 11			

The output of the show frame-relay map command displays the DLCI listings (see Figure 14.10). Notice that no Layer 3 address information is provided. Because the subinterfaces are point-to-point, IOS omitted this information.

The debug frame-relay lmi command shows an indication of both sending and receiving LMI enquiries (see Figure 14.11). The status message is sent by the switch, whereas the status inquiry is sent by the DTE (router). The IOS keepalive setting does not

Figure 14.9 Using the *show frame-relay pvc* Command

```
Atlanta#show frame-relay pvc
PVC Statistics for interface Serial0 (Frame Relay DTE)
DLCI = 52, DLCI USAGE = LOCAL, PVC STATUS = ACTIVE, INTERFACE = Serial0.1
input pkts 843            output pkts 876             in bytes 122723
out bytes 134431          dropped pkts 0              in FECN pkts 0
in BECN pkts 0            out FECN pkts 0             out BECN pkts 0
in DE pkts 0              out DE pkts 0
out bcast pkts 876        out bcast bytes 134431
pvc create time 05:20:10, last time pvc status changed 05:19:31
DLCI = 53, DLCI USAGE = LOCAL, PVC STATUS = ACTIVE, INTERFACE = Serial0.2

input pkts 0              output pkts 875             in bytes 0
out bytes 142417          dropped pkts 0              in FECN pkts 0
in BECN pkts 0            out FECN pkts 0             out BECN pkts 0
in DE pkts 0              out DE pkts 0
out bcast pkts 875        out bcast bytes 142417
pvc create time 05:19:51, last time pvc status changed 04:55:41
DLCI = 54, DLCI USAGE = LOCAL, PVC STATUS = ACTIVE, INTERFACE = Serial0.3

input pkts 10             output pkts 877             in bytes 1274
out bytes 142069          dropped pkts 0              in FECN pkts 0
in BECN pkts 0            out FECN pkts 0             out BECN pkts 0
in DE pkts 0              out DE pkts 0
out bcast pkts 877        out bcast bytes 142069
pvc create time 05:19:52, last time pvc status changed 05:17:42
```

Figure 14.10 Using the *show frame-relay map* Command for Example 2

```
Atlanta#show frame-relay map
Serial0.3 (up): point-to-point dlci, dlci 54(0x36,0xC60), broadcast
          status defined, active
Serial0.2 (up): point-to-point dlci, dlci 53(0x35,0xC50), broadcast
          status defined, active
Serial0.1 (up): point-to-point dlci, dlci 52(0x34,0xC40), broadcast
          status defined, active
```

Figure 14.11   Using the *debug frame-relay lmi* Command

```
Atlanta#debug frame-relay lmi
Frame Relay LMI debugging is on
Displaying all Frame Relay LMI data

Serial0(out): StEnq, myseq 163, yourseen 161, DTE up
datagramstart = 0x45AED8, datagramsize = 13
FR encap = 0xFCF10309
00 75 01 01 01 03 02 A3 A1

Serial0(in): Status, myseq 163
RT IE 1, length 1, type 1
KA IE 3, length 2, yourseq 162, myseq 163
```

cause packets to flow between routers, rather it causes the router to send LMI messages to the switch. It also causes the router to expect LMI messages from the switch.

Example 3:

This last sample network uses both types of subinterfaces. Router A is the only router using both multipoint and point-to-point subinterfaces (see Figure 14.12 and Table 14.9). On the route of Site 1's serial 0.1 interface, multipoint is in use, with DLCIs for the routers at Site 2 and Site 3 listed. On Site 1's other two subinterfaces, which are point-to-point, only a single DLCI needs to be listed. In fact, only one `frame-relay interface-dlci` command is allowed on a point-to-point subinterface because only one VC is allowed. Otherwise, the configurations between the two types are similar (see Tables 14.10 and 14.11).

No mapping statements were required for the configuration because Inverse ARP is enabled on the multipoint subinterfaces by default. The point-to-point subinterfaces do not require mapping statements because after the outgoing subinterface is identified, there is only one possible router to forward the frame to. The show frame-relay map command shows the mapping (see Figure 14.13).

If Inverse ARP was not used at all on any of the three routers, you would have to use the following frame-relay map statements on Router A.

```
frame-relay map ip 140.1.1.2 502 broadcast
frame-relay map ip 140.1.1.3 503 broadcast
frame-relay map ipx 1.0200.bbbb.bbbb 502 broadcast
frame-relay map ipx 1.0200.cccc.cccc 503 broadcast
```

Similar commands would have been required on Routers B and C.

Figure 14.12   Example 3 Using Multipoint and Point-to-Point Connections

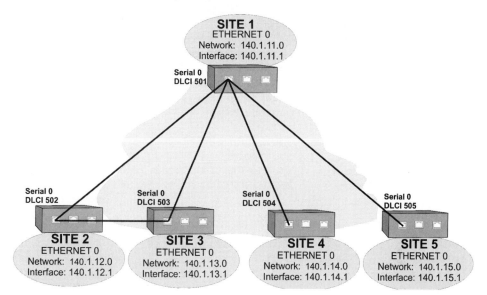

Table 14.9   IP and IPX Addresses for Figure 14.12

	Subnet	IP address	IPX network	IPX address	Subinterface type
Site 1	140.1.1.0/24	140.1.1.1	1	1.0200.aaaa.aaaa	Multipoint
Site 2	140.1.1.0/24	140.1.1.2	1	1.0200.bbbb.bbbb	Multipoint
Site 3	140.1.1.0/24	140.1.1.3	1	1.0200.cccc.cccc	Multipoint
Site 1	140.1.2.0/24	140.1.2.1	2	2.0200.aaaa.aaaa	Point-to-point
Site 4	140.1.2.0/24	140.1.2.4	2	2.0200.dddd.dddd	Point-to-point
Site 1	140.1.3.0/24	140.1.3.1	3	3.0200.aaaa.aaaa	Point-to-point
Site 5	140.1.3.0/24	140.1.3.5	3	3.0200.eeee.eeee	Point-to-point

14.8   CONFIGURING ATM

The first task in configuring ATM is to enable the ATM interface. Then you must configure at least one PVC or SVC. The VCs that you configure must match in three places: (1) On the router, (2) on the ATM switch, and (3) at the remote end of the PVC or SVC connection.

Enabling the ATM interface is done by changing into Global Configuration mode followed by changing into Interface mode. To change into Interface mode, you will use one of the following commands:

```
RouterHostName(config)#interface atm slot/0
RouterHostName(config)#interface atm slot/port-adapter/0
RouterHostName(config)#interface atm number
```

Table 14.10   Multipoint Connections Configuration for Example 3

Site 1	Site 2	Site 3
hostname RouterA ipx routing 0200.aaaa.aaaa interface serial0 encapsulation frame-relay interface serial 0.1 multipoint ip address 140.1.1.1 255.255.255.0 ipx network 1 frame-relay interface-dlci 502 frame-relay interface-dlci 503 interface serial 0.2 point-to-point ip address 140.1.2.1 255.255.255.0 ipx network 2 frame-relay interface-dlci 504 interface serial 0.3 point-to-point ip address 140.1.3.1 255.255.255.0 ipx network 3 frame-relay interface-dlci 505 interface ethernet 0 ip address 140.1.11.1 255.255.255.0 ipx network 11	hostname RouterB ipx routing 0200.bbbb.bbbb interface serial0 encapsulation frame-relay interface serial 0.1 multipoint ip address 140.1.1.2 255.255.255.0 ipx network 1 frame-relay interface-dlci 501 frame-relay interface-dlci 503 interface ethernet 0 ip address 140.1.12.2 255.255.255.0 ipx network 12	hostname RouterC ipx routing 0200.cccc.cccc interface serial0 encapsulation frame-relay interface serial 0.1 multipoint ip address 140.1.1.3 255.255.255.0 ipx network 1 frame-relay interface-dlci 501 frame-relay interface-dlci 502 interface ethernet 0 ip address 140.1.13.3 255.255.255.0 ipx network 13

Use the `interface atm slot/0` command with the AIP on Cisco 7500 series routers, any ATM port adapter on the Cisco 7200 series routers, and the port 1 ATM-25 network module on the Cisco 2600 and 3600 series routers. Use the `interface atm slot/port-adapter/0` command with any ATM port adapter on the Cisco 7500 series routers. Use the `interface atm number` command with the NPM on the Cisco 4500 and 4700 routers. Use `interface atm 0` on the Cisco MC3810.

Table 14.11   Point-to-point Connections Configuration for Example 3

Site 4	Site 5
hostname RouterD ipx routing 0200.dddd.dddd interface serial0 encapsulation frame-relay interface serial 0.1 point-to-point ip address 140.1.2.4 255.255.255.0 ipx network 2 frame-relay interface-dlci 501 interface ethernet 0 ip address 140.1.14.4 255.255.255.0 ipx network 14	hostname RouterE ipx routing 0200.eeee.eeee interface serial0 encapsulation frame-relay interface serial 0.1 point-to-point ip address 140.1.3.5 255.255.255.0 ipx network 3 frame-relay interface-dlci 501 interface ethernet 0 ip address 140.1.15.5 255.255.255.0 ipx network 15

Figure 14.13   Using the *show frame-relay map* Command for Example 3

```
RouterC#show frame-relay map
Serial0.10 (up): ip 140.1.1.1 dlci 501(0x1F5,0x7C50), dynamic,
broadcast,, status defined, active
Serial0.10 (up): ip 140.1.1.2 dlci 502(0x1F6,0x7C60), dynamic,
broadcast,, status defined, active
Serial0.10 (up): ipx 1.0200.aaaa.aaaa dlci 501(0x1F5,0x7C50),
dynamic, broadcast,, status defined, active
Serial0.10 (up): ipx 1.0200.bbbb.bbbb dlci 502(0x1F6,0x7C60),
dynamic, broadcast,, status defined, active
```

If IP routing is enabled on the system, assign a source IP address and subnet mask to the interface:

```
ip address ip-address mask
```

To enable the ATM interface, use the following command in Interface Configuration mode, which begins the segmentation and reassembly operation on the interface:

```
RouterHostName(config-if)#no shutdown
```

To create a PVC on the ATM interface and enter Interface-ATM-VC configuration mode, use the following command beginning in Interface Configuration mode:

```
pvc [name] vpi/vci [ilmi | qsaal | smds]
```

For example, if you want to assign the vpi of *1,* the vci of *40,* and the name of *cisco,* you would use the following command:

```
RouterHostName(config-if)#pvc cisco 1/40
RouterHostName(config-if-atm-vc)#
```

You would then be in Interface-ATM-VC Configuration mode. To exit the Interface-ATM-VC mode, you would use the exit command. Once you specify a name for a PVC, you can reenter the Interface-ATM-VC Configuration mode by simply entering pvc *name.*

The ATM interface supports a static mapping scheme that identifies the network address of remote hosts or routers. To map a protocol address to a PVC, use the following command in Interface-ATM-VC Configuration mode:

```
protocol protocol protocol-address [[no] broadcast]
```

For example,

```
protocol ip 1.1.1.5 broadcast
```

will assign the IP address of 1.1.1.5 and it will forward broadcasts.

To configure the AAL and encapsulation type, use the following command beginning in Interface-ATM-VC Configuration mode:

```
encapsulation aal5encap
```

The encapsulation types are:

- **auto**—For PPP over ATM SVCs only. The *auto* keyword enables an ATM SVC to use either aal5snap or aal5mux encapsulation.
- **ciscoppp**—For Cisco PPP over ATM. Supported on ATM PVCs only
- **mux Apollo**—For a MUX-type VC using the Apollo protocol
- **mux appletalk**—For a MUX-type VC using the AppleTalk protocol
- **mux decent**—For a MUX-type VC using the DECnet protocol
- **mux frame-relay**—For a MUX-type VC for Frame Relay-ATM Network Interworking (FRF.5) on the Cisco MC3810
- **mux fr-atm-srv**—For a MUX-type VC for Frame Relay-ATM Service Interworking (FRF.8) on the Cisco MC3810
- **mux ip**—For a MUX-type VC using the IP protocol
- **mux ipx**—For a MUX-type VC using the IPX protocol
- **mux ppp**—For a MUX-type VC running IETF-compliant PPP over ATM. You must use the virtual template number argument to identify the virtual template.

For more information on configuring ATM on Cisco routers, visit the following website: http://www.cisco.com/univercd/cc/td/doc/product/software/ios122/122cgcr/fwan_c/wcf atm.htm

14.9   TROUBLESHOOTING SERIAL LINE CONNECTIVITY

When troubleshooting serial line problems, Cisco routers provide some commands. They include:

- `show interfaces serial`—The *show interfaces serial* command shows if the serial link is up or down and if the line protocol is up or down. In addition, it will show you the number of dropped packets and the number of CRC errors
- `show controllers`—The show controllers output indicates the state of the interface channels and whether a cable is attached to the interface and the type of cable. In addition, if it cannot identify the type of electrical interface, it may suggest a hardware failure, an improperly connected cable, or a failed cable
- `debug`—The output of the various debug commands provide diagnostic information relating to protocol status and network activity for many internetworking events
- `ping` and `Traceroute`—Used to verify TCP/IP configuration and connectivity.

For more information on troubleshooting serial line problems, see the following websites:

http://www.cisco.com/warp/public/112/chapter15.htm
http://www.cisco.com/univercd/cc/td/doc/cisintwk/itg_v1/tr1915.htm
http://www.cisco.com/warp/public/112/chapter15.pdf

SUMMARY

1. Cisco routers support a wide range of WAN protocols using the serial port.
2. The serial interface will usually be attached to a CSU/DSU type device that provides clocking for the line.
3. If you want to connect two CSU/DSUs back-to-back so that you practice with it in a lab environment, one of the CSU/DSUs must act as a DCE.
4. The show controllers command displays information about the physical interface itself.
5. To access ISDN with a Cisco router, your router needs to have a built-in NT1 (U reference point) or an ISDN modem (called a TA). If your router has a BRI interface (RJ-45 connection specifically designated for a BRI ISDN), you just connect the

ISDN cable to the router. If not, you can use the router's serial interface.
6. The SPIDs are like phone numbers that identify your individual connection. To configure your SPIDs for your router, you would use the `isdn spid1` and `isdn spid2` interface command.
7. DDR is used to allow two or more Cisco routers to dial an ISDN dial-up connection on an as-needed basis. DDR is only used for low-volume, periodic network connections using either a PSTN or ISDN.
8. When enabling Frame Relay on Cisco routers, you need to specify it as an encapsulation on serial interfaces.
9. The first task in configuring ATM is to enable the ATM interface. Then you must configure at least one PVC or SVC.

QUESTIONS

1. What parameters are required in a Frame Relay map command?
   a. two IP addresses; one for each end of the connection
   b. two data-link connection identifiers; one for each end of the connection
   c. an IP address and a data-link connection identifier
   d. a data-link connection identifier and an encapsulation type

2. Which of following commands should be used to define a point-to-point Frame Relay subinterface using DLCI number 24 as its serial interface number?
   a. int s0.24 point-to-point
   b. int s0 point-to-point 24
   c. int s0.24 ppp
   d. int s0 ppp 24

3. Which of the following commands displays active Frame Relay connections on a Cisco router and displays traffic statistics across those connections?
   a. show frame-relay lmi
   b. show frame-relay map
   c. show frame-relay pvc
   d. show interfaces serial

4. Which of the following prompt and command pairs best represents the mode and command that should be used to configure PPP on serial interface s0 for the Cisco router named ROUTER_A?
   a. ROUTER_A#ppp encapsulation
   b. ROUTER_A(config-if)#ppp encapsulation
   c. ROUTER_A#encapsulation ppp
   d. ROUTER_A(config-if)#encapsulation ppp

5. You are configuring Frame Relay between two Cisco routers on an IP internetwork. What process do you use to relate the Layer 3 addresses to the corresponding Layer 2 addresses without relying on an automated process?
   a. inverse ARP
   b. Cisco encapsulation
   c. mapping
   d. IETF encapsulation

6. Which of the following prompt and command pairs best represents the mode and command

that should be used to verify PPP encapsulation on serial interface s1 for the Cisco router HostA?
   a. HostA#show interface s1
   b. HostA#encapsulation ppp
   c. HostA(config-if)#show interface s1
   d. HostA(config-if)#encapsulation ppp

7. Your company is using Frame Relay that connects to Cisco Routers running the Cisco Internetworking Operating System Release 11.2. How does a Frame Relay switch notify routers that the route is congested? (Select all choices that are correct.)
   a. by setting the FECN bit in a Frame Relay packet to any devices receiving the frame
   b. by setting the BECN bit in a Frame Relay packet to any devices receiving the frame
   c. by setting the BECN bit in a Frame Relay packet to the source router
   d. by setting the FECN bit in a Frame Relay packet to the source router

8. You are using PPP to encapsulate multiple protocols on a dial-in asynchronous connection to your network. You have selected Challenge Handshake Authentication Protocol (CHAP) for authentication security. You want to view the exchange sequence to understand how it works through your router. Which of the following commands allows your router to display the CHAP communication?
   a. ppp authentication chap
   b. encapsulation ppp
   c. debug ppp authentication
   d. ppp chap password *password*

9. You are using Frame Relay between branch offices in remote cities. Your local Cisco router is running version 11.2 of the IOS. Which LMI message type should you configure between your router and the Frame Relay switch?
   a. Q.933A   b. ANSI
   c. IETF   d. Cisco
   e. let the router autodetect

10. You connect two Cisco routers with a DTE/DCE cable to simulate a WAN connection. You want to provide clocking at a rate of 64 Kbps. What com-

mand should you use on the router that is acting as a DCE device to accomplish this task?

a. clock rate 64000
b. bandwidth 64000
c. clock rate 64
d. bandwidth 64

11. What is the default LMI message type for Cisco routers?

a. ANSI　　　　　　b. Q.933A
c. Cisco　　　　　　d. IETF

12. Your manager has given you the task of connecting the Cisco routers in several branch offices to a Frame Relay service provider. Your service provider uses StarNet routers to provide this service. Which encapsulation type should you configure the Cisco routers to use?

a. Cisco　　　　　　b. Q.933A
c. IETF　　　　　　d. ANSI

13. What is the default Cisco encapsulation protocol for synchronous serial links?

a. Cisco　　　　　　b. IETF
c. HDLC　　　　　　d. PPP

14. Which of the following prompt and command pairs best represents the mode and command that should be used to enable CHAP authentication on serial interface s0 for the Cisco router named ROUTER_A?

a. ROUTER_A#authentication chap
b. ROUTER_A(config-if)#authentication chap
c. ROUTER_A#ppp authentication chap
d. ROUTER_A(config-if)#ppp authentication chap

15. Once you have defined interesting traffic with the *dialer-list* command, you then must associate an ISDN phone number with the next hop router address. Which IOS command should you use?

a. isdn destination number
b. isdn spid1
c. dialer map
d. isdn line number

16. Which of the following are considered ISDN benefits? (Choose four.)

a. Full time connectivity across the ISDN supported by Cisco IOS routing using DDR.
b. Small office and home office sites can be economically supported with ISDN BRI services.

c. ISDN replaces ss7 in the PSTN backbone.
d. ISDN can be used as a backup service for a lease line connection between remote office and the central office.
e. Modem racking and cabling can be eliminated by integration with digital modem cards on a Cisco IOS NAS.

17. Your company is having trouble connecting a Cisco router to a Nortel router using Frame Relay. What is the default encapsulation type for Frame Relay on a Cisco router?

a. HDLC　　　　　　b. IETF
c. ANSI　　　　　　d. PPP
e. Cisco

18. Cisco supports three different LMI types for Frame Relay. Which of the following are the three LMI types? (Choose three.)

a. IETF　　　　　　b. Q933A
c. CISCO　　　　　　d. Q931
e. IEEE　　　　　　f. ANSI

19. Which show commands can you use to identify the local DLCI number? (Choose two.)

a. Show frame-relay local-dlci
b. Show frame-relay dlci
c. Show ip route
d. Show frame-relay pvc
e. Show frame-relay map

20. When setting up Frame Relay for point-to-point subinterfaces, you enter the following configuration:

```
Router(config)#int s0/0
Router(config-if)#ip address
10.39.0.1 255.255.0.0
Router(config-if)#encapsulation
frame-relay
Router(config-if)#interface
s0/0.39 point-to-point
Router(config-if)#frame-relay
interface-dlci 139
Router(config-if)#exit
Router(config)#exit
Router#copy run start
```

Which of the following must not be configured?

a. The Frame Relay encapsulation on the physical interface.
b. The local DLCI on each subinterface.

c. An IP address on the physical interface.

d. The subinterface type as point-to-point.

21. You are configuring an old router that is running an old IOS that does not support inverse ARP. If a router does not support inverse ARP, how can you set up this Frame Relay connection?

a. Configure static maps.

b. Define an IP address.

c. Disable DHCP on the Frame Relay router.

d. Configure a static route to the remote network.

22. Pat is having trouble configuring Frame Relay subinterfaces. You decide to send Pat an e-mail explaining some of the installation procedures. Which of the following should you include in your e-mail? (Choose three.)

a. Each subinterface is configured either multipoint or point-to-point.

b. Any network address must be removed from the physical interface.

c. The configuration of subinterfaces is done in router Config-(if)# mode.

d. Frame Relay encapsulation must be configured on each subinterface.

23. You need to create a subinterface so that you can support different Frame-Relay encapsulations. Which command specifies a second subinterface on serial interface zero?

a. interface s 0.2 point - to point

b. interface 2 s 0 point to point

c. subinterface 2 s 0 point to point

d. interface 0 sub 2 point to point

e. interface s 0.1 point to point sub 2

24. Frame Relay uses _____ to define the rate, in bits per second, that the Frame Relay switch agrees to transfer data?

a. CR   b. CIR

c. LMI   d. DLCI

e. CRMI

25. You are trying to determine if the connection between your router and the Frame Relay switch is good. Which show command should you use to view Frame Relay LMI traffic statistics?

a. show lmi

b. show interface

c. show frame-relay lmi

d. show ip route

e. show statistics

26. Which command is used to set the bandwidth metric of a Frame Relay connection?

a. Router(Config)# clock rate 56

b. Router(Config-if)# bandwidth 56

c. Router(Config)# bandwidth 56000

d. Router(Config-if)# clock rate 56000

27. When troubleshooting Frame Relay peer problems between two routers, which two commands should you use to show the routers that are reachable? (Choose two.)

a. show IP map

b. show IP route

c. show frame-relay map

d. debug frame-relay map

28. In troubleshooting a Frame Relay link on serial 0/2, which command displays the LMI, DLCI, and bandwidth for that link?

a. show interface serial 0/2

b. show frame-relay serial 0/2

c. show protocol frame-relay serial 0/2

d. show serial 0/2 encapsulation frame-relay

29. Which command verifies encapsulation as well as IP addresses and MAC addresses on a router configured for Frame Relay?

a. show IP   b. show statistics

c. show interface   d. show frame-relay

30. In your test environment, you are connecting two routers together using a back-to-back serial cable. You are not using DSU/CSUs between these devices. Which additional command must be used to be able to establish this connection between these two routers on the router acting as the DCE?

a. serial up   b. clock rate

c. dte rate   d. line protocol up

e. dce rate

31. Consider Frame Relay multipoint subinterfaces. Which is a valid statement?

a. An IP address is required on the physical interface of the central router.

b. All routers are required to be fully meshed.

c. All routers must be in the same subnet to forward routing updates and broadcasts.

d. Multipoint is the default configuration for Frame Relay subinterfaces.

CHAPTER 15

Configuring Routing on Cisco Routers

Topics Covered in this Chapter

Introduction

You have been introduced to routers, the various routing protocols, and the basics of Cisco routers. You have enabled the TCP/IP and IPX protocols and you know how to connect the various interfaces. You are ready to enable the various routing protocols on Cisco routers.

Objectives

- Enable the various routing protocols including RIP, IGRP, and OSPF on a Cisco router.
- Enable static routes on a Cisco router.
- Troubleshoot routing problems on Cisco routers.

15.1   CONFIGURING STATIC IP ROUTING

Static routing occurs when an administrator manually adds routes in each router's routing table. There are both benefits and disadvantages to static routing, as there are for all routing processes. Static routing has the following benefits:

- no overhead on the router CPU
- no bandwidth usage between routers
- security (because the administrator only allows routing to certain networks)

Static routing has the following disadvantages:

- The administrator must understand the internetwork and how each router is connected to configure the routes correctly.
- If one network is added to the internetwork, the administrator must add a route to it on all routers.
- It's not feasible in large networks because it would be a full-time job.

The command used to add a static route to a routing table is:

```
      ip route [destination_network] [mask] [next_hop_address
or exitinterface] [administrative_distance] [permanent]
```

- destination_network—The network you are placing in the routing table
- mask—The subnet mask being used on the network
- next hop address—The address of the next hop router that will receive the packet and forward it to the remote network. This is a router interface that is on a directly-connected network. You must be able to ping the router interface before you add the route. If you type in the wrong next hop address, or the interface to that router

is done, the static route will show up in the configuration of the router but not in the routing table.

- exit_interface—Used in place of the next hop address (if desired). Must be a point-to-point link such as a WAN. This command does not work on a LAN, such as Ethernet.
- Administrative_distance—By default, static routes have an administrative distance of 1. You can change the default value by adding an administrative weight at the end of the command.
- Permanent—If the interface is shut down or the router cannot communicate to the next hop router, the route is automatically discarded from the routing table. Choosing the permanent option keeps the entry in the routing table no matter what happens.

If you want to configure a static IP route for the 172.2.5.0 network with a subnet mask of 255.255.255.0, you would send it through the interface assigned the 168.1.4.2 IP address.

```
ip route 172.2.5.0 255.255.255.0 168.1.4.2
```

After the router is configured, you can type show running-config and show ip route to see the static routes. Remember that if the routes don't appear in the routing table, it is because the route cannot communicate with the next hop address you configured. You can use the *permanent* parameter to keep the route in the route table even if the next hop device cannot be contacted.

Default routing is used to send packets that have a remote destination network not found in the routing table to the next hop router. You can only use default routing on stub networks—networks that have only one exit port out of the network.

To configure a default route, you use wildcards in the network address and mask locations of a static route. To add a default route, you would type the following command:

```
ip route 0.0.0.0 0.0.0.0 next_hop_address
```

For example, to send packets out to the 168.1.4.2 as the default interface, you would type:

```
ip route 0.0.0.0 0.0.0.0 168.1.4.2
```

To remove a static IP address, you would use the following command:

```
no ip route [destination_network] [mask]
[next_hop_address]
```

Therefore, to remove the previous route that was shown:

```
ip route 172.2.5.0 255.255.255.0 168.1.4.2
```

you would use the following command:

```
no ip route 172.2.5.0 255.255.255.0 168.1.4.2
```

Default routing is used to send packets that have a remote destination network not found in the routing table to the next hop router. You can only use default routing on stub networks—networks that have only one exit port out of the network. By using a default route, you would delete any existing static routes from the router and then add one static route:

```
ip route 0.0.0.0 0.0.0.0 168.1.4.2
```

Figure 15.1   Using the *show ip* Route Command with No Routing Protocol Connections

```
Router#sh ip route
Codes: C - connected, S - static, I - IGRP, R - RIP, M - mobile, B - BGP
       D - EIGRP, EX - EIGRP external, O - OSPF, IA - OSPF inter area
       N1 - OSPF NSSA external type 1, N2 - OSPF NSSA external type 2
       E1 - OSPF external type 1, E2 - OSPF external type 2, E - EGP
       i - IS-IS, L1 - IS-IS level-1, L2 - IS-IS level-2, * - candidate default
       U - per-user static route, o - ODR

Gateway of last resort is not set

Router#
```

To show the routing table on a router, you use the show *ip route* command (see Figure 15.1).

All Cisco routers are classful routers, which means that they expect a default subnet mask on each interface on the router. When a router receives a packet for a destination subnet not found in the routing table, it will drop the packet by default. If you are using default routing, you must use the `ip classless` command because no remote subnets will be in the routing table. Recent versions of the IOS have the command on by default. If you are using default routing and this command is not in your configuration, you will need to add it.

15.2   CONFIGURING ROUTING PROTOCOLS

The first task in configuring router-to-router traffic is to assign a routing protocol. Table 15.1 lists the routing protocols that you can set up on your router. Each of the routing protocols in Table 15.1 requires additional information to complete its setup on the router. The most common protocol you will use is RIP. However, in some specific situations you many need to use static routes.

This book will focus on establishing static routes, configuring RIP, and configuring the IGRP protocol. If you would like to learn more on establishing other routing protocols, refer to following websites:

Configuring IP Routing Protocols

http://www.cisco.com/univercd/cc/td/doc/product/software/ios11/cbook/ciproute.htm

Configuring OSPF

http://www.cisco.com/univercd/cc/td/doc/product/software/ios121/121cgcr/ip_c/ipcprt2/1cdospf.htm

Table 15.1 Routing Protocols Used on Cisco Routers

Protocol	Configuration keyword
BGP	bgp
EGP	egp
EIGRP	eigrp
IGRP	igrp
ISO IS-IS	isis
IGRP for OSI Networks	iso-igrp
Mobile routes	mobile
On demand stub routes	odr
OSPF	ospf
RIP	rip
Static routes	static
Traffic-engineered routes	traffic-engineering

Configuring BGP

http://www.cisco.com/univercd/cc/td/doc/product/software/ios113ed/113ed_cr/
np1_c/1cbgp.htm

15.2.1 Configuring the RIP Protocol

RIP is configured with the command `router rip` in Global Configuration mode. After entering the command, the attached network must be defined with the network network-number command:

```
RouterHostName(config)#router rip

RouterHostName(config)#network 168.1.1.0
```

If the router is connected to more than one network, the additional networks also need to be entered. Each network is entered in the same format as the first network. After all networks have been configured, the router is configured and has permission to send routing updates (called advertisements) to other RIP routers associated with each attached network.

To view a router's RIP information, you can use any of the following three commands:

- `Show ip protocol`—This command displays information about routing timers and the network information associated with the entire router. This is a valuable command when attempting to identify a router sending faulty routing information.

- `Show ip route`—This command displays the entire contents of the IP routing table in the RIP router, including codes that indicate how the router learned about each path.
- `debug ip rip`—This command displays RIP routing updates as they come into and are sent out of the router, including information about the interface through which an update arrives. You must be in Privileged Exec mode to use this command.

15.2.2 Configuring the IGRP Protocol

To configure IGRP on a router, you must be in Global Configuration mode. To configure the router, enter the command `router igrp autonomous system number`, where the autonomous system number (ASN) is a globally unique number used to identify your internetwork:

```
router igrp 232
```

After entering this command, you must associate the *network number* (IP address) of all connected networks to the router using the `network network-number` command:

```
network 168.1.1.0
```

This command must be repeated for each network connected to the router in which you want to establish an IGRP link.

After your router is configured for IGRP, you can view the information associated with IRGP functions by entering the following commands:

- `show ip protocols`—Displays parameters, filters, and network information for all networks configured on the router (see Figure 15.2).
- `show ip interfaces`—Displays the status and global parameters associated with available interfaces (see Figure 15.3).
- `show ip route`—Displays the entire contents of the IP routing table contained in the IRGP and RIP router, including codes that indicate how the router learned about each path (see Figure 15.4).
- `debug ip igrp transaction` and `debug ip igrp events`—The debug commands display similar information about transactions and events occurring on the specified networks.

The show commands can be entered from User Exec mode, but the debug commands must be entered from Privileged Exec mode.

15.2.3 Configuring OSPF

The following commands are needed to configure OSPF:

```
RouterHostName(config)#router ospf process_id
RouterHostName(config-router)#network network
wildcard_mask area area-id
```

Figure 15.2 Using the *show ip protocol* Command

```
Router#sh ip route
RouterHostName#show ip protocol
Routing Protocol is "IGRP 10"
    Sending updates every 90 seconds, next due in 55 seconds
    Invalid after 270 seconds, hold down 280, flushed after 630
    Outgoing update filter list for all interfaces is not set
    Incoming update filter list for all interfaces is not set
    Default networks flagged in outgoing updates
    Default networks accepted from incoming updates
    IGRP metric weight K1=1, K2=0, K3=1, K4=0, K5=0
    IGRP maximum hopcount 100
    IGRP maximum metric variance 1
    Redistributing: IGRP 10
    Routing for Networks:
         200.100.0.0
    Routing Information Sources:
         Gateway Distance Last Update
         200.100.20.2 100 0:00:05
    Distance: (default is 100)
```

Figure 15.3 Using the *show ip interface* Command

```
RTR#show ip interface
Ethernet0 is up, line protocol is up
          Internet address is 100.200.50.1 255.255.255.0
          Broadcast address is 255.255.255.255
          Address determined by non-volatile memory
          MTU is 1500 bytes
          Helper address is not set
Directed broadcast forwarding is enabled
          Outgoing access list is not set
          Inbound access list is not set
          Proxy ARP is enabled
          Security level is default
          Split Horizon is enabled
          ICMP redirects are always sent
              ICMP unreachables are always sent
 ICMP masks are never sent
              IP fast switching is enabled
              IP fast switching on the same interface is disabled
          IP SSE switching is disabled
          Router Discovery is disabled
          IP output packet accounting is disabled
          TCP/IP header compression is disabled
          Probe proxy name replies are disabled
```

Figure 15.4   Using the *show ip route igrp* Command

```
RTR#show ip interface
RouterHostName#show ip route igrp
200.100.0.0     255.255.255.0 is subnetted,    4 subnets
I    200.100.50.0 [100/11828] via 200.100.20.2, 00:00:55, Serial0
I    200.100.40.0 [100/11828] via 200.100.20.2, 00:00:55, Serial0
I    200.100.30.0 [100/11828] via 200.100.20.2, 00:00:55, Serial0
```

Figure 15.5   A Basic Multiarea OSPF Scenario

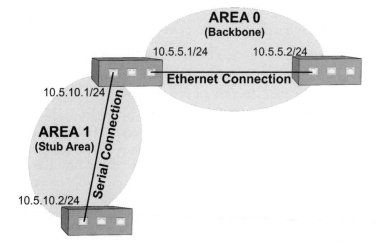

The *process_id* is a number used to distinguish one OSPF process from another OSPF process that might be running on a router. It is not recommended to run more than one OSPF process on a router because of the overhead required to support OSPF. Process IDs do not need to be the same on routers within the same OSPF network. The *network* specifies which attached router interfaces will run OSPF. *Wildcard_mask* is used to specify the network and *area-id* is just a number used to identify the OSPF area.

As an example, review Figure 15.5 and the accompanying configuration. The relevant OSPF configuration on Router R1, which is both an ABR and a backbone router, would be as follows:

```
R1(config)# router ospf 1
R1(config-router)# network 10.5.5.0 0.0.0.255 area 0
R1(config-router)# network 10.5.10.1 0.0.0.0 area 1
```

A wildcard mask of 0.0.0.0 can be used to identify a specific interface instead of a less-specific wildcard mask such as 0.0.0.255. The result is the same, as both the e0 and s0 interfaces participate in the OSPF process on this router.

To configure an OSPF stub area, the following command needs to be entered in OSPF Process Router Configuration mode on all routers within the stub area:

```
RouterHostName(config-router)#area area-id stub
```

To configure a totally stubby area, the following command needs to be entered only on the ABR that is connected to the totally stubby area:

```
RouterHostName(config-router)#area area-id stub no-summary
```

Router R1's relevant OSPF configuration is as follows:

```
R1(config)#router ospf 32
R1(config-router)#network 10.5.5.0 0.0.0.255 area 0
R1(config-router)#network 10.5.10.0 0.0.0.255 area 1
R1(config-router)#area 1 stub
```

Router R3's relevant OSPF configuration is as follows:

```
R3(config)#router ospf 57
R3(config-router)#network 10.5.10.0 0.0.0.255 area 1
R3(config-router)#area 1 stub
```

To configure Area 1 as a totally stubby area, R3 would have the same configuration as in the stub area case but R1's configuration would change slightly. The following shows the relevant configuration needed on R1 to configure Area 1 as a totally stubby area.

```
R1(config)#router ospf 32
R1(config-router)#network 10.5.5.0 0.0.0.255 area 0
R1(config-router)#network 10.5.10.0 0.0.0.255 area 1
R1(config-router)#area 1 stub no-summary
```

Notice that the only change to R1's configuration is the addition of the keyword *no-summary* to the *area stub* command.

To configure a virtual link, the following command must be entered in Router Configuration mode on both routers forming the link:

```
RouterHostName(config-router)#area area-id virtual-link router-id
```

The router ID is the router ID of the other router with which the virtual link is being formed. Figure 15.6 provides an example of a case where a virtual link is needed.

In the case shown in Figure 15.6, Area 2 does not have a physical connection to the backbone Area 0. Thus, a virtual link is needed to connect Area 2 to the backbone area. The following configuration shows the relevant commands needed on Routers R3 and R1 to form the virtual link.

R3's configuration:

```
R3(config)#router ospf 15
R3(config-router)#network 10.5.6.1 0.0.0.0 area 2
R3(config-router)#network 10.5.10.2 0.0.0.0 area 1
R3(config-router)#area 1 virtual-link 10.5.10.1
```

Figure 15.6   Area 2 is Connected to the Backbone by Using a Virtual Link (Area 1)

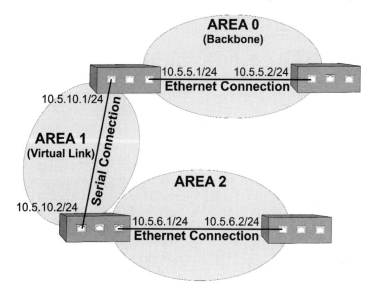

R1's configuration:

```
R1(config)#router ospf 23
R1(config-router)#network 10.5.5.1 0.0.0.0 area 0
R1(config-router)#network 10.5.10.1 0.0.0.0 area 1
R1(config-router)#area1 virtual-link 10.5.10.2
```

The Cisco IOS provides numerous show and debug commands for troubleshooting OSPF. Some useful show commands specific to OSPF are:

- show ip ospf neighbor detail—Displays a list of neighbor routers and their states
- show ip ospf database—Displays the contents of an OSPF database, the router-ID, and the process ID
- show ip ospf interface—Shows the areas to which interfaces have been assigned

As for debug commands, there is really just one that has many options:

- debug ip ospf—Provides many optional keywords for debugging OSPF operation

15.3   MONTORING TCP/IP ON CISCO ROUTERS

Once you think you have everything completed on the routers, there are some commands that can be used to verify their configurations. To view the IP routing tables created on a Cisco router, use the Privileged mode command show ip route (see Figure 15.7).

The show protocol command is useful because it shows you the network layer addresses configured on each interface (see Figure 15.8).

Figure 15.7 Using the *show ip route* Command with Active Connections

```
RouterHostName#show ip route
Codes: C - connected, S - static, I - IGRP, R - RIP, M - mobile, B - BGP
D - EIGRP, EX - EIGRP external, O - OSPF, IA - OSPF inter area
N1 - OSPF NSSA external type 1, N2 - OSPF NSSA external type 2
E1 - OSPF external type 1, E2 - OSPF external type 2, E - EGP
i - IS-IS, L1 - IS-IS level-1, L2 - IS-IS level-2, * - candidate default
U - per-user static route, o - ODR

Gateway of last resort is not set

     134.141.0.0/24 is subnetted, 6 subnets
C       134.141.2.0 is directly connected, TokenRing0
R       134.141.3.0 [120/1] via 134.141.23.3, 00:00:15, Serial1
R       134.141.1.0 [120/1] via 134.141.12.1, 00:00:20, Serial0
C       134.141.12.0 is directly connected, Serial0
R       134.141.13.0 [120/1] via 134.141.12.1, 00:00:20, Serial0
                     [120/1] via 134.141.23.3, 00:00:15, Serial1
C       134.141.23.0 is directly connected, Serial1
```

Figure 15.8 Using the *show protocols* Command

```
RouterHostName#show protocols
Global values:
  Internet Protocol routing is enabled
  IPX routing is enabled
Ethernet0 is up, line protocol is up
  Internet address is 172.16.10.1/24
  IPX address is 10.0060.7015.63d6 (NOVELL-ETHER)
  IPX address is 10A.0060.7015.63dc (SAP)
Ethernet0.10 is up, line protocol is up
  IPX address is 10B.0060.7015.63d6
Ethernet0.100 is up, line protocol is up
  IPX address is 10C.0060.7015.63d6
Serial0 is up, line protocol is up
Internet address is 172.16.20.1/24
IPX address is 20.0060.7015.63d6
```

Figure 15.9   Using the *show ip* Protocol Command

```
RouterHostName>show ip protocol
Routing Protocol is "rip"
  Sending updates every 30 seconds, next due in 23 seconds
  Invalid after 180 seconds, hold down 180, flushed after 240
  Outgoing update filter list for all interfaces is not set
  Incoming update filter list for all interfaces is not set
  Redistributing: rip
  Default version control: send version 1, receive any version
    Interface Send Recv Key-chain
    Serial0 1 1 2
    Serial1 1 1 2
    Ethernet0 1 1 2
  Routing for Networks:

    199.1.1.0
  Routing Information Sources:
    Gateway Distance Last Update
    199.1.1.66 120 00:00:04
    199.1.1.98 120 00:00:14
  Distance: (default is 120)
```

The show ip protocol command shows you the routing protocols that are configured on your router. The show ip protocol command also displays the timers used in the routing protocol. The information included in the show ip protocol command includes the AC, routing timers, networks being advertised, gateways, and administrative distance (see Figure 15.9).

The debug ip rip command sends routing updates as they are sent and received on the router during the console session. If you telnetted into the router, you'll need to use the terminal monitor command to be able to receive the output from the debug commands. As you can see from Figure 15.10, RIP is both sent and received on serial 0, serial 1, and Ethernet interfaces, which can be a great troubleshooting tool.

With the debug IP IGRP command, there are two options: (1) events and (2) transactions. The debug ip igrp events command is a summary of the IGRP routing information that is running on the network. The following router output shows the source and destination of each update as well as the number of routers in each update. Information about individual routes is not generated with the command (see Figure 15.11).

The debug ip igrp transactions command shows message requests from neighbor routers asking for an update and the broadcasts sent from your router towards that neighbor router (see Figure 15.12).

You can use the ping and traceroute commands to test connectivity to remote devices. Both commands can be used with many protocols, not just IP. The ping output displays

Figure 15.10 Using the *debug ip rip* Command

```
RouterHostname#debug ip rip
RIP protocol debugging is on
RouterHostName#
RIP: received v1 update from 163.1.12.202 on Serial0
     163.1.2.128 in 1 hops
     163.1.3.128 in 2 hops
     163.1.23.128 in 1 hops
     163.1.23.203 in 1 hops
RIP: received v1 update from 163.1.13.203 on Serial1
     163.1.2.128 in 2 hops
     163.1.3.128 in 1 hops
     163.1.23.128 in 1 hops
     163.1.23.202 in 1 hops
RIP: sending v1 update to 255.255.255.255 via Serial0 (163.1.12.201)
     subnet 163.1.3.128, metric 2
     subnet 163.1.1.128, metric 1
     subnet 163.1.13.128, metric 1
     host 163.1.23.202, metric 2
RIP: sending v1 update to 255.255.255.255 via Serial1 (163.1.13.201)
     subnet 163.1.2.128, metric 2
     subnet 163.1.1.128, metric 1
     subnet 163.1.12.128, metric 1
     host 163.1.23.203, metric 2
RIP: sending v1 update to 255.255.255.255 via Ethernet0 (163.1.1.201)
     subnet 163.1.2.128, metric 2
     subnet 163.1.3.128, metric 2
     subnet 163.1.12.128, metric 1
     subnet 163.1.13.128, metric 1
     subnet 163.1.23.128, metric 2
     host 163.1.23.203, metric 2
     host 163.1.23.202, metric 2
```

the minimum, average, and maximum times it takes for a ping packet to find a specified system and return. To verify the IP connectivity, you can use the ping command from within Enable mode. Different from the ping command that you use with Windows, a successful ping will be denoted by an exclamation point (!) and a timeout will be denoted by a period (.).

>   *NOTE:* The ping command can be used in User Exec and Privileged Exec modes, but not Configuration mode (see Figure 15.13).

The traceroute command (trace for short) shows the path a packet takes to get to a remote device. To see the protocols that you can use with traceroute, use the traceroute ? command.

Figure 15.11   Using the *debug ip irgrp events* Command

```
RouterHostName#debug ip igrp events

IGRP: sending update to 255.255.255.255 via Ethernet1 (160.89.33.8)
IGRP: Update contains 26 interior, 40 systems, and 3 exterior routes.
IGRP: Total routes in update: 69
IGRP: sending update to 255.255.255.255 via Ethernet0 (160.89.32.8)
IGRP: Update contains 1 interior, 0 system, and 0 exterior routes.
IGRP: Total routes in update: 1
IGRP: received update from 160.89.32.24 on Ethernet0
IGRP: Update contains 17 interior, 1 system, and 0 exterior routes.
IGRP: Total routes in update: 18
IGRP: received update from 160.89.32.7 on Ethernet0
IGRP: Update contains 5 interior, 1 system, and 0 exterior routes.
IGRP: Total routes in update: 6
```

> *NOTE:* In the near future, Cisco will add support to traceroute IPX and AppleTalk. The trace command shows the hop or hops that a packet traverses on its way to a remote device. Three probes are issued; the response time of each probe will be displayed if it is successful. An asterisk (*) indicates a timeout. The trace command returns an *N* if the network is unreachable. A *P* response indicates that the protocol was unreachable. If a router prevents forwarding the packet to the destined host, the traceroute command will be returned three times (see Figure 15.14).

As shown in Chapter 11, for the ping and traceroute commands to perform host name lookup, the router will need to be configured to use a DNS server. The command to specify your DNS name servers is ip name-server *ip_address.*

Host names can be assigned to routers by using the ip host command and specifying a name and one or more IP addresses that exist on the router. You can use the show hosts command to display all of the hostnames and their corresponding IP addresses. If more than one IP address is assigned to the same host name, then all of the IP addresses configured for that name are shown by the show hosts command.

15.4   ENABLING AND CONFIGURING IPX ROUTING

To enable IPX routing, you would use the ipx routing command in Global Configuration mode. Once you enable IPX routing on the router, RIP and SAP also are automatically enabled.

To configure a router to take advantage of multiple IPX paths to another router, you can issue the ipx maximum-paths *paths* command. The maximum number of multiple paths is 512. By default, per-packet load sharing is enabled between equal cost

Figure 15.12   Using the *debug ip igrp transactions* Command

```
RouterHostName#debug ip igrp transactions
IGRP protocol debugging is on
RouterHostName#
IGRP: received update from 170.1.14.4 on Serial0.4
      subnet 170.1.8.0, metric 8539 (neighbor 688)
IGRP: sending update to 255.255.255.255 via Serial0.2 (170.1.10.1)
      subnet 170.1.8.0, metric=8539
      subnet 170.1.14.0, metric=8476
      subnet 170.1.12.0, metric=8476
      subnet 170.1.2.0, metric=688
      subnet 170.1.6.0, metric=8539
IGRP: sending update to 255.255.255.255 via Serial0.3 (170.1.12.1)
      subnet 170.1.10.0, metric=8476
      subnet 170.1.8.0, metric=8539
      subnet 170.1.14.0, metric=8476
      subnet 170.1.2.0, metric=688
      subnet 170.1.4.0, metric=8539
IGRP: sending update to 255.255.255.255 via Serial0.4 (170.1.14.1)
      subnet 170.1.10.0, metric=8476
      subnet 170.1.12.0, metric=8476
      subnet 170.1.2.0, metric=688
      subnet 170.1.6.0, metric=8539
      subnet 170.1.4.0, metric=8539
IGRP: sending update to 255.255.255.255 via Ethernet0 (170.1.3.1)
      subnet 170.1.10.0, metric=8476
      subnet 170.1.8.0, metric=8539
      subnet 170.1.14.0, metric=8476
      subnet 170.1.12.0, metric=8476
      subnet 170.1.6.0, metric=8539
      subnet 170.1.4.0, metric=8539
IGRP: received update from 170.1.10.2 on Serial0.2
      subnet 170.1.4.0, metric 8539 (neighbor 688)
IGRP: received update from 170.1.12.3 on Serial0.3
      subnet 170.1.6.0, metric 8539 (neighbor 688)
```

routes. When static mappings are configured, the `ipx maximum-paths paths` command is required to allow usage of multiple paths.

15.5   MONITORING IPX ON CISCO ROUTERS

Once you have IPX configured and running, there are several ways to verify and track that your router is communicating correctly. The `show ipx servers` command is a lot like the display servers command in NetWare. It displays the contents of the SAP table on

Figure 15.13 Using the *ping* command on Cisco Routers

```
RouterHostName#ping 142.42.52.43

Type escape sequence to abort
Sending 5, 100-byte ICMP echos to 142.42.52.43, timeout is 2 seconds:
!!!!!
Success rate is 100 percent (5/5), route-trip min/avg/max=32/32/32 ms)

RouterHostName#ping router1

Translating "router1"...domain server (192.168.0.70) [OK]
Type escape sequence to abort
Sending 5, 100-byte ICMP echos to 142.42.52.43, timeout is 2 seconds:
!!!!!
Success rate is 100 percent (5/5), route-trip min/avg/max=32/32/32 ms)
```

Figure 15.14 Using the *trace* Command

```
RouterHostName#trace 163.1.13.203

Type escape sequence to abort.
Tracing the route to 163.1.13.203
1 163.1.13.201 16 msec 16 msec 16 msec
2 163.1.13.203 44 msec * 32 msec

RouterHostName#trace router1

Type escape sequence to abort.
Tracing the route to router1 (163.1.13.203)
1 163.1.13.201 16 msec 16 msec 16 msec
2 163.1.13.203 44 msec * 32 msec
```

Cisco routers, so you should see the names of all SAP services. If the router doesn't have entries for remote servers in its own SAP table, local clients will never see those servers. If there are servers missing from this table that should be there, double check your IPX network addresses and encapsulation settings (see Figure 15.15).

The output from the router allows you to see all the IPX servers discovered through the SAP advertisement.

NOTE: Cisco routers that use IPX issue SAP broadcasts every sixty seconds by default. The *Type* field is the type of SAP service being advertised, with 4 being a file service and 7 a print service. The other service numbers listed are specific for that type of application running on the NetWare server. The *Net* and *Address*

Figure 15.15 Using the *show ipx servers* Command

```
Seville#show ipx servers
Codes: S - Static, P - Periodic, E - EIGRP, N - NLSP, H - Holddown, + = detail
2 Total IPX Servers

Table ordering is based on routing and server info

       Type Name               Net     Address      Port    Route Hops Itf
  P      4 Bugs                 1.0000.0000.0001:0451       8/03    3  Se0
  P      4 Daffy                2.0000.0000.0001:0451       8/03    3  Se0
```

Figure 15.16 Using the *show ipx route* Command

```
RouterHostName#show ipx route
Codes: C - Connected primary network,    c - Connected secondary network
       S - Static, F - Floating static, L - Local (internal), W - IPXWAN
       R - RIP, E - EIGRP, N - NLSP, X - External, A - Aggregate
       s - seconds, u - uses

7 Total IPX routes. Up to 1 parallel paths and 16 hops allowed.

No default route known.

C            2 (SAP),          E0_
C         1012 (HDLC),         Se0
C         1023 (HDLC),         Se1
R            1 [07/01] via     1012.0000.aaaa.aaaa,   14s, Se0
R            3 [07/01] via     1023.0200.cccc.cccc,    1s, Se1
R         1001 [08/03] via     1023.0200.cccc.cccc,    1s, Se1
R         1013 [12/01] via     1023.0200.cccc.cccc,    1s, Se1
```

fields are the IPX internal network numbers configured on each server. The *Port* field identifies the upper-layer application. The socket number for the NetWare Core Protocol (NCP) is 451.

The show ipx route command displays the IPX routing table entries that the router knows about. The router reports networks to which it is directly connected, then it reports networks that it has learned of since the router came online. The small *c* in the routing table tells you that it is a secondary configured IPX network (see Figure 15.16).

The show ipx traffic command gives you a summary of the number and type of IPX packets received and transmitted by the router. This command will show you both the IPX RIP and SAP update packets (see Figure 15.17).

Figure 15.17 Using the *show ipx traffic* Command

```
RouterHostName#show ipx traffic
System Traffic for 0.0000.0000.0001 System-Name: Yosemite
Rcvd:    169 total, 0 format errors, 0 checksum errors, 0 bad hop count,
         8 packets pitched, 161 local destination, 0 multicast
Bcast:   160 received, 242 sent
Sent:    243 generated, 0 forwarded
         0 encapsulation failed, 0 no route
SAP:     2 SAP requests, 0 SAP replies, 2 servers
         0 SAP Nearest Name requests, 0 replies
         0 SAP General Name requests, 0 replies
         60 SAP advertisements received, 57 sent
         6 SAP flash updates sent, 0 SAP format errors
RIP:     1 RIP requests, 0 RIP replies, 9 routes
         98 RIP advertisements received, 120 sent
         45 RIP flash updates sent, 0 RIP format errors
Echo:    Rcvd 0 requests, 0 replies
         Sent 0 requests, 0 replies
         0 unknown: 0 no socket, 0 filtered, 0 no helper
         0 SAPs throttled, freed NDB len 0
Watchdog:
         0 packets received, 0 replies spoofed
Queue lengths:
         IPX input: 0, SAP 0, RIP 0, GNS 0
         SAP throttling length: 0/(no limit), 0 nets pending lost route reply
         Delayed process creation: 0
EIGRP:   Total received 0, sent 0
         Updates received 0, sent 0
         Queries received 0, sent 0
         Replies received 0, sent 0
         SAPs received 0, sent 0
NLSP:    Level-1 Hellos received 0, sent 0
         PTP Hello received 0, sent 0
         Level-1 LSPs received 0, sent 0
         LSP Retransmissions: 0
         LSP checksum errors received: 0
         LSP HT=0 checksum errors received: 0
         Level-1 CSNPs received 0, sent 0
         Level-1 PSNPs received 0, sent 0
         Level-1 DR Elections: 0
         Level-1 SPF Calculations: 0
         Level-1 Partial Route Calculations: 0
```

The `show ipx interface` command gives you the interface status of IPX and the IPX parameters configured on each interface. The `show ipx interface e0` command shows you the IPX address and encapsulation type of the interface. If you use the `show interface e0` command, remember that it does not provide the IPX address of the interface—only the IP address. It also shows you the RIP and SAP information received on a certain interface (see Figure 15.18).

The `show protocols` command shows the IPX address and encapsulation type of an interface. This command shows the routed protocols configured on your router and the interface addresses (see Figure 15.19).

The `debug ipx` commands show you IPX as it's running through your internetwork. You can also see the IPX RIP and SAP updates with this command, but be careful when using it because it can consume quite a bit of the routers processor if you don't use wisely. The two commands that are the most useful with IPX are `debug ipx routing activity` and `debug ipx sap activity`.

The `debug ipx routing activity` command shows information about IPX routing updates that are transmitted or received on the router (see Figure 15.20). You can turn this command off by using `undebug all` (`un al` for short), or you can type `undebug ipx routing act`.

The `debug ipx activity` command shows you the IPX SAP packets that are transmitted and received on your router. SAPs are broadcast over every active interface every 60 seconds, just as IPX RIP is. Each SAP packet shows up as multiple lines in the debug output. You can turn the debug command off by using `undebug all` (`un al` for short) or by using the `undebug ipx sap activity` command.

By either telnetting into a remote router or using the `show cdp neighbor detail` or `show cdp entry *` commands, you can find the IPX address of a neighbor router. CDP is explained in the next section. You can ping the router much like you do for the `ping` command used with TCP/IP. It is done by typing `ping ipx` *address* from any router prompt, where *address* is the address of the router that you are trying to ping (see Figure 15.21).

15.6   USING THE CISCO DISCOVERY PROTOCOL

The **Cisco Discovery Protocol (CDP)** is a proprietary protocol designed by Cisco to help administrators collect information about both locally attached and remote devices. By using CDP, which uses Subnetwork Access Protocol (SNAP) to enable neighboring devices to exchange configuration information, you can gather hardware and protocol information about neighbor devices. This information is useful for troubleshooting and documenting the network. Because SNAP functions at the data link layer of the OSI model, it does not rely on a network layer protocol for communication. Instead, CDP broadcasts SNAP packets, which can contain information about the upper-layer protocols, to neighboring devices.

Figure 15.18 Using the *show ipx interface* Command

```
RouterHostName#show ipx interface
Serial0 is up, line protocol is up
  IPX address is 2013.0200.3333.3333 [up]
  Delay of this IPX network, in ticks is 6 throughput 0 link delay 0
  IPXWAN processing not enabled on this interface.
  IPX SAP update interval is 1 minute(s)
  IPX type 20 propagation packet forwarding is disabled
  Incoming access list is not set
  Outgoing access list is not set
  IPX helper access list is not set
  SAP GNS processing enabled, delay 0 ms, output filter list is not set
  SAP Input filter list is not set
  SAP Output filter list is not set
  SAP Router filter list is not set
  Input filter list is not set
  Output filter list is not set
  Router filter list is not set
  Netbios Input host access list is not set
  Netbios Input bytes access list is not set
  Netbios Output host access list is not set
  Netbios Output bytes access list is not set
  Updates each 60 seconds, aging multiples RIP: 3 SAP: 3
  SAP interpacket delay is 55 ms, maximum size is 480 bytes
  RIP interpacket delay is 55 ms, maximum size is 432 bytes
  Watchdog processing is disabled, SPX spoofing is disabled, idle time 60
  IPX accounting is disabled
  IPX fast switching is configured (enabled)
  RIP packets received 53, RIP packets sent 55
  SAP packets received 14, SAP packets sent 25
Serial1 is up, line protocol is up
  IPX address is 2023.0200.3333.3333 [up]
  Delay of this IPX network, in ticks is 6 throughput 0 link delay 0
  IPXWAN processing not enabled on this interface.
  IPX SAP update interval is 1 minute(s)
  IPX type 20 propagation packet forwarding is disabled
  Incoming access list is not set
  Outgoing access list is not set
  IPX helper access list is not set
  SAP GNS processing enabled, delay 0 ms, output filter list is not set
  SAP Input filter list is not set
  SAP Output filter list is not set
  SAP Router filter list is not set
  Input filter list is not set
  Output filter list is not set
  Router filter list is not set
  Netbios Input host access list is not set
```

Continued

Figure 15.18 Continued

```
    Netbios Input bytes access list is not set
    Netbios Output host access list is not set
    Netbios Output bytes access list is not set
    Updates each 60 seconds, aging multiples RIP: 3 SAP: 3
    SAP interpacket delay is 55 ms, maximum size is 480 bytes
    RIP interpacket delay is 55 ms, maximum size is 432 bytes
    Watchdog processing is disabled, SPX spoofing is disabled, idle time 60
    IPX accounting is disabled
    IPX fast switching is configured (enabled)
    RIP packets received 53, RIP packets sent 62
    SAP packets received 13, SAP packets sent 37
  Ethernet0 is up, line protocol is up
    IPX address is 1003. 0000.0cac.ab41, SAP [up]
    Delay of this IPX network, in ticks is 1 throughput 0 link delay 0
    IPXWAN processing not enabled on this interface.
    IPX SAP update interval is 1 minute(s)
    IPX type 20 propagation packet forwarding is disabled
    Incoming access list is not set
    Outgoing access list is not set
    IPX helper access list is not set
    SAP GNS processing enabled, delay 0 ms, output filter list is not set
    SAP Input filter list is not set
    SAP Output filter list is not set
    SAP Router filter list is not set
    Input filter list is not set
    Output filter list is not set
    Router filter list is not set
    Netbios Input host access list is not set
    Netbios Input bytes access list is not set
    Netbios Output host access list is not set
    Netbios Output bytes access list is not set
    Updates each 60 seconds, aging multiples RIP: 3 SAP: 3
    SAP interpacket delay is 55 ms, maximum size is 480 bytes
    RIP interpacket delay is 55 ms, maximum size is 432 bytes
    IPX accounting is disabled
    IPX fast switching is configured (enabled)
    RIP packets received 20, RIP packets sent 62
    SAP packets received 18, SAP packets sent 15
```

Figure 15.19 Using the *show protocols* Command

```
RouterHostName#show protocols
Global values:
  Internet Protocol routing is enabled
  IPX routing is enabled
Ethernet0 is up, line protocol is up
  Internet address is 172.16.10.1/24
  IPX address is 10.0060.7015.63d6 (NOVELL-ETHER)
  IPX address is 10A.0060.7015.63dc (SAP)
Ethernet0.10 is up, line protocol is up
  IPX address is 10B.0060.7015.63d6
Ethernet0.100 is up, line protocol is up
  IPX address is 10C.0060.7015.63d6
Serial0 is up, line protocol is up
Internet address is 172.16.20.1/24
IPX address is 20.0060.7015.63d6
```

The `show cdp` command (`sh cdp` for short) shows information about two CDP global parameters that can be configured on Cisco devices:

- `CDP timer`—How often CDP packets are transmitted to all active interfaces.
- `CDP holdtime`—The amount of time that the device will hold packets received from neighbor devices.

Both Cisco routers and the Cisco switches use the same parameters. The output on the router looks like this:

```
RouterHostName#sh cdp
Global CDP information:
Sending CDP packets every 60 seconds
Sending a holdtime value of 180 seconds.
```

To change `cdp holdtime` and `cdp timer`, use the `cdp holdtime` and `cdp timer` commands. For example, to change the `cdp timer` to ninety seconds, type the following command in Global Configuration mode:

```
RouterHostName(config)#cdp timer 90
```

To change the holdtime to 240 seconds, use the following command:

```
RouterHostName(config)#cdp holdtime 240
```

To turn Off CDP completely, use the `no cdp run` command from Global Configuration mode. To turn CDP OFF or ON in a router interface, use the `no cdp enable` and `cdp enable` commands within the interface mode.

The `show cdp neighbor` command (`sh cdp nei` for short) shows information about directly connected devices. It is important to remember that CDP packets

Figure 15.20 Using the *debug ipx routing activity* Command

```
RouterHostName#debug ipx routing activity
IPX routing debugging is on
Yosemite#
IPXRIP: positing full update to 1002.ffff.ffff.ffff via Ethernet0
(broadcast)
IPXRIP: src=1002.0000.0c24.7841, dst=1002.ffff.ffff.ffff, packet sent
    network 1, hops 4, delay 9
    network 2, hops 4, delay 9
    network 1003, hops 2, delay 8
    network 1001, hops 2, delay 8
    network 2013, hops 2, delay 8
    network 2023, hops 1, delay 2
    network 2012, hops 1, delay 2
IPXRIP: positing full update to 2012.ffff.ffff.ffff via Serial0 (broad-
cast)
IPXRIP: src=2012.0200.2222.2222, dst=2012.ffff.ffff.ffff, packet sent
    network 1003, hops 2, delay 13
    network 2023, hops 1, delay 7
    network 1002, hops 1, delay 7
IPXRIP: positing full update to 2023.ffff.ffff.ffff via Serial1 (broadcast)
IPXRIP: src=2023.0200.2222.2222, dst=2023.ffff.ffff.ffff, packet sent
    network 1, hops 4, delay 14
    network 2, hops 4, delay 14
    network 1001, hops 2, delay 13
    network 2013, hops 2, delay 13
    network 2012, hops 1, delay 7
    network 1002, hops 1, delay 7
IPXRIP: update from 2012.0200.1111.1111
    1 in 3 hops, delay 8
    2 in 3 hops, delay 8
    1003 in 2 hops, delay 13
    2013 in 1 hops, delay 7
    1001 in 1 hops, delay 7
IPXRIP: update from 2023.0200.3333.3333
    1 in 4 hops, delay 14
    2 in 4 hops, delay 14
    1001 in 2 hops, delay 13
IPXRIP: 2012 FFFFFFFF not added, entry in table is static/connected/internal
    2012 in 2 hops, delay 13
    2013 in 1 hops, delay 7
    1003 in 1 hops, delay 7
```

Figure 15.21 Using the *ping ipx* Command

```
RouterHostName#ping ipx 40.000.0c8d.5c9d
Sending 5, 100-byte IPX Novell Echoes to 40.0000.0c8d.5c9d, timeout is 2
seconds
!!!!!
RouterHostName#ping
Protocol [ip]: ipx
Target IPX address: 40.0000.0c8d.5c9d
Repeat count [5]:
Datagram size [100]:
Timeout in seconds [2]:
Verbose [n]
Novell Standard Echo [n]: y
Type escape sequence to abort.
Sending 5, 100-byte IPX Novell Echoes to 40.0000.0c8d.5c9d, timeout is 2
seconds
!!!!!
Success rate is 100 percent (5/5), round-trip min/avg/max=4/7/12 ms
```

Figure 15.22 Using the *show cdp neighbor* Command

```
RouterHostName#show cdp neighbor
Capability Codes: R - Router, T - Trans Bridge, B - Source Route Bridge
                 S - Switch, H - Host, I - IGMP, r - Repeater
Device ID       Local Intrfce    Holdtme    Capability  Platform   Port ID
Router1         Ser 1            172        R           2500       Ser 1
Router2         Ser 0.2          161        R           2500       Ser 0.2
```

are not passed through a Cisco switch, and you only see what is directly attached. On a router connected to a switch, you will not see the other devices connected to the switch. Figure 15.22 shows the output of the show cdp neighbor command used on a router.

The *Device ID* is the hostname of the device directly connected. The *Local Interface* is the port to interface on which you are receiving the CDP packet. The *Holdtime* is the amount of time the router will hold the information before discarding it if no more CDP packets are received. The capability of the neighboring device identifies the type of device it is, such as router, switch or repeater. The *Capability* codes are listed at the top of the command output. The *Platform* is the type of Cisco device. The *Port ID* is the neighbor device's port or interface on which the CDP packets are broadcast.

Another command that provides neighbor information is the show cdp neighbor detail command (show cdp nei de for short) which also can be run on the router or switch. This command shows detailed information about each device connected

Figure 15.23   Using the *show cdp neighbor* Detail Command

```
RouterHostName#show cdp neighbor detail
-----------------------
Device ID: fred
Entry address(es):
  IP address: 163.5.8.3
Platform: cisco 2500, Capabilities: Router
Interface: Serial1, Port ID (outgoing port): Serial1
Holdtime : 164 sec

Version :
Cisco Internetwork Operating System Software
IOS (tm) 2500 Software (C2500-D-L), Version 12.0(6), RELEASE SOFTWARE (fc1)
Copyright 1986-1999 by cisco Systems, Inc.
Compiled Tue 10-Aug-99 23:52 by phanguye
-----------------------
Device ID: Yosemite
Entry address(es):
  IP address: 10.1.5.252
  Novell address: 5.0200.bbbb.bbbb
Platform: cisco 2500, Capabilities: Router
Interface: Serial0.2, Port ID (outgoing port): Serial0.2
Holdtime : 146 sec

Version :
Cisco Internetwork Operating System Software
IOS (tm) 2500 Software (C2500-D-L), Version 12.0(6), RELEASE SOFTWARE (fc1)
Copyright 1986-1999 by cisco Systems, Inc.
Compiled Tue 10-Aug-99 23:52 by phanguye
```

to the device. The output above shows the hostname and IP address of the directly connected devices. In addition to the same information displayed by the show cdp neighbor command, the show cdp neighbor detail command shows the IOS version of the neighbor device (see Figure 15.23).

The show cdp traffic command displays information about interface traffic, including the number of CDP packets sent and received and the errors with CDP (see Figure 15.24).

You can turn a router's CDP OFF by using the no cdp run command. However, CDP can also be turned off per interface with the no cdp enable command (see Figure 15.25). You can enable a port with the cdp enable command. All ports and interfaces default to cdp enable.

The show cdp interface command (sh cdp int for short) shows the CDP status on router interfaces or switch ports including the encapsulation on the line, the timer, and the holdtime for each interface (see Figure 15.26).

Figure 15.24 Using the *show cdp traffic* Command

```
RouterHostName#show cdp traffic
CDP counters :
    Packets output: 41, Input: 21
    Hdr syntax: 0, Chksum error: 0, Encaps failed: 0
    No memory: 0, Invalid packet: 0, Fragmented: 0
```

Figure 15.25 Using the *no cdp enable* Command

```
RouterHostName#config t
Router(config)#int s0
RouterHostName(config-if)#no cdp enable
```

Figure 15.26 Using the *show cdp interface* Command

```
RouterHostName#show cdp interface
Ethernet0 is up, line protocol is down
  Encapsulation ARPA
  Sending CDP packets every 60 seconds
  Holdtime is 180 seconds
Serial0.2 is up, line protocol is up
  Encapsulation FRAME-RELAY
  Sending CDP packets every 60 seconds
  Holdtime is 180 seconds
Serial1 is up, line protocol is up
  Encapsulation HDLC
  Sending CDP packets every 60 seconds
  Holdtime is 180 seconds
```

SUMMARY

1. Static routing occurs when an administrator manually adds routes to each router's routing table.
2. After the router is configured, you can type show running-config and show ip route to see the static routes.
3. Default routing is used to send packets that have a remote destination network not found in the routing table next to the hop router. You can only use default routing on stub networks, which means that they have only one exit port out of the network.
4. Routing protocols are configured in Global Configuration mode.
5. You can use the ping and traceroute commands to test connectivity to remote devices.
6. To enable IPX routing, you would use the ipx routing command in Global Configuration mode.
7. CDP is a proprietary protocol designed by Cisco to help administrators collect information about both locally attached and remote devices.

QUESTIONS

1. What mode should you use when you issue the `ipx routing` command from a Cisco router?
   a. User Exec
   b. Global Configuration
   c. Privileged Exec
   d. Interface Configuration

2. You are the network administrator for a company that has a TCP/IP network with several Cisco routers. You are configuring a static route to a router that is not directly connected to the router that you are configuring. Which of the following most accurately describes the gateway parameter that could be used in the `ip route` command for the router being configured? (Select 2 answers.)
   a. the next hop in the path
   b. the IP address of the destination router interface
   c. the administrative distance to the final destination
   d. the interface used from the source router to reach the destination

3. Pat, a network administrator, is experiencing difficulty reaching the remote host at IP address 10.20.20.2 from his organization's Cisco router. The router's serial interface is configured with the IP address 10.30.68.1. To troubleshoot the connection, Pat would like to send ten consecutive ICMP echo requests to the remote host. Which of the following prompt and command pairs best represents the mode and command that should be used to allow Pat to troubleshoot the connection between Pat's work station and the remote host by sending ten consecutive ICMP echo requests to the remote host?
   a. router>ping
   b. router#ping
   c. router>ping 10.20.20.2 extended
   d. router#ping 10.20.20.2 extended

4. You are the network administrator for your company's network, which contains a Cisco 7500 router that is connected to a Cisco Catalyst 1900 switch. You are currently logged into the switch, but you want to verify the version of the Cisco IOS running on the router. Which of the following commands should you use to accomplish this?
   a. show hosts
   b. show sessions

   c. show cdp entry *
   d. show cdp neighbor detail

5. Your Cisco router currently broadcasts CDP packets every 30 seconds. You want to reduce the frequency at which CDP broadcasts are transmitted from the router to every 2 minutes. Which of the following commands should you use to accomplish this?
   a. cdp holdtime 2
   b. cdp run 2
   c. cdp timer 2
   d. cdp holdtime 120
   e. cdp run 120
   f. cdp timer 120

6. Pat is the network administrator for the Acme Corporation. She centrally administers the Cisco routers on the internetwork by using Telnet. Acme has recently added a few new routers, and Pat is having difficulty remembering all of the IP addresses. She uses the ip host command to configure meaningful names for each router. Which of the following commands can Pat use to display all hostnames and their corresponding IP addresses?
   a. ip host all 255.255.255.255
   b. show hosts
   c. show ip protocol
   d. show running-config

7. You are configuring a Cisco Catalyst 1900 switch to add to your company's network, which contains no other CDP-capable devices. To reduce the amount of network bandwidth consumed by the switch due to CDP broadcasts, you want to disable CDP for the entire device. What command should you use to accomplish this task?
   a. disable
   b. no cdp enable
   c. no cdp run
   d. sh cdp interface

8. Your Cisco router has nothing in NVRAM, nothing in flash memory, and no currently available TFTP servers. What command tells the router where to obtain the IOS?
   a. boot system flash
   b. boot system flash *filename*
   c. boot system ROM
   d. boot system RAM

9. Which protocol does CDP use to exchange configuration information between neighboring routers?
   a. ARP
   b. IP
   c. RIP
   d. ICMP
   e. SNAP

10. Which of the following protocols automatically starts when a Cisco device is started, operates at Layer 2 of the OSI model, and is not forwarded by switches?
    a. BGP
    b. EIGRP
    c. CDP
    d. HDLC

11. Which of the following commands should you issue from a Cisco router to verify the configured name and the hardware platform of neighboring devices? (Select all correct answers.)
    a. show cdp entry *
    b. show cdp interface
    c. show cdp traffic
    d. show hosts
    e. show cdp neighbor

12. Which of the following prompts represents the router command mode that is required to carry out the extended trace command?
    a. Router>
    b. Router(config)#
    c. Router#
    d. Router(config-if)#

13. You want to copy the current running configuration information (in RAM), into the startup configuration file (in NVRAM). Which of the following command can be used to perform the copy? (Select the best choice.)
    a. copy run tftp
    b. copy RAM NVRAM
    c. copy tftp run
    d. copy running-config startup-config

14. What command should you use to enable IPX routing on a Cisco router?
    a. sh ipx route
    b. ipx routing e0
    c. ipx network 50 encapsulation sap
    d. ipx routing

15. Your company maintains two Ethernet segments: (1) Subnet A and (2) Subnet B. Several NetWare 3.11 servers have been installed on Subnet A and several NetWare 4.1 servers have been installed on Subnet B. Subnet A has an IPX number of 1A0F, and Subnet B has an IPX number of 2B0F. All servers use the default Ethernet encapsulation. You are installing a Cisco router to connect the two subnets. Subnet A will be connected to port E0 and Subnet B will be connected to port E1. Which of the following sets of commands should you use to enable the routing of the NetWare servers' IPX packets between your network segments?
    a. ipx routing
       interface ethernet 0
       ipx network 1A0F
       interface ethernet 1
       ipx network 2B0F
    b. ipx routing
       interface ethernet 0
       ipx network 1A0F encapsulation ARPA
       interface ethernet 1
       ipx network 2B0F encapsulation sap
    c. ipx routing
       interface ethernet 0
       ipx network 1A0F encapsulation snap
       interface ethernet 1
       ipx network 2B0F encapsulation novell-ether
    d. ipx routing
       interface ethernet 0
       ipx network 1A0F encapsulation novell-ether
       interface ethernet 1
       ipx network 2B0F encapsulation sap

16. Which of the following commands can you issue on a router to test the connectivity of a remote host? (Select all correct answers.)
    a. show ip
    b. show hosts
    c. ip host
    d. trace
    e. ping

17. Pat is the network administrator for VisionWorx. Users have complained that they are unable to access servers on one of the subnetworks. Pat wants to verify that a suspect router is properly advertising NetWare servers and all of the SAP services. Which of the following commands should Pat use?
    a. show ipx servers
    b. show ipx traffic
    c. show ipx route
    d. ipx maximum-paths

18. Which of the following statements correctly identifies the mode or modes from which you can issue a ping command?
    a. user mode only
    b. configuration mode only
    c. privileged mode only
    d. user mode and privileged mode

19. You have activated IP RIP debugging. Later, you want to minimize the effects of the debug command, so you decide to deactivate the IP debug feature. Which of the following router commands can be used to stop the router from displaying IP RIP routing updates as they occur?
    a. debug ip rip
    b. undebug ip rip
    c. debug ip igrp transactions
    d. undebug all

20. Which router command can be used to display RIP routing updates as they occur?
    a. show ip interface
    b. show ip route
    c. show ip protocol
    d. debug ip rip
    e. trace

21. In an attempt to troubleshoot a communication problem, you ping a known remote host. The ping command returns a *U*. Which of the following is the most likely reason that the *U* is returned?
    a. The ping was successful.
    b. The destination host was unreachable.
    c. The destination network was unreachable.
    d. A timeout occurred.

22. Which command can be used to determine the path a packet takes to reach its destination?
    a. show ip route   b. trace
    c. ipconfig   d. ping
    e. tracert

23. Which of the following pairs of prompts and commands best represents the steps that are required to configure IPX routing on a Cisco router named RouterA? (Select the best choice.)
    a. RouterA#ipx routing
    b. RouterA(config)#ipx routing
    c. RouterA#ipx network 1001
       encapsulation sap
    d. RouterA(config)#ipx network 1001
       encapsulation sap

    e. RouterA#enable ipx routing
    f. RouterA(config-if)#enable ipx routing

24. How often do Cisco routers broadcast SAP information by default?
    a. 30 seconds   b. 90 seconds
    c. 60 seconds   d. 240 seconds

25. Maxwell is the administrator of a TCP/IP internetwork. In an attempt to learn the route taken to reach a remote host, he issues the trace command with a valid host address. What router response will be returned if an access list somewhere along the path prevents a router from forwarding the packet to the host? (Select the best choice.)
    a. *   b. N
    c. P   d. !H

26. You are the network administrator for your company's network, which contains one Cisco router named RouterA. You want to configure IGRP on serial interface S0 with AS 93 and network ID 10.20.30.0. Which of the following prompt and command sequence pairs best represents the steps you should take to accomplish this task?
    a. RouterA(config)#router igrp 93
       RouterA(config-router)#network 10.20.30.0
    b. RouterA(config-if)#router igrp 93
       RouterA(config-router)#network 10.20.30.0
    c. RouterA(config)#router igrp
       RouterA(config-router)#as 93
       RouterA(config-router)#network 10.20.30.0
    d. RouterA(config-if)#router igrp
       RouterA(config-router)#as 93
       RouterA(config-router)#network 10.20.30.0

27. Your company's internetwork includes several Novell NetWare 4.1 servers on multiple network segments. The NetWare servers use only the default protocol and encapsulation type. Users on each segment are reporting difficulty reaching NetWare servers on remote segments. You want to review the appropriate routing table on your Cisco router to verify that all routes are properly defined. Which of the following commands will display the appropriate routing table?
    a. show ip route
    b. ipx maximum-paths
    c. show ipx route
    d. ipx network encapsulation sap

28. Chris is the administrator of a TCP/IP internetwork. He wants to discover the route that is taken to reach a remote network. He issues the *trace* command with a valid IP address. What response will the router return if the network is unreachable?

a. !H

b. P

c. N

d. U

29. Multiple IPX paths exist between two routers in your internetwork. You want to configure the routers to take advantage of the multiple paths. How can you configure the routers to do this?

a. Issue the *show ipx route* command.

b. Issue a static mapping for both routes.

c. Issue the *ipx maximum-paths paths* command.

d. You cannot have multiple IPX paths between two routers.

30. Your company has a small TCP/IP network with two Cisco routers. The subnet mask used throughout your network is 255.255.255.0. You want to configure a static route between Router Z and Router Y. Ethernet interface 0 on Router Z has an IP address of 182.18.10.1. Ethernet interface 1 on Router Z has an IP address of 182.18.20.1. This segment connects to Router Y's Ethernet interface 1, which has an IP address of 182.18.20.2. Router Y's Ethernet interface 0, which has an IP address of 182.18.30.1, connects to network 182.18.30.0.

Which of the following commands configures a static route from Router Z to network 182.18.30.0 and assigns an administrative distance of 90?

a. ip route 182.18.30.1 255.255.255.255 182.18.20.2 90

b. ip route RouterY e0 255.255.255.0 RouterZ e1 90

c. ip route 182.18.30.0 255.255.255.0 182.18.20.2 90

d. ip route 182.18.30.0 182.18.20.2 admin=90

31. You have a TCP/IP network. RIP is currently being used as the routing protocol. Which of the following commands show the routes in the routing table that were learned by RIP?

a. sh ip route

b. sh ip protocol

c. sh ip interface

d. trace

32. Pat is your new assistant network administrator. He is reviewing the configuration settings on one of your company's routers. He issues the *show ip route* command and notices numbers in brackets on the lines starting with an I. Which of the following represents the meaning of the bracketed numbers?

a. administrative distance and number of hops

b. administrative distance and metric

c. number of hops and number of ticks

d. number of hops and administrative distance

33. You are adding a Cisco router to your company's network, and you want to configure IGRP as the routing protocol on the router. The router has two interfaces: E0 and S1. E0 is configured with an IP address of 192.168.0.1, and S1 is configured with an IP address of 10.1.1.0. Which of the following commands configures IGRP on both interfaces of the router?

a. router igrp
   network 50

b. igrp routing
   network 50

c. router igrp 50
   network 192.168.0.0
   network 10.0.0.0

d. router igrp 50
   network 192.168.0.0 10.0.0.0

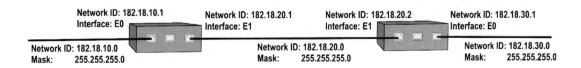

Network ID: 182.18.10.1
Interface: E0

Network ID: 182.18.20.1
Interface: E1

Network ID: 182.18.20.2
Interface: E1

Network ID: 182.18.30.1
Interface: E0

Network ID: 182.18.10.0
Mask: 255.255.255.0

Network ID: 182.18.20.0
Mask: 255.255.255.0

Network ID: 182.18.30.0
Mask: 255.255.255.0

34. Which of the following is the correct syntax for entering a static IP route?

    a. ip route *destination-network mask administrative-distance {next-hop-address | exit-interface}*

    b. ip route *destination-network mask {next-hop-address | exit-interface} administrative-distance*

    c. ip route *administrative-distance {next-hop-address | exit-interface} destination-network mask*

    d. ip route *administrative-distance destination-network mask {next-hop-address | exit-interface}*

35. You have recently configured the RIP protocol on your TCP/IP internetwork. You want to verify whether RIP is being used, how often RIP is transmitting updates, and when the next update is scheduled to occur. Which of the following commands should you use to accomplish these tasks? (Select the best choice.)

    a. show ip route

    b. show ip protocol

    c. show ip route rip

    d. debug ip rip

36. Which of the following commands can you use to enable IGRP?

    a. enable igrp 99

    b. router igrp

    c. passive interface igrp 1

    d. router igrp 99

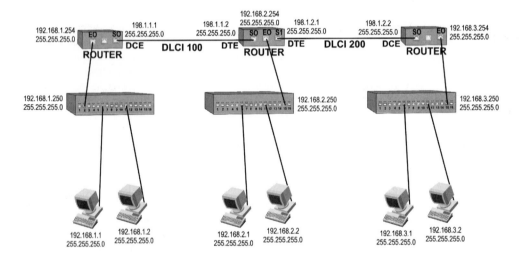

HANDS-ON EXERCISES

Exercise 1: Configuring PPP on a Router

    1. Connect to your router using a telnet session.

    2. Execute the `sh controllers serial 0` command.

    3. If you have a second serial port, execute the `sh controllers serial 1` command.

    4. Enter Global Configuration mode.

5. Enter the Interface mode for serial port 0.
6. Configure your serial port with the IP information shown in the figure. In addition, don't forget to use the `no shutdown` command.
7. If your serial port is designated as a DCE device, set the clock rate to 1000000 by using the `clock rate 1000000`.
8. To support PPP, execute the `encap ppp` command.
9. To support both chap and pap authentication, execute the `ppp authentication chap` and the `ppp authentication pap` commands.
10. To configure the username and password for the link, use the `username remote_router_hostname password cisco` where *remote_router_hostname* is the other router that you are connecting to.
11. Execute the `sh controllers serial 0` command.
12. If you have a second serial port, perform steps 6–11 for the interface.
13. Show the current configuration.
14. Use the `show interface` command.
15. If your router has a second serial port that is connected to another router, perform steps 3–7 for the second serial port.
16. Show the current configuration.
17. From your PC, ping the router port that is nearest to the PC.
18. From your PC, ping another router port on the router.
19. From your PC, try to ping another router and try to ping another PC on another subnet.
20. On Router01, enter Global Configuration mode and execute the `router rip` command. Then execute the `network 192.168.1.0` and `network 198.1.1.0` commands.
21. On Router02, enter Global Configuration mode and execute the `router rip` command. Then execute the `network 198.1.1.0, network 192.168.2.0` and `network 198.1.2.0` commands.
22. On Router03, enter Global Configuration mode and execute the `router rip` command. Then execute the `network 192.168.2.0` and `network 198.168.3.0` commands.
23. On each router, return to Enable mode. Then execute the `show ip route` command to see if all of the networks are listed in the routing table.
24. Execute the `show ip protocols` command and check to see what the RIP update interval is.
25. Execute the `debug ip rip` command.
26. Execute the `no debug all` command to disable all debugging.
27. From your PC, ping another router and try to ping another PC on another subnet.

Exercise 2: Configure the IGRP Routing Protocol

1. Enter Global Configuration mode on each router.
2. Use the `no router rip` command to disable RIP.
3. Execute the `router igrp 100` command to enable IGRP.
4. Use the same `network` commands that you used when configuring the RIP protocol.
5. Execute the `show ip protocols` command. Check to see what the update interval, the hold-down timer interval, and the flush interval are.
6. From your PC, ping a PC from another subnet.

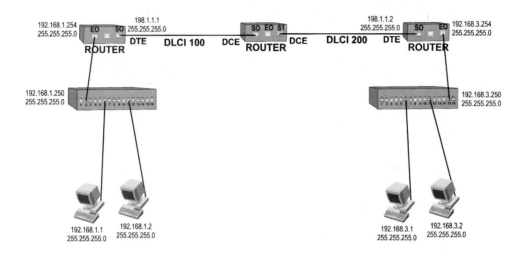

Exercise 3: Configuring a Frame Relay Network

Different from the previous exercises, the connection will be very similar except that the middle router will act as a Frame Relay switch. Therefore, the middle router will be configured as DCE devices.

All Routers

1. Go to Global Configuration mode on each router and execute the `erase start` command.
2. Execute the `reload` command to restart the router with an empty configuration. When asked to enter an initial configuration, press *N* for No. If you are prompted to terminate autoinstall, press *Y* for yes.
3. Set the privilege and vty passwords to *password*.

On the Middle Router

4. To configure the middle router as a Frame Relay switch, enter Global Configuration mode in the middle router and execute the `fr switching` command.
5. To enable Frame Relay encapsulation, change into s0 Interface mode and execute the `encap fr` command.
6. Execute the `no ip address` command.
7. Because the router will act as a Frame Relay switch, it will act as the DCE. Therefore, execute the `clockrate 1000000` command. Then execute the `fr intf-type dce` command.
8. To configure a static route from the first router to the third router through the switch, use the `fr route 100 int s0 200` command.
9. Now activate the interface.
10. Change into the S1 Interface mode and again execute steps 5 through 7.
11. To configure a static route from the third router to the first router through the switch, use the `fr route 200 int s0 100` command.
12. Activate the interface.
13. Exit Global Configuration mode.

On the First and Third Router

1. Configure the Ethernet interfaces with the IP addresses shown in the figure. Don't forget to activate the interface.
2. Change into S0 Interface mode and configure the IP addresses and activate interface.
3. Execute the `encap fr` command.
4. Exit to Global Configuration mode.
5. Configure the router to use IGRP using the autonomous system number 100. Then, use the appropriate network commands to complete the IGRP configuration.
6. Execute the `show fr pvc` command.
7. Execute the `show fr map` command.

On the Middle Router

1. Execute the `show fr route` command.
2. Execute the `show fr pvc` command.

On the PC

1. Ping a computer on another subnet.

CHAPTER 16

Network Security

Topics Covered in this Chapter

Introduction

One of the most important features of any network is network security. The network administrator is ultimately responsible for network security. Modern (network operating systems NOSs) have many levels of security, and to make a network secure, you must look at all levels. While the administrator is ultimately responsible for security, everyone who uses the network must keep the network secure—this job never ends.

Objectives

- Define threat, vulnerability, and exploit. Explain how they relate to each other.
- Given a scenario, determine what the threat and vulnerabilities are and decide how to protect your network from them.
- List and define the different types of firewalls available and explain how each protects its network.

- Given a scenario, determine how you would use a DMZ.
- Compare and contrast private keys and public key encryption.
- Compare and contrast digital envelopes, digital signatures, and digital certificates.
- Explain how a hash encryption protects data.
- Explain how patches can improve the security of a system.

16.1 SECURITY RISKS

By now, you should understand that security is a major concern and a major responsibility for administrators. When you examine your environment, you will need to assess the risks you currently face, determine an acceptable level of risk, and maintain risk at or below that level. Risks are reduced by increasing the security of your environment.

As a general rule, the higher the level of security in an organization, the more costly it is to implement. Unfortunately, at a higher level of security, you may reduce the functionality of the network. Sometimes, extra levels of security will result in more complex systems for users. However, if the authentication process is too complex, some employees will not use the system, which could cost more than attacks the network could suffer.

A **threat** is a person, place, or thing that has the potential to access resources and cause harm. Threats can be divided into three categories:

- **Natural and physical**—Includes fire, flooding, storms, earthquakes, and power failures
- **Unintentional**—Includes uninformed employees and customers
- **Intentional**—Includes attackers, terrorists, spies, and malicious code

A **vulnerability** is a point where a resource is susceptible to attack. It can be thought of as a weakness. Vulnerabilities are often categorized as:

- **Physical**—Such as an unlocked door
- **Natural**—Such as a broken fire suppression system or no UPS
- **Hardware and software**—Such as out-of-date antivirus software
- **Media**—Such as electrical interference
- **Communication**—Such as unencrypted protocols
- **Human**—Such as insecure help desk procedures

An **exploit** is an attack on a resource that is accessed by a threat that makes use of a vulnerability in your environment. Exploitation of resources can be performed in many ways. When a threat uses a vulnerability to attack a resource, some severe consequences can result.

Countermeasures are deployed to counteract threats and vulnerabilities, therefore reducing the risk in your environment. For example, an organization producing fragile electronics may deploy physical security countermeasures such as securing equipment to the building's foundation or adding buffering mechanisms. These countermeasures reduce the likelihood that an earthquake could cause physical damage to their assets. Residual risk is what remains after all countermeasures have been applied.

To analyze all of the ways that a network can be attacked or accessed without proper permission, you first use the OSI model to categorize them. Most of the attacks that you hear about in the news occur at the application layer, going after web servers and browsers

Figure 16.1 Types of Attacks as They Relate to the OSI Model

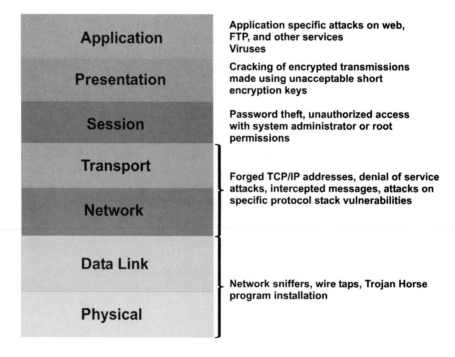

and the information that they have access to, but application-layer attacks on open file shares are also common (see Figure 16.1).

While you can defend against specific threats, please keep in mind that any defense can fail the first time an unanticipated threat shows up. Therefore, you will have to monitor your network constantly.

16.2   USER MANAGEMENT

The username and password is the first line of defense, because every user must have one to gain access to the network and its resources. For the password to be effective, the administrator should set guidelines and policies on how the user should use the network, provide training of these guidelines, and to provide frequent reminders.

16.2.1   Username Policies

As you know by now, the username is the name of the account that represents the person or persons who need to access the network. It is the account through which rights and permissions are given for network resources.

To make it easier to administer, the username should use a consistent naming conventional for all users so that it will be easier to find names that follow a consistent pattern. For example, you can use the first initial, middle initial, and last name; or first name and last initial. Of course, if you have hundreds of employees (or more), you might need to use something like first name, middle initial, and last name to differentiate all of the users. You should create a document stating the naming scheme of user accounts and provide this document to all administrators who might create accounts.

To identify the type of employee, add additional letters at the beginning or end of their name. For example, you can add a T in front of the name or a X at the end of the name to indicate that they are either under contract or temporary.

While standard usernames make it easier for the administrator, they also make it easier to hack. Therefore, to make the network a little bit more secure, you should rename administrator accounts (if possible). For Windows NT, Windows 2000, and Windows Server 2003 servers, the administrator account is *administrator.* For NetWare, it is *admin.* For Linux, it is *root.*

Lastly, when doing everyday activities, you should not be logged in as the administrator of the server. This will help protect the system from carelessness and it will restrict the damage that can be caused while logged in as that account. For example, a virus may spread onto the server and then all of the computers on the network if you accessed a virus while logged in as the administrator. If you are not logged in as the administrator, the rights and permissions to many of the files would be read only and therefore immune to a virus.

16.2.2   Password Policies

When it comes to security, a password is more important than a username. There are very important things that can be done to make passwords more secure. First, establish some common guidelines for the passwords. Second, you then have to educate your users to make sure that they follow those guidelines. Keep giving them reminders to use those passwords. These guidelines should include:

- Always require user names and passwords
- Don't give your password to anyone
- Change your password frequently
- Other people should not see you type in your password
- Do not write your password down near the computer
- When you leave your computer unattended, log off the computer
- Use a password protected screen saver
- Do not use obvious passwords and do not use easy passwords
- Use strong passwords
- If you see a security problem or a potential security problem, report it to the network administrator

Some of these make common sense; for example, you should agree not to give your password to anyone and do not let people see you type in your password. To prevent people from "jumping" onto your computer while you walk away from your desk, you should get in the habit of logging off. Yet, to help protect your computer when you forget to log off, use a password protected screen saver. Therefore, after a short period of time, the screen saver will start. For anyone to get past the screensaver they would have to type in a password. This will automatically protect your system when you leave your computer.

One of the easiest ways to hack into a network is to exploit weak passwords. You would be amazed how many people use easy passwords because it is convenient for the user and easy to remember. Unfortunately, any good hacker will try these first. A weak password would include:

- the word *password*
- the user's name
- the person's first name, middle name, or last name
- the user's pet's name
- a name of a family member
- birthdates or anniversary dates
- any text or label on the PC or monitor
- the company's name
- the user's occupation
- the user's favorite color
- typing keys on the keyboard or numeric keypad as they are placed on the keyboard (examples: qwerty, asdfgh, 123, or 147)
- any derivatives of the above, such as spelling it backwards

One program that hackers use to break into a server is to use a cracker program that uses a dictionary attack to figure out the password. A dictionary attack initially found passwords from a specific list, such as an English dictionary. Today, the lists have been expanded to include combinations of words, such as on-the-fly and common words with digits. The program tries by brute force by going through each item in the list until it figures out the password. Depending on the system, the password, and the skills of the attacker, such an attack can be completed in days, hours, or perhaps only a few seconds. With such programs easily available to anyone who wants them, all users should use strong passwords.

Strong passwords, which are difficult-to-crack, do not have to be difficult to remember. They include a combination of numbers, letters (lower case and upper case), and special characters. Special characters are those that cannot be considered letters or numbers, such as @#$%^&*.

An example of a strong password is:

tqbf4#jotld

Such a password may seem hard to remember, but it is not. This password was actually derived from a common sentence that includes every letter in the alphabet:

The quick brown fox jumped over the lazy dog.

By taking the first letter of each word, and putting the number 4 and a pound (#) symbol in the middle, you have a strong password.

To make passwords more secure, many network operating systems have password management features either built into the operating system or installed as an add-on package. One such example would be that some network operating systems will have an option to enforce strong passwords.

Another option is that you can require a minimum number of characters for the password. A strong password should be at least eight characters, if not more. They shouldn't be any longer than 15 characters because they would then be too difficult for people to remember and create. Having a minimum number of characters requires a much larger number of combinations for a cracker program to try.

To avoid having passwords randomly guessed, some network operating systems offer an automatic account lockout. For example, you could set up a password so that if the wrong password is tried for an account three times within a thirty-minute time period, the network will disable the account for a minimum amount of time—permanently—until a network administrator unlocks the account. In either case, such failure should also be logged somewhere. As the administrator, you should then check these logs on a regular basis to see if there are patterns where someone is trying to hack into a system without the knowledge of the user.

> *NOTE:* If you are the administrator and you accidentally lock yourself out, you will need another administrator to unlock your account. If you are the only administrator, you may not be able to recover.

Another way to avoid passwords from being randomly guessed is to set up password expirations where an account will automatically expire on a certain date or after a certain amount of days, and it forces the users to change passwords every so often. This will also help keep the network secure if someone discovers a password because it will be changed from time to time, making the previous password invalid. Most organizations set up passwords to expire every thirty to forty-five days. After that, users must reset their passwords either immediately or during the allotted grace period. Some systems give users a few grace logins after the password has expired.

Lastly, some systems will require unique passwords. This is when a system will remember a number of recent passwords used and will configure the system so that the same password cannot be used over and over. When implementing a password history policy, be sure to make the password history large enough to contain at least a year's worth of password changes. For a standard thirty-day password, a history of twelve or thirteen passwords will suffice.

Before moving on to user management, login troubleshooting should be discussed. If a person is having trouble logging in, you should always have the user check to see if their keyboard's Caps lock is on. This is the problem most of the time because passwords, and sometimes user names, are case sensitive. If the user is still having problems, it most likely is easier to change the password for the user and have him or her try again. If the problem still persists after changing the password, you should check your encryption scheme. Sometimes passwords are sent in plain text when the program is expecting an encrypted password, or the password could be sent encrypted when the program is expecting a plain text password.

While many of these guidelines are implemented through training and constant reminders, some can be managed or enforced with group policies. For example, with group policies you can enforce strong passwords, how often a person must change their password, and how often a person can reuse the same password.

16.2.3   User Management

A necessary part of securing your network is user management. For example, if you are hiring a temporary employee, most of the network operating systems allow you to create a temporary account and have it automatically disable itself after a certain amount of days or at a certain date. In addition, when someone leaves the company, you either disable or delete a user account.

> *NOTE:* To make sure that the IT department is aware that a person has left the company, make sure that the company has an exit process for the employee that includes recovery of all IT equipment and deletion of the account. Don't forget to set up a checklist for when people leave the company and make sure to gather office keys, pagers, cell phones, company software, laptops, badges, and time cards.

If you decide to use an anonymous account or a guest, you need to treat the accounts with extreme care. It usually is not recommended to use such a generic account because they cannot be audited. If you decide to use such an account, you must make sure that you only give bare minimum access to network resources.

Next, you should limit the amount of concurrent connections or the number of times that a person can log in at one time. For most users, you should only have the user log in once. Therefore, if they want to go to another machine to log in, they must first log out of the first machine. This helps keep the person from leaving a machine unattended.

Lastly, if you have the need, some network operating systems allows you to specify which computer a person can log into and at what time they can log in. Therefore, you can specify that someone cannot log in from 7 AM to 6 PM. If someone tries to hack in after specified hours, they will be automatically denied even if they have a valid username and password.

16.2.4   **Rights and Permissions**

When planning rights and permissions for network resources, there are two main rules that you should follow. First, give only the rights and permissions that are necessary for the user to do his or her job. For example, only give him or her access to necessary files and only give him or her the rights that they need. If he or she needs to read a document but doesn't need to make changes to it, just allow read-only rights.

Second, make sure that the user does have sufficient rights and permissions to do what needs to be done. While you want to keep these resources secure, you want to make sure that the user can get what he or she needs.

Lastly, you need to understand how rights and permissions are assigned for an operating system to a user and a group. For example, you need to understand that if you assign permission to access a network resource to a group, but deny an individual access to the network resource, you must understand the resultant rights and permissions.

You can secure files that are shared over the network in one of two ways:

- share level security
- user level security

In a network that uses share-level security, you assign passwords to individual files or other network resources (such as printers) instead of assigning rights to users. You then give these passwords to all users who need access to the resources. All resources are visible from anywhere in the network, and any user who knows the password for a particular network resource can make changes to it. With this type of security, the network support staff will have no way of knowing who is manipulating each resource. Share-level security is best used in small networks, where resources are more easily tracked. Windows 9X supports share-level security.

In a network that implements user-level security, rights to network resources (such as files, directories, and printers) are assigned to specific users who gain access to the network through individually assigned usernames and passwords. Thus, only users who have a valid username and password and who have been assigned the appropriate rights to network resources can see and access those resources. User-level security provides greater control over who is accessing which resources because users are not supposed to share their usernames and passwords with other users. User-level security is, therefore, the preferred method for securing files. Windows NT, Windows 2000, Windows .NET Server 2003, Windows XP, NetWare, UNIX, and Linux support user-level security.

16.2.5   **Educating Users**

System administrators and help desk people are first level contacts for users in the organization who need system support. It is a good idea for network administrators to educate users and help desk people about basic security issues and practices to follow, either formally or informally. This will help when building secured systems. It is advantageous if users are aware of security issues and implications. Some of the best practices for users are not to leave the terminal logged in, not to share passwords with anyone, to change passwords periodically, not to write down passwords on paper, and to use nondictionary words for passwords. As a system administrator, you should be aware of specific things in your environment so you can educate users.

One point that should be emphasized now is to educate your users about the dangers of social engineering. Typically, the weakest level of a security system is the user level. One of the more successful attempts to break into a network is for someone to try social engineering to gain valuable information about how to access the network. Someone may call a user on the phone and ask them information about the network or how to access the network or the user's password. By educating users of potential scams and informing them of what a user can expect from a network administrator and help desk people, you can reduce this security vulnerability.

16.3   PHYSICAL SECURITY

For larger networks that require switches and routers, you should secure computer servers and other key components, including routers and switches, in a server room or a telecommunication closet that only a handful of people have access to. You should use a locked door into the server room, and you may want to consider camera equipment to monitor the room and/or entrance. In addition, switches and routers should use secure passwords so that no one can reconfigure the equipment without your knowledge. If you are logged into a switch or router, you should always log out when you are not using it.

16.4   DENIAL OF SERVICE

An attacker does not necessarily have to gain access to a system in order to cause significant problems. **Denial of Service (DoS)** is an attack on a network, designed to bring the network to its knees by flooding it with useless traffic. Many DoS attacks, such as the *Ping of Death* and *Teardrop* attacks, exploit limitations in TCP/IP protocols. In the worst cases, for example, a website accessed by millions of people can occasionally be forced to cease operation temporarily. A DoS attack can also destroy programming and files in a computer system. Although usually intentional and malicious, a DoS attack can sometimes happen accidentally (see Table 16.1). For all known DoS attacks, there are software fixes that system administrators can install to limit the damage caused by the attacks. But, like viruses, new DoS attacks are constantly being dreamed up by hackers.

Distributed Denial of Service (DDoS) attacks involve installing programs, known as *zombies,* on various computers in advance of the attack. A command is issued to these zombies, which launch the attack on behalf of the attacker, thus hiding their tracks. The zombies themselves are often installed by using worms. The real danger from a DDoS attack is that the attacker uses many victim computers as host computers to control other zombies that initiate the attack. When the system that is overwhelmed tries to trace the attack, it receives a set of spoofed addresses generated by a series of zombies.

Table 16.1   Forms of DoS Attacks

Form of DoS attack	Description
Buffer overflow attacks	The most common kind of DoS attack is simply to send more traffic to a network address than the programmers who planned its data buffers anticipated that someone might send. The attacker may be aware that the target system has a weakness that can be exploited or the attacker may simply try the attack in case it might work. A few of the better-known attacks based on the buffer characteristics of a program or system include: • Sending e-mail messages that have attachments with 256-character filenames to Netscape and Microsoft mail programs • Sending oversized ICMP packets (this is also known as the *Ping of Death*) • Sending a Pine (e-mail program) user a message with a "From" address larger than 256 characters
SYN attack	When a session is initiated between the TCP client and server in a network, a very small buffer space exists to handle the usually rapid "handshaking" exchange of messages that sets up the session. Session-establishing packets include a SYN field that identifies the sequence in the message exchange. An attacker can send a number of connection requests very rapidly and then fail to respond to the reply. This leaves the first packet in the buffer so that other (legitimate) connection requests can't be accommodated. Although the packet in the buffer is dropped after a certain period of time without a reply, the effect of many of these bogus connection requests is to make it difficult for legitimate requests for a session to get established. In general, this problem depends either on the operating system to provide correct settings or on allowing the network administrator to tune the size of the buffer and the timeout period.
Teardrop attack	This type of DoS attack exploits the way that the IP requires a packet, which is too large for the next router to handle, to be divided into fragments. The fragment packet identifies an offset at the beginning of the first packet that enables the entire packet to be reassembled by the receiving system. In a teardrop attack, the attacker's IP puts a confusing offset value in the second (or later) fragment. If the receiving operating system does not have a plan for this situation, it can cause the system to crash.
Smurf attack	In this attack, the perpetrator sends an IP ping (or "echo my message back to me") request to a receiving site. The ping packet specifies that it be broadcast to a number of hosts within the receiving site's LAN. The packet also indicates that the request is from another site, the target site that is to receive the DoS. (Sending a packet with someone else's return address in it is called spoofing the return address.) The result will be lots of ping replies flooding back to the innocent, spoofed host. If the flood is great enough, the spoofed host will no longer be able to receive or distinguish real traffic.
WinNuke	WinNuke is a Windows program that sends special TCP/IP packets with an invalid TCP header. Windows will crash when it receives one of the packets because of the way that the Windows TCP/IP stack handles bad data in the TCP header. Instead of returning an error code or rejecting the bad data, it sends the computer to the blue screen of death.

Continued

Table 16.1   Continued

Form of DoS Attack	Description
Viruses	Computer viruses, which replicate across a network in various ways, can be viewed as DoS attacks where the victim is not usually specifically targeted. A host is simply unlucky enough to get the virus. Depending on the particular virus, the denial of service can be hardly noticeable or disastrous.
Physical infrastructure attacks	Here, someone may simply snip a fiber optic cable. This kind of attack is usually mitigated by the fact that traffic can sometimes quickly be rerouted.

The following defensive steps will help you prevent these types of attacks:

- Keep systems updated with the latest security patches.
- Block large ping packets at the router and firewall, stopping them from reaching the perimeter network.
- Apply anti-spoof filters on the router; that is, block any incoming packet that has a source address equal to an address on the internal network.
- Filter the ICMP messages on the firewall and router (although this could affect some management tools).
- Develop a defense plan with your ISP, enabling a rapid response to an attack that targets the bandwidth between your ISP and your perimeter network.
- Disable the response to directed broadcasts.
- Apply proper router and firewall filtering.
- Use an intruder detection system to check for unusual traffic and generate an alert if it detects any. Configure the system to generate an alert if it detects `ICMP_ECHOREPLY` without associated `ICMP_ECHO` packets.
- Each week, more DoS attacks are documented and added to bug tracking databases. You should ensure that you always remain current on these attacks and ways in which you can guard against them.

16.5   FIREWALLS AND PROXY SERVERS

Firewalls serve as the primary defense against external threats to an organization's computer network system. A firewall is usually a combination of hardware and software used to implement an organization's security policy governing network traffic. This network traffic is between two or more networks, one of which is under the organization's control. Two objectives common to all firewall systems are (1) to allow the flow of network traffic that has been determined to be consistent with the organization's security policy and (2) to minimize the amount and usefulness of information about the organization's computer network system disclosed to those outside the firewall. A firewall is a barrier to keep destructive forces away from an organization's computer system. The organization's computer system could be directly accessible to anyone on the Internet if a firewall is not in place.

Without a firewall, an organization will not be able to prevent many forms of undesirable access to computer systems and information assets. Undesirable access could lead to loss of confidential business information, loss of availability of mission critical services, exposure of system infrastructure to those who might attack the system, and vandalism of public information services such as the organization's website. Firewall technology provides one of the most effective tools available to manage network risk by providing access control mechanisms that can implement complex security policies.

Firewalls are customizable so that filters can be added or removed based on several conditions. Firewall administrators can control how an organization's employees connect to Internet sites and whether files are allowed to leave the organization via the Internet. A firewall can give the organization tremendous control over how employees use the Internet. For example, a security rule could be implemented to allow only one computer within the organization to be able to receive public FTP traffic.

A firewall can be as simple as a router that filters packets or as complex as a multicomputer, multirouter solution that combines packet filtering and application level proxy services. An organization's network security policy must contain procedures to safeguard the network and its contents against damage or loss. A network security policy identifies network resources and threats, defines network use and responsibilities, and details action plans to follow when policies are violated. The network security policy needs to be strategically enforced at defensible boundaries within the organization's network. These strategic boundaries are called **perimeter networks.**

To establish an organization's perimeter networks, the system administrator first must designate the computers that are to be protected and then define the network security mechanisms that protect them. To establish a successful network security perimeter, the firewall sever must be the gateway for all communication between trusted networks within the organization's control and untrusted external networks such as the Internet. Firewall servers define the point of focus or choke point through which all communication between the internal and external networks must pass. To help monitor network traffic, two main approaches have proven extremely valuable:

- **Packet filters**—You can examine traffic at the network layer, looking at the source and destination addresses. The filter can disallow traffic to or from specific addresses or address ranges and can disallow traffic with suspect address patterns.
- **Firewalls**—You can examine traffic as high as the application layer, checking ports in message addresses or even checking the internal content of specific application messages. Traffic that fails any tests can be rejected.

16.5.1   Packet Filters

As you recall, TCP/IP addresses are composed of both a machine address and, within the machine, a port number identifying the program to handle the message. The combined address/port information is available in every TCP/IP message, with the exception of broadcasts and some messages exchanged while a TCP/IP address is being assigned via the DHCP protocol. The combined address/port information is available for both the sender and the receiver of the message.

Packet filters are based on protecting the network by using an **access control list (ACL).** This list resides on your router and determines which machine (IP address) can use the router and in what direction. Typically, the router will permit all outgoing traffic but will deny any new incoming connections. If a machine on the inside has established a connection with a machine on the outside, it will accept those packets. Therefore, it will reject unsolicited connection attempts from the Internet to your computer.

If your packet filter software is capable enough to examine the subnet of the source address based on which physical port delivers the message to the router, you can set up rules to avoid spoofed TCP/IP addresses. The idea behind spoofing is for messages from the Internet to appear to have originated from your LAN; the spoofing filter prevents this by rejecting messages coming on a port with impossible source addresses.

An anti spoofing filter is an important part of protecting machines on a network in which you've installed filters to limit particular services to machines on your subnet. For instance, suppose that you've installed software on a Linux machine to make it act as a Windows network file server. You can configure Linux to reject all network traffic originating outside your subnet, preventing computers on the Internet from seeing the file server. If an attacker could pretend to be on your LAN, that safeguard would be bypassed. To defeat that attack, you would have to use an antispoofing filter.

An antispoofing filter, also known as Egress and Ingress Filtering, will only route outgoing packets if they have a valid internal IP address. By rule, your routers should disregard and drop any outgoing packets that do not originate from a valid internal IP address. When you perform this setting change, you will effectively prevent your network from becoming a participant in any spoofing attack. The addresses to be filtered are:

Historical low end broadcast: 0.0.0.0/8
Limited broadcast: 255.255.255.255/32
RFC 1918 private networks: 10.0.0.0/8
RFC 1918 private networks: 172.16.0.0/12
RFC 1918 private networks: 192.168.0.0/16
The loop back address: 127.0.0.0/8
Link local networks: 169.254.0.0/16
Class D address: 224.0.0.0/4
Class E reserved address: 240.0.0.0/5
Unallocated address: 248.0.0.0/5

There may be other addresses that need to be blocked by your router. However, the addresses listed above should help protect against DoS and/or spoofing attacks.

One disadvantage of a packet filter is that it generally does not protect against attacks that use the UDP protocol. This is because there is no formal connection opened with UDP as there is with TCP. Therefore, the filter cannot reject the opening message.

Besides analyzing the source and destination TCP/IP address, a filter can also examine the source and destination port numbers and the contents of the packet data. This gives it far more power, such as allowing or disallowing specific application services such as FTP or web pages, and allowing or disallowing access to services based on the contents of the information being transferred. You can even combine these functions, such as allowing incoming FTP access from the Internet but only to a specific, designated server.

When you decide which port numbers to block, you need to choose with care. If you decide to block a specific port, any service or application that uses that port will not function through the firewall. For example, if you block port 80, you will not be able to contact http web servers that use the default port 80.

16.5.2   Dynamic Packet Filters

Some firewalls are considered static packet filters while others are considered dynamic packet filters. With static packet filters, the packet filtering mechanism allows you to set rules based on protocol and port number to control inbound and outbound access on the external interface.

A dynamic packet filter is an extension of packet filtering, and is often referred to as **stateful inspection.** It is a firewall facility that can monitor the state of active connections and use this information to determine which network packets to allow through the firewall. By recording session information, such as IP addresses and port numbers, into a dynamic state list (also known as a state table), a dynamic packet filter can implement a much tighter security posture than a static packet filter.

For example, assume that you wish to configure your firewall so that all users in your company are allowed out to the Internet, but only replies to user data requests are let back in. With a static packet filter, you would need to permanently allow *in replies* from all external addresses, assuming that users were free to visit any site on the Internet. This kind of filter would allow an attacker to sneak information past the filter by making the packet look like a reply (which can be done by indicating "reply" in the packet header). By tracking and matching requests and replies, a dynamic packet filter can screen for replies that don't match a request. When a request is recorded, the dynamic packet filter opens up a small inbound hole so only the expected data reply is let back through. Once the reply is received, the hole is closed. This dramatically increases the security capabilities of the firewall, thus preventing someone from replaying a packet to get access—because it is not part of an active connection.

16.5.3   Circuit-level Gateways

While the application gateway operates on the OSI model's application layer, the circuit level gateway operates on the transport level of the OSI model. As a second-generation firewall, **circuit level gateways** validate TCP and UDP sessions before opening a connection. Because they operate at the transport layer, a circuit-level firewall actually establishes a VC between the client and the host on a session-by-session basis. Once a handshake has taken place, it passes everything through until the session is ended.

A circuit-level gateway translates IP addresses between the Internet and your internal systems. The gateway receives outbound packets and transfers them from the internal network to the external network. Inbound traffic is transferred from the outside network to the internal network. Circuit-level gateways provide a complete break between your internal network and the Internet. Unlike a packet filter, which simply analyzes and routes traffic, a circuit-level gateway translates packets and transfers them between network interfaces. This helps shield your network from external traffic because the packets appear to have originated from the circuit-level gateway's Internet IP address.

To validate and create a session, the circuit-level firewall examines each connection setup to ensure that each follows a legitimate handshake for the transport layer being used, typically TCP. No data packets are forwarded until the handshake is complete. The firewall maintains a table of valid connections, which includes session state and sequencing information, and lets network packets containing data pass through when the network packet information matches an entry in the VC table. When a connection is terminated, the table entry is removed and the VC between the two peers is closed.

Circuit level firewalls permit access through the firewall with a minimum amount of scrutiny by building a limited form of connection state, i.e., handshake—established or closing. Only those packets that are associated with an established connection are allowed through the firewall. When a connection establishment request is received, the circuit-level firewall checks its rule base to determine whether or not the connection should be allowed. If it is allowed, all network packets associated with that connection are routed through the firewall with no further security checks. This method provides very fast service and a minimal amount of state checking.

Circuit level application gateways often provide **network address translation (NAT),** in which a network host alters the packets of internal network hosts so that they can be sent out across the Internet. NAT was introduced in Chapter 5.

NAT allows an Intranet to use addresses that are different from what the Internet sees. NAT allows insiders to get out without allowing outsiders to get in. NAT rewrites the IP headers of internal packets going out, making it appear as if the packets originated from the firewall. Reply packets coming back are translated and forwarded to the appropriate internal machine. With NAT, inside machines are allowed to connect to the outside world but outside machines cannot connect inside the network. Outside machines cannot find internal machines because they are aware of only one IP address: the firewall. The ability to attack internal machines is greatly reduced by employing NAT.

16.5.4   Application Gateways

Application level gateways take requests for Internet services and forward them to the actual services. Application level gateways sit between a user on the internal network and a service on the Internet. Instead of talking to each other directly, each system talks to the gateway. Your internal network never connects directly to the Internet.

Application level gateways help improve security by examining all application layers, bringing context information into the decision process. However, they do this by breaking the client/server model into two connections: (1) one from the client to the firewall and (2) one from the firewall to the server. Unfortunately, because each application gateway requires a different application process, or daemon, you will need to add a different application processor or daemon to support new applications.

In Chapter 5, proxy servers were discussed. If you recall, a proxy server is a server that sits between a client application, such as a web browser, and a real server. It intercepts all requests to the real server to see if it can fulfill the requests itself. If not, it forwards the request to the real server. If it can fulfill the request itself, the user gets increased performance. In addition, it provides a means for sharing a single Internet connection among a number of work stations. While this has practical limits in performance, it can still be a very effective and inexpensive way to provide Internet services, such as e-mail, throughout an office.

> *NOTE:* Proxy servers typically refer to application gateways, but a circuit level gateway is also a form of proxy server.

In addition to increasing performance, a proxy server sits between a client program (typically a web browser) and some external server (typically another server on the web), which acts as an application level firewall. It acts as a type of firewall that manages packet sequence and origin to reduce the chance of hackers hijacking communication sessions.

> *NOTE:* Proxy servers are often used with firewalls and sometimes are the same machine or device as a firewall. Proxy servers can monitor and intercept any and all requests being sent to the external server or coming in from an Internet connection. Therefore, besides improving performance and sharing connections, Proxy servers can also filter requests.

Filtering requests is the security function of and the original reason for having a proxy server. Proxy servers can inspect all traffic (in and out) over an Internet connection and determine if there is anything that should be denied transmission, reception, or access. Because this filtering cuts both ways, a proxy server can be used to keep users out of particular web sites (by monitoring for specific URLs) or restrict unauthorized access to an internal network by authenticating users. Before a connection is made, the server can ask the user to log in. To a web user, this makes every site look like it requires a login. Because proxy servers handle all communications, they can log everything the user does. For HTTP (web) proxies, this includes logging every URL. For FTP proxies, this includes every downloaded file. A proxy can also examine the content of transmissions for "inappropriate" words and scan for viruses, although this may impose serious overhead on performance.

To users, a proxy server is almost totally invisible. All Internet requests and returned responses appear to come directly from the addressed Internet server. The reason that it is not totally invisible is that the IP address of the proxy server has to be specified as a configuration option to the browser or other protocol program.

For the browser to go through a proxy server, the browser must be configured. These configuration settings include automatic configuration, configuring through scripts, or manually specifying the settings. Automatic configuration and configuring through scripts enables you to change settings after you deploy Internet Explorer. By providing a pointer to configuration files on a server, you can change the settings globally without having to change each user's computer. This can help reduce administrative overhead and can potentially reduce help desk calls about browser settings.

To configure the proxy selection and proxy bypass settings in Internet Explorer:

1. Open the *Tools* menu, then click *Internet Options.*
2. Click the *Connections* tab, then click *LAN Settings.*
3. In the Proxy Server area, select the *Use a proxy server* check box.

Figure 16.2   Configuring the Proxy Selection and Proxy Bypass Settings in Internet Explorer

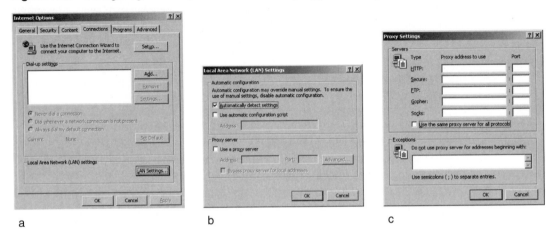

a   b   c

4. Click *Advanced,* then fill in the proxy location and port number for each Internet protocol that is supported (see Figure 16.2).

NOTE: In most cases, only a single proxy server is used for all protocols. In those cases, enter the proxy location and port number for the HTTP setting, then select the *Use the same proxy server for all protocols* check box. If you want to manually set the addresses, enable the *Use a proxy server* check box and specify the address and port number of the proxy server. If you need to specify different addresses and/or port numbers for the various Internet services, click on the *Advanced* button.

For Netscape, the same basic options are available if you:

1. Open the *Edit* menu and select the *Preferences* option.
2. Find and open the *Advanced* option.
3. Click on the *Proxy* option (see Figure 16.3).

16.5.5   Advanced Firewall Features

Most firewalls are hybrids of stateful inspection, circuit level gateways, and application level gateways. Only packets dealing with acceptable activities are allowed in and out of your internal network. Some firewalls provide advanced firewall features that make them more effective in your perimeter.

A firewall is a logical place to install an authentication mechanism to help overcome the limitations of TCP/IP. You can also use a reverse lookup on an IP address to verify that the user is actually at his or her reported location. This activity helps identify and prevent spoofing attacks.

Firewalls can also provide user authentication. Some application level gateways contain an internal user account database or integrate with UNIX and Windows domain ac-

Figure 16.3   Configuring the Proxy Settings for Netscape

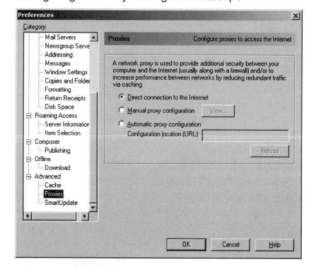

counts. These accounts can be used to limit activities and services by a user or to provide detailed logs of user activity. Because individual users can be easily identified, more granular rule sets can be implemented.

You can also use authentication for remote access. Allowing employees to connect to the internal network from home or while traveling increases productivity, but how can you ensure that the person making the request is who he or she is supposed to be? Most firewalls support third-party authentication methods to provide strong authentication.

Lastly, almost every firewall performs some type of logging. Most packet filters do not enable logging by default because logging degrades performance of traffic analysis. So if you want logging, make sure it is enabled and active. Extensive logging can help you track or capture a hacker. Because your firewall is the single point of entry to your network, an attacker will have to pass through it. Your log files should provide information to show you what the hacker was up to on your systems.

16.5.6   The Demilitarized Zone

If you set a firewall between the Internet and your private network, it provides no good place to locate publicly-accessible servers. If you place the servers out on the Internet in front of the firewall, they will be unprotected. If you have them behind the firewall, you have to create holes in the firewall protection to permit access to the servers. It is those holes that can be exploited on the rest of the network.

To get around this problem, you create a **demilitarized zone (DMZ).** Instead of having two ports: (1) the public network on one port of the firewall and (2) the private network on another port; you have three ports. The third port is the DMZ, which is a less secure area than the private network. The DMZ will include web and FTP servers, and the rest of your computers will be in the private network (see Figure 16.4).

Each segment, whether public, private, or DMZ, that is connected to the firewall has different sets of security rules. The private and public segments are no different from what we already discussed. On a DMZ LAN, you still want to use antispoofing filters, limit the

Figure 16.4   A DMZ

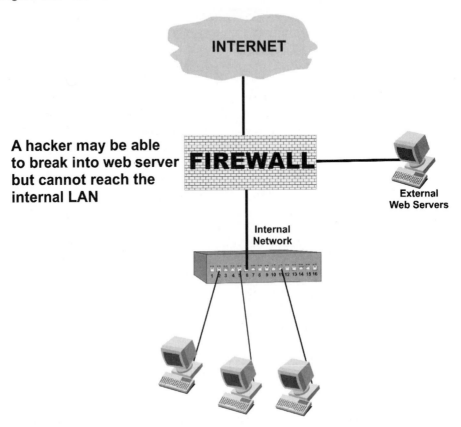

allowable ports to those used by the servers on the LAN, and disallow access from known attacking sites.

> *NOTE:* Remember that firewalls themselves aren't a guarantee of security. You will have to get in the habit of examining firewall logs for suspicious events, and you have to be vigilant about discovering and applying software security patches.

16.6   PROTECTING ROUTERS AND THEIR NETWORKS

Routers are perfect targets for attack because they are always exposed to the rest of the network or the Internet. Routers often use SNMP to manage their feature sets. However, this can be used against them, especially if they utilize SNMP version 1 because hackers can employ widely available network management software to gain access and manipulate the router with little effort.

Another security risk is to leave Telnet open or unprotected on any network resources. The security issue becomes even worse with routers, because with Telnet a hacker can gain access to the unit and access information to help profile the attack against the router. After a hacker has control of a router, he or she has the ability to entirely disable the unit or reconfigure the unit to pass the hurdle that the router can represent, or even change settings that would limit the router's performance.

Filtering Telnet ports on your firewall is an excellent way to protect your routers from outside tampering from the Internet. Telnet uses default ports 161 and 162. By limiting access to these ports in your firewall software, you can help prevent attacks against the router. As a rule, disabling or limiting Telnet access on any router or system is good because you probably don't need to maintain usage of Telnet beyond initial configuration.

Because of the relative ease of use in attacks, many corporate routers and firewalls do not respond to ICMP traffic. For example, if you ping www.microsoft.com, you will receive no ICMP replies.

Make sure that the router isn't vulnerable to DoS or DDoS attacks. A router that is susceptible to these types of attacks can be taken out with relative ease by just about anyone. One way to improve a defense against DoS attacks is to disable broadcasting on the router.

DoS attacks and DDoS attacks often gain more clout if a hacker can use several routers that have been set up to provide directed IP broadcasts; this includes most DoS attacks (including Smurf attacks).

By rule, your routers should disregard and drop any outgoing packets that do not originate from a valid internal IP address. When you perform this setting change, you will effectively prevent your network from becoming a participant in any spoofing attack. Therefore, configure your router to perform Egress and Ingress Filtering as previously explained.

The United States National Security Agency has published the *Router Security Configuration Guide,* which provides technical guidance intended to help network administrators and security officers improve the security of their networks. It contains principles and guidance for secure configuration of IP routers, with detailed instructions for Cisco Systems routers. The information presented can be used to control access, resist attacks, shield other network components, and protect the integrity and confidentiality of network traffic.

Help Defeat Denial of Service Attacks: Step-by-Step

http://www.sans.org/dosstep/index.htm

Router Security Configuration Guide

http://nsa2.www.conxion.com/cisco/download.htm

16.7   ENCRYPTION AND DECRYPTION

In networks, sensitive data gets transmitted across the network, sent as e-mail messages and stored on files on a disk. In all cases, the initial unencrypted data is referred to as plain text. **Encryption** is the process of disguising a message or data in what appears to be meaningless data (ciphered text) to hide and protect the sensitive data from unauthorized access. **Decryption** is the process of converting data from the encrypted format back to its original format. **Cryptography** is the art of protecting information by transforming it (encrypting it) into cipher text. In data and telecommunications, cryptography is necessary when communicating over any untrusted medium. Cryptography not only protects data from theft or alteration, but it can also be used for user authentication.

There are, in general, three types of cryptographic schemes typically used to accomplish these goals:

- **private-key (also known as secret key or symmetric) cryptography**—Uses a single key for both encryption and decryption
- **public-key (or asymmetric) cryptography**—Uses one key for encryption and another key for decryption
- **hash functions**—Uses a mathematical transformation to irreversibly encrypt information

To encrypt and decrypt a file, you must use a key. A **key** is a string of bits used to map text into a code and a code back to text. You can think of a key as a super-decoder ring used to translate text messages to a code and back to text. There are two types of keys: (1) public keys and (2) private keys.

16.7.1   Private Key Encryption

The most basic form of encryption is **private key encryption.** In private key encryption, a single key is used for both encryption and decryption. The sender uses the key (a set of rules) to encrypt the plain text and sends the ciphered text to the receiver. The receiver applies the same key (or rule set) to decrypt the message and recover the plain text. Because a single key is used for both functions, private key encryption is also called symmetric encryption.

This requires that each individual must possess a copy of the key. Of course, for this to work as intended, you must have a secure way to transport the key to other people. You also must keep multiple single keys per person, which can get very cumbersome. Private key algorithms are generally very fast and easily implemented in hardware. Therefore, they are commonly used for bulk data encryption.

There are two general categories of private key algorithms: (1) block cipher and (2) stream cipher. A block cipher encrypts one block of data at a time. A stream cipher encrypts each byte of the data stream individually. The most common secret key cryptography scheme used today is the Data Encryption Standard (DES).

16.7.2   Public Key Encryption

Public key encryption, also known as the asymmetric algorithm, uses two distinct but mathematically related keys: (1) public and (2) private. Public keys are nonsecret keys that are available to anyone you choose, or they could be made available to everyone by posting them in a public place. Often they are made available through a digital certificate. The private key is kept in a secure location used only by you. When data needs to be sent, it is protected with a secret key encryption that was encrypted with the public key of the recipient of the data. The encrypted secret key is then transmitted to the recipient along with the encrypted data. The recipient will use the private key to decrypt the secret key. The secret key will then be used to decrypt the message itself.

For example, if you want to send data to someone, you would retrieve his or her public key and encrypt the data. You encrypt the data and the secret key, then send both the data and the secret key. Because the recipient's private key is the only thing that can decrypt the secret key, which is the only thing that can decrypt the message, the data can be sent over an insecure communications channel.

While public keys may be stored anywhere for easy retrieval by computers, your private key should be carefully guarded. Because it is not convenient (or possible) for most folks to commit the keys to memory, they are stored on your personal computer's hard disk and encrypted by using conventional cryptography and a password. Thus, anyone in possession of your computer would still not be able to use your private key because it is scrambled with your password.

16.7.3   Digital Envelopes, Signatures, and Certificates

A **digital envelope** is a type of security that encrypts the message by using symmetric encryption and encrypts keys to decode the message using public-key encryption. This technique overcomes the problem of public key encryption being slower than symmetric encryption because only the key is protected with public key encryption, providing little overhead.

A **digital signature** is a digital code that can be attached to an electronically transmitted message that uniquely identifies the sender. Like a written signature, the purpose of a digital signature is to guarantee that the individual sending the message really is who he or she claims to be.

A **digital certificate** is an attachment to an electronic message used for security purposes, such as for authentication, and to verify that a user sending a message is who he or she claims to be. Digital certificates also provide the receiver with a means to encode a reply.

A **public key infrastructure (PKI)** enables users of an unsecured public network, such as the Internet, to securely and privately exchange data and money through the use of a public and a private cryptographic key pair that is obtained and shared through a trusted authority. Although the components of a PKI are generally understood, a number of different vendor approaches and services are emerging. Meanwhile, an Internet standard for PKI is being worked on.

An individual wishing to send an encrypted message applies for a digital certificate from a **certificate authority (CA).** The CA issues an encrypted digital certificate containing the applicant's public key and a variety of other identification information. The CA makes its own public key readily available through print publicity or the Internet. The recipient of an encrypted message uses the CA's public key to decode the digital certificate attached to the message, verifies it as issued by the CA, and then obtains the sender's public key and identification information held within the certificate. With this information, the recipient can send an encrypted reply.

16.7.4   Hash Encryption

Hash encryption, also called message digests or one-way encryption, uses algorithms that don't really use a key. Instead, it converts data from a variable length to a fixed length piece of data called a hash value. Theoretically, no two data will produce the same hash value. The hash process is irreversible. You cannot recover the original data by reversing the hash process.

Users must often utilize hashes when there is information they never want decrypted or read. Hash algorithms are typically used to provide a digital fingerprint of a file or message contents, and are often used to ensure that the file has not been altered by an intruder or a virus. Hash functions are also commonly employed by many operating systems to encrypt passwords.

Among the most common hash functions in use today are a family of message digest (MD) algorithms, all of which are byte-oriented schemes that produce a 128-bit ash value form an arbitrary-length message.

16.7.5   RSA and DES Standards

The **RSA standard** (created by Ron **R**ivst, Adi **S**hamir, and Leonard **A**dleman) defines the mathematical properties used in public key encryption and digital signatures. The key length for this algorithm can range from 512 to 2048, making it a very secure encryption algorithm. This algorithm uses a number, known as the public modulus, to come up with the public and private keys. This number is formed by multiplying two prime numbers. The security of this algorithm is found in the fact that while finding large prime numbers is relatively easy, factoring the result of multiplying two large prime numbers is not easy. If the prime numbers used are large enough, the problem approaches being computationally impossible. The RSA algorithm has become the de facto standard for industrial-strength encryption, especially for data sent over the Internet.

The Data Encryption Standard (DES) was developed in 1975 and was standardized by ANSI in 1981 as ANSI X.3.92. It is a popular symmetric key encryption method that uses block cipher. The key used in DES is based on a 56-bit binary number, which allows for 72,057,594,037,927,936 encryption keys. Of these 72 quadrillion encryption keys, a key is chosen at random. If you want to send an encrypted file from one person (source person) to another person (target person), the source person will encrypt the secret key with the target's persons public key, which was obtained from his or her certificate. Because the target person's key was used to encrypt the secret key, only the target person using his or her private key will be able to decrypt the DES secret key and decrypt the DES encrypted data.

> *NOTE:* Until recently, the United States government has banned the export of DES outside of the U.S.

Triple DES is a stronger alternative to regular DES, and is used extensively in conjunction with VPN implementations. Triple DES encrypts a block of data by using a DES secret key. The encrypted data is then encrypted again by using a second DES secret key. Finally, the encrypted data is encrypted a third time by using yet another secret key. Triple DES is of particular importance as the DES algorithm keeps getting broken in shorter and shorter times.

The **Advanced Encryption Standard (AES)** is an encryption algorithm for securing sensitive but unclassified material by U.S. Government agencies and, as a likely consequence, may eventually become the de facto encryption standard for commercial transactions in the private sector. Encryption for the U.S. military and other classified communications is handled by separate, secret algorithms.

In January of 1997, a process was initiated by the National Institute of Standards and Technology (NIST), a unit of the U.S. Commerce Department, to find a stronger than DES and more efficient than 3DES. Efficiency is measured by how fast the algorithm can encrypt and decrypt information, how fast it can present an encryption key and how much information it can encrypt.

The specification called for a symmetric algorithm (same key for encryption and decryption) using block encryption (see block cipher) of 128 bits in size, supporting key sizes of 128, 192 and 256 bits, as a minimum. The algorithm was required to be royalty-free for use worldwide and offer security of a sufficient level to protect data for the next 20 to 30 years. It was to be easy to implement in hardware and software, as well as in restricted environments (for example, in a smart card) and offer good defenses against various attack techniques.

The entire selection process was fully open to public scrutiny and comment, it being decided that full visibility would ensure the best possible analysis of the designs. The end result was that on October 2, 2000, NIST announced that Rijndael had been selected as the proposed standard. On December 6, 2001, the Secretary of Commerce officially approved Federal Information Processing Standard (FIPS) 197, which specifies that all sensitive, unclassified documents will use Rijndael. FIPS are a set of standards that describe document processing, provide standard algorithms for searching, and provide other information processing standards for use within government agencies.

Another type of encryption worth mentioning is **Pretty Good Privacy (PGP).** The name PGP denotes that nothing is 100 percent secure. PGP is one of the most common ways to protect messages on the Internet because it is effective, easy to use, and free. PGP is based on the public key method, which uses two keys. One key is a public key that you disseminate to anyone from whom you want to receive a message. The other is a private key that you use to decrypt received messages.

16.7.6   X.509 Digital Certificates

X.509 digital certificates are the most widely used digital certificates. An X.509 certificate contains information that identifies the user and information about the organization that issued the certificate, including the serial number, validity period, issuer name, issuer signature, and subject (or user) name. The subject can be an individual, a business, a school, or some other organization; including a certificate authority. X.509 describes two levels of authentication: (1) Simple authentication based on a password to verify user identity and (2) strong authentication uses credentials formed by using cryptographic techniques. It is recommended to use strong authentication to provide secure services.

> *NOTE:* X.509 is actually an ITU recommendation, which means that it hasn't been officially defined or approved.

16.8   SECURITY PROTOCOLS

Authentication, which is the layer of network security, is the process by which the system validates the user's log on information. Authentication is crucial to secure communication. Users must be able to prove their identity to those with whom they communicate and must be able to verify the identity of others. Typically, when a user logs on, the user is then authenticated for all network resources that the user has permission to use. The user only has to log on once although the network resources may be located throughout several computers.

16.8.1   Security Protocols for Virtual Tunnels

A **VPN** uses a public or shared network (such as the Internet or a campus intranet) to create a secure, private network connection between a client and a server. The VPN client cloaks each packet in a wrapper that allows it to sneak (or tunnel) unnoticed through the shared network. When the packet gets to its destination, the VPN server removes the wrapper, deciphers the packet inside, and processes the data.

There are two varieties of VPNs, and they differ primarily in their approach to protecting your data: (1) PPTP and (2) L2TP. The oldest and simplest type of VPN uses the point-to-point tunneling protocol (PPTP).

PPTP's data encryption algorithm, Microsoft point-to-point encryption (MPPE), uses the client's log in password to generate the encryption key. This is controversial because hackers are always finding ways to acquire passwords. In addition, early versions of MPPE had flaws that could expose tunneled data to inspection by hackers. Microsoft has since patched MPPE for all versions of Windows. To provide authentication, MPPE requires the use of EAP-TLS, MS-CHAP v1, or MS-CHAP v2. MPPE is available on Windows 2000, Windows Server 2003, Windows XP, Windows NT 4.0, and Windows 9X clients.

The more secure alternative to PPTP is L2TP (Layer 2 Tunneling Protocol). L2TP is another Microsoft development merging elements of PPTP with Layer 2 Forwarding, a Cisco packet encapsulation scheme. L2TP alone is not secure, so it is almost always paired with a fast-growing encryption standard called IPSec (Internet Protocol security), which supports end-to-end encryption between clients and servers.

IPSec supports end-to-end encryption between clients and servers while MPPE only supports link encryption. If implemented properly, IPSec is virtually impenetrable. Ideally, IPSec encryption employs the triple Data Encryption Standard (3DES) based on ANSI X.509 security certificates. Electronic certificates, issued internally or by a public authority such as Verisign Inc., irrefutably identify the client and server. 3DES encryption (ANSI X9.52) stiffens standard 56-bit encryption keys, which can be broken only with considerable effort, by applying the encryption algorithm three times.

16.8.2   IPSec

As mentioned previously, IPSec is a protocol that provide data integrity, authentication, and privacy to data being sent from one point to another point. IPSec works at the IP level and works transparently to protect the data from end-to-end. Besides being used to create a VPN over an unsecure network such as the Internet, it will be built into IP v6 and it is recommended to be used with wireless technology because transmission over the airways can be easily captured. IPSec is documented in a series of Internet RFCs, the overall IPSec implementation is guided by "Security Architecture for the Internet Protocol," RFC 2401.

IPSec is not a single protocol, but is a suite of protocols that can provide either message authentication and/or encryption. IPSec defines a new set of headers to be added to IP datagrams. These new headers are placed after the IP header and before the layer 4 protocol (typically TCP or UDP). The new protocols/headers that provide information for securing the payload of the IP packet are the authentication header (AH) and the encapsulating security payload (ESP).

While AH and ESP provide the means to protect data from tampering, preventing eavesdropping and verifying the origin of the data, it is the Internet Key Exchange (IKE) that defines the method for the secure exchange of the initial encryption keys between the two endpoints. IKE allows nodes to agree on authentication methods, encryption methods, the keys to use, and the lifespan of the keys.

The information negotiated by IKE is stored in a Security Association (SA). A SA is like a contract laying out the rules of the VPN connection for the duration of the SA. A SA is assigned a 32-bit number that, when used in conjunction with the destination IP address, uniquely identifies the SA. This number is called the Security Parameters Index (SPI).

Perfect Forward Secrecy (PFS) ensures that no part of a previous encryption key plays a part in generating a new encryption key. This means that when a new encryption key is generated, the old key does not play any part in the generation of the new key. Under normal circumstances (for performance reasons), an old key will play a part in generating a new key. When using PFS, this requires a little more overhead, as it requires reauthentication every time a new key is generated.

When the AH is added to an IP datagram, the header will ensure the integrity and authenticity of the data, including the fields in the outer IP header. It does not provide confidentiality protection. Thus, while AH provides a method for ensuring the integrity of the packet, it does nothing for keeping its contents secret. In addition, while it provides a mechanism to ensure the integrity of the IP header and the payload of the IP packet that will be transported across an untrusted link (such as the Internet), when used by itself, AH cannot provide a total guarantee of the entire IP header because some of the fields in the IP header are changed by routers as the packet passes through the network. For a truly secure VPN connection, you should use ESP.

AH uses a keyed-hash function rather than digital signatures, because digital signature technology is too slow and would greatly reduce network throughput. If any part of the datagram is changed during transit, this will be detected by the receiver when it performs the same one-way hash function on the datagram and compares the value of the message digest that the sender has supplied. The fact that the one-way hash also involves the use of a secret shared between the two systems means that authenticity can be guaranteed. In addition, AH may also enforce antireplay protection by requiring that a receiving host set the replay bit in the header to indicate that the packet has been seen. Without it, an attacker may be able to resend the same packet many times.

When added to an IP datagram, the ESP header protects the confidentiality, integrity, and authenticity of the data by performing encryption at the IP packet layer. While the default algorithm for IPSec is 56-bit DES, it does support a variety of symmetric encryption algorithms so that it can provide interoperability among different IPSec products.

ESP operates in two modes: (1) transport mode and (2) tunnel mode. When used in transport mode, the ESP header is placed between the IP header and the upper-level (transport layer) header. Any information following the ESP header, including transport layer headers, is encrypted according to the method described by the SA and the packet is sent on its way. This method does not use a gateway, so the clear text IP header at the front of the packet contains the actual destination address of the encapsulated datagram. However, ESP can be used in conjunction with AH to protect the integrity of the IP header information. You would typically use this for encrypting the contents of the IP packet on network connections of limited bandwidth. At the receiving end of the communication path, this clear text header information is saved, the contents of the encrypted packet are decrypted and reassembled with the correct IP header information, and the packet is sent on its way onto the network.

When operating in tunnel mode, ESP is used between two IPSec gateways, such as a set of routers or firewalls. When used in tunnel mode, the ESP header information is inserted directly before the IP or other protocol datagram that is to be protected. Therefore, the entire IP datagram, including the IP header (which has the true source address and destination address), and its payload (usually an upper-level protocol such as TCP or UPD) is encrypted and encapsulated by the ESP protocol. At the destination gateway, this outer wrapper of information is removed, the contents of the packet are decrypted, and the original IP packet is sent out onto the network to which the gateway is attached. This way, the internals of the network are hidden from would-be hackers.

The datagram being protected is encrypted (according to the methods set up by the SA), and additional headers are added in clear text format so that the new IP datagram can be transported to the appropriate gateway. In other words, the original protocol datagram is encrypted, the ESP header is added, and a new IP datagram is created to transport this conglomeration to its destination gateway point. At the receiving gateway, the outer IP header information is stripped off, and according to parameters defined by the SA, the protected payload of original datagram is decrypted.

ESP uses both a header and a trailer to encapsulate datagrams that it protects. The header consists of an SPI, which is used to identify the security association, and a sequence number to identify the packets to ensure that they arrive in the correct order and that no duplicate packets are received. The trailer consists of padding from 0 to 255 bytes to make sure that the datagram ends on a 32-bit boundary. This is followed by a field that specifies the length of the padding that was attached so that it can be removed by the receiver. Following this field is a Next Header field, which is used to identify the protocol that is enveloped as the payload.

Additionally, ESP can include an authentication trailer that contains data used to verify the identity of the sender and the integrity of the message. This Integrity Check Value (ICV) is calculated based on ESP header information as well as the payload and the ESP trailer. The layout of an ESP datagram is shown in Figure 16.5.

Figure 16.5 An ESP Datagram

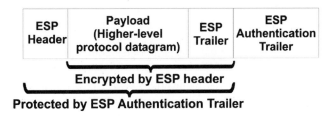

AH and ESP can be used independently or together, although for most applications, one of them is sufficient. IPSec also uses other existing encryption standards to make up a protocol suite.

Any routers or switches in the data path between communicating hosts will simply forward the encrypted and/or authenticated IP packets to their destination. However, if there is a firewall or filtering router, IP forwarding must be enabled for the following IP protocols and UDP port for IPSec to function:

- **IP Protocol ID of 51**—Both inbound and outbound filters should be set to pass AH traffic.
- **IP Protocol ID of 50**—Both inbound and outbound filters should be set to pass ESP traffic.
- **UDP Port 500**—Both inbound and outbound filters should be set to pass ISAKMP traffic.

Until recently, IPSec had some issues working with Network Address Translation (NAT). Transport mode IPSec provides end-to-end security between hosts, while tunnel mode protects encapsulated IP packets between security gateways, for example, between two firewalls or between a roaming host and a remote access server. When TCP or UDP are involved, as they are in transport mode ESP, since NAT modifies the TCP/UDP packet, NAT must also recalculate the checksum used to verify integrity. If NAT updates the checksum, ESP authentication will fail. If NAT does not update the checksum, TCP/UDP verification will fail. If the transport endpoint were under your control, you might be able to turn off checksums. To summarize, ESP can pass through NAT in tunnel mode, or in transport mode with checksums disabled or ignored by the receiver.

IPSec and NAT can function together when NAT occurs before the packet is encrypted. This typically works fine in gateway-to-gateway communications, remote access solutions are problematic because IPSec VPN client on a remote laptop computer will encrypt the packet before it travels to the NAT device, subsequently breaking the IPSec VPN connection.

To enable IPSec VPNs to work with NAT devices, some of the leading technology companies created NAT Traversal. The main technology behind this solution is UDP encapsulation, wherein the IPSec packet is wrapped inside a UDP/IP header, allowing NAT devices to change IP or port addresses without modifying the IPSec packet.

For NAT Traversal to work properly, two things must occur. First the communicating VPN devices must support the same method of UDP encapsulation. Second, all NAT devices along the communication path must be identified.

According to the IETF draft standard, IPSec devices will exchange a specific, known value to determine whether or not they both support NAT Traversal. If the two VPN devices agree on NAT Traversal, they next determine whether or not NAT or NAPT occurs anywhere on the communications path between them. NAT devices are determined by sending NAT-D (NAT Discovery) packets. Both end points send hashes of the source and destination IP addresses and ports they are aware of. If these hashes do not match, indicating that the IP address and ports are not the same, then the VPN devices know a NAT device exists somewhere in between.

Usually, NAT assignments last for a short period of time and are then released. For IPSec to work properly, the same NAT assignment needs to remain intact for the duration of the VPN tunnel. NAT Traversal accomplishes this by requiring any end point communicating through a NAT device to send a "keepalive" packet, which is a one-byte UDP packet sent periodically to prevent NAT end points from being remapped midsession.

All NAT Traversal communications occur over UDP port 500. This works great because port 500 is already open for IKE (Internet Key Exchange) communications in IPsec VPNs, so new holes do not need to be opened in the corporate firewall. This solution does add a bit of overhead to IPSec communications; namely, 200 bytes is added for the Phase 1 IKE negotiation and each IPSec packet has about an additional 20 bytes.

16.9   PATCHES

The last part of security is to make sure that you have the most updated patches and hot fixes for your network operating systems and to make sure that you check with the distributor and vendor of the network operating system (as well as the operating systems on the network) for security holes and the patches to fix the security hole. Microsoft offers a Hfnetchk utility to check if the current configuration on your servers is up to date and has all the appropriate security patches.

Another place that was mentioned when viruses and worms were discussed is the Computer Emergency Response Team (CERT) Coordination Center. The CERT Coordination Center was started in December, 1988 by the Defense Advanced Research Projects Agency (DARPA), which was part of the U.S. Department of Defense, after the Morris Worm disabled about ten percent of all computers connected to the Internet. Cert studies Internet security vulnerabilities, provides services to websites that have been attacked, and publishes security alerts. CERT/CC's research activities include the area of WAN computing and developing improved Internet security. The organization also provides training to incident response professionals.

CERT website

http://www.cert.org/

Symantec Security Advisory List

   http://securityresponse.symantec.com/avcenter/security/Advisories.html

16.10 AUDITING AND INTRUDER DETECTION

Trying to detect intruders can be a very daunting task. It often requires a lot of hard work and a thorough working knowledge of the network operating system and the network as a whole. You should always see what logs (especially the security logs such as those found in Event Viewer) are available with your network operating system (and fire-walls/proxy servers). For example, you can check the log that lists all failed log in attempts. If you see that for several days at late hours, the same account has attempted to log in but has failed. It could be that someone is trying to figure out the password and is trying to login but is failing. Sometimes security logging is enabled by default, other times it has to be enabled. Windows 2000 and Windows Server 2003 have an auditing service by using group policies that allow you to audit a large array of items, including who access which files. These auditing features can also be arranged to check everyone including the administrators—in an attempt to keep the administrators honest as well.

Besides looking at your Audit logs, you can also look at your firewall logs. A typical firewall will generate large amounts of log information. The firewall logs can tell you port scans and unauthorized connection attempts and can identify activity from compromised systems. The real trick in using logs is knowing what to look for.

Traffic moving through a firewall is part of a connection. A connection has two basic components: (1) a pair of IP addresses and (2) a pair of port numbers. The IP addresses identify each computer involved in the communication. The port numbers identify what services or applications are being utilized. More specifically, it is typically the destination port number that will indicate what applications/services are being used. Of course, knowing what port numbers are associated with what services helps identify malicious activity occurring on the firewall.

- **IP addresses that are rejected**—Although a site will be probed from many places many times, knowing that a probe is occurring and what is being probed for proves useful information when trying to secure a network.
- **Unsuccessful logins**—Knowing when someone is trying to gain access to critical systems proves useful to help secure a network.
- **Outbound activity from internal servers**—If there is traffic originating from an internal server, having a good understanding of the normal activity on that server will help an administrator determine if the server has been compromised.
- **Source routed packets**—Source routed packets may indicate that someone is trying to gain access to the internal network. Because many networks have an address range that is unreachable from the internet (10.x.x.x), source routed packets can be used to gain access to a machine with a private address because there is usually a machine exposed to the internet that has access to the private address range.

In addition to the security information documented above, you can get a lot out of firewall logs if you have looked at your logs before, thus you are familiar with normal everyday activities. This way, if you know what is normal, it will be easier to identify malicious activity when they occur.

A **honeypot** is a computer set up as a "sacrificial lamb" on the network. The system is not locked down and has open ports and services enabled. This is to entice a would-be attacker to this computer instead of attacking authentic computers on the network. The honeypot contains no real company information, and will not cause problems if and when it is attacked. The administrator can monitor the honeypot so he or she can see how an attack is occurring without putting your other systems in harms way. It may give the administrator an opportunity to track down the attacker. The longer the hacker stays at the honeypot, the more will be disclosed about his or her techniques.

On your network, you should use virus protection software. For this to be effective, you will need to keep the software up-to-date. In addition, it would be advantageous to have a solid knowledge of what Trojan Horses are in circulation, what ports they are using, how they operate, and what their general purpose is. A nice list of Trojan Horses and their associated ports can be found at http://www.simovits.com/ nyheter9902.html.

16.11   PENETRATION TESTING

Penetration testing is the process of probing and identifying security vulnerabilities in a network and identifying the extent to which they might be exploited by outside parties. It is a necessary tool for determining the current security posture of your network. Such a test should determine both the existence and extent of any risk.

The normal pattern for a malicious user or a person to gain information on a target host or network starts with basic reconnaissance. This could be as simple as visiting an organization's website(s) or using public tools to learn more information about the target's domain registrations. After the attacker has gained enough information, the next logical step is to scan for open ports and services on the target's host or network. The scanning process may yield very important information such as ports open through the router and firewall, available services and applications on hosts or network appliances, and possibly the version of the operation system or application in use. After an attacker has mapped out available hosts, ports, applications, and services; the next step is to test for vulnerabilities that may exist on the target host or network.

When a vulnerability is found and the hacker has gained access to a host, he or she will attempt to keep access and cover their tracks. Covering of tracks most often involves the tampering of logs or logging servers. The defense in-depth strategy should be a layered approach that assumes the perimeter network can be compromised. With this in mind, it is critical to protect logs and logging servers. In the case of an actual intrusion, many times all an organization is left with is their logs. Protect them well because this may be your only evidence of the incident.

16.11.1   Reconnaissance

The reconnaissance phase can be done many different ways depending on the goal of the attacker. Some of the common available tools are:

- **Nslookup**—Available on Unix and Windows platforms
- **Whois**—Available via any Internet browser client
- **ARIN**—Available via any Internet browser client
- **Dig**—Available on most Unix platforms and some websites via a form
- **Web Based Tools**—Hundreds if not thousands of sites offer various reconnaissance tools
- **Target Web Site**—The client's website often reveals too much information
- **Social Engineering**—People are an organization's greatest asset and an organization's greatest risk

16.11.2   Scanning

After the penetration engineer or attacker gathers the preliminary information via the reconnaissance phase, they will try to identify systems that are alive. The live systems will be probed for available services. The process of scanning can involve many tools and varying techniques, depending on what the goal of the attacker is and the configuration of the target host or network is. Remember, each port has an associated service that may be exploitable and may contain vulnerabilities.

The fundamental goal of scanning is to identify potential targets and vulnerabilities of the target host or network. *Nmap* is probably the best known and most flexible scanning tool available today. It is one of the most advanced port scanners. Nmap provides options for fragmentation, spoofing, use of decoy IP addresses, stealth scans, and many other features. Nmap could be downloaded from the http://www.insecure.org/nmap/ website. Another good software package is GFI LANguard Network Security Scanner (evaluation software available from the http://www.gfisoftware.com/ website).

Below is a list of some common tools used to perform scanning:

- **Nmap**—Powerful tool for UNIX that finds ports and services
- **GFI LANguard Network Security Scanner**—Powerful tool for Windows that finds ports and services
- **Telnet**—Can report information about an application or service, (version or platform)
- **Ping**—Available on most every platform and operating system to test for IP connectivity
- **Traceroute**—Maps out the hops of the network to the target device or system
- **Hping2**—Powerful Unix-based tool used to gain important information about a network
- **Netcat**—Some have quoted this application as the "Swiss Army Knife" of network utilities
- **Queso**—Can be used for operating system fingerprinting

16.11.2   Vulnerability Testing

Vulnerability testing is the act of determining which security holes and vulnerabilities may be applicable to the target network or host. The penetration tester or attacker will attempt to identify machines within the target network, open ports, operating systems, and running applications such as the operating system, patch level, and service pack applied.

The vulnerability testing phase is started after some interesting hosts are identified via Nmap scans or another scanning tool and is preceded by the reconnaissance phase. Nmap will determine if a host is alive or not and what ports and services are available even if ICMP is completely disabled on the target network to a high degree of accuracy.

One of the best vulnerability scanners available today just happens to be free. *Nessus* is available at the http://www.nessus.org website. Nessus tool is well supported by the security community and is comparable to commercial products such as ISS Internet Security Scanner and CyberCop by CA. Another powerful utility is the SAINT tool, which is located at the http://www.saintcorporation.com.

Other free vulnerability scanners include SARA, available at http://www-arc.com/sara/. A special version of SARA is available to test specifically for the SANS/FBI Top 20 most critical Internet security vulnerabilities located at http://www.sans.org/top20.htm. SARA and SAINT are both descendants of SATAN, an early security administrator's tool for analyzing networks.

Once an attacker has gained a list of potential vulnerabilities for specific hosts on the target network, they will take this list of vulnerabilities and search for a specific exploit to utilize on their victim. Several vulnerability databases are available to anyone on the Internet:

ISS X-Force

http://www.iss.net/security_center/

Security Focus Database

http://online.securityfocus.com/archive/1

InfoSysSec Database

http://www.infosyssec.com/

Exploit World

http://www.insecure.com/sploits.html

For newer Microsoft operating systems, Microsoft now offers the Microsoft Baseline Security Analyzer (MBSA). It provides a streamlined method of identifying common security misconfigurations. MBSA includes a GUI and a CLI that can perform local or remote scans of Windows systems. MBSA will scan for missing hot fixes and vulnerabilities in the following products: Windows NT 4.0, Windows 2000, Windows .NET Server 2003, Windows XP, Internet Information Server (IIS) 4.0 and 5.0, SQL Server 7.0 and 2000, Internet Explorer (IE) 5.01 and later, and Office 2000 and 2002. MBSA creates and stores individual XML security reports for each computer scanned and will display the reports in the GUI in HTML.

Baseline Security Analyzer Home Page and Download Instructions

http://www.microsoft.com/technet/security/tools/Tools/mbsahome.asp

Baseline Security Analyzer White Paper

http://www.microsoft.com/technet/security/tools/tools/mbsawp.asp

SUMMARY

1. A threat is a person, place, or thing that has the potential to access resources and cause harm.
2. A vulnerability is a point where a resource is susceptible to attack. It can be thought of as a weakness.
3. An exploit is a type of attack on a resource, accessed by a threat that makes use of a vulnerability in your environment.
4. Countermeasures are deployed to counteract threats and vulnerabilities, therefore reducing the risk in your environment.
5. The username and password are the first line of defense because every user needs to have one to get access to the network and its resources.
6. For the password to be effective, the administrator should set guidelines and policies on how the user should use the network, provide training for these guidelines, and provide frequent reminders.
7. Give only the rights and permissions that are necessary for the user to do his or her job.
8. Make sure that the user does have sufficient rights and permissions to do what needs to be done.
9. In a network that uses share-level security, you assign passwords to individual files or other network resources (such as printers) instead of assigning rights to users.
10. In a network that uses user-level security, rights to network resources (such as files, directories, and printers) are assigned to specific users who gain access to the network through individually assigned usernames and passwords.
11. Educate your users about the dangers of social engineering.
12. For larger networks that require switches and routers, you should secure computer servers and other key components, including routers and switches, in a server room or a telecommunications closet to which only a handful of people are allowed access.
13. A DoS is a type of attack on a network. It is designed to bring the network to its knees by flooding it with useless traffic.
14. Firewalls serve as a primary defense against external threats to an organization's computer network system. A firewall is usually a combination of hardware and software used to implement an organization's security policy governing network traffic.
15. A DMZ is a third zone connected to a firewall and is less secure than the private network.
16. Encryption is the process of disguising a message or data in what appears to be meaningless data (ciphered text) to hide and protect the sensitive data from unauthorized access.
17. Decryption is the process of converting data from an encrypted format back to its original format.
18. Cryptography is the art of protecting information by transforming it (encrypting it) into ciphered text.
19. To encrypt and decrypt a file, you must use a key. A key is a string of bits used to map text into a code and a code back to text.
20. The most basic form of encryption is private key encryption. In private key encryption, a single key is used for both encryption and decryption.
21. Public key encryption, also known as the asymmetric algorithm, uses two distinct but mathematically related keys: (1) public and (2) private.
22. A digital envelope is a type of security that encrypts the message by using symmetric encryption and encrypts a key to decode the message by using public key encryption.
23. A digital signature is a digital code that can be attached to an electronically transmitted message that uniquely identifies the sender.
24. A digital certificate is an attachment to an electronic message used for security purposes such as for authentication. It can also verify that a user sending a message is who he or she claims to be and provide the receiver with a means to encode a reply.
25. A CA issues an encrypted digital certificate containing the applicant's public key and a variety of other identification information.
26. Hash encryption, also called message digests or one-way encryption, uses algorithms that don't really use a key. Instead, it converts data from a variable length to a fixed length piece of data called a hash value.
27. X.509 certificates are the most widely used digital certificates.

28. A VPN uses a public or shared network (such as the Internet or a campus intranet) to create a secure, private network connection between a client and a server.
29. The oldest and simplest type of VPN uses PPTP.
30. PPTP's data encryption algorithm, MPPE, uses the client's log in password to generate the encryption key.
31. The more secure alternative to PPTP is L2TP.
32. L2TP is another Microsoft development that merges elements of PPTP with Layer 2 Forwarding, a Cisco packet encapsulation scheme. L2TP alone is not secure, so it is almost always paired with a fast-growing encryption standard called IPSec, which supports end-to-end encryption between clients and servers.
33. IPSec supports end-to-end encryption between clients and servers while MPPE only supports link encryption. If implemented properly, IPSec is virtually impenetrable.
34. Make sure that you have the most updated patches and hot fixes for your network operating systems and check with the distributors and vendors of the network operating system (as well as the operating systems on the network)

for security holes and the patches to fix the security holes.
35. Trying to detect intruders can be a very daunting task. It often requires a lot of hard work and a thorough working knowledge of the network operating system and the network as a whole.
36. In addition to looking at your Audit logs, you can also look at your firewall logs.
37. A honeypot is a computer set up as a "sacrificial lamb" on the network. The system is not locked down and has open ports and services enabled. This is to entice a would-be attacker to this computer instead of authentic computers on the network.
38. You should use virus protection software on your network.
39. A protocol analyzer, also known as a network analyzer, is either software or a hardware/software device that allows you to capture or receive every packet on your media, store it in a trace buffer, and then show a breakdown of each of the packets (by protocol) in the order that they appeared.
40. Penetration testing is the process of probing and identifying security vulnerabilities in a network and the extent to which they might be exploited by outside parties.

QUESTIONS

1. Which device can prevent Internet hackers from accessing a LAN?
   a. a firewall
   b. a MAU
   c. a gateway
   d. a router
2. Pat administers a LAN for the Acme Corporation. Pat has recently connected the LAN to the Internet, but Skip (the CEO) is concerned that hackers will infiltrate the LAN and steal important trade secrets. Skip has also noticed that Internet access is extremely slow, and he wants Pat to improve it. What can Pat use to meet Skip's requirements?
   a. a firewall
   b. a router
   c. an IP proxy
   d. a transceiver

3. For what purpose does a network operating system (NOS) use ACLs?
   a. to determine which users can use resources on the network
   b. to locate hosts on the network
   c. to establish communications between NICs
   d. to determine which TCP/IP service receives data packets
4. Which of the following passwords provides you with the strongest network security?
   a. user1   b. User1
   c. USER1   d. uSEr1#
5. Pat administers a network. He wants to implement a strong password policy. How should Pat accomplish this task? (Choose all correct answers.)
   a. He should configure passwords to expire every 30 days.

b. He should provide users with password hints.

c. He should configure the NOS to lock users out of their accounts after three unsuccessful logon attempts.

d. He should require users to create passwords that contain only alphabetic characters.

e. He should require a minimum password length of eight characters.

6. Spoofing is a method of _____.

a. encrypting a data packet

b. tracking transactions to verify authenticity

c. filtering bad packets

d. fooling a firewall into thinking the packet is friendly

e. translating one IP address to another

7. You manage a small LAN that has a limited bandwidth connection to the Internet. Your users have been complaining of slow access lately. Which of the following could you place on your network to help improve access?

a. a firewall

b. a multiport switch

c. an Internet router

d. a proxy server

8. Which of the following securely transmits data between corporate sites through the Internet?

a. CVP

b. QVP

c. NVP

d. VPN

9. A hardware software device that prevents unauthorized connections to your internal network is called what?

a. a sniffer

b. a packet wall

c. a fluke

d. a firewall

10. What is the best place to put your e-mail router, public web server, and FTP server in your network?

a. PRL

b. CMA

c. TXV

d. DMZ

11. What is DES?

a. data encoded subnetwork

b. double-edged signaling

c. dynamic encoded synchronization

d. data encryption standard

12. Which of the following is a public key encryption utility?

a. PGP

b. QSA

c. RSA

d. GPR

13. Packet filtering allows a router or firewall to see if packets being received match predetermined criteria and drops packets that don't match or fit the current communication session that is established. A list that gives it this ability must be kept on the router. What is this list known as? (Pick two answers.)

a. session table

b. state table

c. dynamic packet list

d. dynamic state list

14. What is the practice of sending packets that have fake source addresses?

a. IP translation

b. packet hopping

c. protocol tunneling

d. IP spoofing

15. What is it called when abnormally large ICMP packets are sent to a system with the intent to bring it down?

a. ping of death

b. WinNuke

c. IP spoofing

d. SYN flood

16. While performing a routing site audit of your wireless network, you discover an unauthorized access point (placed on your network) under the desk of the accounting department secretary. When questioned, she denies any knowledge of it, but informs you that her new boyfriend (of two weeks) has been by to visit her several times, including taking her to lunch one time. What type of attack have you just become a victim of?

a. replay attack

b. SYN flood

c. IP spoofing

d. phone tag

e. social engineering

f. man in the middle attack

g. TCP flood

h. Halloween attack

i. DDoS

17. A honey pot is _____.
   a. something that exists only in theory
   b. a place to store passwords
   c. a false system or network to attract attacks away from your real network
   d. a safe haven for your backup media

18. As the security analyst for your company's network, you are experiencing problems with your Internet facing devices. They are sluggish in response and one of your NT servers has blue screened. You put up a sniffer and are catching a high volume of ICMP traffic. What could be the cause of the problem?
   a. You are seeing a teardrop attack.
   b. You are seeing a fragmentation attack.
   c. You are seeing a brute force attack.
   d. You are seeing a ping of death attack.

19. What kind of attack is a security breach of a computer system that does not usually result in the theft of information or other security loss but does result in a lack of legitimate use of that system?
   a. CRL
   b. ACL
   c. DoS
   d. MD2

20. What is a computer host or small network inserted as a "neutral zone" between a company's private network and the outside public network. Hint: It prevents outside users from getting direct access to a server that has company data.
   a. DMZ
   b. ART
   c. ACL
   d. CERT

21. What two functions does IPSec perform? (Choose two correct answers.)
   a. provides the SSH for data confidentiality
   b. provides the AH for data integrity
   c. provides the ESP for data confidentiality
   d. provides the NH for identity integrity
   e. provides the PAP for user authentication
   f. provides the IP for data integrity

22. As the security analyst for your company's network, you want to use a CA to set up security with digital certificates. Some digital certificates conform to a standard. Which standard is it?
   a. X.507
   b. X.509

   c. Z.509
   d. X.409

23. Users who configure their passwords by using simple and meaningful things such as pet names or birthdays are subject to having their account used by an intruder after what type of attack?
   a. change list attack
   b. dictionary attack
   c. Mickey Mouse attack
   d. man in the middle attack
   e. spoofing attack
   f. random guess attack
   g. rolebased access control attack
   h. brute force attack
   i. replay attack

24. A piece of malicious code that can replicate itself, has no productive purpose, and exists only to damage computer systems or create further vulnerabilities is called a _____.
   a. virus
   b. worm
   c. SYN flood
   d. Trojan Horse
   e. logic bomb

25. By what means can an administrator monitor his network for authorized and unauthorized access without any apparent changes to end users or intruders?
   a. auditing
   b. repudiation
   c. handshaking
   d. authentication
   e. authorization

26. What type of server sits between an internal client and the Internet to help protect the internal client and cache web pages?
   a. port scanner
   b. proxy server
   c. packet inspector
   d. firewall
   e. packet server
   f. web server

27. A device that is placed between the internal network and the Internet to protect internal assets is a _____.
   a. proxy server
   b. firewall
   c. web server

tone pad has sixteen digits, as opposed to ten on a pulse dial. In addition to the numerals 0 to 9, a DTMF has *, #, A, B, C, and D. Although the letters are not normally found on consumer telephones, the IC in the phone is capable of generating them.

The * sign is usually called *star* or *asterisk*. The # sign is often referred to as the *pound sign* but it is actually called an *octothorpe*. Although many phone users have never used these digits, they are used for control purposes such as phone answering machines, bringing up remote bases, electronic banking, and repeater control. The one use of the octothorpe that may be familiar occurs in dialing international calls from phones in the U.S. After dialing the complete number, dialing the octothorpe lets the exchange know you've finished dialing. It can now begin routing your call. Without the octothorpe, it would wait and "time out" before switching your call.

The telephone uses a device to alert you of an incoming call. It may be a bell, a light, or warbling tone. The telephone company sends a ringing signal (which is an AC waveform).

Although the common frequency used in the U.S. is 20 Hz, it can be any frequency between 15 and 68 Hz. Most of the world uses frequencies between 20 and 40 Hz.

17.2 DIGITIZED VOICE NETWORKS

To support voice in its native analog form over a digital network's voice-grade digital channel, the analog signal must be coded or converted into a digital format after leaving your lips and prior to entering the WAN. On the receiving end, the digital signal has to be decoded or converted back into an analog format in order to be intelligible to the human ear.

Those conversion processes are accomplished by using a matching pair of codecs (coder/decoders). The traditional method is to use **Pulse Code Modulation (PCM)** standardized by the ITU as G.711. PCM is based on the **Nyquist Theorem,** which states that, in order to convert analog voice to a digital format, send it over a digital circuit, and reproduce a high-quality analog voice at the receiving end, one must sample the amplitude of the analog sine wave at twice the highest frequency on the line.

Again, if one samples at twice the highest frequency on the line, one samples at a rate of $4000 \times 2 = 8000$ times a second. Each sample that you take will be assigned an 8-bit value (representing one of 256 different values). If you do the math, that is 8000 samples $\times 8$ bits per byte $= 64,000$ bits per second (64 Kbps).

Telephone companies chop their network bandwidth into voice channels or circuits running at 64 Kbps. These voice channels are technically called **digital signal level 0 (DS-0)** circuits and remain the most common type of line leased on a monthly basis or sold to organizations as private lines. This is true even when the DS-0 leased line is used for data purposes, such as to connect routers at two separate locations. Many organizations use a series of DS-0s to connect their private voice switches or private branch exchanges (PBXs). Common groupings of DS-0s used for this purpose gather 6, 12, or 24 voice channels into a single circuit.

The decoded signal, now in analog form once again, is only an approximation of the original analog signal but it's thoroughly understandable to the human ear. A critical component of taking these samples is timing. The network must be in a position to accept, switch, transport, and deliver every voice byte precisely every 125 ms. That means that latency or delay must be minimal and jitter (variation in delay) must be virtually zero.

Today, with newer voice digitization techniques and compression, voice can be achieved at as low as 2 Kbps, but is usually provisioned at 8 Kbps. Methods of generating digitized voice below 64 Kbps PCM voice signals is often referred to as voice compression, but not all digitized voice below 64 Kbps is produced by compressing 64 Kbps PCM voice signals.

For example, let's say that you talk for ten minutes. During this time, the circuit is continuously open between the two phones. Telephone conversations over the PSTN are transmitted at a fixed rate of about 64 kilobits per second (Kbps) in each direction, for a total transmission rate of 128 Kbps. Because there are eight kilobits (Kb) in a kilobyte (KB), this translates to a transmission of sixteen KB each second the circuit is open, and 960 KB every minute it is open. So in a ten-minute conversation, the total transmission is 9600 KB, which is roughly equal to 9.4 megabytes (MB).

If you look at a typical phone conversation, much of this transmitted data is wasted. While you are talking, the other party is listening, which means that only half of the connection is in use at any given time. Based on that, you can surmise that we could cut the file in half, down to about 4.7 MB. In addition, a significant amount of the time in most conversations is "dead air" when neither party is talking. If you could remove these silent intervals, the file would be even smaller. Of course, eight Kbps digitized voice signals use all the bandwidth all the time. But silence suppression converts the digitized voice into a bursty stream of bits.

Voice data can be compressed in order to use shared bandwidth more efficiently; this can be done with little loss in voice quality if everything goes right. If network congestion levels increase, so do latency and jitter, and packet loss may result. If, on the other hand, the ingress gateway has the sense that current congestion levels are such that the quality of the call is likely to be compromised, the call may be routed over the conventional PSTN. Not all service providers offer the PSTN backup option, but many do in order to support business-class users.

17.3   VOICE NETWORKS

All telephone networks consist of a few basic hardware elements, which can be compared to the hardware used on the Internet. The basic hardware elements are:

PSTN Elements
- telephones, modems, or fax machines
- customer premises wiring
- LEC switches
- interexchange carrier switches
- trunks

Internet Elements
- hosts
- LANs
- access routers
- backbone routers
- WAN links

17.3.1   Circuit Switching

As you might have seen in old movies or television shows, switching once was done manually by operators. Besides needing constant attention, this method is extremely slow compared to today's technology. When switching was eventually upgraded to electronic devices, the talking path was no longer an electrically continuous circuit. Instead, the speech being carried was digitized into a stream of 1s and 0s. Of course, on many home systems, the phone call starts as an analog signal, goes to the first switching station along the last mile, and is converted to a digital signal. It will be switched from switching station to switching station until it gets to the last switching station. The phone call is then converted to an analog signal and sent to the destination household.

Whether the system was analog or digital, there was an actual talking path or a circuit from the calling party to the called party. This talking path was established at the beginning of a call and held for the duration of a call. This is called **circuit switching.**

17.3.2   Transmission Media

There are four types of media that can be used to transmit information in the telecommunications world:

- UTP copper wire
- coaxial cable (actually an adaptation of copper wire)
- fiber
- wireless

Most phone systems use UTP. The cable does not have a shield and therefore the signal—primarily the high-frequency part of the signal—was able to leak out. Also, the twisting on the copper pair was very casual, designed as much to identify which wires belonged to a pair as to handle transmission problems. However, this is the way it was done, and for voice communications it was quite satisfactory. Consequently, there are millions of miles of copper in the PSTN.

Not only did the copper cable itself have limitations, but things were done to this cable to make it even more unsuitable for high-speed data transmission. These actions primarily took two forms:

- **Loading**—Load coils were frequently added to loops longer than 18,000 feet. These load coils were essentially low-pass filters. That is, they passed (without attenuation) all voice frequencies but effectively blocked frequencies above the voiceband. This is disastrous for data communications, which depend on high frequencies to achieve the desired speed of transmission.
- **Bridge taps**—A bridge tap is any unterminated portion of a loop that is not in the direct talking path. A bridge tap may be a used cable pair connected at an intermediate point or an extension beyond the customer. For example, a drop wire that provided a second line to a home is left in place even after the second set of CPE is removed. Records of this were not always kept and assigning a particular copper pair to a high-speed data circuit is far from a sure thing. Bridge taps do nasty things to data transmission.

Coaxial cable consists of a single strand of copper running down the axis of the cable. This strand is separated from the outer shielding by an insulator made of foam or other dielectrics. A conductive shield covers the cable. Usually, an outer insulating cover is applied to the overall cable—this has nothing to do with the carrying capacity of the cable. Because of the construction of the coaxial cable, very high frequencies can be carried without leaking out.

Fiber is the third transmission medium, and it is unquestionably the transmission medium of choice. Whereas transmission over copper utilizes frequencies in the MHz range, transmission over fiber utilizes frequencies a million times higher. This is another way of saying that the predominant difference between electromagnetic waves and light waves is the frequency. This difference, in turn, permits transmission speeds of immense magnitudes. Transmission speeds of as high as 9.9 Gbps have become commonplace in the industry. At this speed, the entire fifteen-volume set of Encyclopedia Britannica can be transmitted in well under one second.

Laying fiber on a per-mile basis still costs somewhat more than laying copper. However, on a per-circuit basis there is no contest; fiber wins hands down. If a local loop is being laid to a residence, there is little justification to install fiber—there will never be a need for more than a couple of circuits. So because there is not much need to install fiber for a final several hundred yards, the industry has not implemented fiber-to-the-curb (FTTC). In such a system, fiber would carry a plurality of channels to the curb, whereupon they would be broken down and applied to the copper drop leading to the home. In many cases, even this was overkill, and fiber-to-the-neighborhood (FTTN) is now being used. The message is clear: Apply fiber when it is economical to do so. Otherwise, rely on copper.

Fiber comes in several forms. The two predominant forms are: (1) multimode and (2) single mode. As can be seen, the total strand diameter for both is about 125 microns (a micron is a millionth of a meter). However, the ultrapure glass that forms the core transmission medium is between 50 and 62.5 microns for multimode fiber and about 8 to 10 microns for single mode fiber. One would think that the multimode fiber would have a greater carrying capacity; however, just the opposite is true. With single mode fiber, only one ray or mode can travel down the strand, making for a simpler job in regenerating the signal at points along the span. Single mode fiber makes up the majority of today's long distance network.

The tremendous capacity of fiber certainly makes for more efficient communications; however, placing so much traffic on a single strand makes for greater vulnerability. Most disruptions in the long distance network are a result of physical interruption of a fiber run called *backhoe fade*.

Wireless communication is the fourth transmission medium. This can take several forms: microwave, synchronous satellites, low-earth-orbit satellites, cellular, personal communications service (PCS), etc. Some of these will be described in more detail later. In every case, however, a wireless system necessitates a complex wired infrastructure. In the case of synchronous satellites, transmission can take place across oceans or deserts. With microwave, there is no need to plant cable. In mountainous territories, this is a significant advantage. Cellular and PCS afford mobility. There are advantages and disadvantages to each.

17.3.3   The Hierarchy of Switching Systems

All telephone network customers interact with the voice network by using a telephone, computer modem, or fax machine. The telephone is commonly connected to a CO switch, the network node of the PSTN, by means of a local loop or an access line. The access line is typically a single pair of twisted-pair computer wire.

If you only had a couple of telephones in each area, it would make sense to connect each phone to all other phones and find a simple method of selecting the desired one. However, if there are a few thousand phones in an area, that it would be quite difficult, not to mention probably very confusing. Therefore, it is appropriate to connect each phone to a CO and perform switching there. As we connect each of these thousands of telephones to the CO office, we have a star configuration. All lines are particular to one and only one station, and all terminate on the nucleus of this star at the CO. These connections are called the local exchange plant, and the telephone company handling this function is called the **local exchange carrier (LEC).** These connections were described earlier in the book as the local loop, sometimes referred to as the last mile.

The trunking network forms the backbone on the PSTN in the same way that backbone routers form the global Internet. The trunking network consists of more voice switches and multiplexed links, but there are no access lines attached to the switches on the trunking network. This connectivity is strictly trunk-to-trunk.

The **CO switch's** main job is to connect access lines to each other, based on the network address and the telephone numbers of the destination telephone instrument. The PSTN is a connected-oriented, circuit switched network in which no information can flow from source to destination until a connection is established between a source and destination. If the destination instrument is attached to the same CO switch, this job is easy. It is a more difficult task if the telephone number dialed is at the end of an access line on another switch. The destination can be connected on different switches. The voice connection must be routed onto a trunking network, which is just a network that links telephone switches. Trunks can be individual twisted pairs indistinguishable from access lines, although trunks are more likely to be carried on coaxial cable, fiber optic, or microwave towers.

Each CO is responsible for managing all telephone calls within its area, either switching the call to the called party within the same exchange, or switching the call to a trunk and into another CO's area. The side of the CO closest to the local subscriber is called the line-side interface or local loop. The side of the CO connecting to another CO is called the trunk-side interface. Loop-side interfaces are primarily responsible for battery feed, over-voltage protection, telephone set ringing, call supervision, signal coding, hybrid two-four wire conversion, and circuit testing.

The area covered by a CO is very limited. So there must be a way to connect a phone that has not originated and terminated within the particular CO's coverage area. Because we have thousands and thousands of areas to connect, it was best to organize and connect all of these areas by using a multi-tiered model. The local office, also called the end office, is called a Class-5 office. The office to which it connects is called the Class-4 office. The top level, the Class-1 office, appears in only a few places in the country (see Figure 17.1).

> *NOTE:* The only office that has people as its subscribers is the Class-5 office. The other offices in this hierarchy have lower-level COs as their subscribers. Those lines connecting switching offices to switching offices, rather than to subscribers, are called trunks.

Figure 17.1 The Hierarchy of Switching Systems Used on the PSTN

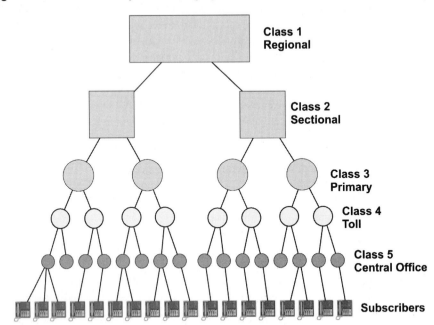

The section leading upward from Class-5 offices is handled not by the LECs but by the **interexchange carriers (IXCs)** (long-distance carriers). This entire structure has been titled the hierarchy of switching systems. The total network is the PSTN.

In days of old, there was only one long-distance carrier—AT&T. Hence, any time a telephone number was dialed with an area code, the LEC knew that it must be handed off to AT&T. But then came MCI, Sprint, and hundreds of other long-distance carriers.

Today, each long-distance company has "equal access," which means that a requesting long-distance carrier could require that the LEC examine the number and hand off the call to the proper long-distance carrier. This handoff was from the CO of the LEC to the point of presence (PoP) of the IXC. This PoP could be in a building adjacent to the telco's CO, or it could be in some convenient site in the suburbs where it could serve several of the telco's COs.

> *NOTE:* Telco is short for telephone company. The pure hierarchy of switching systems was becoming somewhat corrupted; new hierarchies in the long-distance part of the network were being applied on top of the old ones.

17.3.4   Switching Equipment

At a Class 5 CO, a switch receives and interprets the signal from a subscriber's telephone. An end (or local) office switch is known as a local switch, and it will only be found at the end office. All other COs use tandem switches.

In many businesses, the phones are digital phones. Therefore, the voice is digitized immediately by the phone. The signal then travels to a PBX. A **PBX (private branch exchange)** is a telephone system within an enterprise that switches calls between enterprise users on local lines while allowing all users to share a certain number of external phone lines. The main purpose of a PBX is to save the cost of requiring a line for each user to the telephone company's CO. The PBX is owned and operated by the company, supplier, or service provider rather than the telephone company. The PBX is the closest thing that the PBX has to an Internet access router. A PBX includes:

- Telephone trunk (multiple phone) lines that terminate at the PBX
- A computer with memory that manages the switching of calls within the PBX and in and out of it
- The network of lines within the PBX
- A console or switchboard for a human operator
- In some situations, alternatives to a PBX include centrex service (in which a pool of lines are rented at the phone company's CO), key telephone systems, and, for very small enterprises, primary rate ISDN).

Today, almost all PBXs are computers that handle digitized voice—usually at the standard 64 Kbps. Because of the processing power of the computer driving these modern PBXs, most products have an array of features that many users do not even know about. Some companies actually hire consultants to come in and tell the users about the features available on the PBX and how to access them. For instance, many PBXs have a make busy feature that allows a user to set his or her office telephone to give a busy signal to all callers, even if the telephone is not in use. This is good for getting some quiet time to work undisturbed. Enhanced features are common on business PBXs and not as common (or as extensive) on residential systems.

Telephones connected to the PBX have a unique extension number enabling intraswitch phone calls, bypassing the need for an external telephone line. Incoming calls may be sent to an onsite operator or automatically routed using dialed number information provided by the CO switch. PBXs may also be connected to other PBXs over dedicated trunk lines.

An alternative to the PBX is another specialized switch called a **key system.** Key systems are small telephone switches that allow multiple phone sets to share a number of external phone lines. Each line connected to a key system has its own unique number and can be dialed directly from an outside line. Key systems typically connect to standard phone lines from the local CO and provide the same service a standard telephone provides. Additional features are available, depending on the sophistication of the key system controller. Individual telephone sets connect to the key system and have a key (button) for each external phone line. Customers desiring an outside line press the corresponding key to make the connection and receive a dial tone. Incoming calls are typically sent to all phones that have a button for that external line, but may be directed to a single phone or group of phones. Multifeatured key systems often include transfer, speed-dial, memory-dial, park, hold, and paging features.

Centrex is a business telephone service provided by local telephone companies. Instead of a key or PBX system, the switch in the CO provides as many as seventy-five advanced calling features. Unlike key systems and PBXs that require expensive electronic controllers and switches, Centrex only requires phones, which helps to keep system start-up costs down. In addition, telephone companies continually update their switches to add the latest functionality to assure that Centrex will not become obsolete. Centrex systems have unlimited capacity and can grow or decrease as business dictates. Network maintenance is provided by the phone company at no charge.

17.3.5   SS7

On the PSTN, **Signaling System 7 (SS7)** is a system that puts the information required to set up and manage telephone calls in a separate network rather than within the same network that the telephone call is made on. Signaling information is in the form of digital packets.

Using SS7, telephone calls can be set up more efficiently and with greater security. They can also perform routing, especially if one of the channels is overcrowded. Special services such as call forwarding, wireless roaming service, number display, and three-way calling are easier to add and manage. In addition, SS7 can perform billing and allow for toll-free (800 and 888) and toll (900) calls. Lastly, it supports wireless call service including mobile telephone subscriber authentication, PCS, and roaming.

SS7 is now an international telecommunications standard.

Like ISDN lines, SS7 uses what is called out-of-band signaling, meaning that signaling (control) information travels on a separate, dedicated, 56 or 64 Kbps channel rather than within the same channel as the telephone call. Historically, the signaling for a telephone call has used the same voice circuit that the telephone call traveled on (this is known as in-band signaling).

SS7 consists of a set of reserved or dedicated channels known as signaling links and the network points that they interconnect. There are three kinds of network points (which are called signaling points): (1) Service Switching Points (SSPs), (2) Signal Transfer Points (STPs), and (3) Service Control Points (SCPs). SSPs originate or terminate a call and communicate on the SS7 network with SCPs to determine how to route a call or set up and manage some special feature. Traffic on the SS7 network is routed by packet switches called STPs. SCPs and STPs are usually mated so that service can continue if one network point fails.

The signaling network is basically a connectionless, packet switched network with routers as the network nodes, just like the Internet. The signaling network must be connectionless due to the simple fact that the messages that set up connections, known as call setup messages, cannot flow connections if their function is to set up connections (calls) in the first place.

17.4   IP TELEPHONY

IP telephony is a general term for the technologies that use IP's packet-switched connections to exchange voice, fax, and other forms of information that have traditionally been carried over the dedicated circuit-switched connections of the PSTN.

Using the Internet, calls travel as packets of data on shared lines, avoiding the tolls of the PSTN. The challenge in IP telephony is to deliver the voice, fax, or video packets in a dependable flow to the user. Much of IP telephony focuses on that challenge.

IP telephony service providers include (or soon will include) local telephone companies, long-distance providers, cable TV companies, ISPs, and fixed service wireless operators. IP telephony services also affect vendors of traditional handheld devices.

Currently, unlike traditional phone service, IP telephony service is relatively unregulated by government. In the United States, the FCC regulates phone-to-phone connections, but says they do not plan to regulate connections between a phone user and an IP telephony service provider.

17.4.1   Packet Switching Networks

Previously, this chapter discussed that when you are using a circuit switching network, a dedicated path is used during the call. As mentioned earlier in the chapter, you need to realize that this is not the most efficient way to use these lines. When one person is talking and the other person is listening, the circuit is being used in only one direction. Therefore, the circuit is only running at 50 percent efficiency. When no one is talking, the efficiency is 0 percent, although the circuit is maintained.

In a packet-switching network, the information being transmitted (be it data or digitized voice) is not sent in real time over a dedicated circuit; it is stored in a nearby computer until a sufficiently sized packet is on hand. Then, a very smart computer seizes a channel heading in the general direction of the destination, and that packet of data is transmitted at very high speeds. The channel is then released. So, except for some necessary supervisory information (destination, error checking codes) the channel is 100 percent efficient. When the distant station gets the message no more than a few milliseconds later, it responds with the necessary handshaking information—again, by accumulating a packet of data, seizing a channel, and bursting the information out over that channel. Again, it is 100 percent efficient.

Telephone companies offload voice calls from PSTNs to VOIP networks because it is cheaper to carry VOIP networks than over switched circuit networks. In the future, IP telephony networks are expected to enable innovative new multimedia services while working seamlessly with legacy telephone networks.

17.4.2   The Effects of Delay

Circuits give the PSTN two essentials that a network optimized for voice applications needs to preserve quality: (1) guaranteed bandwidth and (2) stable delays. Therefore, if you are going to use a packet switching network for voice communications, the delays must be low enough to satisfy voice users that are exchanging information in real time.

For voice purposes, the ITU has sent this round drip delay at 500 ms. This is a full 1/2 second, and many telephone users comfortable with voice networks that have much smaller round-trip delays are less than pleased when they encounter a voice circuit with very high delays. The "symptom" of high delay voice circuits, such as the circuits provided by satellites for international telephone calls, is that both speakers begin to talk at the same time. This can be quite annoying, and it is important to understand why this symptom occurs, because IP telephony systems tend to have much higher delays than the PSTN.

When two people talk on a voice circuit, they are using a full duplex circuit in a half duplex manner. That is, even though the circuit can easily carry voice in both directions at the same time, most people will listen politely while the other party is speaking.

As it turns out, the pause used to signal an end to a speaker's current "turn" in a conversation in most cultures is about 1/4 second. The "timeout" is not fixed and varies quite a bit, naturally, and also changes from culture to culture. Because on most satellite voice circuits, which rely on geosynchronous Earth orbit (GEO) satellites orbiting a tenth of the way to the moon (at about 22,000 miles), the round-trip delay is almost exactly 1/2 second. It takes 1/4 second for the uplink portion and 1/4 second for the downlink portion of the voice call. The propagation that makes up the 1/4 second comes from the nodal processing delay in the satellite itself.

On shorter, terrestrial circuits, the lines would be nearly horizontal. Even a coast-to-coast call on the PSTN in the U.S. seldom has an end-to-end delay above 30 ms. In most countries, 10 ms or less is the typical delay on domestic PSTN calls. Newer international voice circuits prefer undersea fiber optic links with lower delays, and new satellite voice services use a low-Earth-orbit (LEO) systems.

PSTN voice switches must be able to move voice samples arriving on 64 Kbps input ports to the proper output ports very quickly. The ITU sets an upper bound on switching elements any PSTN component that does more than propagate 64 Kbps voice on a circuit, such as a voice switch). In actuality, a modern CO may contain several switching elements. This is much less than the typical propagation delay on a long voice circuit, and shorter circuits will have fewer switching elements anyway. On a typical coast-to-coast call within the U.S., the propagation delay of the bits on the circuit is generally about 20 ms, and there may be some 15 switching elements along the way. All together, however, they cannot add more than 15×450 µs, or 6.75 ms, to the total delay. Usually, the delay through a modern switching element is much less. Thus variation in nodal processing delay does not significantly change voice quality.

The first impairment caused by delay is the effect of echo. Echo can arise in a voice network due to poor coupling between the earpiece and the mouthpiece in the handset. This is known as acoustic echo. It can also arise when part of the electrical energy is reflected back to the speaker by the hybrid circuit3 in the PSTN. This is known as hybrid echo.

When the one-way end-to-end delay is short, whatever echo that is generated by the voice circuit will come back to the speaker very quickly and will not be noticeable. In fact, the guideline is that echo cancellation is not necessary if the one-way delay is less than 25 ms. In other words, if the echo comes back within 50 ms, it will not be noticeable. However, the one-way delay in a VoIP network will almost always exceed 25 ms, so echo cancellation is always required.

Even with perfect echo cancellation, carrying on a two-way conversation becomes difficult when the delay is too long because of talker overlap. This is the problem that occurs when one party cuts off the other party's speech because of the long delay. G.114 provides the following guidelines regarding the one-way delay limit:

- **0 to 150 ms**—Acceptable for most user application
- **150 to 400 ms**—Acceptable provided that administrations are aware of the transmission time impact on the transmission quality
- **Above 400ms**—Unacceptable for general network planning purposes

When frames are transmitted through an IP network, the amount of delay experienced by each frame may differ. This is because the amount of queuing delay and processing time can vary depending on the overall load in the network. Even though the source gateway generates voice frames at regular intervals (about every 20 ms), the destination gateway typically will not receive voice frames at regular intervals because of jitter. The hybrid circuit converts the two-wire PSTN circuit to a four-wire circuit.

In general, jitter will result in clumping and gaps in the incoming data stream. The general strategy when dealing with jitter is to hold the incoming frames in a playout buffer long enough to allow the slowest frames to arrive in time to be played in the correct sequence. The larger the amount of jitter, the longer some of the frames will be held in the buffer, which introduces additional delay.

To minimize the delay due to buffering, most implementations use an adaptive jitter buffer. In other words, if the amount of jitter in the network is small, the buffer size will be small. If the jitter increases due to increased network load, the buffer size will increase automatically to compensate for it. Therefore, jitter in the network will impair voice quality to the extent that it increases the end-to-end delay due to the playout buffer. Sometimes when the jitter is too large, the playout buffer may choose to allow some frame loss to keep the additional delay from getting too long.

17.5   VOICE OVER FRAME RELAY AND ATM

Frame Relay (FR) is a packet switched WAN protocol widely employed to interconnect company LANs. FR is based on the older X25 WAN technology, but due to improvements in digital line quality, FR has removed the requirement for error protection/correction and offers improved speed and efficiency over X25. Companies can purchase FR services from providers for point-to-point or point-to-multipoint connections and it offers viable alternatives to expensive leased line services. Voice over Frame Relay's (VoFR's) real function is the transmission of voice over WAN links, so it does not scale to the desktop. Nevertheless, many enterprises employ VoFR for the savings made on long distance branch-to-branch calls. Historically, VoFR solutions have been proprietary by vendor, but the establishment of the FRF.11 standard for call setup, coding types, and packet formats will allow future interoperability between vendors' products.

ATM is a high speed backbone technology that offers inherent superior QoS features and is ideally suited for transmission of voice and video. As with VoFR, Voice over ATM (VoA) is primarily for transmission over WAN links and does not scale to the desktop.

Although significant progress has been made in engineering packet networks (IP, FR, and ATM) to carry voice as well as data, today's market is demanding a true convergence of these technologies into a single and ubiquitous communications service that is not limited by the underlying technology. The next challenge, then, is to develop interconnection and internetworking standards in order to deliver voice services ubiquitously over IP, Frame Relay, and ATM.

17.6   VOICE OVER IP

The possibility of voice communications traveling over the Internet, rather than the PSTN, first became a reality in February, 1995 when Vocaltec, Inc. introduced its Internet Phone software. Designed to run on a 486/33 MHz (or higher) PC equipped with a sound card, speakers, microphone, and modem, the software compresses the voice signal and translates it into IP packets for transmission over the Internet. This PC-to-PC Internet telephony works, however, only if both parties are using Internet Phone software.

In the relatively short period of time since then, Internet telephony has advanced rapidly. Many software developers now offer PC telephony software but, more importantly, gateway servers are emerging to act as an interface between the Internet and the PSTN. Equipped with voice processing cards, these gateway servers enable users to communicate via standard telephones.

A call goes over the local PSTN network to the nearest gateway server, which digitizes the analog voice signal, compresses it into IP packets, and moves it onto the Internet for transport to a gateway at the receiving end. With its support for computer-to-telephone calls, telephone-to-computer calls, and telephone-to-telephone calls, Internet telephony represents a significant step toward the integration of voice and data networks.

Originally regarded as a novelty, Internet telephony is attracting more and more users because it offers tremendous cost savings relative to the PSTN. Users can bypass long-distance carriers and their per-minute usage rates and run their voice traffic over the Internet for a flat monthly Internet access fee.

Voice over IP (VoIP) is voice delivered using the Internet Protocol. In general, this means that the technology sends voice information (in digital form) in discrete packets rather than in the traditional circuit-committed protocols of the PSTN. A major advantage of VoIP and Internet telephony is that they avoid the tolls charged by ordinary telephone service. VoIP, now used somewhat generally, derives from the VoIP Forum (an effort by major equipment providers) that includes Cisco, VocalTec, 3Com, and Netspeak to promote the use of ITU H.323, the standard for sending voice (audio) and video using IP on the public Internet and within an intranet. The VoIP Forum also promotes the user of directory service standards so that users can locate other users and the use of touch-tone signals for automatic call distribution and voice mail.

17.6.1   VoIP Applications

One of the most popular IP telephony applications for small and medium-sized businesses is toll bypass, which uses gateways to switch long-distance voice and fax calls to international locations onto IP-based, packet switched networks. IP voice and fax can significantly reduce business long-distance costs, particularly if companies generate high volumes of voice and fax calls to on-network international locations. The range of cost savings can vary according to implementation, but generally speaking, businesses can realize a savings of 50 percent or better with toll bypass as compared to traditional long-distance charges. Voice and fax calls that terminate on another carrier's VoIP network (off-network calls) also save money compared to traditional long-distance charges, but realize only about a 20 to 25 percent savings. Because most IP fax vendors use proprietary routing protocols, interoperability is also an issue with IP faxing.

As a result of the extremely competitive U.S. telecom services market having driven down the cost of long-distance services in the U.S., as well as the U.S. PSTN's high QoS levels, the use of toll bypass for significant cost savings is less applicable domestically than internationally. Toll bypass is also less applicable for large corporations, whose large volume discounts on long-distance services can offset any IP telephony savings.

Web- or network-enabled call centers deploy IP telephony gateways (which interface ACDs to LANs) to enable PC end users with the desktop equipment capability to browse company websites and conduct live telephone conversations with call center agents simultaneously. In this application, end user voice calls to the call center are routed over an IP-based network via IP telephony gateways, saving the call center (in many cases) from 1-800 line charges.

In addition, the advantages of this type of application should be fairly obvious to businesses: Being able to instantly respond to customer needs; close a pending sale through information clarification and end user/agent browser collaboration; and generate interest in or close additional sales almost immediately. In other words, if done right, you will have exceptional customer service.

Unified messaging is the ability for end users to receive and/or retrieve various forms of messaging—voice, e-mail, fax, video mail, etc.—at a single access point. Especially important for mobile employees, unified messaging enables end users to access and manage all messages from a single repository. In these applications, IP telephony gateways are used to provide the interface between the telephone network; the IP network; and voice mail, e-mail, and fax servers.

Benefits include the ability for businesses to provide its employees, especially remote and mobile workers, with single session access to all forms of incoming and outgoing messages. Utilizing a single transport infrastructure provides a potential to save on the equipment, implementation, and management costs associated with having a multitransport (separate voice and data network) infrastructure.

IP conferencing, such as Microsoft NetMeeting, is the most visible IP telephony application on the market today. NetMeeting is client software for the Windows line of operating systems that supports, among other functionality, audio conferencing (i.e., H.323-based voice calls) and IP-based video conferencing over the Internet or IP-based corporate intranets. Opting to route audio and video conferencing calls over IP telephony networks can help businesses reduce the higher costs associated with conferencing.

Many businesses consciously opt not to invest in CPE, but instead lease Centrex services from their local service providers. For these customers, IP-based Centrex services are now a reality from vendors such as Nokia (Nokia IP Centrex) and Nortel (Nortel DMS IP Centrex), among others.

For example, Nortel's IP Centrex solution enables its service provider customers to provision their subscribers with IP access to Nortel DMS-100 Centrex services. The IP Centrex features include a corporate dialing plan (4-digit dialing), AIN (advanced intelligent network) and LNP (local number portability) support, 800 calling, ARS (automatic route selection), multiappearance DNs (directory numbers), and support for many basic calling features such as call hold, call waiting, call transfer, and calling name. Nortel also offers an IP telephone and/or a PC-based softphone client with the service.

Generally speaking, emerging IP telephony applications currently address things like enterprise-wide call control (utilizing a single dialing plan), voice virtual private networks (adding voice to existing VPNs), and help desks (modeled after web-based call centers), among a variety of other pending IP telephony solutions.

17.6.2 Making a Call using VoIP

When a call is made using VoIP, the following occurs:

1. You pick up the receiver and listen for a dial tone. This lets you know that you have a connection to the local office of your telephone carrier.
2. You dial the telephone number. As the digits are accumulated and matched to a configured destination pattern, the telephone number is mapped to an IP host via the dial plan mapper.
3. The call is routed through the switch at your local carrier to the party you are calling. The IP host has a direct connection to either the destination telephone number or a PBX that is responsible for completing the call to the configured destination pattern.
4. A connection is made between your telephone and the other party's line, opening the circuit. The session application then runs the H.323 session protocol to establish a transmission and a reception channel for each direction over the IP network. If the call is being handled by a PBX, the PBX forwards the call to the destination telephone. If Resource Reservation Protocol (RSVP) has been configured, the RSVP reservations are put into effect to achieve the desired QoS over the IP network.
5. The coder-decoder (CODECs) compression schemes are enabled for both ends of the connection and the conversation proceeds using Real-Time Transport Protocol/User Datagram Protocol/Internet Protocol (RTP/UDP/IP) as the protocol stack.
6. You talk for a period of time and then hang up the receiver.
7. When you hang up the circuit is closed, thus freeing your line. This causes the RSVP reservations to be torn down (if RSVP is used) and the session ends. Each end becomes idle, waiting for the next off-hook condition to trigger another call setup.

17.6.3 Components of a VoIP System

Although it will take some time to happen, you can be sure that, eventually, all of the circuit-switched networks will be replaced with packet-switching technology. IP telephony just makes sense, both in terms of economics and infrastructure requirements. More and more businesses are installing VoIP systems, and the technology will continue to grow in popularity as it makes its way into our homes.

The components that make a VoIP system (see Figure 17.2):

- IP telephone
- LAN switch
- IP router
- IP PBX
- PSTN gateway

The IP telephone is a new device that causes some confusion among people accustomed to traditional phones. Although the device resembles a normal phone, which traditionally connects to a proprietary PBX port, the IP phone connects into an Ethernet LAN in the same way a desktop PC does. As IP phones have a unique Ethernet MAC addresses (just like a standard NIC in a desktop PC), they can be plugged in and used anywhere on the LAN after the initial configuration. Some IP phones have a built-in hub that allows connection of the LAN cable into the phone, and then extends to the PC via a patch cable.

Figure 17.2 Enterprise IP Telephony Gateway Configuration

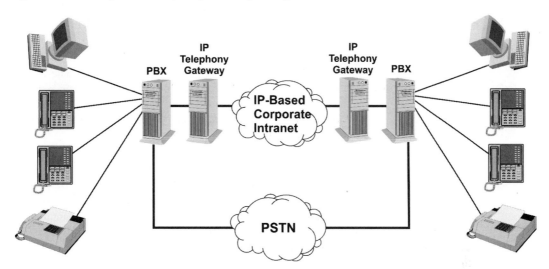

IP phones usually require an external power supply, but some vendors address this issue by developing LAN switches that allow DC voltage supplies to be carried along existing (unused) wires within the Ethernet UTP cables, thereby removing the necessity to have external PSs cluttering the desktop.

In fact, there is no actual need for a physical telephone at all. Softphone is a software simulation of a telephone that runs on the user's PC. With a sound card and connected microphone/headset, the PC can provide all the functionality of a real phone while enabling multimedia communication.

An existing component of the user's LAN, this switch has added importance by keeping delay to a minimum—vital where VoIP is concerned. Only LAN switch connections should be used with IP telephones. Shared media devices such as Ethernet hubs should not be used, as the collisions inherent within such devices can introduce unacceptable delays. It is also paramount that the switch has QoS support (such as the 802.1p standard where a number of bits within the Ethernet frame are used for prioritization) to enable voice packets to receive priority switching across the LAN.

Redundancy is also an important issue that needs to be considered. In an IP telephone-only environment, any failure of a LAN switch or an interswitch link could result in the loss of phone connectivity, with potentially dire consequences for a company. As a result, the LAN infrastructure should feature redundant interswitch links and redundant switches. On larger campus sites, one should also consider implementing layer 3 switching in the backbone in order to provide subnetting and broadcast containment.

As well as being existing components of the user's WAN infrastructure, routers are used for data transmission across company WAN links, commonly in the guise of either leased lines, ISDN, or FR connections. When packet voice is introduced on these WAN links, it may be necessary to increase the bandwidth of the leased line or the CIR in order for the FR connection to cope with the increased traffic. When looking to ensure prioritization for voice packets over data, it also becomes vital to consider the QoS features offered by the router.

The PBX, also known as the Service Control Unit (SCU) or the Call Manager, is essentially the heart of the VoIP system and performs all the functions of a traditional PBX. These functions include call switching and administration and provide 'gatekeeper' functionality such as translating between telephone numbers and IP addresses, call signal processing, and call establishment and management. It will also run core voice applications such as voice mail, auto attendant, and web-based call center applications. The IP PBX can be implemented either in hardware or software. Some vendors offer software implementations that will run on standard platforms such as Windows NT servers, but hardware implementations are vendor specific; usually taking the form of a chassis based system with a modular call processor and a trunk gateway. Hard drives are usually incorporated to provide voice mail capability.

This allows translation between the IP network and the PSTN (between the packet switching domain and the circuit switching domain). This is essential because it is still necessary to route calls originating from IP phones externally to the PSTN. Because gateways can interface to existing PBXs, existing legacy equipment can be retained to coexist alongside the IP telephony system. Gateways can be standalone external devices, modules for routers, or incorporated within chassis-based IP PBXs.

Many major networking vendors now offer integrated IP telephony systems, comprising a chassis-based system housing the IP PBX and PSTN gateway and router, which are also platforms for voice mail, auto attendant, and web-based voice/data converged applications. Hard drives are usually incorporated to provide voice mail capability. These systems are usually bundled with IP phones, which makes them an attractive proposition to customers who need a packaged solution to their VoIP requirements.

17.6.4   Migrating to an IP Telephony System

Migration will be the most common scenario because most sites will already have an existing traditional telephone infrastructure. The first step would be to test voice transmission over existing WAN links. This can be accomplished with existing analog phones, PBXs, and routers. The primary requirement is a gateway to the IP network—in the form of either a module for the router or an external standalone device. The gateway will provide interconnectivity between the phone/PBX system and the router and will provide functionalities such as sampling, digitization and packetization. Initially, two sites should be selected, with just one or two phones at each location. Network managers are then able to analyze WAN traffic to assess the impact upon bandwidth utilization, while an incremental addition of more phones would allow the network manager to predict any need for additional bandwidth capacity. A financial analysis could also be carried out to compare savings made on these intersite calls. With the WAN links successfully transmitting voice traffic between sites, it is possible for the IT staff to implement QoS features on the routers at both ends to test the impact of heavy data traffic upon voice quality. QoS features such as priority queuing and RTP header compression are standard features on most routers and are easily configured to enable experimentation. At this stage, voice and data would only be combined over the WAN links.

The second step would be to incorporate IP telephones. With the LAN suitably prepared for VoIP (hubs having been replaced by 802.1p compliant switches in the wiring closet), IP telephones would now be connected to the LAN, along with the IP PBXs at both sites. No routing changes are required and external phone calls can still be switched via the existing PBX. LAN traffic can be analyzed and with the addition of more IP phones, and engineers can now look at planning the phase out of all remaining analogue/digital phones at the site.

The last step would be the removal of the PBX. With the migration to IP telephones completed, the traditional PBX is removed and replaced with an E-1/T-1 trunk from the gateway to the LEC.

17.7 H.323

There are three major protocols being used for VoIP: (1) H.323, (2) SIP and (3) Media Gateway Control Protocol (MEGACO). All three protocols define ways for devices to connect to each other through VoIP. Also, they include specifications for audio codecs. A codec converts an audio signal into a compressed digital form for transmission, and back into an uncompressed audio signal for replay (see Table 17.1).

The first protocol is H.323, a standard created by the ITU. H.323 was originally created to provide a mechanism for transporting multimedia applications over LANs. Although H.323 is still used by numerous vendors for videoconferencing applications, it has rapidly evolved to address the growing needs of VoIP networks. It provides specifications for real-time interactive videoconferencing, data sharing, and audio applications such as IP telephony. Because of its early availability and its later advancements, H.323 is currently the most widely used VoIP signaling and call-control protocol. International and domestic carriers rely on it to handle billions of minutes of use each year.

Actually a suite of protocols, H.323 incorporates many individual protocols that have been developed for specific applications. It defines all aspects of call transmission, from

Table 17.1 VoIP Protocols

	H.323	SIP	MGCP/H.248/MEGACO
Standards body	ITU	IETF	MGCP/MEGACO—IETF;H.248—ITU
Architecture	Distributed	Distributed	Centralized
Current version	H.323 v4	RFC2543-bis07	MGCP 1.0, Megaco, H.248
Call control	Gatekeeper	Proxy/redirect server	Call agent/media gateway controller
Endpoints	Gateway, terminal	User agent	Media gateway
Signaling transport	TCP UDP	TCP or UDP	MGCP/UDP; Megaco/H.248; or both
Multimedia capable	Yes	Yes	Yes
DTMF—relay transport	H.245 (signaling) or RFC 2833 (media)	RFC 2833 (media) or INFO (signaling)	Signaling or RFC 2833 (media)
Fax—relay transport	T.38	T.38	T.38
Supplemental services	Provided by endpoints or call control	Provided by endpoints or call control	Provided by call agent

call establishment to capabilities exchange to network resource availability. H.323 defines the Registration, Admission, and Status (RAS) Protocol for call routing, H.225 protocols for call set-up, and H.245 protocols for capabilities exchange. This standard is based on the IETF's Real Time Protocol (RTP) and Real Time Control Protocol (RTCP), with additional protocols for call signaling and data and audiovisual communications.

Users can connect with other people over the Internet and use varying products that support H.323, just as people using different makes and models of telephones can communicate over PSTN lines. H.323 defines how audio and video information is formatted and packaged for transmission over the network. Standard audio and video codecs encode and decode input/output from audio and video sources for communication between nodes. A codec converts audio or video signals between analog and digital forms (see Table 17.2 and Figure 17.3).

17.7.1   H.323 Components

The H.323 standard specifies four kinds of components (see Figure 17.4) that, when networked together, provide the point-to-point and point-to-multipoint multimedia communication services:

- terminals
- gateways
- gatekeepers
- multipoint control units (MCUs)

Terminals are used for real-time bidirectional multimedia communications. The H.323 terminal can either be a PC or a standalone device, running a H.323 and the multimedia applications. It supports audio communications and can optionally support video or data communications. Because the basic service provided by a H.323 terminal is audio communications, a H.323 terminal plays a key role in IP telephony services. A H.323 terminal can either be a PC or a standalone device running a H.323 stack and multimedia applications. The primary goal of H.323 is to internetwork with other multimedia terminals. H.323 terminals are compatible with H.324 terminals on SCN and wireless networks, H.310 terminals on B-ISDN, H.320 terminals on ISDN, H.321 terminals on

Table 17.2   The H.323 Protocol Suite

Video	Audio	Data	Transport
H.261	G.711	T.122	H.225
H.263	G.722	T.124	H.235
	G.723.1	T.125	H.245
	G.728	T.126	H.450.1
	G.729	T.127	H.450.2
			H.450.3
			RTP
			X.224.0

Figure 17.3 The H.323 Protocol Suite

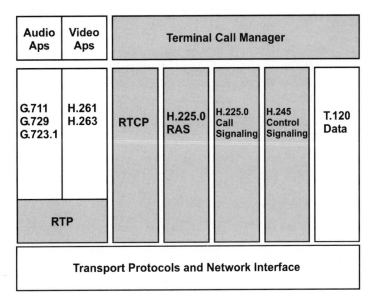

Figure 17.4 The H.323 Network

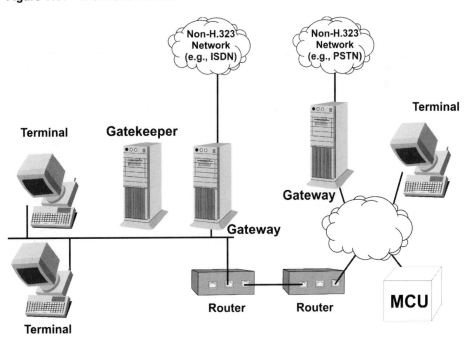

B-ISDN, and H.322 terminals on guaranteed QoS LANs. H.323 terminals may be used in multipoint conferences.

H.323 terminals must support the following:

- **H.245**—Exchanging terminal capabilities and creation of media channels
- **H.225**—Call signaling and call setup
- **RAS**—Registration and other admission control with a gatekeeper
- **RTP/RTCP**—sequencing audio and video packets

H.323 terminals must also support the G.711 audio CODEC. Optional components in an H.323 terminal are video CODECs, T.120 data-conferencing protocols, and MCU capabilities.

A gateway connects two dissimilar networks. A H.323 gateway provides connectivity between a H.323 network and a non—H.323 network. For example, a gateway can connect and provide communication between a H.323 terminal and SCN networks (SCN networks include all switched telephony networks, e.g., the PSTN). Connectivity of dissimilar networks is achieved by translating protocols for call setup and release, converting media formats between different networks, and transferring information between networks connected by the gateway. A gateway is not required, however, for communication between two terminals on a H.323 network.

A gatekeeper can be considered the brain of the H.323 network. It is the focal point for all calls within the H.323 network. Although they are not required, gatekeepers provide important services such as addressing, authorization, and authentication of terminals and gateways; bandwidth management; accounting; billing; and charging. H.323 networks that do not have gatekeepers may not have these capabilities. Gatekeepers may also provide call-routing services. A gatekeeper is a logical component of H.323, but it can be implemented as part of a gateway or MCU.

Calls originating within a H.323 network may use an alias to address the destination terminal. Calls originating outside the H.323 network and received by a gateway may use an E.164 telephone number (e.g., 111-222-3333) to address the destination terminal. The gatekeeper translates this E.164 telephone number or the alias into the network address (e.g., 123.123.123.123 for an IP-based network) for the destination terminal. The destination endpoint can be reached by using the network address on the H.323 network. Therefore, H.323 networks that contain IP telephony gateways should also contain a gatekeeper to translate incoming E.164 telephone addresses into transport addresses.

MCUs provide support for conferences of three or more H.323 terminals. All terminals participating in the conference establish a connection with the MCU. The MCU manages conference resources, negotiates between terminals for the purpose of determining the audio or video CODEC to use, and may handle the media stream. The gatekeepers, gateways, and MCUs are logically separate components of the H.323 standard but can be implemented as a single physical device.

A H.323 zone is a collection of all terminals, gateways, and MCUs managed by a single gatekeeper. A zone includes at least one terminal and may include gateways or MCUs. A zone may be independent of network topology and may be comprised of multiple network segments that are connected through routers or other devices.

17.7.2   CODECs

CODECs define the format of audio and video information and represent the way audio and video are compressed and transmitted over the network. H.323 provides a variety of options for audio and video coding.

An audio CODEC encodes the audio signal from the microphone for transmission on the transmitting H.323 terminal and decodes the received audio code that is sent to the speaker on the receiving H.323 terminal. Because audio is the minimum service provided by the H.323 standard, all H.323 terminals must have at least one audio CODEC support, as specified in the ITU–T G.711 recommendation (audio coding at 64 Kbps). Additional audio CODEC recommendations such as G.722 (64, 56, and 48 Kbps), G.723.1 (5.3 and 6.3 Kbps), G.728 (16 Kbps), and G.729 (8 Kbps) may also be supported.

A video CODEC encodes video from the camera for transmission on the transmitting H.323 terminal and decodes the received video code that is sent to the video display on the receiving H.323 terminal. Because H.323 specifies support of video as optional, the support of video CODECs is optional as well. However, any H.323 terminal providing video communications must support video encoding and decoding as specified in the ITU–T H.261 recommendation.

17.7.3   Transport Protocols

RAS, as defined in H.225, is the protocol between endpoints (terminals and gateways) and gatekeepers. RAS is used to perform registration, admission control, bandwidth changes, status, and disengage procedures between endpoints and gatekeepers. A RAS channel is used to exchange RAS messages. This signaling channel is opened between an endpoint and a gatekeeper prior to the establishment of any other channels.

H.225 call signaling is used to establish a connection between two H.323 endpoints. This is achieved by exchanging H.225 protocol messages on the call-signaling channel. The call-signaling channel is opened between two H.323 endpoints or between an endpoint and the gatekeeper.

H.245 control signaling is used to exchange end-to-end control messages that govern the operation of the H.323 endpoint. These control messages carry information related to the following:

- capabilities exchange
- opening and closing of logical channels used to carry media streams
- flow-control messages
- general commands and indications

Media streams are transported on RTP/RTCP. RTP carries the actual media and RTCP carries status and control information. Signaling is transported reliably over TCP. The following protocols deal with signaling:

- **RAS**—Registration, admission, status
- **Q.931**—Call setup and termination
- **H.245**—Channel usage and capabilities
- **H.235**—Security and authentication

VoIP uses RTP to help ensure that packets get delivered in a timely way. It provides end-to-end network transport functions suitable for applications transmitting real-time data such as audio, video, or simulation data over multicast or unicast network services. Whereas H.323 is used to transport data over IP-based networks, RTP is typically used to transport data via UDP. RTP, together with UDP, provides transport protocol functionality. RTP provides payload type identification, sequence numbering, timestamping, and delivery monitoring. UDP provides multiplexing and checksum services. RTP can also be used with other transport protocols.

RTCP is the counterpart of RTP that provides control services. While RTP does not address resource reservation and does not guarantee QoS for real-time services, the data transport is augmented by a control protocol (RTCP) to allow monitoring of the data delivery in a manner scalable to large multicast networks and to provide minimal control and identification functionality.

The primary function of RTCP is to provide feedback on the quality of the data distribution. RTCP is based on the periodic transmission of control packets to all participants in the session, using the same distribution mechanism as the data packets.

RTP and RTCP are designed to be independent of the underlying transport and network layers. The protocols support the use of RTP-level translators and mixers. Therefore, the underlying protocol must provide multiplexing of the data and control packets, for example, using separate port numbers with UDP. Other RTCP functions include carrying a transport-level identifier for a RTP source, called a canonical name, which is used by receivers to synchronize audio and video.

17.7.4   Connection Procedures

H.225 call signaling is used to set up connections between H.323 endpoints (terminals and gateways), over which the real-time data can be transported. Call signaling involves the exchange of H.225 protocol messages over a reliable call signaling channel. For example, H.225 protocol messages are carried over TCP in an IP-based H.323 network.

H.225 messages are exchanged between the endpoints if there is no gatekeeper in the H.323 network. When a gatekeeper exists in the network, the H.225 messages are exchanged either directly between the endpoints or between the endpoints after being routed through the gatekeeper. The first case is direct call signaling. The second case is called gatekeeper routed call signaling. The method chosen is decided by the gatekeeper during RAS admission message exchange.

Admission messages are exchanged between endpoints and the gatekeeper on RAS channels. The gatekeeper receives the call signaling messages on the call signaling channel from one endpoint and routes them to the call signaling channel of the other endpoint.

During the admission confirmation, the gatekeeper indicates that the endpoints can exchange call signaling messages directly. The endpoints exchange the call signaling on the call signaling channel.

H.245 control signaling consists of the exchange of end-to-end H.245 messages between communicating H.323 endpoints. H.245 control messages are carried over H.245 control channels. The H.245 control channel is the logical channel 0 and is permanently open, unlike the media channels. Messages carried include messages to exchange capabilities of terminals and to open and close logical channels.

Capabilities exchange is a process that uses the communicating terminals' exchange messages to provide their transmit and receive capabilities to the peer endpoint. Transmit capabilities describe the terminal's ability to transmit media streams. Receive capabilities describe a terminal's ability to receive and process incoming media streams.

A logical channel carries information from endpoint-to endpoint (in the case of a point-to-point conference) or multiple endpoints (in the case of a point-to-multipoint conference). H.245 provides messages to open or close a logical channel, which is unidirectional.

If you have two H.323 terminals (T-1 and T-2) connected to a gatekeeper; you have direct call signaling; and the media stream uses RTP encapsulation; the steps involved in creating a H.323 call, establishing media communication, and releasing the call are as follows:

Step 1: T-1 sends the RAS ARQ message on the RAS channel to the gatekeeper for registration. T-1 requests the use of direct call signaling.

Step 2: The gatekeeper confirms the admission of T-1 by sending ACF to T-1. The gatekeeper indicates in ACF that T-1 can use direct call signaling.

Step 3: T-1 sends a H.225 call signaling setup message to T-2 requesting a connection.

Step 4: T-2 responds with a H.225 call proceeding message to T-1.

Step 5: Now T-2 has to register with the gatekeeper. It sends a RAS ARQ message to the gatekeeper on the RAS channel.

Step 6: The gatekeeper confirms the registration by sending a RAS ACF message to T-2.

Step 7: T-2 alerts T-1 of the connection establishment by sending a H.225 alerting message.

Step 8: Then T-2 confirms the connection establishment by sending a H.225 connect message to T-1, and the call is established.

Step 9: The H.245 control channel is established between T-1 and T-2. T-1 sends a H.245 `TerminalCapabilitySet` message to T-2 to exchange its capabilities.

Step 10: T-2 acknowledges T-1's capabilities by sending a H.245 `TerminalCapabilitySetAck` message.

Step 11: T-2 exchanges its capabilities with T-1 by sending a H.245 `TerminalCapabilitySet` message.

Step 12: T-1 acknowledges T-2's capabilities by sending a H.245 `TerminalCapabilitySetAck` message.

Step 13: T-1 opens a media channel with T-2 by sending a H.245 `openLogicalChannel` message. The transport address of the RTCP channel is included in the message.

Step 14: T-2 acknowledges the establishment of the unidirectional logical channel from T-1 to T-2 by sending a H.245 `openLogicalChannelAck` message. Included in the acknowledge message are the RTP transport address allocated by T-2 to be used by T-1 for sending the RTP media stream and the RTCP address received from T-1 earlier.

Step 15: Then, T-2 opens a media channel with T-1 by sending a H.245 `openLogicalChannel` message. The transport address of the RTCP channel is included in the message.

Step 16: T-1 acknowledges the establishment of the unidirectional logical channel from T-2 to T-1 by sending a H.245 `openLogicalChannelAck` message. Included in the acknowledging message are the RTP transport address allocated by T-1 to be used by the T-2 for sending the RTP media stream and the RTCP address received from T-2 earlier. Now the bidirectional media stream communication is established.

Step 17: T-1 sends the RTP encapsulated media stream to T-2.

Step 18: T-2 sends the RTP encapsulated media stream to T-1.

Step 19: T-1 sends the RTCP messages to T-2.

Step 20: T-2 sends the RTCP messages to T-1.

Step 21: T-2 initiates the call release. It sends a H.245 `EndSessionCommand` message to T-1.

Step 22: T-1 releases the call endpoint and confirms the release by sending a H.245 `EndSessionCommand` message to T-2.

Step 23: T-2 completes the call release by sending a H.225 `releasecomplete` message to T-1.

Step 24: T-1 and T-2 disengage with the gatekeeper by sending a RAS DRQ message to the gatekeeper.

Step 25: The gatekeeper disengages T-1 and T-2 and confirms by sending DCF messages to T-1 and T-2.

17.8   THE SESSION INITIATION PROTOCOL

Since its approval in early 1999 as an official standard, the Session Initiation Protocol (SIP) has gained tremendous market acceptance for signaling communications services on the Internet. SIP is an IETF standard protocol for initiating an interactive user session that involves multimedia elements such as video, voice, chat, gaming, and virtual reality. SIP is specified in IETF RFC 2543.

Like HTTP or SMTP, SIP works in the application layer of the OSI model. The application layer is the level responsible for ensuring that communication is possible. SIP can establish multimedia sessions or Internet telephony calls and modify (or terminate) them. The protocol can also invite participants to unicast or multicast sessions that do not necessarily involve the initiator. Because SIP supports name mapping and redirection services, it is possible for users to initiate and receive communications and services from any location and for networks to identify users wherever they are.

SIP is a request/response protocol that deals with requests from clients and responses from servers. Participants are identified by SIP URLs. Requests can be sent through any transport protocol, such as UDP, SCTP, or TCP. SIP determines the end system to be used for the session, the communication media and media parameters, and the called party's desire to engage in the communication. Once these are assured, SIP establishes call parameters at either end of the communication and handles call transfer and termination.

Internet telephony began on the premise that it was cheaper than normal phone calling. Users were willing to tolerate degraded quality or reduced function for lower cost. However, the cost differentials are rapidly disappearing. To continue to exist, Internet telephony must provide other advantages. The answer lies in services provided.

Some of the most exciting applications have become popular on the Internet, through the form of multimedia services. Now think of integrating multimedia communications, such as voice, with web, e-mail, buddy lists, instant messaging, and online games. Whole new sets of features, services, and applications become conceivable.

SIP is ideally suited here. Its use of URLs, its support for MIME and carriage of arbitrary content (SIP can carry images, MP3s, even Java applets), and its usage of e-mail routing mechanisms, means that it can integrate well with other applications. For example, it is just as easy to redirect a user to another phone as it is to redirect a user to a website.

SIP uses the Internet model for scalability—fast and simple in the core, smarter with less volume in the periphery. To accomplish this, SIP defines several types of proxy servers. *Call-stateful* proxies generally live at the edge of the network. These proxies track call state, and can provide rich sets of services based on this knowledge. Closer to the core, *transaction-stateful* (also known stateful) proxies track requests and responses but have no knowledge of session or call state. Once a session invitation is accepted, the proxy forgets about it. When the session termination arrives, the proxy forwards it without needing to know about the session. Finally, *stateless* proxies exist in the core. These proxies receive requests (such as INVITE), forwards them, and immediately forgets about them. SIP provides facilities to ensure that the response can be correctly routed back to the caller. Stateless proxies are very fast, but can provide few services. Call-stateful proxies are not as fast, but they live at the periphery where call volumes are lower.

SIP provides the following functions:

- **Name translation and user location**—To ensure that a call reaches the called party regardless of location, SIP addresses users with an e-mail-like address. Each user is identified through a hierarchical URL built around elements such as a user's telephone number or host name (for example, SIP:user@company.com). Because of this similarity, SIP URLs are easy to associate with a user's e-mail address.
- **Feature negotiation**—SIP allows all parties involved in a call to negotiate and agree on the features supported, recognizing that all participants may not be able to support the same kind of features. For example, a session between a mobile voice-only telephone user and two video-enabled device users would agree to support voice features only. When the mobile telephone user leaves the call, remaining participants may renegotiate session features to activate video communications.
- **Call participant management**—During a session, a participant can bring other users into the call or transfer, hold, or cancel connections.

SIP has two basic components: (1) The SIP user agent and (2) the SIP network server. The user agent is effectively the end-system component for the call and the SIP network server is the network device that handles the signaling associated with multiple calls. The SIP user agent consists of the user agent client (UAC), which initiates calls and the user agent server (UAS), which answers calls. This architecture allows peer-to-peer calls to be made using a client-server protocol.

The SIP network server element consists of three forms of server: (1) The SIP stateful proxy server, (2) the SIP stateless proxy server, and (3) the SIP redirect server. The main function of SIP servers is to provide name resolution and user location, as callers are unlikely to recall the IP address or host name of called parties. Using an easier-to-remember e-mail-like address, the caller's user agent can identify a specific server (or server cluster) to resolve called-party address information.

SIP provides its own reliable transfer mechanism independent of the packet layer. For this reason, SIP does not require the services of the sigtran SCTP protocol and functions reliably over an "unreliable" datagram protocol such as UDP. Sigtran is an abbreviation for signal transport, which is a standards body that enables the integration of the PSTN with IP networks.

The proxy server is responsible for routing and delivering messages to the called party. The called party then sends a response that accepts or rejects the invitation, which is forwarded back through the same set of proxies in reverse order. A proxy can receive a single INVITE request, and send out more than one INVITE request to different addresses. This feature, aptly called "forking," allows a session initiation attempt to reach multiple locations in the hopes of finding the desired user at one of them. A close analogy is the home phone line service, where all phones in the home ring at once.

ISUP, short for ISDN user part, defines the protocol and procedures used to set-up, manage, and release trunk circuits that carry voice and data calls over the PSTN. SIP for telephones (SIP-T) is a mechanism that allows SIP to be used for ISUP call setup between SS7-based PSTNs and SIP-based IP telephony networks. SIP-T carries an ISUP message payload in the body of a SIP message. The SIP header carries translated ISUP routing information. SIP-T also specifies the use of the SIP INFO method for affecting in-call ISUP signaling in IP networks.

Sigtran is not the only IETF working group involved in defining new protocols to enable the integration of the PSTN with IP networks. PINT (PSTN and Internet Interworking) and SPIRITS (Service in the PSTN/IN Requesting Internet Service) are two IETF work group recommendations that address the need to interwork telephony services between the PSTN and the Internet. PINT deals with services originating from an IP network; SPIRITS deals with services originating from the PSTN.

In PINT, PSTN network services are triggered by IP requests. A SIP Java client embedded in a Java servlet on a web server launches requests to initiate voice calls on the PSTN. The current focus of this initiative is to allow web access to voice content and enable click-to-dial/fax services. In SPIRITS, IP network services are triggered by PSTN requests. SPIRITS is primarily concerned with Internet call waiting, Internet caller-ID delivery, and Internet call forwarding.

The IETF's ENUM (telephone number resolution) working group is devising a scheme to map E.164 telephone numbers to IP addresses through the Internet DNS so that any application, including SIP, can discover resources associated with a unique phone number. A SIP phone or proxy server would use number domain translation and DNS resolution to discover a DNS resource that would yield a SIP address at which a dialed number could be reached.

The IPTEL working group is developing TRIP (telephony routing over IP), a policy driven interadministrative domain protocol for advertising the reachability of telephony destinations between location servers, and for advertising attributes of the routes to those destinations. TRIP is designed to allow service providers to exchange routing information to avoid the over provisioning or duplication of gateways using established Internet protocols.

If a telephone number does not have an associated SIP resource, the IP network routes the call to a telephone routing gateway that connects to the PSTN. In an interconnect environment with many peering relationships between service providers, resources in the IP network need to discover which telephone numbers are associated with which gateways.

17.9   MEDIA GATEWAY CONTROL PROTOCOL AND MEGACO

The third set of protocols used to connect devices to each other by using VoIP is the Media Gateway Control Protocol (MGCP) and H.248/MEGACO. Both were designed to provide an architecture where call control and services could be centrally added to a VoIP network. In that sense, an architecture using these protocols closely resembles the existing PSTN architecture and services.

MGCP and H.248/MEGACO define most aspects of signaling by using a model called *packages*. These packages define commonly used functionality, such as PSTN signaling, line-side device connectivity, and features such as transfer and hold. In addition, the Session Definition Protocol (SDP) is used to convey capabilities exchange.

In a centralized architecture, MGCP and H.248/MEGACO allow companies to build large-scale networks that are scalable, resilient, and redundant. It provides mechanisms for interconnecting with other VoIP networks and for adding intelligence and features to the call agent.

SUMMARY

1. PSTNs are based on a circuit switching network.
2. When you make a phone call from a residential area, your phone call starts out as an analog signal. It remains an analog signal as it travels on the last mile to the phone company's first switch. The signal is then converted to a digital signal, then travels switch to switch until it gets to the phone company's last switch before its final destination. The last switch will then convert the signal back to analog and send it to the destination phone.
3. Not all phones found in residential homes are analog phones; some are digital phones.
4. Conversion processes are accomplished by a matching pair of codecs, with the traditional method being PCM, standardized by the ITU as G.711.
5. Telephone companies chop their network bandwidth into voice channels or circuits running at 64 Kbps. These voice channels are technically called DS-0 circuits and remain the most common type of line leased by the month or sold to organizations as private lines.
6. Today, with newer voice digitization techniques and compression, voice can be achieved at as low as 2 Kbps, but is usually provisioned at 8 Kbps.
7. Methods of generating digitized voice below 64 Kbps PCM voice is often referred to as voice compression, but not all digitized voice below 64 Kbps is produced by compressing 64 Kbps PCM voice.
8. Most phone systems use UTP.
9. The CO switch's main job is to connect access lines to each other, based on the network address and the telephone numbers of the destination telephone instrument.
10. The trunking network forms the backbone of the PSTN, in the same way that backbone routers form the global Internet.
11. Like the Internet, the PSTN is a hierarchy network with multiple layers.
12. A PBX is a telephone system within an enterprise that switches calls between enterprise users on local lines while allowing all users to share a certain number of external phone lines. The main purpose

of a PBX is to save the cost of requiring a line for each user to the telephone company's CO. The PBX is owned and operated by the company, supplier, or service provider rather than the telephone company.

13. An alternative to the PBX is another specialized switch called a *key system.*

14. Centrex is a business telephone service, provided by local telephone companies, that would be used instead of a PBX or key system.

15. On the PSTN, SS7 is a system that puts the information required to set up and manage telephone calls in a separate network rather than within the same network that the telephone call is made on.

16. IP telephony is a general term for the technologies that use IP's packet switched connections to exchange voice, fax, and other forms of information that have traditionally been carried over the dedicated circuit-switched connections of the PSTN.

17. Telephone companies offload voice calls from PSTNs to VoIP networks because it is cheaper to carry voice traffic over IP networks than over switched circuit networks.

18. VoIP is voice delivered through IP.

19. The components that make a VoIP system are the IP telephone, a LAN switch, an IP router, an IP PBX, and a PSTN gateway.

20. There are three major protocols being used for VoIP: (1) H.323, (2) SIP, and (3) MGCP MEGACO. All three protocols define ways for devices to connect to each other through VoIP.

21. CODECs define the format of audio and video information and represent the way audio and video information is compressed and transmitted over the network.

QUESTIONS

1. SS7 enables an Internet telephony switch to support which of the following?
   a. toll-free calling
   b. local number portability
   c. calling-card calling
   d. all of the above

2. IP-telephony switches can support calls from which of the following?
   a. the PSTN to the IP network
   b. the PSTN to the PSTN via the IP network
   c. the IP network to the PSTN
   d. the IP network to the IP network
   e. all of the above

3. The signaling of SS7 features _____ signaling.
   a. in-band
   b. both in-band and out-of-band
   c. out-of-band
   d. phase-lock band

4. RTP can be defined as _____.
   a. media stream control
   b. call signaling
   c. registration and admission
   d. control signaling
   e. media stream transport

5. RTCP can be defined as _____.
   a. media stream control
   b. call signaling
   c. registration and admission
   d. control signaling
   e. media stream transport

6. RAS can be defined as _____.
   a. media stream control
   b. call signaling
   c. registration and admission
   d. control signaling
   e. media stream transport

7. H.225 can be defined as _____.
   a. media stream control
   b. call signaling
   c. registration and admission
   d. control signaling
   e. media stream transport

8. H.245 can be defined as _____.
   a. media stream control
   b. call signaling
   c. registration and admission
   d. control signaling
   e. media stream transport

9. The G.723.1 specification for audio CODECs, recommended by the VoIP Forum, requires:
   a. 6.3 Kbps
   b. 7.9 Kbps
   c. 8.4 Kbps
   d. 9.8 Kbps

10. E.164 refers to what?
    a. telephone numbers
    b. proxy services
    c. transport protocol for SIP
    d. CODEC for SIP

11. What class of CO connects the local loop to a carrier's network?
    a. 1   b. 2
    c. 3   d. 4
    e. 5

12. What medium traditionally has been used for local loops?
    a. fiber optic cable
    b. copper wire
    c. aluminum wire
    d. microwave

13. How many wire pairs can a typical RJ-11 jack accept?
    a. 1 or 2   b. 2 or 3
    c. 3 or 4   d. 4 or 6

14. In DTMF, pressing each number on the keypad issues how many different frequencies to the local switch?
    a. 1   b. 2
    c. 3   d. 4

15. Which of the following is an advantage of using a Centrex system over using a PBX system?
    a. lower installation costs
    b. quicker call setup
    c. easier modifications
    d. lower ongoing costs

16. Which type of switching is used for most telephone calls over the PSTN?
    a. circuit switching
    b. message switching
    c. packet switching
    d. time division switching

17. What is the difference between VoIP and Internet telephony?
    a. VoIP uses QoS techniques, but Internet telephony cannot.
    b. VoIP requires IP telephone clients, but Internet telephony allows clients to be computers, analog telephones, or IP telephones.
    c. VoIP applies to any type of network, not just the Internet.
    d. They are the same thing.

18. On a private VoIP network, what device determines how a call should be routed?
    a. IP-PBX   b. router
    c. Access server   d. media gateway

19. What ITU standard waveform CODEC does the PSTN use?
    a. G.711   b. G.723
    c. G.726   d. G.729

20. What function does the H.225 protocol provide as part of the H.323 VoIP specification?
    a. controls communication between media gateways and media gateway controllers
    b. handles call setup, call routing, and call termination
    c. ensures that signals issued to an H.323 terminal are in a format that the terminal can interpret
    d. indicates priority of each IP datagram through the Type of Service field

21. What is one advantage of using SIP over H.323?
    a. SIP uses fewer processing and port resources
    b. SIP enjoys wider acceptance in the industry
    c. SIP supports a broader range of layer 2 protocols
    d. SIP is compatible with more of the newer QoS protocols

22. What does RTP add to packets that compensates for UDP's lack of reliability?
    a. priority indicators
    b. sequence numbers
    c. loss indicators
    d. extended maximum hop counts

CHAPTER **18**

Wireless Technology Used in WANs

Topics Covered in this Chapter

Introduction

As networks advance and get faster, so will wireless technology. Wireless technology can be used for a wide variety of applications including data networks, cell phones, and GPS systems. In addition, wireless technology is useful when certain factors do not allow you to use a wired network.

Objectives

- List and describe the characteristics of the various electromagnetic waves used in wireless communications.
- Compare and contrast the various 802.11 standards.
- Compare and contrast Bluetooth and the 802.11 standard.

18.1   THE WIRELESS SPECTRUM

For decades, radio and television stations have used the atmosphere to transport information via analog signals. The atmosphere is also capable of carrying digital signals. Networks that transmit signals through the atmosphere are known as wireless networks.

All wireless signals are carried through the air along electromagnetic waves. Electromagnetic waves are waves of energy composed of both electric and magnetic components. Sound and light are both examples of electromagnetic waves. Waves that belong to the wireless spectrum (waves used for broadcasting, cellular phones, and satellite transmission) are neither visible nor audible, except by the receiver.

When radio waves are described as the technology used to broadcast radio and TV programs, some people assume radio waves are a little like sound waves. Thus, the term *airwaves* emerged. A sound is made when something causes the air to vibrate. This vibration is transferred to our eardrums when the sound wave arrives. The vibration is then translated into a signal transmitted to our brains, where we perceive the sound.

In reality, radio waves are really not at all like sound waves. They do not create vibrations in our ears. They do not rely on vibrations in the air. In fact, they do not need air for transmission. Instead of being a vibration, they are a form of energy. They are part of what is called the *electromagnetic spectrum.* This energy spectrum includes the full range of radiation created by the interaction of electrons and magnetic fields. Types of radiation include radio waves, microwaves, infrared light, visible light, ultraviolet light, and x-rays.

All are forms of radiation, created by the properties of electromagnetic fields. For example, radio waves are created when electrons are passed through a conductor. Such as an electrical wire. The current creates a magnetic field. Fluctuations in the current produce changes in the magnetic field, creating waves of electromagnetic energy or radiation. Other forms of electromagnetic radiation are produced through other atomic processes.

These changes in the magnetic field are called waves because the energy oscillates, meaning that it rises in intensity to a peak, fades to a minimum, and then rises to its peak level again. The distance between two successive peaks or troughs is called the energy's wavelength.

All of these forms of energy travel at the same speed: The speed of light. The only difference between them is wavelength. Radio waves are the longest. Gamma rays are the shortest. Because gamma rays are shorter, and because they travel the same speed as radio waves, more of them can pass a specified point in a single second. The number of waves passing a point in one second is called the energy's frequency. Gamma rays have significantly higher frequencies than radio waves.

The frequency of a signal is the number of times a signal makes a complete cycle within a given time frame. The length of time interval of one cycle is called its period. The period can be calculated by taking the reciprocal of the frequency:

$$t = \frac{1}{f} \quad f = \frac{1}{t}$$

A wave's number of oscillations per second is called its frequency, and is measured in Hz. Another variable often encountered is the wavelength, which is the distance between two consecutive maxima (or minima) and is measured in meters. There's a fundamental relation between frequency and wavelength:

$$f = \frac{c}{\lambda}$$

λ period or time
f frequency
c speed of light (300,000 kilometers/second)

The greater the frequency, the smaller the wavelength.

Like data transfer rates, frequencies can be very large, so the standard large units are used to note them: kilo (K), mega (M), and giga (G). Radio waves have frequencies from about 150 KHz through 300 GHz. In contrast, light waves are much shorter and have much higher frequencies. Light wave frequencies are in the area of about 100 trillion Hertz, or 100 THz (teraHertz).

It is possible to encode a few bits per Hertz at low frequencies with current technology. However, more bits can be encoded at high frequencies. Therefore, the high frequencies are much more popular. However, it stops at the high end because high frequencies are not able to cover great distances.

The **wireless spectrum** is a continuum of electromagnetic waves that have varying frequencies and wavelengths that are used for telecommunications (see Table 18.1). The wireless spectrum, as defined by the FCC, spans frequencies between 9 KHz and 300,000 GHz. Each type of wireless service is associated with one area of the wireless spectrum. AM broadcasting, for example, involves the low frequency end of the

Table 18.1 The Electromagnetic Spectrum

Band name	Range	Applications
VLF (very low frequency)	3–30 kHz	Used mainly in submarine communications
LF (low frequency)	30–300 kHz	Used mainly in low capacity radio communications
MF (medium frequency)	0.3–3 MHz	Used mainly in low capacity radio communications
HF (high frequency)	3–30 MHz	High capacity long-distance communication; however, contains interference and fading
VHF (very high frequency)	30–300 MHz	Lower VHF frequencies; high capacity long distance communication up to 100 km is possible; higher VHF frequencies, high capacity line of sight communication (40–50 km)
UHF (ultra high frequency)	0.3–3 GHz	High capacity line of sight communication (40–50 km)
SHF (super high frequency)	3–30 GHz	Communication up to 10 km; over longer distances than 10 km, too much interference from rain and obstacles
EHF (extremely high frequency)	30–300 GHz	High capacity communication over short distances
Infrared	300–1000 GHz	Wireless LANs; infrared is not capable of penetrating walls or rain.

wireless communication spectrum, using frequencies between 535 and 1605 KHz. Its wavelengths are between 560 meters and 190 meters long. Infrared waves make use of a wide band of frequencies at the high-frequency end of the spectrum; between 300 GHz and 300,000 GHz. Infrared wavelengths can be between 1 millimeter and 1 micrometer long.

The wireless spectrum is a subset of the spectrum of all electromagnetic waves. Electromagnetic waves with higher or lower frequencies exist in nature, but are not used for telecommunications. Frequencies lower than 9 KHz are used for specialized applications such as wildlife tracking collars and garage door openers.

Frequencies higher than 300,000 GHz are visible to humans, and for that reason, they cannot be used for communications through air. For example, the color red is 428,570 GHz. At the highest end of the electromagnetic spectrum are x-rays and gamma rays.

Wireless networks typically use infrared or radio frequency signaling (see Table 18.2). By using a wireless network, these networks are suited to specialized network environments that require mobility, long distances, or isolated locations.

NOTE: Radio and Infrared are considered unbound media because they are neither carried nor bound with a physical cable.

When two senders use the same frequency for transmitting their information, chaos will be the result. To prevent this chaos, there are national and international agreements about who can use which frequencies. Worldwide, an agency of the ITU (WARC) supervises these agreements. In the U.S., the FCC allocates spectrum. Unfortunately, the FCC is not bound by WARC's recommendations, so some chaos does exist.

Table 18.2 Wireless Technology

Media	Frequency range	Cost	Ease of installation	Capacity range	Attenuation	Immunity for interference and signal capture
Low-power single frequency	Entire RF, high GHz is most common	Moderate (depends on equipment)	Simple	<1 to 10 Mbps	High	Extremely low
High-power single frequency	Entire RF, high GHz is most common	Moderately expensive	Difficult	<1 to 10 Mbps	Low	Extremely low
Spread spectrum radio	Entire RF, 902 to 928 MHz in U.S., 2.4 GHz band is most common	Moderate (depends on equipment)	Simple to moderate	2 to 6 Mbps	High	Moderate
Terrestrial microwave	Low GHz, 4 to 6 or 21 to 23 is most common	Moderate to high (depends on equipment)	Difficult	<1 to 10 Mbps	Variable	Low
Satellite microwave	Low GHz, 11 to 14 GHz most common	High	Extremely difficult	<1 to 10 Mbps	Variable	Low
Point-to-point infrared	100 GHz to 1000 THz	Low to moderate	Moderate to difficult	<1 to 16 Mbps	Variable	Moderate
Broadcast infrared	100 GHz to 1000 THz	Low	Simple	≤1 Mbps	High	Low

18.1.1 Radio Systems

Radio frequency (RF) resides between 10 KHz and 1 GHz of the electromagnetic spectrum. It includes shortwave radio, VHF and UHF. Radio frequencies have been divided between regulated and unregulated bandwidths. Users of regulated frequencies must get a license from the regulatory bodies that have jurisdiction over the desired operating area (the FCC in the U.S. and the CDC in Canada). While the licensing process can be difficult, licensed frequencies typically guarantee clear transmission within a specific area.

The properties of radio waves strongly depend on the frequency used:

- **Low frequencies**—Radio waves pass through obstacles easily, but the power declines sharply with the distance from the transmitter. The main problem with using these low frequencies for data communication is the relative small bandwidth they offer.

- **High frequencies**—Radio waves tend to travel in straight lines and bounce off obstacles like buildings. Transmitters and receivers need a direct line of sight connection. However, the waves that reach the ionosphere, a layer of charged particles circling the earth at a height of about 300 km, are refracted by it and sent back to earth. Amateur radio operators (hams) use these bands to talk long-distance.

At all frequencies, radio waves are subject to interference from other electrical equipment.

In radio network transmissions, a signal is transmitted in one or many directions, depending on the type of antenna that is used. The wave is very short in length with a low transmission strength (unless the transmission operator has a special license for a high-wattage transmission), which means it is best suited to short-range line-of-sight transmissions. A line-of-sight transmission is one in which the signal goes from point-to-point rather than bouncing off the atmosphere over great distances. A limitation of line-of-sight transmissions is that they are interrupted by land masses such as mountains. Due to its ability to travel long distances, interference between users is a problem. Therefore, all governments tightly license users of radio transmitters.

In unregulated bands, you must operate at regulated power levels (under 1 watt in the U.S.) to minimize interference with other signals. If a device broadcast using less power, the effective area will be smaller. The FCC allocated the following bands for unregulated broadcast: 902–928 MHz, 2400–2483.5 MHz and 5752.5–5850 MHz.

> *NOTE:* These are called the ISM bands, short for Industrial, Scientific, and Medical bands (see Table 18.3). While you don't need a license from the FCC to use these frequencies, you must meet FCC regulations, including power limits and interference minimization (antenna gain of 6 dB and 1 watt of radiated power).

Because the bandwidth available increases in the higher frequency ranges, these higher frequencies will support higher data transfer rates. Therefore, many wireless bridge products operate in the 2.4 GHz and 5.7 GHz frequencies. As throughput increases, computer networking becomes more of a real possibility. And with more companies producing RF wireless networking products, prices are continuing to fall, which makes wireless networking a viable alternative to land-based lines in many local areas.

A **band** is a contiguous group of frequencies, used for a single purpose. Commercial radio stations often refer to the band of frequencies they are using as a single frequency. However, typical radio transmissions actually cover a range of frequencies and wavelengths. Because most tuning equipment is designed to address the entire bandwidth at the kilohertz or megahertz level, the distinction between one frequency and another is often overlooked.

A **narrowband radio system** transmits and receives user information on a specific radio frequency. Narrowband radio keeps the radio signal frequency as narrow as possible just to pass the information. Undesirable crosstalk between communication channels

Table 18.3   ISM Bands

Frequency	Range band description	Bandwidth available
902–928 MHz	Industrial band	26.0 MHz
2.40–2.4835 GHz	Scientific band	83.5 MHz
5.725–5.850 GHz	Medical Band	125.0 MHz

is avoided by carefully coordinating different users on different channel frequencies. In a radio system, privacy and noninterference are accomplished through the use of separate radio frequencies. The radio receiver filters out all radio signals except the ones on its designated frequency. Depending on the power and frequency of the radio signal, the range could be a room, an entire building, or long distances. A low power (1–10 watts) single-frequency signal has a data capacity in the range of 1–10 Mbps.

Spread spectrum signals are distributed over a wide range of frequencies and then collected onto their original frequency at the receiver. Different from narrowband signals, spread spectrum signals uses wider bands, which transmit at a much lower spectral power density (measured in Watts per Hertz). Unless the receiver is tuned to the right frequency or frequencies, a spread spectrum signal resembles noise, which makes the signals harder to detect and harder to jam. As an additional bonus, spread spectrum and narrow band signals can occupy the same band, with little or no interference. There are two types of spread spectrum: direct sequence and frequency hopping. Spread spectrum frequency ranges are very high, in the 902–928 MHz range and higher and typically send data at a rate of 2–6 Mbps.

Direct sequence spread spectrum (DSSS) generates a redundant bit pattern for each bit to be transmitted. This bit pattern is called a chip (or chipping code). The intended receiver knows which specific frequencies are valid and deciphers the signal by collecting valid signals and ignoring the spurious signals. The valid signals are then used to reassemble the data. Because multiple subsets can be used within any frequency range, direct sequence signals can coexist with other signals. Although direct sequence signals can be intercepted almost as easily as other RF signals, eavesdropping is ineffective because it is quite difficult to determine which specific frequencies make up the bit pattern, to retrieve the bit pattern, and to interpret the signal. Because of modern error detection and correction methods, the longer the chip, the greater the probability that the original data can be recovered even if one or more bits in the chip are damaged during transmission.

Frequency hopping quickly switches between predetermined frequencies many times each second. Both the transmitter and receiver must follow the same pattern and maintain complex timing intervals to be able to receive and interpret data being sent. Similar to DSSS, intercepting the data being sent is extremely difficult unless they know the signals to monitor and the timing pattern. In addition, dummy signals can be added to increase security and confuse eavesdroppers. The length of time that the transmitter remains on a given frequency is known as the dwell time.

18.1.2   Microwave Signals

Before fiber optics came about, microwaves formed, for many decades, the heart of the long-distance telephone transmission system. Microwave communication is a form of electromagnetic energy that operates at a higher frequency (low GHz frequency range) than radio wave communications. These days, microwaves are widely used for long-distance telephone communication, cellular telephones, television distribution, and many other areas. Because microwaves provide higher bandwidths radio waves, and because microwaves can carry more bits on each eave, microwaves are currently one of the most popular long-distance transmission technologies.

Above 10^8 Hz (or 100 MHz), waves travel in straight lines. Therefore, the signals can be narrowly focused into a small beam by using a parabolic antenna (like the familiar satellite TV dish). The transmitting and receiving antennas must be accurately aligned with each other. Because the microwaves travel in a straight line, repeaters placed in a tower are needed periodically. The higher the towers are, the further apart they can be. Using 100 m towers, 80 km can be covered.

Microwave signals propagate in straight lines and are not significantly affected by the lower atmosphere. In addition, they are not refracted or reflected by ionized regions in the upper atmosphere. The attenuation of microwave systems is highly dependent on atmospheric conditions; for example, both rain and fog can reduce the maximum possible distance. Higher frequency systems are usually affected most by such conditions. In addition, microwaves do not pass through buildings. The systems are not particularly resistant to EMI and protection for eavesdropping can only be achieved by employing encryption techniques.

Terrestrial systems are often used where cabling is difficult or the cost is prohibitively expensive. Relay towers are used to provide an unobstructed path over an extended distance. These line-of-sight systems use unidirectional parabolic dishes that must be aligned carefully.

The cost of these systems is relatively high, and technical expertise is required to install them because accurate alignment is required. Putting up two towers with antennas, however, is sometimes cheaper than getting 100 km of copper cable or fiber into the ground. Often, this service is leased from a service provider, which reduces installation costs and provides the required expertise.

18.1.3   Satellite Signals

Satellite transmission is much like line-of-sight microwave transmission. One of the necessary stations is a satellite orbiting the earth. The sending and receiving antennas must be locked onto each other's locations at all times. The satellite must move at the same speed as the earth so that it seems to remain fixed above a certain spot. These satellites must be in **geosynchronous (GEO) orbits** and must be positioned 22,300 miles (35,800 km) above Earth's equator. Satellite systems provide far bigger areas of coverage than can be achieved through other technologies because they can either relay signals between sites directly or via another satellite. Huge distances covered by the signal result in propagation delays of up to five seconds. The costs of launching and maintaining a satellite are enormous. Consequently, customers usually lease the services from a provider.

For satellite transmission, information sent to Earth from a satellite must first be transmitted to the satellite in an uplink. An uplink is a broadcast from an Earth-based transmitter to an orbiting satellite. Often, uplink information is scrambled before transmission to prevent unauthorized interception. At the satellite, a transponder receives the uplink, then transmits the signals to another Earth-based location in a downlink. A typical satellite contains 24–32 transponders. Each satellite uses unique frequencies for its downlink. Back on Earth, the downlink is picked up by a dish-shaped antenna. The disk concentrates the signal, which has been weakened by traveling over 22,300 miles, so that it can be interpreted by a receiver.

To prevent total chaos in the sky, there have been international agreements about who may use which frequencies. The main frequency bands are shown in Table 18.4.

An alternative to GEO satellites are LEO satellites. LEO satellites orbit the earth with an altitude of between 700 and 1400 kilometers. But different from GEO satellites, LEO

Table 18.4   Satellite Frequency Bands

Band	Frequency range	Applications
C	4–8 GHz	The most heavily used piece of the satellite spectrum The large size of the antennae of the Earth station is a drawback.
X	8–12.5 GHz	Military usage
Ku	12.5–17.7 GHz	Digital direct to home (DTH) services
K	17.7–26.5 GHz	VSAT
Ka	26.5–40 GHz	VSAT

satellites are not placed above the equator. Because their altitude is lower, they can only cover a smaller geographical range than GEO satellites. However, less power is required to issue signals between Earth and a LEO satellite than Earth and a GEO satellite. LEO satellites can be used for data communications, but their primary use is for mobile telephone services.

Medium earth orbiting (MEO) satellites orbit the earth between 10,350 and 10,390 km above its surface. Similar to LEO satellites, they are not placed above the equator. MEOs are used to carry voice and data signals.

18.1.4   Infrared Systems

Another form of wireless technology is **Infrared (IR) systems,** which is based on infrared light (light that is just below the visible light in the electromagnetic spectrum). Similar to your TV or VCR remote controls, infrared links use light emitting diodes (LEDs) or injection laser diodes (ILDs) to transmit signals and photodiodes to receive signals. IR systems transmit in light frequency ranges of 100 GHz–1000 THz. Unfortunately, IR only transmits up to 1 Mbps for omnidirectional communications and 16 Mbps for directional communications.

Because IR is light, it cannot penetrate opaque objects. IR devices work by using either directed or diffused technology. **Directed IR** uses line-of-sight or point-to-point technology. **Diffused** (also known as **reflective** or **indirect**) IR technology spreads the light over an area to create a cell limited to individual rooms. Because infrared light can bounce off walls, ceilings, and any other objects in its path, indirect infrared is not confined to a specific pathway. Unfortunately, because IR is not confined to a specific pathway, the transmission of data is not very secure. Lastly, because infrared signals are not capable of penetrating walls or other opaque objects and are diluted by strong light sources, infrared is most useful in small or open indoor environments.

18.2   COMPONENTS OF A WIRELESS NETWORK

To see how electrical signals get changed into radio signals, look at the two radio components of a wireless data connection: (1) The radio transceiver and (2) the antenna. To create a computer network connection over radio waves, you will first need a network device such as a bridge or a router. The network bridge/router handles data traffic. It routes the appropriate data signals from the computer network in one building to the network at the other end of the radio connection. Second, a radio transmitter and receiver, commonly called a transceiver, is required. The radio transceiver handles radio signal communications between locations.

The interesting part of this marriage of technologies is that radios have always dealt with electrical signals. The radio transmitter modulates (changes) an electrical signal so that its frequency is raised to one appropriate to radio communications. Then the signal is passed on to a radio antenna.

At the other end of the transmission, the receiving portion of the radio transceiver takes the radio signal and demodulates it back to its normal frequency. Then the resulting electrical signal is passed to the bridge/router side for processing by the network. While the actual process of modulation/demodulation is technical, the concept of radio transmission is very simple.

Likewise, when a response is sent back to the originating site, the radio transceiver "flips" from reception mode to transmission mode. The radio transceivers at each end have this characteristic: Transmit-receive, transmit-receive. They change modes as many as thousands of times per second. This characteristic leads to a delay, called latency, communications. It is idiosyncratic to radio communications and negatively affects data throughput.

Two antennas sit in the middle of the radio transmission/reception process: (1) One at the building from which the signal is transmitted and (2) one at the building receiving the signal. It is possible to have one central location and several remote locations connected to the network. For discussion's sake though, let's think of the communication process as a straight line from one antenna to the other. In order to transmit the modulated radio signal, an electrical current passes through the antenna, inducing a magnetic field that oscillates at a given frequency. The variations in the current create slight variations in the radio frequency. These radio waves radiate outward from the antenna in a "beam" according to the antenna's design.

On the other end, when the radio is in receive mode, the antenna is passive. The electromagnetic radiation from the originating antenna passes across the receiving antenna. This creates a magnetic field, that induces an electrical current through the antenna. The current passes through the radio receiver and is demodulated back into an electrical signal with the same form as the original electrical signal from the first network bridge/router. This electrical signal passes to the bridge/router portion of the receiving unit as a normal data signal.

As a result, the data signal is transferred from one network bridge/router to another without the necessity or expense of an interconnecting wire. Because the radio equipment used in wireless networking must by law be very low-powered to minimize interference with other devices, the required antennas are much more focused than those used in radio or television applications. The amount of focus they use in transmitting a signal, and their corresponding ability to "pick out" specific radio signals, is called *gain*. The gain is measured in decibels (dB).

There are two major categories of antennas: (1) Directional and (2) omnidirectional. Directional antennas focus their energy in tight, narrow beams. When receiving signals, directional antennas do not "see" any signals coming from outside the "beam" on which they are focused. This eliminates a great deal of potential interference from other radio sources and contributes to the ability of multiple wireless communication systems to co-exist with a minimum of interference.

Omnidirectional antennas transmit their energy in a full circle. Spreading the radio signal over such a large area reduces the energy in the signal. This severely restricts the distance over which the signal can be transmitted and received effectively. Therefore, transmissions via an omnidirectional antenna do not travel as far before being degraded as do those from directional antennas. However, amplifiers are available to lengthen the transmit distance of both types of antennas.

These characteristics make each type of antenna optimal in different situations. For those networks involving more than two buildings (multipoint connections), an omnidirectional antenna at the central site will be cost-effective.

A directional antenna is installed at each remote site and is aimed back at the central site omnidirectional antenna. Because the omnidirectional antenna transmits in all directions, every remote antenna can pick up its signal and transmit back to it.

On the other hand, some network connections involve only two distinct buildings. These are called point-to-point connections. In these situations, a directional antenna is used at each site—each aimed at the other. Both types of antennas are available with various levels of gain. In addition to the wireless bridge and antenna, there are a few more items required to make a functional wireless network connection. They are:

- **Feature sets**—Some manufacturers sell their wireless bridges in separate units. In such instances, the physical radio/bridge unit has a base cost. Software features, such as individual protocol routing and encryption, are sold as a separate unit. However, these may be required in your implementation. Be sure to define your needs completely to the reseller/integrator/installer who installs your wireless connection.
- **External cables**—For all wireless installations there must be a cable that connects the antenna to the radio in the wireless bridge. Because it runs to the outside of the building, this is called an external cable. When purchasing all the components as part of a kit, an external cable is included. Depending on where the wireless bridge is located inside your building, and where the antenna is mounted, an additional length of cable may be required. In order to keep the wireless system within specifications, it is important to minimize the length of the cable. If necessary, it is possible to locate the wireless bridge at one location in your building and run a network cable from it to your network connection at an alternate location in the building. Be sure to physically secure the bridge if it is located in a public area.
- **Lightning arrestor**—Because external antennas are involved, the threat of a lightning strike can be very real. Make sure that proper measures are implemented to minimize the risk of lightning strikes. Most manufacturers of wireless bridges sell an optional device called a lightning arrestor. It is normally installed between the antenna and the bridge. Also make sure the antenna is properly grounded.
- **Emissions filter**—Some manufacturers provide another optional component known as an emissions filter. It reduces the level of extraneous noise that might interfere with the electrical signal on its way from the antenna to the wireless bridge. It also is installed inline between the antenna and bridge.
- **Mast or tower**—When it is not possible to obtain a clear line-of-sight between the two antennas involved in a wireless connection, a mast or radio tower may provide

additional height for the antenna, clearing obstacles such as trees or buildings that lie in the path of the radio signal. Masts are generally mounted on the roof and may be 10–50 ft. high. If a mast is used in your implementation, be sure it is tied down properly to minimize the risk of wind damage. Radio towers are generally independent structures erected to raise antennas when extended distances are desired. They may also be required when tall buildings (larger than three stories) or topographical features lie directly in the path of the radio signal between two antennas. Towers can be erected at heights of 50 ft. and higher. Obviously, depending on the application, the cost of erecting tall towers can be prohibitive.

■ **Data cable**—A network data cable is required to connect the wireless bridge to your internal network (a hub, switch, or repeater). This cable is generally the responsibility of the individual entity. If the wireless bridge is a significant distance from the network equipment, installation of this cable may require a cable installer. In this case, be sure to discuss the cable run with your wireless installer when the system is being specified.

18.3   WIRELESS LANS (WLANS)

A wireless LAN (WLAN) is a LAN without wires. WLANs have been around for more than a decade, but are just beginning to gain momentum because of falling costs and improved standards. WLANs transfer data through the air through radio frequencies instead of cables. They can reach a radius of 500 feet indoors and 1000 feet outdoors; but antennas, transmitters, and other access devices can be used to widen that area. WLANs require a wired access point that plugs all the wireless devices into the wired network.

Wireless LAN system can provide LAN users with access to real-time information anywhere in their organization. Installing a wireless LAN system can be fast and easy and can eliminate the need to pull cable through walls and ceilings. In addition, wireless technology allows the network to go where wire cannot go. Thus, WLANs combined data connectivity with user mobility, and through simplified configuration, enable movable LANs.

WLAN configurations vary from simple, independent, peer-to-peer connections between a set of PCs, to more complex, intrabuilding infrastructure networks. There are also point-to-point and point-to-multipoint wireless solutions. A point-to-point solution is used to bridge two LANs and to provide an alternative to cable between two geographically distant locations (up to 30 miles). Point-to-multipoint solutions connect several, separate locations to one single location or building. Both point-to-point and point-to-multipoint can be based on the 802.11b standard or on more costly infrared-based solutions that can provide throughput rates up to 622 Mbps (OC-12 speed).

18.4   802.11 WIRELESS STANDARDS

The 802.11 standards can be compared to the IEEE 802.3 standard for Ethernet for wired LANs. A new standard put out by the IEEE called 802.11b or **Wi-Fi** is making WLAN use faster and easier, and the market is growing quickly. The number of IEEE 802.11b users grew from almost zero in early 2001 to more than 15 million at the end of 2002. That still isn't much compared to cell phones and wired Ethernet, but the growth will likely continue.

18.4.1   802.1X

The IEEE 802.1X standard is a relatively recent protocol enhancement that creates a standard for how authentication is performed over an 802 standards-based network. The 802.1X standard is designed to enhance the security of wireless local area networks (WLANs) that follow the IEEE 802.11 standard. 802.1X provides an authentication framework for wireless LANs, allowing a user to be authenticated by a central authority. The actual algorithm that is used to determine whether a user is authentic is left open and multiple algorithms are possible. 802.1X uses an existing protocol, the Extensible Authentication Protocol (EAP), specified in RFC 2284, that works on Ethernet, Token Ring, or wireless LANs, for message exchange during the authentication process.

In a wireless LAN with 802.1X, a user (known as the supplicant) requests access to an access point (known as the authenticator). The access point forces the user (actually, the user's client software) into an unauthorized state that allows the client to send only an EAP start message. The access point returns an EAP message requesting the user's identity. The client returns the identity, which is then forwarded by the access point to the authentication server, which uses an algorithm to authenticate the user and then returns an accept or reject message back to the access point. Assuming an accept was received, the access point changes the client's state to authorized and normal traffic can now take place. The authentication server may use the Remote Authentication Dial-In User Service (RADIUS), although 802.1X does not specify it.

EAP, provides an extensible authentication mechanism for use over PPP, allowing new authentication mechanisms (biometrics, smart cards, etc.) to be "plugged in" without the PPP protocol needing to understand them. EAP on LAN (EAPOL) is an adaptation of EAP. It allows authentication information to be passed in network frames, rather than requiring that it be embedded in a higher-level protocol such as PPP. This reduces network overhead for authentication, and removes the necessity for the network to be running a particular protocol suite such as TCP/IP.

The potential network client passes authentication information through a wireless access point to a centralized authentication server, who validates the logon and permits certain network activities based on the identity of the client. For instance, the authentication server may install a certain set of firewall security rules or a specific VPN configuration for that client's address, based on user identity. Until a user is authenticated, the wireless network will only forward 802.1X traffic for that connection. Nothing else, such as attempts to browse the web, send mail, or obtain a local IP address via DHCP, will be permitted.

Optionally, it can be used to improve the privacy of wireless LAN communication by dynamically varying the keys used to encrypt the wireless traffic. It does this by return encryption keys to users, allowing the network to dynamically vary the encryption used by each connection, rather than requiring that all stations be pre-configured with a fixed key (currently a time-consuming activity).

802.1X is only the framework allowing EAP transactions to be passed on the media. It is not EAP itself. To get authentication functionality, you must choose a particular flavor of EAP, and install it on your authentication server. Here's a listing of the choices:

- Transport Layer Security (EAP-TLS)
- EAP Tunneled Transport Layer Security (EAP-TTLS)

- RADIUS
- LEAP

You can change the flavor of EAP that you use at any time, without needing to replace 802.1X-compliant access points, because the exact mechanics of EAP are transparent to the access points.

18.4.2   802.11 Physical Layer and Architecture

The 802.11 standard defines three physical layers for WLANs, two radio frequency specifications (RF - direct sequence and frequency hopping spread spectrum) and one infrared (IR). Most WLANs operate in the 2.4 GHz license-free frequency radio band and have throughput rates up to 2 Mbps.

> *NOTE:* The 2.4 GHz band is particularly attractive because it enjoys worldwide allocations for unlicensed operations.

The most popular 802.11 types are:

- **802.11a**—Operate in the 5 GHz license-free frequency band and is expected to provide throughput rates up to 54 Mbps in normal mode or 75 Mbps in turbo mode but most commonly, communications takes place at 6 Mbps, 12 Mbps, or 24 Mbps. It uses a modulation scheme known as orthogonal frequency-division multiplexing (OFDM).
- **802.11b (Wi-Fi)**—standard is direct sequence only, and initially provided throughputs rates up to 11 Mbps with the potential of three simultaneous channels, but has been recently increased to 22 Mbps. The modulation method selected for 802.11b is known as complementary code keying (CCK), which allows higher data speeds and is less susceptible to multipath-propagation interference. 802.11b is the clear leader in business and institutional wireless networking and is gaining share for home applications as well.
- **802.11g**—Has a nominal maximum throughput of 54 Mbps. But because it is using the 2.4 GHz frequency band, its products should be compatible with 802.11b products.

For other 802.11 types, see Table 18.5.

There are two operation modes defined in IEEE 802.11:

- Ad hoc mode
- Infrastructure mode

The ad hoc network, also referred to as the Independent Basic Service Set (IBSS), stands alone and is not connected to a base. Wireless stations communicate directly with each other without using an access point or any connection to a wired network. This basic topology is useful in order to quickly and easily set up a wireless network anywhere a wireless infrastructure does not exist such as a hotel room, a convention center, or an airport.

In infrastructure mode, also known as Extended Service Set (ESS), the wireless network consists of at least one access point (AP) connected to the wired network infrastructure and a set of wireless end stations (see Figure 18.1). An access point controls encryption on the network and may bridge or route the wireless traffic to a wired Ethernet network (or the Internet). Access points that act as routers can also assign an IP address to your PCs by using DHCP services. APs can be compared with a base station used in cellular networks.

Table 18.5   802.11 Standards

IEEE Working Group	Primary Task	Status of Work
802.11a	Worked to establish specification for wireless data transmission in the 5 GHz band.	Approved 1999
802.11b	Worked to establish specifications for wireless data transmission in the 2.4 GHz band.	Approved 1999
802.11c	Worked to establish wireless MAC bridging functionality	Folded into 802.1d
802.11d	Working to determine requirements that will allow 802.11 to operating outside the United States	The work of this group is ongoing
802.11e	Working to add multimedia and quality of service (QoS) capability to wireless MAC layer	Proposal in draft form
802.11f	Working to allow for better roaming between multivendor access points and distribution systems.	The work of this group is ongoing.
802.11g	Working to provide raw data throughput over wireless networks at a rate of up to 54 Mbps.	Draft created in January 2002 and final approval expected soon.
802.11h	Worked to allow for European implementation requests regarding the 5 GHz band.	The work of this group is ongoing.
802.11i	Worked to fix security flaws in WLANs by developing new security standards	The work of this group is ongoing.
802.11j	Worked to create a global standard in the 5 GHz band by making high-performance LAN (HiperLAN) and 802.11 interoperable	Disbanded

An ESS consists of two or more BSSs forming a single subnetwork. Traffic is forwarded from one BSS to another to facilitate movement of wireless stations between BSSs that use cellular topology. The distribution system that connects these networks is almost always an Ethernet LAN. Because most corporate WLANs require access to the wired LAN for services (file servers, printers, and Internet links) they will operate in infrastructure mode.

One of the requirements of IEEE 802.11 is that it can be used with existing wired networks. 802.11 solved this challenge with the use of a portal. A **portal** is the logical integration between wired LANs and 802.11. It also can serve as the access point to the DS. All data going to an 802.11 LAN from an 802.X LAN must pass through a portal. It thus functions as a bridge between wired and wireless.

Today, 802.11a still has some issues to work out, particularly in the area of compatibility. Currently, products aren't backward compatible with 802.11b products, which clearly dominate the market. Although all 802.11a products use the same chip set, implementation by each manufacturer differs enough to make them incompatible. Until an interoperability standard is established, 802.11a products from one company may not be able to communicate with those of another.

The Wireless Ethernet Compatibility Alliance (WECA) is an industry consortium that tests for interoperability. Those 802.11b products that pass WECA's tests are given

Figure 18.1   A Wireless End Station and a Wireless Access Point

the wireless fidelity (Wi-Fi) seal of approval. WECA is working on an 802.11a certification called WiFi5.

18.4.3   Framing

Frame formats are specified for wireless LAN systems by 802.11. Each frame consists of a MAC header, a frame body, and a FCS. The MAC header consists of seven fields and is thirty bytes long. The fields are frame control, duration, address 1, address 2, address 3, sequence control, and address 4. The frame control field is two bytes long and is comprised of eleven subfields.

The duration/ID field is two bytes long. It contains the data on the duration value for each field, and for control frames it carries the associated identity of the transmitting station. The address fields identify the basic service set, the destination address, the source address, and the receiver and transmitter addresses. Each address field is six bytes long. The sequence control field is two bytes and is split into two subfields: (1) fragment number and (2) sequence number. The fragment number is four bits and tells how many fragments the MSDU is broken into. The sequence number field is twelve bits, which indicate the sequence number of the MSDU. The frame body is a variable length field from 0–2312. This is the payload. The frame check sequence is a 32 bit CRC that ensures there are no errors in the frame.

Figure 18.2   The Hidden Node Problem

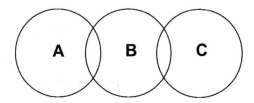

18.4.4   The Medium Access Control Protocol

Most wired LAN products use CSMA/CD as the MAC protocol. *Carrier sense* means that the station will listen before it transmits. If there is already someone transmitting, then the station waits and tries again later. If no one is transmitting, then the station goes ahead and sends what it has. When two stations send at the same time, the transmissions will collide and the information will be lost. This is where collision detection comes into play. The station will listen to ensure that the transmission made it to the destination without collisions. If a collision occurred, the stations wait and try again later. The time the station waits is determined by a different random amount of time. This technique works very well for wired LANs, but wireless topologies can create a problem for CSMA/CD. The problem is the hidden node.

The hidden node problem is shown in Figure 18.2. Node C cannot hear Node A. So, if Node A is transmitting, Node C will not know and may transmit as well. This will result in collisions. The solution to this problem is Carrier Sense Multiple Access with Collision Avoidance (CSMA/CA). In CSMA/CA, the station listens before it sends. If someone is already transmitting, it will wait for a random period and try again. If no one is transmitting then it sends a short message called the RTS message. This message contains the destination address and the duration of the transmission. Other stations now know that they must wait that long before they can transmit. The destination then sends a short message, the CTS message. This message tells the source that it can send without fear of collisions. Each packet is acknowledged. If an acknowledgement is not received, the MAC layer retransmits the data. This entire sequence is called the 4-way handshake and is illustrated by Figure 18.3. This is the protocol that 802.11 chose for the standard.

18.4.5   Wireless Application Protocol

WAP (Wireless Application Protocol) is a specification for a set of communication protocols to standardize the way that wireless devices with limited capability, such as cellular telephones and radio transceivers, can be used for Internet access, including e-mail, the World Wide Web, newsgroups, and Internet Relay Chat (IRC). While Internet access has been possible in the past, different manufacturers have used different technologies. In the future, devices and service systems that use WAP will be able to interoperate.

Wireless Application Protocol (WAP) is a universal open standard developed by the WAP forum and governs wireless communication. The programming used for WAP is

Figure 18.3 The 4-way Handshake

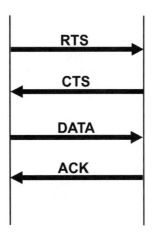

based on the WWW programming model. The model has three components: the client, the gateway, and the original server. HTTP is used between the gateway and the original server to transfer the content of the message, and the gateway acts as a proxy server for the wireless domain.

Another component of the WAP is the wireless markup language (WML). WML documents are subdivided into small well-defined units of user interaction known as cards. The users navigate by moving from card to card. The communications protocol stack of WAP has six layers—application, session, transaction, security, transport, and network—which can adapt to the standard Web protocols.

The WAP layers are:

- **Wireless application environment (WAE)**—Defines the user interface on the phone.
- **Wireless Session Layer (WSL)**—The WAP equivalent of HTTP. This layer links the WAE to two session services: a connection oriented operating over the WTP, and a connectionless service operating above the WDP.
- **Wireless Transport Layer Security (WTLS)**—incorporates security features that are based on TLS.
- **Wireless Transport Layer (WTP)**—the WAP equivalent of TCP or UDP, that provides reliable or unreliable communications. WTP supports Protocol Data Unit concatenation and delayed acknowledgment to help reduce the number of messages sent.
- **Wireless Datagram Protocol (WDP)**—allows WAP to be bearer independent by adapting the transport layer of the underlying bearer. WDP presents a consistent data format to the higher layers of the WAP protocol stack.
- **Network Carrier Method**—Type of wireless signal.

The WAP was conceived by four companies: Ericsson, Motorola, Nokia, and Unwired Planet (now Phone.com). The Wireless Markup Language (WML) is used to create pages that can be delivered using WAP.

18.4.6   Accessing the Wireless LAN

The way 802.11b works is that if you possess a couple pieces of information, which are shared among network users, you can access the network. There is generally no individual authentication when gaining access to the network. The two pieces of information required to communicate over an 802.11b LAN are the SSID and, if encryption is enabled, the WEP key. The Service Set Identifier (SSID) is a 32-character identifier that is attached to each packet, identifying the wireless LAN to which the traffic belongs, so that multiple wireless LANs can exist in the same physical area. Much like multiple Windows, workgroups can exist on a single physical LAN, and an individual can select the workgroup to join by setting its name in their system configuration; a user can select the 802.11b LAN to participate in by setting the proper SSID. All users who desire to communicate with each other typically set their SSID to the same value. Since the SSID can be "sniffed" from the network via programs that monitor wireless LAN activity, and once known, anyone can set their wireless network adapter's SSID to the desired value, the SSID really is only a LAN selection feature for user convenience, not an access control feature designed to add security.

To protect an 802.11b network from unauthorized, use and "snooping", you can enable packet encryption via WEP. Different cards have different levels of support for WEP. WEP works by using a RC4 encryption scheme (Refer to encryption for details on RC4) with a key that can be 40, 64, 128 or 256 bits in length. The design in 802.11 for RC4 uses a shared key. The access point sends a random number at the registration request. The receiving node assigns the key with a secret key that was pre-shared. The access point checks the results and allows the node to sign on.

Data between the devices is encrypted by one of the values listed. The method described is known as one-way authentication. Stated another way, the access point knows it is from some group of computers that has the pre-shared key and cannot identify a specific computer. Given this, it is possible for a rogue computer to pretend it is an access point. When enabling WEP (Wired Equivalent Privacy) on a network, the encryption key must be the same among all the devices, including the wireless base station providing network connectivity.

Another difficulty with WEP is that it is possible to "break" this WEP encryption and gain access to the network. Another issue with WEP is RC4 being used in wireless. RC4 was designed for a synchronous stream. The nature of wireless communications is such that the signal can be dropped very easily. The designers address this challenge by changing the key for every packet. This uses up unique keys very rapidly, which forces key reuse, which hurts security. In addition, RC4 is part of the logic and a number known as an initialization vector is not encrypted. Because of this, anyone can capture a bunch of packets and figure out the WEP pattern.

18.4.7   Security

War driving is the act of locating and possibly exploiting connections to wireless local area networks while driving around a city or elsewhere. To do war driving, you need a vehicle, a computer (which can be a laptop), a wireless Ethernet card set to work in promiscuous mode, and some kind of an antenna which can be mounted on top of or positioned inside the car. Because a wireless LAN may have a range that extends beyond an office building, an outside user may be able to intrude into the network, obtain a free Internet connection, and possibly gain access to company records and other resources.

Some people have made a sport out of war driving, in part to demonstrate the ease with which wireless LANs can be compromised. With an omnidirectional antenna and a geophysical positioning system (GPS), the war driver can systematically map the locations of 802.11b wireless access points. Companies that have a wireless LAN are urged to add security safeguards that will ensure only intended users have access.

Wireless Transport Layer Security (WTLS) is the security level for Wireless Application Protocol (WAP) applications. Based on Transport Layer Security (TLS) v1.0 (a security layer used in the Internet, equivalent to Secure Socket Layer 3.1), WTLS was developed to address the problematic issues surrounding mobile network devices – such as limited processing power and memory capacity, and low bandwidth – and to provide adequate authentication, data integrity, and privacy protection mechanisms.

Wireless transactions, such as those between a user and their bank, require stringent authentication and encryption to ensure security to protect the communication from attack during data transmission. Because mobile networks do not provide end-to-end security, TLS had to be modified to address the special needs of wireless users. Designed to support datagrams in a high latency, low bandwidth environment, WTLS provides an optimized handshake through dynamic key refreshing, which allows encryption keys to be regularly updated during a secure session.

Wired Equivalent Privacy (WEP) is a security protocol, specified in the IEEE Wireless Fidelity (Wi-Fi) standard, 802.11b, that is designed to provide a wireless local area network (WLAN) with a level of security and privacy comparable to what is usually expected of a wired LAN. A wired local area network (LAN) is generally protected by physical security mechanisms (controlled access to a building, for example) that are effective for a controlled physical environment, but may be ineffective for WLANs because radio waves are not necessarily bound by the walls containing the network. WEP seeks to establish similar protection to that offered by the wired network's physical security measures by encrypting data transmitted over the WLAN. Data encryption protects the vulnerable wireless link between clients and access points; once this measure has been taken, other typical LAN security mechanisms such as password protection, end-to-end encryption, virtual private networks (VPNs), and authentication can be put in place to ensure privacy.

A research group from the University of California at Berkeley recently published a report citing "major security flaws" in WEP that left WLANs using the protocol vulnerable to attacks (called wireless equivalent privacy attacks). In the course of the group's examination of the technology, they were able to intercept and modify transmissions and gain access to restricted networks. The Wireless Ethernet Compatibility Alliance (WECA) claims that WEP - which is included in many networking products - was never intended to be the sole security mechanism for a WLAN, and that, in conjunction with traditional security practices, it is very effective.

Minimum steps that should be taken to protect your network should include:

■ Change the default network name, ESSID, and the default password which is needed to sign on to a WLAN on your access points. Each manufacturer's defaults settings are commonly known by hackers.

- Disable the ESSID broadcast in the Access Point Beacon. By default access points periodically transmit their ESSID values. Wireless utilities including with Windows XP and as freeware programs can capture these values to present a list of available networks to the user. Disabling this broadcast makes it more difficult for intruders to recognize your network.
- Enable Wired Equivalent Privacy (WEP). Without encryption, your data is transmitted in readable form. Anyone within radio range using a wireless protocol analyzer or a promiscuous-mode network adapter may capture the data without joining the network. REP employs RC4 encryption, the same algorithm used for secure online shopping. WEP encryption can generally be found in 64-bit or 128-bit flavors. Of course, use the 128-bit variety if available.
- Change your encryption keys periodically. While the WEP is reasonably strong, the algorithm can be broken in time. The relationship between breaking the algorithm is directly related to the length of time that a key is in use. So WEP allows changing of the key to prevent brute force attach of the algorithm. Note: WEP can be implemented in hardware or in software. One reason that WEP is optional is because encryption may not be exported from the United States. This allows 802.11 to be a standard outside the U.S. albeit without the encryption.
- Enable Media Access Control (MAC) filtering on your access point (AP). Each wireless PC Card has a unique identifier known as the MAC address. Many access points let you build a list of MAC addresses that are allowed on the network. Those not listed are denied.

While WEP is probably adequate for most home use, depending on the confidentiality of the data, corporate administrators should add strong encryption to the WLAN. Virtual private networks (VPNs) can be used so that you can also use IPSec or PPTP encryption over the wireless segment.

802.11i is a developing IEEE standard for security in a wireless local area network (WLAN). A subset of the 802.11i is Wi-Fi Protected Access (WPA), which solves the problem by abandoning WEP in favor of 802.11i's vastly improved Temporal Key Integrity Protocol (TKIP). WPA ensures that TKIP keys vary for each packet through key mixing. WPA also increases part of the keyspace and adds encrypted packet integrity to reject inserted packets. Current Wi-Fi puts weak integrity outside the encrypted payload. WPA includes full support for server-based authentication using the 802.1X protocol and EAP (Extensible Authentication Protocol).

WPA requires the user to provide a master key, but this does not become a static encryption key. Instead, the master key is simply a password used as a starting point through which WPA derives the key it will use to encrypt network traffic. Moreover, the key is regularly and automatically changed (and never reused), reducing the likelihood that it will be compromised. The master key also serves as a password by which users can be authenticated and granted network access.

Temporal Key Integrity Protocol (TKIP, pronounced tee-kip) fixes the key reuse problem of WEP, that is, periodically using the same key to encrypt data. The TKIP process begins with a 128-bit "temporal key" shared among clients and access points.

TKIP combines the temporal key with the client's MAC address and then adds a relatively large 16-octet initialization vector to produce the key that will encrypt the data. This procedure ensures that each station uses different key streams to encrypt the data. TKIP uses RC4 to perform the encryption, which is the same as WEP. A major difference from WEP, however, is that TKIP changes temporal keys every 10,000 packets. This provides a dynamic distribution method that significantly enhances the security of the network. TKIP also includes a message integrity check.

An advantage of using TKIP is that companies having existing WEP-based access points and radio NICs can upgrade to TKIP through relatively simple firmware patches. In addition, WEP-only equipment will still interoperate with TKIP-enabled devices using WEP. TKIP is a temporary solution, and most experts believe that stronger encryption is still needed.

In addition to the TKIP solution, the 802.11i standard will likely include the Advanced Encryption Standard (AES) protocol. An issue, however, is that AES requires a coprocessor (additional hardware) to operate. This means that companies need to replace existing access points and client NICs to implement AES. Based on marketing reports, the installed base today is relatively small compared to what future deployments will bring. As a result, there will be a very large percentage of new wireless LAN implementations that will readily take advantage of AES when it becomes part of 802.11. Companies having installed wireless LANs, on the other hand, will need to determine whether it's worth the costs of upgrade for better security.

A number of third-party manufacturers have stepped into the breach to offer a new class of hardware-based VPN products designed specifically for wireless networks. In addition, IEEE formed a task group, TGi, specifically to tighten up WLAN security in a nonproprietary systematic format.

TGi proposed a stopgap measure called the Temporary Key Integrity Protocol (TKIP) which is intended to work with existing and legacy hardware. Your WLAN provider may add this feature through a firmware revision. TKIP uses a mechanism called fast-packet rekeying, which changes the encryption keys frequently.

In addition, TGi also ratified the use of 802.1X, that requires a WLAN client to initiate an authorization request to the access point, which authenticates the client with an Extensible Authentication Protocol (EAP)-compliant RADIUS server. This RADIUS server may authenticate either the user (via passwords) or the machine (by MAC address). In theory, the wireless client is not allowed to join the network until the transaction is complete.

One form of EAP that was created by Cisco and is now supported by Microsoft is PEAP. PEAP, short for Protected Extensible Authentication Protocol, is a form of EAP that is combined with Transport Layer Security (TLS) to create a TSL-encrypted channel between client and server. To provide mutual authentication, PEAP uses Microsoft Challenge Authentication Protocol (MS-CHAP) Version 2. Because the challenge/response packets are sent over a TLS encrypted channel, the password and the key are not exposed to offline dictionary attacks.

The first step in a successful wireless installation is to conduct a site survey. It's virtually impossible to identify the ideal wireless solution and location of wireless access points without first conducting a site survey. Wireless site surveys analyze the conditions required to provide an optimal radio link, including:

- The users, applications and equipment on the LANs that need to be internetworked.
- The wireless system best suited for the application (e.g the level of security, speed and distance required).
- The line-of-sight requirements between antennas (using calculations for antenna size and cable length).
- The specific places where each component should be located (e.g. keeping access points as close to clients as possible).
- Whether to use a point-to-point or multipoint configuration. Typically, point-to-point configuration is used when two buildings need to communicate to one another, while multipoint is ideal when two or more buildings need to communicate in a "triangle" configuration.
- Potential sources of interference, in alternative RF bands (e.g cordless phones, microwaves, natural interference, or other access points using the same channel).
- Any federal, state and local regulations (e.g. FCC regulations and right-of-way mandates).

When considering location issues, a prime area of concern is wireless networking because too little attention paid to wireless network positioning can increase the likelihood that your network is available to unauthorized individuals. When considering wireless network components, minimizing transmission power reduces the chances your data will leak out of the intended area. Careful antenna placement will also have an effect. Attempt to place antennas as far from exterior walls as possible. Consider the RF pattern options with different types of antennas.

Typically the interface between the wired network and the transceiver is placed in a corner in an effort to hide the electronics. If that corner is along the outside of your building, that places the network signal outside and easy to intercept. In effect, you have put an Ethernet jack for your network in the parking lot.

Wireless networks can also be interrupted by EMI or RFI and the only real countermeasure to that is a strong signal. This is done by either purchasing an amplifier or new APs that offer a stronger signal. Of course, when installing your wireless network, you should ensure that you don't place workstation or APs near any obvious sources of EMI and RFI. Lastly, if another business or person uses wireless networking near your wireless network, you may need to use a different channel than their network. Of course, you should not use the default channel that is set on your wireless equipment.

Shielding (paint with metal and Mylar window covering can attenuate the RF signals) reduces the distance that radio and other electronic waves can travel, decreasing the chance someone can get to your network. In addition, shielding reduces the risk of a wireless denial of service attack (such as using a heavy duty antenna or even using a consumer microwave and disabling the safety interlock). The downside could be a negative impact on pagers and cellular phones.

More sensitive environments may wish to hire someone to perform a Technical Surveillance Counter Measures (TSCM) sweep on a periodic basis. Extremely sensitive sites would be wise to consider installing in-place monitoring in addition to periodic searches for unauthorized Infra-Red (IR) or cellular phone based equipment.

18.5   BLUETOOTH

Bluetooth refers to a short-range radio technology aimed at simplifying communications among Internet devices and between devices and the Internet. It also aims to simplify data synchronization between Internet devices and other computers. An advantage of Bluetooth is its similarity to many other specifications already deployed and its borrowing of many features from these specifications. The Bluetooth standard is becoming more and more of a short time network between devices for a small amount of information.

Bluetooth has a present nominal link range of 10 cm–10 m, which can be extended to 100 m, with increased transmitting power. Bluetooth operates in the 2.4 GHz ISM band and uses a frequency hop spread spectrum technology in which packets are transmitted in defined time slots on defined frequencies. A full duplex information interchange rate of up to 1 Mbps may be achieved when a Time-Division Duplex (TDD) scheme is used. The second generation of Bluetooth supports up to 2 Mbps.

Work on the Bluetooth specification is progressing and is primarily the responsibility of the Bluetooth Special Group (SIG).This is an industry group consisting of leaders in telecommunications and computing industries. The promoter group within the SIG currently consists of 3Com, Ericsson, IBM, Intel, Lucent Technologies, Microsoft, Motorola, Nokia and Toshiba.

A Bluetooth system is comprised of the following four major components:

- **Radio unit**—Consisting of a radio transceiver that provides the radio link between Bluetooth devices.
- **Baseband unit**—Hardware consisting of flash memory and a CPU. This interfaces with the radio unit and the host device electronics.
- **Link management software**—A driver software or firmware that enables the application software to interface with the baseband unit and radio unit.
- **Application software**—This implements the user interface and is the application that can run on wireless. For example, this could be chat software that allows two laptop users in a conference hall to talk to each other through wireless technology.

Each device has a unique 48-bit address from the IEEE 802 standard. In addition, a frequency hop scheme allows devices to communicate even in areas with a great deal of electromagnetic interference and it includes built-in encryption and verification.

One Bluetooth standard is **HomeRF SWAP** (SWAP is an acronym for Shared Wireless Access Protocol). It is designed specifically for wireless networks in homes, while 802.11 was created for use in businesses. HomeRF networks are designed to be more affordable to home users than other wireless technologies. It is based on frequency hopping and using radio frequency waves for the transmission of voice and data, with a range of up to 150 feet.

SWAP works together with the PSTN network and the Internet through existing cordless telephone and wireless LAN technologies to enable voice-activated home electronic systems, accessing the Internet from anywhere in the home, and to forward fax, voice, and e-mail messages. SWAP uses TDMA for interactive data transfer and CSMA/CA for high-speed packet transfer. SWAP operates in the 2400 MHz band at 50 hops per second to provide a data rate between 1 and 2 Mbps.

SUMMARY

1. For decades, radio and television stations have used the atmosphere to transport information via analog signals. The atmosphere is also capable of carrying digital signals.

2. Networks that transmit signals through the atmosphere are known as wireless networks.

3. All wireless signals are carried through the air along electromagnetic waves.

4. The wireless spectrum is a continuum of electromagnetic waves, with varying frequencies and wavelengths that are used for telecommunications.

5. RF resides between 10 KHz and 1 GHz of the electromagnetic spectrum. It includes shortwave radio, VHF, and UHF.

6. In unregulated bands, you must operate at regulated power levels (under one watt in the U.S.) to minimize interference with other signals.

7. A band is a contiguous group of frequencies used for a single purpose. Commercial radio stations often refer to the band of frequencies they are using as a single frequency.

8. A narrowband radio system transmits and receives user information on a specific radio frequency.

9. Spread-spectrum signals are distributed over a wide range of frequencies and then collected onto their original frequency at the receiver. Unless the receiver is not tuned to the right frequency or frequencies, a spread spectrum signal resembles noise, making the signals harder to detect and harder to jam.

10. DSSS generates a redundant bit pattern for each bit to be transmitted. The intended receiver knows which specific frequencies are valid and deciphers the signal by collecting valid signals and ignoring the spurious signals. Valid signals are then used to reassemble the data.

11. Frequency hopping quickly switches between predetermined frequencies many times each second. Both the transmitter and receiver must follow the same pattern and maintain complex timing intervals to be able to receive and interpret the data being sent.

12. Before fiber optics came about, microwaves formed the heart of the long-distance telephone transmission system. Microwave communication is a form of electromagnetic energy that operates at a higher frequency (low GHz frequency range) than radio wave communications.

13. Satellite transmission is similar to line-of-sight microwave transmission, in which one of the stations is a satellite orbiting the Earth. This requires the sending and receiving antennas to be locked onto each other's location at all times.

14. Another form of wireless technology is IR systems, which are based on IR light (light that is just below the visible light in the electromagnetic spectrum).

15. IR devices work by using either directed or diffused technology.

16. A WLAN is a LAN without wires.

17. A new standard put out by the IEEE, called 802.11b or Wi-Fi, is making WLAN use faster and easier. The market is growing quickly.

18. The ad-hoc network, also referred to as the IBSS, stands alone and is not connected to a base. Wireless stations communicate directly with each other without using an AP or any connection to a wired network.

19. In infrastructure mode, also known as ESS, the wireless network consists of at least one AP connected to the wired network infrastructure and a set of wireless end stations.

20. While WEP is probably adequate for most home use, depending on the confidentiality of the data, corporate administrators should add strong encryption to the WLAN. VPNs can be used so that you can also use IPSec or PPTP encryption over the wireless segment.

21. Bluetooth refers to a short-range radio technology aimed at simplifying communications among Net devices and between devices and the Internet. It also aims to simplify data synchronization between Net devices and other computers.

22. One Bluetooth standard is HomeRF SWAP. It is designed specifically for wireless networks in homes, while 802.11 was created for use in businesses.

23. The new 802.11b standard is direct sequence only and initially provided throughput rates up to 11 Mbps but has been recently increased to 22 Mbps.

24. The new standard, 802.11a, will operate in the 5 GHz license-free frequency band and is expected to provide throughput rates up to 54 Mbps in normal mode or 75 Mbps in turbo mode.

25. The newest standard is the 802.11g standard, which has a nominal maximum throughput of 54 Mbps.

QUESTIONS

1. Network transmission of data via radio, laser, infrared, or microwave is said to be sent on what?
a. switching media
b. bound media
c. pulse media
d. unbounded media

2. What is the acronym for the specification developed by the HomeRF work group for wireless voice and data networking at home?
a. SWAP
b. WEB
c. WEPPA
d. WPPA

3. Which of the following represents an advantage of spread spectrum technology?
a. reduced interference
b. lower admin cost
c. higher speed
d. lower maintenance cost

4. In the US, what organization regulates the radiation rating of computers?
a. WIHI
b. SETS
c. FCC
d. WHIFI
e. WANA

5. You need to provide wireless network connectively to a portion of a building that cannot be wired and cannot be reached by a low power antenna. What type of antenna should you use to connect the two parts of the building through a wall?
a. omnidirectional
b. multicast
c. highly directional
d. semidirectional
e. unidirectional

6. Which of the following types of antennas issues signals with equal strength and clarity in all directions?
a. directional
b. bidirectional
c. tridirectional
d. omnidirectional

7. Which of the following wireless services uses the lowest range of frequencies?
a. AM radio
b. FM radio
c. cellular telephone service
d. wireless LANs

8. What type of transmission path does a fixed wireless signal require?
a. line-of-sight
b. non-line-of-site
b. omnidirectional
d. code divided

9. Which of the following is an advantage of using spread spectrum signaling over narrowband signaling?
a. Spread spectrum is easier to install.
b. Spread spectrum is more secure.
c. Spread spectrum is less expensive to deploy.
d. Spread spectrum can achieve higher throughput.

10. The 802.11g WLAN standard is compatible with what other WLAN standard?
a. Bluetooth
b. 802.11a
c. 802.11b
d. HomeRF

11. What frequency band does 802.11b, 80211g, Bluetooth, and HomeRF WLANs share?
a. 1.25 GHz
b. 2.4 GHz
c. 5 GHz
d. 12.5 GHz

12. At what altitude does a GEO satellite orbit the earth?
a. 700 km
b. 1400 km
c. 10,400 km
d. 34,800 km

Glossary

100BaseFX—A form of fast Ethernet that operates over multimode fiber optic cabling. It provides 100 Mbps of throughput.

100BaseT4—A form of fast Ethernet that runs over existing category 3 UTP by using all four pair. Three pairs are to transmission simultaneously and the fourth pair is used for collision detect. It provides 100 Mbps of throughput.

100BaseTX—A form of fast Ethernet that uses two pairs of standard category 5 UTP to provide 100 Mbps of throughput.

100VG-ANYLAN—A 100 Mbps half duplex transmission that allows 100 Mbps on a four pair category 3 cabling system. Allows for Voice over IP (VoIP).

10Base2—A simplified version of the 10Base5 Ethernet network. The name describes a 10 Mbps baseband network with a maximum cable segment length of approximately 200 meters (actually 185 meters). Instead of having external transceivers, the transceivers are on the network card, which attaches to the network through a BNC T-connector. The cable used is a 50 Ω RG-58 A/U coaxial type cable. 10Base2 does not use a drop cable. (Also known as *thinnet*.)

10Base5—A form of Ethernet. A 10 Mbps baseband network that can have cable segments up to 500 meters long. It uses 50 Ω RG-8 and RG-11 as backbone cables. 10Base5 uses physical and logical bus topology. (Also known as *thicknet*.)

10BaseT—A form of Ethernet that uses UTP to form a logical bus topology while actually being a physical star topology. Therefore, network devices connect to a hub (or switch).

5-4-3 Rule—An important rule used on Ethernet networks: They must not exceed five segments connected by four repeaters. Of these segments, only three of them can be populated by computers. This means that the distance of a computer cannot exceed five segments and four repeaters when communicating with other computers on the network.

802.11 Standard—A wireless standard.

A

access control list (ACL)—A set of data that informs a computer's operating system which permissions (access rights) each user or group has to a specific system object such as a directory or file. Each object has a unique security attribute that identifies which users have access to it. The ACL is a list of objects and user access privileges such as read, write, or execute.

access method—The set of rules defining how a computer puts data onto the network cable and takes data from the cable.

acknowledgment (ACK)—A special message that is sent back when data packets make it to their destinations.

adapter unit interface (AUI) connector—A female, 15-pin, D connector used to connect to an Ethernet 10Base5 network. (Also known as a *DIX (Digital-Intel-Xerox) connector.*)

Address Resolution Protocol (ARP)—A TCP/IP protocol that is used to obtain hardware addresses (MAC addresses) of hosts located on the same physical network.

addressing—A method used to identify senders and receivers.

administrative share—A shared folder typically used for administrative purposes. To make a shared folder or drive into an administrative share, the share name must have a "$" at the end of it. Because the shared folder or drive cannot be seen during browsing, you would have to use a UNC name that includes the share name (including the $).

administrative distance (AD)—A value used to rate the trustworthiness of routing information received on a router from a neighbor router

ADSL Lite—A DSL specification, also known as g.lite. A low-cost, easy-to-install version of ADSL specifically designed for the consumer marketplace. ADSL Lite is a lower-speed version of ADSL (Up to 1.544 Mbps downstream, up to 512 Kbps upstream) that will eliminate the need for the telephone company to install and maintain a premises-based POTS splitter.

always on/dynamic ISDN (AO/DI)—A networking application that uses the 16 Kbps ISDN D-channel X-25 packet service to maintain an "always on" connection between an ISDN end user and an information service provider.

American Standard Code for Information Interchange (ASCII)—An alphanumeric code.

amplitude—(1) Represents the peak voltage of the sine wave. (2) Loudness or intensity of sound.

amplitude modulation (AM)—An encoding technique that changes the amplitude of sine waves.

analog signal—The opposite of a digital signal. Instead of having a finite number of states, it has an infinite number of values that change constantly. Analog signals are typically sinusoidal waveforms characterized by amplitude and frequency.

analog-to-digital converter (ADC)—A device that performs analog to digital conversion.

anycast—Packets sent when communication between any sender and the nearest of a group of receivers in a network.

AppleTalk—A protocol and networking software found on Apple Macintosh computers.

application layer—The highest layer of the OSI reference model, which initiates communication requests. It is responsible for interaction between operating systems and it provides an interface to the system. It provides the user interface to a range of network-wide distributed services, including file transfer, printer access, and e-mail.

application programming interfaces (APIs)—A set of routines, protocols, and tools for building software applications.

application server—A server that is similar to a file and print server except that the application server also does some of the processing.

application level gateway—A gateway or firewall that sits between a user on the internal network and a service on the Internet. Instead of talking to each other directly, each system talks to the gateway.

arbitration—See *access method.*

area border router (ABR)—A router that has interfaces in multiple areas, and routes packets between those areas. In OSPF autonomous areas, the routers that attach an area to the backbone.

area—A term used for the OSPF routing protocol. A grouping of contiguous networks.

AS boundary router (ASBR)—A router that exchanges routing information with routers in other autonomous systems.

Asymmetrical DSL (ADSL)—A form of DSL that transmits an asymmetric data stream. Much more goes downstream to the subscriber than what comes back.

asynchronous—Devices that use intermittent signals. They can occur at any time and at irregular intervals. They do not use a clock or timing signal.

asynchronous transfer mode (ATM)—Both a LAN and a WAN technology. Generally implemented as a backbone technology. It is a cell switching and multiplexing technology that combines the benefits of circuit switching and packet switching.

AT commands—See *Hayes command set.*

attenuation—When the strength of a signal falls off with distance over a transmission medium. This loss of signal strength is caused by several factors, such as the signal converted to heat due to the resistance of the cable or the energy is reflected as the signal encounters impedance changes throughout the cable.

autonomous area (AS)—Areas or a grouping of contiguous networks that usually correspond to an administrative domain such as a department, a building, or a geographic site. An AS can be a single network or a group of networks, owned and administered by a common network administrator or group of administrators.

available bit rate (ABR)—A specification that provides a guaranteed minimum capacity but allows data to be bursted at higher capacities when the network is free. This is used for applications, such as file transfer and e-mail, that can tolerate delays.

B

backbone cable—(1) A backbone can be used as a main cable segment such as that found in a bus topology network. (2) A backbone can refer to as the main network connection through a building, campus, WAN, or the Internet.

backbone cabling—Provides interconnections between telecommunications closets, equipment rooms, and entrance facilities and includes the backbone cables, intermediate and main cross-connects, terminations, and patch cords for backbone-to-backbone cross-connections.

backbone router—An interface on the backbone area.

backbone wiring—The system of cables that are often designed to handle a higher bandwidth. It is used to interconnect wiring closets, server rooms, and entrance facilities (telephone systems and WAN links from the outside world).

back end—In client/server applications, services provided by the server.

backup—An extra copy of data and/or programs. As a technician, consultant, or support person, you need to emphasize backup procedures for servers and client systems.

band—A contiguous group of frequencies used for a single purpose.

bandwidth—The amount of data that can be carried on a given transmission media.

baseband systems—A system that uses the transmission medium's entire capacity for a single channel.

basic rate interface (BRI)—A form of ISDN that defines digital communication lines consisting of three independent channels: Two bearer (or B) channels that each carry 64 Kbps and one Data (or D) channel at 16 Kbps. For this reason, the ISDN BRI is often referred to as 2B+D.

basket systems—Baskets or trays used on the back of office furniture. They are used to hold and hide network cables without using cable ties.

baud rate—The modulation rate or the number of times per second that a line changes state.

bearer channels (B channels)—A channel used in ISDN lines to transfer data at a bandwidth of 64 Kbps for each channel.

bend radius—The radius of the maximum arc into which you can loop a cable before you will impair data transmission. Generally, a cable bend radius is less than four times the diameter of the cable.

binary digits (bits)—A piece of information that can represent the status of an ON/OFF switch. When several bits are combined together, they can signify a letter, a digit, a punctuation mark, a special graphical character, or a computer instruction.

binary number system—The simplest number system based on only two digits: A zero (0) and a one (1).

bind—A method that links the protocol stack to the NIC.

BIND—The most widely used name server (DNS server).

bit error rate (BER)—The percentage of bits that have errors relative to the total number of bits received in a transmission, usually expressed as ten to a negative power.

blackouts—Total power failures.

Bluetooth—A form of short-range radio technology aimed at simplifying communications among devices and the Internet. It also aims to simplify data synchronization between Net devices and other computers.

BNC connector—Short for British Naval Connector, Bayonet Nut Connector, or Bayonet Neill Concelman. It is a type of connector used with coaxial cables. The basic BNC connector is a male type connector mounted at each end of a cable. This connector has a center pin connected to the center cable conductor and a metal tube connected to the outer cable shield. A rotating ring outside the tube locks the cable to any female connector.

BNC T-connectors—Used with 10Base-2 systems. They are female devices for connecting two cables to a NIC.

Bootstrap protocol (BOOTP)—A TCP/IP protocol that enables a booting host to configure itself dynamically.

bridge—A device that works at the data link OSI layer. Connects two LANs and makes them appear as one or is used to connect two segments of the same LAN. The two LANs being connected can be alike or dissimilar such as an Ethernet LAN connected to a Token Ring LAN.

bridge protocol data unit (BPDU)—Packets used with bridges and switches that use the spanning tree algorithm to determine the spanning tree topology.

bridge router (brouter)—A device that functions as both a router and a bridge. A brouter understands how to route specific types of packets (routable protocols), such as TCP/IP packets. For other specified packets (nonroutable protocols), it acts as a bridge that simply forwards the packets to other networks.

broadband system—A system that uses the transmission medium's capacity to provide multiple channels by using FDM.

broadcast—Packets that are sent to every computer on a network or a subnet.

broadcasting—A method that sends unaddressed packets to everyone on the network.

brownouts—Drops in power that can force the computer to shut down, introduce memory errors, or cause unsaved work to be lost.

bus topology—A topology that looks like a line where data is sent along the single cable. The two ends of the cable do not meet and the two ends do not form a ring or a loop.

byte—Eights bits of data. One byte of information can represent one character.

C

cable modem—A device that is located in subscriber homes to create a VLAN connection over a cable system.

cable system—A system that delivers broadcast television signals efficiently to subscriber homes through a sealed coaxial cable line.

cable testers—A device designed to test a cable.

cable ties—Small devices used to bundle cables traveling together and to pull the cables off the floor so that they will not get trampled or run over by office furniture.

cables—A physical transmission medium that has a central conductor of wire or fiber surrounded by a plastic jacket. Used to carry electrical or light signals between computers and networks.

cabling system—The veins of the network that connect all of the computers together and allow them to communicate with each other.

carrier detect signal—A signal that remains ON throughout the modem connection. If the carrier is gone, the connection is broken.

carrier sense multiple access (CSMA)—The most common form of contention (access method) used on networks.

carrier sense multiple access with collision avoidance (CSMA/CA)—The access mechanism used in Apple's LocalTalk network. Collision avoidance uses time slices to make network access smarter and avoid collisions.

carrier sense multiple access with collision detection (CSMA/CD)—The access method utilized in Ethernet and IEEE 802.3. The collision detection approach listens to the network traffic as the NIC transmits. By analyzing network traffic, it detects collisions and initiates retransmissions.

CD-ROM File System (CDFS)—The read-only file system used to access resources on a CD-ROM. Windows supports CDFS so as to allow CD-ROM file sharing. Because a CD-ROM is read only, you cannot assign specific permissions to files through CDFS.

cell relay—A form of packet switching network that uses relatively small, fixed-size packets called cells.

cell—A relatively small, fixed-size packet.

cellular topology—A topology used in wireless technology. Each area is divided into cells. A broadcast device located at the center broadcasts in all directions to form an invisible circle (cell). All network devices located within the cell communicate with the network through the central station or hub, which are interconnected with the rest of the network infrastructure. If the cells are overlapped, devices may roam from cell to cell while maintaining connection to the network as the devices.

central office (CO)—The place on a PSTN that connects access lines to each other based on the network address and the telephone numbers of the destination telephone instrument.

centralized computing—When the processing is done for many people by a central computer.

centrex—A business telephone service provided by local telephone companies. Instead of a key or PBX system, the switch in the phone company central office provides as many as seventy-five advanced calling features.

certificate authority (CA)—A trusted, third-party organization or company that issues digital certificates used to create digital signatures and public/private key pairs. The role of the CA in this process is to guarantee that the individual granted the unique certificate is, in fact, who he or she claims to be. Usually, this means that the CA has an arrangement with a financial institution, such as a credit card company, which provides the CA with information to confirm an individual's claimed identity. CAs are a critical component in data security and electronic commerce because they guarantee that the two parties exchanging information are really who they claim to be.

Challenge Handshake Authentication Protocol (CHAP)—The most common dial-up authentication protocol used. Uses an industry MD5 hashing scheme to encrypt authentication.

channel service unit (CSU)—A device that connects a terminal to a digital line and provides the LAN/WAN connection.

Channel Service Unit/Data Service Unit (CSU/DSU)—Two devices packaged as a single unit. The DSU is a device that performs protective and diagnostic functions for a telecommunications line. The CSU is a device that connects a terminal to a digital line. You can think of it as a very high-powered and expensive modem.

checksum—A form of error control.

circuit level gateways—A second generation firewall that validates TCP and UDP sessions before opening a connection. Because it operates at the transport layer, a circuit-level firewall actually establishes a VC between the client and the host on a session-by-session basis. Once a handshake has taken place, it passes everything through until the session is ended.

circuit switching—A technique that connects the sender and the receiver by a single path for the duration of a conversation. Once a connection is established, a dedicated path exists between both ends. The path is always consuming network capacity, even when there is no active transmission taking place (such as when a caller is put on hold). Once the connection has been made, the destination device acknowledges that it is ready to carry on a transfer. When the conversation is complete, the connection is terminated.

Cisco Discovery Protocol (CDP)—A proprietary protocol designed by Cisco to help administrators collect information about locally attached and remote devices.

classical IP over ATM (CIP)—A mature standard that enables you to route IP packets over an ATM network or cloud by using ATM as either a backbone technology or a workgroup technology.

Classless InterDomain Routing (CIDR)—A new IP addressing scheme that replaces the older system based on classes A, B, and C. With CIDR, a single IP address can be used to designate many unique IP addresses. A CIDR IP address looks like a normal IP address except that it ends with a slash followed by a number called the IP prefix.

Classless Internetwork Domain Routing (CIDR)—An addressing method that does not use the standard classes (Class A, B, or C). Provides a flexible subnetting scheme with an organization's IP addresses.

clear text—In cryptography, clear text refers to any message that is not encrypted.

client—A computer that requests services.

client software—Software that allows a work station attached to the network to communicate with others.

client/server network—A network that is made of servers and clients. Typically used on medium or large networks.

clipper chip—An encryption chip designed under the auspices of the U.S. government. The government's idea was to enforce use of this chip in all devices that might use encryption.

cloud—A logical network with multiple pathways is illustrated by a black box. The subscribers that connect to the cloud don't worry about the details inside the cloud. Instead, the only thing that the subscriber needs to know is that they connect at one edge of the cloud and the data is received at the other edge of the cloud.

clustering—Connecting two or more computers, known as nodes, together in such a way that they behave like a single computer. Used for parallel processing, load balancing, and fault tolerance. The computers that form the cluster are physically connected by cable and are logically connected by cluster software. As far as the user is concerned, the cluster appears as a single system to end users.

clustering—Software and services that enable two or more servers to work together to keep server-based applications available. See *fault tolerance.*

coaxial cable (COAX)—A cable that has a center wire surrounded by insulation and then a grounded shield of braided wire (mesh shielding). The copper core carries the electromagnetic signal, and the braided metal shielding acts as both a shield against noise and a ground for the signal. The shield minimizes electrical and radio frequency interference and provides a connection to ground.

CODEC—The format of audio and video information. Represents the way audio and video are compressed and transmitted over the network.

collision—The situation that occurs when two or more devices attempt to send a signal along the same channel at the same time. The result of a collision is generally a garbled message. All computer networks require some sort of mechanism to either prevent collisions or to recover from collisions when they do occur.

collision domain—A network segment in which all devices share the same bandwidth.

COM+—An extension of COM. COM+ is both an object-oriented programming architecture and a set of operating system services. It adds a new set of system services for application components while they are running, such as notifying them of significant events or ensuring they are authorized to run. COM+ is intended to provide a model that makes it relatively easy to create business applications that work well with the MTS in a Windows NT system.

command line interface (CLI)—A command driven interface used on Cisco routers and switches.

committed information rate (CIR)—A value that specifies the maximum average data rate that the network undertakes to deliver under normal conditions.

common Internet file system (CIFS)—A public or open variation of the SMBP used by Windows. Currently used by Linux with Samba, Novell Netware 6.0, and AppleTalkIP.

communication server—A remote access server.

Component Object Model (COM)—An object-based programming model designed to promote interoperability by allowing two or more applications or components to easily cooperate with one another, even if they were written by different vendors, at different times, in different programming languages, or if they are running on different OSs. COM is the foundation technology upon which broader technologies, such as OLE and ActiveX can be built.

Computer Emergency Response Team Coordination Center (CERT/CC)—CERT/CC was started in December 1988 by DARPA, part of the U.S. Department of Defense, after the Morris Worm disabled about 10% of all computers connected to the Internet. CERT/CC is located at the Software Engineering Institute, a federally funded research center operated by Carnegie Mellon University. CERT/CC studies Internet security vulnerabilities, provides services to websites that have been attacked, and publishes security alerts. CERT/CC's research activities include WAN computing and developing improved Internet security. The organization also provides training to incident response professionals.

connectionless—A type of protocol that neither requires an exchange of messages with the destination host before data transfer begins nor makes a dedicated connection, or VC, with a destination host. Instead, connectionless protocols rely upon upper-level, not lower-level protocols for safe delivery and error handling.

connection-oriented network—A network in which you must establish a connection through an exchange of messages or a preestablished path-way between a source point and a destination point before you can transmit packets.

constant bit rate (CBR)—Specifies a fixed bit rate so that data is sent in a steady stream for applications and services that require a small amount of bandwidth at all times. Sensitive to delay and cell loss.

container—In directory services, an object that can hold other objects.

contention—When two or more devices contend (compete) for network access. Any device can transmit whenever it needs to send information. To avoid data collisions (two devices sending data at the same time), specific contention protocols, which require the device to listen to the cable before transmitting data were developed.

continuity check—A test done with a device such as an ohmmeter. Because a wire or fuse is a conductor, you should measure no resistance (0 ohms) to show that there is no break in the wire or fuse.

cooperative multitasking—Each program can control the CPU for as long as it needs it. If a program is not using the CPU, however, it can allow another program to use it temporarily.

count to infinity—A problem that typically happens when a network has slow convergence. A loop that happens when a link in a network goes down and routers on the network update their routing tables with incorrect hop counts that eventually reach the number 16. Number 16 is considered unreachable.

countermeasures—A step or method that is deployed to counteract threats and vulnerabilities, therefore reducing the risk in your environment.

crossed pairs—When two wires are connected improperly, causing the two wires to be crossed.

crossover cable—A cable that can be used to connect from one NIC to another NIC or a hub to a hub, reverses the transmit and receive wires.

crosstalk—When signals induct (law of induction) or transfer from one wire to the other.

current state—A digital signal periodically measured for the specific state.

cut-through processing—Used with switches. The first bits of the frame are sent out the outbound port before the last bit of the incoming frame is received instead of waiting for the entire frame to be received.

cyclic redundancy check (CRC)—A form of error control.

D

daemon—A background process or service that monitors and performs many critical system functions and services.

data—The raw facts, numbers, letters, or symbols that the computer processes into meaningful information.

data channel (D channel)—A channel used in ISDN lines used for transmitting control information.

data circuit terminating equipment (DCE)—Special communication devices that provide the interface between the DTE and the network. Examples include modems and adapters. The purpose of the DCE is to provide clocking and switching services in a network and to transmit data through the WAN. Therefore, the DCE controls data flowing to or from a computer.

data encryption standard (DES)—A popular symmetric key encryption method developed in 1975 and standardized by ANSI in 1981 as ANSI X.3.92. DES uses a 56-bit key and is illegal to export out of the U.S. or Canada if you don't meet BXA requirements.

data link control (DLC)—A special, nonroutable protocol that enables computers running Windows 2000 to communicate with computers running a DLC protocol stack such as IBM mainframes, IBM AS/400 computers, and Hewlett-Packard network printers connected directly to the network through older HP JetDirect network cards.

data link layer—The OSI layer that is responsible for providing error free data transmission. Establishes local connections between two computers or hosts. Divides received data from the network layer into distinct frames that can then be transmitted by the physical layer and it packages raw bits from the physical layer into blocks of data called frames.

data Service Unit (DSU)—A device that performs all error correction, handshaking, protective, and diagnostic functions for a telecommunications line.

data terminal equipment (DTE)—A device used on end systems that communicate across the WAN. They control data flowing to or from a computer. They are usually terminals, PCs, or network hosts located on the premises of individual subscribers.

datagram—A packet on an IP network.

data-link connection identifier (DLCI)—An addressing protocol used in Frame Relay networking that identifies the originating and terminating ends. A DLCI is a 10-bit address (with 1024 different combinations) that identifies a particular permanent VC.

***de jure* standard**—A standard that has been dictated by an appointed committee (by law standard).

decibels (dB)—A scale based on a logarithmic curve. It is often used with sound.

decimal number system—The most commonly-used numbering system in which each position contains ten different possible digits. Because there are ten different possible digits, the decimal number system contains numbers with base 10. These digits are 0, 1, 2, 3, 4, 5, 6, 7, 8, and 9.

decryption—The process of converting data from an encrypted format back to its original format.

cryptography—The art of protecting information by transforming it (encrypting it) into ciphered text.

dedicated link—Point-to-point connections that are preestablished WAN communication paths from the CPE, through the DCE switch, to the CPE of the remote site. The advantage of a dedicated link is that they are always available to communicate at any time with no set up procedures before transmitting data. Examples include T-1 and T-3 lines.

default gateway—In TCP/IP, an address that specifies the local address of a router. If the default gateway is not specified, you will not be able to communicate with computers on other networks.

demand priority—An access method that uses a device that makes request to the hub. The hub grants permission. High priority packets are serviced before normal priority packets.

demarcation point (demarc)—The point where the local loop ends at the customer's premises.

Demilitarized Zone (DMZ)—An area used by a company that wants to host its own Internet services without sacrificing unauthorized access to its private network. The DMZ sits between the Internet and an internal network's line of defense, usually some combination of firewalls and bastion hosts. Typically, the DMZ contains devices accessible to Internet traffic, such as web (HTTP) servers, FTP servers, SMTP (e-mail) servers, and DNS servers.

demultiplexing—The function that occurs when the destination computer receives the data stream and separates and rejoins the application's segments. See *multiplexing.*

Denial of Service (DoS)—An attack on a network that is designed to bring the network to its knees by flooding it with useless traffic.

designator—Keeps track of which drive designations are assigned to network resources.

device drivers—Programs that control a device. Acts like a translator between the device and programs that use the device. Each device has its own set of specialized commands that only its driver knows. While most programs access devices by using generic commands, the driver accepts generic commands from the program and translates them into specialized commands for the device.

device manager—The software that allows you to manage your devices and device drivers in Windows.

DHCP relay agent—A computer that relays DHCP and BOOTP messages between clients and servers on different subnets. This way, you can use a single DHCP server to handle several subnets without the DHCP server being connected directly to those subnets.

dial-on-demand routing (DDR)—A protocol/software that allow two or more routers to dial an ISDN dial-up connection on an as-needed basis.

dial-up networking—A method used when a RAC makes a nonpermanent, dial-up connection to a physical port on a RAS by using the service of a telecommunications provider such as analog phone, ISDN, or X.25.

differential phase modulation—An encoding method in which the modem shifts the phase of each signal a certain number of degrees for a "0" (90 degrees, for example) and a different number of degrees for a "1" (270 degrees, for example). This method is easier to detect than phase modulation.

diffused IR—Infrared that spreads the light over an area to create a cell. Limited to individual rooms.

digital certificate—An attachment to an electronic message. Used for security purposes such as for authentication and verification that a user sending a message is who he or she claims to be. Provides the receiver with a means to encode a reply.

digital envelope—A type of security that encrypts the message by using symmetric encryption and encrypts a key to decode the message by using public-key encryption.

digital multimeter (DMM)—A device that combines several measuring devices including a voltmeter and an ohmmeter.

digital signal—A system that is based on a binary signal system produced by pulses of light or electric voltages. The site of the pulse is either On/high or Off/low to represent 1s and 0s. Digital signals are the language of computers.

digital signature—A digital code that can be attached to an electronically transmitted message that uniquely identifies the sender. Like a written signature, the purpose of a digital signature is to guarantee that the individual sending the message really is who he or she claims to be.

digital subscriber line (DSL)—A special communication line that uses sophisticated modulation technology to maximize the amount of data that can be sent over plain twisted pair copper wiring that already carries phone service to subscriber homes.

digitizing—A method that takes samples of the electrical signal and assigns a binary value to the amplitude of the signal.

directed IR—Infrared that uses line-of-sight or point-to-point technology.

directory number (DN)—The ten-digit phone number that the telephone company assigns to any analog line.

directory service—A network service that identifies all resources on a network and makes those resources accessible to users and applications. Resources can include e-mail addresses, computers, and peripheral devices (such as printers).

directory service servers—A server used to locate information about the network—such as domains (logical divisions of the network) and other servers.

direct-sequence spread-spectrum (DSSS)—A technique that generates a redundant bit pattern for each bit to be transmitted. This bit pattern is called a chip (or chipping code). The intended receiver knows which specific frequencies are valid and deciphers the signal by collecting valid signals and ignoring the spurious signals. The valid signals are then used to reassemble the data.

diskless work station—A computer that does not have its own hard disk. Instead, the computer stores files on a network file server.

distance vector based routing—A routing protocol that periodically advertises or broadcasts routes in routing tables to neighboring routers.

distributed computing—Processing is done by individual PCs rather than a central computer.

distributed denial of service (DDoS)—A DOS attack that involves installing programs known as

zombies on various computers in advance of the attack. A command is issued to these zombies, which then launch the attack on behalf of the attacker, thus hiding the attacker's tracks.

Digital-Intel-Xerox (DIX) connector—A female, 15-pin D connector used to connect to an Ethernet 10Base5 network. (Also known as an *AUI connector*.)

DNS zone—A portion of the DNS namespace in which database records exist and are managed in a particular DNS database file.

domain—A logical unit of computers and network resources that define a security boundary. It is typically found on medium or large networks or on networks that require a secure environment. Different from a work group, a domain uses one database to share its common security and user account information for all computers within the domain. Therefore, it allows centralized network administration of all users, groups, and resources on the network.

domain controller—A Windows server that contains the domain database.

domain name service (DNS)—A service that provides mapping between names and IP addresses and distributing network information (i.e., mail servers).

domain user account—In Windows NT family domains, an account that can log onto a domain to gain access to network resources.

DS0 channel—A channel that can carry 64 Kbps of data. Sufficient to carry voice communication.

dumb terminal—A display monitor and keyboard that has no processing capabilities. A dumb terminal is simply an output device that accepts data from another computer such as a main frame.

duplex cables—A cable that has two optical fibers inside a single jacket. The most popular use for duplex fiber optic cable is as a fiber optic LAN backbone cable. Duplex cables are perfect because all LAN connections need a transmission fiber and a reception fiber.

Dynamic Host Configuration Protocol (DHCP)—A TCP/IP server that is used to automatically assign TCP/IP addresses and other related information to clients. An extention of BOOTP.

dynamic IP addresses—IP addresses that are dynamically assigned and configured by a DHCP server.

dynamic packet filter—An extension of packet filtering that can monitor the state of active connections and use this information to determine which network packets to allow through the firewall. (Also known as *stateful inspection*).

E

E-1 line—A digital line with thirty-two 64 Kbps channels for a bandwidth of 2.048 Mbps.

E-3 line—A digital line with five hundred twelve 64 Kbps channels for a bandwidth of 34.368 Mbps.

EAP transport level security (EAP-TLS)—An EAP type that is used in certificate-based security environments. The EAP-TLS exchange of messages provides mutual authentication, negotiation of the encryption method, and secured private key exchange between the RAC and the authenticating server.

E-carrier systems—An entire digital system that consists of permanent dedicated point-to-point connections. It is typically used in Europe.

EIA-232F—The current incarnation of the RS-232 standard, an interface standard for connecting a DTE to a voice-grade modem for use on analog public telecommunication systems.

electromagnetic interference (EMI)—Signals caused by large electromagnets used in industrial machinery, motors, fluorescent lighting, and power lines that cause interference to other signals.

electronic mail (e-mail)—A sophisticated tool that allows you to send text messages and file attachments (documents, pictures, sound, and movies) to anyone who has an e-mail address.

electrostatic discharge (ESD)—Electricity generated by friction—like when your arm slides on a table top or when you walk across a carpet. Electronic devices, including NICs and computer components can be damaged by electrostatic discharge.

emulated LAN (ELAN)—A set of LANE clients that reside as ATM endpoints. The ELAN is equivalent to a VLAN.

Enable Exec mode—Accessed from User Exec mode through the `enable` command and a password on Cisco routers and switches. If an Enable Exec mode password has not been set, this mode can be accessed only from the router console port. You can perform all User Exec mode functions from within Enable Exec mode. In addition, you have access to higher-level testing and debugging, detailed probing of router functions, and the ability to update or change configuration files. (Also known as *Privileged* or *Privileged Exec. Priviledged mode—see Enable Exec mode. Priviledged Exec mode—see Enable Exec mode*)

encapsulation—The concept of placing data behind headers (and before trailers) for each layer.

encoding—The process of changing a signal to represent data.

encryption—The process of disguising a message or data in what appears to be meaningless data (ciphered text) to hide and protect the sensitive data from unauthorized access.

enhanced interior gateway routing protocol (EIGRP)—A routing protocol that combines the advantages of link-state protocols with those of distance-vector protocols.

enterprise—Any large organization that utilizes computers, usually consisting of multiple LANs.

enterprise WAN—A WAN that is owned by one company or organization.

entity—Identifies the hardware and software that fulfills the role of a server.

entrance facility—Where the outside telecommunication service enters the building and interconnects with the building's telecommunication systems in a campus or multibuilding environment. It may also contain the building's backbone cross-connections.

equipment room—The area in a building where telecommunication equipment is located and the cabling system terminates.

error control—The notification of lost or damaged data frames.

Ethernet—The most widely used LAN technology. Uses a logical bus topology.

Exec command interpreter—The working name of the CLI used for Cisco routers.

exploit—A type of attack on a resource, accessed by a threat, that makes use of a vulnerability in your environment.

extended network prefix—Part of an IP address (specifically, part of the network number or network prefix) that identifies a subnet. The subnet mask is used to define which bits represent the network prefix (including the subnet number) and which bits represent the host address.

extensible authentication protocol (EAP)—An authentication protocol that allows new authentication schemes to be plugged in as needed. Therefore, EAP allows third-party vendors to develop custom authentication schemes such as retina scans, voice recognition, finger print identification, smart card, Kerberos, and digital certificates.

external IPX address—An 8-digit (4-byte) hexadecimal number used to identify the network on an IPX network.

extranet—An intranet that is partially accessible to authorized outsiders. While an intranet resides behind a firewall and is accessible only to people who are members of the same company or organization, an extranet provides various levels of accessibility to outsiders.

F

facsimile (fax) transmission—A machine or device that takes a piece of paper, digitizes the contents, and sends the data over a telephone line. A fax machine on the other end reassembles the contents and prints them on paper.

fast Ethernet—An extension of the 10BaseT Ethernet standard that transports data at 100 Mbps but still keeps using the CSMA/CD protocol used by 10 Mbps Ethernet.

fat client—A client that performs the bulk of the data processing operations. The data itself is stored on the server. Although a fat client usually refers to software, it can also apply to a network computer that has relatively strong processing abilities.

FAT32—A file system that is an enhancement of the FAT/VFAT file system. Uses 32-bit FAT entries. It supports hard drives up to two terabytes.

fault tolerance—The ability of a system to respond gracefully to an unexpected hardware or software failure. There are many levels of fault tolerance, the lowest being the ability to continue operation in the event of a power failure. Many fault-tolerant computer systems mirror all operations—that is, every operation is performed on two or more duplicate systems, so if one fails the other can take over.

fax server—A server that manages fax messages sent into and out of the network through a fax modem.

fiber distributed data interface (FDDI)—A MAN protocol that provides data transport at 100 Mbps and can support up to 500 stations on a single network.

fiber optic—A cable that consists of a bundle of glass or plastic threads, each capable of carrying data signals in the form of modulated pulses of light.

file allocation table (FAT)—A simple and reliable file system that uses minimal memory. It supports file names of eleven characters, which includes eight characters for the file name and three characters for the file extension.

file attribute—A characteristic about each file. Attributes can be either ON or OFF. The most common attributes include read-only, hidden, system, and archive.

file server—A server that manages user access to files stored on a server. When a file is accessed on a file server, the file is downloaded to the client's RAM. For example, if you are working on a report using a word processor, the word processor files will be executed from your client computer and the report will be stored on the server. As the report is accessed from the server, it would be downloaded or copied to the RAM of the client computer. All of the processing done on the report is done by the client's microprocessors.

file sharing—A network server that allows you to access files, which are on another computer, without using a floppy disk or other forms of removable media. To ensure that the files are secure, most networks can limit the access to a directory or file and what kind of access (permissions or rights) that a person or a group of people have.

file transfer protocol (FTP)—A TCP/IP protocol that allows a user to transfer files between local and remote host computers.

firewall—A system designed to prevent unauthorized access to or from a private network. Firewalls can be implemented in both hardware and software, or a combination of both. Firewalls are frequently used to prevent unauthorized Internet users from accessing private networks connected to the Internet, especially intranets. All messages entering or leaving the intranet pass through the firewall, which examines each message and blocks those that do not meet the specified security criteria.

flash memory—A form of nonvolatile RAM that will retain information after losing power. Can be erased and reprogrammed as needed.

flow control—The process of controlling the rate at which a computer sends data.

foil twisted-pair (FTP)—See *screened twisted-pair (ScTP) cable.*

forest—In active directory, a grouping of one or more trees that are connected by two-way, transitive trust relationships that allow users to access resources in the other domain/tree.

forwarders—DNS servers configured to send all recursive queries to a selected list of servers. Servers used in the list of forwarders provide recursive lookup for any queries that a DNS server receives that it cannot answer based on its own zone records. During the forwarding process, a DNS server configured to use forwarders behaves as a DNS client to its forwarders. Typically, forwarders are used on remote DNS servers that use a slow link to access the Internet.

fox and hound—See *tone generator and probe.*

FragmentFree processing—Used with switches. The 64 bytes of an incoming frame are received before forwarding the first bytes of the outgoing frame.

frame—A structured package for moving data. Includes not only the raw data (payload), but also the sender's and receiver's network addresses and error checking and control information.

Frame Relay—A packet switching protocol designed to use high-speed digital backbone links to support modern protocols that provide for error handling and flow control for connecting devices on a WAN.

Frame Relay access device (FRAD)—It multiplexes and formats traffic for entering a Frame Relay network. (Also known as *Frame Relay Assembler/Disassembler.)*

frame type—The format for the completed packet. (Also known as *encapsulation method*).

frequency—The number of times that a single wave will repeat over any period. Measured in Hz (cycles per second).

frequency hopping—A technique that quickly switches between predetermined frequencies, many times each second. Both the transmitter and receiver must follow the same pattern and must maintain complex timing intervals to be able to receive and interpret the data being sent.

frequency shift keying (FSK)—The earliest form of encoding data over telephone lines. Very similar to frequency modulation used with FM radios. FSK sends a logical 1 at one particular frequency (usually 1750 Hz) and a logical 0 is sent at another frequency (often 1080 Hz).

frequency division multiplexing (FDM)—A method that uses a transmission medium's capacity to provide multiple channels. Each channel uses a carrier signal, which runs at a different frequency than the other carrier signals used by the other channels.

front end—The interface used in client/server applications. Provided to a user or another program.

The part that the user or program will see and interact with.

full-duplex dialog—A form of dialog that allows every device to transmit and receive simultaneously.

fully qualified domain names (FQDN)—Used to identify computers on a TCP/IP network. Examples include Microsoft.com and Education. Novell.com. (Also known as *domain names*).

G

gateway—Hardware and/or software that links two different types of networks by repackaging and converting data from one network to another network or from one network OS to another.

geosynchronous (GEO) orbit—The path used by satellites that are positioned 22,300 miles (35,800 km) above Earth's equator.

giant—A frame greater than 1518 bytes. Typically formed by faulty or out-of-specification LAN drivers.

gigabit Ethernet—A form of Ethernet that has a bandwidth of a Gigabit throughput.

global WAN—A WAN, not owned by any one company, that could cross national boundaries. The best known example of a global WAN is the Internet, which connects millions of computers.

GNU—A UNIX-compatible software system developed by the FSF. As GNU was started, hundreds of programmers created new, open source versions of all major UNIX utility programs with Linux providing the kernel. Many of the GNU utilities were so powerful that they have become the virtual standard on all UNIX systems. For example, gcc became the dominant C compiler, and GNU emacs became the dominant programmer's text editor.

gopher—A system that predates the WWW for organizing and displaying files on Internet servers. A Gopher server presents its contents as a hierarchically-structured list of files.

group—A collection of user accounts. Groups are not containers. They list members but they do not contain the members.

guard tone—A certain frequency used to identify the device on the other end as a modem.

H

H.323—A standard approved by the ITU. Defines how audiovisual conferencing data is transmitted across networks. In theory, H.323 should enable users to participate in the same conference even though they are using different videoconferencing applications.

half duplex dialog—A form of dialog that allows each device to transmit and receive but not at the same time. Only one device in a dialog can transmit at a time.

handshaking—The process through which two devices initiate communication. For some devices, handshaking enables negotiation of a common data rate and other transmission parameters.

hardware handshaking—Handshaking or flow control accomplished by sending electrical signals through additional wires.

hashing scheme—A method that scrambles information in such a way that it's unique and can't be reversed back to the original format.

Hayes command set—A set of commands that control the modem. (Also known as *AT commands*.)

Hertz (Hz)—Cycles per second.

hexadecimal number system—A number system based on sixteen digits (0, 1, 2, 3, 4, 5, 6, 7, 8, 9, A, B, C, D, E, and F). One hexadecimal digit is equivalent to a four-digit binary number (4 bits or a nibble) and two hexadecimal digits are used to represent a byte (8 bits).

high level data link control (HDLC) protocol—The protocol used with PPP protocols that encapsulate data during transmission.

hold down—A set time limit in which a router should not change its routing tables in response to turmoil over the network. If a router receives a message that a particular route has gone down, it will start a hold down timer, during which time it will not transmit any info about that route but will instead listen to the network for other reports. This will prevent flapping when a connection seems to be flaky and the link goes up and down.

home directory—A folder used to hold or store a user's personal documents.

HomeRF SWAP—A form of Bluetooth. Designed specifically for wireless networks in homes.

honeypot—A computer set up as a sacrificial lamb on the network. The system is not locked down and has open ports and services enabled. This is to entice a would-be attacker to this computer instead of authentic computers on the network.

hop—The trip a data packet takes from one router to another router or a router to another intermediate point to another in the network.

hop count—The number or routers that a data packet takes to its destination.

horizontal cabling—The cabling system covers from the work area receptacle to the horizontal cross-connect in the telecommunications closet. It includes the receptacle and optional transition connector (such as undercarpet cable connecting to round cable).

horizontal wiring system—The system of cables that extend from wall outlets throughout the building to the wiring closet or server room.

host—Computer or device that connects to the network and is the source or final destination of data.

host number—Part of an IP address that identifies the host.

HOSTS file—A text file that lists the IP address followed by the host name. Used to resolve host names to IP addresses.

hub—A device that works at the physical OSI layer. It is a multiported connection point used to connect network devices via a cable segment. (Also known as a *concentrator*).

hybrid fiber coaxial (HFC) network—A telecommunication technology in which optical fiber cable and coaxial cable are used in different portions of a network to carry broadband content (such as video, data, or voice).

hybrid topology—A topology scheme that combines two of the traditional topologies, usually to create a larger topology. In addition, hybrid topology allows you to use the strengths of various topologies to maximize the effectiveness of the network.

hyperlink—An element in an electronic document that links to another place in the same document or to an entirely different document. Typically, you click on the hyperlink to follow the link. Hyperlinks are the most essential ingredient of all hypertext systems, including the WWW.

HyperText Markup Language (HTML)—The authoring language used to create documents on the WWW.

Hypertext Transfer Protocol (HTTP)—A TCP/IP protocol that is the basis for exchange over the WWW.

I

IMAP-4—A standards-based message access protocol. It follows the online model of message access, although it does support offline and disconnected modes. IMAP-4 offers an array of up-to-date features, including support for the creation and management of remote folders and folder hierarchies, message status flags, new mail notification, retrieval of individual MIME body parts, and server-based searches to minimize the amount of data that must be transferred over the connection.

independent computing architecture (ICA)—A protocol that allows multiple computers to take control of a virtual computer and use it as if it was a desktop (thin client).

infrared (IR)—Light that is just below visible light in the electromagnetic spectrum.

integrated services digital network (ISDN)—A planned replacement for POTS that can provide voice and data communications worldwide, using circuit switching, and using the same wiring that is currently being used in homes and businesses. Because ISDN is a digital signal from end to end, it is faster, much more dependable, and has no line noise. ISDN has the ability to deliver multiple simultaneous connections, in any combination of data, voice, video or fax, over a single line. Allows for multiple devices to be attached to the line.

interexchange carriers (IXCs)—Long-distance carriers used on a PSTN.

interference—When undesirable electromagnetic waves affect the desired signal.

interior gateway protocols (IGPs)—The routing protocols that manage routing information within an autonomous system.

interior gateway routing protocol (IGRP)—A distance vector routing protocol used within an AS. Have arbitrarily complex topology and consist of media with diverse bandwidth and delay characteristics. Allows gateways to build up routing tables by exchanging information with other gateways.

internal IPX network number—An 8-digit (4-byte) hexadecimal number used to identify a server on an IPX network.

Internet control message protocol (ICMP)—A TCP/IP protocol that sends messages and reports errors regarding the delivery of a packet.

Internet group management protocol (IGMP)—A TCP/IP protocol that is used by IP hosts to report host group membership to local multicast routers.

Internet protocol (IP)—Connectionless protocol primarily responsible for addressing and routing packets between hosts.

Internet protocol telephony (IP telephony)—A general term for the technologies that use IP's packet switched connections to exchange voice, fax, and other forms of information that have traditionally been carried over the dedicated circuit switched connections of the PSTN.

Internet service provider (ISP)—A company that provides access to the Internet.

internetwork—A network that is internal to a company and is private. It is often a network consisting of several LANs linked together. Smaller LANs are known as subnetworks or subnets.

internetwork operating system (IOS)—The operating system of the Cisco router and switch.

internetwork packet exchange (IPX)—A networking protocol used by Novell NetWare operating systems. Like UDP/IP, IPX is a datagram protocol used for connectionless communications. Higher-level protocols, such as SPX and NCP, are used for additional error recovery services.

internetworking—The art and science of connecting individual LANs to create WANs and connecting WANs to form even larger WANs by using routers, bridges, and gateways.

intranet—A network based on the TCP/IP protocol, the same protocol that the Internet uses. Unlike the Internet, an intranet belongs to a single organization, accessible only by the organization's members. An intranet's websites look and act just like any other websites, but they are isolated by a firewall to stop illegal access. An intranet could have access to the Internet, but does not require it.

inverse query—A DNS query provides the IP address and requests a FQDN.

IP address—A logical address used to uniquely identify a connection on a TCP/IP address.

IP Security (IPSec)—A set of protocols developed by the IETF to support secure exchange of packets at the IP layer. IPsec has been deployed widely to implement VPNs. Supports two encryption modes: Transport and Tunnel. Transport mode encrypts only the data portion (payload) of each packet, but leaves the header untouched. The more secure Tunnel mode encrypts both the header and the payload. On the receiving side, an IPSec compliant device decrypts each packet. For IPsec to work, the sending and receiving devices must share a public key. This is accomplished through a protocol known as Internet Security Association and Key Management Protocol/Oakley (ISAKMP/Oakley), which allows the receiver to obtain a public key and authenticate the sender with digital certificates.

IPng—See *IP v6*.

IPv6—A new version of the IP. Currently being reviewed in IETF standards committees. Designed to allow the Internet to grow steadily, both in terms of the number of hosts connected and the total amount of data traffic transmitted. (Also known as *IPng.*)

iterative query—A DNS query that gives the best answer it currently has back as a response. The best answer will be the address being sought or an address of a server that would have a better idea of its address.

J

jabber—An error in which a faulty device (usually a NIC) continuously transmits corrupted or meaningless data onto a network. This may keep the entire network from transmitting data because other devices will perceive the network as busy.

jitter—Instability in a signal wave caused by signal interference.

K

Kerberos—An authentication system designed to enable two parties to exchange private information across an otherwise open network. It works by assigning a unique key, called a ticket, to each user that logs onto the network. The ticket is then embedded in messages to identify the sender of the message.

kernel—The central module of an operating system. The part of the OS that loads first and remains in RAM. Because it stays in memory, it is important for the kernel to be as small as possible while still providing all the essential services required by other parts of the OS and applications. Typically, the kernel is responsible for memory management, process and task management, and disk management.

Kernel mode—A Windows NT family mode that runs in Ring 0 of the Intel 386 microprocessor protection model. While User mode components are protected by the OS, Kernel mode components are protected by the processor. It has direct access to all hardware and all memory including, the address space of all User mode processes. It includes the Windows NT family executive hardware abstraction layer (HAL) and the Microkernel.

key—A string of bits used to map text into a code and a code back to text. You can think of the key as a super decoder ring used to translate text messages to a code and back to text. There are two types of keys: Public keys and private keys.

key system—Small telephone switches that allow multiple phone sets to share a number of external phone lines. Each line connected to a key system has its own unique number and can be dialed directly from an outside line.

L

LAN emulation (LANE)—An ATM standard that emulates an Ethernet or Token Ring LAN on top of an ATM network.

last mile—The telephone line that runs from your home or office to the telephone company's CO or neighborhood switching station (often a small building with no windows). (Also known as *local loop* and *last mile.*)

latency—The time it takes for a packet to cross the network.

layer 3 switch—A device that combines a router and a switch. Optimized for high-performance LAN support. Not meant to service wide area connections.

layer 4 switch—A switch that refers to an added feature and capability of layer 3 switches. It enhances their ability to control and forward network traffic based on the information that can be derived from protocols that operate at layer 4 of the OSI model.

layer two tunneling protocol (LTP2)—An extension of the PPP protocol, which enables ISPs to operate VPNs. L2TP merges the best features of two other tunneling protocols: PPTP from Microsoft and L2F from Cisco. Like PPTP, L2TP requires that the ISP's routers support the protocol.

learning bridging—See *transparent bridging.*

lightweight directory access protocol (LDAP)—A set of protocols used for accessing information directories. LDAP is based on the standards contained within the X.500 standard but is significantly simpler.

line conditioner—A device that uses the inductance of transformers to filter out noise and capacitors (and other circuits) and to fill-in brownouts. In addition, most line conditioners include surge protection.

link control protocol (LCP)—A PPP subprotocol that establishes, configures, maintains, and terminates point-to-point links (including MP sessions) and tests link quality prior to data transmission. User authentication is generally performed by LCP as soon as the link is established. It can also increase throughput by using compression.

link-state algorithms—A routing protocol that sends updates directly (or by using multicast traffic) to all routers within the network. Each router, however, sends only the portion of the routing table that describes the state of its own links. In essence, link-state algorithms send small updates everywhere. (Also known as *shortest path first* algorithms.)

LMHOSTS file—A text file, similar to a HOSTS file, used to resolve computer names to IP addresses.

load sharing—See *round robin*.

local area network (LAN)—A network in which computers are connected within a geographical close network, such as a room, a building, or a group of adjacent buildings.

local exchange carrier (LEC)—The connections between the local exchange plant and the telephone company. (Also known as the *local loop* or *last mile*.)

local loop—The telephone line that runs from your home or office to the telephone company's CO or neighborhood switching station (often a small building with no windows). (Also known as *subscriber loop* and *last mile*.)

local management interface (LMI)—A signaling standard between a CPE device (router) and a frame switch that adds extensions onto the Frame Relay protocol used to manage complex internetworks.

local procedure call (LPC)—A mechanism used to transfer information between applications on the same computer.

local user account—In Windows NT family domains, an account that allows users to log on at and gain resources only from the computer where you create the local user account. The local user account is stored in the local security database. When using a local user account, you will not be able to access any network resources. In addition, for security reasons, you cannot log on as a local user account on a domain controller.

LocalTalk—Apple's own network interface and cable system. Because AppleTalk can operate at only 230 Kbps, it is not commonly used.

logical link control (LLC)—A sublayer of the data link layer of the OSI model. Manages the data link between two computers within the same subnet.

logical topology—Part of the data link layer. Describes how data flows through the physical topology or the actual pathway of the data.

long frame—A frame greater than 1518 bytes. These frames are typically formed by faulty or out-of-specification LAN drivers. (Also known as a *giant*.)

loopback testing—Testing method used to verify that a link is good by looping received data back onto the transmit path.

M

mail server—A server that manages e-mail between users.

mailslot—Connectionless messaging in which messaging is not guaranteed. Useful for identifying other computers or services on a network, such as the Browser service offered in Windows 2000.

mainframes—Large, centralized computers used to store and organize data.

management information base (MIB)—A database of objects that can be monitored by a network management system. Both SNMP and

RMON use standardized MIB formats that allow any SNMP and RMON tools to monitor any device defined by a MIB.

Manchester signal encoding—The encoding method used on Ethernet networks.

media access control (MAC) address—A hardware address (physical address) identifying a node on the network. It is a unique hardware address (unique on the LAN/subnet) burned onto a ROM chip assigned by the hardware vendors or selected with jumpers or DIP switches.

media access control (MAC) sublayer—The lower sublayer of the data link layer of the OSI model that communicates directly with the NIC. It defines the network logical topology, which is the actual pathway (ring or bus) of the data signals being sent. In addition, it allows multiple devices to use the same media and it determines how the NIC gets access or control of the network media so that two devices don't trample each other.

member server—A server that is not a domain controller and does not have a copy of the domain database.

mesh topology—A topology in which every computer is linked to every other computer.

message transfer agent (MTA)—The program responsible for receiving incoming e-mail and delivering the messages to individual users. Transfers messages between computers. Hidden from the average user, it is responsible for routing messages to proper destinations. Receive messages from both MUAs and other MTAs, although single user machines more often retrieve mail messages by using POP. Commonly referred to as the mail server program. UNIX sendmail and Microsoft Exchange Server are two examples of MTAs.

metric—A standard of measurement, such as hop count, used by routing algorithms to determine the optimal path to a destination.

metropolitan area network (MAN)—A network designed for a town or city. Usually uses high-speed connections such as fiber optics.

Microcom networking protocols (MNP)—A set of successful proprietary modem protocols used with modems for compression, error control, and other features.

microsegmentation—The process of creating smaller collision domains by segmenting a LAN rather than creating additional subnets.

Microsoft challenge handshake authentication protocol (MS-CHAP)—An authentication protocol that is Microsoft's proprietary version of CHAP. Unlike PAP and SPAP, it lets you encrypt data that is sent by using PPP or PPTP connections that use MPPE.

microwave—A form of electromagnetic energy that operates at a higher frequency (low GHZ frequency range) than radio wave communications. Because it provides higher bandwidths than those available for radio waves, it is currently one of the most popular long-distance transmission technologies.

modulation—The process of changing a signal to represent data.

modulator-demodulator (modem)—A device that enables a computer to transmit data over telephone lines. Because the computer information is stored and processed digitally, and the telephone lines transmit data using analog waves, the modem converts digital signals to analog signals (modulates) and analog signals to digital signals (demodulates).

MT-RJ connector—A fiber optic connection that is similar to a RJ-45 connector. It offers a new, small form factor, two-fiber connector that is lower in cost and smaller than the duplex SC interface.

multicast—Packets sent when communication is between a single sender and multiple receivers.

Multifiber cable—A cable that has anywhere from three to several hundred optical fibers, typically in multiples of two.

multimode fiber (MMF)—Fiber optic cable that is capable of transmitting multiple modes (independent light paths) at various wavelengths or phases.

multiplexer (mux)—A device that sends and receives several data signals at different frequencies.

multiplexing—The technique that allows data from different applications to share a single data stream.

multipoint—A connection that links three or more devices together through a single communication medium.

multiprotocol over ATM (MPOA)—A method developed by the ATM Forum to route protocols such as IP, IPX, and NetBIOS from traditional LANs over a switched ATM backbone.

Multipurpose Internet Mail Extensions (MIME)—A specification for formatting non-ASCII messages so that they can be sent over the Internet. Many e-mail clients now support MIME, which enables them to send and receive graphics, audio, and video files via the Internet mail system. In addition, MIME supports messages in character sets other than ASCII.

multistation access unit (MAU or MSAU)—A physical layer device, unique to Token Ring networks, that acts as a hub. While a hub defines a logical bus, the MAU defines a logical ring. Named pipes and mailslots are high-level interprocess communication mechanisms used by network computers. Different from the other mechanisms, both are written as file system drivers.

N

namespace—A set of names in a naming system.

narrowband radio system—A radio system that transmits and receives user information on a specific radio frequency.

narrowband radio system—A radio system that transmits and receives user information on a specific radio frequency. Narrowband radio keeps the radio signal frequency as narrow as possible just to pass the information.

nearest active upstream neighbor (NAUN)—Each node of a Token Ring network acts as a repeater that receives token and data frames from its neighbors.

NetBIOS Enhanced User Interface (NetBEUI)—Provides the transport and network layers for the NetBIOS protocol. Usually found on Microsoft networks. NetBEUI is a protocol used to transport data packets between two nodes. While NetBEUI is smaller than TCP/IP or IPX and is extremely quick, it will only send packets within the same network. Unfortunately, NetBEUI is not a routable protocol, which means that it cannot send a packet to a computer on another network.

network—Two or more computers connected together to share resources such as files or a printer. For a network to function, it requires a network service to share or access a common media or pathway to connect the computers. To bring it all together, protocols give the entire system common communication rules.

network address—An address that uniquely identifies a network.

network address translation (NAT)—A method of connecting multiple computers to the Internet (or any other IP network) using one IP address. With a NAT gateway running on a single computer, it is possible to share that single address between multiple local computers and connect them all at the same time. The outside world is unaware of this division and thinks that only one computer is connected.

network analyzer—See *protocol analyzer.*

network basic input/output system (NetBIOS)—A common program that runs on most Microsoft networks. It is used by applications to communicate with NetBIOS-compliant transports such as NetBEUI, IPX, or TCP/IP. It is responsible for establishing logical names (computer names) on the network, establishing a logical connection between two computers, and supporting reliable data transfer between computers that have established a session.

network control protocol (NCP)—A PPP subprotocol that is used to configure the different communications protocols, including TCP/IP and IPX, which are allowed to be used simultaneously.

network device interface specification (NDIS)—Microsoft specification that allows multiple protocols to use a single NIC at the same time.

network interface card (NIC)—A device used to connect computers to the network by using a special expansion card (or built into the motherboard). The NIC will then communicate by sending signals through a cable (twisted-pair, coaxial, or fiber optic) or by using wireless technology (IR or radio waves). The role of the NIC is to prepare and send data to another computer, receive data from another computer, and control the flow of data between the computer and the cabling system.

network layer—The OSI model layer that is concerned with addressing and routing necessary to move data (known as packets or datagrams) from one network (or subnet) to another. This includes establishing, maintaining, and terminating connections between networks, making routing decisions, and relaying data from one network to another.

network number—Part of an IP address that identifies the entire network. (Also known as *network prefix.*)

network operating system (NOS)—An operating system that includes special functions for connecting computers and devices into a LAN, to manage the resources and services of the network and to provide network security for multiple users.

network prefix—Part of an IP address that identifies the entire network. (Also known as *network number.*)

network time protocol (NTP)—An Internet standard protocol that assures accurate synchronization (to the millisecond) of computer clock times in a network of computers.

network attached storage (NAS)—Hard disk storage that is set up with its own network address rather than being attached to the department computer that is serving applications to a network's work station users.

network node interface (NNI)—Used in packet switching and cell relay network. Interfaces used to connect different types of networks.

nodes—Devices connected to the computer, including network computers, routers, and network printers.

noise—Interference or static that destroys the integrity of signals. Noise can come from a variety of sources, including radio waves, nearby electrical wires, lightning, other power fluctuations, and bad connections.

non-real-time variable bit rate (nrt-VBR)—Provides a specified throughput capacity when services and applications require high bandwidth but data is not sent evenly. Different from real-time variable bit rate, it does not have any latency requirements.

nonvolatile RAM (NVRAM)—Memory that will retain information after losing power.

NTFS—A file system for the Windows NT Family OSs. Designed for both the server and work station. It provides a combination of performance, reliability, security, and compatibility.

NTLM authentication—The client selects a string of bytes, uses the password to perform a one-way encryption of the string, and sends both the original string and the encrypted one to the server. The server receives the original string and uses the password from the account database to perform the same one-way encryption. If the result matches the encrypted string sent by the client, the server concludes that the client knows the username/password pair.

NWLink—Microsoft's NDIS-compliant, 32-bit implementation of IPX, SPX, and NetBIOS protocols used in Novell networks. NWLink is a standard network protocol that supports routing and can support NetWare client/server applications where NetWare-aware socket-based applications communicate with IPX/SPX socket-based applications.

Nyquist theorem—A theorem that states to ensure accuracy, a signal sample should be taken at least twice the rate of its frequency. It can also be used to calculate the data transfer rate of a signal, given its frequency and the number of signaling levels.

O

ohm meter—A device that can check wires and connectors and measure the resistance of an electronic device.

open—A conductor with a break in it or wires that are unconnected, preventing electricity from flowing.

open architecture—Specifications of the system or standard are public.

open data link interface (ODI)—Developed by Apple and Novell. Allows multiple protocols to use a single NIC.

open shortest path first (OSPF)—A link state route discovery protocol where each router periodically advertises itself to other routers.

open systems interconnection (OSI) reference model—The world's most prominent networking architecture model.

optical time domain reflectometer (OTDR)—The fiber optic equivalent of the TDR that is used to test copper cables. The OTDR transmits a calibrated signal pulse over the cable to be tested and monitors the signal that returns back to the unit. Instead of measuring signal reflections caused by electrical impedance as a TDR does, however, the OTDR measures the signal returned by backscatter—a phenomenon that affects all fiber optic cables.

P

packet—A piece of a message transmitted over a packet switching network. One of the key features of a packet is that it contains the destination address in addition to the data.

packet filters—A method typically found on firewalls. Based on protecting the network by using an ACL. This list resides on your router and determines which machine (IP address) can use the router and in what direction.

packet switching—A technique in which messages are broken into small parts called packets. Each packet is tagged with source, destination, and intermediary node addresses as appropriate.

Packets can have a defined maximum length and can be stored in RAM instead of on a hard disk. Packets can take a variety of possible paths through the network in an attempt to keep the network connections filled at all times.

parity—A method that provides an error check on the bits that are being sent.

password authentication protocol (PAP)—An authentication protocol that has passwords sent across the link as unencrypted plain text.

patch—A temporary fix to a program bug. A patch is an actual piece of object code that is inserted into (patched into) an executable program.

patch panels—A panel with numerous RJ-45 ports. The wall jacks are connected to the back of the patch panel to the individual RJ-45 ports. You can then use patch cables to connect the port in the front of the patch panel to a computer or a hub. As a result, you can connect multiple computers with a hub located in a wiring closet or server room.

peer-to-peer network—A network that does not have dedicated servers. Instead, all computers are equal. Therefore, they provide services and request services. Because a person's resources are kept on his or her own machine, a user manages his or her own shared resources. A peer-to-peer network is sometimes referred to as a work group.

penetration testing—The process of probing and identifying security vulnerabilities in a network and the extent to which they might be exploited by outside parties. It is a necessary tool for determining the current security posture of your network. Such a test should determine both the existence and extent of any risk.

permanent virtual circuit (PVC)—A permanently established VC that consists of one mode: data transfer. PVCs are used in situations in which data transfer between devices is constant.

permission—Defines the type of access granted to an object or object attribute. The permissions available for an object depend on the type of object.

personal computer (PC)—A computer meant to be used by one person. The first PC produced by IBM was called the *PC,* and the term *PC* came to mean IBM or IBM-compatible PCs, excluding Macintosh computers. In recent years, the term *PC* applies to any PC based on an Intel microprocessor, or on an Intel-compatible microprocessor.

phase—Measured in degrees to specify how close two sinusoidal waves are to each other.

phase modulation (PM)—A process where two sinusoidal waveforms are compared with each other.

physical layer—The OSI model that is responsible for the actual transmission of the bits sent across a physical media. It allows signals, such as electrical signals, optical signals, or radio signals, to be exchanged among communicating machines. Therefore, it defines the electrical, physical, and procedural characteristics required to establish, maintain, and deactivate physical links.

physical topology—Part of the physical layer. Describes how the network actually appears.

ping—A utility used to determine whether a specific IP address is accessible. It works by sending a packet to the specified address and waiting for a reply. Ping is used to troubleshoot Internet connections.

plain old telephone service (POTS)—The PSTN/standard telephone service in most homes.

plenum—The space above the ceiling and below the floors. Used to circulate air throughout the workplace.

plenum cable—A special cable that gives off little or no toxic fumes when burned.

point-to-point—A topology that connects two nodes directly together.

point-to-point protocol (PPP)—The predominant protocol for modem-based access to the Internet. Provides full duplex, bidirectional operations between hosts and can encapsulate multiple network layer LAN protocols to connect to private networks.

point-to-point tunneling protocol (PPTP)—A new technology for creating VPNs, developed jointly by Microsoft Corporation, U.S. Robotics, and several remote access vendor companies known collectively as the PPTP Forum. A VPN is a private network of computers that uses the public Internet to connect some nodes. Because the Internet is essentially an open network, the PPTP is used to ensure that messages transmitted from one VPN node to another are secure. With PPTP, users can dial in to their corporate network via the Internet.

poison reverse—In a computer network that uses RIP or other distance vector routing protocols, a poison reverse is a way in which a gateway node tells its neighbor gateways that one of the gateways is no longer connected. To do this, the notifying gateway sets the number of hops to the unconnected gateway to a number that indicates "infinite." Because RIP allows up to fifteen hops to another gateway, setting the hop count to sixteen would mean "infinite."

policies—In Windows NT family networks, a tool used by administrators to define and control how programs, network resources, and the operating system behave for users and computers in a domain or active directory structure.

polling—An access method that has a single device (sometimes referred to as a channel-access administrator) designated as the primary device. The primary device polls or asks each of the secondary devices (known as "slaves") if they have information to be transmitted.

port—An address on a host where an application makes itself available to incoming data.

post office protocol (POP)—A TCP/IP protocol that defines a simple interface between a user's mail client software and his or her e-mail server. It is used to download mail from the server to the client and allows the user to manage his or her mailbox.

postal, telegraph, and telephone (PTT)—A group that is responsible for providing combined postal, telegraph, and telephone services.

power on self test (POST)—A series of tests that are performed when a machine or device (such as a switch, router, or PC) first starts up.

PPP over Ethernet (PPPoE)—A protocol that was designed to bring the security and metering benefits of PPP to Ethernet connections such as those used in DSL.

preemptive multitasking—The operating system parcels out CPU time slices to each program.

presentation layer—The OSI layer that ensures that information sent by an application layer protocol of one system will be readable by the application layer protocol on the remote system. It also provides encryption/decryption and compression/decompression of data and network redirectors.

pretty good privacy (PGP)—A technique for encrypting messages developed by Philip Zimmerman. PGP is one of the most common ways to protect messages on the Internet because it is effective, easy to use, and free. PGP is based on the public key method, which uses two keys. One is a public key that you disseminate to anyone from whom you want to receive a message. The other is a private key that you use to decrypt messages that you receive.

primary domain controller (PDC)—The server that contains the master copy of the domain database on Windows NT networks.

primary memory—Memory used in Cisco routers that contains a running copy of the Cisco IOS, which is loaded into RAM from Flash at startup. It also contains a running copy of the configuration file, which is loaded into RAM from NVRAM at startup. Lastly, the primary memory stores the routing tables, ARP tables, and other IOS data structures.

primary name server—A DNS name server that stores and maintains the zone file locally. Changes to a zone, such as adding domains or hosts, are done by changing files at the primary name server.

primary rate interface (PRI)—A form of ISDN that includes twenty-three B channels (thirty in Europe) and one 64 Kb D Channel. PRI service is generally transmitted through a T-1 line (or an E-1 line in Europe).

print server—A server that manages user access to printer resources connected to the network, allowing one printer to be used by many people.

print sharing—A network service that allows several people to send documents to a centrally located printer in the office.

private branch exchange (PBX)—A telephone system within an enterprise. Switches calls between enterprise users on local lines while allowing all users to share a certain number of external phone lines.

private network—A network that is not connected to the Internet.

private key encryption—The most basic form of encryption that requires each individual to possess a copy of the key. Of course, for this to work as intended, you must have a secure way to transport the key to other people. You must keep multiple single keys per person, which can get very cumbersome. Private key algorithms are generally very fast and easily implemented in hardware. Therefore, they are commonly used for bulk data encryption.

Priviledged mode—See *Enable Exec mode*.

Priviledged Exec mode—See *Enable Exec mode*.

process—An executing program.

Project 802—A set of standards that have several areas of responsibility, including the NIC, WAN components, and media components.

propagation delay—The amount of time that passes between when a signal is transmitted and when it is received at the opposite end of the copper or optical cable.

proprietary system—A system or architecture that is privately owned and controlled by a company and that has not divulged specifications that would allow other companies to duplicate the product.

protocol analyzer—Software or a hardware/software device that allows you to capture or receive every packet on your media, stores it in a trace buffer, and then shows a breakdown of each of the packets by protocol in the order that they appeared. Therefore, it can help you analyze all levels of the OSI model to determine the cause of the problem. (Also known as *network analyzer.*)

protocols—The rules or standards that allow computers to connect to one another and enable computers and peripheral devices to exchange information with as little error as possible.

protocol suite—A set of protocols that work together.

proxy—Any device that acts on behalf of another.

proxy server—A server that performs a function on behalf of other computers. It is typically used to provide local intranet clients with access to the Internet, while keeping the local intranet free from intruders.

public key encryption—Nonsecret keys that are available to anyone you choose, or made available to everyone by posting them in a public place. It is often made available through a digital certificate. Private keys are kept in a secure location and are used only by you. When data needs to be sent, it is protected with a secret key encryption that was encrypted with the public key of the recipient of the data. The encrypted secret key is then transmitted to the recipient along with the encrypted data. The recipient will use the private key to decrypt the secret key. The secret key will then be used to decrypt the message itself.

public key infrastructure (PKI)—An infrastructure that enables users of an unsecured public network, such as the Internet, to securely and privately exchange data and money through the use of a public and a private cryptographic key pair that is obtained and shared through a trusted authority.

public switched telephone network (PSTN)—The international telephone system based on copper wires (UTP cabling) that carry analog voice data.

pulse code modulation (PCM)—The method of digitizing analog voice signals.

punch down block—A device used to connect several cable runs to each other without going through a hub.

Q

quadrature amplitude modulation (QAM)—An encoding method that allows the transmission of data using both the phase shift of phase modulation and the signal magnitude of amplitude modulation simultaneously. The more phase shifts and magnitude levels used, the more data the technique can be used to transmit.

quality of service (QoS)—Guaranteed bandwidth that has connection-oriented networks. Provides sufficient bandwidth for audio and video without jitters or pauses and enables the transfer of important data within a timely manner.

query—A request for information from a database.

R

rackmount cabinet—A cabinet designed to hold several servers.

radio frequency (RF)—Electromagnetic waves that reside between 10 KHz and 1 GHz in the electromagnetic spectrum. It includes shortwave radio, VHF, and UHF. Can be used to transmit data through air.

radio frequency interference (RFI)—Transmission sources, such as a radio station, may cause interference with other signals.

read only memory (ROM)—A form of nonvolatile memory that will retain information after losing power.

real-time variable bit rate (rt-VBR)—Provides a specified throughput capacity when services and applications require high bandwidth but data is not sent evenly. This is a popular choice for voice and videoconferencing data.

recursive query—A query that asks the DNS server to respond with the requested data, with an error stating that the requested data doesn't exist, or an error stating that the domain name specified doesn't exist.

redirectors—Intercepts file input/output requests and directs them to a drive or resource on another computer.

redundant array of independent (or inexpensive) disks (RAID)—A category of disk drives that employ two or more drives in combination for fault tolerance and performance. RAID disk drives are used frequently on servers but aren't generally necessary for personal computers.

remote access server (RAS)—A server that hosts modems for inbound requests to connect to the network. The computer and associated software that is set up to handle users seeking remote access to a network.

remote access service (RAS)—A service that allows users to connect remotely through various protocols and connection types.

remote authentication dial-in user service (RADIUS)—An industry standard client/server protocol and software that enables RASs to communicate with a central server to authenticate dial-in users and authorize their access to the requested system or service.

repeater—A device that works at the physical OSI layer. A network device used to regenerate or replicate a signal or to move packets from one physical media to another.

request for comments (RFC)—A series of documents that specify TCP/IP standards.

requesters—A program or part of a program that requests services.

reverse address resolution protocol (RARP)—A TCP/IP protocol that permits a physical address, such as an Ethernet address, to be translated into an IP address.

reverse query—A DNS query that is used by a resolver (an IP address) and wants to know the host name.

right—(1) Authorizes a user to access a file or directory on a network server. (2) Authorizes a user to perform certain actions on a computer, such as logging on to a system interactively/log on locally to the computer, backing up files and directories, performing a system shutdown, or adding/removing a device driver.

ring topology—A topology that has all devices connected to one another in a closed loop. Each device is connected directly to two other devices.

riser cable—Cable intended for use in vertical shafts that run between floors.

risers—Vertical connections between floors.

RJ-45—A connector that supports 10Base-T/100Base-TX (UTP) cabling.

rollover cable—A cable used to connect to Cisco routers and switches to a console port.

root bridge—Used with bridges and switches that employ the STA, which will act as the default pathway from one segment to another based on the lowest cost assigned to each link.

root domain—The top of the DNS tree. It is sometimes shown as a period (.) or as empty quotation marks (" "), indicating a null value.

round robin—Rotates the order of resource records data returned in a query answer in which multiple resource records exist of the same resource record type for a queried DNS domain name. Because the client is required to try the first IP address listed, a DNS server configured to perform round robin rotates the order of the A resource records when answering client requests. (Also known as *load sharing.*)

router—A device that works at the network OSI layer. It connects two or more LANs. In addition, it can break a large network into smaller, more manageable subnets. As multiple LANs are connected together, multiple routes are created to get from one LAN to another. Routers then share status and routing information to other routers so that they can provide better traffic management and bypass slow connections.

router information protocol (RIP)—A distance vector route discovery protocol where the entire routing table is periodically sent to all other routers on the network.

RS-232—An interface between a terminal or computer (the DTE) and its modem (the DCE).

RSA—A public-key encryption technology based on the fact that there is no efficient way to factor very large numbers. Deducing a RSA key, therefore, requires an extraordinary amount of computer processing power and time. The RSA algorithm has become the *de facto* standard for industrial-strength encryption, especially for data sent over the Internet. It is built into many software products, including Netscape Navigator and Microsoft Internet Explorer.

RSA standard—A public key encryption technology developed by RSA Data Security, Inc. The acronym stands for Rivest, Shamir, and Adelman, the inventors of the technique. The RSA algorithm is based on the fact that there is no efficient way to factor very large numbers. Deducing an RSA key, therefore, requires an extraordinary amount of computer processing power and time.

runt—A frame that is less than 64 bytes with a valid CRC. These frames are typically formed by faulty or out-of-specification LAN drivers. (Also known as a *short frame.*)

S

sags—Usually are not a problem. Very short drops in power lasting only a few milliseconds.

Samba—Software used on a Linux computer that provides file and print sharing like a Windows NT server using the CIFS protocol.

sampling—A method that takes samples of the electrical signal and assigns a binary value to the amplitude of the signal.

satellite systems—A microwave system that provides far bigger areas of coverage than can be achieved through other technologies. Microwave dishes are aligned to GEOs that can either relay signals between sites directly or via another satellite. The huge distances covered by the signal result in propagation delays of up to five seconds.

schema—The structure of a database system, described in a formal language supported by the DBMS. In a relational database, the schema defines the tables, the fields in each table, and the relationships between fields and tables. Schemas are generally stored in a data dictionary. Although a schema is defined in text database language, the term is often used to refer to a graphical depiction of the database structure.

screened twisted-pair (ScTP) cable—Foil surrounds all four conductors. It is a hybrid of STP and UTP cable, which contains four pairs of 24 AWG, 100 ÉΩ wire surrounded by a foil shield or wrapper and a drain wire for bonding purposes. (Also known as *foil twisted pair (FTP).*)

search engine—A program that searches documents for specified keywords and returns a list of the documents where the keywords were found.

secondary name server—A DNS name server that gets the data from its zone from another name server, either a primary name server or another secondary name server. The process of obtaining this zone information across the network is referred to as *zone transfer.*

second level domain names—Part of the DNS system. Variable length names registered to an individual or organization for use on the Internet.

Secure Sockets Layer (SSL)—A protocol developed by Netscape for transmitting private documents via the Internet. SSL works by using a public key to encrypt data that's transferred over the SSL connection. Both Netscape Navigator and Internet Explorer support SSL, and many websites use the protocol to obtain confidential user information such as credit card numbers. By convention, URLs that require an SSL connection start with https: instead of http:.

segment—A single cable, such as a backbone cable or a cable that connects a hub to a computer.

Sequenced Packet Exchange (SPX)—A transport layer protocol (layer 4 of the OSI model) used in Novell Netware networks. The SPX layer sits on top of the IPX layer (layer 3) and provides connection-oriented services between two nodes on the network. SPX is used primarily by client/server applications.

serial interface—An interface that can only send and receive one bit at a time.

serial line interface protocol (SLIP)—A simple protocol in which you send packets down a serial link delimited with special END characters. Used for a computer to connect to a server (such as those used by an ISP) via a serial line such as a modem to become an actual node on the Internet.

server—A service provider that provides access to network resources.

server message block (SMB)—The SMB protocol, which was jointly developed by Microsoft, Intel, and IBM, defines a series of commands used to pass information between networked computers. Clients connected to a network using NetBIOS over TCP/IP, NetBEUI, or IPX/SPX can send SMB commands. Microsoft refers to NetBIOS over TCP/IP as NBT.

server rack—A rack designed to hold several servers.

service—A program, routine, or process that performs a specific system function to support other programs.

service access point (SAP)—Used by the LLC to identify which protocol it is.

service advertising packet (SAP)—An IPX protocol used to advertise the services of all known servers on the network, including file servers, print servers, and so on. Servers periodically broadcast their service information while listening for SAPs on the network and storing the service information. Clients then access the service information table when they need to access a network service.

service level agreement (SLA)—A contract between a provider of WAN services and a buyer of those services. SLAs differs from ordinary, generic service agreements in that they obligate service providers to maintain a certain grade or level of service that is contractually guaranteed.

service profile identifier (SPID)—A directory number and additional identifier used to identify the ISDN device to the telephone network.

session—A reliable dialog between two computers.

session initiation protocol (SIP)—A standard that is used for signaling communication services on the Internet. For initiating an interactive user session that involves multimedia elements such as video, voice, chat, gaming, and virtual reality.

session layer—The OSI model layer that allows remote users to establish, manage, and terminate a connection (sessions).

Shannon's formula—A formula that calculates the maximum data transfer rate of an analog signal (with any number of signal levels). It also incorporates noise.

shared memory—Memory on Cisco routers used for buffering. This is a temporary storage area where packets go when they are waiting to be processed.

share-level security model—A model for which a network administrator assigns passwords to network resources.

sharing—The process of making a drive, directory, or printer available to users on the network.

shell—Shell is a term for an interactive user interface with an operating system. The shell is the layer of programming that understands and executes the commands a user enters. In some systems, the shell is called a command interpreter. A shell usually implies an interface with a command syntax (think of the DOS operating system and its "C:>" prompts and user commands such as "dir" and "edit").

shielded twisted pair (STP)—Similar to UTP except that it is usually surrounded by a braided shield that serves to reduce both EMI sensitivity and radio emissions.

Shiva password authentication protocol (SPAP)—An authentication protocol that sends passwords across links in a reversibly encrypted form. It is typically used when connecting to a Shiva LanRover, or when a Shiva client connects to a Windows 2000-based remote access server.

short—When a circuit has a zero or an abnormally low resistance path between two points, resulting in excessive current. In Networking cables, a short is an unintentional connection made between two conductors (such as wires) or pins/contacts.

short frame—A frame that is less than 64 bytes with a valid CRC. These frames are typically formed by faulty or out-of-specification LAN drivers. (Also known as a *runt.*)

shortest path first algorithms—See *link-state algorithms.*

S-HTTP—An extension to the HTTP protocol to support sending data securely over the WWW.

signaling—The method for using electrical energy, light energy, or radio waves to communicate.

Signaling System 7 (SS7)—The system that puts the information required to set up and manage telephone calls in a separate network rather than within the same network that the telephone call is made on.

signal-to-noise ratio (SNR or S/N)—A measure of signal strength relative to background noise in analog signals. The ratio is usually measured in dB.

simple mail transfer protocol (SMTP)—A TCP/IP protocol for the exchange of e-mail over the Internet. It is used between e-mail servers on the Internet or to allow an e-mail client to send mail to a server.

simple network management protocol (SNMP)—A TCP/IP protocol that defines procedures and management information databases for managing TCP/IP-based network devices.

simplex dialog—A form of dialog that allows communications on the transmission channel to occur in only one direction. One device is allowed to transmit and all of the other devices receive.

simplex fiber optic cable—A type of cable that has only one optical fiber inside the cable jacket. Because simplex cables only have one fiber inside them, there is usually a larger buffer and a thicker jacket to make the cable easier to handle.

single mode fiber (SMF)—Fiber optic cable that can transmit light in only one mode, but the narrower diameter yields less dispersion, resulting in longer transmission distances.

small office/home office (SOHO)—Small networks used primarily in home offices that might be part of a larger corporation but yet remain apart from it. SOHO networks are usually peer-to-peer networks.

smart permanent virtual circuit (SPVCs)—A hybrid of a PVC and a SVC.

SNMP agent—A client or device that returns the appropriate information to a SNMP manager.

SNMP community—A collection of hosts grouped together for administrative purposes. Deciding what computers should belong to the same community is generally, but not always, determined by the physical proximity of the computers. Communities are identified by the names you assign to them.

SNMP manager—The console through which the network administrator performs network management functions.

socket—A logical address assigned to a specific process running on a host computer. It forms a virtual connection between the host and the client and it identifies a specific upper-layer software process or protocol.

software handshaking—Handshaking that involves sending flow control signals as signal bytes embedded with the data bytes. Therefore, no hardware handshaking lines are necessary.

Solid cable—Cable used for the cabling that exists throughout the building. This should include cables that lead from the wall jacks to the server room or wiring closet.

sound—Vibrations of compressed air. As sound starts out, it travels in all directions away from the source. When the sound reaches the human ear, it causes the eardrum to vibrate, allowing you to hear the sound.

source route bridging (SRB)—A bridging method used on Token Ring networks. Responsible for determining the path to the destination node. Placed on the sending node, not on the bridge.

spanning tree algorithm (STA)—A method used with Ethernet bridges. Designates a loop-free subset of the network's topology by placing those bridge ports that, if active, would create loops into a standby (blocking condition) mode.

spike—Overvoltage that occurs. May damage the computer. (Also known as *transient.*)

split pair—Incorrect pinouts that cause data-carrying wires to be twisted together, resulting in additional crosstalk. Split pairs can be the result of mistakes during installation. The solution is to reattach the connectors at both ends using either the T568-A or T568-B pinouts.

split-horizon—A route-advertising algorithm that prevents the advertising of routes in the same direction in which they were learned so that it will prevent count to infinity problems.

spread spectrum signals—Signals that are distributed over a wide range of frequencies and then collected onto their original frequency at the receiver. Different from narrowband signals, spread spectrum signals use wider bands, which transmit at a much lower spectral power density (measured in Watts per Hertz).

SQL server—A server that is a DBMS that can respond to queries from client machines formatted in the SQL language (a database language).

standards—A dictated specification that a PC, hardware, or software follow or a PC, hardware, or software that has become popular.

standby power supply—A device consisting of the battery hooked up parallel to the PC. When the SPS detects a power fluctuation, the system will switch over to the battery to power the PC. The SPS requires a small (but measurable) amount of time to switch over (usually one-half of one cycle of the AC current or less than 10 milliseconds). Most SPSs will include built in surge protection devices.

star topology—The most popular topology in use. It has each network device connect to a central point such as a hub, which acts as a multipoint connector.

stateful inspection filter—An extension of packet filtering that can monitor the state of active connections and use this information to determine which network packets to allow through the firewall. (Also known as *dynamic packet filter.*)

static IP addresses—IP addresses that are manually assigned and configured.

static routing—A method that uses table mappings established by the network administrator prior to the beginning of routing. These mappings do not change unless the network administrator alters them.

statistical time-division multiplexing (SDTM)—A modified method of TDM that analyzes the amount of data that each device needs to transmit and determines (on-the-fly) how much time for each device should be allocated for data transmission on the cable or line. As a result, SDTM uses the bandwidth more efficiently.

storage area networks (SAN)—A high-speed subnetwork of shared storage devices. A SAN's architecture works in a way that makes all storage devices available to all servers on a LAN. If an individual application in a server cluster fails (but the node does not), the cluster service will typically try to restart the application on the same node. If that fails, it moves the application's resources and restarts them on another node of the server cluster. This process is called fail over.

store-and-forward operation—A method used on transparent bridging devices. Copies the entire frame onto its onboard buffers and then computes the CRC before forwarding it to its destination.

straight tip (ST) connector—Probably the most widely used fiber optic connector. It uses a BNC attachment mechanism similar to the ThinNet connector mechanism.

straight-through cable—A cable that can be used to connect a NIC to a hub. Has the same sequence of colored wires at both ends of the cable.

stranded cable—Cable that is typically used as patch cables between patch panels and hubs and between the computers and wall jacks. Because the stranded wire isn't as firm as solid wire, it is a little easier to work with.

stub area—An area used with OSPF that has only one area border router.

subdomain names—Part of the DNS system, additional names that an organization can create. Derived from the registered second-level domain name. The subdomain allows an organization to divide a domain into a department or geographical location, allowing the partitions of the domain name space to be more manageable. A subdomain must have a contiguous domain name space. This means that the domain name of a zone (child domain) is the name of that zone added to the name of the domain or parent domain.

subnet—A simple network or smaller network used to form a larger network.

subnet mask—Numbers used to define which bits represent the network address (including the subnet number) and which bits represent the host address.

subscriber connector (SC)—Typically latched connectors. This makes it impossible for the connector to be pulled out without releasing the connector's latch (usually by pressing some kind of button or release). (Also known as *square connectors.*)

subscriber loop—The telephone line that runs from your home or office to the telephone company's CO or neighborhood switching station (often a small building with no windows). (Also known as *local loop* and *last mile.*)

supernetting—The process of combining multiple IP address ranges into a single IP network such as combining several class C networks.

surge—Overvoltage that can stretch into milliseconds and that may damage the computer.

surge protector—A device designed to prevent most short duration, high-intensity spikes and surges from reaching your PC by absorbing excess voltages.

switch—See *switching hub.*

switched multimegabit data service (SMDS)—A high-speed, cell relay, WAN service designed for LAN interconnection through the PSTN.

switched virtual circuit (SVC)—See *temporary virtual circuit* (TVC).

switching hub—A fast multiported bridge, that builds a table of the MAC addresses of all the connected stations. It then reads the destination address of each packet and forwards the packet to the correct port. (Also known as *switch* or *layer 2 switch.*)

symmetric multiprocessing (SMP)—A computer that uses two or more microprocessors that share the same memory. If software is written to use the multiple microprocessors, several programs can be executed at the same time or multithreaded applications can be executed faster.

synchronous—Devices that use a timing or clock signal to coordinate communications between the two devices.

Synchronous Digital Hierarchy (SDH)—An international standard that specifies synchronous data transmission over fiber optic cables.

Synchronous Optical Network (Sonet)—The North American equivalent of SDH that specifies synchronous data transmission over fiber optic cables.

SYS volume—The primary volume on a NetWare server.

T

T-1 line—A digital line that has twenty-four 64 Kbps channels for a bandwidth of 1.544 Mbps.

T-3 line—A digital line that has six hundred seventy two 64 Kbps channels for a bandwidth of 44.736 Mbps.

tape drives—A device that reads from and writes to a long magnetic tape. Relatively inexpensive and offer large storage capacities, making tape backup drives ideal for backing up hard drives on a regular basis.

T-carrier system—The first successful system that converted an analog voice signal to a digital bit stream. While the T-carrier system was originally designed to carry voice calls between telephone company COs, today it is used to transfer voice, data, and video signals between different sites and to connect to the Internet.

telecommunication network (TELNET)—A virtual terminal protocol (terminal emulation) allowing a user to log on to another TCP/IP host to access network resources (RFC 854).

telecommunication closet—The floor serving facilities for horizontal cable distribution. Can be used for intermediate and main cross-connects.

telephony server—A server that functions as an intelligent answering machine for the network. It can also perform call center and call routing functions.

temporary virtual circuit (TVC)—Virtual circuits that are dynamically established on demand and terminated when transmission is complete. Communication over a TVC consists of three phases: Circuit establishment, data transfer, and circuit termination.

terrestrial system—A microwave system that uses relay towers to provide an unobstructed path over an extended distance. These line-of-sight systems use unidirectional parabolic dishes that must be aligned carefully.

thicknet—See *10Base5*.

thin client—A computer that is between a dumb terminal and a PC. A thin client is a client designed to be especially small so that the bulk of the data processing occurs on the server.

threat—A person, place, or thing that has the potential to access resources and cause harm.

vulnerability—A point where a resource is susceptible to attack. It can be thought of as a weakness.

time domain reflectometer (TDR)—The primary tool used to determine the length of a copper cable and to locate the impedance variations that are caused by opens, shorts, damaged cables, and interference with other systems. The TDR works much like radar, by transmitting a signal on a cable with the opposite end left open and measuring the amount of time it takes for the signal's reflection to return to the transmitter.

When you have this elapsed time measure, called the nominal velocity of propagation (NVP), and you know the speed at which electrons move through the cable, you can determine the length of the cable.

time-division multiplexing (TDM)—A method that divides the single channel into short time slots, allowing multiple devices to be assigned time slots.

token—A packet that is passed around the network in an orderly fashion from one device to the next to inform devices that they can transmit data.

token passing—A special authorizing packet of information used to inform devices that they can transmit data. These packets, called tokens, are passed around the network in an orderly fashion from one device to the next.

token passing—An access method that specifies that a network device only communicates over the network when it has the token (a special data packet that is generated by the first computer that comes online in a Token Ring network). The token is passed from one station to another around a ring. When a station gets a free token and transmits a packet, it travels in one direction around the ring, passing all of the other stations along the way.

Token Ring—A network technology that is a ring logical topology. For computers to access the network, they use a token.

tone generator and probe—Consists of a unit that you connect to a cable with a standard jack or an individual wire with alligator clips, which transmits a signal over the cable or wire. The other unit is a penlike probe that emits an audible tone when touched to the other end of the cable or wire or even its insulating sheath. (Also called a *"fox and hound" wire tracer.*)

top-level domains—Immediately below the root domain, found on the top of the NDS tree. They indicate a country, region, or type of organization. Three-letter codes indicate the type of organization. For example, *com* indicates commercial (business) and *edu* stands for educational institution.

topology—Describes the appearance or layout of the network. Depending on how you look at the network, there is the physical topology and the logical topology.

traceroute—A utility that traces a packet from your computer to an Internet host, showing how many hops the packet requires to reach the host and how long each hop takes. If you're visiting a website and pages are appearing slowly, you can use traceroute to figure out where the longest delays are occurring.

transceivers—Devices that transmit and receive analog or digital signals.

transition state—A digital signal that represents data by how the signal transitions from high to low or low to high. A transition indicates a binary 1 while the absence of a transition represents a binary 0.

translational bridging—Bridging that provides translation between the formats and transit principles of different media types (usually Ethernet and Token Ring).

transmission control protocol (TCP)—A protocol that provides connection-oriented, reliable communications for applications that typically transfer large amounts of data at one time or that require an acknowledgement for data received.

transparent bridging—A type of bridging based on a spanning tree. Called transparent because the endpoint devices do not need to know that the bridge(s) exists. In other words, the computers attached to the LAN do not behave any differently in the presence or absence of transparent bridges. (Also known as *learning bridge*.)

transport layer—An OSI model layer that can be described as the middle layer that connects the lower and upper layers together. In addition, it is responsible for reliable transparent transfer of data (known as segments) between two end points. Because it provides end-to-end recovery of lost and corrupted packets and flow control, it deals with end-to-end error handling, dividing messages into smaller packets, numbers of the messages, and the repackaging of messages.

transport layer security (TLS)—The successor to the secure sockets layer (SSL), TLS is composed of two layers: the TLS record protocol and the TLS handshake protocol. The TLS record protocol provides connection security by using an encryption method, such as DES. The TLS record protocol can also be used without encryption. The TLS handshake protocol allows the server and client to authenticate each other and to negotiate an encryption algorithm and cryptographic keys before data is exchanged.

trap—An unsolicited message sent by SNMP agent to a SNMP management system when the agent detects that a certain type of event has occurred locally on the managed host. The SNMP management console receives a trap message known as a trap destination. For example, a trap message might be sent when a system restarts or when a router link goes down.

trellis coded quadrature amplitude modulation (TCQAM or TCM)—A method that uses QAM to encode 6 bits for every baud.

triggered updates—A method that allows a router to announce changes in metric values almost immediately rather than waiting for the next periodic announcement. The trigger is a change to a metric in an entry in the routing table.

trivial file transfer protocol (TFTP)—A simple form of the FTP. TFTP uses UDP and provides no security features. It is often used by servers to boot diskless work stations, X-terminals, and routers.

trunk—The single cable usually designed to carry the bulk of network traffic to other sites or to connect multiple network or buildings at a site.

trust relationship—A relationship between domains that makes it possible for users in one domain to access resources in another domain. The domain that grants access to its resources is known as the trusting domain. The domain that accesses the resources is known as the trusting domain.

tunnel—The logical connection through which the packets travel in a VPN.

tunneling—The method for transferring data packets over the Internet or other public network, providing the security and features formerly available only on private networks. A tunneling protocol encapsulates the data packet in a header that provides routing information to enable the encapsulated payload to securely traverse the network.

twisted pair—Consists of two insulated copper wires twisted around each other. While each pair acts as a single communication link, twisted pairs are usually bundled together into a cable and wrapped in a protective sheath.

U

unicast—Packets sent when a single sender communicates with a single receiver over the network.

uniform naming convention (UNC)—See *Universal Naming Convention (UNC)*.

uninterruptible power supply—A device that has a battery connected in series with the PC. The AC power is connected directly to the battery. Because the battery always provides clean power, the PC is protected against overvoltages and undervoltages.

universal asynchronous receiver/transmitter (UART)—A single IC chip that is the translator between the serial device and the system bus and is the component that processes, transmits, and receives data.

universal naming convention (UNC)—A PC format for specifying the location of resources on a LAN. UNC uses the \\server-name\shared-resource-pathname format.

universal security group—A Windows NT family group that is only available in native mode. It can contain users, universal groups, and global groups from any domain and it can be assigned rights and permissions to any network resource in any domain in the domain tree or forest.

unmodulated carrier tone—A tone that routers use to query each other about their capabilities, such as speed.

unshielded twisted pair (UTP)—The same type of cable that is used with telephones. The most common cable used in networks. UTP cable consists of two pairs or four pairs of twisted wires.

unspecified bit rate (UBR)—A specification that does not guarantee any throughput levels. It is for non-real-time traffic with no required service guarantees.

user account—An account that represents the user and enables a user to log on to a network.

user datagram protocol (UDP)—A TCP/IP protocol that provides connectionless communications and does not guarantee that packets will be delivered. Applications that use UDP typically transfer small amounts of data at once. Reliable delivery is the responsibility of the application.

User Exec mode—The first mode on a Cisco router or switch after you successfully log into the router, meaning that you entered the appropriate password correctly. In this mode, you can connect to other devices (such as another router) to perform simple tests and display system information.

user profile—In Windows, a collection of folders and data that stores the user's current desktop environment and application settings.

user level security model—A model in which a user has a user account that includes a user name and password. The user account is provided with an ACL each time the user logs on to the network. A user can only access a network resource if that resource is on the ACL. A user cannot access a network resource if a resource is not on the ACL. The user level security model allows a network administrator to manage network security from a central network location. An administrator would normally assign users to group accounts and then grant the group accounts permissions to use resources on the network.

user network interface (UNI)—Used in packet switching and cell relay networks, a user's interface to the network.

V

V.90—A modem standard, which is actually two standards in one, that defines a digital modem and analog modem pair capable of transmitting data at up to 56 Kbps downstream and up to 33.6 Kbps upstream. In this case, downstream means from the digital to the analog modem.

value added network (VAN)—A network with special services such as EDI or financial services such as credit card authorization or ATM transactions.

vampire tap—A mechanical device that uses conducting teeth to penetrate the insulation and attach directly to the wire conductor.

variable length subnet mask (VLSM)—In TCP/IP, a network with more than one subnet mask.

vertical cabling system—Cable system that connects between floors.

virtual circuit (VC)—A logical circuit created to ensure reliable communications between two network devices. To provide this, it provides a bidirectional communications path from one device to another and is uniquely identified by some type of identifier. A number of VCs can be multiplexed into a single physical circuit for transmission across the network.

virtual link—A logical link between a backbone area border router, an unspecified number of routers, and a second border router that is not connected to the backbone.

virtual local area network (VLAN)—A collection of nodes that are grouped together in a single broadcast domain that is based on something other than physical location. A VLAN is a switched network that is logically segmented on an organizational basis, by functions, project teams, or applications rather than on a physical or geographical basis.

virtual private network (VPN)—A protocol that uses a public or shared network (such as the Internet or a campus intranet) to create a secure, private network connection between a client and a server. The VPN client cloaks each packet in a wrapper that allows it to sneak (or tunnel) unnoticed through the shared network. When the packet gets to its destination, the VPN server re-

moves the wrapper, deciphers the packet inside, and processes the data.

virus—A program designed to replicate and spread, generally without the knowledge or permission of the user.

virus hoax—A letter or e-mail message warning you about a virus that does not exist.

Voice over IP (VoIP)—Voice communication sent over an IP network.

volt meter—A device that measures voltage output or voltage signal.

volume—A fixed amount of storage on a disk or tape. The term "volume" is often used as a synonym for the storage medium itself, but it is possible for a single disk to contain more than one volume or for a volume to span more than one disk.

W

web browser—The client program/software that you run on your local machine to gain access to a web server. It receives the HTML commands, interprets the HTML, and displays the results.

web server—A computer equipped with the server software that uses Internet protocols such as HTTP and FTP to respond to web client requests on a TCP/IP network via web browsers.

web server—A server that runs WWW and FTP services for access through an intranet or the Internet.

wide area network (WAN)—A network that uses long-range telecommunication links to connect network computers over long distances. Often consists of two or more smaller LANs. Typically, LANs are connected through public networks, such as the PSTN.

Windows 2000—A newer operating system based on Windows NT architecture.

windows driver model (WDM)—A driver technology developed by Microsoft to create drivers that are source-code compatible for Windows 98, 2000, Me and XP. WDM works by channeling some of the work of the device driver into portions of code that are integrated into the operating system. These portions of code handle all of the low-level buffer management, including DMA and Plug and Play device enumeration. The WDM device driver becomes more streamlined with less code and works at greater efficiency.

windows Internet naming service (WINS)—A system that contains a database of IP addresses and NetBIOS (computer names) that update dynamically. It is used to resolve IP addresses from computer names.

winsock—A programming interface and supporting program that handles input/output requests for Internet applications in a Windows operating system. It's called Winsock because it's an adaptation for Windows of the Berkeley UNIX sockets interface.

wire map tester—A device that uses a wire map testing, which transmits signals through each wire in a copper twisted-pair cable to determine if it is connected to the correct pin at the other end.

Wired Equivalent Privacy (WEP)—A form of encryption used by wireless communication.

wireless fidelity (Wi-Fi)—Another name for IEEE 802.11b. Wi-Fi is used in place of 802.11b in the same way that Ethernet is used in place of IEEE 802.3.

wireless LAN (WLAN)—A LAN without wires that transfer data through the air by using radio frequencies.

wireless spectrum—A continuum of electromagnetic waves, with varying frequencies and wavelengths, that are used for telecommunications.

work area—The area that includes the station equipment, patch cable, and adapters (such as a media filter).

work group—A peer-to-peer network.

work station—(1) In networking, *work station* refers to any computer connected to a LAN. It could be a work station or a PC. (2) Type of computer used for engineering applications (CAD/CAM), desktop publishing, software development, and other types of applications that require a moderate amount of computing power and relatively high-quality graphics capabilities.

worm—A program or algorithm that replicates itself over a computer network and usually performs malicious actions, such as using up the computer's resources and shutting the system down. Typically, a worm enters the computer because of vulnerabilities available in the computer's operating system.

X

X.400—A set of standards relating to the exchange of electronic messages (messages can be e-mail, fax, voice mail, telex, etc.). It was designed to let you exchange e-mail and files with the confidence that no one besides the sender and the recipient will ever see the message, that delivery is assured, and that proof of delivery is available if desired.

X.500—A directory service in which objects are organized similar to the files and folders on a hard drive.

X.509 certificates—The most widely used digital certificates.

Z

zone transfer—The process of obtaining DNS zone information across a network.

Index

boldface page numbers indicate the primary pages for an entry.